RENTON'S METAPHORS

Third Edition

A Dictionary of 4,000 Picturesque Idiomatic Expressions

N E Renton

THE BOOK THAT LEAVES NO STONE UNTURNED

UNICORN BOOKS

Publishers
UNICORN BOOKS
J-3/16, Daryaganj, New Delhi-110002
☎ 23275434, 23272783/84 • Fax: 011-23260518
E-mail: unicornbooks@vsnl.com • *Website:* www.unicornbooks.in

Distributors
Pustak Mahal®, Delhi
J-3/16, Daryaganj, New Delhi-110002
☎ 23276539, 23272783, 23272784 • *Fax:* 011-23260518
E-mail: info@pustakmahal.com • *Website:* www.pustakmahal.com

Sales Centres
■ 10-B, Netaji Subhash Marg, Daryaganj, New Delhi-110002
☎ 23268292, 23268293, 23279900 • *Fax:* 011-23280567
E-mail: salespmahal@airtelmail.in • *E-mail:* rapidexdelhi@indiatimes.com

■ **Hind Pustak Bhawan**
6686, Khari Baoli, Delhi-110006
☎ 23944314, 23911979

Branch Offices
Bengaluru: ☎ 22234025 • *Telefax:* 22240209
E-mail: pustak@airtelmail.in • pustak@sancharnet.in
Mumbai: ☎ 22010941
E-mail: rapidex@bom5.vsnl.net.in
Patna: ☎ 3294193 • *Telefax:* 0612-2302719
E-mail: rapidexptn@rediffmail.com
Hyderabad: *Telefax:* 040-24737290
E-mail: pustakmahalhyd@yahoo.co.in

The first edition of this book was published as *Metaphors: an Annotated Dictionary* by Schwartz and Wilkinson, Melbourne, 1990. The second edition was published as *Metaphorically Speaking* by Warner Books, New York, 1992. Third edition was published as *Renton's Metaphors* by Bas Publishing, Australia, 2005

ISBN 978-81-7806-173-3

Edition : 2009

Printed at : Param Offsetters, Okhla, New Delhi

To all the people who think
that they never use any metaphors

Some Words on Words

Dictionary

A malevolent literary device for cramping the growth of a language and making it hard and inelastic

Ambrose Bierce, *Devil's Dictionary*

Lexicographer

A writer of dictionaries, a harmless drudge

Samuel Johnson

Words

Words, words, mere words, no matter from the heart

Shakespeare, Troilus and Cressida

A spade is a spade

Early today the senator called a spade a spade. He later issued a retraction.

Anonymous

Playing dice

God does not play dice with the universe

Albert Einstein

Déjà vu

It's déjà vu all over again

Yogi Berra

Economist

An economist is a tea-leaf reader who drinks only coffee

Anonymous, from an Internet site

Laying an egg

Wall Street Lays an Egg

Headline announcing the stock market crash of 1929

Engineers

Question: What does an engineer do when he sees the light at the end of the tunnel?

Answer: He extends the tunnel.

From a lecture on metaphors given by the present author

Money matters

When someone says to a person: 'A penny for your thoughts,' and that person puts in his two cents' worth, what happens to the change?

Anonymous

Exaggeration

To say that they 'gilded the lily' is an understatement. What they did was to dip the lily in a gold solution.

Ron Mulock, in the New South Wales Parliament

Every Man and his Dog Uses Metaphors

Metaphors that have the community's seal of approval roll off the tongue so readily that, by any yardstick, they are invariably thick on the ground.

A person in the pink who plays his cards right and who takes up the cudgels for the cause will, without going overboard or changing tack, find an avalanche of metaphors under his very nose. Unless he puts a foot wrong or goes off half-cocked he will take the bull by the horns, bite the bullet, and regard them all as useful tools and as grist to his mill. He will already be in the picture and will not need to engage in a witchhunt or rely on the grapevine in order to put his finger on them.

Without matters getting out of hand or losing any momentum it stands out a mile that metaphors are in the blood of every Tom, Dick, and Harry worth his salt and willing to show the flag.

Many expressions have been gathering dust for donkey's years and are so much a hallmark of our society that their down-to-earth use at the drop of a hat does not ring a bell or cause any eyebrows to be raised.

About the Author

Nick Renton is a consulting actuary, commercial arbitrator, company director, and writer. He was born in 1931 and qualified as a fellow of the Faculty of Actuaries in 1957. He is also a fellow of the Institute of Actuaries of Australia.

He holds an investment adviser's licence and qualifications as a commercial arbitrator. In 1975 he was elected a fellow of the Securities Institute of Australia for his services to the industry.

After fifteen years as principal officer of a life insurance company he became the first executive director of the Life Offices' Association of Australia from 1975 to 1979. He was executive director of the Life Insurance Federation of Australia from its formation in 1979 until 1986. In those capacities he acted as the official spokesman for the life insurance industry.

He is now an independent business consultant to leading stockbrokers, insurance companies, employer organisations, government agencies, and others. He also serves on the boards of several financial institutions and is in great demand as a speaker at seminars and conferences.

He was the founder and first president of the Australian Shareholders' Association and has been federal president of the Australian Society of Security Analysts and Victorian chairman of the Commercial Law Association of Australia.

Nick Renton has been published by 11 different publishers in Australia and the United States. He has written books about more different topics than any other Australian author.

His *Guide for Meetings and Organisations*, published by the Law Book Company, has been widely used as a reference work on all aspects of chairmanship and the running of voluntary associations since it first appeared in 1961. It deals with many practical aspects of meetings procedure not covered in Joske and is now in a two-volume seventh edition.

He is also the author of books on the stock exchange, managed investments, taxation, wills, good writing, public relations, the Internet and the Australian economy, as well as of numerous papers to professional bodies.

He has published well over 500 articles in newspapers and financial journals in the last 10 or so years.

In 1992 he was awarded the prestigious H M Jackson Memorial Prize for two of his works, *Understanding Dividend Imputation* and the *Retirement Handbook*.

In 1995 he received the Ken Millar Award for his best-selling *Understanding the Stock Exchange* and his highly controversial *Company Directors: Masters or Servants?*

Nick Renton maintains his own web site of over 80 pages at http://users.bigpond.net.au/renton

He was made a Member of the Order of Australia in 2004.

He is married and has three children. He lives in Melbourne, Australia.

Contents

Foreword

In a time when the visual image is such a powerful influence on our attitude and thoughts, it is well to be reminded of the miracle of language. How and when was it invented? How do we explain its richness and variety? By what extraordinary transformation did words which have quite literal and specific meanings take on metaphysical significance? Which expression conveys the most vivid meaning, 'the top dog', or its definition, 'the person in the most powerful position'?

The metaphor wins every time.

For metaphor is the spice of language. It also activates the reader's or listener's inner eye to produce images which are just as vivid as visual ones. Without its colour, wit and concreteness would disappear.

Here is a dictionary and thesaurus of metaphors which is both a practical guide to meaning and a stimulus to enquiry. Only a person in love with words could have compiled it; and there are surprises in it for even the most knowledgeable student of language. Mr Renton achieves the aim that Sir Philip Sidney saw as the central principle of poetry – to teach by delighting.

Leonie Kramer

Preface

'The question is,' said Alice, 'whether you can make words mean so many different things."

'The question is,' said Humpty Dumpty, 'which is to be master – that's all.

Lewis Carroll
Through the Looking Glass

This handy word-book with its original format is intended as a useful yet entertaining reference tool for writers, editors, publishers, students, migrants and those engaged in public speaking.

It is a work for all users of words, whether as readers or writers – effectively the whole English-speaking community. It will also have a special appeal to the many people who specifically regard themselves as lovers of words.

This new edition is a revised and expanded version of its predecessors. Further notes on metaphors and illustrations of their use have been added to the text.

With minor exceptions all the metaphors listed are commonly found in current usage.

Many topical and interesting expressions have been included for the first time, although it must be pointed out that a book of this type, by its very nature, can never hope to be complete.

Nick Renton
http://users.bigpond.net.au/renton
nrenton@bigpond.net.au

Introduction

CHAPTER ONE

Preamble

It is one of the maxims of the civil law that definitions are hazardous

Samuel Johnson
The Rambler

I am a Bear of Very Little Brain and long words bother me

A. A. Milne
Winnie-the-Pooh

What is a Metaphor?

A cynic once defined a metaphor as 'a simile with the words of comparison left out'. Less frivolously, the *Concise Oxford Dictionary* puts it as the 'application of name or descriptive term to an object to which it is not literally applicable'. The word is derived from two Greek roots – *meta* (with, after) and *pherein* (bear) – which, in combination, denote 'transfer' (of meaning).

The modern English language – as employed in ordinary conversation, as used on radio and television, as seen in newspaper and magazine articles and headlines, and as found in more serious literature – is remarkably full of metaphors. Some of these have been in currency for a hundred years or more, giving rise to the description 'fossil poetry'.

Many metaphors involve colourful analogies. Every day one talks of 'missing the bus', of 'being in the same boat' as someone else, of 'getting down to brass tacks', or of 'not having a crystal ball'. People are always 'getting a feather in their cap', 'earning brownie points', 'building bridges', 'clasping at straws', 'muddying the waters', 'cutting the Gordian knot', and 'missing something by a whisker'.

For the most part such *figures of speech* involve combinations of words sounding very familiar to their audience, and their non-literal use is quite subconscious.

In practice, very few metaphors are ever written inside inverted commas (quotation marks). Such a tell-tale sign is generally absent, thus clearly indicating that the writers were not focusing on the fact that their words did not represent the literal truth. Fowler, in *Modern English Usage*, characterises such phrases as 'dead metaphors'.

A metaphor is often used because it can convey a particular shade of meaning much more succinctly than can other words. The present book demonstrates that metaphors serve to enrich both speech and writing – although at the price of making communication in English much more difficult both for foreigners and for computers used on translation tasks.

Objectives

This book includes, as self-contained listings, a dictionary (Part I), a thematic section (Part II), and a thesaurus (Part III). It is intended as a handy reference tool for both general readers and educational institutions in all English-speaking countries.

The book is designed to serve a number of assorted purposes, including the following:

1. to set out the meanings of the various metaphors in a style that is popular and easy to read;
2. to help persons for whom English is a second language;

3. to assist writers and public speakers to become more articulate;
4. to provide resource material for teachers of English who wish to design imaginative courses;
5. to give an overall perspective of the subject;
6. to show the richness and diversity of the living English language to students and lovers of words;
7. to refresh memories of half-remembered phrases;
8. to provide some amusement from the patterns presented by the different categorisations;
9. to illustrate that some particular words and concepts are especially prevalent in figurative use; and
10. to provide raw material for party games, advertising copy, church sermons, crossword puzzles, and other specialist applications.

The lists can be used for many different purposes – including inspiring pithy headlines for newsletter articles, helping speakers to devise alliterative oratory, and assisting fans to solve cryptic crosswords.

The book takes into account the fact that English can rightly be described as 'the language of buried metaphors' and that this feature, while doubtless fascinating to word-buffs, must be very frustrating to non-native speakers. Even secondary students for whom English is their first language tend to see things very literally.

Each metaphor has been given a separate entry – thus avoiding the practice (seen in many dictionaries) of jumbling up related material, which saves space but causes inconvenience to users. The form of presentation in this book also allows similar-sounding figurative formations to be compared and contrasted with each other easily.

Although the nature of the subject matter of this work inevitably involves some overlap with other books on idioms or picturesque expressions, the present book is original in terms of the selection of the phrases included, of their presentation and analysis, and of the simplicity of the definitions given.

Coverage

This short word-book, despite its specialised nature, makes no pretence to being complete. That would be an impossible task – particularly because people with an eye out for resemblances are free to coin their own metaphorical expressions at will. However, the book contains 15,000 dictionary-style alphabetical entries listing more than 4,000 different metaphors commonly found in current usage, selected from the wide range available on the basis of the criteria described above. Many of these could be described as 'classical' expressions, but the book also includes some other metaphors of special interest or appeal because of their origins in fields such as history, mythology, religion, commerce, science, or classical literature, or because they are illustrative of typical modern innovations.

Minor instances of figurative phrases based on local customs and circulating only in some communities can be found – for example, the Australian expressions 'to stir the possum', 'to be up the creek', 'to have Buckley's chance', and 'to get the wrong end of the pineapple'. However, most of the tabulated metaphors will be readily understood throughout the entire English-speaking world. This is, no doubt, due to the common origins of the language in the case of metaphors of long standing, and to their use in films and television in the case of the more recent formations.

There is some overlap between metaphors, clichés, idioms, colloquialisms, and even pithy sayings and proverbs. No attempt has been made to draw very fine distinctions – although similes, jargon, and euphemisms have, for the most part, been deliberately excluded. Many outright slang terms have also been ignored, although a few borderline cases have been admitted. Some common picturesque expressions which might not, strictly speaking, be metaphors have been included where it seemed likely that this would be of convenience to users of this book.

Phrases such as 'the chair upheld the point of order', 'he has a good pen', or 'the land belonged to the crown' are examples of the figure of speech known as *metonymy* and are also outside the scope of this book. In the same vein, expressions such as 'I want a *word* with you' (in reference to a desired lengthy discussion), a subdivision of the figure of speech called *synecdoche* (see Chapter 7), have been disregarded.

Prepositions used metaphorically have also been excluded: 'to be *in* difficulties', 'to be *within* one's rights', 'to be *beyond* help', and so on.

The main criterion for listing an expression was that, in normal contexts, its words are not used in their true or literal sense. However, in each case the user's intention would have been to convey a message which was meant to be readily understood by his or her particular public and which expressed a specific idea in a picturesque or emphatic way.

To enable the book to remain of a reasonable length, obscure phrases occasionally found in textbooks and traditional dictionaries but which are not actually in current circulation have, for the most part, been excluded. On the other hand, some very obviously modern metaphors have been included – especially where they seemed colourful. However, a living language being what it is, it is likely that some of these expressions might not last.

The richness of the English language can be demonstrated and put into perspective by comparing the number of metaphors mentioned above as included in this book even on this limited basis – namely, over 4,000 – with the number of words in 'Basic English' – a mere 850. (Basic English was invented by C. K. Ogden between 1926 and 1930, as a first step towards the teaching of English as a foreign language. The initials are said to stand for British, American, Scientific, International, Commercial.).

Arrangement

The bulk of this book is in three separate parts.

First of all there is the main dictionary list (Part I). This sets out each metaphor dealt with, and gives a deliberately brief (yet concise) explanation of its import.

In many cases, further background information has been added where this seemed appropriate – for example, in relation to biblical or literary allusions, or scientific aspects. This edition includes a much greater number of such notes than the earlier editions. In addition, many of the definitions have been extensively rewritten, so as to improve their clarity and/or accuracy.

Of course, the fact that a particular quotation illustrating the use of a metaphor is mentioned is not meant to imply that this was the first definitive use of the metaphor. The quotations and notes are supplied as matters of general historical interest, rather than as formal definitive statements of derivation.

This listing is followed in the thematic section (Part II) by subsidiary lists showing the relevant metaphors occurring in each of a number of readily identifiable categories.

The thesaurus (Part III) is a special section, not normally found in dictionaries. It is designed more for writers than for readers, although the latter will still find it of interest. It contains lists showing metaphors classified according to the broad subject areas in which the metaphors express ideas or concepts. These lists will also be of particular relevance to public speakers when preparing their material.

In addition, some general comments – relating to metaphors at large and dealing with historical and other interesting aspects of the subject – are made in this Introduction (Chapters 1–7). Some of these comments are based on a computer analysis made while researching this project. In particular, the categories relevant to Part II are discussed further in Chapter 4. They have regard to the *literal* or original meaning of the words – not to their *figurative* or borrowed usage.

The basis of the thesaurus in Part III is explained in Chapter 5. A number of miscellaneous case studies is presented in Chapter 6. Some aspects of grammar and punctuation are dealt with in Chapter 7.

Chapter 2 deals with some of the more important sources of metaphors under a number of general headings. Some other interesting sources are mentioned elsewhere – for example, sport in Chapter 4 and computers in Chapter 6.

Of course, short definitions – while no doubt convenient to most users – do suffer from one disadvantage, in that they cannot readily cover exhaustively all the various shades of meaning being attributed to some phrases in actual practice.

The main list is in alphabetical order of the 'keyword' of the phrase – usually the noun or the verb but, on occasions where appropriate, an adjective or an adverb. Simple verbs occurring frequently – *be, get, give, have, let, put, take,* and so on – have, however, been ignored. For the convenience of readers, many metaphors and their explanations have been set out in the alphabetical sequence under more than one keyword. This eliminates the need for a separate index or extensive cross references. This presentation thus overcomes a weakness and an annoying feature of the few other books in this area. (Transitive verbs are usually shown with an appropriate object, such as 'someone' or 'something'.) With minor exceptions – for special reasons – pronouns, prepositions, conjunctions and interjections are not listed.

It should be recognised that, because English is a living language, most metaphors can occur in numerous variations – depending on the taste or the mood of the writer or speaker. For instance, words of qualification or of emphasis can be added or omitted. Many subjects can also be approached from more than one angle. For example, the expressions 'something *coming* to light' and 'someone *bringing* something to light' were both regarded as involving the same figurative concept, and only the latter version was included in the list. Similarly, 'to *run* for cover' and 'to *duck* for cover' were treated as really being the one metaphor – despite the use of a different verb in the two versions.

In some instances a pair of opposite metaphors exists. For example:

- 'to run off the rails' and 'to be back on the rails';
- 'to give a thumbs up' and 'to give a thumbs down';
- 'to be on the right track' and 'to be on the wrong track';
- 'cold-hearted' and 'warm-hearted';
- 'to be the first cab off the rank' and 'to be the last [or latest] cab off the rank';
- 'to give someone the green light' and 'to give someone the red light';

and so on.

In other instances, two related words exist – for example, 'crusade' and 'crusader'. In other instances, the same word is used as two different parts of speech – for example, 'to snowball' and 'the snowball effect'.

For space reasons, some editorial selection has had to be made in many such cases. Thus, if a phrase is not found at the first attempt, a different keyword should be tried – such as a synonym or an antonym, a derivative or related term, or a word from a different part of the phrase. (In a few selected cases two alternative versions of a particular keyword or a particular phrase have been included for ease of reference.)

Hyphenated and unhyphenated compound words that are not tabulated as such will be found shown under their components. In practice, the words 'one', 'someone', and so on (used for convenience in the listings) can be replaced by other appropriate words – nouns or pronouns, and so on.

The subsidiary lists in the thematic section (Part II) are each in alphabetical order of the keyword relevant to the category concerned. This approach should assist readers who wish to locate metaphors momentarily forgotten. Where appropriate, a phrase is included in more than one category or even more than once in the same category. The lists themselves are in alphabetical order of category.

The subsidiary lists in the thesaurus (Part III) are each in alphabetical order of the full metaphor in the form in which it appears in Part I. The lists themselves are in alphabetical order of subject area.

This book is essentially a practical work, more concerned with examples of metaphors actually being encountered in daily use rather than with the obscure theories of metaphor devised by some academic commentators. Writers – whether amateurs or professionals, whether using existing metaphors or coining new ones, and whether setting out to do so deliberately or acting subconsciously – are not really assisted by theoretical considerations. Nor is such theory of much interest to readers coming across metaphors, whether or not they understand the underlying message.

Borderline Cases

A number of phrases such as 'to jump at the opportunity', 'to swallow one's pride', 'to sift the evidence' and 'to have a sweet tooth' contain some words used literally as well as other words employed figuratively. Other examples are 'to be bankrupt of ideas', 'to shoulder the blame', 'to sing someone's praises', 'not to mince words' and 'a passport to success'. In such cases, only the figurative components have usually been treated as giving rise to tabulated keywords – although, for ease of reference, some exceptions to this principle were made.

One of the difficulties faced by compilers of dictionaries such as this one is how to draw a clearcut and unambiguous dividing line between words having more than one literal meaning and words used figuratively. For example, although the verb 'to stand' has a primary literal meaning of 'to have or take up an upright position', it also has over twenty secondary meanings, found in expressions such as 'to stand on one's dignity', 'to stand up for one's rights', 'to stand a case over', 'to stand firm', 'to stand for tax reform', 'to stand on ceremony', 'to stand one's ground', and so on. Most expressions of this type have been regarded as being literal, in contradistinction to expressions which can – and are intended to – convey a mental picture of an erect person, such as 'to stand up and be counted', 'to stand out from the crowd', and 'to stand on one's own two feet'.

Common Keywords

The most common keywords relate to the parts of the human body – 'head', 'hand', 'eye', 'back', 'heart', 'foot', 'ear', 'blood', and so on. Some of these words are, of course, also used in other contexts – for example, 'head' in 'head of steam', 'head of the pack', the 'head of a nail', 'heads and tails' on coins, heads of animals, and so on. The noun 'hand' is also used in three different senses – a part of the human body; an employee or worker; and the cards dealt to a player in a game of cards. There is also the verb 'to hand'.

Among the tabulated metaphors, the most common noun that is not related to the human body is 'water', and the animal referred to most often is, unsurprisingly, the dog. Phrases containing these very common keywords might, in some cases, be found more easily if the search is based on one of the secondary keywords.

More Background

This chapter opened with an attempt to define what a metaphor really is. The author of this work felt that it might be more helpful to readers to illustrate the concept by putting a few familiar examples together. This led him to create the 'Every Man and his Dog' passage at the front of this book. For those who are wondering just how many metaphors this illustration actually contains, the answer is 35 (not including the heading).

CHAPTER TWO

Sources of Metaphors

The greatest thing by far is to have a command of metaphors

Aristotle
The Poetics

Much matter decocted into a few words

Thomas Fuller
definition of a proverb in
The Worthies of England

Metaphors from Literature

Metaphors abound in poetry, but such a specialised usage is dealt with by many other analysts and is outside the scope of this book.

Many interesting metaphors in contemporary use by the general public have their apparent origins in major (or sometimes minor) literary works – or derived their popularity at least in part from such usages. William Shakespeare was responsible, *inter alia*, for 'something is rotten in the State of Denmark' (in *Hamlet*), 'the devil can cite scripture for his purpose' and 'to want one's pound of flesh' (both in *The Merchant of Venice*). The picturesque euphemism for sexual intercourse, 'to make the beast with two backs', comes from *Othello*. Of course, other Shakespearian passages, such as 'all the world's a stage', are sometimes quoted by people, but these have not really passed into the modern language as living metaphors.

Cervantes contributed 'to tilt at windmills' and 'neither fish, flesh nor good red herring' (both from *Don Quixote*). Hans Christian Andersen wrote a story entitled 'The Ugly Duckling', and the expression 'curate's egg' dates back to a *Punch* cartoon, first published in the nineteenth century, which featured a curate's response to his bishop, a response to the effect that parts of his breakfast egg were excellent! The phrase 'to be a bear of very little brain' comes from A. A. Milne's *Winnie-the-Pooh.* Sir Walter Scott wrote 'O, what a tangled web we weave' (in a line continuing 'When first we practise to deceive!'). 'To do a Jekyll and Hyde' refers to a book by Robert Louis Stevenson. *Catch 22* and *The Last of the Mohicans* are the titles of novels by Joseph Heller and James Fenimore Cooper respectively. *Box and Cox* is the name of a play.

The concept of somebody being a real Scrooge refers to a character in Charles Dickens' *A Christmas Carol.* 'To be a Svengali' refers to the evil hypnotist of that name in George du Maurier's book, *Trilby.* It is curious that the name of the person who did the controlling has passed into the language, but that of the victim whom he manipulated has not – there is no corresponding metaphor, as logically there could be, 'to be a Trilby'.

Many well-known quotations are, of course, literally true and thus do not rank as metaphors – for example, John Donne's famous 'no man is an island'.

The works of Shakespeare also lend themselves to the coining of brand new expressions. For instance, a writer recently mentioned the 'Macbeth Principle', in reference to the view that if something unpleasant needs to be done, then it should be done without delay (or, as the immortal bard himself put it, 'if it were done when 'tis done, then 'twere well it were done quickly').

Virgil, who died in 19 BC, probably originated the two modern expressions involving the Trojan horse and the Greeks bearing gifts. However, as the so-called Trojan horse was actually a large gift horse full of Greek soldiers used to bring about the fall of Troy, it might have been more logical to refer to it as a Greek horse.

Metaphors from Radio and Television

In more modern times, the electronic media have had some influence – for example, in regard to terms such as 'soap opera'. This refers to low-quality radio or television serials, often based on exaggerated domestic situations of no great importance. The word 'soap' derives from the frequent sponsorship, originally, of such programs by manufacturers of soap products.

A pertinent but very difficult question can be labelled a 'sixty-four thousand dollar question', in reference to a radio quiz show in which an initial $1000 prize doubled with the successful answering of progressively more difficult questions.

Metaphors from Politics

Although politicians no doubt invent numerous metaphors in the course of their daily speech-making, few of these seem to survive.

Oliver Cromwell's famous direction to Sir Peter Lely to paint his portrait 'warts and all' has, however, become a contemporary idiom.

Benjamin Disraeli once told a conference that he was 'on the side of the angels'. Sir Winston Churchill used the term 'the iron curtain', but the Churchillian ring to some of his other sayings has probably militated against their use in ordinary situations. Churchill is also credited with describing his successor, Clement Attlee, as a 'sheep in sheep's clothing'.

In America at the turn of the century, President Theodore Roosevelt coined the oft-quoted expression 'speak softly and carry a big stick'. Two phrases attributed to another United States president – this time Harry S. Truman – are 'if you can't stand the heat, get out of the kitchen' and 'the buck stops here'. The latter expression built up on a much earlier metaphor, 'to pass the buck' which, in turn, referred to the buckhorn knife passed around the table during certain card games in order to indicate who the dealer was.

A well-chosen political metaphor can be remarkably powerful in its psychological effect – consider, for example, the expression 'the cold war'.

Clever politicians can also use existing classical metaphors to good advantage – for instance, Harold Macmillan once said of an opponent: 'If Harold Wilson ever went to school without any boots, it was merely because he was too big for them'. A commentator once described a politician as a 'candidate for the Moscow Circus' – in a clever reference to the large number of backflips that he had made!

Metaphors from Religious Sources

The ancient non-Christian European religions gave rise to a number of current expressions, such as 'to be in the lap of the gods' and 'Delphic'. Primitive tribes in Africa originated the term 'mumbo jumbo', and Australian Aboriginal culture was the source of the expression 'to point the bone' at someone.

Both the Old and the New Testaments of the Bible contribute a number of phrases that are used by both believers and non-believers in circumstances far removed from those of their origin. Some of these phrases sound distinctly biblical, but many others do not. Of course, the Bible in its English translation exists in many different editions. The classical expressions often come from the King James Version. To illustrate, the Old Testament uses the oft-quoted 'to hold out an olive branch', 'the writing is on the wall', 'to cast one's bread upon the waters', and 'an eye for an eye, a tooth for a tooth'. Somewhat surprisingly, the very modern term 'to be in an ivory tower' also comes from this source. Other Old Testament passages which give rise to currently used expressions involve 'forbidden fruit', 'David and Goliath', 'the walls of Jericho', 'a fly in the ointment', 'the tower of Babel', 'the mark of Cain', 'feet of clay', 'manna from heaven', 'the fleshpots of Egypt', and 'the wisdom of Solomon'.

'To sell one's birthright for a mess of pottage' (in other words, for a mere portion of soup) is another contemporary expression – although one that admittedly sounds rather quaint because of its archaic language. The famous test word shibboleth has also passed into the language as the term for an outdated political principle. (It is actually a Hebrew word meaning 'stream in flood'. Its significance in biblical times was that the way in which it was pronounced made it possible to tell an Ephraimite from a member of another tribe, because of his inability to pronounce the initial 'sh' sound in some words correctly.)

The New Testament uses the popular 'by their fruits ye shall know them', and the New Testament also refers to 'a wolf in sheep's clothing', 'the salt of the earth', 'putting one's hand to the plough', 'turning the other cheek', 'killing the fatted calf', being 'a doubting Thomas', 'separating the sheep from the goats', being 'a good Samaritan', 'the road to Damascus', and seeing 'the mote in another person's eye'.

For metaphors which are derived from the Bible, the chapter and verse citations pertaining to them are set out following the definitions given in this book. (However, in the case of expressions which are found in more than one place in the Bible – as is frequently the case – only one of the multiple references is given.)

A special classification called 'Religion and Biblical' is included in Part II. This lists:

- biblical metaphors, regardless of their modern meanings;
- non-biblical metaphors involving words such as *angel, devil, saint, soul, heaven,* and *hell,* regardless of any actual religious origins.

Incidentally, the use of such terms raises an interesting philosophical point that is best illustrated by an example.

Consider the expression 'to send someone to Coventry'. This can clearly be used literally in relation to the English city of that name, and those employing the expression would no doubt believe that such a place really existed. However, the same expression can also be used figuratively in the sense of 'to ignore a person ostentatiously and collectively by way of punishment'. In contrast, whether heaven and hell really exist is a question of faith rather than a matter of fact. In these circumstances, can phrases such as 'manna from heaven' (unexpected benefits) or 'on a cold day in hell' (never) be truly regarded as metaphors by those who do not ascribe any literal meaning to the words 'heaven' or 'hell'?

On a different aspect, religious practices have also inspired some interesting figurative expressions – for example, 'every Pancake Tuesday' (only on occasions). This refers to Shrove Tuesday, the day before the start of Lent in the Christian calendar, when pancakes are traditionally eaten.

Metaphors Based on Historical Incidents

Various expressions from history are listed under that heading in Part II.

Even now, an unrealistic financial venture can be described as being a 'South Sea bubble', in reference to the time when a prospectus was issued soliciting funds ' ... for carrying on an undertaking of great advantage, but nobody to know what it is'.

Various eminent persons – including Edmund Burke (1729–97), Thomas Carlyle (1795–1881), and Lord Macaulay (1800–59) – are attributed with dubbing the press the 'fourth estate', a term still in popular use today. The reference was to the three estates of the realm – the Lords Spiritual (the bishops), the Lords Temporal (the peers) and the Commons, which together make up the United Kingdom parliament. The implication was that the press was equally powerful, by virtue of the enormous influence that it could assert.

Metaphors Based on Legal Precepts

A number of expressions relating to the law are listed under that heading in Part II.

The term 'scot free' refers to the local rates or taxes formerly payable by the inhabitants of an English borough, which were known as 'scot and lot'. The expression has no connection with Scotland.

The relatively modern term, 'rule of thumb' – meaning a simple yet useful approximation – is often said to come from the old English common law principle that a man could not beat his wife with a stick any thicker than the diameter of his own thumb. However, this appears to be a good example of *folk etymology*.

Another suggestion is that the term comes from the brewing industry. In the days before thermometers, brewers were supposed to have gauged the temperature of the fermenting liquor with their thumbs (in the same way as mothers often test the temperature of their baby's bath water with their elbows). However, the thumb is not particularly sensitive, and the range of temperatures for fermentation between 'too cool' and 'too hot' is quite small.

The more likely explanation is that the saying comes from the length of the first joint of the thumb, which is about an inch – in much the same way as twelve inches were given the name 'foot' because of the use of that limb as a rough measuring instrument.

Metaphors from Heraldry

Metaphors derived from heraldry are comparatively rare and those that exist are not without their controversy.

For instance, the phrase 'blue ribbon' (of superb quality) probably refers to the insignia of the Order of the Garter, the highest of the ancient British Orders of Chivalry. However, many heraldry experts feel that the expression really refers to the ribands used in agricultural shows or at race meetings rather than to the blue ribbons worn by knights on ceremonial occasions.

The 'blot on the escutcheon' (a blemish on a person's character, in reference to one of nine possible marks of disgrace placed on a shield in earlier days) is better known in heraldry as an 'abatement of honour'. The expression actually refers to the charges (that is, to the designs, figures or symbols) placed on coats of arms to show that the bearer has been guilty of some unknightly conduct or dishonourable action. Few examples were encountered in practice because, understandably enough, men would rather not display arms at all than show their disgrace to the world. Blots were in any case regarded as only temporary, as they could be erased by some compensating deed of honour.

The term 'bar sinister' in reference to illegitimacy has not been regarded as a true metaphor but, in any case, the expression is heraldic nonsense, because bars (horizontal stripes on a coat of arms) can, from their very nature, be neither 'dexter' nor 'sinister'. Furthermore, the various symbols used for denoting bastardy in heraldry include the bend, the baton, and the border – but never the bar.

The Role of Foreign Languages

Although it is not widely realised, some ordinary English words originate from the metaphorical use of certain Latin terms – 'companions', from *cum panis*, people who eat bread together; 'colleagues', from *cum* and *legere*, persons who are chosen with each other; 'to conspire', from *cum* and *spirare*, to breathe together; and so on.

In a few instances, English has actually borrowed current metaphors from a foreign language. The following twelve French phrases are examples of this:

- 'avant garde'
- 'carte blanche'
- 'crème de la crème'
- 'enfant terrible'
- 'faux pas'
- 'tour de force'
- 'bête noire'
- 'coup de grâce'
- 'danse macabre'
- 'esprit de corps'
- 'touché'
- 'volte face'

The Italian *prima donna* and the Latin *sub rosa* are further examples.

In a slightly different class is the Swedish word *smorgasbord* which is used both literally of food and figuratively of other things. Similar remarks also apply to the Latin phrase *post mortem*, which is used both literally as a medical term and figuratively in other contexts. From German comes a chess term, *zugzwang*.

CHAPTER THREE

The Metaphor in Daily Use

The sole aim of the metaphor is to call up a visual image

Aristotle

The intolerable wrestle with words and meanings

T. S. Eliot
Burnt Norton

The Prevalence of Metaphors

Metaphors are so prevalent that if one were to specifically look out for them it would spoil completely one's reading and listening, and thus detract from the author's purpose.

There are only a few areas of writing in which metaphors are excluded deliberately and carefully. Two examples are material prepared specifically for non native speakers and material intended for translation into foreign languages. Another example is legislation and legal documents generally, where precision is essential and where beauty of expression is an unaffordable luxury. Even the modern trend towards 'plain English' drafting does not make metaphors acceptable in such contexts.

Metaphors are, of course, less likely to be used in technical materials such as car or computer manuals than in, say, ordinary conversation or literary works, whether prose or poetry.

Figurative expressions have, on occasion, had their opponents. In 1670, Samuel Parker went so far as to seriously advocate an Act of Parliament actually forbidding the use of 'fulsome and luscious' metaphors in England!

The Graphic Nature of Longer Metaphors

The standard metaphors listed in this book range from single words to longer phrases and, on rare occasions, even to complete sentences (see also Chapter 7).

Many idiomatic expressions depend for their effect on the ideas represented by the *combination* of words rather than by the words individually – consider, for example, the metaphors 'to pour oil on troubled waters', 'lean and hungry', 'a storm in a teacup', and 'to shut the stable door after the horse has bolted'.

Writers can, of course, create graphic messages by incorporating metaphorical ideas into longer passages of their own. For example, the plain 'a chink of light' can be built up into 'a welcome ray of light piercing the gloom'. Or one can express despair or disillusionment by saying: 'we cannot yet see the tunnel, let alone the light at its end'. Alternatively, one can register a protest based on the same metaphor with a phrase on the lines of: 'due to the recent budget cuts the light at the end of the tunnel has just been cut off'.

Again, one can draw attention to the ravages of inflation by sentences such as: 'money saved for a rainy day now buys a much smaller umbrella than it used to'.

Similarly:

- the ever-increasing government regulation, with its many anomalies, can be criticised by pointing out that the 'level playing field is getting more bumpy all the time';
- legislative changes can be ridiculed by labelling them as having been made 'at the stroke of a parliamentary pen';

- unreal ambitions can be put in place by statements such as: 'if you want to paint high ceilings then you need to knock around with the Pope';
- overreaction can be characterised as 'using a water cannon to put out a lighted match';
- incompetence can be rubbished by saying that someone 'could not find an elephant trail in the snow';
- a person's stupidity can be emphasised by commenting that 'the lights are on but no one is home';
- superficial change can be lampooned by words such as: 'you are only calling the rose by another name'; and
- the notion of high quality but at a high cost can be highlighted by describing the law courts as involving a 'Rolls-Royce system of justice'.

The well-known phrase 'waiting for the other shoe to drop' can be expanded by adding further words such as 'especially when dealing with a centipede'. Newspapers can cast doubt on a political process by the use of phrases such as 'potholes in the road to peace'. A barrister discussing the nature of certain evidence once made his point to the court very neatly in the following terms: 'If there is a large elephant on your front doorstep, then it is not a bad idea to take notice of it, even if you cannot weigh it exactly'.

Taking particular care can be described as 'checking whether every *i* has been dotted and making sure that every *t* is crossed'. A narrow or unexpected win can be described as 'snatching victory from the jaws of defeat'. A politician once claimed: 'one swallow does not make a summer, but we have seen the first few swallows'.

Original metaphors drawing on contemporary practices can also be very effective. For example, something particularly large or unusual can be described as 'justifying an entry in the *Guinness Book of Records*'.

On a different tack, well-known expressions can also be brought in quite factually. For example: 'The comparison here with merely shifting the deckchairs on the *Titanic* is incontrovertible'.

Short Metaphors

In contrast to the above, there are many effective metaphors that consist basically of only one word, very often a noun.

Some examples of this pattern are:

- 'angel'
- 'avalanche'
- 'backwater'
- 'catalyst'
- 'copycat'
- 'drawcard'
- 'gambit'
- 'hiccup'
- 'witchhunt'
- 'zugzwang'
- 'architect'
- 'avenue'
- 'bedfellow'
- 'chameleon'
- 'draconian'
- 'fiefdom'
- 'heresy'
- 'tsar'
- 'yardstick'

Mixed Metaphors

An anonymous author once wrote 'never mix your drinks or your metaphors', and this accords with the traditional advice on this subject given to young writers. However, mixed metaphors frequently arise in practice without any intention on the part of their creators and without their absurdity necessarily distracting readers.

For example, a government official investigating a fraud case was recently reported as saying: 'When the music stops the house of cards collapses and the emperor is found to be wearing no clothes'.

Again, a politician has criticised his opponents for 'orchestrating the emasculation' of a particular law.

A newspaper even reported recently that a person's testimony had 'opened up a Pandora's floodgate of worms'.

An employer told his employee: 'You have cooked your goose and you must now lie in it'.

A theatre critic once asked rhetorically: 'Just how many swan songs can a lame duck deliver?'

The most frequently quoted mixed metaphor comes from a speech by Sir Boyle Roche to the Irish parliament two hundred years ago: 'Mr Speaker, I smell a rat; I see him forming in the air and darkening the sky; but I'll nip him in the bud.'

One further example: 'While the iron is hot, stay on your toes, keep the ball rolling, and don't throw a spanner in the works.'

Of course, even a single metaphor can sound absurd – for example, a reference to the Yiddish Art Theatre as a 'Mecca for Jewish theatre-goers'.

Further examples of an unintended clash of ideas are found in the following sentences:

- 'The whole chain of events consists entirely of missing links.'
- 'The officials kept the boatrace on an even keel.'

It is also possible to deliberately create amusing results by twisting and parodying commonly used metaphors, as in: 'Mr Smith is all *tip* and no *iceberg*; he always has his head buried under the desk'.

The lists in this book will provide raw material for party games (see Appendix 3), and also for scriptwriters seeking to achieve comic effects by stringing together chains of unrelated or inconsistent metaphors, as in the following two illustrative passages:

- 'Keep your back to the wall, your shoulder to the wheel, your ear to the ground, your nose to the grindstone, your eye out for trouble, your chin up, your head down, and your feet firmly on the ground.'
- 'Our staff get exercise by jumping to conclusions, flying off the handle, carrying things too far, juggling the books, dodging responsibility, and pushing their luck.'

Metaphors in Transition

Sometimes expressions which originally started off in figurative usage later on make a complete transition and, over time, virtually become accepted words. For instance:

- 'to be petrified'
- 'to unmask someone'
- 'to be in the limelight'
- 'to have overtones'
- 'to set up a smokescreen'
- 'to be in the pipeline'
- 'a watchdog role'
- 'a snowball effect'
- 'a pastor and his flock' (both components having become accepted metaphors)

Possible further examples of this trend include the nouns:

- 'a backlash'
- 'a catalyst'
- 'a pipedream'
- 'a whitewash'
- 'a framework'
- 'an avalanche'
- 'a loophole'
- 'a crusade'
- 'a sounding-board'
- 'a nightmare'
- 'a yardstick'
- 'a stalemate'
- 'a blueprint'
- 'a bottleneck'
- 'a watershed'
- 'a scenario'

- 'a stumbling block'
- 'a stereotype'
- 'a bread-winner'
- 'a nosedive'
- 'a figurehead'
- 'fanfare'
- 'chickenfeed'
- 'imprimatur'
- 'a footing'
- 'a scapegoat'
- 'a windfall'
- 'a deadline'
- 'heresy'
- 'pecking order'
- 'spectrum'

The adjectives:

- 'pedestrian'
- 'apocryphal'
- 'short-sighted'
- 'fruitless'
- 'halfbaked'

And the verbs:

- 'to encapsulate'
- 'to crystallise'
- 'to choreograph'
- 'to undermine a person'
- 'to hand-pick'
- 'to pontificate'
- 'to crucify a person'
- 'to backfire'
- 'to polarise'
- 'to highlight'
- 'to ferret something out'
- 'to paralyse a city'
- 'to back pedal'
- 'to pre-empt something'

Other such verbs are mentioned later in the section headed 'Metaphors Involving a Change to the Parts of Speech' in Chapter 7.

It seems likely that many of the other terms in this book, particularly those lacking short synonyms, are heading in the same direction and will become 'regular' words in due course.

CHAPTER FOUR

Metaphors in Various Categories

Words are, of course, the most powerful drug used by mankind

Rudyard Kipling

That's nothing to what I could say if I chose

Lewis Carroll
(as spoken by the Duchess in)
Alice's Adventures in Wonderland

The Thematic Section

The different sets of tabulations in the Thematic Section (Part II) reflect the attempt at classification referred to in Chapter 1. They are included mainly as a matter of general interest, but also because, in some cases, the category gives a shorthand indication as to the origin of the metaphor concerned.

Of necessity, the categorisation process involves the making of a number of arbitrary decisions. There is, for example, some overlap among certain animals and plants viewed as such, or alternatively regarded as food, or alternatively again as a product of farming.

Some words were accordingly allocated to the *nearest* available category. However, despite this roughness, the examples go some way towards demonstrating the unevenness of the literal subject matter that gives rise to the phrases listed. The comments below will serve as a brief general introduction to this aspect, but the detailed listings really speak for themselves. Some metaphors are included under more than one heading. For example, 'to hold a sword at someone's throat' appears under both 'war and military' and 'human body'.

Sport

Understandably, analogies based on sport are fairly common:

- 'to be given riding instructions'
- 'to be slow off the mark'
- 'to hit someone below the belt'
- 'to throw in the towel'
- 'to get a guernsey'
- 'hook, line, and sinker'
- 'track record'
- 'to be right behind the eight ball'
- 'to play by the book'
- 'to give a blow-by-blow description'
- 'to jump the gun'
- 'saved by the bell'
- 'to be a master stroke'

to name just a few.

Cricket terms are particularly prevalent in the countries favouring that game. For example:

- 'it's not cricket'
- 'to have had a good innings'
- 'until stumps are drawn'
- 'to open the batting'
- 'to be on a sticky wicket'
- 'to have the runs on the board'
- 'to let something go to the keeper'
- 'to break one's duck'

- 'to hit someone for six'
- 'the second eleven'

and so on.

The Human Body

However, the most frequent references involve parts of the human body. Over a thousand different examples are tabulated, including:

- 'to scratch one's head'
- 'to twist someone's arm'
- 'to burn one's fingers'
- 'to have broad shoulders'
- 'to keep an ear to the ground'
- 'to step on someone's toes'

and so on.

Some people get 'itchy feet' whereas others merely get 'cold feet'.

About 21 per cent of all entries relate to just this one important category.

Animals

The next most popular category is the one based on animals:

- 'to let sleeping dogs lie'
- 'to be an ostrich'
- 'to take the bull by the horns'
- 'to throw a cat among the pigeons'
- 'to stir up a hornets' nest'
- 'to buy a pig in a poke'

Then there are 'black sheep', 'red herrings', 'dark horses', 'underdogs', 'sacred cows', 'guinea pigs', 'sacrificial lambs', 'flies in the ointment', 'cans of worms', and the well-known 'dog in the manger'.

The range of animals found in metaphors is quite uneven. Some less common species – such as giraffes, platypuses, and zebras – are not represented at all.

The term 'animal' has been used in its correct sense, including birds, fish, insects, and so on, and not merely mammals. In some cases it is not clear whether a particular expression refers to human beings or to animals. For example, the analogy in 'to put flesh and bone on something' could have either in mind.

The World of Sail

The era of sailing ships has left its legacy in phrases such as:

- 'to learn the ropes'
- 'to change tack'
- 'to nail one's colours to the mast'
- 'to sail close to the wind'
- 'the calm before the storm'
- 'to trim one's sails'
- 'to be plain sailing'
- 'to take the wind out of someone's sails'
- 'I like the cut of his jib'

There is also the pair of opposites, 'to sail under false colours' and 'to show one's true colours'.

One of the expressions mentioned above, 'to be plain sailing' (to be quite straight forward and very easy), is actually a corruption of 'plane sailing', in reference to navigation by means of a 'plane chart' on which meridians and parallels of latitude are represented by equidistant straight lines, an approximate method that ignores the curvature of the earth and which is therefore simpler for short distances.

Sailing expressions are shown in the 'Nautical' category.

Music

Music is another rich source. Examples include:

- 'to change one's tune'
- 'to sing for one's supper'
- 'to hit a sour note'
- 'to soft pedal'
- 'to be a one-man band'
- 'to face the music'
- 'to have another string to one's bow'

There are also two that are rather similar in meaning – 'to beat one's drum' and 'to blow one's own trumpet' – presumably in contrast to the position of the person who 'plays second fiddle' to somebody else.

The listings include two similar examples based on the verb 'to strike' and the adjective 'right' – namely, 'to strike the right chord' (to appeal successfully to someone's emotions) and 'to strike the right key/note' (to make comments that set the appropriate tone in a speech or conversation).

Whereas these definitions have been given to demonstrate the shades of meaning that are possible, the phrases may well be being used more-or-less interchangeably in practice.

Other variations to this theme are 'to strike a responsive chord' (to get a favourable reaction to a proposal) and the plain 'to strike a chord' (to sound familiar or to recall something to mind). The last-mentioned idea can also be rendered as 'to ring a bell'.

Commerce

Some expressions have come into wider usage from the world of commerce. These include:

- 'A1 at Lloyds'
- 'a Rolls-Royce solution'
- 'the other side of the coin'
- 'to show dividends'

- 'to give someone a blank cheque'
- 'to be below par'

There is also the concept of something 'not adding up'.

The terms 'to burn one's fingers' and 'to fly a kite' – the latter in the sense of issuing uncovered cheques in the hope of covering them before clearance – have moved in the reverse direction, although this particular phrase is also used in a different way in politics (the testing of public reaction to contemplated legislation by leaking broad details of it to the media in advance of an official announcement).

Amusements Generally

Apart from sport and music, as discussed above, many other forms of popular amusement also are, understandably enough, noteworthy sources of metaphors – for instance, art, theatre, circuses, gambling, and various indoor games such as cards and chess.

The origins of some of the expressions relating to cards that are in popular use today might not be obvious on the surface. For example, a 'showdown' occurs in poker games when the players put their cards down on the table face-up to show the strength of their hands, and 'level pegging' refers to the marking of the score with pegs in cribbage. 'To be a laid-down misère' refers to the declaration in certain card games undertaking to win no tricks. Two other cards phrases, 'passing the buck' and 'the buck stops here', have already been mentioned in Chapter 2.

Statistics of Usage

The five largest of the Part II categories in a representative sample of metaphors were as follows:

1. Human Body (21% of total)
2. Animals (8% of total)
3. Food and Drink (7% of total)

4. Farming (6% of total)
5. Sport (5% of total)

Such statistics have a fascination of their own – although admittedly their practical use is probably confined to being used as throwaway lines in conversations over dinner and the like.

However, these figures do provide an interesting sociological commentary on the activities that most readily spring to mind when writers and speakers wish to make a point by using an analogy. In most cases the association will be readily understood by readers and listeners with a twenty-first century English-speaking cultural background.

CHAPTER FIVE

Metaphors Expressing Ideas in Certain Subject Areas

Let thy speech be short, comprehending much in few words

Ecclesiasticus 32:8

Be not the slave of words

Thomas Carlyle
Sartor Resartus

The Thesaurus

The Thesaurus (Part III) is, to some extent, the reverse of the Dictionary (Part I). Instead of starting with metaphors and then presenting their meanings, it starts with base words (summarising the meanings) and then sets out the various metaphors relevant to the broad subject-area concerned.

To illustrate further, the expression 'to be a dog in the manger' – which was included in the 'animal' category in Part II because it involved a (hypothetical) dog – is shown in Part III under the subject area 'refusal and rejection'.

Sometimes for convenience several different subject areas are shown together, where the base word has more than one meaning. More than a hundred subject areas, arranged alphabetically from 'abuse' to 'worry', have been adopted – although, admittedly, this particular categorisation is somewhat arbitrary.

To take another example, 'taking a risk' is an area in which many metaphorical expressions abound, although they all have slightly different connotations:

- 'to go out on a limb'
- 'to take the plunge'
- 'to go through fire and water'
- 'to chance one's arm'
- 'to play Russian roulette'
- 'to be sitting on a volcano'
- 'to stick one's neck out'
- 'to play with dynamite'
- 'to rush in where angels fear to tread'
- 'to jump in feet first'
- 'to take a punt'

and so on.

The opposite of this concept is 'to play it safe'. These and various other such phrases are shown under 'Risk' in Part III.

Of course, the main alphabetical list in Part I also contains some entries that deal with subject concepts – for instance, phrases relating to 'newness' can be obtained by looking up 'new' and 'old' in Part I, and some phrases implying completeness will be found under 'all' and 'every'.

In some cases, the listings contain both positive and negative usages. Thus entries actually relating to 'Lack of Enthusiasm' will be found under the general heading 'Enthusiasm', and so on.

The subject areas chosen for tabulation are set out alphabetically in the Table of Contents. As there is some overlap between the subject areas, users interested in a particular subject might need to consult more than one list – depending on the shade of meaning desired. For example, it might be appropriate to look at the two lists headed 'Risk' and 'Danger'; or alternatively at the two lists headed 'Risk' and 'Chance'.

Again, the unevenness of metaphorical usage causes some surprise. For instance, why should there be nearly three times as many expressions for the *end* of various activities as for the *start* of something? Actually, some metaphors (for example, 'big bang') can be used for either meaning – depending on the context.

'Difficulty' as a Concept

To take a further example, the concept of 'difficulty' gives rise to a great many figurative expressions. On the first encounter with a difficulty one 'runs into a road block', 'strikes a snag', or 'runs into heavy weather'. In fact, one 'has a job in front of one' and might need 'to put one's thinking cap on' to solve the problem.

If the difficulty is shared with other people, they are all 'in the same boat'. As one prepares to overcome the difficulty, one decides that 'the show must go on' or one 'sharpens one's axe' or, alternatively, 'battens down the hatches'.

The actual attempt to overcome the difficulty involves 'grasping the nettle', 'taking the bull by the horns', 'grabbing the devil by the tail', or 'biting the bullet'.

After that, one 'jumps the hurdle', 'irons out' the problem, or 'makes a good fist' of trying to fix it. If one fails, one 'sinks deeper into the mire' (or 'into the mud'). If one succeeds, one has 'fallen on one's feet'. One is then 'out of the woods' and can 'heave a sigh of relief'.

To take unfair advantage of someone already in difficulty is 'to kick a man when he is down'. To desert a person who is in difficulty is 'to leave him in the lurch'. A period fraught with difficulties is 'a sticky patch'. Something particularly difficult can be said to be 'sheer murder'.

There are well over a dozen different expressions for actually 'being in difficulty'. Some involve shades of additional meaning:

- from (a): to just being agitated because one is in a slight muddle;
- through (b): to being stuck in a delicate situation or experiencing bad luck;
- all the way to (c): to facing near despair because some task is beyond one's capabilities.

In rough order of severity (least at the top to most at the bottom) these expressions are as follows:

- 'to be in a pickle'
- 'to be in a jam'
- 'to be out of one's depth'
- 'to have a hard row to hoe'
- 'to have the cards' (or 'the odds') 'stacked against one'
- 'to be in a quagmire'
- 'to be in a stew'
- 'to be in a hole'
- 'to be on a sticky wicket'
- 'to be pushing uphill' (or 'fighting an uphill battle')
- 'to be in deep water' (or 'in hot water')
- 'to be in the soup'

A difficult query is a 'sixty-four thousand dollar question'. If, on the other hand, one encounters no difficulties at all, then one is said to be having a 'dream run'.

The above illustrations do not, of course, exhaust all the possibilities.

Money Matters

Part III lists a number of expressions relating to 'money' under that heading.

Financial journals use ordinary metaphors all the time. For example, share prices can 'head south' or they can either 'skyrocket' or 'go into a tailspin', takeovers are made 'with much fanfare', and new chief executives 'take the helm'. Special metaphors with technical meanings also exist. For example, securities held by investors can be said to be 'above the water' (above cost price).

Political allusions to spending taxpayers' funds occur in expressions such as 'to pork barrel' and 'to engage in pump-priming'. For a humorous effect, large sums of money can be referred to as 'telephone numbers'.

The actual word 'money' used in its literal sense is found in the partly figurative phrases 'money for jam', 'to see the colour of someone's money', 'to have money burning a hole in one's pocket', 'putting one's money where one's mouth is', 'money down the drain', and 'the money is rolling in'.

When a purely figurative expression for 'money' is desired, words such as 'pocket', 'purse', or 'penny' are often used, as in:

- 'to have deep pockets'
- 'to line one's pocket'
- 'to button up one's purse'
- 'to cost a pretty penny'

However, not all terms fall into this pattern. People can be 'in the black'. They can also 'feather their nest', or they might 'burn their fingers'.

Not surprisingly, a number of metaphors use the word 'gold'.

Sometimes colours are used in conjunction with the word 'dollar' to convey particular ideas. For example:

- 'pink dollars' – profits generated from marketing goods and services to the homosexual community
- 'blue dollars' – profits generated from the sale of soft pornography
- 'grey dollars' – profits generated from marketing goods and services to older persons

Strange things happen when a country's sterling currency is decimalised. Phrases such as 'in for a penny, in for a pound', 'the penny dropped', 'a ha'p'orth of tar', 'penny-pinching', and the ungrammatical 'he doesn't have two pennies to rub together', remain unchanged.

On the other hand, 'to throw in one's six-pennies' worth' (sometimes rendered as '... one's two bobs' worth') becomes 'to throw in one's two cents' worth', whereas 'to have two bob each way' is converted to the version 'to have fifty cents each way' – hardly close decimal equivalents.

Similarly, expressions involving imperial distances or weights do not always get metricated. For example:

- 'to drain every ounce out of something'
- 'to go the extra mile'
- 'a milestone'
- 'to stand out a mile'
- 'to get mileage out of some matter'
- 'a yardstick'
- 'not to give an inch'
- 'to inch forward'

Some expressions in current use even involve obsolete units of measurement. For example, 'give him an inch and he will take an ell', in reference to an old unit of length (45 inches or 1143 millimetres). Of course, everyone with even 28.3 grams of common sense realises that *exact* metric conversions would not be appropriate in all circumstances.

Metaphors Used Euphemistically

Metaphors can be used as a device for being tactful or to soften a harsh message. For example, instead of saying to a person 'you are an unmitigated liar' one can put it more gently – but just as effectively – in the form of 'that is just a cock-and-bull story'.

Similarly one can say 'a cobbler should stick to his last' (rather than saying 'you are a fool for trying this'); 'your friend is a slippery customer' (rather than 'your friend tried to cheat me'); and 'it was under your very nose' (rather than 'you are an idiot for not spotting the obvious'). Again, in a business context, a short reference to a 'new broom' can sound much more positive than a formal utterance about 'changed management practices'.

Whether this tactic really works, and whether the words sound less 'hard' can, of course, depend on other factors – such as accompanying the message by suitable body language, by a smile, or by a twinkle in the eye of the speaker.

Other euphemisms will be found in Part III under headings such as:

- 'Mistake' – 'to put the cart before the horse', etc.
- 'Naïveté' – 'to be babes in the wood', etc.
- 'Slowness' – 'to drag one's heels', etc.
- 'Stupidity' – 'to put forward a cock-eyed proposal', etc.
- 'Unrealistic Ideas' – 'to have one's head in the clouds', etc.

Some old-established metaphors are no longer in common use because in this enlightened age they are widely regarded as being likely to give offence to certain people. An example of this is the expression 'the nigger in the woodpile' (the factor spoiling an otherwise satisfactory arrangement).

CHAPTER SIX

Selected Case Studies

Proper words in proper places make the true definition of style

Jonathan Swift
Letter to a Young Clergyman

'When I use a word,' Humpty Dumpty said in rather a scornful tone, 'it means just what I choose it to mean – neither more nor less.'

Lewis Carroll
Through the Looking Glass

The Living English Language

The origins of most of the figurative expressions currently in circulation are lost in antiquity and their authors are unknown. However, the heterogeneous nature of English metaphors, and the power that they add to the language, can best be demonstrated by examining some actual cases. The undermentioned illustrations are taken, more or less at random, from the vast collection used to compile this book.

It is, for example, intriguing to note that words which, when taken literally, are quite inoffensive, often acquire not only colour but also pejorative overtones, when engaged as figures of speech – for example, 'to split hairs'.

Many metaphors represent a shorthand way of expressing an idea. However, sometimes the figurative version is longer than the literal one. For example, 'one man's meat is another man's poison' (people's tastes differ) uses seven words rather than only three.

On another tack (!), interesting effects can also be obtained by deliberately misquoting well-known expressions, producing renditions such as 'every silver cloud has a dark lining'.

Sometimes a political happening can start off an expression which then acquires a much more general meaning. For example, 'to have a nuclear-ships policy', in reference to the United States' policy of neither confirming nor denying a proposition (in the original case, as to whether a particular ship is carrying nuclear arms).

The word 'metaphor' itself can be used in a non-literal way. For example, a film on 'home entertainments and theatre' was given the subtitle 'metaphors of decadence and blurred reality', and one writer coined the phrase 'metaphors of evil' in connection with 'contemporary German literature and the shadow of Nazism'.

It is hard to predict whether any specific newly formed metaphors will survive. For example, a new proprietary drug was released recently to help male patients to get or maintain erections. Thus 'to be handed Viagra' now means 'to be given a new lease of life'. But will that expression last as the novelty of this particular scientific advance wears off?

Again, 'to have more holes than a teenager's jeans' might become meaningless when the particular fashion fad to which it refers disappears.

Computer Aspects

It will be interesting to see whether the new computer technology inspires any additional metaphors for the wider community.

As regards the reverse situation, many computer terms, such as those that follow and some others, are ordinary English words given special meanings, rather than, strictly speaking, figures of speech:

- 'bandwidth';
- 'bit'
- 'boot'
- 'browser'
- 'bug'
- 'card'
- 'chip'
- 'client'
- 'cookie'
- 'disk'
- 'drive'
- 'environment'
- 'fingerprint'
- 'firewall'
- 'flag'
- 'frames'
- 'gateway'
- 'handshake'
- 'heartbeat'
- 'host'
- 'icon'
- 'master'
- 'memory'
- 'mouse'
- 'packet'
- 'patch'
- 'path'
- 'portal'
- 'proxy'
- 'sandbox'
- 'site'
- 'slave'
- 'software'
- 'surfing'
- 'syntax'
- 'virus'
- 'web'
- 'wild card'
- 'window'
- 'word'
- 'worm'

Perhaps the term 'garbage' is a true metaphor – 'garbage in, garbage out' or 'GIGO' (if there are errors in the input data there will inevitably be errors in the output data).

The term 'Trojan horse' (a type of computer virus) is an interesting example of a computer metaphor made out of an ordinary English metaphor.

Words can also go the full circle – for example, 'firewall'. Literally, this means a partition erected in a building – a device designed to prevent the spread of a fire from one side to the other. As a computer metaphor, it means a special computer program which is designed to prevent access by unauthorised persons into a database kept electronically and the like. As an ordinary English metaphor made out of this computer metaphor, it now refers to any device designed to keep private confidential data even in a manually maintained database.

The word *software* (meaning a computer program) is, despite its appearance, actually an artificially coined term of comparatively recent origin, based on the long-established word *hardware* (meaning building materials, tools, and so on in ordinary usage, but also adopted by the computer industry to mean the physical components of a computer, as distinct from the programs).

The metric prefix *giga*, meaning '1 000 000 000 times', is rarely used in ordinary conversation, but is encountered by computer users in regard to gigabyte drives and the like. This has inspired phrases in other contexts – organisations no longer make superprofits or even megaprofits; instead they now make gigaprofits.

The term 'butterfly effect' has passed into the language. It comes from chaos theory and was discovered by a meteorologist (Edward Lorenz) in 1960 when doing computer simulations. It is said that a butterfly's light-winged flight in one part of the world can set off an avalanche of effects that lead to hurricanes and other weather events somewhere else. In figurative use it refers to the way complex systems can be radically affected by minute changes in their parameters.

Some further examples of figurative computer terms are set out in Appendix 2.

Less-pleasing metaphors surfaced in a recent press release from a leading computer company. It read as follows: 'The integration of Microsoft Mail with HP DeskManager allows customers of HP DeskManager to migrate their desktops to Microsoft Windows while leveraging their existing investments in an enterprise-wide messaging backbone'.

These days the human brain is often likened to a computer. In earlier times a different analogy would have been used. The brain might, for example, have been described as a type of telephone exchange.

The phenomenon often called the 'millennium bug' or 'Y2K' refers to the fact that many computer systems treat calendar years according to their last two digits and thus think that '00' means '1900' rather than '2000'. Many people were concerned that this 'bug' would seriously disrupt commerce and industry around 1 January 2000 and would have all sorts of other unpleasant consequences – for example, aircraft falling out of the sky and the like. Large sums of money and many hours of professional time were devoted to fixing this problem and, in the end, the changeover from 1999 to 2000 passed relatively smoothly.

However, from the perspective of a lexicographer, the expression 'millennium bug' was very poorly formed, for no less than three different reasons:

- the feature was not a 'bug' at all, as it was created quite deliberately to conserve space;
- it related to the change of century (two digits) rather than to the change of millennium (three digits); and
- the main problems were expected to occur twelve months before the true start of the third millennium on 1 January 2001 anyway.

The media sometimes referred to this problem as a 'virus' – which was even less accurate than 'bug'.

Duplications

On occasions, a whole series of commonly used metaphors is evolved to express just one simple idea – such as 'to be within a bull's roar of something', 'to be within a hair's breadth of something', and 'to be within an ace of something'. A similar phenomenon is seen when speakers refer to only 'a postage stamp' (or alternatively 'a cigarette paper', or alternatively again 'a wafer' or 'a tissue') separating either two objects or two close contestants in a race.

Again, wishful thinking has inspired several different phrases – those referring to the impossibility of turning the clock back, of unscrambling an omelette, or of putting the genie back in the bottle.

Some further examples of this pattern are 'to miss the boat', 'to miss the bus', and 'to miss the train' – three transport phrases which all mean much the same thing. Similarly, 'to hold a winning hand', 'to hold all the aces', and 'to hold the trump card' are three phrases from the world of cards which, again, have an identical meaning.

One can also be in something 'up to one's shoulder', 'up to one's neck', 'up to one's freckles', or even 'up to one's eyeballs'.

There are also many pairs of duplicates. To name just a few:

- 'to give a hand' and 'to lend a hand';
- 'to escape by the skin of one's teeth' and 'to escape by the skin of one's nose';
- 'to bore someone to tears' and 'to bore someone to death';
- 'a thorn in one's side' and 'a thorn in one's flesh';
- 'to tremble in one's shoes' and 'to quake in one's boots'; and
- 'a drop in the ocean' and 'a drop in the bucket'.

One common metaphor even exists in at least four separate forms: 'to clasp at straws', 'to clutch at straws', 'to grasp at straws', and 'to catch at straws'.

'To be on the wrong tack' (another sailing term) parallels 'to be on the wrong track' and 'to be on the wrong tram' (from on-shore activities).

Plays on Words

Although similes, in general, are outside the scope of this book, special mention should be made of those which amount to a play on words rather than a true comparison – for example, 'to charge like a wounded bull' (to impose excessive prices) and 'to be flat out like a lizard drinking' (to be hard at work).

Emphasis

Particular attention is drawn to a series of phrases that contain some words used quite literally in combination with figurative fancy expressions and elaborations inserted purely for the purpose of greater emphasis. Some examples of this pattern are as follows:

- 'to vanish into thin air'
- 'crystal clear'
- 'to be the end of the road'
- 'to confront something head on'
- 'to save a bundle'
- 'why in the world?'
- 'in every nook and cranny'
- 'short and sweet'
- 'at a break-neck pace'
- 'every man and his dog'
- 'to get away with murder'
- 'a long time between drinks'
- 'to refuse point blank'
- 'no way!'
- 'enough to sink a battleship'
- 'alive and kicking'

- 'the last of the Mohicans'
- 'to go post haste'
- 'to cost an arm and a leg'

Again, it is sometimes said that prices are 'going through the roof' or that some innovation is 'the hottest thing since sliced bread'. Incidentally, this raises the intriguing question: 'What was the hottest thing *before* sliced bread was invented?'

In a slightly different class is the picturesque insult in which a person is described as being 'lower than a snake's belly'!

Some metaphors used by way of elaboration really add little of substance – for example, 'for my sins'.

The Need for Precision

In many metaphors, the precise words do not matter – and synonyms or other variations according to the speaker's preferences can readily be used. In other cases, however, the exact word is essential. For example, the two words 'street' and 'road' are not interchangeable in either direction in:

- 'to be streets ahead';
- 'not to be in the same street as someone';
- 'to be on the right road'; and
- 'to be at the cross roads'.

Similarly, something can be 'up one's street' or more commonly 'up one's alley', but never 'up one's road'.

Again, a person can 'pull himself up' either 'by his bootstraps' or 'by his own shoelaces'. But a person is 'British to his bootstraps' without such an alternative.

Overlap

Is a 'shot in the dark' really different from a 'stab in the dark'? There are, no doubt, differences in the shades of meaning that might make one term or the other better in some particular circumstances. In the listings, the former has been defined as a 'hopeful attempt at the unknown; a sheer guess', and the latter simply as a 'sheer guess'.

In the context of a living language spoken by millions of people, it should not be assumed that clearcut distinctions are made every time people use these expressions. These remarks apply not only to the specific illustration just given but also in the general case.

Again, some rather similar combinations of words occur in two or more really quite distinct metaphors. Thus, 'that is a fine kettle of fish' (that is a terrible muddle) can be distinguished from 'that is a very different kettle of fish' (that is something very dissimilar).

Again, 'to undermine a person' (to injure his or her reputation) has only a small overlap with 'to undermine a proposal' (to sabotage it).

'That is all water under the bridge' (that no longer matters) is not quite the same as 'a lot of water has passed under the bridge since they came' (much has happened since they came).

'To give someone a hand' (to assist a person) is significantly different from 'to give someone a free hand' (to authorise a person to act as that person sees fit).

'To rekindle an old flame' (to inspire the reinstatement of a former loving relationship) might even refer to 'an old flame' (a former lover).

'An activity on the horizon' (one expected, but not immediately) differs both from 'a cloud on the horizon' (a faint indication of possible future trouble), and from the worse still 'black clouds on the horizon' (anticipated bad news).

A person can either 'see the light' (understand the real situation) or 'see the light at the end of the tunnel' (perceive relief at the imminent end of a period of prolonged difficulty), and a document can 'see the light of day' (be made public). Again, a matter can be 'brought to light' (drawn to general attention) so that those responsible can 'shed light on it' (give explanations about it).

A person can 'keep his or her own eyes open for something' (be on the lookout for useful information) or can 'open someone else's eyes to something' (alert another person to the truth of some matter). A person can also receive a real 'eye-opener' (surprise) or can go into something 'with his or her eyes wide open' (fully conscious of the ramifications).

The expression 'to put one's feet up' (to relax) can be contrasted with the expression 'to put one's foot down' (to assert one's authority and insist on something).

In the area of near slang, 'to have a shot at someone' (to tease a person) is very different from 'to have a shot at something' (to make an attempt at achieving some goal).

Negative Expressions

A great number of rather colloquial expressions seems to work only in the negative. For instance:

- 'it is not the end of the world'
- 'he is not Robinson Crusoe'
- 'that is not cricket'
- 'it does not matter a row of beans'
- 'that is not my cup of tea'
- 'he held a gun with no bullets'
- 'it's not over until the fat lady sings'
- 'don't hold your breath for the outcome'
- 'you're not here to win prizes'
- 'she didn't give an inch'
- 'I would not touch that with a forty-foot barge pole'
- 'he didn't miss a beat'
- 'he is not the only pebble on the beach'
- 'don't lose any sleep over this'

- 'he did not turn a hair'
- 'she did not bat an eyelid'
- 'I would not know him from Adam'
- 'he did not put a foot wrong'
- 'I cannot for the life of me ... '
- 'you haven't a leg to stand on'
- 'nothing is sacred'
- 'not for love or money'
- 'he didn't have a dog's chance'
- 'she didn't pull any punches'
- 'to make no bones about it ... '

In most cases the corresponding affirmative phrase would just not be idiomatic.

However, it is of interest that the negative expression 'that cuts no ice with me' does have a positive version – namely, 'that cuts little ice with me'.

On a slightly different tack, the expression 'he is no angel' (he has many faults) is not at all the opposite of 'he is an angel' (he is very helpful).

Nonsense Expressions

Then there are also some 'nonsense' metaphors, such as:

- 'since the year dot'
- 'to move at a rate of knots'
- 'to the *n*th degree'
- 'to increase exponentially'
- 'to exceed something by several orders of magnitude'

These are all expressions which, when taken literally, are actually quite meaningless. To explain further, 'exponential growth' does not mean 'fast growth'. Rather, the term refers to growth proportional to the size of an existing amount – for example, money growing at compound interest. The actual *rate* of growth can be quite small. Again, the expression 'to the *n*th degree' is not, as popularly thought, a synonym for 'to the utmost extent'. The term refers to a mathematical proposition which is true for all values of *n*.

'To fly in the face of my specific orders' contains not one but, rather, two quite absurd terms.

There is also the expression 'with 20/20 hindsight', which sounds more impressive and plausible than is really justified.

The television phrase, 'back to back', in reference to two programs screened on after the other, is also absurd. The reality is that the *end* of the first program is adjacent to the *start* of the second, not that the two ends are near each other.

Then there is the curious thought that a sphere can actually have corners – an inherent contradiction that is found in the popular expression 'the four corners of the globe'.

There is also the interesting 'to eat humble pie' (to be prepared to humiliate oneself and apologise), which actually confuses the concept of humility with the entrails of a deer – the *umble pie* once eaten by persons of low rank.

In a different category is the phrase 'to compound the felony'. Despite the way this metaphor is widely used, this legal term does not really mean 'to make matters worse'. Compounding a felony is actually the crime of agreeing for money not to prosecute a person for felony. In reality it is therefore an offence by a different person – not a second and worse offence by the original culprit.

Colloquialisms

Some phrases can be used orally – although they would be regarded as unacceptable in some literary pieces. For instance:

- 'stiff cheese'
- 'fair crack of the whip'

- 'shoot!' (in the sense of 'speak')
- 'if I've told you once I've told you a thousand times'
- 'buzz off'
- 'I'll nail him'
- 'I have to fly'
- 'he can get lost'
- 'between you and me and the gatepost'
- 'you can go and jump in the lake'
- 'you can eat your heart out'
- 'more power to your elbow'
- 'that is your funeral'
- 'keep your shirt on!'
- 'that is on your head'

Another 'negative only' expression, 'no dice', is also in the same category.

A rather different example is 'if he were alive today he would turn in his grave'.

Sexist Language

Many metaphors involve sexist language, having been coined long before attention was paid to such matters. Examples include 'the man in the street', 'a man-size job', 'soul brother', 'to separate the men from the boys', 'as every schoolboy knows', and 'he is your man'.

Of course, not every reference to males paints that sex in a good light – consider, for example, the expression 'a man of straw'. However, the relatively few references in metaphors to females tend to be unflattering – for instance, 'witchhunt' and 'it's not over until the fat lady sings'.

The phrase 'to wear the pants' can be used literally of either sex. However, it is often used figuratively of females in order to label the wife as the dominant party in a marriage.

Double Metaphors

The expression 'a back-seat driver' is a rare example of a *double metaphor.* Clearly, the word 'driver' is not being used literally – even when the phrase is employed in the context of motoring. When it is used with the figurative meaning of 'a person seeking to exercise control', the whole phrase becomes yet a further metaphor.

A more modern example is the radio term 'feedback'. Originally it referred to the interaction between amplifiers and speakers, which must have suggested to its early users some analogy to food. The secondary concept, in turn, gave rise to the contemporary meaning of the phrase (a response from a target audience to those trying to influence it) – an analogy based on an analogy.

The word 'cocktail', in the sense of mixed drinks, is clearly a metaphor. However, it can be taken one step further, to represent some other type of mixture in a double metaphor, as in: 'Fast cars and aggressive teenagers make up a dangerous cocktail'.

Words are Fun!

Because of the convention that maps are always drawn with north at the top, it has been customary to talk of 'coming *down* to X' where X is a place which is *south* of a journey's starting point. However, this analogy can be taken one step further. For example, some investors like to refer to share prices as metaphorically 'heading south' when they are falling.

Finally, another curiosity. Sometimes an interesting reversal of the normal pattern occurs. A humorous effect can be achieved by actually employing a commonly used figurative expression in its literal sense – as in the caption to an amusing press photograph published recently. This showed two policemen exchanging their official headgear with two pretty female party-goers wearing Mickey Mouse hats. The imaginative caption was 'If the cap fits ... '

Words are fascinating and their study can be fun. One enthusiast summarised this neatly by creating a bumper sticker reading: 'Metaphors be with you'!

Metaphors can almost be regarded as an art form. Readers who might never have become aware of the multitude of metaphorical usages, even in their own speech will, it is hoped, find the analysis and examples in this book both entertaining and instructive.

CHAPTER SEVEN

Some Grammatical Aspects

Terminological inexactitude

Winston Churchill

And torture one poor word ten thousand ways

John Dryden
Mac Flecknoe

Grammatical Form of the Metaphor

Metaphors can take a great variety of different grammatical forms, including:

- nouns by themselves – for example, 'a figurehead', 'a honeymoon';
- nouns qualified by adjectives – 'a round robin', 'a lame dog';
- adjectives by themselves – 'apocryphal', 'ham-fisted'; and
- adjectival phrases – 'off the cuff', 'for the long haul'.

Nouns qualified by adjectival phrases with or without other adjectives are relatively common:

- 'an ocean full of fish'
- 'a knight in shining armour'
- 'the other side of the coin'
- 'a share of the cake'

- 'a trap for young players'

and so on.

A few metaphors are adverbial phrases:

- 'with a heavy heart'
- 'with a flourish of trumpets'

Or adverbial clauses:

- 'when the chips are down'
- 'when it comes to the crunch'
- 'when one's ship comes in'

Some metaphors are mini-sentences:

- 'his name is mud'
- 'there is no such animal'

Others are exclamations:

- 'chalk it up!'
- 'tell it to the marines!'

Some are even questions:

- 'just what is his game?'
- 'were your ears burning?'

Some sentences start with the impersonal pronoun 'it':

- 'it takes two to tango'
- 'it will all come out in the wash'

Some metaphors are direct conditional statements:

- 'if the cap fits, then wear it'
- 'if the mountain will not go to Muhammad, then Muhammad will go to the mountain'

Others merely imply conditions:

- 'first in, best dressed'
- 'love me, love my dog'

About 70 per cent of all the expressions listed in this book commence with a verb, although it can be argued in some cases that only the words following the infinitive comprise the real metaphor. Metaphors can involve:

- a verb by itself – 'to ruminate', 'to pan out'
- a verb with a noun or an adjective as a complement – 'to be a tonic', 'to be kosher')
- a verb with an object – 'to throw a long shadow', 'to trump a person', 'to beard the lion in his den'
- a verb modified by an adverb or an adverbial phrase – 'to ebb away', 'to be in hand'

  and so on.

Sometimes only the passive voice gives an idiomatic expression – for example, 'to be cheesed off'.

There are really no limits to the grammatical forms which a metaphor can take. Furthermore, no logical rules govern this aspect.

Principles Used in the Listings

Where the infinitive is shown in the listings, all forms of the verb concerned are normally usable except where specifically stated otherwise – for example, 'to rest on one's laurels' extends to 'she rested on her laurels', and 'are you just going to rest on your laurels?', and so on.

On occasions, however, an expression involving a verb exists in a more restricted way – such as 'I could eat a horse', which is used mainly in the first person. Another example is the near-slang 'join the club!' – which is found only in the imperative mood. In such cases the listings show the commonly used form of the metaphor.

Nouns shown with either the definite or the indefinite article in the listings are usually encountered only in that form.

No attempt has been made to correct the language of ungrammatical or inelegant expressions in popular use – for example, 'fast and furious' (when used as an adverb) or 'this is nothing to write home about'.

Metaphors Involving a Change to the Part of Speech

Some expressions are based on nouns when used literally, but on verbs when used figuratively – as in 'a white ant' and 'to white-ant someone', respectively.

Other examples of this phenomenon include the following:

- 'to snowball'
- 'to cave in'
- 'to earmark'
- 'to mushroom'
- 'to mothball'
- 'to pinpoint'
- 'to rubber stamp'
- 'to grandstand'
- 'to spearhead'

Some examples of phrases that moved in the reverse direction – namely, verbs when used literally and nouns when used figuratively – are as follows:

- 'a breakthrough'
- 'a standstill'
- 'a walkover'

Verbs Requiring Special Subjects

Some verbs used as metaphors can be combined with only a narrow range of nouns as their subjects in their figurative applications. For example:

- only a *price* or a *value* can 'skyrocket';
- only a *telephone* or some similar piece of equipment can 'run hot';
- only *alleged facts* can be 'taken at face value';
- only an *unpleasant incident* can 'come back to haunt a person';
- only a *joke* or a *funny* story can 'fall flat';
- only an *argument* can be 'shot to ribbons'; and
- only *information* can be brought 'out into the open'.

Again, only the participants in some contest such as an election can be said to be 'level pegging' or 'running neck and neck'.

The Use of Inverted Commas

The metaphors listed in this book can, generally speaking, be regarded as perfectly respectable. As mentioned in Chapter 1, they are therefore not usually written inside quotation marks. Such punctuation would not really be appropriate, as it would indicate to readers either that the author felt guilty and apologetic about the use of the expression (in the case of slang), or that the author was feeling particularly proud for having invented something brilliant and wanted to draw special attention to it.

Idioms

Outside the scope of this book are a large number of colourful idioms that represent the literal truth – picturesque expressions such as:

- 'this is not the end of the world' (you will get over this setback);
- 'he does not wear horns' (he is much more like you than you expect);
- 'you should practise what you preach' (you should do yourself what you tell others to do); and

- 'you got it in one' (your first hypothesis, as just enunciated, is correct).

Some Further Non-Metaphors

Technically speaking, the phrase 'a rose by any other name would smell as sweet' – actually, another quotation from Shakespeare, this time from *Romeo and Juliet* – is not a metaphor. Clearly, the statement is literally true. However, speakers using it would not be referring to roses, or to smelling, or to sweetness. The phrase taken as a whole is clearly much more powerful than its separate components might suggest.

In a similar category is the rhetorical question: 'How long is a piece of string?' – often used to imply that somebody's query cannot be answered in any meaningful way.

A plea to someone not to act stupidly can be illustrated by pointing out that 'if you own a car, you do not put oil where the petrol goes'.

Unrealistic assumptions can be highlighted by comments to the effect that 'no matter how long the runway, pigs still can't fly'.

Recklessness can be put in perspective with: 'You should never bet the whole farm on one deal'.

A promise of stability can be indicated by a statement on the lines of: 'We are not going to change that every five minutes'.

A person's imminent death can be rendered euphemistically as: 'He has seen his last gum tree'.

Other examples of phrases that are literally true but that are really meant to convey a completely different picture from that implied by the actual words include the following:

- 'I would not be seen dead doing that'
- 'I will shed no tears over that'
- 'I can live with that'
- 'Keep your shirt on!'

- 'I will not lift a finger to help him'
- 'Rome was not built in a day'
- 'It's not a hanging offence'
- 'Wild horses could not drag that name out of me'
- 'One does not have to be a Rhodes scholar to know that'
- 'One can hear a pin drop'
- 'She let him have his head'
- 'You don't get your hair cut at the butcher's'
- 'As sure as eggs is eggs'
- 'There is no law against this'
- 'You can chew gum and walk at the same time'
- 'You can count them on the fingers of one hand'

Fortune magazine has published extracts from some actual United States' military performance-appraisal reports. The more imaginative ones included the following:

- 'He is not the sharpest knife in the drawer';
- 'One-celled organisms would outscore him in IQ tests';
- 'If brains were taxed, he'd get a rebate' (also attributed to the Australian politician Artie Fadden); and
- 'If you gave him a penny for his thoughts, you'd get change'.

Synecdoche

In some metaphors the abstract is treated as though it were the concrete, as when a proposal is 'thrown out of the window' or 'swept under the carpet' or 'taken with a grain of salt'.

Again, one can 'pour cold water' on an idea or 'knock it on the head'. A person can 'come to grips' with a problem, 'bare' his soul, 'unveil' a plan, 'eat' his words, or know something 'inside out'.

Such phrases are further examples of the figure of speech called *synecdoche.*

Personification

Other metaphors involve ***personification***, for instance, 'to break the back' of a task, a 'glaring error' and 'the kiss of death'. Again, the solution to a problem can 'stare someone in the face'.

Hyperbole

The expression 'light years' is both a metaphor and an *hyperbole.* It can legitimately be used to mean 'a great distance'. However, it is also frequently used – quite incorrectly, as it happens – in the sense of 'a long time'.

On the other hand, 'breathing space', despite appearances, does refer to an interval of time. The expression 'if I've told you once I've told you a thousand times' also involves an hyperbole. Some metaphors comprise deliberate oversimplifications or understatements, as 'to dot the i's and cross the t's', and 'to turn an honest penny'.

Irony

Some metaphors involve elements of irony. For example:

- 'a deafening silence'
- 'people stayed away in droves'
- 'the doors of the Ritz are open to all'

It is also possible to invent metaphors in order to be ironical. For instance, a copper coin tendered in mistake for a silver coin can be described as being 'rather sunburnt'.

Part I
Dictionary

A

a

from a to z
from start to finish

A1

to be A1 at Lloyd's
to be in perfect order
refers to the classification of ships in Lloyd's register in London

abandon

to abandon ship
to abrogate one's responsibilities or to abandon a project
refers to the order given when a ship is about to sink

able

to be able to chew gum and walk at the same time
to be able to do two relatively simple things simultaneously
used ironically to disparage a person of limited capacities

to be able to do something standing on one's head
to be able to do something very easily

to be able to do something with one hand behind one's back
to be able to do something very easily

to be able to eat someone for breakfast
to be able to outwit a person very easily

to be able to hear a pin drop
to experience silence

to be able to lay one's hands on something
to be able to locate something

to be able to spot trouble a mile away
to be able to perceive problems before they actually occur

Abbott

to be an Abbott and Costello act
to involve two persons working together as a team

about

nothing to make a song or dance about
unexciting or unimportant

nothing to write home about
unimpressive

to bandy something about
to discuss something in a light-hearted manner

to be nuts about someone
to be infatuated with a person

to beat about the bush
to fail to come to the point
refers to hunters flushing game from cover by beating of the vegetation in which animals are hidden

to do an about face
to reverse a previously enunciated policy

to have a blind spot about something
to have a lack of understanding and perception about something
refers to that part of the retina insensitive to light, at the point of entry of the optic nerve

to know a thing or two about something
to have acquired a lifetime of cunning about a subject

to make a noise about something
to complain or express dissatisfaction about something

to make no bones about it
to be brutally frank

to see a man about a dog
to do something unspecified

you wouldn't read about it!
that is unbelievable

above

to be above board
to be quite legitimate
refers to gambling

to be above water
(of securities) to have a market value in excess of the cost price

to be a cut above the rest
to be plainly superior

to be head and shoulders above the rest
to be significantly more capable than others

to hold one's head just above water
to cope with problems but with little margin to spare or to stay solvent

abyss

to be close to the abyss
to face imminent total destruction

accept

to accept something with both hands
to accept something eagerly

according

according to Hoyle
with authority
Edmond Hoyle (1671–1769) codified the laws of games — including card games (especially whist), backgammon, and chess — and wrote a number of treatises that were accepted as authoritative, leading to common use of the phrase 'according to Hoyle'; a book entitled *According to Hoyle* was published in 1965 containing the rules of 300 games

to cut one's coat according to the cloth
to accommodate oneself to limitations beyond one's control and to do the best in the circumstances

ace

to be within an ace of something
to be extremely close to something
from Latin *as* ('unity', that is 'one' or 'a single point')

to have an ace up one's sleeve
to hold an impressive counter-argument in reserve
refers to card games; from Latin *as* ('unity', that is 'one' or 'a single point')

aces

to hold all the aces
to be in an unbeatable position to defeat others
refers to playing cards; from Latin *as* ('unity', that is 'one' or 'a single point')

ache

heartache
sadness
William Blake (1757–1827), *To Hayley*, 'Thy friendship oft has made my heart to ache'

Achilles

to be someone's Achilles' heel
to represent a weakness in an otherwise strong position
refers to Achilles, Greek warrior and hero of Homer's *Iliad*, who was invulnerable except for his heel

acid

to be the acid test
to establish something beyond doubt
refers to test for gold with *aqua fortis* (nitric acid)

to put the acid on someone
to make demands on a person
refers to test for gold with *aqua fortis* (nitric acid)

acorns

tall oaks from little acorns grow
even major enterprises have to have small beginnings
David Everett (1769–1813), *Lines Written for a School Declamation*, 'Large streams from little fountains flow, / tall oaks from little acorns grow'

across

across the board
over the whole range of activity

shots across the bow
warnings
nautical metaphor

act

to act as a devil's advocate
to put a point of view that one does not hold in order to draw out the best arguments regarding a proposition
refers to a church official vetting a candidate for sainthood (and ultimately to the testing of Job by Satan, *Job* 1:9 ff)

to act as a safety valve
to be a procedure that allows persons with grievances to ventilate them in an orderly fashion

to act as a sounding board
to give, on request, constructive criticisms of ideas tentatively held
refers, originally, to a board placed behind a speaker (esp. a preacher) to reflect the speaker's voice forwards to the congregation or audience

to act out a charade
ostentatiously to pretend to be doing something; a pretence
refers to a parlour game of pretence

to be a hard act to follow

to be an impressive performance, not easily matched by the next person

to be an Abbott and Costello act
to involve two persons working together as a team

to clean up one's act
to fix up the deficiencies in one's affairs

to get in on the act
to participate in some activity started by others

to get one's act together
to organise one's activities so as to make them efficient

to read the riot act
to reprimand persons who are excessively noisy or otherwise misbehaving

refers to the police reading out to a rowdy crowd extracts from a law requiring the crowd's dispersement

action

to galvanise someone into action
forcefully to shock or rouse someone into action

refers to Luigi Galvani (1737–98), Italian physiologist, whose name was applied to the shock received from a direct electric current

to have a piece/slice of the action
to be one of several parties to a project

Adam

not to know someone from Adam
to be unable to recognise a person

refers to the name of the first man as recorded in *Genesis* 2

since Adam was a boy
for a very long time

refers to the name of the first man as recorded in *Genesis* 2

add

to add apples to oranges
to lump unconnected things together quite illogically

to add fuel to the fire
to make a bad situation worse

added

that takes on added colour
there are now further facts that alter the appearance of a matter

address

keynote address
opening address, designed to set the theme of a conference

refers to music

adds

it adds up
it makes sense

adrift

to come adrift
(of a plan) not to work out as intended

advocate

to act as a devil's advocate
to put a point of view that one does not hold in order to draw out the best arguments regarding a proposition

refers to a church official vetting a candidate for sainthood (and ultimately to the testing of Job by Satan, *Job* 1:9 ff)

afloat

to stay afloat
to remain solvent

after

to be after someone's blood
to be keen to make a person the victim of an angry confrontation

to be after someone's scalp
to be keen to penalise a person

refers to the savage practice of removing the scalp of a killed person as a trophy

to be someone after one's own heart
to be a person who shares one's beliefs

1 Samuel 13:14 'A man after his own heart'

to look after number one
to act selfishly

to shut the stable door after the horse has bolted
to take preventive action only after the relevant event

to throw good money after bad
to waste further money in a vain attempt to recover money already lost

against

something goes against the grain
something is completely and frustratingly against a person's inclination

refers to woodworking

the dice are loaded against someone
a person is unlikely to succeed in something
refers to cheating in gambling with dice

to bang one's head against a brick wall
to fight an unwinnable case

to be up against a brick wall
to be unable to achieve anything because of intractable opposition or apathy

to be up in arms against something
to express violent opposition to a proposal

to have a black mark against one's name
to have a tarnished reputation

to have the cards stacked against one
to be faced with many difficulties frustrating a project
refers to playing cards

to have the odds stacked against one
to be faced with many difficulties frustrating a project
refers to betting

to sail against the wind
to oppose the views currently being held by others

to set one's face against something
to oppose some matter

to steel one's heart against something
to determine that, notwithstanding one's natural compassion, something shall not happen

to swim against the tide
to take up a minority position

to throw a pebble against the window
gently to draw attention to oneself

ahead

ull-bore ahead!
proceed forward at full power!

full-steam ahead!
get going as fast as possible!
refers to a steam engine (especially in a ship or train)

to be ahead by a country mile
to be in a comfortable lead
in the long distances of certain rural areas, a 'country mile' is jocularly believed to be a very long mile

to be ahead of the field
to be better than one's competitors

to be streets ahead
to outperform one's competitors by a wide margin

to face a rocky road ahead
to be likely to encounter difficulties

aid

a band-aid
help that is superficial or ephemeral rather than substantial or permanent
refers to a commercial brand of plastic adhesive dressing for wounds

air

a castle in the air
a desirable imagining, but an impracticable proposition

a feeling in the air
a premonition held by many people

to be a breath of fresh air
to be a pleasant change from the past

to be full of hot air
to make unsubstantiated empty statements; to be bombastic

to clear the air
to remove any possible misunderstandings

to have too many balls in the air
to attempt to do more than can be coped with
refers to juggling

to leave something up in the air
to have an unresolved problem

to pluck figures out of the air
to make figures up arbitrarily

to produce something out of thin air
to get hold of something in circumstances where this seemed impossible
Shakespeare, *The Tempest* IV:i, ' … are melted into air, into thin air'

to throw one's cap/hat into the air
to express joy; OR to celebrate some achievement

to vanish into thin air
unexpectedly to disappear

Shakespeare, *The Tempest* IV:i, ' ... are melted into air, into thin air'

to walk on air
to be joyful

airs

to put on airs and graces
to act in an affected manner

aisles

to have an audience rolling in the aisles
to amuse an audience

Aladdin

an Aladdin's cave
a place full of unexpected treasure
refers to a character and events in *Arabian Nights' Entertainments* alarm

the alarm bells are ringing
it is unwise to proceed

to sound alarm bells
to give warning

albatross

to be an albatross around someone's neck
to be a great burden
refers to a mythical mariner who suffered terrible ordeals as a result of killing an albatross; Samuel Taylor Coleridge (1772–1834), *The Ancient Mariner*, 1798, 'Why look'st thou so? — with my cross-bow, I shot the albatross'

Alec

to be a smart Alec
to give witty but cheeky responses to one's superiors or customers
origin obscure, but dates back to 1860s in USA

alive

to be alive and kicking
to be in good form

to eat someone alive
to defeat a person soundly

all

a Jack of all trades
an amateur who can do many different tasks'

all hands on deck
everybody is requested to help out
nautical metaphor

all hands to the pumps
everybody is requested to help out
nautical metaphor

all hell broke loose
great confusion erupted
John Milton (1608–74) *Paradise Lost*, 'Wherefore with thee came not all hell broke loose?'

all roads lead to Rome
all alternatives will have the same outcome
refers to roads radiating from the great imperial capital to all parts of the Roman empire

all that glisters/glitters is not gold
things are not always what they seem
Shakespeare, *Merchant of Venice*, II:vii, 'All that glisters is not gold'

all the dogs are barking
this news is being widely disseminated

all their Christmases came at once
they were overjoyed

I would not do so-and-so for all the tea in China
I will never do so-and-so no matter how large the inducement

it is all grist to the mill
this is all useful material for the task at hand

it will all come out in the wash
the facts will emerge as work proceeds

not to be all beer and skittles
not to be all pleasant and easy

not to put all one's eggs in the one basket
to spread one's risks

someone's fingerprints are all over this
it is obvious that a particular person was solely responsible for this

someone's fingers are all thumbs
a person is clumsy with his or her hands

to all sing from the same hymnal
to act consistently with each other
refers to a book of hymns

to be all ears
to be very attentive

to be all eyes
to observe very closely

to be all over bar the shouting
to be virtually finished

to be all systems 'go'

to be ready to proceed as fast as possible

to be all that it is cracked up to be
to be as good as the claims made for something

to be all washed out
to feel feeble

to compete on all fours with someone
to strive on equal terms
refers to the four limbs of the body

to get the worst of all worlds
to get a series of disadvantages without achieving any corresponding advantages

to go the way of all flesh
to die
Joshua 23:14, 'And, behold, this day I am going the way of all flesh'

to hold all the aces
to be in an unbeatable position to defeat others
refers to playing cards; from Latin *as* ('unity', that is 'one' or 'a single point')

to hold all the cards
to be assured of victory
refers to playing cards

to laugh all the way to the bank
to appreciate one's good fortune

to let it all hang out
to be uninhibited; to unburden oneself

to pull out all stops
to make maximum effort
refers to organ playing at maximum volume

to spark on all cylinders
to work extremely well

to walk all over someone
to act in a way that completely disregards another person's sensibility

to want to jump all one's fences at once
unrealistically to want to solve all problems at once, rather than sequentially
refers to steeplechasing on horseback

warts and all
with the unfavourable features as well as the favourable ones
Oliver Cromwell's reported direction to the artist, Sir Peter Lely, painting his portrait

alley

to be up one's alley
to be right within a person's expertise or area of interest

to rush into a blind alley
to make a precipitate move that does not lead one anywhere

alliance

an unholy alliance
a working relationship for a nefarious purpose between unlikely partners

almost

to drive someone almost to tears
to act in such a way as to cause someone significant distress

along

to go along for the ride
to seek to benefit from a project in which others contribute the effort

to pass the ball along
to cooperate with others

not to get along with someone in a fit
not to get along with a person in any circumstances

alpha

from alpha to omega
from start to finish
refers to the first and last letters of the Greek alphabet

altar

to sacrifice something on the altar of some belief
to give up some benefit as a matter of principle

always

one's door is always open
people can take their problems to one at any time

amendment

to plead the fifth amendment
to refuse to answer an unwelcome question
refers to the fifth amendment of the United States constitution, which provides protection against self-incrimination

ammunition

ammunition
arguments helpful to a case

anchor

the sheet anchor
the ultimate of one's confidence
refers to a large ship's anchor used in an emergency

to anchor
to fix firmly

to weigh anchor
to move to another address
nautical metaphor

angel

a fallen angel
a previously trusted person who has transgressed
refers to the fallen spirits who rebelled against God (Milton *Paradise Lost* Bk I, 392)

someone's guardian angel
someone's friend, watching over them and advancing their interests
Shakespeare, *Hamlet* IV:i, 'Angels and ministers of grace defend us!'

to be an angel
to be very helpful

to be no angel
to have a great many serious faults

angels

fools rush in where angels fear to tread
unsophisticated persons take unwise risks in circumstances where more knowledgeable persons would exercise caution
Alexander Pope (1688–1744), *An Essay on Criticism* 1:625, 'For fools rush in where angels fear to tread'

to be on the side of the angels
to be on the side of righteousness
Benjamin Disraeli (1804–81), 'Is man an ape or an angel? Now I am on the side of the angels' (speech debating theory of evolution, Diocese of Oxford, 25 November 1864)

animal

there is no such animal
that does not exist

to be a political animal
to be a person who thinks and acts politically in all aspects of life

anointed

the anointed one
the desired successor
refers to use of anointing oil to indicate and sanctify a chosen perso; *Exodus* 28:41, 'and shalt anoint them, and consecrate them, and sanctify them, that they may minister unto me in the priest's office'

answer

the answer is a lemon
there is no appropriate answer to that sort of proposition

the answer to a maiden's prayer
an unexpected but very welcome happening

ant

to white-ant someone
surreptitiously to seek to destroy a person
refers to the damage done to timber structures by white ants

antediluvian

antediluvian
very outmoded
literally 'before the flood' — refers to the time before the flood described in *Genesis* Chapter 6ff

antlers

to lock antlers with someone
to have an argument with another person
refers to fighting between male horned animals

anything

not to do anything by halves
to do everything extremely well

apart

to be miles apart
to have great philosophical differences

to be poles apart
to have ideas that are very different

to come apart at the seams
(of an arrangement) to break down

to drift apart
to lose contact or to change feelings once held in common

to tear someone apart
ruthlessly to destroy another person's case

apocryphal

apocryphal

fictitious but resembling truth and illustrating a point

Greek: *apocrypha*, 'hidden'

apology

to be an apology for something

to be a poor substitute for something

apparent

heir apparent

the person likely to succeed another

appetite

to whet one's appetite

to arouse one's curiosity, interest, or desire

apple

a rotten apple

an isolated dishonest person in an otherwise honest group

in apple-pie order

in perfect order and condition

to be the apple of someone's eye

to be a much cherished person

refers to the pupil of the eye — 'the apple of the eye' as being the centre of visual perception and therefore especially cherished and much-valued

apples

to add/compare apples with oranges

to lump unconnected things together quite illogically

to compare apples with apples

to make a valid comparison

applecart

to upset the applecart

to engage in conduct disturbing a peaceful state of affairs and thereby to cause discomfort

apply

to apply pressure on someone

to induce a person to do something that that person would otherwise not do by implying adverse consequences if the person does not cooperate

to apply the blowtorch to something

to apply very strong pressure to some person

approval

a seal of approval

confirmation that something is satisfactory

apron

to be tied to someone's apron strings

to be excessively influenced by one's mother

architect

to be the architect of something

to be the person devising something innovative

area

to be a grey area

to be in an undefined position straddling two or more possibilities

refers to something being neither black nor white

argue

to argue the toss

to dispute a decision

refers to the tossing of a coin

argument

to buy into some argument

to seek to participate in some discussion

to parry some argument

to deflect some argument

refers to fencing

that argument is wearing a bit thin

that case has been heard so often that it is losing its effect

refers to clothes or similar beginning to fail from continued use

arm

a shot in the arm

something to revive a person's enthusiasm

refers to medical injections

at arm's length

between parties who are strangers bearing no special duty to each other and who have no financial or other relationship with each other

a legal term

I would give my right arm for something

I am very keen to acquire something

to chance one's arm

to take a great risk

refers to the stripes on the uniforms of non-commissioned officers

to cost an arm and a leg
to be excessively expensive

to have a long arm
to have far-reaching power

to lose one's right arm
to lose some highly valued assistance

to twist someone's arm
to coerce another person to do something against that person's will or better judgment

armchair

to get an armchair ride
to be given a particularly easy time

armed

to be armed to the teeth
to carry many weapons
perhaps refers to carrying a knife in the teeth

armour

a chink in someone's armour
a weakness in someone's defences that creates an opportunity to do something that otherwise could not be done

a knight in shining armour
a person who comes to the rescue; a champion
derived from mediaeval tales of valiant knights rescuing those in distress

armpits

to be in something up to one's armpits
to be involved very deeply in something

arms

to be up in arms against something
to express violent opposition to a proposal

with open arms
enthusiastically

around

a millstone around someone's neck
a great burden

to be an albatross around someone's neck
to be a great burden
refers to a mythical mariner who suffered terrible ordeals as a result of killing an albatross; Samuel Taylor Coleridge (1772–1834), *The Ancient Mariner*, 1798, 'Why look'st thou so? — with my cross-bow, I shot the albatross'

to be around the corner
to be imminent

to be hedged around
(of a statement) to be surrounded by qualifications

to fall around someone's ears
to collapse utterly around someone

to get around some difficulty
to use an approach that overcomes some difficulty

to get around someone
to induce a person to do as one wishes; to circumvent a person's opposition

to kick some proposal around
to examine a proposal from all angles
refers to football

to kick someone around
to abuse a person

to push someone around
to exercise, in an obnoxious manner, one's superiority over another person

to pussyfoot around
to take stealthy, cautious, non-committal steps
refers to a cat prowling

to put a wall around someone
to stop a person associating with others

to run around in circles
to engage in excited but useless activity

to run rings around someone
to outwit another person easily

to shop around
to explore alternatives

to skate around some subject
by diversionary tactics to avoid discussing some subject

to skirt around the difficulties
to proceed with care and avoid problems

to be around the corner
to be imminent

to throw one's weight around
to assert one's real or assumed authority excessively

to tip-toe around the difficulties

to act with discretion and care to conceal difficulties, or to prevent problems occurring

to turn around 180 degrees
completely to reverse a stance

to twist someone around one's little finger
to exert easy control over a person

arrive

to arrive on the dot
to turn up at the exact scheduled time

arrow

another arrow in one's quiver
an additional reason

arrows

slings and arrows
adverse fortunes in life; hurtful experiences
Shakespeare, *Hamlet* III:i, 'Whether 'tis nobler in the mind to suffer / the slings and arrows of outrageous fortune, / or to take arms against a sea of troubles, / and by opposing end them?'

art

to raise something to a fine art form
to refine a thing or a process to the point where doing it is a highly skilled task

Arthur

I don't know whether I'm Arthur or Martha
I'm confused

article

an article of faith
a fundamental belief on which certain behaviour is based

ascertain

to ascertain the lie of the land
to establish the pertinent facts and opinions

ashes

to rise from the ashes like a phoenix
to be the replacement for something destroyed in some disaster
refers to a mythical bird that was supposed to rise from the ashes of its funeral pile/pyre with renewed youth

to wear sackcloth and ashes
humbly to demonstrate repentance
Esther 4:3, 'There was great mourning ... and many lay in sackcloth and ashes'

asked

someone asked for it
a person deserves a certain fate

ass

to make an ass of oneself
to act stupidly in public

asses

asses and little pitchers have long ears
children have a tendency to overhear things

assume

to assume someone's mantle
to take over another person's role
refers to the passing of Elijah's mantle to Elisha: *2Kings* 2:13, 'He took up also the mantle of Elijah that fell from him ... '

atmosphere

atmosphere
psychological environment

in a rarefied atmosphere
in ignorance of the real world

one could have cut the atmosphere with a knife
those present were very tense

attached

to have strings attached
to be subject to conditions

attack

to attack with a vengeance
to attack strongly

attention

to jump to attention
to show respect

attitude

a holier-than-thou attitude
excessive righteousness

attract

to attract flak
to attract criticism
refers to anti-aircraft fire — abbrev. of German *fliegerabwehrkanone* (lit. 'aviator-defence-gun')

Aunt

an Aunt Sally

a person who can readily be singled out and criticised as the proxy for a group
refers to an old game in which objects were thrown at the figure of the head of a woman

avalanche

avalanche
a great volume manifesting itself in a short time

avenue

avenue
method of approach

awash

to be awash with something
to have plenty of something

away

people stayed away in droves
few people came
refers to a moving group of cattle, sheep, or other animals

something is but a hop, skip, and jump away
something is nearby

the cheering could be heard a block away
there was great rejoicing

to be able to spot trouble a mile away
to be able to perceive problems before they actually occur

to be carried away
to be excited by something imaginative

to be miles away
to have one's mind on other matters

to be unable to keep people away with a big stick
to be faced with a large crowd or much demand

to beaver away
to work diligently at some task
refers to the industriousness of the beaver

to blow the cobwebs away
to revive an old issue

to chisel away at something
to reduce the size of something in a series of small stages

to ebb away
to decline gradually

to get away with murder
to do something outrageous without penalty

to give the game away
to cease involvement with some activity; OR to reveal the nature of a hidden activity or plan

to give the show away
indiscreetly to reveal sensitive information
perhaps refers to revealing the plot of a theatre play

to send someone away with a flea in the ear
to give a person frank, but unwelcome, facts
perhaps refers to fleas trapped in the armour of ancient knights, or perhaps from the discomfort felt by a dog with a flea in its ear; or perhaps, figuratively, to any lingering irritation in the ear

to take one's breath away
to surprise greatly, or astonish

to tear oneself away
to leave despite a great desire to stay

to tuck something away in a drawer
to put something aside for the time being

to walk away from something
to abrogate one's responsibilities in regard to some matter

to walk away with a profit
to achieve a profit on concluding a project

when the cat is away the mice will play
in the absence of supervision discipline will be lax

axe

an old battle-axe
a hostile woman

the axe has fallen
it is now too late
refers to execution by decapitation

to axe
to cancel

to have an axe to grind
to have a vested interest; to pursue a personal objective

to sharpen one's axe
to get ready for a difficult task

where the axe falls

who suffers the consequences

B

babes

out of the mouths of babes and sucklings
(as indiscreetly revealed) the truth
Psalms 8:2, 'Out of the mouths of babes and sucklings hast thou ordained strength ... '

to be babes in the wood
to be excessively naVve and inexperienced and thus ripe for exploitation
based on the folk legend of the babes in the wood of Wayland Hall, Norfolk

Babel

a tower of Babel
a noisy and confused assembly
Genesis 11:9, 'Therefore is the name of it called Babel; because the Lord did there confound the language of all the earth' (from which the word 'babble' is also derived)

baby

to be left holding the baby
to be forced to accept responsibility for someone else's problems

to be one's baby
to be one's area of responsibility; to be one's special object of devotion or doting

to throw out the baby with the bathwater
to discard a major benefit in the course of obtaining a comparatively minor advantage

back

a back-seat driver
a person seeking to exercise control when it is not that person's responsibility

a thought in the back of one's mind
an undeveloped idea

as soon as someone's back was turned
at the moment it became possible to do something without a person's knowledge

back-breaking
overburdening

behind someone's back
in a way that deliberately conceals an activity from a person

feedback
response from a target audience to those seeking to influence it
refers (originally) to the interaction between amplifiers and speakers

it fell off the back of a truck
(of an item of goods) it was stolen; (of a politically sensitive document) it was leaked to me

on the back of something
by virtue of something

put your back into it!
work energetically!

so-and-so would give you the shirt off his or her back
so-and-so is very generous
Luke 6:29 (RSV), ' ... and from him who takes away your coat do not withhold even your shirt'

something is on the back burner
consideration is postponed pending further research

the straw that broke the camel's back
the latest step that, when added to a large number of seemingly harmless previous steps, sets off a sudden significant event resulting from the cumulative effect

through the back door
unofficially or surreptitiously

to back pedal
to reverse to some extent previously applied policies
refers to riding a cycle

to back someone into a corner
to leave a person no option

to back the wrong horse
to have faith in, give support to, and/or invest in a project that proves to be unsuccessful
refers to betting on racehorses

to be able to do something with one hand behind one's back
to be able to do something very easily

to be back in the trenches
to be made to carry out menial tasks
military metaphor

to be back on deck
to have returned after an absence
nautical metaphor

to be back to scratch
to have to start all over again
perhaps refers to the scratch mark in a boxing ring used to indicate an ability or willingness to fight, or perhaps refers to a starting line in a race from which competitors not receiving an advantage begin the race

to be fed up to the back teeth
to be disgusted after prolonged provocation

to be home on the sheep's back
to be doing well

to be like water off a duck's back
(of advice or criticism) to be completely ignored

to break the back of a task
to complete the bulk of the work

to bring someone back to the pack
to make a person conform to

bounce back
to resume a cheerful existence after some setback

to cover one's back
to take precautions

to engage in back-biting
to criticise in a trivial, annoying unfriendly manner

to get back on one's feet
to recover from an illness or some other set-back

to get off someone's back
to leave a person alone to carry on without constant criticism

to get one's own back on someone
to extract revenge

to go back into the melting pot
to be up for reconsideration from the beginning
refers to a vessel for melting and mixing metals

to go back to square one
to start all over again
refers to board games

to go back to the well
to go to the original source
Genesis 24:20, 'And [Rebekah] ran again unto the well to draw water'

to have eyes at/in the back of one's head
to know more of what is going on than is generally realised

to have one hand tied behind one's back
to work with a handicap

to have one's back to the wall
to be hard-pressed by creditors or opponents

to make a rod for one's own back
to make a handicap for oneself

to make the beast with two backs
to engage in sexual intercourse
Shakespeare, *Othello* I:i, 'Your daughter and the Moor are now making the beast with two backs'

to need to watch one's back
to find it necessary to take care in case others act against one's interests

to pat oneself on the back
immodestly to congratulate oneself

to pat someone on the back
to congratulate a person or to reassure a person

to pay someone back in that person's own coin
to retaliate in kind

to pay something back with interest
to return a small favour with a bigger favour; or to extract retribution of greater value than the circumstances warrant

to plough profits back
to retain profits in a business

to put one's back into something
to work hard at achieving some goal

to put someone back in his or her box/place
to require a person to act in accordance with that person's level of seniority

to put someone back on his or her feet
to restore to a functioning condition

to put someone on the back foot
to make a person less confident of that person's position

to put something back on its feet
to restore to a functioning condition

to ride on the back of someone
without effort to benefit from the prior efforts of others

to ride on the sheep's back
to benefit from the production of wool
to see the back of someone
to know that a person is no longer involved in something
to stab someone in the back
deliberately and surreptitiously to harm a person who regarded one as a friend
to take a back seat
not to involve oneself actively
to tie someone's hands behind that person's back
to make it impossible for a person to act at all
to turn back the clock
to have another opportunity to do something that should have been done already; or to attempt to undo something that cannot be undone
to turn one's back on someone
to decline to assist or deal with a person
with one's ears pinned back
chastened
refers to the aggressive attitude of horses

back-handed
a back-handed compliment
a polite expression seemingly of praise but really intended as an insult

backbone
backbone
chief strength or character

backfire
to backfire
to be counterproductive

background
background information
(relating to some matter) supplementary information that enables the main information to be seen in context and understood better
one's background
the environment in which one grew up

backlash
a backlash
adverse reaction to some move

backroom
a backroom boy
someone who works behind the scenes
Lord Beaverbrook (24 April 1941), 'to whom must praise be given ... to the boys in the backroom' (referring to the anonymous laboratory workers who contributed so much to scientific warfare and war production in World War II)

backs
to scratch one another's backs
to help each other

backwards
to bend over backwards to do something
to go to great trouble to accommodate another person's wishes
to take a step backwards
to move further away from one's goal

backwash
backwash
consequence

backwater
a backwater
a place of little activity

backyard
in one's own backyard
in one's own domain

bacon
to bring home the bacon
to be successful
refers to bringing home a valued prize
to save one's bacon
to escape harm
refers to the value attached to bacon as a stored food

bad
bad blood
animosity
to be a bad egg
to be a dishonest or disreputable person
to give a dog a bad name
to malign a person
to make bad blood between two parties
to cause ill feeling between two parties
to throw good money after bad

to waste further money in a vain attempt to recover money already lost

bag

a mixed bag
some advantages and some disadvantages

a whole bag of tricks
a series of articles or a series of artificial devices

it is in the bag
the enterprise has succeeded or surely will succeed

to let the cat out of the bag
to reveal an embarrassing secret
refers to the practice of selling a person a cat (purported to be a pig) in a bag (or poke) — hence 'a pig in a poke'; if the person opened the bag and looked inside, that person 'let the cat out of the bag'

baggage

to carry baggage
to handicap oneself

bags

to pack one's bags
to signal one's intention to depart

yes sir, yes sir, three bags full!
(in servile response to some request) yes, very willingly!
refers to old nursery rhyme

bail

to bail someone out
to render assistance to someone unable to help himself or herself

bailiwick

to be in someone's bailiwick
to be some other person's responsibility
refers to a region under the jurisdiction of a particular bailiff

to defend one's bailiwick
to protect one's power, influence, or authority in regard to a particular activity
refers to a region under the jurisdiction of a particular bailiff

bait

to swallow the bait
to succumb to a temptation deliberately put in one's way
refers to angling

baked

halfbaked
not well thought out

balance

to balance the books
to get one's own back
refers to accountancy

to balance the picture
to quote facts or arguments in contradiction

to tip the balance
to be further information or argument that results in an issue, that could have been decided either way, being determined in a particular way
refers to balance scales

to weigh two alternative propositions in the balance
to assess the relative significance of two alternative propositions
Daniel 5:27, 'Thou art weighed in the balances and art found wanting'

bale

to bale out of something
to abandon an enterprise in anticipation of disaster
refers to emergency parachute jump from an aeroplane

ball

a crystal ball
accurate knowledge of the future
refers to ancient means of divining the future

the ball is in someone's court
it is some other person's responsibility
refers to tennis

to be a new ball game
to be subject to completely revised rules or very different conditions

to be in the right ballpark
to be approximately correct
refers to baseball

to be line ball
to be equal or to be a matter about which it is very difficult to make a definitive decision one way or the other
refers to sport (especially tennis)

to be on the ball
to be fully informed

to be right behind the eight ball

to be in a position of extreme disadvantage
refers to US game of pool in which the ultimate objective is to pot the black ball (which is numbered 8)

to blackball someone
to reject a person as unsuitable
refers to a vote against someone by secretly placing a black ball in a box (as opposed to a white or red ball which indicated approval); the voting procedure was common in ancient Rome and Greece — hence 'ballot' (French, *ballotte*, 'a little ball')

to have a ball
to have an enjoyable time

to have the ball at one's feet
to have unlimited opportunity
refers to football games

to have too many balls in the air
to attempt to do more than can be coped with
refers to juggling

to keep an eye on the ball
to monitor a fast-changing situation

to keep the ball rolling
to take advantage of the existing momentum or to participate actively

to keep up with the ball
to maintain awareness of a situation

to pass the ball along
to cooperate with others

to play ball
to cooperate

to run with the ball
to make the most of the opportunity
refers to rugby

to start the ball rolling
to commence and advance enthusiastically an activity

to take one's bat and ball home
as a gesture of spite to remove an essential ingredient that one has contributed to a joint enterprise, and to refuse to take any further part in its activities
refers to cricket

to throw the ball back to someone
to return responsibility for something to another person

balloon

to go down like a lead balloon
to receive a very cool reception

when the balloon goes up
when the adverse facts come to light

banana

a banana republic
a country with a poor economy

band

a one-man band
a person performing many different roles singlehandedly

band-aid

a band-aid
help that is superficial or ephemeral rather than substantial or permanent
refers to a commercial brand of plastic adhesive dressing for wounds

bandwagon

to hop onto the bandwagon
to subscribe to an emerging majority opinion

bandy

to bandy something about
to discuss something in a light-hearted manner
perhaps from French *bander*, 'to take sides at tennis'

bang

a big bang
a sudden major change in the environment

to bang one's head against a brick wall
to fight an unwinnable case

to finish with a bang
to conclude something in grand style

bank

to laugh all the way to the bank
to appreciate one's good fortune

bankrupt

to be bankrupt of ideas
to be bereft of ideas

baptism

a baptism of fire
the commencement of an operation that presents great difficulty
refers to religious ceremonial washing as an initiation ceremony; metaphorical use (as here) attributed to Napoleon III in referring to to a soldier's first battle

bar

not to have a bar of something

to be totally opposed to something

to slide under the bar
not to arouse suspicion

bare

the bare bones
(of a story) nothing but the essential elements

the cupboard is bare
the wished-for resources are not available

to bare one's soul
talkatively to give a revealing insight into oneself

to bare one's teeth
to imply threats
refers to savage animals

barefaced

barefaced
shameless

bargained

to be more than one bargained for
to be more than one expected

bargaining

bargaining chips
benefits that can be conceded in negotiations to obtain some advantage

barge

not to touch something with a forty-foot barge pole
to go out of one's way to avoid something

bark

the bark is worse than the bite
the harsh words belie the reality of mild action

to bark up the wrong tree
to reach an incorrect conclusion and/or to pursue an erroneous course of action

why keep a dog and bark oneself?
it is silly to pay for assistance and then do things personally

barking

all the dogs are barking
this news is being widely disseminated

to feed the dogs while they are barking
to do something while the opportunity is available

barn

horses are out of the barn
it is now too late

barnstorm

to barnstorm
to travel around and actively promote one's cause or performance
refers to itinerant actors who performed in barns

barred

no holds barred
without any limitation
refers to wrestling

barrel

a barrelful of something
many of something

lock, stock and barrel
entirely
the lock, stock and barrel of a gun is the complete firearm

to have someone over a barrel
to take advantage of someone's weakened position in relation to oneself

to look down the barrel of a gun
to be given little choice in a matter

to pork barrel
to spend taxpayers' money in one area in order to attract political support
refers to times of slavery in America when pork was provided to slaves gathered around the pork barrel

to scrape the bottom of the barrel
to be forced to use the last available resources; to lower one's standards because one is short of resources

barrels

with both barrels blazing
with great intensity

barricades

to go to the barricades for something
to believe in something very strongly and to be willing to go to great lengths in support of that belief

barriers

to break down the barriers
to do away with the prejudice preventing something

barrow

to push a barrow
to promote a particular cause

base

to get to first base
to succeed in achieving the first stage in any undertaking
refers to baseball

to touch base with someone
to make an initial contact
refers to baseball

basher

a bible basher
a person who makes unwelcome attempts to force religious beliefs on others

basket

a basket case
a poorly performing enterprise probably doomed to failure
perhaps refers to the practice of foundlings hospitals leaving baskets on the doorstep to receive abandoned infants

not to put all one's eggs in the one basket
to spread one's risks

to put something into the 'too-hard' basket
to defer consideration of a difficult issue

bastard

a bastard
(by itself, or in expressions such as 'you bastard', or when qualified by pejorative adjectives) an unpleasant person; OR (in other contexts, especially when preceded by adjectives such as 'poor' or 'stupid') a person to be pitied or held in ridicule (often with elements of sympathy or endearment)

bastion

the last bastion
the only remaining defensive measure

bat

not to bat an eyelid
to fail to express any surprise

off one's own bat
on a person's own initiative and without outside help
refers to cricket

to bat on
to continue an activity
refers to cricket

to go in to bat for someone
to carry out a task on another person's behalf
refers to cricket

to maintain a straight bat
to operate in orthodox fashion, avoiding risk
refers to cricket

to take one's bat and ball home
as a gesture of spite to remove an essential ingredient that one has contributed to a joint enterprise, and to refuse to take any further part in its activities
refers to cricket

bated

to wait with bated breath
to be excited in anticipation of some event

bath

a bloodbath
catastrophic losses

to give someone a bath
to defeat a person comprehensively

bathwater

to throw out the baby with the bathwater
to discard a major benefit in the course of obtaining a comparatively minor advantage

bâton

to have a field marshal's bâton in one's kit
to be ambitious
variously attributed:
Louis XVIII (1755–1824), 'There is not one of you who has not in his knapsack the field marshal's bâton; it is up to you to bring it out' (speech to the Saint-Cyr cadets, 9 Aug. 1819, *Moniteur*, 10 Aug. 1819);
Napoleon I (1769–1821), 'Every French soldier carries in his cartridge-pouch the bâton of a marshal of France'; Mark Pattison (1813–84), 'Every private in the French army carries in his haversack the bâton of a marshal'

to pass on the bâton
to hand over to a successor

bats

to have bats in the belfry
to be mad
literally refers to a tower or attic, or, figuratively, the head

batten

to batten down the hatches
to get ready for expected difficulties
nautical metaphor

batteries

to recharge one's batteries
to have a recuperative break

batting

to open the batting
to be the first in a series of persons speaking or doing something
refers to cricket

battle

a battle royal
a fight or argument with many simultaneous participants
refers to cockfighting

an old battle-axe
a hostile woman

to fight an uphill battle
to face difficulties or to have formidable opposition
refers to military battle

battleship

enough to sink a battleship
much more than sufficient

bay

to hold someone at bay
successfully to resist an attacker
James Thomson (1700–48), *Autumn*, 'He stands at bay, and puts his last weak refuge in despair' — description of a stag

to keep the jackals at bay
to pay one's creditors just sufficient to avoid repercussions
James Thomson (1700–48), *Autumn*, 'He stands at bay, and puts his last weak refuge in despair' — description of a stag

baying

to set the hounds baying
to excite the gossips by providing material that they can use
Shakespeare, *Julius Caesar*, 'I had rather be a dog, and bay the moon, than such a Roman'

beach

not to be the only pebble on the beach
not to be the only person available for some task, or affected by some set of circumstances

beadledom

beadledom
stupid officiousness
refers to a church official (a beadle) appointed to deal with petty offenders

beady

to have one's beady eyes on something
to await the chance to acquire something to which one is not properly entitled

beak

to be a sticky beak
to show excessive curiosity into matters not of one's concern

beam

to be off-beam
to be mistaken

bean

not to have a bean
to have no money

beans

not to matter a row of beans
to be utterly unimportant

to be full of beans
to be very cheerful

to know how many beans make five
to have common sense
refers to an old riddle

to spill the beans
indiscreetly to reveal sensitive information

bear

I fear the Greeks even when they bear gifts
I am suspicious of generous behaviour from traditional opponents
Virgil (70–19 BC), *Aeneid* II:49, *Timeo Danaos et dona ferentis* ('I fear the Greeks even when they bring gifts'), in reference to the Trojan horse

to be a bear of very little brain
to have little intelligence
refers to A. A. Milne's *Winnie-the-Pooh*

to be a cross that one has to bear
to be a difficulty that one has to endure
Luke 14:27, 'And whosoever doth not bear his cross, and come after me, cannot be my disciple'

to bear fruit
to result in success

to grin and bear it
to suffer adversity cheerfully

beard

to beard the lion in his den
to tackle a daunting opponent in that person's own familiar surroundings
Sir Walter Scott (1771–1832), *Marmion*, 'And darest thou then to beard the lion in his den ... ' (probably a reference to the story of Daniel in the den of lions as related in *Daniel* 6:16)

bearer

a standard bearer
a highly visible activist for a cause
military metaphor

beast

the nature of the beast
the reality of the situation
Revelation 13:17, ' ... he that had the mark, or the name of the beast, or the number of his name'

to make the beast with two backs
to engage in sexual intercourse
Shakespeare, *Othello* I:i, 'Your daughter and the Moor are now making the beast with two backs'

beat

any stick to beat a dog
any excuse will do if it serves one's purpose

not to miss a beat
to carry on without the slightest interruption

one can't beat City Hall
the ordinary citizen is powerless against bureaucracy

to beat a drum for someone
to propagate another person's cause

to beat a path to someone's door
to seek a person out in great numbers
Ralph Waldo Emerson (1803–82), *Sarah S. B. Yule, Borrowings*, 'If a man write a better book, preach a better sermon, or make a better mouse-trap than his neighbour, tho' he build his house in the woods, the world will make a beaten path to his door'

to beat a retreat
to abandon some project
military metaphor

to beat about the bush
to fail to come to the point
refers to hunters flushing game from cover by beating of the vegetation in which animals are hidden

to beat by a long shot
to defeat very convincingly

to beat each other over the head
to be always fighting

to beat one's breast
to express sorrow
refers to traditional expression of grief

to beat one's drum
to publicise immodestly one's own attributes

to beat someone at that person's own game
to outwit a person in that person's own specialisation

to beat someone to the punch
to get to some objective ahead of some keen rival
refers to boxing

to beat the odds
to do better than could reasonably have been expected
refers to betting on horse races or similar

beaten

to be off the beaten track
to do unconventional things; to be travelling along relatively unused routes

beatify

to beatify someone
to describe a person as worthy of honour
refers to a step in the process towards canonisation as a saint

beauty

beauty is in the eye of the beholder
some things are matters for subjective judgments
Shakespeare *Love's Labour Lost* II:i, 'Beauty is bought by judgment of the eye'

beaver

an eager beaver

a person with great drive and enthusiasm even if this causes annoyance to others

refers to the industriousness of the beaver, and adapted as World War II US expression for a very keen person who habitually volunteered

to beaver away

to work diligently at some task

refers to the industriousness of the beaver bed

a hotbed of crime

a place where illegal activity flourishes

refers to a bed of earth, heated by fermenting manure, for artificially raising plants; hence, figuratively, a place that encourages the rapid growth of (usually undesirable) matter

one has made one's bed and one will now have to lie on it

one has to bear the consequences of one's actions

to be no bed of roses

to be difficult or uncomfortable

Robert Louis Stevenson (1850–94), *Virginibus Puerisque* I:i, 'Marriage is like life in this — that it is a field of battle, and not a bed of roses'

to be on one's death bed

(of a person, organisation or piece of equipment) to be about to cease effectiveness

to get out of bed on the wrong side

to be grumpy

to jump into bed with someone

to enter into a joint enterprise with another person

to put something to bed

finally to dispose of something

bedding

feather bedding

(in industrial relations) creating unnecessary jobs solely to increase employment; OR (in economics) assisting an inefficient industry by government grants or excessive tariff protection

bedfellow

bedfellow

collaborator

bedlam

bedlam

a scene of uproar

refers to the Hospital of St Mary of Bethlehem ('Bedlam'), which was used as a lunatic asylum from 1547 onwards

bedrock

bedrock price

lowest possible price

bee

to be a busy bee

to work with great diligence

to have a bee in one's bonnet

to have an obsession

beeline

to make a beeline for something

to go straight to something with great enthusiasm or to head for some goal by the most direct route

beer

not to be all beer and skittles

not to be all pleasant and easy

to be small beer

to be quite unimportant

to cry in one's beer

to show remorse

before

before one can say 'knife'

very quickly

before one can say 'Jack Robinson'

very quickly

origin of phrase is disputed, but dates from at least the eighteenth century

one needs to crawl before one can walk

skills are best developed in logical stages

the calm before the storm

the quiet period before an expected or inevitable crisis

to cast pearls before swine

to confer valuable benefits on someone who neither recognises nor appreciates them

Matthew 7:6, 'Neither cast ye your pearls before swine'

to count one's chickens before they are hatched

to treat as fact the expected results of a future proposal

originally attributed to Erasmus (1466–1536) in slightly different form

to put the cart before the horse
to do things in the wrong order
Rudyard Kipling (1865–1936), *The Conundrum of the Workshops*, 'We know the tail must wag the dog, for the horse is drawn by the cart'

to think twice before doing something
to consider with particular care

beg

to beg on bended knees
to request in great earnestness

begins

charity begins at home
a person's first responsibility should be to that person's family
John Fletcher (1579–1625), *The Wild-Goose Chase*, 'Charity and beating begins at home'

behind

behind someone's back
in a way that deliberately conceals an activity from a person

behind the scenes
out of public view or awareness
refers to the theatre

the power behind the throne
a person exercising the real authority but without having the official right to do so
William Pitt, Earl of Chatham (1708–78) ('Pitt the Elder'), 'There is something behind the throne greater than the king himself'

to be able to do something with one hand behind one's back
to be able to do something very easily

to be right behind the eight ball
to be in a position of extreme disadvantage
refers to US game of pool in which the ultimate objective is to pot the black ball (which is numbered 8)

to be wet behind the ears
to be excessively naVve and inexperienced

to have one hand tied behind one's back
to work with a handicap

to start from behind scratch
to be faced with a handicap
refers to the starting mark (with no handicap advantage) in a race

to tie someone's hands behind that person's back
to make it impossible for a person to act at all

beholder

beauty is in the eye of the beholder
some things are matters for subjective judgments
Shakespeare *Love's Labour Lost* II:i, 'Beauty is bought by judgment of the eye'

belfry

to have bats in the belfry
to be mad
literally refers to a tower or attic, or, figuratively, the head

believe

to believe in the tooth fairy
to be particularly gullible
refers to the mythical figure who exchanges children's milk teeth for a small sum of money

bell

bell-wether
first indication
refers to the leading sheep (wether) of a flock, this sheep having a bell hung around its neck

right on the bell
at the last possible moment
refers to boxing

saved by the bell
rescued before disaster strikes
refers to boxing

to be a warning bell
to be a warning

to bell the cat
to do some dangerous but highly useful mission
refers to a fable in which none of the mice was willing to put a warning bell on a cat

to ring a bell
to sound familiar or recall something to mind

bells

bells and whistles
imaginative variations, or with ostentatious embellishments

the alarm bells are ringing
it is unwise to proceed

to sound alarm bells

to give warning

belly

a fire in someone's belly
ambition or driving force producing great enthusiasm

I've had a belly full
I have had enough of this

below

below the salt
in a subordinate position
refers to the seating order at ancient Roman dining tables

to be below par
to be less than the desired standard

to hit someone below the belt
to act unfairly towards another person
refers to boxing

belt

a belt-and-braces approach
action backing up other action by way of excessive caution
refers to wearing a belt as well as braces

to belt someone over the head
to override someone's views or arguments, often involving the use of heavy pressure

to get something under one's belt
to add to one's experience by achieving something worthwhile

to hit someone below the belt
to act unfairly towards another person
refers to boxing

to tighten one's belt
to lower one's rate of spending

benchmark

a benchmark
a standard by which something is measured
refers to a mark (and associated bench) used in ancient building practices as a reference point for measuring and levelling

bend

to be round the bend
to be crazy
refers to the Kew Asylum in Victoria, Australia; the institution was built on the banks the River Yarra, on a curved part of the river originally known as the 'Old Bend'

to bend over backwards to do something
to go to great trouble to accommodate another person's wishes

to bend the rules
to overlook minor infractions of the rules

bended

to beg on bended knees
to request in great earnestness

bent

to be hell bent on something
to be very determined to achieve something, regardless of the adverse consequences

berth

to give someone a wide berth
to go out of one's way to avoid contact with a person
nautical metaphor

beside

to be beside oneself
to be very agitated

best

father knows best
as an expert, I know better than you do what is most suitable for you

first in best dressed
persons acting early will do better than latecomers

level best
making all possible effort
perhaps refers to railways

the very best of British luck
you will have a hard time of it, but you carry my best wishes

to claim that something is the best thing since sliced bread
to have a high opinion of the importance or novelty of an invention or practice

to give one's best shot
to make the best attempt possible

to put one's best face on something
to focus on the positive features surrounding a basically disastrous situation

to put one's best foot forward
to make a special effort

to want the best of both worlds

unreasonably to desire to get some advantage without incurring a corresponding disadvantage

bet

a good bet
a good proposition

you bet!
definitely!

you can bet your life on something
something is certain to happen

bLte

to be someone's bLte noire
to be a person whose ideas and actions cause upset and loathing in another person
French, *bLte noire* ('black beast')

bets

to hedge one's bets
to insure against a losing bet or investment by also investing on the opposite outcome

better

to be better than a poke in the eye with a burnt stick
to be not particularly welcome, but better than other alternatives

between

a rose between two thorns
something beautiful in the midst of ugliness

between you and me and the gatepost
confidentially

it is a long time between drinks
activity is occurring only very spasmodically

only a cigarette paper between them
virtually equal or close together

only a postage stamp between them
virtually equal or close together

only a tissue between them
virtually equal or close together

the choice is between eating well or sleeping well
one can invest for maximum yield or maximum security, but not both

to be between a rock and a hard place
to be faced with two equally difficult and uncomfortable choices

to be between Scylla and Charybdis
to be faced with two equally unpalatable alternatives that cannot both be avoided
refers to the voyage of Ulysses

to be between the devil and the deep blue sea
to be faced with two equally unpalatable alternatives that cannot both be avoided

to drive a wedge between two persons
to set out to cause a division between two persons
refers to the use of wedges in timber work

to fall between the cracks
to be ineligible for something because one does not fit neatly into any of several relevant categories

to fall between two stools
not to fit neatly into either of two available alternatives, and to waver between them

to have one's tail between one's legs
to be dejected or humiliated
refers to dogs

to hit someone right between the eyes
to be brutally frank
refers to fighting

to make bad blood between two parties
to cause ill feeling between two parties

to read between the lines
to appreciate the true significance of something not put into words

to take the bit between one's teeth
to face up to a problem
refers to riding or racing horses

beyond

to be beyond the pale
to be socially unacceptable, especially for unacceptable standards or behaviour
'the Pale' originally (fourteenth century and later) referred to that part of Ireland

under British rule (Latin *palus* 'a stake', marking a fence or boundary)

to be successful beyond one's wildest dreams
to be far more successful than one could have expected

bible

a bible basher
a person who makes unwelcome attempts to force religious beliefs on others

to be the bible
to be the authority

big

a big bang
a sudden major change in the environment

a big shot
an important person

a big wheel
an important person

speak softly and carry a big stick
be polite to your potential enemies but maintain an active and visible defensive and offensive capability
from a speech by US President Theodore Roosevelt in 1901

the big smoke
the big city

to be a big fish in a little pond
to be a person holding an important office but in an unimportant organisation

to be a big mouth
to lack discretion in one's conversation

to be too big for one's boots
to have an unwarranted belief in one's capabilities or status

to be too big for one's breeches
to have an exaggerated idea of one's own importance

to be unable to keep people away with a big stick
to be faced with a large crowd or much demand

to stand over someone with a big stick
to intimidate a person in order to get that person to act in a particular way

to wield a big stick
to assert power

bigger

someone's eyes are bigger than that person's stomach
a person is unrealistic in regard to that person's ability to cope with something

bill

to fit the bill
to meet all the requirements

to get a clean bill of health
after proper investigation to be found not wanting

bind

to bind someone hand and foot
completely to limit a person's freedom to act

to catch someone in a bind
to find a person in a difficulty from which that person cannot readily extricate himself or herself

binding

spellbinding
fascinating to an audience

bird

a bird in the hand is worth two in the bush
a benefit currently available is more valuable than a seemingly much larger benefit that might or might not be achieved in the future

a bird's-eye view
a general overview or summary of a subject, emphasising the major features

a little bird told me
I heard from an informant who cannot be named
Ecclesiastes 10:20, 'Even in your thought do not curse the king ... for a bird of the air will carry your voice or some winged creature tell the matter'

the bird has flown
the person sought is no longer about

the bird is carved
the necessary action has been taken

the early bird gets the worm
a person who acts ahead of others gets an advantage over them

to be a rare bird
to be an unusual type of individual

to have a bird brain

to be stupid

birds

birds of a feather flock together
persons of like interests gather in the same place
Samuel Rutherford (?1600–61), 'Fowls of a feather flock together'

that is strictly for the birds
that is trivial nonsense appealing only to the naVve and the gullible

to kill two birds with one stone
to achieve a second objective in the course of achieving the first objective

birth

to give birth to something
to create or invent something

birthright

to sell one's birthright for a mess of pottage
through foolishness to exchange something of substance for something of little value
Genesis 25:34, 'Then Jacob gave Esau bread and pottage of lentils ... thus Esau despised his birthright'

bit

that argument is wearing a bit thin
that case has been heard so often that it is losing its effect
refers to clothes or similar beginning to fail from continued use

that is a bit rich
that is very cheeky

to champ at the bit
to be impatient
refers to horses keen to begin

to give someone a bit of stick
to criticise a person mildly

to have a hair of the dog that bit one
to drink more alcohol in an attempt to overcome the effects of alcohol already consumed
refers to the belief that the hair of the rabid dog that bit a person was a cure for the madness that can ensue

to take the bit between one's teeth
to face up to a problem
refers to riding or racing horses

bite

the bark is worse than the bite
the harsh words belie the reality of mild action

to bite
to respond predictably to a remark designed to provoke

to bite off more than one can chew
to be over ambitious and thus unrealistic as to one's capabilities

to bite one's fingernails
anxiously to await a decision

to bite one's lip
to control emotion such as anger or mirth

to bite one's tongue
to resist from criticising

to bite someone's head off
rudely and excessively to express displeasure at a person

to bite someone's nose off
to speak to a person with excessive aggression

to bite the bullet
to face up to the difficulties of a situation
refers to the use of biting on a bullet as a means of controlling one's reaction to pain in a surgical procedure without anaesthetic (for example, following a military battle)

to bite the dust
to fall, to fail, to die

to bite the hand that feeds one
to show ingratitude
Edmund Burke (1729–97), *Thoughts and Details on Scarcity* (1797), 'And having looked to government for bread, on the very first scarcity they will turn and bite the hand that fed them'

to get only one bite at the cherry
to receive no further opportunity

to start to bite
to start to be effective

biting

to engage in back-biting
to criticise in a trivial, annoying unfriendly manner

bitten

hard-bitten
toughened by experience
refers to horses that are 'hard' in the mouth or bite (and thus difficult to control)

I could have bitten my tongue off

I wish that I had not made such an inappropriate remark

to be bitten

to be swindled

to be bitten with something

to become very enthusiastic over something

bitter

to be a bitter pill to swallow

to be a great humiliation or disappointment that has to be endured

black

a black hole

a place where things disappear without trace; OR an intermediate range of values producing anomalous results; OR a particularly obnoxious prison cell

the first and second definitions refer to an astronomical black hole — an area of extreme density from which even light cannot escape; the third definition refers to the infamous 'black hole of Calcutta'

a black sheep

a disreputable member of an otherwise reputable group

in black and white

in writing, spelling out all the details

Ben Jonson (1573–1637), *Every Man in hisHonour*, 'I have it here in black and white'

the pot calling the kettle black

criticising another person without realising one's own even greater shortcomings

there are black clouds on the horizon

bad news is expected

things look black

there is little hope of success or prosperity or a favourable outcome

to be a black-and-white issue

to involve very clear distinctions

Ben Jonson (1573–1637), *Every Man in his Honour*, 'I have it here in black and white'

to be black magic

to lack any scientific or logical basis

refers to witchcraft

to be in someone's black books

to be out of favour with a person

biblical allusion: refers to God's judgment and the desirability of having one's name entered in the book of life; *Rev* 20: 12, 'and the books were opened ... and the dead were judged out of those things that were written in the books, according to their works'

to be in the black

to have money

refers to the black ink used to indicate a credit in a manuscript accounting ledger

to blackball someone

to reject a person as unsuitable

refers to a vote against someone by secretly placing a black ball in a box (as opposed to a white or red ball which indicated approval); the voting procedure was common in ancient Rome and Greece — hence 'ballot' (French, *ballotte*, 'a little ball')

to give someone a black look

to indicate one's displeasure with a person

to have a black mark against one's name

to have a tarnished reputation

to paint a black picture

to state a set of unfavourable factors

to paint someone black

to ruin a person's reputation

blame

to shoulder the blame

to accept the responsibility for error

blanche

carte blanche

freedom to use one's discretion on behalf of another person

French, literally 'white card' (that is, a blank sheet of paper on which to write)

blank

to draw a blank

to be unsuccessful

refers to playing cards

to give someone a blank cheque

to give another person unlimited delegated authority

to have a blank canvas

freedom to create anything

refers to an artist's canvas

to refuse point blank

to refuse outright

refers to pointing at the white spot (blank, French blanc) in the centre of an archery target

to start with a blank sheet of paper

to commence an exercise without being bound by any established practices

blanket

to be a wet blanket
to be a spoil sport

to be born on the wrong side of the blanket
to be illegitimate

to throw a blanket over a proposal
to refuse to proceed with a proposal

blaze

to blaze a trail
to be the first person to do something
refers to marking a course to be followed by making blazes on a tree

blazing

with both barrels blazing
with great intensity

with all guns blazing
using all available devices

bleed

to bleed to death slowly
to be heading in gradual steps towards total ruin

bleeding

to stem the bleeding
to put a stop to the financial losses of a project

bleeds

one's heart bleeds for someone
one feels truly sad for a person's fate
derived from the Christian Church's veneration of the sacred heart of Jesus (*sacré couer*) which was symbolised by a bleeding heart — sacrificed for the sake of humanity

blessing

a blessing in disguise
an unwelcome but salutary experience
James Hervey (1696–1743), *Reflections on a Flower Garden*, 'Ee'en crosses from his sov'reign hand are blessings in disguise'

to be a mixed blessing
to be an outcome with some desirable and some undesirable features

to give one's blessing to something
to indicate one's approval of something

blew

the affair blew up
certain unwelcome facts have become publicly available

blind

a nod is the same as a wink to a blind horse
fine distinctions are not appropriate here
Captain Marryat (1792–1848), *Peter Simple*, 'But you're a dutiful son, so I'll say no more about it — a nod's as good as a wink to a blind horse'

blind Freddy could see that something is such-and-such
it is very obvious that something is such-and-such

the blind leading the blind
persons without the necessary skills for a task purporting to impart those skills to others
Matthew 15:14, 'And if the blind lead the blind, both shall fall into the ditch'

to be blind to something
to be unaware of some matter and its significance

to fly blind
to do something in ignorance of the relevant facts
refers to pilots flying without visual guidance (and relying on instruments)

to have a blind spot about something
to have a lack of understanding and perception about something
refers to that part of the retina insensitive to light, at the point of entry of the optic nerve

to rush into a blind alley
to make a precipitate move that does not lead one anywhere

to turn a blind eye to something
to pretend that something obvious does not exist
refers to action by Horatio, Lord Nelson (1758–1805), when disregarding Admiralty signals: 'I have only one eye — I have a right to be blind sometimes — I really do not see the signal!' (at the Battle of Copenhagen, reported in Southey, *Life of Nelson*, ch. 7)

blindly

to follow someone blindly
to follow a person unquestioningly

blinkers

to take one's blinkers off
to face reality
refers to the use of leather screens on a bridle to prevent a horse seeing sideways

block

someone's head is on the block
a person is in danger of being condemned; OR a person is in danger of having an appointment terminated
refers to execution by decapitation

stumbling block
an impediment or difficulty preventing the easy completion of some project; OR a dilemma involving a moral issue
1 Corinthians 8:9, 'But take heed lest by any means this liberty of yours become a stumbling block to them that are weak'

the cheering could be heard a block away
there was great rejoicing

to be a chip off the old block
to resemble one's father in behaviour and/or appearance

to be the new kid on the block
to lack the experience of others

to block someone's path
to interfere with a person's opportunity to advance

to put one's head on the block
to have the courage of one's convictions
refers to execution by decapitation

blocks

road blocks
difficulties

blood

a blueblood
a person of high birth
refers to the appearance of the blood of certain Spanish noble families — supposed to be more of a blue colour due to a lack of Moorish blood

bad blood
animosity

blood, sweat, and tears
hard work and much effort
Winston Churchill, House of Commons, 13 May 1940, 'I have nothing to offer but blood, toil, tears, and sweat'

bloodshed
serious harm that is deliberately caused

fresh blood
newly joined members of some organisation

one's own flesh and blood
one's own offspring, ancestors, or close relatives
Genesis 2:23, 'Bone of my bones, and flesh of my flesh'

that person's blood is worth bottling
that person is very clever or competent

the lifeblood
the main or essential ingredient; OR the person or factor instilling enthusiasm

there is blood in the streets
much damage has been done to a cause

there is blood in the water
something is likely to cause a person to go into a frenzy

there is blood on the floor
this has caused great anguish

to be after someone's blood
to be keen to make a person the victim of an angry confrontation

to be in someone's blood
to be something about which a person is inherently very knowledgeable or keen

to curdle one's blood
to be horrific

to do something in cold blood
to be cruel without feeling any emotion about it

to draw blood from a stone
to do the impossible

to draw first blood
to get an early advantage

to give something a blood transfusion
to give something new enthusiasm

to have blood on one's hands
to be the person responsible for someone else's predicament

Matthew 27:24, 'He [Pilate] took water and washed his hands in full view of the crowd. "My hands are clean of this man's blood," he declared'

to introduce new blood
to recruit new members to some organisation

to let blood
to allow some harm as the price for achieving some greater benefit
refers to surgical removal of a patient's blood

to make bad blood between two parties
to cause ill feeling between two parties

to make someone's blood boil
to make a person very angry

to see blood
to be very angry
refers to a frenzy excited in some animals by the sight of blood

to smell blood
to divine imminent victory

to thirst for blood
to be eager for revenge

bloodbath

a bloodbath
catastrophic losses

blooded

full-blooded
vigorous, with every effort

hot-blooded
very passionate
Horace (65–8 BC), '*Non ego hoc ferrem calidus iuventa consule planco* (I shouldn't have put up with this when I was a hot-blooded youth, and Plancus was consul)'

bloodletting

bloodletting
removal (perhaps violent) of persons from office or employment
refers to surgical removal of a patient's blood

bloody

to get a bloody nose
to suffer an undignified rebuff

blossom

to blossom
(of a person's attributes) to develop

blot

to be a blot on someone's escutcheon
to be a blemish on a person's character
refers to the shield on which a coat of arms is depicted; hence, a sign of dishonour on the symbol of one's name and honour

to blot one's copybook
to spoil one's previously good reputation or record

blow

a blow-by-blow description
a very detailed word picture of some event
refers to boxing

a body blow
a very damaging event

death blow
incident that results in the destruction of something

to be a severe blow
to be a great disappointment

to blow hot and cold
to vacillate
Revelations 3:15, 'I know thy works, that thou art neither cold nor hot'

to blow one's own trumpet
immodestly to publicise one's own attributes
refers to the trumpet as an instrument of triumph; *Joshua* 6:20, 'When the priests blew with the trumpets ... the wall fell down flat'

to blow one's top
to show anger
refers to a volcano

to blow something
unintentionally to destroy some opportunity

to blow something out of the water
to destroy something

to blow the cobwebs away
to revive an old issue

to blow the lid off something
to expose something no matter how embarrassing this might be

to blow the whistle on someone
to report a person's improper behaviour to the authorities or to publicise it

to blow up
(of a person) to express rage

to blow up in someone's face
to rebound on a person

to soften the blow
to take action to reduce the trauma of bad news

to strike a blow
to begin or resume work

to strike a blow for some principle
to work towards the attainment of some principle

blowing

to see which way the wind is blowing
to establish the factors relevant to a situation

John Seldon (1584–1654), 'Take a straw and throw it up into the air, you shall see by that which way the wind is'

blown

to get one's head blown off
to be abused very soundly

blows

it is an ill wind that blows no good
even a seeming misfortune leads to some blessings

blowtorch

to apply the blowtorch to something
to apply very strong pressure to some person

blue

a blueblood
a person of high birth

refers to the appearance of the blood of certain Spanish noble families — supposed to be more of a blue colour due to a lack of Moorish blood

blue ribbon
of superb quality

refers to the insignia of the Order of the Garter, or perhaps to the ribands used in agricultural shows and at race meetings

blue sky
unrealistic optimism

blue-eyed boy
person shown unjustified favouritism

once in a blue moon
very rarely

refers to the volcanic eruption at Krakatoa in 1883 when volcanic dust caused the moon to appear blue

to be a blue-chip stock
to be of excellent quality

to be a bolt from the blue
to be a totally unexpected event

to be between the devil and the deep blue sea
to be faced with two equally unpalatable alternatives that cannot both be avoided

to be in a blue funk
to be terrified

to come out of the blue
to be totally unexpected

to feel blue
to feel depressed

to go on until one is blue in the face
to do something difficult for a long time without being able to complete it

to have a blue fit
to be very agitated

to scream blue murder
to make serious allegations; OR to protest violently

perhaps refers to the French *morbleu* (altered version of *mort Dieu*, 'God's death'), a comic oath attributed to French speakers

true blue
superbly loyal

refers to the traditional blue colour of the Conservative Party in the UK

blueprint

blueprint
a master plan for some activity or a model that others can copy

refers to a detailed architectural or engineering drawing — originally consisting of white lines on a blue background

blush

at first blush
at first sight

refers to Middle English term *blusche*, 'a gleam, a glimpse'

board

a springboard
a situation from which one is able to make a rapid advance

across the board
over the whole range of activity

back to the drawing board
to start again from the very beginning

to act as a sounding board

to give, on request, constructive criticisms of ideas tentatively held
refers, originally, to a board placed behind a speaker (esp. a preacher) to reflect the speaker's voice forwards to the congregation or audience

to be above board
to be quite legitimate
refers to gambling

to be on the drawing board
to be being planned from the very beginning

to go overboard
to act foolishly and in an excessive way

to have the runs on the board
to have a demonstrable record of achievement
refers to scoring in cricket

to pipe someone on board
to welcome a person
nautical metaphor

to take something on board
to offer to give further consideration to a matter
nautical metaphor

boarders

to repel boarders
to keep out unwanted persons
refers to naval battles

boat

to be in the same boat
to share a common set of difficulties

to get off the boat
to dissociate oneself from some project

to miss the boat
to fail to exploit an opportunity

to rock the boat
to disturb the comfortable status quo

Bob

Bob's your uncle!
that solves the problem!
refers to the many preferments given in the nineteenth century by UK Prime Minister (Robert) Lord Salisbury to his nephew A. J. Balfour (and to a number of other relatives of the prime minister)

bob

not to be the full two bob
not to be very intelligent
refers to slang term for two shillings

to have two bob each way
to equivocate
refers to the slang term for two shillings, and to betting for a win or a place body

a body blow
a very damaging event

over my dead body
never

to keep body and soul together
barely to stay alive

boggles

the mind boggles
this is astonishing

boil

to bring something to the boil
to bring something to a climax

to come off the boil
to require urgent attention no longer

to make someone's blood boil
to make a person very angry

boiled

hard-boiled
toughened by experience
refers to cooking (esp. eggs)

boiling

to keep the pot boiling
to ensure that an issue stays current
refers to cooking

to reach boiling point
to reach a climax; OR to be close to losing one's temper boiler

not to bust one's boiler
not to exert oneself unduly
refers to a steam boiler

boils

it boils down to this
the essential features are as follows

bolt

to be a bolt from the blue
to be a totally unexpected event

to shoot one's bolt
to waste one's only opportunity; to have expended all one's effort
refers to an arrow, especially one for a crossbow

bolted

to shut the stable door after the horse has bolted
to take preventive action only after the relevant event

bolts

nuts and bolts
basic ingredients

bomb

a bombshell
an unpleasant surprise

a time bomb
a source of serious problems that are certain to surface later on

to be a bomb
to be grossly defective

to put a bomb under someone
to induce a person to take some action

bombard

to bombard someone with something
to overwhelm a person with material or to assail a person persistently with words of argument or abuse

bone

a bone of contention
the subject matter of violent disagreement
probably refers to dogs fighting over a bone

backbone
chief strength or character

to cut costs to the bone
to economise strictly

to get close to the bone
to cause discomfort by being accurate

to gnaw one's fingers to the bone
to fret

to have a bone to pick
to have a grievance that requires discussion

to point the bone at someone
to accuse a person
an Australian Aboriginal method of applying a curse

to put flesh and bone on something
to supply details of a proposal previously revealed only in outline

to throw someone a bone
to fob a person off with a symbolic but unimportant gesture
refers to feeding a dog

to work one's fingers to the bone
to work very hard

boneheaded

boneheaded
stupid

bones

to feel something in one's bones
to suspect something without having any real evidence for it

to make no bones about it
to be brutally frank

the bare bones
(of a story) nothing but the essential elements

bonnet

to have a bee in one's bonnet
to have an obsession

boo

to be too frightened to say 'boo' to a goose
to be excessively shy

booby

to win the booby prize
to do worse than all others

book

to be a closed book
to be a secret

to close the book on something
to terminate an activity

to judge a book by its cover
foolishly to go only by superficial appearances

to play by the book
to apply the rules strictly

to take a leaf out of someone's book
to model oneself on another person
refers to taking a page from the 'Book of Life' — *Rev* 20: 12, 'and the books were opened ... and the dead were judged out of those things that were written in the books, according to their works'

to talk one's book
to present arguments that, although plausible, are really designed to foster one's vested interest

to throw the book at someone
to prosecute a person with all the vigour allowed by law

to use every trick in the book
to try very hard and use every conceivable argument

books

to balance the books
to get one's own back

refers to accountancy

to be a turn-up for the books
to be a surprising development
refers to bookmaking and gambling

to be in someone's black books
to be out of favour with a person
biblical allusion: refers to God's judgment and the desirability of having one's name entered in the book of life; *Rev* 20: 12, 'and the books were opened … and the dead were judged out of those things that were written in the books, according to their works'

to be in someone's good books
to be well regarded by another person
biblical allusion: refers to God's judgment and the desirability of having one's name entered in the book of life; *Rev* 20: 12, 'and the books were opened … and the dead were judged out of those things that were written in the books, according to their works'

to be on some organisation's books
to be a member or client of some organisation

to cook the books
fraudulently to maintain false records of financial transactions

bookworm

a bookworm
a person who likes reading and study

boom

to lower the boom
to bring to account and punish

boot

the boot is on the other foot
the advantage is reversed

to give someone the boot
to terminate a person's appointment

to put the boot in
to issue a severe (possibly sadistic) reprimand to a person

boots

to be too big for one's boots
to have an unwarranted belief in one's capabilities or status

to go in boots and all
to do something very roughly
refers to fighting violently

to hang up one's boots
to retire

to have one's heart in one's boots
to be afraid or dejected

to lick someone's boots
to show humility

to quake in one's boots
to be afraid

bootstraps

to be British to one's bootstraps
to be very demonstrative about one's Britishness

to pull oneself up by one's bootstraps
to make a praiseworthy effort to better oneself unaided

bore

full-bore ahead!
proceed forward at full power!

to bore someone to death
to weary a person greatly by dull and uninteresting conversation or by lack of action

to bore someone to tears
to weary a person by dull and uninteresting conversation or by lack of action

to bore the pants off someone
to weary a person by dull and uninteresting conversation

born

not to have been born yesterday
not to be naVve

to be born on the wrong side of the blanket
to be illegitimate

to be born with a silver spoon in one's mouth
to be brought up by wealthy parents
refers to the traditional gift of a silver spoon (an 'apostle spoon') to a child at baptism — the child born of wealthy parents is assured of riches from the moment of birth and thus does not have to await baptism to receive a valuable gift

borrowed

to live on borrowed time
to live longer than expected

bottle

a bottleneck
a factor obstructing an even flow

to be a full bottle on something

to be very knowledgeable about a subject

to bottle-up some feeling
to keep some feeling entirely to oneself

to let the genie out of the bottle
to cause something irreversible to take place
'genie' was adopted (to refer to a spirit released from a bottle) by the French translators of *Arabian Nights' Entertainments*

to put the genie back in the bottle
to undo something that cannot be undone
'genie' was adopted (to refer to a spirit released from a bottle) by the French translators of *Arabian Nights' Entertainments*

bottling

that person's blood is worth bottling
that person is very clever or competent

bottlewasher

to be chief cook and bottlewasher
to perform a range of duties single-handedly — ranging from important to menial

bottom

from the bottom of one's heart
very sincerely

rock bottom
very low

the bottom line
the conclusion that matters or the net effect of a series of developments
refers to the last line is a series of calculations or accounts

to be at the bottom of the food chain
to be at the lowest level in a hierarchy

to be at the bottom of the heap
to be in the lowest position in a hierarchy

to be at the bottom of the ladder
to be in the most junior position in some hierarchy

to be at the bottom of the totem pole
to be in the most junior position in some hierarchy
refers to a pole with emblems or carvings having religious significance

to scrape the bottom of the barrel
to be forced to use the last available resources; to lower one's standards because one is short of resources

bounce

to bounce back
to resume a cheerful existence after some setback

bounds

by leaps and bounds
with surprisingly fast progress

bow

shots across the bow
warnings
nautical metaphor

to bow down
to succumb to pressure

to bow out
to retire from some activity

to draw a long bow
to state a conclusion that, although possible, is unlikely on the known facts
refers to archery

to have a second string to one's bow
to have an additional qualification appropriate to the task
refers to archery

to take a bow
to receive recognition

bowl

to be in a goldfish bowl
to be very open to view

Box

Box and Cox
two persons who are never around at the same time
refers to the name of a play by J. M. Morton (1811–91), *Box and Cox* (adapted from the French)

box

the whole box and dice
all relevant components

to be in the box seat
to be in a very powerful position to control activity
refers to the driver's seat in a horse-drawn carriage

to be on one's soap box
to hold forth on an issue about which one feels keenly
refers to orators standing on soap boxes (strong wooden boxes) as a platform

to be one out of the box
to be unexpectedly superb
refers to magician's trick

to open a Pandora's box
to do something that produces all sorts of undesired and unexpected side-effects
refers to the woman in Greek mythology who brought misery to the world; Pandora's box contained all human ills and, when opened, it released uncontrollable misery on humanity

to put someone back in his or her box
to require a person to act in accordance with that person's level of seniority

to shadow box
to go through the motions without achieving or intending to achieve anything
refers to training for boxing by punching at one's own moving shadow

boy

a backroom boy
someone who works behind the scenes
Lord Beaverbrook (24 April 1941), 'to whom must praise be given ... to the boys in the backroom' (referring to the anonymous laboratory workers who contributed so much to scientific warfare and war production in World War II)

a whipping boy
a person made to suffer for the faults of others
refers to a boy kept for whipping when a king or prince deserved punishment

as every schoolboy knows
as is recognised by everyone
Jonathon Swift (1667–1745), *The Country Life*, 1:81,'How haughtily he cocks his nose, / To tell what every schoolboy knows'; Lord Macaulay (1800–59), *Lord Clive* (Jan. 1840), 'Every schooboy knows who imprisoned Montezuma, and who strangled Atahualpa'

blue-eyed boy
person shown unjustified favouritism

since Adam was a boy
for a very long time
refers to the name of the first man as recorded in *Genesis* 2

to be a good boy
to be cooperative

to send a boy on a man's errand
to engage a person to do a task beyond that person's capabilities

boys

to separate the men from the boys
to distinguish between those with and without certain skills

brace

to splice the main brace
to serve an extra ration of rum
nautical metaphor

braces

a belt-and-braces approach
action backing up other action by way of excessive caution
refers to wearing a belt as well as braces

brain

anyone with even half a brain
anyone with any degree of common sense or knowledge

to be a bear of very little brain
to have little intelligence
refers to A. A. Milne's *Winnie-the-Pooh*

to have a bird brain
to be stupid

to have something on one's brain
to be obsessed with some notion

to pick someone's brain
to get the benefit of another person's knowledge and experience

brainchild

brainchild
inspired original idea

brained

hare-brained
wildly stupid
Benjamin Disraeli (1804–81), speech 1878, 'The hare-brained chatter of irresponsible frivolity'

brainstorm

to brainstorm
to pool thoughts in the course of a session designed to generate fresh ideas and especially to build up on the ideas of others

brainwash

to brainwash someone
systematically and forcibly to instil certain attitudes in place of previous ideas in the mind of a person

brainwave

a brainwave
a suddenly occurring bright idea

brake

to put the brake on someone
to stop or slow down a person

branch

to hold out an olive branch
to make peace overtures
the olive branch was recognised as a symbol of peace and prosperity in many ancient civilisations; *Genesis* 8:11, 'And the dove came in to him in the evening; and lo, in her mouth was an olive leaf plucked off: so Noah knew that the waters were abated off the earth'

brass

not to have a brass razoo
to be very poor
refers to an imaginary coin of trivial value

to get down to brass tacks
to discuss the aspects that really matter
perhaps refers to Cockney rhyming slang ('brass tacks' = 'facts')

brave

to be a brave soldier
courageously to do one's duty

to brave the water
to enter a venture with courage and determination

to put a brave face on it
to face adversity cheerfully

breach

once more unto the breach
let us get on and undertake the task again
Shakespeare, *Henry V* III:i, 'Once more unto the breach, dear friends, once more; / Or close the wall up with our English dead!'

to stand in the breach
to fill a gap in the defences and bear the brunt of an attack or criticism
Shakespeare, *Henry V* III:i, 'Once more unto the breach, dear friends, once more; / Or close the wall up with our English dead!'

bread

a bread-and-butter issue
a basic issue that is of importance to many people

a bread-winner
a person earning by personal exertion the income of a household
Deuteronomy 8:3, 'Man doth not live by bread alone, but by every word that proceedeth out of the mouth of the Lord' (see also *Matthew* 5:4)

to be someone's bread and butter
to be a person's livelihood or to be a person's everyday experience

to cast one's bread upon the waters
to give generously because one will eventually be rewarded for one's generosity
Ecclesiastes 11:1, 'Cast thy bread upon the waters: for thou shalt find it after many days'

to claim that something is the best thing since sliced bread
to have a high opinion of the importance or novelty of an invention or practice

to know on which side one's bread is buttered
to be aware of the important personally advantageous considerations

to put jam on someone's bread
to make a good situation even better

breadth

to be within a hair's breadth of something
to be extremely close to something

break

at a break-neck pace
very fast
refers to horseriding at great speed

heartbreak
despair
Psalms 69:21, 'Thy rebuke hath broken my heart; I am full of heaviness'; Shakespeare *Hamlet* I:ii, 'But break my heart ... '

not to break someone's door down
to be unenthusiastic about someone's goods or services

to break a drought

to resume supplies after an interval

to break down the barriers
to do away with the prejudice preventing something

to break new ground
to do something for which there is no precedent
refers to ploughing of ground

to break one's duck
to end a spell that had no results
refers to cricket in which a 'duck' represents no score

to break one's neck to do something
to be particularly keen
refers to reckless enthusiasm

to break ranks
to identify oneself as having separate interests or views from the rest of a group
military metaphor

to break the back of a task
to complete the bulk of the work

to break the ice
to take the initiative in starting discussions
Francis Bacon (1561–1626), *Of Cunning*, 'In things that are tender and unpleasing, it is good to break the ice by some whose words are of less weight ...'

to break someone's heart
to act in a way causing great upset to another person
Psalms 69:21, 'Thy rebuke hath broken my heart; I am full of heaviness'; Shakespeare *Hamlet* I:ii, 'But break my heart ... ')

to break the spell
to spoil the effect

to make or break someone
to be a factor leading either to a person's success or to that person's failure, with no intermediate position

breaker

a circuit-breaker
an event that breaks the tension in a dispute
refers to electrical circuits

breakfast

to be a dog's breakfast
to be a very messy arrangement

to be able to eat someone for breakfast
to be able to outwit a person very easily

breaking

back-breaking
overburdening

one cannot make an omelette without breaking eggs
the desired end dictates the means even if they cause harm to others

breakthrough

a breakthrough
major success in overcoming obstacles to knowledge or a proposal

breast

to beat one's breast
to express sorrow
refers to traditional expression of grief

to make a clean breast of something
to confess

breath

not to hold one's breath for something
to give up all expectation

to be a breath of fresh air
to be a pleasant change from the past

to draw a deep breath
to get ready for exertion or for emotional news

to take one's breath away
to surprise greatly, or astonish

to wait with bated breath
to be excited in anticipation of some event

to waste one's breath
to talk and request something without achieving anything

breathe

to breathe down someone's neck
to cause annoyance to another person by remaining in that person's vicinity or by supervising that person too closely; OR to be narrowly behind another person in some competitive situation

to breathe easy
(following some crisis) to relax

to breathe life into a corpse
to revive something moribund

breathing

to get some breathing space
to get more time in which to accomplish something

breeches

to be too big for one's breeches
to have an exaggerated idea of one's own importance

breeze

it's a breeze
it is easy

brick

it is London to a brick on
it is virtually certain
a metaphor coined by the Australian horse-race caller, Ken Howard, to indicate that one could bet the whole of London against a single brick — in the confident expectation of winning

to bang one's head against a brick wall
to fight an unwinnable case

to be up against a brick wall
to be unable to achieve anything because of intractable opposition or apathy

to drop a brick
to make a socially embarrassing or inappropriate announcement

brickbats

to throw brickbats at someone
to express displeasure with a person
refers to portions of brick, esp. ones used as missiles

bricks

one cannot make bricks without straw
one cannot achieve results in the absence of adequate resources
Exodus 6:7 'Ye shall no more give the people straw to make bricks … let them go and gather straw for themselves'

bride

to be off like a bride's nightie
to act promptly

willing bride
(commerce) keen partner

bridge

a lot of water has flowed under the bridge since then
much has happened since then

to be water under the bridge
to matter no longer

to bridge a gap
to fill a need or make up a shortfall

to bridge a gulf
to overcome a wide divergence in views
Luke 16:26, 'Between us and you there is a great gulf fixed'

to cross a bridge only when one comes to it
to await the crystallisation of a situation before sorting it out

bridgehead

a bridgehead
an advance post set up to facilitate further access to some new market, etc.
military metaphor

bridges

to build bridges
to work at improving relationships

to burn one's bridges
to do something irreversible

to mend bridges
to restore a broken-up relationship

bridle

to make a wigwam for a goose's bridle
to do something unspecified
nonsense said to children

bright

bright-eyed and bushy-tailed
naVve but enthusiastic

the bright side
the favourable aspects

the one bright spot on the horizon
the only hopeful aspect

bring

to bring a fact home to someone
to make a person recognise a fact despite that person's inclination to the contrary

to bring a plate
to take food to a party

to bring home the bacon
to be successful
refers to bringing home a valued prize

to bring someone back to the pack
to make a person conform to bring someone down to earth

to disillusion a person

to bring someone to heel
to make a person conform
refers to the training of dogs

to bring something into focus
to put some matter into its proper context and explain its true significance

to bring something to the boil
to bring something to a climax

to bring out one's biggest guns
to use the most impressive persons or arguments

to bring something to light
to draw to public attention

to bring the house down
to obtain rapturous applause
refers to the theatre

to labour mightily and bring forth a mouse
to be quite ineffective

brink

to push someone over the brink
by a small action to cause the absolute ruin (financially or emotionally) of someone already in peril

British

the very best of British luck
you will have a hard time of it, but you carry my best wishes

to be British to one's bootstraps
to be very demonstrative about one's Britishness

broad

a broad-brush approach
the handling of a situation with a deliberate lack of attention to detail
rough justice

a broad church
an organisation willing to accept members with a wide variety of different views

it is as broad as it is long
it does not really matter

to have broad shoulders
to be able to cope well with responsibility

broaden

to broaden someone's mind
to expose a person to a greater variety of experiences and interests than that person had previously experienced

broadside

a broadside
a short verbal attack
refers to all the guns situated or able to fire on one side of a ship

broke

all hell broke loose
great confusion erupted
John Milton (1608–74) *Paradise Lost*, 'Wherefore with thee came not all hell broke loose?'

the straw that broke the camel's back
the latest step that, when added to a large number of seemingly harmless previous steps, sets off a sudden significant event resulting from the cumulative effect

broken

to be a broken reed
to be a weak and unreliable person
Isaiah 36:6 and *2 Kings* 18:21, 'Lo, thou trustest in the staff of this broken reed, on Egypt; whereon if a man lean, it will go into his hand and pierce it'

bronze

to be cast in bronze
to be virtually unalterable

broom

a new broom
a changed regime that is likely to alter the status quo

broth

too many cooks spoil the broth
more than one leader can confuse and harm a project brother

a soul brother
a person of similar ideals

brow

highbrow
intellectual or cultural

brows

to knit one's brows
to indicate one's displeasure

browned

to be browned off
to be fed up

brownie

to get brownie points

to receive credit for being very well behaved, or for meritorious achievement

refers to junior girl guide members; the metaphor is often used jocularly or sarcastically with respect to adults

bruises

to nurse one's bruises

to adjust oneself to defeat

brush

a broad-brush approach

the handling of a situation with a deliberate lack of attention to detail

to be tarred with the same brush

to be damned merely because of one's association with another person

refers to treating cuts on sheep with a tarbrush

to brush someone aside

to pass over and ostentatiously ignore a person

to give someone the brush-off

to make it clear that one does not want dealings or conversation with a person

bubble

a South Sea bubble

an unrealistic financial venture that is bound to result in total loss

refers to a notorious financial scandal involving the South Sea Company (UK) in 1720

froth and bubble

superficially attractive but really insignificant items

'Life is mainly froth and bubble ... ' (folk rhyme)

the bubble has burst

the inevitable has occurred, or the scheme has come to ruination

buck

the buck stops here

I accept full responsibility

hand-lettered sign on desk of US President Harry S. Truman (Phillips, *The Truman Presidency*, Ch. 12)

to pass the buck

to shift responsibility to someone else

refers to the buckhorn knife passed around the table to indicate the dealer while playing poker

bucket

to be only a drop in the bucket

to be quite insignificant in the total scene

to kick the bucket

to die

to tip a bucket on someone

to point out, in a humiliating way, another person's faults

Buckley

to have Buckley's chance

to have no expectation at all

a pun, a reference to what follows 'Buckley' in 'Buckley & Nunn', the name of a well-known former Melbourne retailer

bud

to nip something in the bud

to stop some activity in its early stages when stopping it is still relatively easy

refers to the first signs of growth in plants

buggy

the horse-and-buggy days

long ago

build

to build bridges

to work at improving relationships

to build up a war chest

to accumulate cash in readiness for some move

building

to engage in empire building

to set out to expand the size of the business or bureaucratic unit for which one is responsible, especially as a means of increasing one's own importance

built

Rome was not built in a day

complicated things require time

bull

a bull in a china shop

a careless person likely to cause great damage

a cock-and-bull story

an explanation that is completely unbelievable and unacceptable

Laurence Sterne (1713–68), *Tristram Shandy*, 'Said my mother, "What is this story all about?" — "a cock and a bull," said Yorick.'

to be a red rag to a bull
to be something that makes a person very angry and very excited
refers to the erroneous belief that the colour red, rather than the motion of waving, excites a bull

to be within a bull's roar of something
to be very close to something

to charge like a wounded bull
to impose excessive prices
a play on words; not a simile

to hit the bull's eye
to be extremely accurate in an activity; to score derived from archery

to take the bull by the horns
to come to grips with the realities of a difficult problem

bulldoze

to bulldoze some proposal through
to ensure the passage of some measure in complete disregard of criticism or opposition

bullet

a magic bullet
a highly effective guaranteed remedy to bite the bullet
to face up to the difficulties of a situation
refers to the use of biting on a bullet as a means of controlling one's reaction to pain in a surgical procedure without anaesthetic (for example, following a military battle)

to have a bullet that can be fired
to have available an effective weapon that can be used at will

bullets

a gun with no bullets
something incomplete and therefore useless for the desired purpose

bump

to bump into someone
to meet a person accidentally

bundle

to drop one's bundle
to become despondent

to save a bundle
to save much money

bunfight

a bunfight
a social gathering; a tea party

burden

to put a burden on someone's shoulders
to impose responsibilities on a person

buried

dead and buried
(of some issue) definitely concluded, especially so long ago as to be nearly forgotten

burn

heartburn
distress or regret at some disappointment
originally referred to passion, as in *Luke* 24:32, 'Did not our hearts burn within us, while he talked with us by the way?'

to burn one's bridges
to do something irreversible

to burn one's fingers
to suffer (esp. loss of money) through foolishness or meddling
refers to taking chestnuts from a fire

to burn oneself out
to overexert oneself

to burn the candle at both ends
to exhaust one's resources through working excessive hours'

to burn the midnight oil
to work late into the night
Francis Quarles (1592–1644), *Emblems*, 'We spend our midday sweat, our midnight oil; / we tire the night in thought, the day in toil'

burner

something is on the back burner
consideration is postponed pending further research

burning

a burning question
a much discussed question

to have money burning a hole in one's pocket
to be impatient to spend or invest available funds

to keep the home fires burning
to maintain normal domestic activity during the temporary absence of the main provider of the household

were your ears burning?
we were discussing you
Pliny: 'When our ears do glow and tingle, some do talk of us in our absence'

burns

to fiddle while Rome burns
to neglect important considerations while concentrating on trivial side-issues
refers to Nero's behaviour during the burning of Rome (AD 64) when he played a lyre and watched the spectacle from a height

burnt

to be better than a poke in the eye with a burnt stick
to be not particularly welcome, but better than other alternatives

burst

the bubble has burst
the inevitable has occurred, or the scheme has come to ruination

the dam burst
the cumulative effect of many things caused a disaster

bursting

to be bursting at the seams
to be very crowded

bury

to bury one's head in the sand
to refuse to face up to an unpleasant truth
refers to the reputed habit of ostriches in danger

to bury the hatchet
to abandon hostilities
refers to tradition of North American indigenous peoples to symbolise cessation of hostilities

bus

the wheels are back under the bus
normal activity has been resumed

to jump on the bus
to join an activity already well under way

to miss the bus
to fail to exploit an opportunity

bush

a bird in the hand is worth two in the bush
a benefit currently available is more valuable than a seemingly much larger benefit that might or might not be achieved in the future

a bush lawyer
a person without legal qualifications who has a reasonable, although not perfect, knowledge of the law, and who likes to make technical points in arguments

to beat about the bush
to fail to come to the point
refers to hunters flushing game from cover by beating of the vegetation in which animals are hidden

bushed

to be bushed
to be lost or exhausted or puzzled or confused

bushel

to hide one's light under a bushel
to keep others in ignorance of one's skills and experience
Luke 11:33, 'No man, when he hath lighted a candle, putteth it in a secret place, neither under a bushel'

bushfires

to fight bushfires
to deal with crises as they arise rather than take preventive action

bushy

bright-eyed and bushy-tailed
naVve but enthusiastic

business

monkey business
mischievous or underhand activity

to mean business
to demonstrate a serious intent to do something

busman

a busman's holiday
leisure time spent in a way not significantly different from one's normal business activities

bust

not to bust one's boiler
not to exert oneself unduly
refers to a steam boiler

busy

to be a busy bee
to work with great diligence

butt

to butt in
to involve oneself, uninvited, in someone else's conversation
refers to the aggressive action of animals with the head

to get up off one's butt
to cease being apathetic
refers to US slang for the buttocks

butter

a bread-and-butter issue
a basic issue that is of importance to many people

a butter fingers
a person unable to catch and/or hold on to an object

someone looks as if butter would not melt in his or her mouth
a person looks sweet and innocent

to be someone's bread and butter
to be a person's livelihood or to be a person's everyday experience

buttered

to know on which side one's bread is buttered
to be aware of the important personally advantageous considerations

butterflies

to have butterflies in one's stomach
a feeling of anxiety

butterfly

to have a butterfly mind
not to concentrate on the matter on hand

button

to button up one's purse
to refuse to spend money

to hit the panic button
to act hastily and irrationally

to press a button
to make something happen

buy

I buy that
I accept that idea

to buy a pig in a poke
to buy goods of unknown quality
refers to the practice of selling a person a cat (purported to be a pig) in a bag (or poke); if the person opened the bag and looked inside, that person 'let the cat out of the bag'

to buy into some argument
to seek to participate in some discussion

to buy something for a song
to buy something very cheaply

to buy straw hats in winter
to buy in a depressed market when most other people are sellers

buzz

to buzz off
to go away

C

cab

to be the first cab off the rank
to be the first chosen or tried out

cabbage

to be on someone's cabbage patch
to engage in a competitive activity in a territory regarded by someone already there as rightfully belonging exclusively to that person

Cain

the mark of Cain
disgrace
refers (wrongly) to a supposed mark of disgrace placed upon Cain as punishment for the killing of his brother; the mark was, in fact, a sign of God's protection against anyone attempting to kill Cain; *Genesis* 4:15, 'And the Lord set a mark upon Cain, lest any finding him should kill him'

to raise Cain
to create a disturbance
Genesis 4:5, 'And Cain was very wroth, and his countenance fell'

cake

a share of the cake
a portion of the total available for distribution

that takes the cake
that is quite absurd or outrageous or excessively cheeky

to be a piece of cake
to be very easy or greatly to one's liking

to be icing on top of the cake
to be an additional benefit in an already satisfactory scenario
to want to have one's cake and eat it too
to want two mutually exclusive alternatives

calf
to kill the fatted calf
to demonstrate welcome and complete acceptance of another person
Luke 15:23. 'And bring hither the fatted calf and let us eat, and be merry'

call
a clarion call
a strong signal that is an unmistakable invitation to do something
port of call
one of a series of places being visited
nautical mataphor
to call a spade a spade
to speak bluntly; not to use euphemisms
to call it a day
to cease involvement with some activity
to call off the dogs
to abandon a pursuit or inquiry
refers to hunt master calling off the dogs if they are on the wrong scent
to call the shots
to have the direction over a project

calling
the pot calling the kettle black
criticising another person without realising one's own even greater shortcomings

calls
he who pays the piper calls the tune
a person contributing money or resources to a project is entitled to control it

calm
the calm before the storm
the quiet period before an expected or inevitable crisis

came
all their Christmases came at once
they were overjoyed
that person came unstuck
that person's plans did not work out

camel
the straw that broke the camel's back
the latest step that, when added to a large number of seemingly harmless previous steps, sets off a sudden significant event resulting from the cumulative effect

camp
in our camp
in the group, representing our vested interest

camps
to have one's feet in both camps
to have good relations with two opponents

can
a can of worms
a collection of complex intertwined problems
the empty can makes the most noise
the least worthy arguments often attract the most publicity
to carry the can for someone
to accept the blame for another person's actions or inactions
to kick the communist can
to take every opportunity to exacerbate fear of communism in others
cancer
a cancer
an evil that is likely to spread

candle
not fit to hold a candle to someone
greatly inferior to another person
refers to a servant holding a candle to assist a more senior person
not to be worth the candle
to be too expensive in relation to the true value; AND/OR not to be worth the effort required
to burn the candle at both ends
to exhaust one's resources through working excessive hours'

caning
to take a caning
to suffer the adverse consequences of one's acts or omissions

cannon

a loose cannon on the deck
a person or factor out of control and likely to cause trouble
nautical metaphor

canoe

to paddle one's canoe
to do something unaided and in one's own way
phrase first used by Captain Marryat (1792–1848) *Settlers in Canada*, ch. viii (1844)

canter

to win the prize in a canter
to win very easily
refers to horse racing

canvas

to get off the canvas
to recover after near defeat
refers to boxing

to have a blank canvas
freedom to create anything
refers to an artist's canvas

cap

a feather in one's cap
a meritorious personal achievement
refers to the practice in a number of cultures of adding a feather to the headgear of a person in recognition of a significant personal achievement

cap
upper permitted limit

if the cap fits then wear it
if that description corresponds with your characteristics, then you are in that category

to cap a story
to tell an even funnier story than the one just told

to earn a dunce's cap
to do something stupid
a 'dunce' being derived from the name of Duns Scotus (1265–1308) and his followers ('Dunsers') whose hair-splitting theology was later perceived to be opposed to learning and enlightenment; Thomas Fuller (1608–61), 'a dunce, void of learning but full of books'

to go cap in hand
to show humility while soliciting a favour

to put one's thinking cap on
to concentrate on finding a solution to a difficult problem

to set one's cap at someone
(of females) to try to attract a person as a marriage partner

to throw one's cap into the air
to express joy; OR to celebrate some achievement

caravan

the caravan will roll on
the activity will continue

carbon

a carbon copy
an exact imitation
refers to the practice of producing a copy of a document by typing the original with carbon paper beneath, thus simultaneously making a copy

card

a three-card trick
an extremely simple yet effective ruse used by a dishonest person to induce victims to hand over some of their assets

a wild card
(in general) an unexpected unpredictable development; OR (in playing cards) a card of a value specified by the player holding it; OR (in sport) a player or a team given entrance to a competition by the organisers, even if the entry is not strictly merited; OR (in computing) a character that will match any other character in a search string

drawcard
feature expected to attract a crowd

to have a card up one's sleeve
secretly to have information relevant to a transaction
refers to card games

to hold the trump card
to be in an unbeatable position to defeat others
refers to playing cards

to play every card in the pack
to try very hard and use every conceivable argument
refers to playing cards

to play the last card in the pack
to be forced to use one's last expedient

refers to playing cards

to play the trump card
to make a final move, thereby defeating one's opponents
refers to playing cards

cards

a house of cards
an organisation that gives a misleading impression of solidity

let the cards fall where they may
irrespective of what happens
refers to playing cards

to be on the cards
to be likely

to have the cards stacked against one
to be faced with many difficulties frustrating a project
refers to playing cards

to hold all the cards
to be assured of victory
refers to playing cards

to hold one's cards close to one's chest
to keep one's plans and strategies secret
refers to playing cards

to lay one's cards on the table
to be utterly frank and open or to honestly disclose one's position
refers to playing cards

to play one's cards right
to approach a matter sensibly
refers to playing cards

to play the cards as they fall
to deal with problems as they arise
refers to playing cards

without any cards to play
without the means to achieve something
refers to playing cards

care

a devil-may-care attitude
a reckless attitude

not to care a hoot
not to show the slightest concern or enthusiasm

not to care a pin for something
not to have the slightest interest in something

carpet

the red-carpet treatment
courtesies extended to a person to make that person feel important and welcome
refers to the welcome accorded a visiting dignitary

to be on the carpet
to be lectured in regard to one's alleged misdeeds

to get a magic carpet ride to something
to be given an easy and fortunate passage to an objective
refers to the magic carpet (of Oriental legend) that transported its owners wherever they wished

to sweep something under the carpet
to pretend that some blemish does not exist

carried

to be carried away
to be excited by something imaginative

carrots

sticks and carrots
disincentives and incentives in combination
refers to the handling of donkeys

carry

speak softly and carry a big stick
be polite to your potential enemies but maintain an active and visible defensive and offensive capability
from a speech by US President Theodore Roosevelt in 1901

to carry a spare tyre
to be fat

to carry a torch for someone
to harbour (perhaps secret and unrequited) desires for love and marriage
refers to the torch of love

to carry coals to Newcastle
to do something ridiculously unnecessary
refers to the coal-mining district of Newcastle, UK

to carry the can for someone
to accept the blame for another person's actions or inactions

to carry the world on one's shoulders
to perform a huge task alone

refers to Atlas, who was condemned to bear the heavens on his shoulders for leading the Titans against the gods

to carry weight
to be influential

cart

to put the cart before the horse
to do things in the wrong order
Rudyard Kipling (1865–1936), *The Conundrum of the Workshops*, 'We know the tail must wag the dog, for the horse is drawn by the cart'

to upset the applecart
to engage in conduct disturbing a peaceful state of affairs and thereby to cause discomfort

carte

carte blanche
freedom to use one's discretion on behalf of another person
French, literally 'white card' (that is, a blank sheet of paper on which to write)

carve

to carve out a niche for oneself
deliberately to create an opportunity to use one's talents effectively

carved

the bird is carved
the necessary action has been taken

to be carved in granite/marble
to be virtually unalterable

case

a basket case
a poorly performing enterprise probably doomed to failure
perhaps refers to the practice of foundlings hospitals leaving baskets on the doorstep to receive abandoned infants

to be an open-and-shut case
to be an unarguable proposition

to have a cast-iron case
to be assured absolutely of victory in a dispute, an argument, or in legal proceedings

to make a federal case out of something
to attach far too much significance to a trivial issue

cash

a cash cow
a source of ready money

cast

the die is cast
the course of action is irreversible

to be cast in bronze
to be virtually unalterable

to be cast in someone's mould
to take after another person

to cast a chill over something
to be a depressing influence over something

to cast a cloud over something
to spoil the pleasure of an occasion

to cast a shadow over something
to introduce a note of warning or sadness in regard to some matter

to cast an eye over something
to look at something critically

to cast one's bread upon the waters
to give generously because one will eventually be rewarded for one's generosity
Ecclesiastes 11:1, 'Cast thy bread upon the waters: for thou shalt find it after many days'

to cast prudence to the winds
to cease being careful or wise

to cast sheep's eyes at someone
to look at a person amorously

to cast pearls before swine
to confer valuable benefits on someone who neither recognises nor appreciates them
Matthew 7:6, 'Neither cast ye your pearls before swine'

cast-iron

to give a cast-iron guarantee
to give a very secure undertaking to do something

to have a cast-iron case
to be assured absolutely of victory in a dispute, an argument, or in legal proceedings

castle

a castle in Spain
a desirable imagining, but an impracticable proposition

a castle in the air
a desirable imagining, but an impracticable proposition

cat

a cat-and-dog existence

a life full of frequent squabbles

a cat may look at a king

don't give yourself airs!

a copycat

a person who imitates another person's ideas

a fat cat

a well-remunerated politician, public servant, or businessperson

a game of cat and mouse

negotiations between two parties of unequal bargaining power during which the stronger makes some temporary concessions to the weaker without, however, affecting the latter's eventual total defeat

there is more than one way to skin a cat

this can be achieved in a variety of ways

there is no room to swing a cat

this place is very small

refers to the swinging of a whip (a cat-o'-nine-tails) in the confined space of a ship's hull

to be a cat's paw

to be a person who is being used as a tool by others

refers to the fable of the monkey who used the paw of his friend, the cat, to extract roasted chestnuts from the fire

to be the cat's pyjamas

to be the very best, to be superlatively good

American slang (origin obscure)

to bell the cat

to do some dangerous but highly useful mission

refers to a fable in which none of the mice was willing to put a warning bell on a cat

to kick the cat

to take out one's anger on some innocent party

to let the cat out of the bag

to reveal an embarrassing secret

refers to the practice of selling a person a cat (purported to be a pig) in a bag (or poke) — hence 'a pig in a poke'; if the person opened the bag and looked inside, that person 'let the cat out of the bag'

to see which way the cat jumps

to await developments

to throw a cat among the pigeons

to cause consternation and upset

when the cat is away the mice will play

in the absence of supervision discipline will be lax

wild cat

(of a strike) unofficial; OR (of an oil well) drilled as a pure prospect; OR (of a financial scheme) very hazardous

cats

to rain cats and dogs

to rain heavily

derived from ancient northern mythology in which cats and dogs were symbolically linked to weather: the cat can be taken as a symbol of falling rain and the dog as a symbol of wind gusts

catalyst

a catalyst

a factor causing something to happen

in chemistry, a catalyst is strictly, a factor that facilitates (but does not initiate) a chemical reaction

catapult

to catapult

(of sales, etc.) to increase rapidly

to catapult to fame

to achieve fame unexpectedly quickly

catch

catch 22

a condition or consequence that precludes success; a dilemma where the victim cannot win

title of a 1961 novel by Joseph Heller in which a man pleads insanity to escape war service, but whose plea of insanity demonstrates his inherent sanity

first catch your hare

do things in logical order and after proper preparation

generally attributed to Hannah Gleese, habit-maker to the Prince of Wales and co-author of *The Art of Cookery Made Plain and Easy* (1747)

to catch someone flat-footed

to take someone unawares or making mistakes

to catch someone in a bind

to find a person in a difficulty from which that person cannot readily extricate himself or herself

to catch someone in the net
unexpectedly to involve a particular person in the course of activity designed to involve many others

to catch someone off guard
to surprise a person
refers to fencing

to catch someone on the hop
to take a person by surprise

to catch someone red-handed
to apprehend a person in the course of committing a wrongdoing
refers originally to being caught with blood on one's hands

to catch someone with his pants/trousers down
to act when another person least expects it

to catch someone's eye
to attract the attention of another person, or to seek permission to address that person

to throw a sprat to catch a mackerel
to risk a little in the hope of gaining much

caught

I wouldn't be caught dead without some object
I regard some object as very important

to be caught by the tide
to be dealt with by something inevitable

cause

one's heart is not in some cause
one has little enthusiasm for some cause

to cause waves
to disturb the status quo

cave

an Aladdin's cave
a place full of unexpected treasure
refers to a character and events in *Arabian Nights' Entertainments*

to cave-in
to yield to pressure

ceiling

ceiling
upper permitted limit

glass ceiling
an unstated but definite limit (resulting from prejudice) to promotion in employment

cement

to cement a relationship
to do something in an endeavour to make a relationship permanent

centre

the centre of gravity
the natural point of importance to which things are attracted
refers to physics

to be centre stage
to have everyone's attention
refers to the theatre

to be the centre of the spider's web
to control an operation that involves numerous and/or complex ingredients

centrepiece

the centrepiece
(of a proposal) the highlight or the main ingredient

cents

to have fifty cents each way
to equivocate
refers to betting for a win or a place

to throw in one's two cents' worth
modestly to supply one's own facts or views

chaff

to separate the wheat from the chaff
to separate the worthy from the unworthy
Matthew 3:12, 'His winnowing fork is in his hand, and he will clear his threshing floor and gather his wheat into the granary, but the chaff he will burn with unquenchable fire'

chain

the weakest link in the chain
the least efficient component in a project the overall efficiency of which is governed by the efficiency of the least efficient component

to be at the bottom of the food chain
to be at the lowest level in a hierarchy

to drag the chain

to perform unduly slowly

refers to a horse or bullock that is not pulling its weight, thus causing its chains to drag on the ground

chair

to get an armchair ride

to be given a particularly easy time

chairs

to play musical chairs

to be a part of a general reshuffling (of duties or functions) that is not necessarily to everyone's liking

refers to a parlour game culminating in a sudden scrambling for positions

chalice

to hand someone a poisoned chalice

to confer a seeming benefit on a person that will turn out to be a significant detriment

chalk

chalk it up!

the success was unexpected

refers to scoring in a contest by making chalk marks on a score board

to win by a long chalk

to win very conclusively

refers to scoring in a contest by making chalk marks on a score board

chameleon

a chameleon

a person without character who changes stance repeatedly to reflect the current circumstances

champ

to champ at the bit

to be impatient

refers to horses keen to begin

chance

a fat chance

little hope

not a dog's chance

virtually no hope at all

not the ghost of a chance

no hope at all

Katherine Mansfield (1888–1923), 'he hadn't a ghost of a chance, he hadn't an earthly'

to chance one's arm

to take a great risk

refers to the stripes on the uniforms of non-commissioned officers

to have a snowflake's chance in hell

to have no hope or possibility at all

to have Buckley's chance

to have no expectation at all

a pun, a reference to what follows 'Buckley' in 'Buckley & Nunn', the name of a well-known former Melbourne retailer

change

a leopard cannot change its spots

each person is born with certain unalterable characteristics

Jeremiah 13:23, 'Can the Ethiopian change his skin, or the leopard his spots?'

a sea-change

a significant transformation

Shakespeare, *The Tempest* I:ii, 'Nothing of him that doth fade / but doth suffer a sea-change / into something rich and strange

if you gave that person a penny for that person's thoughts you would get change

that person is extremely stupid

the cold wind of change

the unpleasant realities of new circumstances

to change horses in mid-stream

to alter that upon which one is reliant during the course of a project

to change one's mind

to alter the views that one had previously formed

to change one's tune

to alter one's publicly expressed views

to change tack

to alter one's direction

refers to sailing

to change the whole picture

to alter the major assumptions on which some assessment was based

to have a change of heart

to form a new view in place of a strongly held prior view

changed

to be short-changed

to be given less than is due to one

changes

to ring the changes
to exhaust the number of different ways of doing something
refers to the permutations used for ringing peals of church bells

chapter

to quote chapter and verse
to authenticate the information
refers to quoting the full details of a scriptural reference

charade

to act out a charade
ostentatiously to pretend to be doing something; a pretence
refers to a parlour game of pretence

charge

to charge a mint
to impose very high prices

to charge like a wounded bull
to impose excessive prices
a play on words; not a simile

to charge the earth
to impose very high prices

to recharge one's batteries
to have a recuperative break

charity

charity begins at home
a person's first responsibility should be to that person's family
John Fletcher (1579–1625), *The Wild-Goose Chase*, 'Charity and beating begins at home'

Charlie

tailend Charlie
a person who habitually comes last
refers to the nickname given to the rear gunner in RAF aircraft during World War II

charm

to charm the pants off someone
to delight a person

Charybdis

to be between Scylla and Charybdis
to be faced with two equally unpalatable alternatives that cannot both be avoided
refers to the voyage of Ulysses

chase

a wild-goose chase
a futile chase or search
refers to old game of 'follow-the-leader' on horses in which the objective was to follow a winding and difficult course without ever catching up

to chase a corpse
to harp on something long ago resolved or a lost cause

to chase every hare
to be easily sidetracked

to chase rainbows
to be quite unrealistic

checkmate

checkmate
defeat
refers to chess

cheek

cheek by jowl
close to each other

to turn the other cheek
to refuse, on moral grounds, to retaliate to provocation in like manner
Matthew 5:38, 39, 'Ye have heard that it hath been said an eye for an eye and a tooth for a tooth: but I say unto you … whosoever shall smite thee on the right cheek, turn to him the other also'

tongue in cheek
full of irony

cheering

the cheering could be heard a block away
there was great rejoicing

cheese

cheese paring
miserly

stiff cheese!
circumstances that might be unwelcome but will not be altered, and in respect of which no great sympathy is felt

cheesed

to be cheesed off
to be disgusted

chemistry

good chemistry
an ability to work closely together

cheque

to give someone a blank cheque
to give another person unlimited delegated authority

cherry

to engage in cherry picking
(in business) to accept only the potentially most lucrative deals

to get only one bite at the cherry
to receive no further opportunity

chess

to be a chess game
to be a complex, skilful exercise involving moves and countermoves

chessmaster

a chessmaster
a clever strategist

chest

to build up a war chest
to accumulate cash in readiness for some move

to get something off one's chest
to confess

to hold one's cards close to one's chest
to keep one's plans and strategies secret
refers to playing cards

to lock something up in the old oak chest
to put in a safe place and out of mind

chestnuts

to pull someone's chestnuts out of the fire
to retrieve a situation for someone else
refers to fable of a monkey getting roasting chestnuts out of a fire by using the cat's paw to achieve the desired result

chew

to be able to chew gum and walk at the same time
to be able to do two relatively simple things simultaneously
used ironically to disparage a person of limited capacities

to bite off more than one can chew
to be over ambitious and thus unrealistic as to one's capabilities

to chew fat
to discuss a matter, often with grumbling and unhappiness

to chew someone's ear
to force one's conversation on an unwilling listener

to chew the cud
to reflect on something
refers to the chewing of the cud by ruminant animals

to have something to chew on
to have firm facts on which to base a decision

chicken

chicken and egg
a situation involving two factors each of which causes the other, making it impossible to decide which came first

chicken-hearted
showing little courage

to be chicken feed
to be small and unimportant

chickens

the chickens are coming home to roost
the consequences of a person's past actions are now being felt by that person
Robert Southey (1774–1843), *The Curse of Kehama* (1810), 'Curses are like young chickens, they always come home to roost'

to count one's chickens before they are hatched
to treat as fact the expected results of a future proposal
originally attributed to Erasmus (1466–1536) in slightly different form

chief

to be chief cook and bottlewasher
to perform a range of duties single-handedly — ranging from important to menial

chiefs

more chiefs than Indians
a disproportionately large number of supervisors

child

a problem child
a source of unnecessary difficulty

brainchild
inspired original idea

to be child's play
to be easy or to require only elementary skills and knowledge

childhood

second childhood

dotage

Shakespeare, *As You Like It* II:vii, 'Last scene of all, / that ends this strange eventful history, / is second childishness, and mere oblivion'

children

to take food out of the mouths of children
cruelly to deprive the needy

chill

to cast a chill over something
to be a depressing influence over something

to send a chill down someone's neck
to be worrying news

chin

to keep one's chin up
to maintain one's morale

to lead with one's chin
by one's brash behaviour to virtually invite one's opponents to take action against one

refers to boxing

to rub one's chin
to muse

to take it on the chin
to accept a misfortune cheerfully

China

I would not do so-and-so for all the tea in China
I will never do so-and-so no matter how large the inducement

china

a bull in a china shop
a careless person likely to cause great damage

Chinese

Chinese walls
a system to ensure that different parts of some organisation do not gain access to each other's confidential information

a Chinese puzzle
a perplexing enigma

chink

a chink in someone's armour
a weakness in someone's defences that creates an opportunity to do something that otherwise could not be done

a chink in the wall
an opportunity to do something that otherwise could not be done

a chink of light
a small hope of a solution or breakthrough

chip

to be a blue-chip stock
to be of excellent quality

to be a chip off the old block
to resemble one's father in behaviour and/or appearance

to chip in
to contribute financially

to have a chip on one's shoulder
unreasonably to resent something

chips

bargaining chips
benefits that can be conceded in negotiations to obtain some advantage

that is the way the chips fall
that is the way that the benefits and detriments are distributed after an event

to have had one's chips
to have received all that is going to be forthcoming

to turn one's chips in
to convert one's assets or entitlements into cash

when the chips are down
when all facts are known and taken into consideration

chisel

to chisel away at something
to reduce the size of something in a series of small stages

choice

Hobson's choice
no right at all to select

refers to Thomas Hobson, a Cambridge horsekeeper, who offered customers seeking a change of horses a single beast on a 'take it or leave it' basis

the choice is between eating well or sleeping well
one can invest for maximum yield or maximum security, but not both

chop

to chop someone off at the socks

to stop someone's proposals prematurely

chops

to lick one's chops
to look forward to something with pleasurable anticipation
refers to salivation in anticipation of food

chord

to strike a chord
to sound familiar or recall something to mind
refers to music

to strike a responsive chord
to get a favourable reaction to a proposal
refers to music

to strike the right chord
to appeal successfully to someone's emotions
refers to music

choreograph

to choreograph something
to organise the detail of who does what and when in a project

Christmases

all their Christmases came at once
they were overjoyed

chum

a green chum
an inexperienced person
Shakespeare, *Antony & Cleopatra* I:v, 'my salad days, when I was green in judgment'

church

a broad church
an organisation willing to accept members with a wide variety of different views

chute

to be on a slippery chute
to court disaster
refers to an opening in the side of a shearing shed known as the porthole or chute (spelling variations include shoot and shute); after a sheep is shorn it is pushed through the porthole and slides down

cigarette

only a cigarette paper between them
virtually equal or close together

circle

the wheel has turned the complete/full circle
things are now back to where they were before

to do a full circle
to be back to where one was before or (in error) to go in the opposite direction

to try to square the circle
to attempt the impossible
refers to a classical problem in geometry, namely, to construct with a compass a square of the same area as a given circle

circles

to run around in circles
to engage in excited but useless activity

circuit

a circuit-breaker
an event that breaks the tension in a dispute
refers to electrical circuits

to short-circuit something
to do something, eliminating various intermediate steps
refers to electrical circuits

circus

to be a real circus
to be a highly disorganised affair

cite

the devil can cite scripture for his purpose
a person can quote a respectable or hostile authority while advocating a disreputable cause of that person's own
Shakespeare, *The Merchant of Venice* I:ii, 'The devil can cite scripture for his purpose'

citizen

a second-class citizen
a person not treated as an equal

City

one can't beat City Hall
the ordinary citizen is powerless against bureaucracy

civil

to keep a civil tongue in one's head

to be polite, especially under provocation

claim

to stake a claim
to indicate one's desire to obtain something
refers to placing a series of stakes in the ground as a sign of claiming a place for gold mining

clad

ironclad
firm or rigorous
refers to armour-plated naval vessels

clanger

to drop a clanger
to do something that is indiscreet or that offends social conventions

clap

to clap eyes on something
to catch sight of something

clarion

a clarion call
a strong signal that is an unmistakable invitation to do something

clasp

to clasp at straws
desperately to resort to any expedient in a hopeless situation
refers to a drowning person

class

a second-class citizen
a person not treated as an equal
to be first class
to be of the highest standard

clay

to have feet of clay
to be vulnerable or not as good as thought
Daniel 2:42, 'And as the toes of the feet were part of iron and part of clay, so the kingdom shall be partly strong and partly broken'

clean

a clean sweep
a complete clearing out; OR winning all available prizes or awards
a cleanskin
a person without a criminal record or other blemish on that person's reputation
probably refers to an unblemished animal skin
to clean up a mess
to sort out mistakes or neglect
to clean up one's act
to fix up the deficiencies in one's affairs
to come clean
to confess
to get a clean bill of health
after proper investigation to be found not wanting
to have clean hands
to be innocent or to act ethically
Matthew 27:24, 'He [Pilate] took water and washed his hands in full view of the crowd. "My hands are clean of this man's blood," he declared'
to keep one's nose clean
to act with circumspection and honesty despite temptation to do otherwise
to make a clean breast of something
to confess
to wipe the slate clean
to forgive past indiscretions

cleaners

to take someone to the cleaners
to cheat a person financially

cleaning

a Herculean cleaning of the stables
a thorough revision of operating procedure
refers to the labours of Hercules (Heracles in Greek) who had twelve labours imposed upon him by Eurystheus — one of which was the cleaning of the stables of King Augeas in a single day
a spring cleaning
a regular (usually annual) review with a view to discarding the obsolete and retaining that which is useful

clear

the coast is clear
there are no observers to one's activity around
to be crystal clear
to have a very obvious meaning
to be in the clear

to be exonerated or free from suspicion

to clear a hurdle
to overcome a problem or difficulty

to clear the air
to remove any possible misunderstandings

to clear the decks
to get ready for action
nautical metaphor

to clear the ground
to dispose of the preliminaries
refers to clearing of ground in preparation for ploughing

to come through loud and clear
to be well understood
refers to radio reception

to have a clear picture of something
to have a good understanding of something

to clear a hurdle
to overcome a problem or difficulty

clearcut

clearcut
not borderline

clears

when the smoke clears
when sufficient time has passed to see what is going on

cleft

to be in a cleft stick
to be in a fix that allows for no alternatives

cliff

to be a cliff-hanger
to be very exciting with the result in doubt
refers to episodes of early serial films that ended with the hero in a hazardous plight to attract cinema-goers to the next episode

climate

climate
commercial, political, or other environment

cling

to cling on by one's fingertips
to have only a slender hold

clip

to clip someone's wings
to reduce another person's freedom to act as that person thinks fit
refers to clipping the wings of birds, especially poultry

cloak

cloak-and-dagger activity
secret activity
originally referred to as 'cloak-and-sword' comedies (Spanish: *comedias de capa y espada*) — plays by seventeenth-century Spanish dramatists involving swashbuckling adventure; later adapted to refer to intrigue and secrecy ('cloak and dagger')

to cloak something
to disguise the true nature of something

clock

the clock is ticking
time is running out

to turn back the clock
to have another opportunity to do something that should have been done already; or to attempt to undo something that cannot be undone

close

to be a close shave
to be a narrow escape

to be close to one's heart
to be a project about which one is very keen

to be close to the abyss
to face imminent total destruction

to be too close to home
to be too near the truth to be welcome

to close ranks
to sink minor differences in order to present a unified front to a common enemy
military metaphor

to close the book on something
to terminate an activity

to close the door on someone
to deny another person a desired opportunity

to close the gate
to deny an opportunity that was previously available

to get close to the bone
to cause discomfort by being accurate

to sail close to the wind

to take a considered risk; to test the limits of what is possible or acceptable

refers to sailing in a manner such that sails remain filled while keeping the boat headed as near as possible into the wind

closed

to be a closed book

to be a secret

closer

to draw the nets closer

to intensify one's efforts

closet

a skeleton in the closet

an unpleasant truth the knowledge of which has been deliberately suppressed

William Makepeace Thackeray (1811–63), *The Newcomers* (1855), '... they have a skeleton or two in their closets as well as their neighbours'

to come out of the closet

to admit publicly one's homosexuality

cloth

to cut one's coat according to the cloth

to accommodate oneself to limitations beyond one's control and to do the best in the circumstances

clothes

to steal someone's clothes

to plagiarise another person's ideas

clothing

to be a wolf in sheep's clothing

to be a hypocrite; to be dangerous although masquerading as something harmless

Matthew 7:15, 'Beware of false prophets, which come to you in sheep's clothing, but inwardly they are ravening wolves'

cloud

every cloud has a silver lining

there are consolations and potential benefits even in seemingly adverse situations

to be in cloud-cuckoo land

to be mad or to have unrealistic expectations

'cloud-cuckoo land' was an imaginary city built in the air by the birds (according to the *Nephelococcygia* of *The Birds* by Aristophanes) — hence any utopian fantastic scheme

to be on cloud nine

to be very happy

to be under a cloud

to be under suspicion or to be out of favour

to cast a cloud over something

to spoil the pleasure of an occasion

to cloud one's mind

to allow irrelevant or extraneous factors to affect one's impartiality or judgment

to have a cloud hanging over one's head

there is doubt as to one's future

refers to the pillar of cloud (God) passing judgment on the Hebrews; the pillar of cloud is described in *Exodus* 13:21 *et seq.*

clouds

there are black/storm clouds on the horizon

bad news is expected

to have one's head in the clouds

to be unrealistic

clover

to be in clover

to enjoy a life of ease and luxury

refers to grazing animals in rich pasture

club

join the club!

you are only one of many people with similar problems

coach

an opening wide enough to drive a coach and four through

an excellent opportunity to demonstrate the major errors or absurdities of something

the saying seems sometimes also to have referred to six horses: Sir Stephen Rice (1673–1715), as quoted by W. King, *State of the Protestants of Ireland* (1672), 'I will drive a coach and six horses through the Act of Settlement'

to drive a coach and horses through something

to demonstrate the major errors or absurdities of something

Sir Stephen Rice (1673–1715), as quoted by W. King, *State of the*

Protestants of Ireland (1672), 'I will drive a coach and six horses through the Act of Settlement'

coal

to be at the coal face
to be in the place where the real work is done

coals

to carry coals to Newcastle
to do something ridiculously unnecessary
refers to the coal-mining district of Newcastle, UK

to haul someone over the coals
to reprimand a person
refers to church punishment of heretics

to rake over old coals
to seek to reopen a matter decided on long ago

coast

the coast is clear
there are no observers to one's activity around

coaster

a roller-coaster ride
a series of successes followed by failures

coat

a turncoat
a person changing sides
refers to the practice of mercenary soldiers switching to the winning side and displaying that side's colours by turning their coats inside out

to cut one's coat according to the cloth
to accommodate oneself to limitations beyond one's control and to do the best in the circumstances

coat-tails

to hang onto someone's coat-tails
to rely excessively on another's initiatives and achievements

to trail one's coat-tails
to invite a quarrel
refers to old Irish custom of trailing one's coat inviting a fight with anyone bold enough deliberately to tread on one's coat-tails

cobbler

a cobbler should stick to his last
a person should confine himself or herself to activities for which that person has been trained

cobwebs

to blow the cobwebs away
to revive an old issue

cock

a cock-and-bull story
an explanation that is completely unbelievable and unacceptable
Laurence Sterne (1713–68), *Tristram Shandy*, 'Said my mother, "What is this story all about?" — "a cock and a bull," said Yorick.'

cock-eyed
stupid

to cock one's eye at someone
to glance knowingly at a person

cocked

to go off half-cocked
to act without adequate thought or preparation
refers to a gun at the half-ready

to knock something into a cocked hat
to defeat easily in a game or contest of skill
refers to a game of nine-pins in which the pins were arranged in a triangle like a cocked hat

cockles

to warm the cockles of someone's heart
to delight a person
refers to the cockle shell which looks like a heart; the formal name for bivalve molluscs (such as cockles) is *cardium* (Latin for 'heart')

cocktail

a cocktail
a mixture of several components contributing to a result
refers to an aperitif; origin of name obscure

cocoon

in a cocoon
in a safe and isolated environment

coffin

to be another nail in someone's coffin

to represent a further step towards someone's downfall

cog

to be a small cog in a large wheel
to be a relatively unimportant person in a large organisation

coin

the other side of the coin
the arguments for the opposite point of view

to pay someone back in that person's own coin
to retaliate in kind

cold

cold turkey
the sudden cessation of drugs to an addict and, by extension, the sudden cessation of any habitually pleasurable activity

probably refers to the appearance of the skin of drug addicts experiencing withdrawal symptoms (similarity to the skin of a plucked cold turkey)

in the cold light of day
in an unemotional atmosphere at a later stage

on a cold day in hell
never

that is cold comfort
that appears on the surface to be reassurance and consolation but really it is not

the cold war
the unfriendly relations between the communist nations and the rest of the world

phrase first used by Bernard M. Baruch (1870–1965) in a speech before the South Carolina legislature, although Baruch said that the phrase was suggested to him by H. B. Swope, former editor of the New York *World*; Baruch, 16 April 1947, 'Let us not be deceived — we are today in the midst of a cold war'

the cold wind of change
the unpleasant realities of new circumstances

to be a cold fish
to be an unemotional person

to be in a cold sweat
to be afraid

to blow hot and cold
to vacillate

Revelations 3:15, 'I know thy works, that thou art neither cold nor hot'

to come in out of the cold
to be welcomed into a group

to do something in cold blood
to be cruel without feeling any emotion about it

to get cold feet
to become scared

to give someone the cold shoulder
ostentatiously to ignore a person

to leave someone cold
to fail to impress a person

to leave someone out in the cold
to be excluded, ignored or neglected

to pour cold water on some idea
to be unenthusiastic about some proposal or scornful of its apparent weaknesses

to put something into cold storage
to put something aside to be dealt with at some indeterminate future time

to send a cold shiver down someone's spine
to horrify a person

cold-hearted

cold-hearted
cruel or mean or unmoved

Edmund Burke (1729–97), *Reflections on the Revolution in France*, 'This barbarous philosophy, which is the offspring of cold hearts ... '

collar

to be hot under the collar
to be very agitated

collision

to be on a collision course
to be headed for a clash with an opponent

colour

that is a horse of a very different colour
that is a different matter altogether

Shakespeare, *Twelfth Night*, 'My purpose is, indeed, a horse of that colour'

that takes on added colour
there are now further facts that alter the appearance of a matter

to see the colour of someone's eyes

to see how a person matches expectations or requirements

to see the colour of someone's money

to get evidence of the sincerity of a person's proposal

colours

to nail one's colours to the mast

publicly to declare one's position and to maintain it in the face of criticism

nautical metaphor

to pass with flying colours

to be very successful in a test or contest

refers to ships returning to port with colours flying triumphantly

to sail under false colours

to pretend that one's real character or beliefs are different from what they really are

refers to a ship concealing its true identity

to show one's true colours

to disclose one's real character or beliefs

nautical metaphor

columnist

a fifth columnist

a person using a position of trust to work for a rival cause

refers to an extra body of supporters claimed by General Mola as being within Madrid when he besieged the city with four columns of nationalist forces during the Spanish Civil War in 1936

comb

to go through something with a fine-tooth comb

to conduct an extremely thorough investigation

come

till the cows come home

for a very long time, perhaps forever

Francis Beaumont (1584–1616) & John Fletcher (1579–1625), *The Scornful* Lady, 'Kiss till the cow comes home'

to come adrift

(of a plan) not to work out as intended

to come apart at the seams

(of an arrangement) to break down

to come back to haunt someone

(of an unpleasant incident) to be a constant reminder to a person

to come clean

to confess

to come down with a thud

to be suddenly disillusioned

to come in out of the cold

to be welcomed into a group

to come in thick and fast

to arrive quickly and in great volume

to come out into the open

to start being frank

to come out of one's ears

to be plentiful

to come out of the blue

to be totally unexpected

to come out of the closet

to admit publicly one's homosexuality

to come through loud and clear

to be well understood

refers to radio reception

to come to a full stop

to cease activity completely

to come to a head

to reach culmination

medical metaphor; refers to abscess formation

to come to grips with some problem

to be on the way to solving a problem

to come to someone's ears

to come to someone's attention

to come off the boil

to require urgent attention no longer

to come to the party

to agree to someone's terms

to come up smelling like a rose

not to have a stain on one's character

to have come down in the last shower

to be naVve

refers to someone having just arrived with the last shower of rain

comes

to cross a bridge only when one comes to it

to await the crystallisation of a situation before sorting it out

when one's ship comes in

when one's business venture is successfully completed; OR when luck arrives

when the crunch comes
when the inevitable conclusion is reached

when the wash comes through the machine
in due course

comedy

a comedy of errors
a series of separate mistakes in relation to some matter
refers to the title of a Shakespearean play

comes

to jump that hurdle when one comes to it
to deal with a particular problem only when it becomes necessary to do so

comfort

that is cold comfort
that appears on the surface to be reassurance and consolation but really it is not

coming

the chickens are coming home to roost
the consequences of a person's past actions are now being felt by that person
Robert Southey (1774–1843), *The Curse of Kehama* (1810), 'Curses are like young chickens, they always come home to roost'

command

to be in command
to be on top of a situation

commanding

to be in a commanding position
to have a strategic advantage

commandment

eleventh commandment
unwritten rule
refers to the ten commandments (*Exodus* 20:1–17)

common

the lowest common denominator
the highest level of taste found among all the members of some target audience
this mathematical phrase is used despite the fact that 'the highest common multiple' would be more logical

communist

to kick the communist can
to take every opportunity to exacerbate fear of communism in others

company

to have shares in a paper company
to institute unnecessary clerical procedures

compare

to compare apples with apples
to make a valid comparison

to compare apples with oranges
to lump unconnected things together quite illogically

to compare notes
to exchange information about some subject of mutual interest

compete

to compete on all fours with someone
to strive on equal terms
refers to the four limbs of the body

complaint

the cure is worse than the complaint
the remedy involves more disadvantages than if it were not applied
Francis Bacon (1561–1626), *Of Seditions and Troubles*, 'The remedy is worse than the disease'

complete

the wheel has turned the complete circle
things are now back to where they were before

to turn a complete somersault
to reverse one's established policy

compliment

a back-handed compliment
a polite expression seemingly of praise but really intended as an insult

a left-handed compliment
a thinly disguised insult

to return the compliment
to reciprocate; OR to extract revenge

compound

to compound the felony

having already acted improperly to make matters worse

concert

to be up to concert pitch
to be ready

conclusion

to jump to a conclusion
to infer something without proper consideration

concrete

to set something in concrete
to make something virtually unalterable

conduct

to conduct a post mortem on something
to review past actions with a view to learning lessons for the future
Latin, *post mortem*, 'after the death'

confront

to confront someone head on
to meet and face up to someone in a hostile and direct fashion

conjure

to conjure up a picture
to use words to convey a vivid impression

to conjure up something
to produce something in circumstances where this seemed impossible

consign

to consign something to limbo
to consider something as being in a temporary state of inaction pending future developments
refers to the region (in Christian belief) on the border of hell; neither heaven nor hell

contain

to contain much meat
to contain much material worthy of consideration

contemplate

to contemplate one's navel
to be introspective
refers to a contemplative posture (as in yoga)

contention

a bone of contention
the subject matter of violent disagreement
probably refers to dogs fighting over a bone

continental

not to be worth a continental
to have no value
refers to currency notes of early US issue which quickly depreciated in value
converted

to preach to the converted
to say something to those who already believe in it

Cook

a Cook's tour
a guided tour of inspection
refers to Thomas Cook, who established the world's first travel/tourist company, and the first commercial guided tours

cook

there are many ways to cook eggs
there are many ways to achieve an objective

to be chief cook and bottlewasher
to perform a range of duties single-handedly — ranging from important to menial

to cook one's goose
to make a fatal mistake; to ruin one's plans
nineteenth-century street ballad: 'If they come here we'll cook their geese'

to cook the books
fraudulently to maintain false records of financial transactions

cookie

that is the way the cookie crumbles
that is the actual situation

cooking

to be cooking with gas
to be fully operational and on the way to success

cooks

too many cooks spoil the broth
more than one leader can confuse and harm a project cool

cool it!
calm down!

to cool one's heels
to be kept waiting

to keep a cool head
to stay calm and rational in a crisis
Rudyard Kipling (1865–1936), *If*, 'If you can keep your head when all about you are losing theirs ... '

to play it cool
to take a low-key and rational approach

coop

to fly the coop
to grow up and become independent
refers to a cage or pen for confining poultry and other birds

cop

to cop it in the neck
to be severely castigated or reprimanded
refers to death by decapitation

copy

a carbon copy
an exact imitation
refers to the practice of producing a copy of a document by typing the original with carbon paper beneath, thus simultaneously making a copy

copybook

to blot one's copybook
to spoil one's previously good reputation or record

copycat

a copycat
a person who imitates another person's ideas

cord

to cut the cord
to sever a connection
refers to the umbilical cord

to cut the umbilical cord
to free a person from the excessive influence of another; OR to separate a person from an essential source of supplies

core

rotten to the core
completely corrupt

to be the hard core
to be the central and most difficult problem

corner

cornerstone
key ingredient

to back someone into a corner
to leave a person no option

to be around the corner
to be imminent

to be in a tight corner
to have little or no chance of escape from a difficult situation

to paint oneself into a corner
foolishly to put oneself into a position from which escape is impossible

to see something out of the corner of one's eye
only just to see something

to turn the corner
to commence being successful after initial failures

corners

from the four corners of the globe
from everywhere

to cut corners
to lower one's standards in order to complete something more quickly

cornerstone

cornerstone
key ingredient

corns

to step/tread on someone's corns
to upset another person by interfering in that person's area of responsibility

corps

esprit de corps
a feeling of camaraderie and concern for the good name of some organisation of which one is a member
French, 'vital breath of a body'

corpse

to breathe life into a corpse
to revive something moribund

to chase a corpse
to harp on something long ago resolved or a lost cause

cost

to cost a pretty penny
to be very expensive

to cost an arm and a leg
to be excessively expensive

costs

to cut costs to the bone
to economise strictly

Costello

to be an Abbott and Costello act
to involve two persons working together as a team

cotton

to be out of one's cotton-picking mind
to act irrationally

to keep one's cotton-picking fingers off something
not to interfere (in a meddlesome fashion) with something

to wrap someone in cotton wool
to be overprotective towards a person

count

the final countdown
the last stages of something
refers to the launch of space vehicles

to count one's chickens before they are hatched
to treat as fact the expected results of a future proposal
originally attributed to Erasmus (1466–1536) in slightly different form

countdown

the final countdown
the last stages of something
refers to the launch of space vehicles

counted

to stand up and be counted
publicly to announce one's position on some issue

country

one looks for elephants in elephant country
one needs to search in the right place

to be ahead by a country mile
to be in a comfortable lead
in the long distances of certain rural areas, a 'country mile' is jocularly believed to be a very long mile

coup

to receive the coup de grâce
to be finished off by an opponent
French, 'mercy stroke'

course

in the course of a day's march
while carrying out one's normal activities
military metaphor

to be on a collision course
to be headed for a clash with an opponent

to be on course
to be progressing satisfactorily towards one's goal

to be par for the course
to be normal
refers to golf

to plot a safe course through troubled waters
to make a plan that overcomes certain difficulties
nautical metaphor

to run its course
to come to a natural end

courses

it is horses for courses
the correct means to an end needs to be chosen
refers to horse racing

court

a friend at court
a person with influence who is willing to use it on one's behalf
refers to royal courtiers

the ball is in someone's court
it is some other person's responsibility
refers to tennis

to laugh something out of court
to ridicule a proposition as having no basis whatsoever
refers to courts of law

to put oneself out of court
to disqualify oneself from being considered for something
refers to royal courtiers

Coventry

to send someone to Coventry
ostentatiously and collectively to ignore a person by way of punishment
refers to the refusal of the citizens of Coventry (UK) to have any social contact whatsoever with royalist soldiers in the English Civil War

cover

to cover one's back
to take precautions

to cover one's hide
to provide excuses or take other evasive action in an attempt to avoid the

adverse consequences of one's actions

to cover one's tracks
to hide the evidence of one's involvement

to cover oneself
to create evidence so that if one is criticised or accused later on one can clear one's name

to cover the field
to be comprehensive

to duck/run for cover
to seek to avoid blame

to judge a book by its cover
foolishly to go only by superficial appearances

cow

a cash cow
a source of ready money

a milch cow
an easy and plentiful source of some desired benefit

a sacred cow
an institution, person, idea, custom, etc. treated as being immune from criticism and change
refers to Hindu veneration of the cow

cows

till the cows come home
for a very long time, perhaps forever
Francis Beaumont (1584–1616) & John Fletcher (1579–1625), *The Scornful Lady*, 'Kiss till the cow comes home'

Cox

Box and Cox
two persons who are never around at the same time
refers to the name of a play by J. M. Morton (1811–91), *Box and Cox* (adapted from the French)

crack

a hard nut to crack
a difficult problem to be solved; OR someone not easily influenced

the crack of dawn
at the exact moment of sunrise

to be a crack in the wall
to represent a small opportunity that can be exploited

to be a fair crack of the whip
to be just; to provide a fair opportunity

to crack
to have a mental break-down

to crack down on something
to seek to eradicate something

to crack the whip
to assert one's authority
refers to the use of a whip in riding or driving animals

to have a crack at something
to attempt something

to use a sledgehammer to crack a nut
to devote vastly more resources to a project than is warranted by all the circumstances

cracked

to be all that it is cracked up to be
to be as good as the claims made for something

cracks

to fall between the cracks
to be ineligible for something because one does not fit neatly into any of several relevant categories

to paper over the cracks
to institute extremely superficial and basically ineffective remedies
refers to placing wallpaper over cracks in a wall

to slip through the cracks
to be overlooked

cradle

to be the cradle of something
to be the place where some idea was first nurtured

cranny

in every nook and cranny
everywhere

crawl

one needs to crawl before one can walk
skills are best developed in logical stages

to crawl out of the woodwork
(referring to something unwelcome) to emerge from hiding or obscurity

cream

to be cream on top of the milk
to be an additional benefit in an already satisfactory scenario

create

to create a Frankenstein
to create something wicked and out of control
a reference to the fictional creator of a monster, in mistake for a reference to the monster itself; from the novel *Frankenstein: the Modern Prometheus* (1818), by Mary Wollstonecraft Shelley (1797–1851), second wife of British poet, Percy Bysshe Shelley (1792–1822)

to create a storm
to cause a fuss

creek

to be up the creek
to be mistaken completely

to be up the creek without a paddle
to be in trouble

creep

to make someone's flesh creep
to frighten a person with something horrific

crPme

crPme de la crPme
something quite superlative
French, 'the cream of the cream'

crest

to be on the crest of a wave
to enjoy success that might not last

crestfallen

crestfallen
dejected
refers to the crest of a fighting cock

cricket

a cricket team
eleven people

not to be cricket
to be unfair

crime

a hotbed of crime
a place where illegal activity flourishes
refers to a bed of earth, heated by fermenting manure, for artificially raising plants; hence, figuratively, a place that encourages the rapid growth of (usually undesirable) matter

crocodile

to shed crocodile tears
hypocritically to show concern or sympathy for a person in distress
refers to the reflex lacrimation of a crocodile while eating

crook

by hook or by crook
by fair means or foul
perhaps refers to collection of firewood by different implements

cross

to be a cross that one has to bear
to be a difficulty that one has to endure
Luke 14:27, 'And whosoever doth not bear his cross, and come after me, cannot be my disciple'

to be at the cross-roads
to need to choose between several mutually exclusive alternatives

to cross a bridge only when one comes to it
to await the crystallisation of a situation before sorting it out

to cross one's mind
to occur to one

to cross one's mind
to think of something

to cross someone's path
to meet another person by chance

to cross swords with someone
to have a disagreement with another person

to cross the Rubicon
to make an irreversible decision in regard to some commitment
refers to Caesar's crossing of the Rubicon River in Gaul in 49 BC thus declaring war on Pompey

to dot the i's and cross the t's
to be meticulous in completing documentation

crossed

to have one's wires crossed
to be mistaken about key facts
refers to a short-circuit in electrical wiring

to keep one's fingers crossed
to hope for a good outcome
refers to making the sign of the Christian cross to protect against ill-fortune

crow

as the crow flies

by the shortest distance

to eat crow
to act in a humiliating fashion to achieve a desired outcome
from an incident in New England (North America) in the Anglo–American War of 1812–14

to have a crow's eye
to be cunning or alert

crowd

to stand out from the crowd
to be noticeably better than one's competitors

crown

the jewel in someone's crown
the most significant component

to wear one's crown of thorns
to have one's own difficulties
John 19:2, 'And the soldiers plaited a crown of thorns, and put it on his [Jesus'] head'

uneasy lies the head that wears a crown
leadership involves some risks and some burdens (esp. the risk of being deposed)
Shakespeare, *Henry IV*, Part 2, III:i, 'Uneasy lies the head that wears a crown'

crowning

the crowning point
the height of a person's achievement

crucify

to crucify someone
to do severe damage unfairly to a person's reputation or credibility
Mark 15:13, 'And they cried out again, Crucify him'

cruel

to cruel someone's pitch
to spoil a person's chances

crumbles

that is the way the cookie crumbles
that is the actual situation

crumbs

to throw someone a few crumbs
to fob a person off with a few symbolic but unimportant concessions
Luke 16:21, 'a certain beggar ... desiring to be fed with the crumbs which fell from the rich man's table'

crunch

when it comes to the crunch
when the matter comes up for decision

when the crunch comes
when the inevitable conclusion is reached

crusade

a crusade
an aggressive campaign to achieve some political or social objective
refers to the wars undertaken in the Middle Ages in an attempt to secure the rights of Christians to visit the Holy Land (from Latin *crus*, 'cross')

Crusoe

not to be Robinson Crusoe
to be one of a large number of people with a common problem
refers to Daniel Defoe's *Robinson Crusoe*

crutch

a crutch
an artificial non-permanent support

cry

a cry for help
a subconscious or indirect indication that a person is in need of psychological counselling

a shoulder to cry on
sympathy

to be a far cry from something
to be a long way from something; to be quite dissimilar

to cry in one's beer
to show remorse

to cry one's eyes out
to express great sadness at a situation

to cry 'wolf'
repeatedly to raise an unjustified concern with the result that one will be ignored when the circumstances change and a real threat emerges

crying

it is no use crying over spilt milk
there is nothing to be gained by lamenting over an irredeemable error

crystal

a crystal ball
accurate knowledge of the future

refers to ancient means of divining the future

to be crystal clear

to have a very obvious meaning

crystallise

to crystallise

to emerge in its final form

cuckoo

to be a cuckoo in the nest

to purport to be a member of a group of people although having no such right and, in the process, to usurp the rights of those entitled to be there

refers to a cuckoo depositing its eggs in the nests of other birds

to be in cloud-cuckoo land

to be mad or to have unrealistic expectations

'cloud-cuckoo land' was an imaginary city built in the air by the birds (according to the *Nephelococcygia* of *The Birds* by Aristophanes) — hence any utopian fantastic scheme

cud

to chew the cud

to reflect on something

refers to the chewing of the cud by ruminant animals

cudgels

to take up the cudgels for someone

to defend a person

refers to a thick short stick used as a weapon

cuff

off the cuff

impromptu

perhaps refers to notes scribbled on the shirt cuff for use during a speech

cup

a storm in a teacup

a controversy about a minor matter but one that looms large in the minds of the parties

not to be someone's cup of tea

not to be to a person's liking; OR to be outside a person's expertise or area of interest

cupboard

a skeleton in the cupboard

an unpleasant truth the knowledge of which has been deliberately suppressed

William Makepeace Thackeray (1811–63), *The Newcomers* (1855), '... they have a skeleton or two in their closets as well as their neighbours'

the cupboard is bare

the wished-for resources are not available

curate

to be a curate's egg

to be good only in parts

refers to a cartoon (*Punch*, vol. cix, p. 222, 1895) showing the nervous young curate (Jones) in conversation with the Lord Bishop:

'I'm afraid you've got a bad egg, Mr Jones.'

'Oh no, my Lord, I assure you! Parts of it are excellent!'

curdle

to curdle one's blood

to be horrific

cure

the cure is worse than the complaint/disease

the remedy involves more disadvantages than if it were not applied

Francis Bacon (1561–1626), *Of Seditions and Troubles*, 'The remedy is worse than the disease'

curl

to make someone's hair curl

(of news) to give someone a shock

W. S. Gilbert, *Ruddigore* (1887), 'when he's excited he uses language that would make your hair curl'

curly

to get someone by the short and curly hairs

to have domination over a person

current

an undercurrent

a barely noticeable feeling of dissent that is not being vocalised

curse

not worth a tinker's curse

worthless

from a tinker's custom of blocking up a hole with a pellet of bread before soldering, the pellet of bread being discarded as worthless after the soldering was completed

curtain

curtain raiser
introduction
refers to the theatre

the curtain rises on something
something is about to start
refers to the theatre

the iron curtain
the border between the communist nations and the rest of the world
used famously by Winston Churchill in a speech in 1946, but also attributed before this to Ethel Snowden (1920), Goebbels (1945), and by Churchill himself in 1945 (before his famous 1946 speech)

to ring down the curtain on something
to treat something as concluded

curtains

it's curtains!
this is the end!

customer

a slippery customer
a shifty person

cut

clearcut
not borderline

cut it out!
stop doing that!

cut-throat
highly competitive

one could have cut the atmosphere with a knife
those present were very tense

the cut of someone's jib
someone's personal appearance
Sir Walter Scott (1771–1832), 'If she disliked what the sailor calls the cut of their jib'; refers to the recognition of ships at sea by noting the appearance of their foresail

to be a cut above the rest
to be plainly superior

to be cut and dried
to be well settled or long established
refers to timber cut and dried, and ready for use

to be cut off at the knees
to have a pet project aborted

to be cut to pieces
to be very upset; OR to be completely overrun and defeated

to be cut up
to be distressed

to cut both ways
to involve both advantages and disadvantages of similar significance

to cut corners
to lower one's standards in order to complete something more quickly

to cut costs to the bone
to economise strictly

to cut no ice with someone
to have little effect on a person
perhaps refers to ice-skating

to cut one's coat according to the cloth
to accommodate oneself to limitations beyond one's control and to do the best in the circumstances

to cut one's nose off to spite one's face
to act in pique in a way that harms only oneself

to cut one's own throat
to act in a way that damages one's own interests

to cut one's teeth on something
to get one's first experience by doing something

to cut someone dead
to snub a person

to cut someone off with a shilling
to exclude a person as a beneficiary under one's will
refers to the mistaken belief that a will cannot be upset in favour of a person actually named in a will and clearly not overlooked

to cut tall poppies down to size
to diminish the self-importance of haughty persons

to cut the cord
to sever a connection
refers to the umbilical cord

to cut the Gordian knot
to solve, especially by force, a virtually insoluble problem
refers to a complicated knot tied by Gordius and eventually cut by Alexander the Great

to cut the ground from under someone's feet

to withdraw support unexpectedly and, in the process, to cause embarrassment; OR to demolish a person's case and cause defeat, especially by anticipating that person's arguments or plans

to cut the painter
to become separated
nautical metaphor; refers to cutting a boat loose from its moorings

to cut the umbilical cord
to free a person from the excessive influence of another; OR to separate a person from an essential source of supplies

to have one's work cut out to do something
to have a difficult task to achieve something

cuts

death of a thousand cuts
a slow, unpleasant ending

to take short cuts
to do something by a faster but less thorough method

cutting

to be at the cutting edge of something
to be in a position where important decisions are made

cylinders

to spark on all cylinders
to work extremely well

czar

czar
a person exercising excessive power over others

D

D-Day

D-Day
the long-awaited time at which some action commences
refers to the Allied invasion of Europe in World War II

daddy

the daddy of them all
the biggest and/or best example of something

dagger

cloak-and-dagger activity
secret activity
originally referred to as 'cloak-and-sword' comedies (Spanish: *comedias de capa y espada*) — plays by seventeenth-century Spanish dramatists involving swashbuckling adventure; later adapted to refer to intrigue and secrecy ('cloak and dagger')

daggers

to look daggers at someone
to look at a person in a way that indicates great animosity
Shakespeare, *Hamlet* III:ii, 'I will speak daggers to her, but use none'

dam

the dam burst
the cumulative effect of many things caused a disaster

Damascus

a road to Damascus experience
a sudden, dramatic conversion
refers to the sudden conversion of Paul (Saul) — *Acts* 9:3, 'And as he journeyed, he came to Damascus: and suddenly there shined around him a light from heaven: And he fell to the earth'

Damocles

to have a sword of Damocles hanging over one
to be in imminent danger despite normal activity going on all around one
refers to Damocles who had the sword of Dionysius hanging, by a slender thread, over his head — as a symbol of perpetual risk in life; the story is told in Cicero, *Tusculanae Disputationes*

damp

a damp squib
disappointingly ineffective action
refers to fireworks that fail to go off

dance

nothing to make a song or dance about
unexciting or unimportant

to lead someone a merry dance
to mislead a person
refers to the complex dances of earlier centuries when one person led another through complex steps

to make a song and dance about something
to create a fuss

danse

danse macabre
gruesome final step
French, 'ghastly dance'; now used to describe a gruesome literary or theatrical production (refers to fourteenth-century religious art depicting persons being led to the grave by death)

dark

a dark horse
a person with unsuspected talents
Benjamin Disraeli (1804–81), *The Young Duke*, 'A dark horse, which had never been thought of, and which the careless St James had never even observed in the list, rushed past the grandstand in sweeping triumph'

a leap in the dark
a decisive move into the unknown
Thomas Hobbes (1588–1679), 'I am about to take my last voyage, a great leap in the dark' (quoted by Watkins, *Anecdotes of Men of Learning*)

a shot in the dark
a hopeful attempt at the unknown; a sheer guess

a stab in the dark
a sheer guess

to be in the dark
to be uninformed

to keep someone in the dark
deliberately to keep a person uninformed

to keep something dark
to keep something secret

to look on the dark side
to be pessimistic

to whistle in the dark
to feign greater confidence than one really has
John Dryden (1631–1700), *Amphitryon* II:i, 'Whistling to keep myself from being afraid'

darken

never darken my door again
do not ever return
refers to the shadow cast by a person's presence in a doorway

David

a David and Goliath battle
a struggle between two parties who are not evenly matched
refers to *1 Samuel* 17:23 ff

dawn

a false dawn
an incident giving rise to unjustified hope
refers to a transient light that precedes the true dawn by about an hour

the crack of dawn
at the exact moment of sunrise

to be the dawn of a new day
to be the start of a different regime

dawns

light dawns
the point is understood

day

a field day
a very enjoyable and successful occasion
refers (originally) to an army's practice manoeuvres

a nine-day wonder
an exciting event, but one that will cease to arouse interest when the novelty has worn off
old English proverb: 'a wonder lasts nine days, and then the puppy's eyes are open'; Shakespeare was probably alluding to this proverb (or similar) in *Henry VI Pt III*, III:ii, 'That would be ten days' wonder, at the least / That's a day longer than a wonder lasts'

a red-letter day
an important occasion
refers to the colour used to indicate days of obligation in the Christian Church missal — as opposed to black-letter days, which are optional days

at the end of the day
in due course, or at the conclusion of a project

D-Day
the long-awaited time at which some action commences
refers to the Allied invasion of Europe in World War II

every dog has its day
persons being criticised or persecuted will have their opportunity to reverse the situation; good luck comes sooner or later

Charles Kingsley (1819–75). *Young and Old*, 'Young blood must have its course, lad, and every dog his day'

in the cold light of day
in an unemotional atmosphere at a later stage

in the course of a day's march
while carrying out one's normal activities
military metaphor

late in the day
when a project is well advanced

on a cold day in hell
never

Rome was not built in a day
complicated things require time

that person would not give one the time of day
that person is unwilling to help anybody

the order of the day
the customary behaviour

to be the dawn of a new day
to be the start of a different regime

to call it a day
to cease involvement with some activity

to keep something for a rainy day
to keep something in reserve for bad times

to see the light of day
to be made public

days

in halcyon days
in past happier times
Shakespeare, *Henry V*, *Part 1*, I:ii, 'Expect St Martin's summer, halcyon days' refers to the fourteen days about the winter solstice when winds were calm, and to the mythical bird said to breed in a floating nest at that time

one's days are numbered
one is about to be abolished
Daniel 5:26, 'God hath numbered thy kingdom, and finished it'

the horse-and-buggy days
long ago

daylight

daylight robbery
the charging of grossly excessive prices

to see daylight
to discern the way ahead towards the right answer

dead

a dead-end position
a job with no prospects of advancement

a dead letter
a rule still in existence but no longer observed in practice

dead and buried
(of some issue) definitely concluded, especially so long ago as to be nearly forgotten

drop dead!
go away, I want no dealings with you

I wouldn't be caught dead without some object
I regard some object as very important

over my dead body
never

to be a dead duck
to have failed; OR to be in a hopeless situation

to cut someone dead
to snub a person

to flog a dead horse
misguidedly to do something patently useless

to get rid of the dead wood
to terminate the services of unsatisfactory personnel
refers to pruning of bushes

to kill some proposal stone dead
to take action that stops a proposal completely
refers to death by stoning

to leave others for dead
to be vastly superior

to make noise enough to wake the dead
to be excessively noisy

to run into a dead end
to get nowhere in an investigation

deadline

deadline
time by which something must be completed
refers to a line drawn around a military prison, beyond which a prisoner might be shot dead — hence, an absolute limit

deaf

to fall on deaf ears
to be totally disregarded

deafening

deafening silence
great apathy and lack of enthusiasm

deal

a raw deal
unfair treatment

a sweetheart deal
an agreement negotiated in private to the special benefit of those involved in the negotiations

to deal the final hand
to take steps that conclude a matter
refers to playing cards

to stitch up a deal
successfully to conclude a deal

to sweeten a deal
to offer some concessions or incentives

to wheel and deal
energetically to enter into commercial transactions of dubious propriety
refers to US slang: 'wheel' = important person or operator

to wrap up a deal
to bring a deal to a successful conclusion

dealer

sharp dealer
person engaging in barely honest or mildly unethical practices
refers to poker

death

a death wish
the contemplation or commission of action so foolish that it is likely to lead to utter disaster

death blow
incident that results in the destruction of something

death of a thousand cuts
a slow, unpleasant ending

sudden death
instantaneously or without phasing in

to be in at the death
to be present at the conclusion of something
refers to fox hunting — when the fox is caught and killed

to be on one's death bed
(of a person, organisation or piece of equipment) to be about to cease effectiveness

to be the kiss of death
to be something intended to be helpful but resulting in total destruction

to bore someone to death
to weary a person greatly by dull and uninteresting conversation or by lack of action

to die a natural death
by virtue of changed circumstances or the effluxion of time to be no longer relevant

to sign one's own death warrant
foolishly to do something that is inevitably bound to lead to utter disaster

to bleed to death slowly
to be heading in gradual steps towards total ruin

to sound the death knell of something
to indicate the impending end of something
refers to the knell (sound) of a bell rung at a funeral; Shakespeare, *Macbeth* II:i, 'The bell invites me ... it is a knell that summons thee to heaven or to hell'

deathknock

on the deathknock
at the last possible moment
refers to the mythical figure of 'Death' knocking on the door to claim a victim

debate

to hijack a debate
to involve oneself in discussion on some matter and turn that discussion to one's advantage

decimate

to decimate
to reduce in size greatly
strictly refers to reducing by one tenth — originally a punishment inflicted on Roman legions whereby one tenth of the soldiers were selected by lot and executed

decipher

to decipher something
to understand the significance of something

deck

a loose cannon on the deck
a person or factor out of control and likely to cause trouble
nautical metaphor

all hands on deck
everybody is requested to help out
nautical metaphor

to be back on deck
to have returned after an absence
nautical metaphor

decks

to clear the decks
to get ready for action
nautical metaphor

deckchairs

to rearrange the deckchairs on the Titanic
to take an initiative that is quite useless because it does not take much greater change into account
refers to the liner *Titanic* which struck an iceberg and sank in 1912

deep

deep-rooted
firmly established, strongly felt

still waters run deep
a person with a quiet manner might have many unrecognised characteristics — both good and bad
W. H. Auden (1907–73), *Twelve Songs VIII*, 'Still waters run deep, my dear, there's never smoke without fire'

to be in deep water
to be in great difficulty

to be between the devil and the deep blue sea
to be faced with two equally unpalatable alternatives that cannot both be avoided

to draw a deep breath
to get ready for exertion or for emotional news

to go off the deep end
to lose one's temper

to have deep pockets
to have large financial resources and to be willing to use them if the circumstances seem right

to jump straight in at the deep end
to do something without proper preparation

to play a deep game
to show cunning

deeper

to sink deeper into the mud/mire
to get into even greater difficulty

defend

to defend one's bailiwick
to protect one's power, influence, or authority in regard to a particular activity
refers to a region under the jurisdiction of a particular bailiff

deflower

to deflower
to deprive of virginity

defy

to defy gravity
to go up when the expectation is to go down

degree

to give someone the third degree
to apply pressure while questioning closely a person under suspicion

to the nth degree
with great precision
refers to mathematics

degrees

to have more degrees than a thermometer
to be too academic
a play on the word 'degree'

to turn around 180 degrees
completely to reverse a stance

deliver

to deliver the goods
to achieve the objective; to supply what is required

delivered

delivered in spades
to a considerable degree; in large numbers

Delphic

Delphic
deliberately obscure
refers to the Oracle at Delphi

den

to beard the lion in his den
to tackle a daunting opponent in that person's own familiar surroundings

Sir Walter Scott (1771–1832), *Marmion*, 'And darest thou then to beard the lion in his den … ' (probably a reference to the story of Daniel in the den of lions as related in *Daniel* 6:16)

Denmark

something is rotten in the state of Denmark

the situation is corrupt and unacceptable

Shakespeare, *Hamlet* III:iv, 'Something is rotten in the state of Denmark'

denominator

the lowest common denominator

the highest level of taste found among all the members of some target audience

this mathematical phrase is used despite the fact that 'the highest common multiple' would be more logical

depth

to be out of one's depth

to find that some issue is too complicated or too difficult

derail

to derail some strategy

to cause a strategy to fail

description

a blow-by-blow description

a very detailed word picture of some event

refers to boxing

despond

a slough of despond

a feeling of hopelessness

refers to a swamp; John Bunyan (1628–88), *The Pilgrim's Progress* Pt I, 'The name of the slough was despond'

destined

to be destined for the scrapheap

to face a future in which one will have no meaningful role

destroying

soul-destroying

breaking the spirit or will to continue

devastated

to be devastated

to be extremely disappointed

develop

to develop a head of steam

to gain momentum

refers to a steam engine or boiler

devil

a devil-may-care attitude

a reckless attitude

be a devil!

take a chance!

he must have a long spoon that sups with the devil

great care is needed when negotiating with disreputable parties

Shakespeare apparently alludes to an old proverb in *The Tempest* II:ii, 'Mercy! mercy! this is a devil … I will leave him, I have no long spoon!'

poor devil

person to be pitied

speak/talk of the devil

here is the person we were just discussing

the devil can cite scripture for his purpose

a person can quote a respectable or hostile authority while advocating a disreputable cause of that person's own

Shakespeare, *The Merchant of Venice* I:ii, 'The devil can cite scripture for his purpose'

the devil one knows is better than the devil one does not know

the status quo is more comfortable than change

to act as a devil's advocate

to put a point of view that one does not hold in order to draw out the best arguments regarding a proposition

refers to a church official vetting a candidate for sainthood (and ultimately to the testing of Job by Satan, *Job* 1:9 ff)

to be between the devil and the deep blue sea

to be faced with two equally unpalatable alternatives that cannot both be avoided

to give the devil his due

to be fair

to grab the devil by the tail

to face up to difficulties

diamond

to be a rough diamond

to have many attributes, but an uncultivated manner lacking social polish

dice

no dice
the proposal is totally unacceptable

the dice are loaded against someone
a person is unlikely to succeed in something
refers to cheating in gambling with dice

the final throw of the dice
one last, desperate gamble

the whole box and dice
all relevant components

Dick

every Tom, Dick, and Harry
virtually all ordinary people
appears to have been coined in Victorian times

dictionary

someone has swallowed a dictionary
a person uses excessively long words

die

the die is cast
the course of action is irreversible

those who live by the sword shall die by the sword
those that are rough with others must accept the likelihood of unfavourable treatment in return
Matthew 26:52, 'All they that take the sword shall perish by the sword'

to be the throw of a loaded die
to be an act of deceit
refers to cheating in gambling with dice

to die a natural death
by virtue of changed circumstances or the effluxion of time to be no longer relevant

to die hard
stubbornly to refuse to give up a belief or theory; not to give up easily

diehard

to be a diehard
to be a person who refuses to change, an obdurate person

difference

to make a world of difference
to make a great deal of difference

different

that is a horse of a very different colour
that is a different matter altogether
Shakespeare, *Twelfth Night*, 'My purpose is, indeed, a horse of that colour'

to be a different kettle of fish
to be something very dissimilar
refers to a riverside picnic where freshly caught fish is cooked and eaten

to have one's fingers in many different pies
to be engaged in a variety of separate activities

to march to a different drum
to show an independent approach
military metaphor

difficulty

to get around some difficulty
to use an approach that overcomes some difficulty

dig

to dig one's heels in
to become even more stubborn than at first

to dig one's own grave
to take action that results in an unintended disaster for oneself

to dig one's toes in
to become even more stubborn than at first

dilemma

the horns of a dilemma
two unpalatable alternatives between which a choice must be made
dilemma: Greek for 'two assumptions'

dim

to take a dim view of something
not to regard something favourably

dinner

to be done like a dinner
to be defeated and humiliated

dinners

I have had more of these than I have had hot dinners
I have had a very large number of these

dinosaur

a dinosaur
someone or something with incredibly outmoded ideas

dip

to dip one's toe in the water

gently to explore an opportunity

dire

in dire straits
in great need

direction

a step in the right direction
the first in a series of measures designed to correct some problem

it is pointing in the right direction
it is proceeding towards success

to head someone in the right direction
to assist a person to achieve something

dirt

to strike pay dirt
to become successful
refers to soil containing gold or other precious metal

dirty

dirty
unfair

to do someone's dirty work
to do something unethical on behalf of another person

to get one's hands dirty
to do the necessary but unpleasant or menial parts of a task

to wash one's dirty linen in public
to expose one's embarrassing domestic affairs to the world at large'

disaster

a pit of disaster
great and unexpected misfortune

a recipe for disaster
a certain way of achieving disaster

disclose

to disclose one's hand
to give away information regarding one's intention
refers to playing cards

disease

the cure is worse than the disease
the remedy involves more disadvantages than if it were not applied
Francis Bacon (1561–1626), *Of Seditions and Troubles*, 'The remedy is worse than the disease'

disguise

a blessing in disguise
an unwelcome but salutary experience
James Hervey (1696–1743), *Reflections on a Flower Garden*, 'Ee'en crosses from his sov'reign hand are blessings in disguise'

dispatches

to be mentioned in dispatches
to be favourably mentioned
refers to military recognition for bravery

disseminate

to disseminate ideas
to spread ideas to a wide audience
literally, 'to scatter seeds in various places'

distance

to be within striking distance
to be fairly close

to keep one's distance
to avoid familiarity

distant

distant fields look greener
activities of which one has no experience seem more attractive than is really the case
Psalms 23:1, 'The Lord is my shepherd ... he shall feed me in a green pasture'

ditch

to make a last-ditch stand
to make a brave effort to stave off final defeat
King William III (1650–1702), 'There is one way never to see it lost ... and that is to die in the last ditch' (quoted by Burnet, *History of His Own Times*,1715)

dive

to take a nose dive
to fall steeply, suddenly and unexpectedly

dividends

to show dividends
to be successful

dock

to be in the dock
to need to defend one's stance
refers to a courtroom

to be in the dry dock
to be out of action while undergoing repairs
refers to ship repairs

doctor

just what the doctor ordered
exactly right
to go for the doctor
to go all out or to make a desperate bid for something

dog

a cat-and-dog existence
a life full of frequent squabbles
a dogfight
a confused fight, especially between aeroplanes
a lame dog
a person under some disadvantage needing attention and assistance
a shaggy dog story
a laborious, far-fetched, amusing story
refers to the shaggy dog that originally featured in many of these stories
a sly dog
a knowing, cunning, clever person (esp. one who discreet about that person's own personal weaknesses)
a watchdog
a person or organisation monitoring behaviour
any stick to beat a dog
any excuse will do if it serves one's purpose
dog-eared
(of pages) well-thumbed
refers to the turned-down appearance of the ears of many dogs
dog-tired
tired out
every dog has its day
persons being criticised or persecuted will have their opportunity to reverse the situation; good luck comes sooner or later
Charles Kingsley (1819–75). *Young and Old*, 'Young blood must have its course, lad, and every dog his day'
every man and his dog
everybody
love me, love my dog
if you accept me then you must also accept my associates
Latin proverb: *Qui me amat, amat et canem meam*, quoted by St Bernard of Clairvaux (1090–1153)
not a dog's chance
virtually no hope at all
one cannot teach an old dog new tricks
people become set in their ways irreversibly
the tail wagging the dog
a minor aspect with disproportionate effect on a major aspect
the top dog
the person in the most powerful position
refers to the dominant dog in a pack
to be a dog in the manger
spitefully to deny something to others, notwithstanding its uselessness to oneself
from *Aesop's Fables*
to be a dog's breakfast
to be a very messy arrangement
to be a gay dog
to lead an idle life while flaunting the symbols of wealth
to be in the doghouse
to be in disgrace
to give a dog a bad name
to malign a person
to have a hair of the dog that bit one
to drink more alcohol in an attempt to overcome the effects of alcohol already consumed
refers to the belief that the hair of the rabid dog that bit a person was a cure for the madness that can ensue
to lead a dog's life
to be ill-treated
to see a man about a dog
to do something unspecified
to try something out on the dog
to test the feasibility or safety of a dubious remedy or project
two men and a dog
very few people
underdog
a person or team that is likely to lose a contest and therefore likely to be the object of sympathy
why keep a dog and bark oneself?
it is silly to pay for assistance and then do things personally

dogs

all the dogs are barking

this news is being widely disseminated

to call off the dogs
to abandon a pursuit or inquiry
refers to hunt master calling off the dogs if they are on the wrong scent

to feed the dogs while they are barking
to do something while the opportunity is available

to go to the dogs
to be ruined

to let sleeping dogs lie
to refrain from raising an issue that is not obviously requiring attention

to rain cats and dogs
to rain heavily
derived from ancient northern mythology in which cats and dogs were symbolically linked to weather: the cat can be taken as a symbol of falling rain and the dog as a symbol of wind gusts

to throw something to the dogs
to discard something as useless and worthless
Shakespeare, *Macbeth* v:iii, 'Throw physic to the dogs, I'll none of it'

doldrums

to be in the doldrums
to be depressed or to show no activity
refers to a region of little wind near the equator, becalming sailing ships

dollar

a sixty-four thousand dollar question
a pertinent but very difficult question
refers to a radio quiz show in which an initial $1000 prize doubled with the successful answering of progressively more difficult questions

dollars

to hold out a fistful of dollars
to offer money by way of inducement

domino

a domino effect
a series of events, each of which is precipitated by the one before
refers to a series of domino pieces falling over in sequence

Don

to be a Don Juan
to be a libertine
refers to Don Juan Tenorio, legendary fourteenth-century libertine of Seville, who features in many plays and operas

donkey

donkey work
necessary but uninspiring routine work
refers to the laborious work done by a donkey

for donkey's years
for a long time

to pin the tail on the donkey
to put the blame on a person who has with some effort been identified as responsible
refers to children's parlour game

to talk the hind leg off a donkey
to talk excessively

donna

a prima donna
a person with an exaggerated opinion of that person's own importance making relations with others needlessly difficult
Italian, 'first lady'

door

a foot in the door
the opportunity to do business

never darken my door again
do not ever return
refers to the shadow cast by a person's presence in a doorway

not to break someone's door down
to be unenthusiastic about someone's goods or services

one's door is always open
people can take their problems to one at any time

through the back door
unofficially or surreptitiously

to be out the door
to have one's position terminated

to beat a path to someone's door
to seek a person out in great numbers
Ralph Waldo Emerson (1803–82), *Sarah S. B. Yule, Borrowings*, 'If a man write a better book, preach a better sermon, or make a better mouse-trap than his neighbour, tho' he build his house in the woods, the world will make a beaten path to his door'

to close the door on someone

to deny another person a desired opportunity

to keep the wolf from the door
to struggle to survive (esp. with respect to hunger)

to leave the door open
to provide an opportunity

to put something at someone's door
to blame a person

to show someone the door
to ask a person to leave

to shut the door on someone
to deny another person a desired opportunity

to shut the stable door after the horse has bolted
to take preventive action only after the relevant event

to slam the door in someone's face
ostentatiously to refuse to have any dealings with a person

doors

the doors of the Ritz are open to all
despite rhetoric to the contrary wealthy people have many advantages over poor people
refers to the Ritz Hotel, London, founded in 1906 by César Ritz

to knock on doors
to seek out opportunities

to open doors
to create opportunities

doorstep

on one's own doorstep
in one's own domain

dot

from the year dot
for a long time
refers to the year one — hence, colloquially, a time in the remote past

to arrive on the dot
to turn up at the exact scheduled time

to dot the i's and cross the t's
to be meticulous in completing documentation

dotted

to sign on the dotted line
to confirm one's agreement

doubting

a doubting Thomas
a person who refuses to believe claims in the absence of proof
John 20:25, 'But he [Thomas] said ... except I shall see in his hands the print of the nails ... I will not believe'

doughnut

watch the doughnut — not the hole
look for the positive aspects

down

a down-to-earth solution
a realistic solution

it boils down to this
the essential features are as follows

low-down
confidential information relevant to something

not to break someone's door down
to be unenthusiastic about someone's goods or services

that is money down the drain
money has been wastefully lost on a failed project

to batten down the hatches
to get ready for expected difficulties
nautical metaphor

to be a laid-down misPre
to be very easily accomplished and/or to be certain of outcome
refers to card playing where one player undertakes not to win any tricks while playing with the disadvantage of having that player's cards exposed to observation by others

to be down in the mouth
to be depressed
refers to facial expression

to be down the track
to be making progress

to be further down the line
to have a low priority; OR to be further advanced in a project, at a later stage

to be on the down grade
to be of deteriorating quality

to be tied down
to have responsibilities precluding alternative activities

to bow down
to succumb to pressure

to break down the barriers

to do away with the prejudice preventing something

to breathe down someone's neck
to cause annoyance to another person by remaining in that person's vicinity or by supervising that person too closely; OR to be narrowly behind another person in some competitive situation

to bring someone down to earth
to disillusion a person

to bring the house down
to obtain rapturous applause
refers to the theatre

to catch someone with his pants/trousers down
to act when another person least expects it

to come down with a thud
to be suddenly disillusioned

to crack down on something
to seek to eradicate something

to cut tall poppies down to size
to diminish the self-importance of haughty persons

to downgrade
to put into a lower category or priority to dress someone down
to scold a person

to get down to brass tacks
to discuss the aspects that really matter
perhaps refers to Cockney rhyming slang ('brass tacks' = 'facts')

to get down to taws
to discuss the aspects that really matter

to go down a particular road
to adopt a particular strategy

to go down a particular track
to make decisions aimed at a particular goal

to go down like a lead balloon
to receive a very cool reception

to go down memory lane
to reminisce

to go down on one's hands and knees to someone
with great humility to ask a favour of a person

to go down the gurgler
to be ruined
refers to plumbing

to go down the tube
to fail

to happen down the road
to happen later

to have come down in the last shower
to be naVve
refers to someone having just arrived with the last shower of rain

to jump down someone's throat
to react angrily to the remarks of the other party to a conversation

to jump up and down
to show excitement or anger or frustration

to keep one's head down
to stay out of trouble, AND/OR to work very diligently

to kick a man when he is down
to take unfair advantage of a person already in difficulty

to lay down the law
to be officious

to let one's hair down
to relax

to look down the barrel of a gun
to be given little choice in a matter

to look down the nose at something
to treat a matter with obvious contempt

to move down a notch
to accept a lower position
refers to gradations of notches on a measuring stick

to nail something down
to define something precisely

to pin someone down
to find a person willing to accept blame or responsibility; OR to force a person to announce a decision or concede a point
refers to wrestling

to play down something
to seek to have less emphasis or attention given to something

to put one's foot down
to assert one's authority and insist on something

to put one's roots down
to settle in

to ram something down someone's throat
to pressure another person into accepting an idea with which that person does not agree

to ring down the curtain on something
to treat something as concluded

to sell someone down the river
to betray a person who has placed trust in one
refers to selling slaves to owners further down the river

to send a chill down someone's neck
to be worrying news

to shake down
to sleep on an improvised bed

to shoot someone down in flames
utterly to destroy another person's arguments
refers to loss of aircraft in battle

to step down
to retire from some position

to take someone down a peg or two
to humble a person (especially a conceited person)
refers to scoring in backgammon or cribbage; Samuel Butler (1612–80), *Hudibras* II:ii, 'And took your grandees down a peg'

to take something lying down
to accept a disadvantage without protest

to throw down the gauntlet
to issue a challenge
refers to the glove worn by a knight; OFr *gantelet* (diminutive of 'glove')

to turn something upside down
to revolutionise something

to water down something
to reduce the severe impact of something

to win hands down
to win very convincingly
refers to a jockey riding confidently with hands low when a race is as good as won

when the chips are down
when all facts are known and taken into consideration

downfall

downfall
ruination

downgrade

to downgrade
to put into a lower category or priority

downhill

to go downhill
to deteriorate

dozen

it is six of one and half a dozen of the other
it does not matter either way
Captain Marryat (1792–1848), *The Pirate* ch. 4, 'I never knows the children. It's just six of one and halfa dozen of the other.'

to talk nineteen to the dozen
to speak very quickly

draconian

draconian
excessively severe
refers to an especially harsh code of laws drawn up by the Athenian legislator, Drako (620 BC)

drag

to drag one's feet
to be deliberately uncooperative or slow to act

to drag one's heels
to perform unduly slowly

to drag someone by the head and ears
to force a person to reveal the true facts

to drag someone kicking and screaming to do something
to force a person into some action that the person is most reluctant to undertake

to drag the chain
to perform unduly slowly
refers to a horse or bullock that is not pulling its weight, thus causing its chains to drag on the ground

wild horses would not drag that out of me
I refuse absolutely to reveal that
refers to a form of torture in which persons were dragged behind horses

drain

that is money down the drain
money has been wastefully lost on a failed project

to drain every ounce out of something
to get the maximum use or pleasure out of something

drakes

to play ducks and drakes
not to treat the matter seriously
derived from the old name given to the game of throwing a stone such that it skips across the surface of water; hence: 'to throw away idly and carelessly

draught

to feel the draught
to experience unfavourable conditions

draw

to be quick on the draw
to act precipitately
refers to drawing a firearm

to be the luck of the draw
to be a chance result
refers to card games or a raffle

to draw a blank
to be unsuccessful
refers to playing cards

to draw a deep breath
to get ready for exertion or for emotional news

to draw a line in the sand
to indicate clearly the limits of acceptability beyond which people should not go

to draw a long bow
to state a conclusion that, although possible, is unlikely on the known facts
refers to archery

to draw a veil over something
pointedly to avoid discussing something

to draw blood from a stone
to do the impossible

to draw fire
to act in a way that attracts criticism

to draw first blood
to get an early advantage

to draw the line at that
to refuse to go any further

to draw the nets closer
to intensify one's efforts

to draw the short straw
to be chosen (perhaps by lot) to undertake an undesired task

drawbridge

to pull up the drawbridge
defensively to withdraw and refuse to cooperate'
refers to the drawbridge over a defensive moat around a castle

drawcard

drawcard
feature expected to attract a crowd

drawer

to tuck something away in a drawer
to put something aside for the time being

top drawer
first class

drawing

back to the drawing board
to start again from the very beginning

to be on the drawing board
to be being planned from the very beginning

drawn

until stumps are drawn
until the end of the day's activities
refers to cricket

dream

a pipedream
a fanciful notion, wished for but unlikely
probably derived from smoking opium in pipes

to dream up some story
to concoct a false story naVvely or maliciously

to have a dream run
to encounter no difficulties

dreams

to be successful beyond one's wildest dreams
to be far more successful than one could have expected

dress

dress rehearsal

a preliminary practice or experience before the real thing

to dress someone down

to scold a person

dressed

first in best dressed

persons acting early will do better than latecomers

to be dressed to kill

to be very smartly dressed with the intention of making a striking impression — usually with a view to a romantic or sexual conquest

to be dressed up to the nines

to be attired in garments of the highest standard

perhaps a corruption of 'to then eyen' ('to the eyes'); Thomas Hardy (1840–1928), 'She's dressed up to the nines for some grand party'

to be mutton dressed up as lamb

foolishly to pretend to be younger

dressing

to engage in window dressing

to present someone or something in a falsely favourable light

refers to displays in shop windows

dried

to be cut and dried

to be well settled or long established

refers to timber cut and dried, and ready for use

drift

to drift apart

to lose contact or to change feelings once held in common

drink

one can lead a horse to water, but one can't make it drink

one can give advice to a person but cannot ensure that it will be acted on

to be meat and drink

to be very pleasurable; or to be basic, familiar, and essential to one's experience of life'

Matthew 25:35, 'For I was an hungred, and ye gave me meat: I was thirsty and ye gave me drink'; Shakespeare, 'It is meat and drinke to me to see a clowne'

drinks

it is a long time between drinks

activity is occurring only very spasmodically

drive

an opening wide enough to drive a coach and four through

an excellent opportunity to demonstrate the major errors or absurdities of something

the saying seems sometimes also to have referred to six horses: Sir Stephen Rice (1673–1715), as quoted by W. King, *State of the Protestants of Ireland* (1672), 'I will drive a coach and six horses through the Act of Settlement'

to drive a coach and horses through something

to demonstrate the major errors or absurdities of something

Sir Stephen Rice (1673–1715), as quoted by W. King, *State of the Protestants of Ireland* (1672), 'I will drive a coach and six horses through the Act of Settlement'

to drive a wedge between two persons

to set out to cause a division between two persons

refers to the use of wedges in timber work

to drive someone almost to tears

to act in such a way as to cause someone significant distress

to drive someone from pillar to post

to send a person to a series of places in a vain attempt to achieve something

originally a term from royal tennis, referring to the balls being struck and banging about structures in the (indoors) court

to drive someone out of that person's mind

to produce insanity in a person

often used jocularly, with exaggeration

to drive someone to the wall

to ruin a person

to drive someone up the wall

by one's actions, to cause extreme annoyance to the point of desperation

to drive the lesson home

to take certain action that is unpleasant but that has the effect of registering a message

driver
a back-seat driver
a person seeking to exercise control when it is not that person's responsibility
to be in the driver's seat
to be in charge

drone
a drone
an idle person

drop
at the drop of a hat
very readily
from the practice of signalling the beginning of a race or fight with the drop of a hat
drop dead!
go away, I want no dealings with you
to be able to hear a pin drop
to experience silence
to be only a drop in the bucket/ocean
to be quite insignificant in the total scene
to drop a brick
to make a socially embarrassing or inappropriate announcement
to drop a clanger
to do something that is indiscreet or that offends social conventions
to drop into one's lap
to turn up fortuitously
to drop names
to slip names of celebrities allegedly known to the speaker into a conversation in an attempt to impress
to drop one's bundle
to become despondent
to squeeze the last drop out of something
to get the maximum advantage out of some favourable situation
to wait for the other shoe to drop
to await the seemingly imminent and inevitable
refers to a person being disturbed by a neighbour who drops one shoe on the floor, the listener then being frustrated when the sound of the other shoe being dropped is not heard

dropped
the penny dropped
a person has just realised a fact that should have been obvious
refers to old-fashioned pay toilets
someone's jaw dropped
someone registered obvious astonishment and/or disappointment

drought
to break a drought
to resume supplies after an interval

droves
people stayed away in droves
few people came
refers to a moving group of cattle, sheep, or other animals

drown
to drown one's sorrows
to drink by way of solace and in an attempt to forget some misfortune

drug
to be a drug on the market
to be in overplentiful supply

drum
to beat a drum for someone
to propagate another person's cause
to beat one's drum
to publicise immodestly one's own attributes
to drum someone out of some organisation
to terminate in ignominy a person's employment or membership
refers to the ceremonial cashiering in the army to the beating of parade drums
to drum-up support
actively to seek out support
to march to a different drum
to show an independent approach
military metaphor

drunk
to be punch drunk
to be stupefied by repeated setbacks or bad news
refers to a form of brain damage suffered by boxers who have received repeated blows to the head

dry
a dry hole
an exercise that, after much effort, proves fruitless
refers to drilling for oil
a dry run

a trial exercise

refers to a creek bed that is dry until heavy rain causes it to become a stream

the ink is hardly dry

this involves indecent haste

refers to acting promptly, as soon as a document is signed

to be in the dry dock

to be out of action while undergoing repairs

refers to ship repairs

to dry up

to cease

to keep one's powder dry

to retain key arguments or resources in reserve for use later

refers to gunpowder in battle

to leave someone high and dry

to isolate a person from a desired involvement; to withdraw all support from a person

nautical metaphor referring to a boat stranded out of water

to squeeze the lemon dry

to get the maximum advantage out of some favourable situation

Sir Eric Geddes (1875–1937), 'The Germans ... are going to pay every penny; they are going to be squeezed, as a lemon is squeezed — until the pips squeak. My only doubt is not whether we can squeeze hard enough, but whether there is enough juice.' (10 December 1918)

duck

a lame duck

a person unable to fend for himself or herself

a 'lame-duck president' is a president still in office but without influence because the commencement of the successor's term is imminent

in two shakes of a duck's tail

in an instant

to be a dead duck

to have failed; OR to be in a hopeless situation

to be a sitting duck

to be vulnerable to exploitation

to be like water off a duck's back

(of advice or criticism) to be completely ignored

to break one's duck

to end a spell that had no results

refers to cricket in which a 'duck' represents no score

to duck for cover

to seek to avoid blame

duckling

an ugly duckling

an unprepossessing person or thing, the characteristics of which change in time to become attractive

refers to a cygnet in a brood of ducks in a children's story of that name by Hans Christian Andersen

ducks

to play ducks and drakes

not to treat the matter seriously

derived from the old name given to the game of throwing a stone such that it skips across the surface of water; hence: 'to throw away idly and carelessly

due

to give the devil his due

to be fair

dump

to dump something in someone's lap

to impose an unwelcome responsibility on another person

dumps

to be in the dumps

to feel depressed

dunce

to earn a dunce's cap

to do something stupid

a 'dunce' being derived from the name of Duns Scotus (1265–1308) and his followers ('Dunsers') whose hair-splitting theology was later perceived to be opposed to learning and enlightenment; Thomas Fuller (1608–61), 'a dunce, void of learning but full of books'

dust

to bite the dust

to fall, to fail, to die

to dust some idea off

to revive some proposal

to gather dust

not to be acted upon, but without being formally rejected

to throw dust into someone's eyes

to deceive a person by presenting inaccurate or misleading information

Koran: 'Neither didst thou, O Muhammad, cast dust into their eyes; but it was God who confounded them'

when the dust settles
when sufficient time has passed to allow matters to be perceived clearly

duster

today a rooster, tomorrow a feather duster
when circumstances change, an important person can, immediately, become unimportant

dyed

dyed in the wool
very loyal and partisan

refers to a garment in which the wool itself (from which the garment is woven) is dyed, rather than the completed garment being dyed as a piece (and thus less thoroughly)

dying

to be dying to do something
to be extremely keen to do something

dynamite

to be dynamite
to cause outrage or to have the potential to lead to danger or controversy

to play with dynamite
to invite trouble by virtue of one's risky conduct

E

each

not to live in each other's pockets
to each follow his or her own lifestyle

to be at each other's throats
to be always fighting

to beat each other over the head
to be always fighting

to have two bob each way
to equivocate

refers to the slang term for two shillings, and to betting for a win or a place

to have fifty cents each way
to equivocate

refers to betting for a win or a place

eager

an eager beaver
a person with great drive and enthusiasm even if this causes annoyance to others

refers to the industriousness of the beaver, and adapted as World War II US expression for a very keen person who habitually volunteered

eagle

to have an eagle eye
to be able very readily to notice small mistakes or fine details missed by others

ear

a word in someone's ear
a confidential discussion

one can't make a silk purse out of a sow's ear
it is impossible to manufacture something of a high standard from inferior raw materials

Malcolm Bradbury (1932–), 'For the mass of men, you can't make a silk purse out of a sow's ear'

to be out on one's ear
to be ejected from a situation or place or to have one's services abruptly terminated

to chew someone's ear
to force one's conversation on an unwilling listener

to get the wrong sow by the ear
to reach an incorrect conclusion

to go in one ear and out the other
to leave no impression

to have someone's ear
to have a person's attention

Shakespeare, *Julius Caesar* III:ii, 'Friends, Romans, countrymen, lend me your ears'; *Hamlet* I: iii, 'Give every man thine ear, but few thy voice'

to keep an ear to the ground
to be well informed as to current developments

refers to listening for distant sound by applying one's ear to the ground

to lend someone an ear
to pay attention to a person

Shakespeare, *Julius Caesar* III:ii, 'Friends, Romans, countrymen, lend me your ears'

to play it by ear

to develop one's strategy to always fit in with circumstances as they change from time to time

refers to playing music without the benefit of a written score

to send someone away with a flea in the ear

to give a person frank, but unwelcome, facts

perhaps refers to fleas trapped in the armour of ancient knights, or perhaps from the discomfort felt by a dog with a flea in its ear; or perhaps, figuratively, to any lingering irritation in the ear

to turn something on its ear

to reverse something

ears

asses and little pitchers have long ears

children have a tendency to overhear things

music to one's ears

comments that one is very pleased to hear

Shakespeare, *Romeo and Juliet* II:i, 'How silver-sweet sound lovers' tongues by night, / like softest music to attending ears!'

to be all ears

to be very attentive

to be up to one's ears in something

to be involved very deeply in something

to be wet behind the ears

to be excessively naVve and inexperienced

to come out of one's ears

to be plentiful

to come to someone's ears

to come to someone's attention

to drag someone by the head and ears

to force a person to reveal the true facts

to fall around someone's ears

to collapse utterly around someone

to fall on deaf ears

to be totally disregarded

to have money flowing out of one's ears

to be very rich

to keep one's ears open

to be alert for useful information

to prick up one's ears

suddenly to start paying attention to a conversation in progress as a result of a half-heard phrase

refers to horses and dogs

walls have ears

someone may be overhearing

words on wartime posters, reminding people of the existence of spies; might also refer to certain rooms in the Louvre, constructed so that conversations could be heard in other rooms

were your ears burning?

we were discussing you

Pliny: 'When our ears do glow and tingle, some do talk of us in our absence'

with one's ears pinned back

chastened

refers to the aggressive attitude of horses

eared

dog-eared

(of pages) well-thumbed

refers to the turned-down appearance of the ears of many dogs

early

early in the piece

at an early stage of some activity

the early bird gets the worm

a person who acts ahead of others gets an advantage over them

earmark

to earmark

to allocate to a specific purpose

refers to marking animals

earn

to earn a dunce's cap

to do something stupid

a 'dunce' being derived from the name of Duns Scotus (1265–1308) and his followers ('Dunsers') whose hair-splitting theology was later perceived to be opposed to learning and enlightenment; Thomas Fuller (1608–61), 'a dunce, void of learning but full of books'

to earn one's stripes

to deserve promotion

refers to military rank

to earn peanuts

to get a reward that is far too small in relation to the value of the services rendered

earth

a down-to-earth solution
a realistic solution

earth-shattering
very significant

how on earth?
just how?

the salt of the earth
special people who make a vital contribution to society
Matthew 5:13, 'Ye are the salt of the earth'

to bring someone down to earth
to disillusion a person

to charge the earth
to impose very high prices

to move heaven and earth
to do everything possible
Revelation 21:1, 'And I saw a new heaven and a new earth, for the first heaven and the first earth had passed away'; a reference to the apocalyptic vision of the greatest possible change to all creation

to promise the earth
to give extravagant assurances
Matthew 5:5, 'Blessed are the meek, for they shall inherit the earth'

to run someone to earth
to locate a person
refers to fox hunting

easy

to be easy meat
to be an opponent who is readily outwitted

to be easy on the eye
to be visually attractive

to breathe easy
(following some crisis) to relax

eat

I could eat a horse
I am very hungry

I'll eat my hat if so-and-so happens
I do not believe that so-and-so will happen

to be able to eat someone for breakfast
to be able to outwit a person very easily

to eat crow
to act in a humiliating fashion to achieve a desired outcome
from an incident in New England (North America) in the Anglo–American War of 1812–14

to eat humble pie
to be prepared to humiliate oneself and apologise
a play on words — derived from the eating of 'umble pie' (entrails of a deer) by lowly persons

to eat one's head off
to eat excessively

to eat one's heart out
to suffer bitterly
Shakespeare, *Othello* IV:i, 'O God! That I were a man! I would eat his heart in the market place'

to eat one's words
to retract in a humiliated fashion

to eat out of someone's hands
to be very compliant and submissive

to eat someone alive
to defeat a person soundly

to eat someone out of house and home
to ruin a person by eating all that that person has
used in an exaggerated, humorous sense

to want to have one's cake and eat it too
to want two mutually exclusive alternatives

you can eat your heart out
I don't care if you are intensely aggrieved or jealous

eaten

moth-eaten
antiquated, shabby

eating

the choice is between eating well or sleeping well
one can invest for maximum yield or maximum security, but not both

the proof of the pudding is in the eating
the success of a venture will be measured by its results

eavesdrop

to eavesdrop

deliberately to listen to conversations to which one is not a party

originally — by standing beneath the eaves of a house; James Shirley (1596–1666), 'It is not civil to eavesdrop him'

ebb

ebb and flow

fluctuations

to ebb away

to decline gradually

echo

to echo someone's words

to repeat another person's views as though they were one's own

eclipse

to eclipse someone

to make dim in comparison (in effect, to outshine a person)

edge

a leading edge

an advantage through possession of the latest technology or knowledge

refers to the foremost edge of an aircraft's wings

to be at the cutting edge of something

to be in a position where important decisions are made

to be on a knife edge

to be in danger; OR to be a very close result

to be on edge

to be nervous

to be on the edge of one's seat

to be very excited or anxious regarding what is currently happening

to be on the razor's edge

to be critically balanced; OR to be in danger

to give someone the edge

to give a person an advantage over others

to push someone over the edge

by a small action to cause the absolute ruin (financially or emotionally) of someone already in peril

to set someone's teeth on edge

to cause a person intense irritation or discomfort

Ezekiel 18:2, 'The fathers have eaten sour grapes, and the children's teeth are set on edge'; Shakespeare, *Henry IV Pt 1* III:i, 'And that would set my teeth nothing on edge, nothing so much as mincing poetry'

to take the edge off something

to weaken the force or impact of something

to tip someone over the edge

to cause someone to exceed that person's limit of tolerance or endurance

edged

gilt-edged

very safe

nineteenth century; refers to certificates for government stock that were printed with a gold edging

to be a two-edged sword

to involve both advantages and disadvantages of similar significance

Psalms 149:6, 'Let the high praises of God be in their mouth, and a two-edged sword in their hand'

edges

to fiddle at the edges

to do some relatively minor things that do not deal with the substance of a problem

to become frayed at the edges

to become tatty, lacking clear definition; no longer quite appropriate

to tinker at the edges

to make minor or cosmetic changes without affecting the substance

refers to the common assumption that a tinker was an unreliable tradesman

edgeways

to get words in edgeways

to manage to interrupt a conversation or monologue in order to say something oneself

effect

a domino effect

a series of events, each of which is precipitated by the one before

refers to a series of domino pieces falling over in sequence

egg

a nest egg

a sum of money set aside in case of need; a nucleus of savings

derived from the custom of placing an egg in a hen's nest as an inducement for the hen to lay more

chicken and egg
a situation involving two factors each of which causes the other, making it impossible to decide which came first

to be a bad egg
to be a dishonest or disreputable person

to be a curate's egg
to be good only in parts
refers to a cartoon (*Punch*, vol. cix, p. 222, 1895) showing the nervous young curate (Jones) in conversation with the Lord Bishop:
'I'm afraid you've got a bad egg, Mr Jones.'
'Oh no, my Lord, I assure you! Parts of it are excellent!'

to have egg on one's face
to be embarrassed by the results of one's own stupidity

eggs

as sure as eggs is eggs
with great certainty
perhaps a corruption of the logician's formula: 'x is x'

not to put all one's eggs in the one basket
to spread one's risks

one cannot make an omelette without breaking eggs
the desired end dictates the means even if they cause harm to others

there are many ways to cook eggs
there are many ways to achieve an objective

to kill the goose that lays the golden eggs
through excessive greed, to sacrifice future gains for a short-term advantage
based on a Greek fable about a man who killed the goose that laid golden eggs; his aim was to collect the whole stock of eggs at once but, in doing so, he ended his future supply

to teach one's grandmother how to suck eggs
to try to tell a much more experienced person something very obvious to that person

eight

to be right behind the eight ball
to be in a position of extreme disadvantage
refers to US game of pool in which the ultimate objective is to pot the black ball (which is numbered 8)

elbow

elbow grease
hard manual work
old jocular saying, in existence for several centuries, referring to the vigorous use of the elbow in rubbing, polishing, scrubbing, etc.

more power to your elbow
may your praiseworthy efforts continue and be strengthened

to elbow someone out
to force a person to move aside and thus enable oneself to assume that person's position

elbows

to be up to one's elbows in something
to be very busy and involved with something

element

to be in one's element
to be very comfortable in familiar surroundings or in an environment in which one can cope very readily

elephant

a rogue elephant
a person of vicious temper who does not function as part of the group and who acts in an undisciplined way

a white elephant
an expensive and useless luxury
refers to gifts of sacred elephants by the King of Siam to persons then ruined by the expense of their upkeep

to get an elephant stamp
to receive praise

elephants

one looks for elephants in elephant country
one needs to search in the right place

eleven

the second eleven
the second rank of persons who are performing a function less important than that performed by others
refers to a second-level sporting team, esp. cricket

eleventh

at the eleventh hour
at the last moment
Matthew 20:9: 'And when they came that were hired about the eleventh hour, they received every man a penny'; refers to the last hour of the working day in biblical times, and therefore the last opportunity to secure work — hence the very last opportunity

eleventh commandment
unwritten rule
refers to the ten commandments (*Exodus* 20:1–17)

ell

give someone an inch and that person will take an ell
make a small concession to a person and that person will abuse it by taking much more
derived from old measure of length (ell) originally based on the length of the forearm (the Old English word *eln* being cognate with the Latin *ulna*–a long bone of the forearm)

emasculate

to emasculate something
to delete the essential features of something

emollient

to be an emollient
to be a measure designed to make people more favourably disposed to one's wishes

empire

to engage in empire building
to set out to expand the size of the business or bureaucratic unit for which one is responsible, especially as a means of increasing one's own importance

empty

the empty can makes the most noise
the least worthy arguments often attract the most publicity

encapsulate

to encapsulate some idea
to reduce the essential points of a complicated proposal to a small number of words

end

a dead-end position
a job with no prospects of advancement

at the end of the day
in due course, or at the conclusion of a project

the tail end of something
the very end of something

this is the end of the road for someone
a person will have no further opportunity to do something

to be at the end of one's tether
to be frustrated because one is at the very limit of one's resources of knowledge, authority, or patience
refers to tethering of animals with a rope

to be on the losing end of the stick
to be worse off while the other party to a transaction becomes correspondingly better off

to be the thin end of the wedge
to be a small action or thing that has the potential to cause much larger undesirable consequences
refers to wedges used for splitting wood

to come to a sticky end
to endure an unpleasant fate

to come to the end of the road
to come to the point where hope and endeavour are finished

to go off the deep end
to lose one's temper

to have hold of the wrong end of the pineapple
to be utterly mistaken

to hold the wrong end of the stick
to be completely mistaken about something

to jump straight in at the deep end
to do something without proper preparation

to look though the wrong end of the telescope
completely to miss the point

to make someone's hair stand on end
to give a person shocking news
Job 4:15, 'Then a spirit passed before my face; the hair of my flesh stood up'; Shakespeare, *Hamlet* I:v, 'would harrow

up thy soul … and each particular hair to stand an end'

to run into a dead end
to get nowhere in an investigation

to see the light at the end of the tunnel
to perceive relief at the imminent end of a period of prolonged difficulty

to seek the pot of gold at the end of the rainbow
to have naVve expectations
refers to the proverbial belief in the existence of a pot of gold at the end of a rainbow

ends

to burn the candle at both ends
to exhaust one's resources through working excessive hours'

to make ends meet
to live within one's income
Thomas Fuller (1608–61), 'Worldly wealth he cared not for, desiring only to make both ends meet', referring to Edmund Grindall, in *The History of the Worthies of England* (1662), *Worthies of Cumberland*

to tie up the loose ends
to complete the minor outstanding items of some substantially finished project

enfant

an enfant terrible
a person who causes embarrassment by inappropriate action, or by inappropriate speech about unpalatable issues'
French for 'terrible child'

engage

to engage in cherry picking
(in business) to accept only the potentially most lucrative deals

to engage in pump priming
to spend public money with the aim of attracting parochial electoral support
refers to priming a water pump

enough

enough to sink a battleship
much more than sufficient

enshrine

to enshrine
to incorporate as an important part of something

enter

to enter a long road
to commence a task that will take a long time

to enter the home stretch
to commence the last stage
refers to horse racing

to enter treacherous waters
to engage in an enterprise with risks that are not obvious
nautical metaphor

errand

to send a boy on a man's errand
to engage a person to do a task beyond that person's capabilities

errors

a comedy of errors
a series of separate mistakes in relation to some matter
refers to the title of a Shakespearean play

escape

to escape by the skin of one's teeth
to only just avoid some disaster
Job 19:20, 'I am escaped with the skin of my teeth'

escutcheon

to be a blot on someone's escutcheon
to be a blemish on a person's character
refers to the shield on which a coat of arms is depicted; hence, a sign of dishonour on the symbol of one's name and honour

esprit

esprit de corps
a feeling of camaraderie and concern for the good name of some organisation of which one is a member
French, 'vital breath of a body'

estate

the fourth estate
the press
refers to the fourth 'power' in the realm (after the Lords Temporal, the Lords Spiritual, and the Commons); variously attributed to Edmund Burke (1729–97), Thomas Carlyle (1795–1881), and Lord Macaulay (1800–59)

eve

to be on the eve of something
to occur just before some event
refers to the evening of the day before

even

anyone with even half a brain
anyone with any degree of common sense or knowledge

I fear the Greeks even when they bear gifts
I am suspicious of generous behaviour from traditional opponents
Virgil (70–19 BC), *Aeneid* II:49, *Timeo Danaos et dona ferentis* ('I fear the Greeks even when they bring gifts'), in reference to the Trojan horse

to even the score
to respond by way of retribution for some past action of another person

to keep something on an even keel
to ensure that something is kept balanced and stable
nautical metaphor

every

as every schoolboy knows
as is recognised by everyone
Jonathon Swift (1667–1745), *The Country Life*, 1:81,'How haughtily he cocks his nose, / To tell what every schoolboy knows'; Lord Macaulay (1800–59), *Lord Clive* (Jan. 1840), 'Every schooboy knows who imprisoned Montezuma, and who strangled Atahualpa'

every cloud has a silver lining
there are consolations and potential benefits even in seemingly adverse situations

every dog has its day
persons being criticised or persecuted will have their opportunity to reverse the situation; good luck comes sooner or later
Charles Kingsley (1819–75). *Young and Old*, 'Young blood must have its course, lad, and every dog his day'

every galah in the petshop
everybody

every man and his dog
everybody

every Pancake Tuesday
only on occasions
refers to Shrove Tuesday, when pancakes are traditionally eaten

every Tom, Dick, and Harry
virtually all ordinary people
appears to have been coined in Victorian times

in every nook and cranny
everywhere

to chase every hare
to be easily sidetracked

to drain every ounce out of something
to get the maximum use or pleasure out of something

to play every card in the pack
to try very hard and use every conceivable argument
refers to playing cards

to resist something every inch of the way
to resist something utterly

to use every trick in the book
to try very hard and use every conceivable argument

everything

everything in the garden is lovely
everything is fine
Genesis 2:8–9, 'And the Lord God planted a garden ... to grow every tree that is pleasant to the sight'

everything but the kitchen sink
virtually all things

everything under the sun
absolutely everything

to do everything by halves
to do everything imperfectly or incompletely

exercise

a soul-searching exercise
a deep and penetrating examination of personal motives and conscience

exhaust

to exhaust the field
to use up all the possibilities

exhibition

to make an exhibition of oneself
to behave in a way that invites ridicule

existence

a cat-and-dog existence
a life full of frequent squabbles

expedition

a fishing expedition

an exercise that sets out to gather incriminating information without knowing its exact nature or location

experience

a road to Damascus experience
a sudden, dramatic conversion
refers to the sudden conversion of Paul (Saul) — *Acts* 9:3, 'And as he journeyed, he came to Damascus: and suddenly there shined around him a light from heaven: And he fell to the earth'

explode

to explode
(of a person) to express rage

expose

to expose holes
to expose weaknesses in an argument

to expose one's flank
to leave oneself open to the possibility of having advantage taken

extra

to go the extra mile
to work beyond the call of duty
Matthew 5:41, 'Whosoever shall compel thee to go a mile, go with him twain'

eye

a bird's-eye view
a general overview or summary of a subject, emphasising the major features

a mote in someone's eye
a fault in another person that is trifling in comparison with an unrecognised major fault in oneself
Matthew 7:3, 'Why beholdest thou the mote that is in thy brother's eye, but considerest not the beam that is in thine own eye?'

a smack in the eye
a rebuff

an eye for an eye
retaliation of equal magnitude to the original offence
Exodus 21:24, 'Eye for eye, tooth for tooth, hand for hand, foot for foot'; see also 'to turn the other cheek'

beauty is in the eye of the beholder
some things are matters for subjective judgments
Shakespeare *Love's Labour Lost* II:i, 'Beauty is bought by judgment of the eye'

in one's mind's eye
using a vivid imagination

one would give one's eye teeth for something
a person would very much like to achieve some objective
refers to the (valued) canine teeth directly under the eye

to be an eye-opener
to be a surprise

to be better than a poke in the eye with a burnt stick
to be not particularly welcome, but better than other alternatives

to be easy on the eye
to be visually attractive

to be eye wash
to be nonsense

to be in the eye of the storm
to be at the centre of a controversy

to be in the public eye
to have one's every action subject to scrutiny by the community

to be one in the eye for someone
to represent an unexpected and unwelcome defeat

to be only a gleam in someone's eyes
not yet conceived, let alone achieved

to be the apple of someone's eye
to be a much cherished person
refers to the pupil of the eye — 'the apple of the eye' as being the centre of visual perception and therefore especially cherished and much-valued

to cast an eye over something
to look at something critically

to catch someone's eye
to attract the attention of another person, or to seek permission to address that person

to cock one's eye at someone
to glance knowingly at a person

to do someone in the eye
to cheat a person

to have a crow's eye
to be cunning or alert

to have an eagle eye
to be able very readily to notice small mistakes or fine details missed by others

to have an eye for something

to have particular expertise in assessing something

to hit the bull's eye
to be extremely accurate in an activity; to score
derived from archery

to keep a weather eye out for something
to look out with particular care
nautical metaphor; refers to the eye that is turned towards the wind

to keep an eye on the ball
to monitor a fast-changing situation

to keep one's eye on someone
to supervise a person

to keep one's eye on something
to monitor a situation

to see eye to eye with someone
to agree
Isaiah 52:8, 'For they shall see eye to eye, when the Lord shall bring again Zion'

to see something out of the corner of one's eye
only just to see something

to see something with half an eye
to sum up a matter instantly
refers to taking note with a mere glance

to turn a blind eye to something
to pretend that something obvious does not exist
refers to action by Horatio, Lord Nelson (1758–1805), when disregarding Admiralty signals: 'I have only one eye — I have a right to be blind sometimes — I really do not see the signal!' (at the Battle of Copenhagen, reported in Southey, *Life of Nelson*, ch. 7)

with an eye towards doing something
with the intention that something particular be done

eyeball

eyeball to eyeball
confronting each other and taking account of each other's reactions

eyeballs

to be up to the eyeballs in something
to be involved very deeply in something

eyebrows

to raise one's eyebrows
to show surprise or disbelief

eyed

blue-eyed boy
person shown unjustified favouritism

bright-eyed and bushy-tailed
naVve but enthusiastic

cock-eyed
stupid

lynx-eyed
having acute vision

one-eyed
biased

eyeful

to get an eyeful of something
to obtain a very good view of something

eyelid

not to bat an eyelid
to fail to express any surprise

eyelids

to hang on by the eyelids
to have only a slender hold

eyes

all eyes are on something
everyone's attention is focused on something

in someone's eyes
in a person's judgment

someone's eyes are bigger than that person's stomach
a person is unrealistic in regard to that person's ability to cope with something

someone's eyes popped
a person expressed great surprise

to be a sight for sore eyes
to be something welcome

to be all eyes
to observe very closely

to cast sheep's eyes at someone
to look at a person amorously

to clap eyes on something
to catch sight of something

to cry one's eyes out
to express great sadness at a situation

to have eyes at/in the back of one's head

to know more of what is going on than is generally realised

to have one's beady eyes on something
to await the chance to acquire something to which one is not properly entitled

to have one's eyes glued to something
to concentrate on looking at something to the exclusion of other competing calls for attention

to have stars in one's eyes
to receive a blow on the head that affects one's vision; OR to have unrealistic expectations of one's position and prospects

to hit someone right between the eyes
to be brutally frank
refers to fighting

to keep one's eyes open
to be on the lookout for useful information

to keep one's eyes open for something
to be on the lookout for an opportunity to do something

to keep one's eyes peeled for something
to be on the constant lookout for something
refers to keeping the eyelids open

to make eyes at someone
to look at a person amorously

to open someone's eyes to something
to alert another person to the truth of something
Matthew 9:30, 'And their eyes were opened'

to pick the eyes out of something
to choose the most valuable items from among a large number

to pull the wool over someone's eyes
to deceive or deliberately mislead another person
derived from the inability of some sheep to see clearly if wool is across their eyes

to rub one's eyes
to express astonishment

to see the colour of someone's eyes
to see how a person matches expectations or requirements

to shut one's eyes to something
deliberately to take no notice of something, especially in dereliction of one's duty

to throw dust into someone's eyes
to deceive a person by presenting inaccurate or misleading information
Koran: 'Neither didst thou, O Muhammad, cast dust into their eyes; but it was God who confounded them'

with one's eyes wide open
fully conscious of the ramifications

eyesore

eyesore
extremely ugly object

F

face

a poker face
a facial expression that does not reveal one's thoughts during negotiations
refers to playing cards

a slap in the face
a calculated insult or action amounting to a rebuke

a straight face
a facial expression that does not reveal one's thoughts in a humorous situation

someone's face fell
someone registered obvious disappointment

to be at the coal face
to be in the place where the real work is done

to blow up in someone's face
to rebound on a person

to cut one's nose off to spite one's face
to act in pique in a way that harms only oneself

to do an about face
to reverse a previously enunciated policy

to face a rocky road ahead
to be likely to encounter difficulties

to face the music
to accept responsibility when confronted by one's critics
refers to the theatre

to fall flat on one's face
to fail or to be seriously embarrassed by a bad error of judgment

to fly in the face of some rule
blatantly to disregard some rule

to go on until one is blue in the face
to do something difficult for a long time without being able to complete it

to have a long face
to look miserable

to have egg on one's face
to be embarrassed by the results of one's own stupidity

to hurl something in someone's face
to reproach a person in regard to something

to lose face
to experience embarrassment by an affront to one's dignity

to present a happy face to the world
bravely to gloss over one's problems and to appear contented to others

to put a brave face on it
to face adversity cheerfully

to put a new face on something
to alter the way something should be regarded

to put one's best face on something
to focus on the positive features surrounding a basically disastrous situation

to save face
to avoid humiliation or loss of reputation

to set one's face against something
to oppose some matter

to show one's face
to appear

to slam the door in someone's face
ostentatiously to refuse to have any dealings with a person

to stare someone in the face
to be obvious

to take something at face value
(of alleged facts) to accept something without question or challenge

to wipe the smile off someone's face
to destroy a person's complacency

volte face
a reversal of previously held beliefs
French, 'a turning around'; the term 'volte' originally had use in both fencing and horsemanship

wipe that smile off your face!
treat this matter more seriously!

you will laugh on the other side of your face
you will regret this

faced

to be left red-faced
to be embarrassed

two-faced
insincere

fact

to bring a fact home to someone
to make a person recognise a fact despite that person's inclination to the contrary

failure

heart failure
a shock

fair

a fair-weather friend
a person purporting to be a friend who offers no support in difficult times

to be a fair crack of the whip
to be just; to provide a fair opportunity

to be fair game
to be someone who can be attacked legitimately
refers to hunting

fairy

a fairy godmother
a person who provides for one's needs
based on the mythical magical figure

to believe in the tooth fairy
to be particularly gullible

refers to the mythical figure who exchanges children's milk teeth for a small sum of money

faith

an article of faith
a fundamental belief on which certain behaviour is based

faithful

the old faithful
a greatly loved article

fall

downfall
ruination

let the cards fall where they may
irrespective of what happens
refers to playing cards

that is the way the chips fall
that is the way that the benefits and detriments are distributed after an event

to be riding for a fall
to act in a reckless manner
refers to riding horses in a dangerous manner likely to result in a fall

to fall around someone's ears
to collapse utterly around someone

to fall between the cracks
to be ineligible for something because one does not fit neatly into any of several relevant categories

to fall between two stools
not to fit neatly into either of two available alternatives, and to waver between them

to fall by the wayside
to be abandoned and to therefore drop out; to fail to stay the course
Matthew 13:4, 'And when he sowed, some seeds fell by the wayside, and the fowls came and gobbled them up'

to fall flat
(of a joke) to be unappreciated by the audience

to fall flat on one's face
to fail or to be seriously embarrassed by a bad error of judgment

to fall head-over-heels in love
to fall very much in love

to fall in a heap
to collapse utterly

to fall in love with something
to have lost detachment in assessing the merits of some matter

to fall into line
to conform with others
military metaphor

to fall on deaf ears
to be totally disregarded

to fall on one's feet
surprisingly to succeed despite difficulties

to fall on one's sword
voluntarily to sacrifice one's position as a result of a sense of responsibility for an error
refers to suicide of Roman soldiers

to fall over one's own feet
to be very clumsy

to fall through
not to eventuate as expected

to fall to pieces
to collapse

to fall to the ground
to fail
Matthew 10:29, 'Are not two sparrows sold for a farthing? And one of them shall not fall on the ground without your Father ... '

to play the cards as they fall
to deal with problems as they arise
refers to playing cards

windfall
unexpected good fortune
refers to fruit falling from a tree without having to be picked

fallen

a fallen angel
a previously trusted person who has transgressed
refers to the fallen spirits who rebelled against God (Milton *Paradise Lost* Bk I, 392)

crestfallen
dejected
refers to the crest of a fighting cock

the axe has fallen
it is now too late
refers to execution by decapitation

the roof has fallen in
an enterprise has collapsed

falls

where the axe falls
who suffers the consequences

false

a false dawn
an incident giving rise to unjustified hope
refers to a transient light that precedes the true dawn by about an hour

to sail under false colours
to pretend that one's real character or beliefs are different from what they really are
refers to a ship concealing its true identity

fame

to catapult to fame
to achieve fame unexpectedly quickly

family

to sell off the family silver
to sell off one's prized possessions

famine

to be either feast or famine
to go from one extreme to the other

fan

to fan the flames
to increase unrest

fancy

to give rein to one's fancy
to let one's imagination have free scope
refers to riding or driving horses

fancyfree

footloose and fancyfree
unmarried and without any romantic attachments

fanfare

with much fanfare
with great enthusiasm and public acclaim

far

to be a far cry from something
to be a long way from something; to be quite dissimilar

fast

fast and furious
in an exciting way, in quick succession

life in the fast lane
existence full of exciting, high-pressure activity

to come in thick and fast
to arrive quickly and in great volume

to have to run fast just to stand still
competition is such that merely to maintain one's relative position one needs to make positive progress

to play fast and loose
to ignore one's obligations, be unreliable
refers to old fairground game in which the player was cheated

to pull a fast one
to gain an advantage by questionable means

fat

a fat cat
a well-remunerated politician, public servant, or businessperson

a fat chance
little hope

it's not over until the fat lady sings
it is not finished yet
probably refers to operatic performances, but during a radio broadcast made by the present author, a listener suggested that the metaphor refers to Kate Smith singing the US national anthem

the fat is in the fire
action with certain unstoppable consequences has now been initiated

to chew fat
to discuss a matter, often with grumbling and unhappiness

to trim the fat
to increase efficiency by reducing outlays

fatal

to be fatal
to be sufficient to destroy some proposal

fate

the hand of fate
chance

to be sentenced to some fate
to be condemned by circumstances to endure some fate

to seal someone's fate
to cause a certain final outcome adversely affecting a person'

father

father knows best

as an expert, I know better than you do what is most suitable for you

fatted

to kill the fatted calf
to demonstrate welcome and complete acceptance of another person
Luke 15:23. 'And bring hither the fatted calf and let us eat, and be merry'

faux

faux pas
something indiscreet or offending social conventions
French: 'false step'

favourite

favourite son
person preferred by many people for some office

fear

fools rush in where angels fear to tread
unsophisticated persons take unwise risks in circumstances where more knowledgeable persons would exercise caution
Alexander Pope (1688–1744), *An Essay on Criticism* 1:625, 'For fools rush in where angels fear to tread'

I fear the Greeks even when they bear gifts
I am suspicious of generous behaviour from traditional opponents
Virgil (70–19 BC), *Aeneid* II:49, *Timeo Danaos et dona ferentis* ('I fear the Greeks even when they bring gifts'), in reference to the Trojan horse

in fear and trembling
in a state of apprehension
Philippians 2:12, 'Work out your own salvation with fear and trembling'

to put the fear of God into someone
to frighten a person into behaving properly
Ecclesiates 12:13, 'Fear God, and keep his commandments; for this is the whole duty of man'

feast

a movable feast
an event not customarily held on a set date
refers to the feast days of the Christian Church, some of which are held on fixed days ('immovable feasts') and some of which vary with the date of Easter ('movable feasts')

to be either feast or famine
to go from one extreme to the other

feather

a feather in one's cap
a meritorious personal achievement
refers to the practice in a number of cultures of adding a feather to the headgear of a person in recognition of a significant personal achievement

birds of a feather flock together
persons of like interests gather in the same place
Samuel Rutherford (?1600–61), 'Fowls of a feather flock together'

feather bedding
(in industrial relations) creating unnecessary jobs solely to increase employment; OR (in economics) assisting an inefficient industry by government grants or excessive tariff protection

to feather one's own nest
improperly to appropriate things for oneself (especially in financial transactions)

to show the white feather
to indicate cowardice
refers to cross-bred birds, not regarded as useful in cock fighting

to thrash with a feather
to impose only a minor punishment for a very serious offence

today a rooster, tomorrow a feather duster
when circumstances change, an important person can, immediately, become unimportant

feathers

to make feathers fly
to cause a flurry of consternation and vigorous activity
refers to the fighting of cock birds

to ruffle someone's feathers
to engage in behaviour that irritates another person

fed

to be fed up to the back teeth
to be disgusted after prolonged provocation

federal

to make a federal case out of something
to attach far too much significance to a trivial issue

feed

to be chicken feed
to be small and unimportant

to feed the dogs while they are barking
to do something while the opportunity is available

to feed the fire
to exacerbate a situation

feedback

feedback
response from a target audience to those seeking to influence it
refers (originally) to the interaction between amplifiers and speakers

feeds

to bite the hand that feeds one
to show ingratitude
Edmund Burke (1729–97), *Thoughts and Details on Scarcity* (1797), 'And having looked to government for bread, on the very first scarcity they will turn and bite the hand that fed them'

feel

to feel blue
to feel depressed

to feel one's oats
to be energetic and lively (UK and Australia); to be self-important (USA)
refers to an energetic horse fed on oats

to feel something in one's bones
to suspect something without having any real evidence for it

to feel the draught
to experience unfavourable conditions

to feel the pinch
to be adversely affected by stringency (esp. financial)

to feel the rough side of someone's tongue
to be verbally abused by a person

feeling

a feeling in the air
a premonition held by many people

a gut feeling
a belief based purely on intuition and unsupported by facts or evidence

feet

itchy feet
a desire to travel

not to let grass grow under one's feet
not to let inertia or delay spoil something

to be quick on one's feet
cleverly to take advantage of a situation

to be rushed off one's feet
to be overwhelmed with tasks to perform and services to provide

to be six feet under
to be dead
refers to the depth of a grave

to cut the ground from under someone's feet
to withdraw support unexpectedly and, in the process, to cause embarrassment; OR to demolish a person's case and cause defeat, especially by anticipating that person's arguments or plans

to drag one's feet
to be deliberately uncooperative or slow to act

to fall on one's feet
surprisingly to succeed despite difficulties

to fall over one's own feet
to be very clumsy

to find one's feet
to develop one's skills in a previously unfamiliar situation

to get back on one's feet
to recover from an illness or some other set-back

to get cold feet
to become scared

to get one's feet wet
to do the necessary initial parts of a task, despite their being unpleasant and menial
refers to nautical tasks

to have feet of clay
to be vulnerable or not as good as thought

Daniel 2:42, 'And as the toes of the feet were part of iron and part of clay, so the kingdom shall be partly strong and partly broken'

to have one's feet firmly on the ground
to be very practical

to have one's feet in both camps
to have good relations with two opponents

to have the ball at one's feet
to have unlimited opportunity
refers to football games

to have two left feet
to be clumsy

to jump in feet first
to take a calculated risk

to put one's feet up
to relax

to put someone back on his or her feet
to restore to a functioning condition

to put something back on its feet
to restore to a functioning condition

to run someone off that person's feet
to keep a person very busy on some physical task

to stand on one's own two feet
not to require the help of others

to sweep someone off that person's feet
to cause a person to lose all discernment (esp. with respect to romance)

to vote with one's feet
to express one's attitude by one's physical movement towards or away from something

fell

in one fell swoop
all at the same time
Shakespeare, *Macbeth* IV:iii, 'What! all my pretty chickens and their dam, at one fell swoop?'

it fell off the back of a truck
(of an item of goods) it was stolen; (of a politically sensitive document) it was leaked to me

someone's face fell
someone registered obvious disappointment

the sky fell in
a very serious problem arose
Matthew 24:29, 'Immediately after the distress of those days the sun will be darkened, and the moon will not give its light; the stars will fall from the sky, and the heavenly bodies will be shaken'

the wheels fell off
the plan failed

they fell over themselves to do something
they showed great keenness while doing something

felony

to compound the felony
having already acted improperly, to make matters worse

fence

that person has some palings off the fence
that person is mentally disturbed

on our side of the fence
in the group representing our vested interest

to be on the other side of the fence
to have an opposing point of view or position

to be over the fence
to be unreasonable

to sit on the fence
to refuse to choose between two alternatives

fences

to mend fences
to achieve a reconciliation

to rush one's fences
to act precipitately
refers to steeplechasing on horseback

to want to jump all one's fences at once
unrealistically to want to solve all problems at once, rather than sequentially
refers to steeplechasing on horseback

ferret

to ferret something out
by diligent research to discover some secret
refers to a ferret pursuing rabbits in their burrows

festering

to open up a festering sore

to upset a person by drawing attention to a long-standing grievance apparently forgotten

fetter

to fetter someone

to stop a person acting on that person's own initiative

fever

to be at fever pitch

to be in a state of excited activity

fiddle

to fiddle at the edges

to do some relatively minor things that do not deal with the substance of a problem

to fiddle while Rome burns

to neglect important considerations while concentrating on trivial side-issues

refers to Nero's behaviour during the burning of Rome (AD 64) when he played a lyre and watched the spectacle from a height

to play second fiddle

to fulfil a subordinate role

refers to playing in an orchestra

fiefdom

fiefdom

a sphere of operation in which a person exercises absolute control regardless of the wishes of others

field

a field day

a very enjoyable and successful occasion

refers (originally) to an army's practice manoeuvres

a level playing field

competition on equal terms

a minefield

a source of great hidden danger or of difficulties not obvious at first

to be ahead of the field

to be better than one's competitors

to be in the field

to be out in the working environment as opposed to headquarters, a laboratory, etc.

to cover the field

to be comprehensive

to exhaust the field

to use up all the possibilities

to have a field marshal's bâton in one's kit

to be ambitious

variously attributed:

Louis XVIII (1755–1824), 'There is not one of you who has not in his knapsack the field marshal's bâton; it is up to you to bring it out' (speech to the Saint-Cyr cadets, 9 Aug. 1819, *Moniteur*, 10 Aug. 1819);

Napoleon I (1769–1821), 'Every French soldier carries in his cartridge-pouch the bâton of a marshal of France'; Mark Pattison (1813–84), 'Every private in the French army carries in his haversack the bâton of a marshal'

to hold the field

not to be superseded

to play the field

to distribute one's favours among more than one person

fields

distant fields look greener

activities of which one has no experience seem more attractive than is really the case

Psalms 23:1, 'The Lord is my shepherd ... he shall feed me in a green pasture'

fifth

a fifth columnist

a person using a position of trust to work for a rival cause

refers to an extra body of supporters claimed by General Mola as being within Madrid when he besieged the city with four columns of nationalist forces during the Spanish Civil War in 1936

to be a fifth wheel

to be superfluous

to plead the fifth amendment

to refuse to answer an unwelcome question

refers to the fifth amendment of the United States constitution, which provides protection against self-incrimination

fifty

to have fifty cents each way

to equivocate

refers to betting for a win or a place

fig

one would not give a fig for something

one regards something as worthless

fight

a bunfight
a social gathering; a tea party

a dogfight
a confused fight, especially between aeroplanes

to fight an uphill battle
to face difficulties or to have formidable opposition
refers to military battle

to fight bushfires
to deal with crises as they arise rather than take preventive action

to fight fire with fire
to counter a dangerous situation by making an equally dangerous move

to fight tooth and nail
to strive very hard to win

to have a fight on one's hands
to encounter resistance or opposition to a proposal

figurehead

a figurehead
the ceremonial chief officer of some organisation without any real power
refers to the ornamental carving at the front of a ship

figures

to pluck figures out of the air
to make figures up arbitrarily

fill

to fill a vacuum
to take advantage of an opportunity not acted on by others

to fill in the fine print
to provide the precise details in respect of something presently existing in broad outline only

to fill someone's shoes
to be a good successor

filter

to filter through to someone
(of information) to reach a person eventually

final

the final (or last) straw
the latest step that, when added to a large number of seemingly harmless previous steps, sets off a significant event resulting from the cumulative effect
see 'the straw that broke the camel's back'

the final throw of the dice
one last, desperate gamble

to deal the final hand
to take steps that conclude a matter
refers to playing cards

find

to find one's feet
to develop one's skills in a previously unfamiliar situation

to find one's niche
to find the opportunity to use one's talents

to find one's tongue
to overcome one's shyness and speak

to find out the state of play
to ascertain the current position of some project

water will find its own level
people will reach an appropriate position relative to others

fine

not to put too fine a point on it
speaking bluntly
Charles Dickens (1812–70) *Bleak House* ch. 11, '"not to put too fine a point upon it" — a favourite apology for plain-speaking with Mr Snagsby'

to be a fine kettle of fish
to be a terrible muddle
refers to a riverside picnic where freshly caught fish is cooked and eaten

to fill in the fine print
to provide the precise details in respect of something presently existing in broad outline only

to fine-tune something
to adjust something in order to bring it to perfection or to make it fit the circumstances in a much more appropriate fashion

to go through something with a fine-tooth comb
to conduct an extremely thorough investigation

to raise something to a fine art form
to refine a thing or a process to the point where doing it is a highly skilled task

to tread a fine line
cautiously to take action in circumstances where either too much or too little will cause difficulties

finger

not to lay a finger on someone
to refrain from hurting a person

not to lift a finger to help someone
to refuse to assist

to have a finger in something
to be involved in something

to have a finger in the pie
to have an interest in a project, especially an officious involvement

to point the finger at someone
to accuse a person or allege some indiscretion on that person's part

to put one's finger on something
to identify the essential features of something

to stir a finger
to make some minimum effort

to twist someone around one's little finger
to exert easy control over a person

to wave a finger at someone
to indicate mild displeasure at another person's actions

fingered

light-fingered
habitually likely to steal
William Makepeace Thackeray (1811–63), 'The light-fingered gentry pick pockets furiously'

fingernails

to bite one's fingernails
anxiously to await a decision

to hang on by one's fingernails
to have only a slender hold

fingerprints

someone's fingerprints are all over this
it is obvious that a particular person was solely responsible for this

fingers

a butter fingers
a person unable to catch and/or hold on to an object

someone's fingers are all thumbs
a person is clumsy with his or her hands

to burn one's fingers
to suffer (esp. loss of money) through foolishness or meddling
refers to taking chestnuts from a fire

to gnaw one's fingers to the bone
to fret

to have green fingers
to be good at gardening

to have itchy fingers
to be impatient

to have one's fingers in many different pies
to be engaged in a variety of separate activities

to have one's fingers in the till
to steal from one's employer

to have one's fingers on the pulse
to know what is going on
medical/nursing metaphor

to have sticky fingers
to be dishonest; OR to be very adept at catching a ball

to keep one's cotton-picking fingers off something
not to interfere (in a meddlesome fashion) with something

to keep one's fingers crossed
to hope for a good outcome
refers to making the sign of the Christian cross to protect against ill-fortune

to let something slip through one's fingers
to allow something to escape from one's ownership or control

to pull one's fingers out
to cease indolence and get on with a job with alacrity

to snap one's fingers
to gesture contemptuously, especially in the expectation of immediate obedience

to work one's fingers to the bone
to work very hard

fingertips

to cling on by one's fingertips
to have only a slender hold

to have a subject at one's fingertips
to be very familiar with a subject

finish

a photo finish
a close result in a contest

refers to horse racing

to finish with a bang

to conclude something in grand style

fire

a baptism of fire

the commencement of an operation that presents great difficulty

refers to religious ceremonial washing as an initiation ceremony; metaphorical use (as here) attributed to Napoleon III in referring to to a soldier's first battle

a fire in someone's belly

ambition or driving force producing great enthusiasm

fire sale

a forced sale, realising bargain prices

refers to the sale of goods damaged by fire

out of the frying pan into the fire

from one bad situation to an even worse one

sure-fire

guaranteed

refers to firearms

the fat is in the fire

action with certain unstoppable consequences has now been initiated

to add fuel to the fire

to make a bad situation worse

to draw fire

to act in a way that attracts criticism

to feed the fire

to exacerbate a situation

to fight fire with fire

to counter a dangerous situation by making an equally dangerous move

to fire a parting shot/shaft

to make a defiant or cutting gesture or remark on leaving

sometimes also referred to as a 'Parthian shot/shaft' — refers to missiles shot backwards by fleeing Parthian horsemen

to fire a salvo at someone

to present a series of criticisms to a person

refers to simultaneous discharge of firearms in a battle or as a salute (Italian *salva*, 'salutation')

to fire a volley at someone

to send a series of angry messages to someone

refers to a volley of missiles in battle; Alfred, Lord Tennyson (1809–92), *The Charge of the Light Brigade*, 'Cannon to right of them, cannon to left of them, cannon in front of them, volley'd and thunder'd'

to go through fire and water

to undertake all attendant risks

perhaps refers to ordeals of fire and water — ancient Anglo-Saxon ordeals of torture used to ascertain guilt or innocence

to hang fire

to take no immediate action

refers to use of old guns in which there was a delay between ignition and firing of the charge

to have other irons in the fire

to have the opportunity to do something else as an alternative

Francis Beaumont (1584–1616) & John Fletcher (1579–1625), *The Faithful Friends* I:ii, 'It is always good when a man has two irons in the fire'

to hold fire

to defer criticising or attacking

to hold one's fire

to delay proposed action

to play with fire

to invite trouble by meddling with dangerous matters

to pull someone's chestnuts out of the fire

to retrieve a situation for someone else

refers to fable of a monkey getting roasting chestnuts out of a fire by using the cat's paw to achieve the desired result

to pull something out of the fire

to salvage something in a seemingly hopeless situation

to set the Thames on fire

to do something noteworthy

similar sayings exist regarding setting fire to the Rivers Seine, Tiber, and Rhine

to set the world on fire

to do something remarkable

where there is smoke there is fire

if there is a hint of trouble, then it is highly likely that there really is trouble

W. H. Auden (1907–73), *Twelve Songs* VIII, 'Still waters run deep, my dear, there's never smoke without fire'

fireman

a visiting fireman
an important person calling on business to whom certain courtesies need to be paid
US slang

fired

to have a bullet that can be fired
to have available an effective weapon that can be used at will

fires

to keep the home fires burning
to maintain normal domestic activity during the temporary absence of the main provider of the household

to stoke the fires
to provoke a violent reaction

firestorm

to run into a firestorm
to be faced with many protests

fireworks

fireworks
a spectacular display or effect (including anger, panic, confusion, etc.)

firing

to be in the firing line
to be among the first to be under attack

first

at first blush
at first sight
refers to Middle English term *blusche*, 'a gleam, a glimpse'

at first hand
personally

first catch your hare
do things in logical order and after proper preparation
generally attributed to Hannah Gleese, habit-maker to the Prince of Wales and co-author of *The Art of Cookery Made Plain and Easy* (1747)

first in best dressed
persons acting early will do better than latecomers

head first
precipitately

to be first class
to be of the highest standard

to be first off the mark
to start ahead of all others
refers to the starting mark of a race

to be the first cab off the rank
to be the first chosen or tried out

to draw first blood
to get an early advantage

to get to first base
to succeed in achieving the first stage in any undertaking
refers to baseball

to jump in feet first
to take a calculated risk

fish

a queer fish
an unusual type of person

an ocean full of fish
plenty of opportunity

neither fish flesh nor good red herring
unclassifiable by virtue of being neither one thing nor another
Miguel de Cervantes (1547–1616), *Don Quixote*

that has nothing to do with the price of fish
that is quite irrelevant

to be a big fish in a little pond
to be a person holding an important office but in an unimportant organisation

to be a cold fish
to be an unemotional person

to be a different kettle of fish
to be something very dissimilar
refers to a riverside picnic where freshly caught fish is cooked and eaten

to be a fine kettle of fish
to be a terrible muddle
refers to a riverside picnic where freshly caught fish is cooked and eaten

to be a fish out of water
to be in difficulty by virtue of being in a strange environment

to be in a goldfish bowl
to be very open to view

to fish for compliments
to drop hints in the hope that one will receive praise or recognition

to fish in troubled waters
to profit from a disturbed situation
refers to angling

to have more important fish to fry
to have more important things to do

what has that to do with the price of fish?
what is the relevance of this?

fishing

a fishing expedition
an exercise that sets out to gather incriminating information without knowing its exact nature or location

fishy

to be a fishy situation
to be a suspicious situation

fist

hand over fist
rapidly overtaking each other during progress towards a common goal
refers to movement of the hands in climbing a rope or similar

fist

to lose money hand over fist
to lose money very fast and comprehensively

to make a good fist of something
to make a good attempt at, or to succeed in, a difficult task

to rule with an iron fist
to keep strict discipline

fisted

ham-fisted
undiplomatic and clumsy
refers to having large and clumsy hands

hard-fisted
mean

tight-fisted
mean

fistful

to hold out a fistful of dollars
to offer money by way of inducement

fit

not fit to hold a candle to someone
greatly inferior to another person
refers to a servant holding a candle to assist a more senior person

not to get along with someone in a fit
not to get along with a person in any circumstances

to fit the bill
to meet all the requirements

to have a blue fit
to be very agitated

to have a fit
to be in a state of great agitation

to have a fit of the vapours
to demonstrate exaggerated anxiety, hysteria, nervousness or similar

fits

if the cap fits then wear it
if that description corresponds with your characteristics, then you are in that category

if the shoe fits then wear it
if a general proposition describes your specific circumstances, then consider that it applies to you

five

at five minutes to midnight
almost at the last moment

to know how many beans make five
to have common sense
refers to an old riddle

flag

to rally to the flag
to show support for a cause under attack
refers to military battle

to show the flag
to visit a place in order to boost morale there
military metaphor

to wave a flag for someone
to promote a person's cause

flagship

flagship
most important member of a group of related entities
refers to the ship carrying an admiral's flag

flak

to attract flak
to attract criticism
refers to anti-aircraft fire — abbrev. of German *Fliegerabwehrkanone* (lit. 'aviator-defence-gun')

flame

an old flame
a former lover

keepers of the flame
persons entrusted to maintain old traditions and keen to do so

refers to those entrusted with keeping a sacred flame of remembrance alight

to inflame a situation
to aggravate a situation
Shakespeare, *Julius Caesar* III:ii, 'It will inflame you, it will make you mad'

to rekindle an old flame
to inspire the reinstatement of a former loving relationship
David Garrick (1717–79), 'Kitty, a fair, but frozen maid, kindled a flame I still deplore'

flames

to fan the flames
to increase unrest

to pour petrol on the flames
to make a bad situation worse

to shoot someone down in flames
utterly to destroy another person's arguments
refers to loss of aircraft in battle

flank

to expose one's flank
to leave oneself open to the possibility of having advantage taken

flash

a flash in the pan
something that begins promisingly but does not last
refers to the priming of old guns

in a flash
in an instant

flashing

to see red lights flashing
to be conscious of the danger
refers to the 'stop' signal on roads and rail, or perhaps to lights on an emergency vehicle

flat

to be flat out like a lizard drinking
to be hard at work
a play on words, not strictly a simile

to be in a flat spin
to be in a state of agitation or panic
refers to an aircraft that is falling while spinning in a horizontal plane

to catch someone flat-footed
to take someone unawares or making mistakes

to fall flat
(of a joke) to be unappreciated by the audience

to fall flat on one's face
to fail or to be seriously embarrassed by a bad error of judgment

flavour

to be the flavour of the month
to be a person or commodity temporarily popular
refers to sales or marketing of foods of a particular flavour

flea

to send someone away with a flea in the ear
to give a person frank, but unwelcome, facts
perhaps refers to fleas trapped in the armour of ancient knights, or perhaps from the discomfort felt by a dog with a flea in its ear; or perhaps, figuratively, to any lingering irritation in the ear

fleece

to fleece someone
to cheat a person out of some asset
Thomas Carlyle (1795–1881), 'To divide what they fleeced from these poor drudges'

flesh

neither fish flesh nor good red herring
unclassifiable by virtue of being neither one thing nor another
Miguel de Cervantes (1547–1616), *Don Quixote*

one's own flesh and blood
one's own offspring, ancestors, or close relatives
Genesis 2:23, 'Bone of my bones, and flesh of my flesh'

one's pound of flesh
that which is strictly due to one, albeit excessive and lacking in compassion
Shakespeare, *Merchant of Venice* IV:i, 'The pound of flesh, which I demand of him, is dearly bought; 't is mine, and I will have it!'

the spirit is willing but the flesh is weak
the body is not up to the demands made on it–physically or morally
Matthew 26:41: 'Watch and pray, that ye enter not into temptation: the spirit indeed is willing but the flesh is weak

to be a thorn in someone's flesh

to be a constant annoyance or affliction

2 Corinthians 12:7, 10: 'There was given to me a thorn in the flesh … I will glory in my infirmities'

to be more than flesh can stand

to be more than a person reasonably can be expected to endure

to flesh out the skeleton

to supply the missing pertinent details

to go the way of all flesh

to die

Joshua 23:14, 'And, behold, this day I am going the way of all flesh'

to make someone's flesh creep

to frighten a person with something horrific

to put flesh and bone on something

to supply details of a proposal previously revealed only in outline

to see someone in the flesh

to see someone in person

fleshpots

fleshpots

sumptuous living

Exodus 16:3, ' … in the land of Egypt, when we sat by the fleshpots and when we did eat bread to the full'

flex

to flex one's muscles

to assert one's personality or powers

flies

as the crow flies

by the shortest distance

there are no flies on someone

a person is alert and astute

time flies

time passes very quickly but, if wasted, can never be recovered

Virgil (70–19 BC) *Georgics* III:284, '*Fugit irreparabile tempus*' ('Time, which cannot be retrieved, is flying')

flip

flip side

the arguments for the other point of view

flit

a moonlight flit

an escape from creditors

flock

birds of a feather flock together

persons of like interests gather in the same place

Samuel Rutherford (?1600–61), 'Fowls of a feather flock together'

flock

congregation in the charge of a religious official

numerous biblical references incl.: *Isaiah* 40:11, 'He shall feed his flock like a shepherd: he shall gather the lambs with his arm, and carry them in his bosom, and shall gently lead those that are with young'

flog

to flog a dead horse

misguidedly to do something patently useless

floodgates

to open the floodgates

to take action that will have massive consequences

Shakespeare, *Othello* I:iii, 'My particular grief is of so flood-gate and o'erbearing nature that it engluts and swallows other sorrows'

floor

there is blood on the floor

this has caused great anguish

to get in on the ground floor

to invest on very favourable terms

to hold the floor

to dominate a conversation

to wipe the floor with someone

to inflict a humiliating defeat on a person

flotsam

flotsam and jetsam

persons or things in an unfixed and disordered state, and considered worthless

refers, respectively, to goods found floating, and to goods thrown overboard deliberately

flourish

with a flourish of trumpets

triumphantly

refers to the trumpet as an instrument of triumph; *Joshua* 6:20, 'When the priests blew with the trumpets … the wall fell down flat'

flow

ebb and flow

fluctuations

flowed

a lot of water has flowed under the bridge since then
much has happened since then

flowing

to have money flowing out of one's ears
to be very rich

flown

the bird has flown
the person sought is no longer about

flush

to flush out the facts
to ascertain, after some effort, the truth of some matter

flux

to be in a state of flux
to be subject to continuous change

fly

a fly in the ointment
a minor flaw that spoils a thing
Ecclesiastes 10:1, 'Dead flies cause the ointment of the apothecary to send forth a stinking savour: so doth a little folly him that is in reputation for wisdom and honour'

a fly-by-night operator
a person who disappears suddenly and without warning in an attempt to avoid the payment of debts or compensation or the obligations under some contract

I would love to be a fly on the wall
I would love to observe what goes on without those under observation being aware of my presence

someone wouldn't hurt a fly
someone is very gentle and kind-hearted
William Hazlitt (1778–1830). 'He would not hurt a fly'

to fly a kite
to issue uncovered cheques in the hope that they will be covered before clearance; OR to test public reaction to a measure in contemplation by leaking broad details of it to the media

to fly blind
to do something in ignorance of the relevant facts
refers to pilots flying without visual guidance (and relying on instruments)

to fly by the seat of one's pants
to act by instinct in the absence of specific knowledge or instructions

to fly high
to be ambitious

to fly in the face of some rule
blatantly to disregard some rule

to fly off the handle
to show irrational anger

to fly out the window
to become irretrievably and wastefully lost

to fly the coop
to grow up and become independent
refers to a cage or pen for confining poultry and other birds

to have to fly
to need to leave in order to reach the next destination quickly

to let fly at someone
to launch a verbal or physical assault on a person

to make feathers fly
to cause a flurry of consternation and vigorous activity
refers to the fighting of cock birds

to make sparks fly
to inflame or cause friction in a situation
Job 5:7, 'Man is born unto trouble, as the sparks fly upward'

to make the fur fly
to create a disturbance
refers to animals fighting

flyer

a highflyer
an ambitious and/or successful person

flying

to achieve a flying start
to get operational very quickly

to pass with flying colours
to be very successful in a test or contest
refers to ships returning to port with colours flying triumphantly

foam

to foam at the mouth
to show extreme uncontrollable anger

refers to a rabid animal; Washington Irving (1783–1859), 'Fall down in convulsions [and] foam at the mouth'

focus

to bring something into focus
to put some matter into its proper context and explain its true significance

to focus on something
to concentrate attention on something

fog

to be in a fog
to be in a state of confusion

foggiest

not to have the foggiest notion
to know nothing at all about the subject

fold

the fold
the body of believers
refers to an enclosure for sheep; *John* 10:16, 'Other sheep I have, which are not of this fold'

quietly to fold up one's tent
surreptitiously to abandon a previously cherished stance
Henry Wadsworth Longfellow (1807–82), *The Day is Done*, 'The cares that infest the day shall fold their tents, like the Arabs, and as silently steal away'

follow

to be a hard act to follow
to be an impressive performance, not easily matched by the next person

to follow in someone's footsteps
to do as another person did

to follow one's nose
to act intuitively

to follow someone blindly
to follow a person unquestioningly

to follow the herd
to do what most other people are doing

to follow suit
to do the same as others
refers to playing cards

food

food for thought
material for examination in one's mind
Robert Southey (1774–1843), 'A lively tale, and fraught with ... food for thought'

to be at the bottom of the food chain
to be at the lowest level in a hierarchy

to take food out of the mouths of children
cruelly to deprive the needy

fool

to live in a fool's paradise
to delude oneself into a state of happy contentment when reality is quite different

fools

fools rush in where angels fear to tread
unsophisticated persons take unwise risks in circumstances where more knowledgeable persons would exercise caution
Alexander Pope (1688–1744), *An Essay on Criticism* 1:625, 'For fools rush in where angels fear to tread'

foot

a foot in the door
the opportunity to do business

not to put a foot wrong
to behave impeccably
refers to dancing steps

the boot is on the other foot
the advantage is reversed

to bind someone hand and foot
completely to limit a person's freedom to act

to get off on the wrong foot with someone
to make an unfavourable initial impression on a person
refers to dancing

to go hot foot
to do something fast

to have one foot in the grave
to be very old or dying
W. S. Gilbert 1836–1911, HMS *Pinafore* (1878), 'A greenery-yallery, Grosvenor Gallery/ Foot-in-the-grave young man!'

to have one's foot on something
to be about to acquire something or to be able to acquire something
perhaps refers to limbering-up exercises before Roman footraces in which competitors were said to 'have their foot in (or on)' — meaning that they were ready to begin the task

to pussyfoot around

to take stealthy, cautious, non-committal steps
refers to a cat prowling

to put one's best foot forward
to make a special effort

to put one's foot down
to assert one's authority and insist on something

to put one's foot in it
to make a foolish mistake

to put one's foot in one's mouth
to say something foolish

to put someone on the back foot
to make a person less confident of that person's position

to shoot oneself in the foot
to act in a foolish way and thus harm one's own cause

to start off on the right foot
to commence an operation with great care to do it correctly
refers to marching

to tread someone under foot
to oppress a person

to wait hand and foot on someone
to serve a person's every real or imagined whim

football

a political football
a political issue that is being exploited for political point-scoring and gamesmanship, rather than being debated on its merits

footed

nimble-footed
quick to change the direction of one's activities when circumstances warrant

to catch someone flat-footed
to take someone unawares or making mistakes

foothold

to gain a foothold
to achieve a position from which further advances can readily be made

footloose

footloose and fancyfree
unmarried and without any romantic attachments

footnote

a footnote
a passing comment by way of elaboration

footprints

without leaving any footprints
without making any impression

footsteps

to follow in someone's footsteps
to do as another person did

for

a tooth for a tooth
retaliation of equal magnitude to the original offence
Exodus 21:24, 'Eye for eye, tooth for tooth, hand for hand, foot for foot'; see also 'to turn the other cheek'

an eye for an eye
retaliation of equal magnitude to the original offence
Exodus 21:24, 'Eye for eye, tooth for tooth, hand for hand, foot for foot'; see also 'to turn the other cheek'

forbidden

forbidden fruit
something particularly desired because it is not allowed
Genesis 2:17, 'but of the tree of the knowledge of good and evil, thou shalt not eat of it'

force

to force someone's hand
to take action causing another person to react
refers to playing cards

to force someone on to that person's knees
to inflict a humiliating defeat on a person

tour de force
feat of skill or strength
French, 'feat of strength'

forces

to join forces
to cooperate with one another in order to achieve a common objective

forelock

to tug one's forelock
to pay obeisance to someone

forgiven

anyone could be forgiven for believing that

it is understandable that people would believe that

fork

fork in the road
time or place for decision

forked

to speak with a forked tongue
to utter halftruths with the intention of misleading the listener

form

not to do something in any shape or form
not to do something in any way at all

to raise something to a fine art form
to refine a thing or a process to the point where doing it is a highly skilled task

fort

to hold the fort
to be in charge during the temporary absence of a superior
Philip Paul Bliss (1838–76), *The Charm*, 'Hold the fort, for I am coming'

fortune

fortune's wheel
the vicissitudes of life
refers to the traditional representation of the goddess Fortuna with a wheel in her hand, symbolising her fickleness

forty

not to touch something with a forty-foot barge pole
to go out of one's way to avoid something

forward

to give something a nudge forward
to give modest encouragement to something

to inch forward
to make slow progress
William Golding (1911–93), 'He inched along the path, with shuffling steps'

to put one's best foot forward
to make a special effort

to take a giant step forward
to make a significant advance
Genesis 6:4, 'There were giants in the earth in those days'

foul

foul play
treachery or murder
Shakespeare: *Hamlet* II:i, 'All is not well; I doubt some foul play'

to foul one's own nest
to disparage or bring discredit on one's home or workplace

found

the river found its mark
equilibrium between two pressures has been achieved

founder

to founder on the shoals of something
to come to grief because of unexpected dangers
refers to a ship running aground in undetected shallow water

fountainhead

fountainhead
chief or prime source of something (wisdom, knowledge, etc.)

four

an opening wide enough to drive a coach and four through
an excellent opportunity to demonstrate the major errors or absurdities of something
the saying seems sometimes also to have referred to six horses: Sir Stephen Rice (1673–1715), as quoted by W. King, *State of the Protestants of Ireland* (1672), 'I will drive a coach and six horses through the Act of Settlement'

four square
honest and reliable
refers to a solid building construction

from the four corners of the globe
from everywhere

to scatter something to the four winds
permanently to get rid of something
refers to the north, south, east, and west winds

fours

to compete on all fours with someone
to strive on equal terms
refers to the four limbs of the body

fourth

the fourth estate

the press
refers to the fourth 'power' in the realm (after the Lords Temporal, the Lords Spiritual, and the Commons); variously attributed to Edmund Burke (1729–97), Thomas Carlyle (1795–1881), and Lord Macaulay (1800–59)

fox

a fox hole
a small space of refuge and shelter (especially in battle)
Matthew 8:20, 'the foxes have holes, and the birds of the air have nests; but the son of man hath not where to lay his head'

framework

framework
outline of a proposal, upon which further details can be developed

Frankenstein

to create a Frankenstein
to create something wicked and out of control
a reference to the fictional creator of a monster, in mistake for a reference to the monster itself; from the novel *Frankenstein: the Modern Prometheus* (1818), by Mary Wollstonecraft Shelley (1797–1851), second wife of British poet, Percy Bysshe Shelley (1792–1822)

frayed

to become frayed at the edges
to become tatty, lacking clear definition; no longer quite appropriate

freckles

to be up to one's freckles in something
to be very deeply involved in something

Freddy

blind Freddy could see that something is such-and-such
it is very obvious that something is such-and-such

free

a free kick
an advantageous opportunity accorded to a person
refers to football

to get off scot-free
to go unpunished
refers to an exemption from tax; scot (from old norse *skot*) means tax

to give someone a free hand
to authorise a person to act as that person sees fit

to give someone free rein
to confer complete discretion on another person
refers to riding or driving horses

freeze

to freeze someone out
deliberately to exclude a person

fresh

fresh blood
newly joined members of some organisation

to be a breath of fresh air
to be a pleasant change from the past

friend

a fair-weather friend
a person purporting to be a friend who offers no support in difficult times

a friend at court
a person with influence who is willing to use it on one's behalf
refers to royal courtiers

frighten

to frighten hell out of someone
to cause great alarm to a person

to frighten the horses
to scare people off by one's ill-considered tactics
Mrs Patrick Campbell (1865–1940), quoting oral tradition, 'I don't mind where people make love, so long as they don't do it in the street and frighten the horses'

frog

to have a frog in one's throat
to have a transient hoarseness, or a trivial throat obstruction

to leap-frog something
to overtake something, with the likelihood of, in turn, being overtaken
refers to a game in which participants jump over each other in turn

front

front runner
person expected to win; OR someone who performs well only when holding an advantage

to have a job in front of one

to have all or much of a difficult task still to be completed

froth

froth and bubble
superficially attractive but really insignificant items
'Life is mainly froth and bubble ... ' (folk rhyme)

frown

to frown on something
to disapprove of some matter

fruit

forbidden fruit
something particularly desired because it is not allowed
Genesis 2:17, 'but of the tree of the knowledge of good and evil, thou shalt not eat of it'

to bear fruit
to result in success

fruitless

fruitless
yielding no benefit

fruits

by their fruits ye shall know them
their true nature will be revealed by their results
Matthew 7:20, 'wherefore by their fruits ye shall know them'

fry

to have more important fish to fry
to have more important things to do

frying

out of the frying pan into the fire
from one bad situation to an even worse one

fuel

to add fuel to the fire
to make a bad situation worse

full

an ocean full of fish
plenty of opportunity

full-bore ahead!
proceed forward at full power!

full-steam ahead!
get going as fast as possible!
refers to a steam engine (especially in a ship or train)

full-blooded
vigorous, with every effort

I've had a belly full
I have had enough of this

not to be the full quid
not to be very intelligent

not to be the full two bob
not to be very intelligent
refers to slang term for two shillings

the wheel has turned the full circle
things are now back to where they were before

to be a full bottle on something
to be very knowledgeable about a subject

to be full of beans
to be very cheerful

to be full of hot air
to make unsubstantiated empty statements; to be bombastic

to be in full play
to be fully operational

to be in full swing
to be very active and going as well as possible

to come to a full stop
to cease activity completely

to do a full circle
to be back to where one was before or (in error) to go in the opposite direction

to get full marks for something
to receive the highest praise for something

to have one's hands full
to be fully occupied

yes sir, yes sir, three bags full!
(in servile response to some request) yes, very willingly!
refers to old nursery rhyme

fun

fun and games
light-hearted amusement and games (esp. flirtatious and/or naughty)

to be no fun
to be difficult; to be lacking in levity

funeral

that is your funeral!
that is the fate that you will have to suffer

funk

to be in a blue funk
to be terrified

fur

to make the fur fly
to create a disturbance
refers to animals fighting

furious

fast and furious
in an exciting way, in quick succession

furniture

to be part of the furniture
to be so familiar that one's presence goes completely unnoticed

further

to be further down the line
to have a low priority; OR to be further advanced in a project, at a later stage

fuse

to have a short fuse
to lose one's temper very readily
refers to explosives

to light a fuse
to set in train processes that will cause a serious reaction
refers to explosives

fuss

to kick up a fuss
to create a commotion

future

to mortgage the future
to get benefits now but at a cost in due course
refers to a charge over property recognised by the law

G

gain

to gain a foothold
to achieve a position from which further advances can readily be made

to gain ground
to advance one's position relative to others
originally military; Shakespeare *Hamlet* IV:iv, 'we go to gain a little patch of ground'

to gain the upper hand
to attain, after some effort, an advantage over another person

gains

what one loses on the swings one gains on the roundabouts
there are advantages and disadvantages that offset each other
Patrick Reginald Chalmers (1872–1942), *Green Days and Blue Days: Roundabouts and Swings*, 'what's lost upon the roundabouts we pulls up on the swings!'

galah

every galah in the petshop
everybody

gall

gall
impudence

gallery

to play to the gallery
to do something that appeals to unrefined opinion rather than something that is right
refers to the theatre

galvanise

to galvanise someone into action
forcefully to shock or rouse someone into action
refers to Luigi Galvani (1737–98), Italian physiologist, whose name was applied to the shock received from a direct electric current

gambit

a gambit
(in a competitive situation) an opening move that involves short-term losses in the expectation of long-term gains
Italian *gambetto*, literally 'tripping up'

opening gambit
the first in a series of strategic moves
usually refers to chess (see also *gambit*); Italian *gambetto*, literally 'tripping up'

game

a game of cat and mouse
negotiations between two parties of unequal bargaining power during which the stronger makes some temporary concessions to the weaker without, however, affecting the latter's eventual total defeat

a game of poker
negotiations in which the parties try to bluff each other
refers to playing cards
a game of snakes and ladders
a series of ups and downs
refers to a board game
a mug's game
an activity that wise persons eschew
perhaps refers to the practice of representing faces (often humorous) on drinking mugs
game, set, and match
completion
refers to tennis
I'll soon stop that person's little game
that person's activities are not tolerated and I will ensure that they cease
it is just a game to someone
it is an exercise that a person does not take seriously
so-and-so is the name of the game
so-and-so is the essential element of the exercise
the game is up
the plan is no longer able to succeed
the only game in town
the only event worthy of attention
to be a chess game
to be a complex, skilful exercise involving moves and countermoves
to be a new ball game
to be subject to completely revised rules or very different conditions
to be fair game
to be someone who can be attacked legitimately
refers to hunting
to beat someone at that person's own game
to outwit a person in that person's own specialisation
to give the game away
to cease involvement with some activity; OR to reveal the nature of a hidden activity or plan
to lift one's game
to raise the standard of one's performance
to play a deep game
to show cunning
to play the game
to observe the letter and the spirit of the rules; to act honourably
to stick to one's game
to confine oneself to activities in areas in which one has knowledge and expertise
two can play at that game
it is possible to retaliate
what is that person's game?
what is the significance of that person's actions?

games

don't play games with me!
do not insult my intelligence by that sort of conduct
fun and games
light-hearted amusement and games (esp. flirtatious and/or naughty)

gamekeeper

to appoint a poacher to be gamekeeper
to engage, perhaps foolishly, a formerly dishonest person to a position where that person's specialised knowledge can assist the prevention of similar dishonest activity by others

gamut

the whole gamut
the whole range of some activity
refers to the whole range of notes in music

gander

what is sauce for the goose is sauce for the gander
arguments that apply in one case also apply in another

gap

to bridge a gap
to fill a need or make up a shortfall

garage

garage sale
sale of miscellaneous assets at cheap prices

garden

everything in the garden is lovely
everything is fine
Genesis 2:8–9, 'And the Lord God planted a garden ... to grow every tree that is pleasant to the sight'
to lead someone up the garden path

to mislead a person by deliberately fallacious arguments

garters

I will have that person's guts for garters

I am extremely angry and dissatisfied with that person

gas

to be cooking with gas

to be fully operational and on the way to success

gate

to close the gate

to deny an opportunity that was previously available

gatecrash

to gatecrash a gathering

to attend a gathering without any right to be there

gatepost

between you and me and the gatepost

confidentially

gateway

gateway to something

method of achieving something

gather

to gather dust

not to be acted upon, but without being formally rejected

gathers

a rolling stone gathers no moss

a person who keeps changing jobs will not have a successful career

Tusser, *Five Hundred Points of Good Husbandrie* (1573), 'The stone that is rolling can gather no moss. / For master and servant oft changing is loss'

gauntlet

to run the gauntlet

to be subjected to criticism

from Swedish *gantlopp* ('laneway') in reference to a military punishment inflicted on delinquents made to run between two files of soldiers, as used in Thirty Years' War, Holy Roman Empire, 1618–48

to throw down the gauntlet

to issue a challenge

refers to the glove worn by a knight; OFr *gantelet* (diminutive of 'glove')

gave

if you gave that person a penny for that person's thoughts you would get change

that person is extremely stupid

gay

to be a gay dog

to lead an idle life while flaunting the symbols of wealth

gear

to be in top gear

to be making excellent progress

refers to mechanics

geared-up

to be geared up to do something

to have equipment, labour, and know-how in place adequate for some task

refers to mechanics

gel

to gel

to settle into a coherent state and thus make sense

genie

to let the genie out of the bottle

to cause something irreversible to take place

'genie' was adopted (to refer to a spirit released from a bottle) by the French translators of *Arabian Nights' Entertainments*

to put the genie back in the bottle

to undo something that cannot be undone

'genie' was adopted (to refer to a spirit released from a bottle) by the French translators of *Arabian Nights' Entertainments*

getting

it is getting to me

it is affecting me psychologically

ghost

not the ghost of a chance

no hope at all

Katherine Mansfield (1888–1923), 'he hadn't a ghost of a chance, he hadn't an earthly'

to give up the ghost

to die

Mark 15:39, 'He so cried out and gave up the ghost' (refers to the use of 'ghost' to indicate one's spirit)

giant

a giant

a person whose ability and achievements exceed that of most other people

Genesis 6:4, 'There were giants in the earth in those days'

to take a giant step forward

to make a significant advance

Genesis 6:4, 'There were giants in the earth in those days'

giddy

to play the giddy goat

to act the fool

'giddy' derived from Old English *gidig* ('possessed by a god')

gift

to look a gift horse in the mouth

to be suspicious about a benefit that has been volunteered

Samuel Butler (1612–80), *Hudibras*, 'He ne'er consider'd it, as loth to look a gift horse in the mouth'; refers to the examination of a horse's teeth for an accurate assessment of its age

gifts

I fear the Greeks even when they bear gifts

I am suspicious of generous behaviour from traditional opponents

Virgil (70–19 BC), *Aeneid* II:49, *Timeo Danaos et dona ferentis* ('I fear the Greeks even when they bring gifts'), in reference to the Trojan horse

gild

to gild the lily

to add superfluous ornamentation to something already beautiful

Shakespeare *King John* IV:i, 'to gild refined gold, to paint the lily'

gilt

gilt-edged

very safe

nineteenth century; refers to certificates for government stock that were printed with a gold edging

to take the gilt off the gingerbread

to strip something of its main attraction

gingerbread

to take the gilt off the gingerbread

to strip something of its main attraction

gird

to gird up one's loins

to get ready for action

Job 38:3 'Gird up thy loins now like a man'

give

give someone an inch and that person will take an ell

make a small concession to a person and that person will abuse it by taking much more

derived from old measure of length (ell) originally based on the length of the forearm (the Old English word *eln* being cognate with the Latin *ulna*–a long bone of the forearm)

give someone an inch and that person will take a mile

make a small concession to a person and that person will abuse it by taking much more

he wouldn't give you the shine off his suit

he is very mean

I would give my right arm for something

I am very keen to acquire something

not to give an inch

not to budge or concede to the slightest degree despite pressure to do so

one would give one's eye teeth for something

a person would very much like to achieve some objective

refers to the (valued) canine teeth directly under the eye

one would not give a fig for something

one regards something as worthless

so-and-so would give you the shirt off his or her back

so-and-so is very generous

Luke 6:29 (RSV), ' … and from him who takes away your coat do not withhold even your shirt'

that person would not give one the time of day

that person is unwilling to help anybody

that person wouldn't give you the steam off his or her sausages that person is very mean

to give a dog a bad name
to malign a person

to give a thumbs up
to approve or grant permission
refers to sign given by Roman emperor sparing a life

to give birth to something
to create or invent something

to give ground
to make some concessions or to retreat or to concede some arguments
refers to military battle

to give one's best shot
to make the best attempt possible

to give one's blessing to something
to indicate one's approval of something

to give rein to one's fancy
to let one's imagination have free scope
refers to riding or driving horses

to give someone a bath
to defeat a person comprehensively

to give someone a bit of stick
to criticise a person mildly

to give someone a black look
to indicate one's displeasure with a person

to give someone a blank cheque
to give another person unlimited delegated authority

to give someone a free hand
to authorise a person to act as that person sees fit

to give someone a hand
to assist a person

to give someone a leg up
to give a person some assistance
refers to mounting a horse

to give someone a piece of one's mind
to abuse another person

to give someone a wide berth
to go out of one's way to avoid contact with a person
nautical metaphor

to give someone enough rope to hang himself or herself
to give a person the opportunity to do something that is likely to get that person into severe trouble

to give someone heart
to cause a person to cheer up

to give someone hell
to make life extremely difficult for a person

to give someone his or her head
to let a person do as that person wishes

to give someone a piece of one's mind
to abuse another person

to give someone a rocket
to reprimand a person severely

to give someone short shrift
to be impatient with a person; to give a person little of one's time
'shrift' refers to prescribing penance and giving absolution after a confession; hence 'short shrift' refers to the brevity of the penance and absolution pronounced by a priest after a confession by a condemned person just before an execution

to give someone the boot
to terminate a person's appointment

to give someone the brush-off
to make it clear that one does not want dealings or conversation with a person

to give someone the cold shoulder
ostentatiously to ignore a person

to give someone the edge
to give a person an advantage over others

to give someone the third degree
to apply pressure while questioning closely a person under suspicion

to give someone too much rope
to give a person too much latitude
refers to tethering of animals

to give something a blood transfusion
to give something new enthusiasm

to give something a label
to classify something

to give something a nudge forward
to give modest encouragement to something

to give the devil his due
to be fair

to give the game away

to cease involvement with some activity; OR to reveal the nature of a hidden activity or plan

to give the green light
to grant permission
refers to the 'go' signal on roads and rail

to give the show away
indiscreetly to reveal sensitive information
perhaps refers to revealing the plot of a theatre play

to give up the ghost
to die
Mark 15:39, 'He so cried out and gave up the ghost' (refers to the use of 'ghost' to indicate one's spirit)

glaring

glaring error
patently obvious mistake

glass

glass ceiling
an unstated but definite limit (resulting from prejudice) to promotion in employment

people in glass houses should not throw stones
those who are less than perfect are foolish to criticise others
John 8:7, 'He that is without sin among you, let him first cast a stone at her' (refers to ancient condemnation and punishment of people by stoning)

glasses

to see something through rose-coloured glasses
to appreciate only the advantages and to disregard completely the disadvantages

gleam

to be only a gleam in someone's eyes
not yet conceived, let alone achieved

glee

to rub one's hands with glee
to express great satisfaction

glisters

all that glisters is not gold
things are not always what they seem
Shakespeare, *Merchant of Venice*, II:vii, 'All that glisters is not gold'

glitters

all that glisters is not gold
things are not always what they seem
Shakespeare, *Merchant of Venice*, II:vii, 'All that glisters is not gold'

globe

from the four corners of the globe
from everywhere

glove

to work hand in glove with someone
to work in close cooperation with a person or to be in collusion with a person to the detriment of others

with an iron hand in a velvet glove
with a hard attitude made to seem soft

gloves

the gloves are off
there are now no restrictions on how we resolve our differences
refers to bare-knuckle fighting before the introduction of the 'Marquis of Queensberry rules'

to take off the gloves
to fight mercilessly or to debate with great ferocity
refers to bare-knuckle fighting before the introduction of the 'Marquis of Queensberry rules'

to treat someone with kid gloves
to handle a person with great discretion
refers to very soft leather gloves made from the skin of young goats

glow

a warm inner glow
satisfaction at some achievement
Joseph Conrad (1857–1924), *Youth*, 'the heat of life ... that glow in the heart that with every year grows dim, grows cold'

glued

to have one's eyes glued to something
to concentrate on looking at something to the exclusion of other competing calls for attention

glutton

to be a glutton for punishment
a person who is eager to work very hard even without the prospect of commensurate reward

Rudyard Kipling (1865–1936), 'He's honest, and a glutton for work'

gnash

to gnash one's teeth
to express frustration
Matthew 8:12, 'There shall be weeping and gnashing of teeth'

gnat

to strain at a gnat
to be scrupulous about trifles
Matthew 23:23, '... that strain at a gnat, and swallow a camel'

gnaw

to gnaw one's fingers to the bone
to fret

go

from go to whoa
from start to finish
refers to the commands given to horses

from the word 'go'
from the beginning
John 1:1, 'In the beginning was the word'

if the mountain will not come to Muhammad then Muhammad will go to the mountain
on recognising that one has insufficient power to effect one's most desired solution one decides to make do with the next best alternative
refers to the story of Muhammad humbly submitting to the greater power of God when Mt Safa did not obey the prophet's command to come to him

it was touch and go
there were considerable risks —- the objective was achieved, but only just
perhaps refers to the touching of the wheels of two moving vehicles

the show must go on
despite difficulties the action in contemplation has to proceed
refers to the theatre

to be all systems 'go'
to be ready to proceed as fast as possible

to be itching to go
to be highly enthusiastic and keen to start

to be on a merry-go-round
to be a circular exercise ending in no definite result

to go along for the ride
to seek to benefit from a project in which others contribute the effort

to go back into the melting pot
to be up for reconsideration from the beginning
refers to a vessel for melting and mixing metals

to go back to square one
to start all over again
refers to board games

to go back to the well
to go to the original source
Genesis 24:20, 'And [Rebekah] ran again unto the well to draw water'

to go cap in hand
to show humility while soliciting a favour

to go down a particular road
to adopt a particular strategy

to go down a particular track
to make decisions aimed at a particular goal

to go down like a lead balloon
to receive a very cool reception

to go down memory lane
to reminisce

to go down on one's hands and knees to someone
with great humility to ask a favour of a person

to go down the gurgler
to be ruined
refers to plumbing

to go down the tube
to fail

to go downhill
to deteriorate

to go for the gold
to aim for victory
refers to Olympic medals

to go for the jugular
to attack a very vital and vulnerable point with a view to a decisive victory

to go hammer and tongs
to do something with great energy
refers to energetic work of a blacksmith

to go haywire
to function in a disordered and strange fashion
refers to difficulty in handling coils of hay-binding wire

to go hot foot
to do something fast

to go in one ear and out the other
to leave no impression

to go off at a tangent
to depart from the main matter under consideration and follow instead some other matter only marginally related to it
refers to a line touching, but not intersecting, another geometrical figure

to go off half-cocked
to act without adequate thought or preparation
refers to a gun at the half-ready

to go off one's head
to lose one's temper

to go off the deep end
to lose one's temper

to go in boots and all
to do something very roughly
refers to fighting violently

to go over someone's head
to bypass lower levels of authority and approach someone more senior instead; OR to be beyond a person's ability to understand

to go out on a limb
to put oneself in an isolated or stranded position

to go over someone's head
to bypass lower levels of authority and approach someone more senior instead; OR to be beyond a person's ability to understand

to go overboard
to act foolishly and in an excessive way

to go post haste
to go very fast
refers to urgent postal messages (originally carried on horseback)

to go the extra mile
to work beyond the call of duty
Matthew 5:41, 'Whosoever shall compel thee to go a mile, go with him twain'

to go the way of all flesh
to die
Joshua 23:14, 'And, behold, this day I am going the way of all flesh'

to go the whole hog
to do something very thoroughly
origin uncertain; alternative explanations include: (i) Muslim divines attempting to ascertain how much of the whole hog could be eaten according to Islamic law (Cowper, 1779, 'but for one piece they thought it hard/from the whole hog to be debarred'); (ii) colloquial term for a shilling — that is, to spend the whole hog (or shilling) at one time; (iii) refers to the close shearing of lambs

to go through fire and water
to undertake all attendant risks
perhaps refers to ordeals of fire and water — ancient Anglo-Saxon ordeals of torture used to ascertain guilt or innocence

to go through something with a fine-tooth comb
to conduct an extremely thorough investigation

to go through the roof
(of a person) to be very upset; OR (of prices) to escalate greatly

to go to great lengths
to take much trouble

to go to ground
to become unavailable to those seeking a person
refers to fox hunting

to go to rack and ruin
to face downfall or destruction
'rack' was originally spelt 'wrack' (a variant of wreck)

to go to sleep
to become inactive

to go to someone's head
to cause a person to get an exaggerated idea of that person's abilities or status

to go to the barricades for something
to believe in something very strongly and to be willing to go to great lengths in support of that belief

to go to the dogs
to be ruined

to go to the wall
to become bankrupt

to go to town
to do something enthusiastically, extravagantly, to the full

to go to water
to succumb to pressure

to go up in smoke
to come to nothing

to let one's head go
to do as one wants to

refers to letting a horse have its head (and run as it wishes to)

to let something go to the keeper
to deliberately ignore a particular incident
refers to cricket

to make the wheels go round
to cause something to happen

goal

to move the goal posts
unfairly to alter the rules after some action (that relied on the old rules) has already started
refers to sporting games

to score a goal
to achieve an objective

to score an own goal
to make a foolish mistake that counts against oneself
refers to soccer

goat

a scapegoat
a person who is forced to take the blame for something not their fault
Leviticus 16:10, 'But the goat, on which the lot fell to be the scapegoat ... to make an atonement'

to play the giddy goat
to act the fool
'giddy' derived from Old English *gidig* ('possessed by a god')

goats

to separate the sheep from the goats
to distinguish between the worthy and the unworthy
Matthew 25:32, 'and he shall separate them one from one another, as a shepherd divideth his sheep from the goats'

God

the mills of God grind slowly
retribution might be delayed but is inevitable
Friedrich von Logau (1604–55), *Sinngedichte* (translated by H. W. Longfellow), 'Though the mills of God grind slowly, yet they grind exceeding small; though with patience he stands waiting, with exactness grinds he all'

to put the fear of God into someone
to frighten a person into behaving properly
Ecclesiates 12:13, 'Fear God, and keep his commandments; for this is the whole duty of man'

god

a little tin god
a petty tyrant

godforsaken

godforsaken
dismal and without any redeeming feature

godmother

a fairy godmother
a person who provides for one's needs
based on the mythical magical figure

gods

to be in the lap of the gods
to be a matter of apparent chance beyond human control
refers to wax tablets inscribed with requests and placed on the knees of statues of Greek gods

goes

when the balloon goes up
when the adverse facts come to light

going

going the rounds
(of a rumour) being spread

gold

a pot of gold
wealth, especially a reward long wished-for

a rich vein of gold
much useful information; a good source of something desirable

all that glisters/glitters is not gold
things are not always what they seem
Shakespeare, *Merchant of Venice*, II:vii, 'All that glisters is not gold'

to be a river of gold
to be a source of ongoing great profitability

to be worth one's weight in gold
to be very valuable or useful

to go for the gold
to aim for victory
refers to Olympic medals

to have a heart of gold
to have a generous disposition
Hilaire Belloc (1870–1953), 'With hearts of gold and lungs of bronze'

to seek the pot of gold at the end of the rainbow
to have naVve expectations
refers to the proverbial belief in the existence of a pot of gold at the end of a rainbow

to strike gold
to have one's efforts suddenly rewarded by great success
refers to gold-mining

golden

golden handshake
a large payment in connection with, or as an inducement to, retirement

golden mean
a moderate compromise between two extremes
from mathematics: the division of a straight line into two portions so that the ratio of the smaller to the larger equals the ratio of the larger to the whole

golden opportunity
an unparalleled chance or occasion

golden parachute
(in a remuneration package) generous provisions that come into play in certain circumstances

golden shackles
financial arrangements designed to discourage employees changing from one employer to another

silence is golden
peace and quiet is valued; it is better to keep one's own counsel
Swiss proverb, 'speech is silvern; silence is golden' (quoted by Thomas Carlyle (1795–1881)

to kill the goose that lays the golden eggs
through excessive greed, to sacrifice future gains for a short-term advantage
based on a Greek fable about a man who killed the goose that laid golden eggs; his aim was to collect the whole stock of eggs at once but, in doing so, he ended his future supply

goldfish

to be in a goldfish bowl
to be very open to view

what is this — a bunch of grapes or a bowl of goldfish?
surely you know what this is?

goldmine

a goldmine
a source of much wealth or of many facts

Goliath

a David and Goliath battle
a struggle between two parties who are not evenly matched
refers to *1 Samuel* 17:23 ff

a Goliath
a giant or a person whose ability and achievements exceed that of most other people
refers to *1 Samuel* 17:23 ff

Gomorrah

a Sodom and Gomorrah
a place of vice
Genesis 18:20, 'Sodom and Gomorrah ... their sin is very great'

good

a good bet
a good proposition

a good Samaritan
a person going out of that person's way to do a kindness to others
Luke 10:33, 'But a certain Samaritan, as he journeyed, came where he was: and when he saw him, he had compassion on him'

good chemistry
an ability to work closely together

it is an ill wind that blows no good
even a seeming misfortune leads to some blessings

neither fish flesh nor good red herring
unclassifiable by virtue of being neither one thing nor another
Miguel de Cervantes (1547–1616), *Don Quixote*

this does my heart good
I rejoice at this
Shakespeare, *A Midsummer Night's Dream* I:ii, ' ... will do any man's heart good to hear'

to be a good boy
to be cooperative

to be a good old stick
to be a kind and thoughtful person

to be in [or of] good heart
to be cheerful, especially in adversity

to be in someone's good books

to be well regarded by another person
biblical allusion: refers to God's judgment and the desirability of having one's name entered in the book of life; *Rev* 20: 12, 'and the books were opened ... and the dead were judged out of those things that were written in the books, according to their works'

to get the good oil
to receive useful, reliable and timely information

to have a good nose for business
to be able to identify profitable business situations

to have had a good innings
to have enjoyed satisfactory time and success in an undertaking; to have had a successful life
refers to cricket

to make a good fist of something
to make a good attempt at, or to succeed in, a difficult task

to see someone in a good light
to regard a person favourably

to throw good money after bad
to waste further money in a vain attempt to recover money already lost

good-bye

to kiss something good-bye
to give something up as permanently lost

goods

to deliver the goods
to achieve the objective; to supply what is required

goose

a wild-goose chase
a futile chase or search
refers to old game of 'follow-the-leader' on horses in which the objective was to follow a winding and difficult course without ever catching up

to be too frightened to say 'boo' to a goose
to be excessively shy

to cook one's goose
to make a fatal mistake; to ruin one's plans
nineteenth-century street ballad: 'If they come here we'll cook their geese'

to kill the goose that lays the golden eggs
through excessive greed, to sacrifice future gains for a short-term advantage
based on a Greek fable about a man who killed the goose that laid golden eggs; his aim was to collect the whole stock of eggs at once but, in doing so, he ended his future supply

to make a wigwam for a goose's bridle
to do something unspecified
nonsense said to children

what is sauce for the goose is sauce for the gander
arguments that apply in one case also apply in another

gooseberry

to play gooseberry
to act as an unwelcome chaperon

Gordian

to cut the Gordian knot
to solve, especially by force, a virtually insoluble problem
refers to a complicated knot tied by Gordius and eventually cut by Alexander the Great

gospel

to spread the gospel
to propagate principles or attitudes that one believes to be true
Mark 16:15, 'Go ye into the world and preach the gospel to every creature'

to take something as gospel
to believe that something is true

government

petticoat government
rule by women

grab

to grab an opportunity with both hands
to seize an opportunity with great enthusiasm

to grab the devil by the tail
to face up to difficulties

grabs

to be up for grabs
to be available virtually for the asking

grâce

to receive the coup de grâce
to be finished off by an opponent
French, 'mercy stroke'

graces

to put on airs and graces
to act in an affected manner

grade

to be on the down grade
to be of deteriorating quality

to downgrade
to put into a lower category or priority

to make the grade
to succeed

grail

search for the Holy Grail
work towards a difficult goal
refers to a vessel or platter supposedly used by Christ at the Last Supper and featuring in the Arthurian legends

grain

something goes against the grain
something is completely and frustratingly against a person's inclination
refers to woodworking

to take something with a grain of salt
to regard the facts in a statement with considerable scepticism

grandmother

to teach one's grandmother how to suck eggs
to try to tell a much more experienced person something very obvious to that person

grandstand

to grandstand
to put on an ostentatious performance designed to draw attention to oneself

granite

to be carved in granite
to be virtually unalterable

grapes

that is just sour grapes
those are disparaging remarks made only because that person is peeved and resentful at someone else's better fortune
derived from Aesop's fable of 'the fox and the grapes' about expressing deliberate disparagement of a desired but unattainable object; 'sour grapes' also occurs in *Ezekiel* 18:2, 'the fathers have eaten sour grapes, and the children's teeth are set on edge'

what is this — a bunch of grapes or a bowl of goldfish?
surely you know what this is?

grapevine

to hear on the grapevine
to learn unofficially
the earlier form of the metaphor was a 'grapevine telegraph' as a means of communicating private information

grasp

to grasp at straws
desperately to resort to any expedient in a hopeless situation
refers to a drowning person

to grasp the nettle
to deal with an unpleasant difficulty by decisive action
Aaron Hill (1685–1750), 'Tender-hearted stroke a nettle, / And it stings you for your pains; / Grasp it like a man of mettle, / And it soft as silk remains'

grass

a snake in the grass
a person of low character who manages to disguise that trait
Virgil, *Eclogue*, 'There's a snake hidden in the grass'

grass roots
at the lowest level of a hierarchy

not to let grass grow under one's feet
not to let inertia or delay spoil something

grasshopper

since that person was knee-high to a grasshopper
since that person was a very young child

grave

someone would turn in his or her grave
someone would have been very surprised or displeased if he or she had known while still alive

to dig one's own grave
to take action that results in an unintended disaster for oneself

to have one foot in the grave
to be very old or dying

W. S. Gilbert 1836–1911, HMS *Pinafore* (1878), 'A greenery-yallery, Grosvenor Gallery/ Foot-in-the-grave young man!'

gravity

the centre of gravity
the natural point of importance to which things are attracted
refers to physics

to defy gravity
to go up when the expectation is to go down

gravy

to get on a gravy train
to take steps to become a recipient of benefits that are available but undeserved

grease

elbow grease
hard manual work
old jocular saying, in existence for several centuries, referring to the vigorous use of the elbow in rubbing, polishing, scrubbing, etc.

to grease someone's palms
to bribe a person
Francis Quarles (1592–1644), English poet, *The Virgin Widow* IV:i, 'grease my fist with a tester or two, and you shall find it in your pennyworth'

great

the great unwashed
the general public

to be going great guns
to be making very successful progress

to be great guns at something
to be very skilled at something

to go to great lengths
to take much trouble

Greek

something is all Greek to someone
something is incomprehensible to a person
Shakespeare, *Julius Caesar*, I:ii, 'but, for mine own part, it was Greek to me'

Greeks

I fear the Greeks even when they bear gifts
I am suspicious of generous behaviour from traditional opponents
Virgil (70–19 BC), *Aeneid* II:49, *Timeo Danaos et dona ferentis* ('I fear the Greeks even when they bring gifts'), in reference to the Trojan horse

green

a green chum
an inexperienced person
Shakespeare, *Antony & Cleopatra* I:v, 'my salad days, when I was green in judgment'

to be green
to be naVve
Shakespeare, *Antony & Cleopatra* I:v, 'my salad days, when I was green in judgment'

to give the green light
to grant permission
refers to the 'go' signal on roads and rail

to have green fingers
to be good at gardening

to turn green
to become very envious
Shakespeare, *Othello* III:iii, 'O! beware, my Lord, of jealousy;/it is the green-ey'd monster ... '

greener

distant fields look greener
activities of which one has no experience seem more attractive than is really the case
Psalms 23:1, 'The Lord is my shepherd ... he shall feed me in a green pasture'

to move on to greener pastures
to move to a better environment; to commence a new, better career
Psalms 23:1, 'The Lord is my shepherd: therefore can I lack nothing. he shall feed me in a green pasture: and lead me forth beside the waters of comfort'

grey

to be a grey area
to be in an undefined position straddling two or more possibilities
refers to something being neither black nor white

greyhound

move over and let the greyhound see the rabbit
stand aside to allow things to get under way
refers to hunting with greyhounds

grin

to grin and bear it
to suffer adversity cheerfully

grind

the mills of God grind slowly
retribution might be delayed but is inevitable
Friedrich von Logau (1604–55), *Sinngedichte* (translated by H. W. Longfellow), 'Though the mills of God grind slowly, yet they grind exceeding small; though with patience he stands waiting, with exactness grinds he all'

the wheels of justice grind slowly
it takes a long time to get a decision from the courts of law
Friedrich von Logau (1604–55), *Sinngedichte* (translated by H. W. Longfellow), 'Though the mills of God grind slowly, yet they grind exceeding small; though with patience he stands waiting, with exactness grinds he all'

to grind to a halt
to have an activity gradually cease to function despite expectations that it would continue

to have an axe to grind
to have a vested interest; to pursue a personal objective

grinder

to want the organ-grinder, not the monkey
to wish to deal with the person in authority rather than an underling
refers to a street musician using a barrel-organ, often accompanied by a pet monkey

grindstone

to keep one's nose to the grindstone
to work with particular diligence
refers to having one's head down low while working on a grindstone sharpening tools

grip

to have something in an iron grip
to hold something very securely

grips

to come to grips with some problem
to be on the way to solving a problem

grist

it is all grist to the mill
this is all useful material for the task at hand

grit

to grit one's teeth
to get ready to suffer pain

groaned

the table groaned
the food was plentiful

ground

ground rules
basic principles
refers to the rules observed at a particular playing ground

stamping ground
one's favourite place for certain activities

to be on shaky ground
not to have strong arguments

to be thin on the ground
to be scarce

to break new ground
to do something for which there is no precedent
refers to ploughing of ground

to clear the ground
to dispose of the preliminaries
refers to clearing of ground in preparation for ploughing

to cut the ground from under someone's feet
to withdraw support unexpectedly and, in the process, to cause embarrassment; OR to demolish a person's case and cause defeat, especially by anticipating that person's arguments or plans

to fall to the ground
to fail
Matthew 10:29, 'Are not two sparrows sold for a farthing? And one of them shall not fall on the ground without your Father ... '

to gain ground
to advance one's position relative to others
originally military; Shakespeare *Hamlet* IV:iv, 'we go to gain a little patch of ground'

to get in on the ground floor
to invest on very favourable terms

to get something off the ground
to take a project beyond its initial stages and make it operational
refers to flying aircraft

to give ground

to make some concessions or to retreat or to concede some arguments
refers to military battle

to go to ground
to become unavailable to those seeking a person
refers to fox hunting

to have one's feet firmly on the ground
to be very practical

to have the high ground
to have an advantage in moral terms
refers to military battle

to keep an ear to the ground
to be well informed as to current developments
refers to listening for distant sound by applying one's ear to the ground

to kiss the ground
to revere or bless the land; OR to be overthrown

to plough new ground
to engage laboriously in an untried activity

to prepare one's ground
to get ready for a confrontation
refers to military battle

to run someone to ground
to discover the whereabouts of a person
refers to fox hunting

to stand one's ground
to maintain a stance in the face of opposition
refers to military battle

grow

not to let grass grow under one's feet
not to let inertia or delay spoil something

growing

growing pains
problems encountered by virtue of expansion
refers to the pains sometimes felt in the limbs by children and adolescents

grows

something grows on one
one becomes gradually more favourably impressed with something

guarantee

to give a cast-iron guarantee
to give a very secure undertaking to do something

guard

new guard
changed regime

to catch someone off guard
to surprise a person
refers to fencing

to slip under one's guard
to cause a mistake to be made despite care being taken to prevent this
refers to fencing

guardian

someone's guardian angel
someone's friend, watching over them and advancing their interests
Shakespeare, *Hamlet* IV:i, 'Angels and ministers of grace defend us!'

guernsey

stick it up your guernsey!
I have absolutely no interest in you and what you saying!
refers to the jumpers worn by members of football teams

to get a guernsey
to be given the opportunity to do something
refers to the jumpers worn by members of football teams

guiding

guiding light
a principle or example to follow in any activity
Exodus 13:21, 'And the Lord went before them by day in a pillar of a cloud, to lead them the way; and by night in a pillar of fire, to give them light'

guinea

a guinea pig
a person on whom some new practice is tried out
refers to use of guinea pigs in medical experimentation

gulf

to bridge a gulf
to overcome a wide divergence in views
Luke 16:26, 'Between us and you there is a great gulf fixed'

gum

to be able to chew gum and walk at the same time
to be able to do two relatively simple things simultaneously
used ironically to disparage a person of limited capacities

to be up a gum tree
to be in difficulty; OR at the end of one's resources

to gum up the works
to cause an activity to cease by preventing normal functioning of the necessary processes

gun

a gun with no bullets
something incomplete and therefore useless for the desired purpose

a scatter-gun approach
an effort going here, there and everywhere, instead of being properly targeted

a shotgun wedding
a wedding held to ensure that an impending birth will be legitimate
refers to threats by the bride's father to kill the bridegroom

smoking gun
damning evidence

to be a gun for hire
to be a person willing to undertake assignments for a fee

to hold a gun at someone's head
to put pressure on a person to make a particular decision regardless of that person's desires in the matter

to jump the gun
to start before one is meant to
refers to a starting pistol in a race

to look down the barrel of a gun
to be given little choice in a matter

to outgun someone
to assert superiority over another person by use of more powerful devices

guns

to be going great guns
to be making very successful progress

to be great guns at something
to be very skilled at something

to bring out one's biggest guns
to use the most impressive persons or arguments

to spike someone's guns
to sabotage (or negate the effect of) an opponent's devices

to stick to one's guns
to continue to hold certain beliefs notwithstanding opposition by others
refers to military battle

to turn one's guns on someone
to direct an attack or criticism at a person

with all guns blazing
using all available devices

gurgler

to go down the gurgler
to be ruined
refers to plumbing

gut

a gut feeling
a belief based purely on intuition and unsupported by facts or evidence

gutful

to have had a gutful
to have experienced something to the point of utter intolerance to any more

gutless

gutless wonder
coward

guts

I will have tha person's guts for garters
I am extremely angry and dissatisfied with that person

something has no guts in it
something has no substance to it

to kick someone in the guts
to take action needlessly hurtful to another person

H

ha'p'orth

to spoil the ship for a ha'p'orth of tar
to engage in a false economy
the current word 'ship' is actually a mistake for the original word 'sheep', and the tar refers to the treatment of wounds

hackles

to raise someone's hackles
to make a person angry
refers to feathers raised in anger on the back of the neck of certain birds; also, by analogy, refers to hairs raised in anger on the neck of dogs

haemorrhage

to stem the haemorrhage
to put a stop to the financial losses of a project

hair

hair-raising
scary
Job 4:15, 'Then a spirit passed before my face; the hair of my flesh stood up'; Shakespeare, *Hamlet* I:v, 'would harrow up thy soul ... and each particular hair to stand an end'

not to touch a hair on someone's head
not to harm a person
Matthew 10:30, 'the very hairs of your head are all numbered'

not to turn a hair
to remain composed

to a hair
exactly
Matthew 10:30, 'the very hairs of your head are all numbered'

to be within a hair's breadth of something
to be extremely close to something

to have a hair of the dog that bit one
to drink more alcohol in an attempt to overcome the effects of alcohol already consumed
refers to the belief that the hair of the rabid dog that bit a person was a cure for the madness that can ensue

to keep one's hair on
to remain calm in a crisis
Shakespeare, *Macbeth* I:iii, ' ... whose horrid image doth unfix my hair'

to keep out of someone's hair
to let someone get on with that person's work in his or her own way

to let one's hair down
to relax

to make someone's hair curl
(of news) to give someone a shock
W. S. Gilbert, *Ruddigore* (1887), 'when he's excited he uses language that would make your hair curl'

to make someone's hair stand on end
to give a person shocking news
Job 4:15, 'Then a spirit passed before my face; the hair of my flesh stood up'; Shakespeare, *Hamlet* I:v, 'would harrow up thy soul ... and each particular hair to stand an end'

to tear one's hair out
to be frustrated and extremely agitated
refers to ancient demonstration of grief and mourning

to wear a hair shirt
to practise self-discipline
refers to a shirt worn next to the skin by ascetics and penitent persons

hairs

to get someone by the short and curly hairs
to have domination over a person

to split hairs
to draw absurdly fine distinctions

halcyon

in halcyon days
in past happier times
Shakespeare, *Henry V, Part 1*, I:ii, 'Expect St Martin's summer, halcyon days'; refers to the fourteen days about the winter solstice when winds were calm, and to the mythical bird said to breed in a floating nest at that time

half

anyone with even half a brain
anyone with any degree of common sense or knowledge

half a loaf is better than none
it is more advantageous to accept less than is really desired than risk missing out completely
John Heywood (1546), 'Throw no gift at the giver's head;/better is half a loaf than no bread

it is six of one and half a dozen of the other
it does not matter either way
Captain Marryat (1792–1848), *The Pirate* ch. 4, 'I never knows the children. It's just six of one and halfa dozen of the other.'

to have half a mind to do something
to be tempted or mildly inclined to do something

to see something with half an eye
to sum up a matter instantly
refers to taking note with a mere glance

halfbaked

halfbaked
not well thought out

halfcocked

to go off half-cocked
to act without adequate thought or preparation
refers to a gun at the half-ready

half-hearted

half-hearted
unenthusiastic

halfpenny

a twopenny-halfpenny outfit
a quite insignificant operation

halfway

a halfway house
an intermediate position
refers to an inn situated situated halfway between two towns on a journey

Hall

Liberty Hall
a place where one is free to do as one wishes
Oliver Goldsmith (1730–74), *She Stoops to Conquer* ii, 'This is Liberty Hall gentlemen'

one can't beat City Hall
the ordinary citizen is powerless against bureaucracy

hallmark

a hallmark
a standard
refers to the official assay mark on gold and silver, originally put on at the Goldsmiths' Hall, London

halt

to grind to a halt
to have an activity gradually cease to function despite expectations that it would continue

halves

not to do anything by halves
to do everything extremely well

to do everything by halves
to do everything imperfectly or incompletely

ham

ham-fisted
undiplomatic and clumsy
refers to having large and clumsy hands

to be the ham in the sandwich
to be caught in the middle of a dispute between other parties
refers to the food snack popularised by the fourth Earl of Sandwich (1718–92)

hammer

to go hammer and tongs
to do something with great energy
refers to energetic work of a blacksmith

to use a sledgehammer to crack a nut
to devote vastly more resources to a project than is warranted by all the circumstances

hamstrung

to be hamstrung
to have limited freedom to act as one would wish
refers to ancient practice of disabling a person or animal by cutting the hamstring muscles of the thigh

hand

a bird in the hand is worth two in the bush
a benefit currently available is more valuable than a seemingly much larger benefit that might or might not be achieved in the future

at first hand
personally

hand over fist
rapidly overtaking each other during progress towards a common goal
refers to movement of the hands in climbing a rope or similar

on the one hand
putting one side of the proposition

on the other hand
putting the opposing side of the proposition

one's right-hand person
one's chief aide
Hebrews 1:1, 'His son … by whom he also made the worlds … sat down on the right hand of the majesty in heaven'

sleight of hand
deceit by trickery
Daniel Defoe (1660–1731), 'All the artifice and sleight of hand they were masters of'

the hand of fate
chance

the left hand does not know what the right hand is doing
a person or an organisation is not aware of inconsistencies in conduct
Matthew 6:3, 'But when you give alms, do not let your left hand know what your right hand is doing'

to be able to do something with one hand behind one's back
to be able to do something very easily

to be at hand
to be in the vicinity, ready to help

to be in hand
to be under control

to bind someone hand and foot
completely to limit a person's freedom to act

to bite the hand that feeds one
to show ingratitude
Edmund Burke (1729–97), *Thoughts and Details on Scarcity* (1797), 'And having looked to government for bread, on the very first scarcity they will turn and bite the hand that fed them'

to deal the final hand
to take steps that conclude a matter
refers to playing cards

to disclose one's hand
to give away information regarding one's intention
refers to playing cards

to force someone's hand
to take action causing another person to react
refers to playing cards

to gain the upper hand
to attain, after some effort, an advantage over another person

to get out of hand
to get out of control

to give someone a free hand
to authorise a person to act as that person sees fit

to give someone a hand
to assist a person

to go cap in hand
to show humility while soliciting a favour

to hand on the torch
to pass on the traditions and aspirations of life
Lucretius (94?–55 BC), ' ... the generations of living creatures are changed and like the runners relay the torch of life'

to hand over something on a silver platter
to provide a valuable benefit for virtually nothing
refers to first-class service

to hand someone a poisoned chalice
to confer a seeming benefit on a person that will turn out to be a significant detriment

to hand-pick someone
to choose a person carefully for that person's individual attributes

to have a hand in something
to be one of the participants in some project

to have one hand tied behind one's back
to work with a handicap

to have the whip hand
to be in control of a situation
refers to the hand holding the whip in controlling horses, and perhaps slaves

to hold a winning hand
to be in an unbeatable position to defeat others
refers to playing cards

to hold someone's hand
to give detailed on-the-job training and supervision

to hold the power to do something in the hollow of one's hand
to have the right to make crucial decisions
Isaiah 40:12, ' ... who hath measured the waters in the hollow of his hand ... '

to keep one's hand in
to engage in activities that reinforce skills that one has previously acquired

to lend a hand
to assist

to live from hand to mouth
being in poor financial circumstances to survive (with little safety margin)

refers to immediate consumption of whatever one has in one's hand

to lose money hand over fist
to lose money very fast and comprehensively

to put one's hand to the plough
voluntarily to undertake some task
Luke 9:62. 'No man, having put his hand to the plough, and looking back, is fit for the Kingdom of God'

to put one's hand up
to identify oneself or to volunteer

to put one's hand in one's pocket
to provide money from one's own resources, especially for a charitable purpose

to rule with an iron hand
to keep strict discipline

to stir a hand
to volunteer assistance

to strengthen someone's hand
to give a person additional authority or greater moral support or more facts to support that person's case

to take something in hand
to assume control over something

to throw in one's hand
to give in or to give up
refers to playing cards

to tip one's hand
to disclose details of one's position
refers to playing cards

to try one's hand at something
to attempt a new activity, especially by way of experiment

to turn one's hand to something
to tackle some project (especially an unfamiliar project)

to wait hand and foot on someone
to serve a person's every real or imagined whim

to work hand in glove with someone
to work in close cooperation with a person or to be in collusion with a person to the detriment of others

with a heavy hand
in an oppressive fashion

with a high hand
arrogantly
Exodus 14: 8 'And the children of Israel went out with an high hand'

with an iron hand in a velvet glove
with a hard attitude made to seem soft

with an open hand
generously

hand-pick

to hand-pick someone
to choose a person carefully for that person's individual attributes

handed

a back-handed compliment
a polite expression seemingly of praise but really intended as an insult

a left-handed compliment
a thinly disguised insult

high-handed
overbearing

to catch someone red-handed
to apprehend a person in the course of committing a wrongdoing
refers originally to being caught with blood on one's hands

handedly

single-handedly
without help from other persons

handful

a handful
a small number or amount

to be a handful
to be difficult to manage
P. G. Wodehouse (1881–1975), 'Bailey will find her rather a handful. Does she ever sit still, by the way?'

handle

to fly off the handle
to show irrational anger

to get a handle on something
to acquire understanding of something

hands

all hands on deck
everybody is requested to help out
nautical metaphor

all hands to the pumps
everybody is requested to help out
nautical metaphor

to accept something with both hands
to accept something eagerly

to be able to lay one's hands on something
to be able to locate something

to be in someone's hands
to be being dealt with by someone with the necessary authority
Ecclesiasticus 2:11, 'We will fall into the hands of the Lord, and not into the hands of men: for as his majesty is, so is his mercy'

to be out of someone's hands
to be up for decision by a different person
Ecclesiasticus 2:11, 'We will fall into the hands of the Lord, and not into the hands of men: for as his majesty is, so is his mercy'

to be putty in someone's hands
to be far too easily influenced by another person
refers to material able to be fashioned into various shapes

to eat out of someone's hands
to be very compliant and submissive

to get one's hands dirty
to do the necessary but unpleasant or menial parts of a task

to go down on one's hands and knees to someone
with great humility to ask a favour of a person

to grab an opportunity with both hands
to seize an opportunity with great enthusiasm

to have a fight on one's hands
to encounter resistance or opposition to a proposal

to have blood on one's hands
to be the person responsible for someone else's predicament
Matthew 27:24, 'He [Pilate] took water and washed his hands in full view of the crowd. "My hands are clean of this man's blood," he declared'

to have clean hands
to be innocent or to act ethically
Matthew 27:24, 'He [Pilate] took water and washed his hands in full view of the crowd. "My hands are clean of this man's blood," he declared'

to have one's hands full
to be fully occupied

to join hands with someone
to cooperate with a person

to lay one's hands on something
to acquire or find something

to play right into someone's hands
to act so as to give a person an unintended advantage

to rub one's hands with glee
to express great satisfaction

to sit on one's hands
deliberately to do nothing

to throw up one's hands
to give up or quit (perhaps in frustration)

to tie someone's hands
to prevent a person from acting as that person sees fit

to tie someone's hands behind that person's back
to make it impossible for a person to act at all

to wash one's hands of something
emphatically to decline future responsibility
Matthew 27:24, 'He [Pilate] took water and washed his hands in full view of the crowd. "My hands are clean of this man's blood," he declared'

to win hands down
to win very convincingly
refers to a jockey riding confidently with hands low when a race is as good as won

to wring one's hands
to express despair

handshake

golden handshake
a large payment in connection with, or as an inducement to, retirement

handstands

to turn handstands
to express great joy

hang

a peg to hang a hat on
something that provides a convenient or plausible excuse for some particular action

to get the hang of something
to learn how to do something

to give someone enough rope to hang himself or herself
to give a person the opportunity to do something that is likely to get that person into severe trouble

to hang by a slender thread
to be in a precarious situation

refers to Damocles who had the sword of Dionysius hanging, by a slender thread, over his head — as a symbol of perpetual risk in life; the story is told in Cicero, *Tusculanae Disputationes*

to hang fire
to take no immediate action
refers to use of old guns in which there was a delay between ignition and firing of the charge

to hang on by one's fingernails [or nails]
to have only a slender hold

to hang on by the eyelids
to have only a slender hold

to hang on by the skin of one's teeth
to be barely surviving
Job 19:20, 'I am escaped with the skin of my teeth'

to hang one's head
to be ashamed of oneself; OR to be disappointed and lacking in morale
Shakespeare, *Henry VIII* III:i, 'Even the billows of the sea, / hung their heads and then lay by'

to hang onto someone's coat-tails
to rely excessively on another's initiatives and achievements

to hang up one's boots
to retire

to hang up one's shingle
to go into business offering expert personal services
refers to an external notice advertising one's name and qualifications

to let it all hang out
to be uninhibited; to unburden oneself

hanging

not to be a hanging matter
to be only a minor mistake

there is a big question mark hanging over someone's head
there are considerable doubts about a person's competence, integrity, or suitability
refers to Damocles who had the sword of Dionysius hanging, by a slender thread, over his head — as a symbol of perpetual risk in life; the story is told in Cicero, *Tusculanae Disputationes*

to have a cloud hanging over one's head
there is doubt as to one's future
refers to the pillar of cloud (God) passing judgment on the Hebrews; the pillar of cloud is described in *Exodus* 13:21 *et seq*.

to have a sword of Damocles hanging over one
to be in imminent danger despite normal activity going on all around one
refers to Damocles who had the sword of Dionysius hanging, by a slender thread, over his head — as a symbol of perpetual risk in life; the story is told in Cicero, *Tusculanae Disputationes*

to have a threat hanging over one's head
to fear some intimated unpleasant action
refers to Damocles who had the sword of Dionysius hanging, by a slender thread, over his head — as a symbol of perpetual risk in life; the story is told in Cicero, *Tusculanae Disputationes*

hanged

one might as well be hanged for a sheep as for a lamb
further action will not increase the adverse consequences already in train
refers to the stealing of either sheep or lambs being capital crimes under old English law

hanger

to be a cliff-hanger
to be very exciting with the result in doubt
refers to episodes of early serial films that ended with the hero in a hazardous plight to attract cinema-goers to the next episode

happen

to happen down the road
to happen later

happy

to be a happy ship
to have a contented workforce

to be trigger-happy
to be impetuous
refers to firing guns

to present a happy face to the world
bravely to gloss over one's problems and to appear contented to others

hard

a hard nut to crack

a difficult problem to be solved; OR someone not easily influenced

this is hard to take
it is difficult to face up to the reality of this

to be a diehard
to be a person who refuses to change, an obdurate person

to be a hard act to follow
to be an impressive performance, not easily matched by the next person

to be between a rock and a hard place
to be faced with two equally difficult and uncomfortable choices

to be hard to swallow
not to be readily acceptable or believable
Matthew 23:23, '… that strain at a gnat, and swallow a camel'

to be hard on the heels of something
to pursue something closely

to be the hard core
to be the central and most difficult problem

to die hard
stubbornly to refuse to give up a belief or theory; not to give up easily

to have a hard row to hoe
to have a difficult assignment
refers to agriculture; James Russell Lowell (1819–91), *The Biglow Papers*, 'You've a darned long row to hoe'

to hit someone hard
greatly to affect a person emotionally; OR to cost a person a lot of money

to put something into the 'too-hard' basket
to defer consideration of a difficult issue

to take a hard line
to be uncompromising

hard-bitten

hard-bitten
toughened by experience
refers to horses that are 'hard' in the mouth or bite (and thus difficult to control)

hard-boiled

hard-boiled
toughened by experience
refers to cooking (esp. eggs)

hard-fisted

hard-fisted
mean

hard-headed

hard-headed
realistic

hard-hearted

hard-hearted
unsympathetic
Exodus 7:3, '… and I will harden Pharaoh's heart'

hard-mouthed

hard-mouthed
uncontrollable
refers to horses that are 'hard' in the mouth or bite (and thus difficult to control)

hard-nosed

hard-nosed
tough in negotiations

hare

first catch your hare
do things in logical order and after proper preparation
generally attributed to Hannah Gleese, habit-maker to the Prince of Wales and co-author of *The Art of Cookery Made Plain and Easy* (1747)

hare-brained
wildly stupid
Benjamin Disraeli (1804–81), speech 1878, 'The hare-brained chatter of irresponsible frivolity'

to chase every hare
to be easily sidetracked

to run with the hare and hunt with the hounds
to keep in with two opposing sides
refers to hunting

to set a hare running
to initiate an activity to achieve a related and desired effect
refers to hunting

harmonise

to harmonise several things
to make several things function cooperatively and effectively together

harmony

to be in harmony with someone

to work cooperatively and effectively together

harness

in harness
to be constrained and in work

Harry

every Tom, Dick, and Harry
virtually all ordinary people
appears to have been coined in Victorian times

harvest

harvest
end result of labour
Matthew 8:37, 'The harvest truly is plenteous, but the labourers are few'

haste

to go post haste
to go very fast
refers to urgent postal messages (originally carried on horseback)

hat

a peg to hang a hat on
something that provides a convenient or plausible excuse for some particular action

at the drop of a hat
very readily
from the practice of signalling the beginning of a race or fight with the drop of a hat

I'll eat my hat if so-and-so happens
I do not believe that so-and-so will happen

not to just pick something out of a hat
to choose carefully, after weighing all the considerations
refers to choosing by lot by choosing things unseen from a hat

to be old hat
to be old-fashioned; OR well known to the point of tedium

to keep something under one's hat
to maintain a confidence

to knock something into a cocked hat
to defeat easily in a game or contest of skill
refers to a game of nine-pins in which the pins were arranged in a triangle like a cocked hat

to pull a rabbit out of the hat
to produce an unexpected and seemingly miraculous but highly desirable solution
refers to magician's trick

to score a hat trick
to have three successive favourable outcomes
refers to a bowler in cricket taking three wickets in three balls; such a feat being originally rewarded with the prize of a new hat

to take one's hat off to someone
to be full of admiration for a person
refers to deferential gesture of removing one's hat

to talk through one's hat
to say things that demonstrate the speaker's ignorance of the subject

to throw one's cap/hat into the air
to express joy; OR to celebrate some achievement

to throw one's hat into the ring
publicly to announce one's interest in some position
refers to custom of throwing one's hat into a ring to indicate a willingness to take part in a boxing challenge

to wear a particular hat
to act in a particular capacity or for a particular vested interest

hats

to buy straw hats in winter
to buy in a depressed market when most other people are sellers

hatched

to count one's chickens before they are hatched
to treat as fact the expected results of a future proposal
originally attributed to Erasmus (1466–1536) in slightly different form

hatches

to batten down the hatches
to get ready for expected difficulties
nautical metaphor

hatchet

to bury the hatchet
to abandon hostilities
refers to tradition of North American indigenous peoples to symbolise cessation of hostilities

to do a hatchet job
to destroy some existing activity or to ruin a person's credibility

haul

for the long haul
as a long-term proposition

to haul someone over the coals
to reprimand a person
refers to church punishment of heretics

haunt

to come back to haunt someone
(of an unpleasant incident) to be a constant reminder to a person

hay

to hit the hay
to go to sleep
refers to sleeping on beds of hay

to look for a needle in a haystack
to attempt something with a very small chance of success

to make hay while the sun shines
to utilise an opportunity before it disappears
John Betjeman (1906–84), *The Last Laugh*, 'I made hay while the sun shone'

haystack

to look for a needle in a haystack
to attempt something with a very small chance of success

haywire

to go haywire
to function in a disordered and strange fashion
refers to difficulty in handling coils of hay-binding wire

head

a hothead
an impetuous person

a swelled head
an exaggerated idea of one's abilities or status

an old head on young shoulders
experience, knowledge, and maturity in a young person

head first
precipitately

head over heels
to be turned upside down; OR to be very excited

not to touch a hair on someone's head
not to harm a person
Matthew 10:30, 'the very hairs of your head are all numbered'

off the top of one's head
impromptu, based on experience or intuition, but without detailed consideration

pull your head in!
do not interfere in this! you are advised to withdraw from this situation

someone's head is on the block
a person is in danger of being condemned; OR a person is in danger of having an appointment terminated
refers to execution by decapitation

that is on your head
you will have to accept responsibility for that
Shakespeare, *Merchant of Venice*, IV:i, 'My deeds upon my head'

there is a big question mark hanging over someone's head
there are considerable doubts about a person's competence, integrity, or suitability
refers to Damocles who had the sword of Dionysius hanging, by a slender thread, over his head — as a symbol of perpetual risk in life; the story is told in Cicero, *Tusculanae Disputationes*

to bang one's head against a brick wall
to fight an unwinnable case

to be able to do something standing on one's head
to be able to do something very easily

to be at the head of the pack
to be the best of many, or the *de facto* leader

to be head and shoulders above the rest
to be significantly more capable than others

to be off one's head
to be crazy

to be over someone's head
to be beyond a person's ability to understand

to be unable to make head nor tail of something
to be unable to understand how something functions or what something means

to beat each other over the head
to be always fighting

to belt someone over the head
to override someone's views or arguments, often involving the use of heavy pressure

to bite someone's head off
rudely and excessively to express displeasure at a person

to bury one's head in the sand
to refuse to face up to an unpleasant truth
refers to the reputed habit of ostriches in danger

to come to a head
to reach culmination
medical metaphor; refers to abscess formation

to confront someone head on
to meet and face up to someone in a hostile and direct fashion

to develop a head of steam
to gain momentum
refers to a steam engine or boiler

to drag someone by the head and ears
to force a person to reveal the true facts

to eat one's head off
to eat excessively

to fall head-over-heels in love
to fall very much in love

to get one's head blown off
to be abused very soundly

to give someone his or her head
to let a person do as that person wishes

to go off one's head
to lose one's temper

to go over someone's head
to bypass lower levels of authority and approach someone more senior instead; OR to be beyond a person's ability to understand

to go to someone's head
to cause a person to get an exaggerated idea of that person's abilities or status

to hang one's head
to be ashamed of oneself; OR to be disappointed and lacking in morale
Shakespeare, *Henry VIII* III:i, 'Even the billows of the sea, / hung their heads and then lay by'

to have a cloud hanging over one's head
there is doubt as to one's future
refers to the pillar of cloud (God) passing judgment on the Hebrews; the pillar of cloud is described in *Exodus* 13:21 *et seq.*

to have a head start
to have an advantage over others
refers to horse racing

to have a threat hanging over one's head
to fear some intimated unpleasant action
refers to Damocles who had the sword of Dionysius hanging, by a slender thread, over his head — as a symbol of perpetual risk in life; the story is told in Cicero, *Tusculanae Disputationes*

to have eyes at/in the back of one's head
to know more of what is going on than is generally realised

to have one's head in the clouds
to be unrealistic

to have one's head screwed on
to be shrewd

to have rocks in the head
to be stupid or mentally unbalanced

to head north
(of prices, etc.) to go up

to head someone in the right direction
to assist a person to achieve something

to head south
(of prices, etc.) to go down

to hit the nail right on the head
astutely to come to the correct conclusion

to hold a gun/pistol at someone's head
to put pressure on a person to make a particular decision regardless of that person's desires in the matter

to hold one's head high
to stay unruffled and to maintain one's dignity despite attempts by others to embarrass

to hold one's head just above water
to cope with problems but with little margin to spare or to stay solvent

to keep a civil tongue in one's head
to be polite, especially under provocation

to keep a cool head
to stay calm and rational in a crisis
Rudyard Kipling (1865–1936), *If*, 'If you can keep your head when all about you are losing theirs ... '

to keep a level head
to stay calm and rational in a crisis
Rudyard Kipling (1865–1936), *If*, 'If you can keep your head when all about you are losing theirs ... '

to keep one's head
to remain calm in a crisis or unexpectedly to retain an elected or appointed position
Rudyard Kipling (1865–1936), *If*, 'If you can keep your head when all about you are losing theirs ... '

to keep one's head down
to stay out of trouble, AND/OR to work very diligently

to knock an idea on the head
utterly to reject a proposal

to laugh one's head off
to enjoy something greatly

to let one's head go
to do as one wants to
refers to letting a horse have its head (and run as it wishes to)

to let one's heart rule one's head
to act on emotion rather than on reason
George Colman the younger (1762–1836), *Who Wants a Guinea?*, 'His heart runs away with his head'

to lose one's head
to become agitated or confused
Rudyard Kipling (1865–1936), *If*, 'If you can keep your head when all about you are losing theirs ... '

to need something like a hole in the head
to be confronted with a completely undesired problem

to need to have one's head read
to engage in behaviour so foolish that a psychiatric examination seems called for

to pull one's head in
to retreat from a previously held stance
refers to habit of a tortoise in avoiding danger

to put one's head in the noose
to expose oneself to great danger likely to lead to one's downfall
refers to death by hanging

to put one's head into the lion's mouth
recklessly to expose oneself to great danger
refers to circus performance

to put one's head on the block
to have the courage of one's convictions
refers to execution by decapitation

to rear its ugly head
to make an unwelcome appearance

to scratch one's head
to be amazed or puzzled

to scream one's head off
to utter loud and piercing cries as if in great pain

to shake one's head
to indicate disbelief or wonder or disapproval
Shakespeare, *Macbeth* III:iv, 'Never shake thy gory locks at me'

to snap someone's head off
to speak to a person with excessive aggression

to tackle someone head on
to confront a person directly

to turn someone's head
to cause a person to get an exaggerated idea of that person's abilities or status

to turn something on its head
to reverse something

uneasy lies the head that wears a crown
leadership involves some risks and some burdens (esp. the risk of being deposed)
Shakespeare, *Henry IV*, Part 2, III:i, 'Uneasy lies the head that wears a crown'

you need your head read

your behaviour is so foolish that you require psychiatric examination

headache

a headache
a cause for worry

headed

a hydra-headed monster
an evil that is not readily destroyable
refers to the hydra — in Greek legend, a multiple-headed monster that grew two more heads whenever one was cut off; it was killed by Heracles

hard-headed
realistic

level-headed
rational

pig-headed
unduly obstinate

woolly-headed
slightly muddled

heads

heads I win, tails you lose
whichever way this matter goes I will benefit at your expense
refers to the tossing of a coin

heads will roll
transgressors will be punished
refers to execution by decapitation

to kick heads in
to demonstrate extreme annoyance at, or dislike of, certain persons

to knock two heads together
to make two persons come to their senses and deal with each other

to promote someone over the heads of others
to promote a person to a position more senior than that held by some persons previously outranking the promoted person

to put several heads together
to confer and pool ideas

headway

to make headway
to make progress

heal

to heal wounds
to effect a reconciliation
Shakespeare, *Two Gentlemen of Verona*, I:ii, 'Poor wounded name! my bosom, as a bed, shall lodge thee till thy wound be thoroughly healed'

health

to get a clean bill of health
after proper investigation to be found not wanting

heap

to be at the bottom of the heap
to be in the lowest position in a hierarchy

to be destined for the scrap-heap
to face a future in which one will have no meaningful role

to fall in a heap
to collapse utterly

hear

to hear a whisper
to learn of a rumoured fact
Shakespeare, *Macbeth*, V:i, 'Foul whisperings are abroad'; William Congreve (1670–1729), *Love for Love*, 'I know that's a secret, for it's whispered everywhere'

to hear on the grapevine
to learn unofficially
the earlier form of the metaphor was a 'grapevine telegraph' as a means of communicating private information

heard

the cheering could be heard a block away
there was great rejoicing

heart

from the bottom of one's heart
very sincerely

heart and soul
with great energy
Matthew 22:36–40, 'Thou shalt love the Lord thy God with all thy heart and with all thy soul and with all thy mind'

heart failure
a shock

heart-stopping
exciting

one's heart bleeds for someone
one feels truly sad for a person's fate
derived from the Christian Church's veneration of the sacred heart of Jesus (*sacré couer*) which was symbolised by a bleeding heart — sacrificed for the sake of humanity

one's heart is not in some cause

one has little enthusiasm for some cause

one's heart sank

one realised the extent of some disaster

this does my heart good

I rejoice at this

Shakespeare, *A Midsummer Night's Dream* I:ii, ' ... will do any man's heart good to hear'

to be close to one's heart

to be a project about which one is very keen

to be in [or of] good heart

to be cheerful, especially in adversity

to be someone after one's own heart

to be a person who shares one's beliefs

1 Samuel 13:14 'A man after his own heart'

to break someone's heart

to act in a way causing great upset to another person

Psalms 69:21, 'Thy rebuke hath broken my heart; I am full of heaviness'; Shakespeare *Hamlet* I:ii, 'But break my heart ... ')

to eat one's heart out

to suffer bitterly

Shakespeare, *Othello* IV:i, 'O God! That I were a man! I would eat his heart in the market place'

to give someone heart

to cause a person to cheer up

to have a change of heart

to form a new view in place of a strongly held prior view

to have a heart

to have compassion

to have a heart of gold

to have a generous disposition

Hilaire Belloc (1870–1953), 'With hearts of gold and lungs of bronze'

to have a heart of oak

to be brave

refers to a famous sea song and naval march from the pantomime, *Harlequin's Invasion* (1759), by Garrick and Boyce.

to have a heart of stone

to be unfeeling

Shakespeare, *Othello*, 'My heart is turned to stone'

to have a heart-to-heart talk

to have a confidential discussion on a highly personal matter

John Henry Newman (1801–90), 'Heart speaks to heart' (*cor ad cor loquitur*), motto on coat-of-arms as cardinal

to have one's heart in one's boots

to be afraid or dejected

to have one's heart in one's mouth

to be very apprehensive

to have one's heart in something

to be enthusiastic about and committed to a cause

to have one's heart in the right place

to have good intentions, to mean well

to have one's heart set on something

to be very keen to achieve something

to know something in one's heart of hearts

to know something — although reluctant to admit it, even to oneself

Shakespeare, *Hamlet* III:ii, 'In my heart's core, ay, in my heart of heart'

to let one's heart rule one's head

to act on emotion rather than on reason

George Colman the younger (1762–1836), *Who Wants a Guinea?*, 'His heart runs away with his head'

to lose heart

to be discouraged

to pour one's heart out to someone

to reveal one's innermost hopes and fears to another person

to pull at one's heart strings

to affect one emotionally

to search one's heart

to seek after one's innermost feelings and motivations

Jeremiah 17:10, 'I, the Lord, search the heart ... to give every man according to his ways, and according to the fruit of his doings'

to steal someone's heart

to move someone's affections towards another person or cause

Shakespeare, *Julius Caesar* III:ii, 'I come not, friends. to steal away your hearts'

to steel one's heart against something

to determine that, notwithstanding one's natural compassion, something shall not happen

to take heart from something
to be encouraged by something

to take something to heart
to learn to appreciate the significance of something; or to be much saddened by something

to warm the cockles of someone's heart
to delight a person
refers to the cockle shell which looks like a heart; the formal name for bivalve molluscs (such as cockles) is *cardium* (Latin for 'heart')

to wear one's heart on one's sleeve
to lack the reserve expected of one
refers to the fashion of wearing a sign of romantic attachment on one's sleeve; Shakespeare *Othello* I:i, 'But I will wear my heart upon my sleeve'

with a heavy heart
in sorrow
Johann Wolfgang von Goethe (1749–1832), *Gretchen am Spinnrad*, 'My peace is gone, my heart is heavy'

with a sinking heart
with growing despondency

you can eat your heart out
I don't care if you are intensely aggrieved or jealous

heartache

heartache
sadness
William Blake (1757–1827), *To Hayley*, 'Thy friendship oft has made my heart to ache'

heartbreak

heartbreak
despair
Psalms 69:21, 'Thy rebuke hath broken my heart; I am full of heaviness'; Shakespeare *Hamlet* I:ii, 'But break my heart ... '

heartburn

heartburn
distress or regret at some disappointment
originally referred to passion, as in *Luke* 24:32, 'Did not our hearts burn within us, while he talked with us by the way?'

hearted

chicken-hearted
showing little courage

cold-hearted
cruel or mean or unmoved
Edmund Burke (1729–97), *Reflections on the Revolution in France*, 'This barbarous philosophy, which is the offspring of cold hearts ... '

half-hearted
unenthusiastic

hard-hearted
unsympathetic
Exodus 7:3, ' ... and I will harden Pharaoh's heart'

open-hearted
cordial
Ecclesiasticus 8:19, 'Open not thine heart to every man'

warm-hearted
affectionate or generous

heat

if one can't stand the heat one should stay out of the kitchen
if one cannot put up with the pressure of a situation, one should get out of it
US President Harry S. Truman (1884–1972), *Mr Citizen*, ch. 15, 'If you can't stand the heat, get out of the kitchen'

to take the heat off someone
to remove pressure or harassment from someone

to turn the heat on something
to intensify the investigation of some matter

to turn up the heat on someone
to increase the pressure on a person
Shakespeare, *Macbeth* II, i, 'Proceeding from the heat-oppressed brain'

heave

to heave a sigh of relief
to express satisfaction at the achievement of a solution to a difficult problem
John Keats (1795–1821), *I stood tip-toe upon a little hill*, 'born of the very sigh that silence heaves'

heaven

heaven help you!
you are in trouble

Psalms 121:1, 'My help cometh even from the Lord: who hath made heaven and earth'

heaven only knows
it is not known to me or anyone else

manna from heaven
unexpected benefits

derived from Hebrew *man-hu* ('what is this?'); *Exodus* 16:15, 'It is manna: for they wist not what it was. And Moses said unto them: this is the bread which the Lord hath given you to eat'

to be in a seventh heaven
to be ecstatically happy in a state of bliss

refers to the highest state of heavenly bliss in Judaism, Christianity, and Islam

to move heaven and earth
to do everything possible

Revelation 21:1, 'And I saw a new heaven and a new earth, for the first heaven and the first earth had passed away'; a reference to the apocalyptic vision of the greatest possible change to all creation

to reek to high heaven
to be patently unethical

Shakespeare, *Hamlet* III:iii, 'O! my offence is rank, it smells to heaven'

heavy

to make heavy weather of something
to struggle excessively with a relatively simple task

nautical metaphor

to run into heavy weather
to encounter difficulties

nautical metaphor

with a heavy hand
in an oppressive fashion

with a heavy heart
in sorrow

Johann Wolfgang von Goethe (1749–1832), *Gretchen am Spinnrad*, 'My peace is gone, my heart is heavy'

heavyweight

a heavyweight
a person of importance or influence

refers originally to boxing

hedge

to hedge one's bets
to insure against a losing bet or investment by also investing on the opposite outcome

hedged

to be hedged around
(of a statement) to be surrounded by qualifications

heel

to be someone's Achilles' heel
to represent a weakness in an otherwise strong position

refers to Achilles, Greek warrior and hero of Homer's *Iliad*, who was invulnerable except for his heel

to bring someone to heel
to make a person conform

refers to the training of dogs

heeled

well-heeled
rich

heels

head over heels
to be turned upside down; OR to be very excited

to be hard/hot on the heels of something
to pursue something closely

to fall head-over-heels in love
to fall very much in love

to cool one's heels
to be kept waiting

to dig one's heels in
to become even more stubborn than at first

to drag one's heels
to perform unduly slowly

to kick one's heels
to be kept waiting

to snap at someone's heels
to be in very close pursuit

refers to hounds pursuing a fox

heir

heir apparent
the person likely to succeed another

hell

all hell broke loose
great confusion erupted

John Milton (1608–74) *Paradise Lost*, 'Wherefore with thee came not all hell broke loose?'

come hell or high water
regardless of the difficulties or obstacles

on a cold day in hell

never

to be hell bent on something
to be very determined to achieve something, regardless of the adverse consequences

to frighten hell out of someone
to cause great alarm to a person

to give someone hell
to make life extremely difficult for a person

to have a snowflake's chance in hell
to have no hope or possibility at all

to raise merry hell
to cause an uproar by outlandish, reckless, or larrikinish behaviour

in the eighteenth century there were clubs of reckless young men, known as 'hell-fire clubs', who were said to 'raise merry hell'

helm

to be at the helm
to be in charge

nautical metaphor

help

a cry for help
a subconscious or indirect indication that a person is in need of psychological counselling

heaven help you!
you are in trouble

Psalms 121:1, 'My help cometh even from the Lord: who hath made heaven and earth'

not to lift a finger to help someone
to refuse to assist

hemmed

to be hemmed in
to be limited in the choice of actions available

John Dryden (1631–1700), 'Hemm'd in with warlike foes'

hen

a mother hen
an over-protective person

Matthew 12:37, 'Even as a hen gathereth her chickens under her wings'

hen-pecked
subject to domination by one's wife

Lord Byron (1788–1824), *Don Juan*, 'But — oh! ye lords of ladies intellectual, inform us truly, have they not hen-peck'd you all?'

Herculean

a Herculean cleaning of the stables
a thorough revision of operating procedure

refers to the labours of Hercules (Heracles in Greek) who had twelve labours imposed upon him by Eurystheus — one of which was the cleaning of the stables of King Augeas in a single day

to be a Herculean task
to be laborious

refers to the labours of Hercules (Heracles in Greek) who had twelve labours imposed upon him by Eurystheus — one of which was the cleaning of the stables of King Augeas in a single day

herd

to follow the herd
to do what most other people are doing

here

the buck stops here
I accept full responsibility

hand-lettered sign on desk of US President Harry S. Truman (Phillips, *The Truman Presidency*, Ch. 12)

to be neither here nor there
to be irrelevant or unimportant

heresy

heresy
views different from those held by the majority

originally referred only to church orthodoxy, but now generalised metaphorical use

hero

to make a hero of oneself
to do something for personal glorification

herring

neither fish flesh nor good red herring
unclassifiable by virtue of being neither one thing nor another

Miguel de Cervantes (1547–1616), *Don Quixote*

to be a red herring
to be something designed to divert attention away from the main question

refers to hunting with hounds — a red herring was dragged across the scent trail to train hounds to ignore distractions and follow the correct trail

hiccup

a hiccup
a temporary minor holdup

hide

to cover one's hide
to provide excuses or take other evasive action in an attempt to avoid the adverse consequences of one's actions

to have a thick hide
to be impervious to criticism

to have the hide of a rhinoceros
to be unaffected by, and unresponsive to, valid criticism

to hide one's light under a bushel
to keep others in ignorance of one's skills and experience
Luke 11:33, 'No man, when he hath lighted a candle, putteth it in a secret place, neither under a bushel'

to hide under someone's skirts
to let someone else take the consequences of one's actions
refers to childish seeking for protection

to want someone's hide
to be keen to penalise a person

hidebound

hidebound
narrow-minded

high

come hell or high water
regardless of the difficulties or obstacles

high-handed
overbearing

high-water mark
the best or highest level achieved by an enterprise

since that person was knee-high to a grasshopper
since that person was a very young child

the high priest of something
the leading advocate of something
refers to religious leaders

to be for the high jump
to face dismissal or the end of one's career
refers to death by hanging

to be on one's high horse
to be excessively pompous
refers to persons of high rank riding on tall horses; John Brown (1715–66), *Letter to Garrick*, 'Altogether upon the high horse'

to fly high
to be ambitious

to have the high ground
to have an advantage in moral terms
refers to military battle

to hold one's head high
to stay unruffled and to maintain one's dignity despite attempts by others to embarrass

to leave someone high and dry
to isolate a person from a desired involvement; to withdraw all support from a person
nautical metaphor referring to a boat stranded out of water

to reek to high heaven
to be patently unethical
Shakespeare, *Hamlet* III:iii, 'O! my offence is rank, it smells to heaven'

to ride high
to be successful but vulnerable
refers to riding a horse while sitting high and upright — a posture likely to result in a fall

with a high hand
arrogantly
Exodus 14: 8 'And the children of Israel went out with an high hand'

highbrow

highbrow
intellectual or cultural

highflyer

a highflyer
an ambitious and/or successful person

highlight

a highlight
a particularly important item
originally refers (1658) to a a term from art (painting)

to highlight something
to draw particular attention to a matter
originally refers (1658) to a a term from art (painting)

highway

highway robbery
the charging of grossly excessive prices
refers to robbery by armed brigands on the highways

hijack

to hijack a debate
to involve oneself in discussion on some matter and turn that discussion to one's advantage

hill

light on the hill
distant goal acting as an inspiration
usually attributed to Australian prime minister, Ben Chifley (1949)

to be over the hill
to be old, or past one's prime

to be pushing uphill
to face difficulties

to fight an uphill battle
to face difficulties or to have formidable opposition
refers to military battle

to go downhill
to deteriorate

to push water uphill
foolishly to attempt the impossible

hills

to head for the hills
to seek to escape one's commitments

hilt

to the hilt
to the maximum extent
refers to swords

Himalayan

of Himalayan proportions
huge
refers to Himalayan mountains (Sanskrit: 'snow abode')

hind

to stand up on one's hind legs
to assert one's authority
refers to animals adopting aggressive posture

to talk the hind leg off a donkey
to talk excessively

hindsight

with 20/20 hindsight
with the benefit of knowing what happened
refers to American system of expressing perfect visual acuity

hip

the hip-pocket nerve
the assessment of issues by their financial effects on one

to shoot from the hip
to speak without careful assessment of the situation

hire

to be a gun for hire
to be a person willing to undertake assignments for a fee

hit

to hit a sour note
to say or do something inappropriate to a situation
refers to music

to hit one's stride
to settle down to some task
refers to horses in harness

to hit someone below the belt
to act unfairly towards another person
refers to boxing

to hit someone for six
to damage a person's cause severely
refers to cricket

to hit someone hard
greatly to affect a person emotionally; OR to cost a person a lot of money

to hit someone right between the eyes
to be brutally frank
refers to fighting

to hit the bull's eye
to be extremely accurate in an activity; to score
derived from archery

to hit the hay
to go to sleep
refers to sleeping on beds of hay

to hit the jackpot
to be very lucky
refers to draw-poker, in which a pot or pool accumulates until one of the players can open the betting with a pair of jacks or better

to hit the mark
to achieve one's object or to make the correct decision
refers to archery

to hit the nail right on the head

astutely to come to the correct conclusion

to hit the panic button
to act hastily and irrationally

to hit the roof
to be very angry

to hit the straps
to really get going
refers to horses in harness

hits

it hits one
one suddenly realises something

hobby

to be on one's hobby horse
to dominate a conversation by insisting on talking about subjects in which one has an obsessive interest
refers to a person who dressed with a figure of a horse around the waist or on the head in Morris dancing — hence a figure of fun, a jester, a buffoon

Hobson

Hobson's choice
no right at all to select
refers to Thomas Hobson, a Cambridge horsekeeper, who offered customers seeking a change of horses a single beast on a 'take it or leave it' basis

hoe

to have a hard row to hoe
to have a difficult assignment
refers to agriculture; James Russell Lowell (1819–91), *The Biglow Papers*, 'You've a darned long row to hoe'

hog

a road hog
an inconsiderate motorist
refers to gluttonous swine

to go the whole hog
to do something very thoroughly
origin uncertain; alternative explanations include: (i) Muslim divines attempting to ascertain how much of the whole hog could be eaten according to Islamic law (Cowper, 1779, 'but for one piece they thought it hard/from the whole hog to be debarred'); (ii) colloquial term for a shilling — that is, to spend the whole hog (or shilling) at one time; (iii) refers to the close shearing of lambs

to make a hog of oneself
to demonstrate greed
refers to gluttonous swine

hogwash

hogwash
nonsense
refers to 'hog wash' — meaning kitchen swill for pigs (and therefore worthless)

hoist

to be hoist with one's own petard
to have one's own case used against one
refers to being blown up by one's own petard (bomb); Shakespeare, *Hamlet* III:iv, 'for 'tis sport to have the engineer hoist with his own petard'

hold

hold your horses!
just wait a little!

not fit to hold a candle to someone
greatly inferior to another person
refers to a servant holding a candle to assist a more senior person

not to hold one's breath for something
to give up all expectation

to have hold of the wrong end of the pineapple
to be utterly mistaken

to hold a gun/pistol at someone's head
to put pressure on a person to make a particular decision regardless of that person's desires in the matter

to hold a knife/sword at someone's throat
to assert undue pressure on another person in an endeavour to achieve a result that would otherwise not be forthcoming

to hold a winning hand
to be in an unbeatable position to defeat others
refers to playing cards

to hold all the aces
to be in an unbeatable position to defeat others
refers to playing cards; from Latin *as* ('unity', that is 'one' or 'a single point')

to hold all the cards
to be assured of victory
refers to playing cards

to hold fire
to defer criticising or attacking

to hold one's cards close to one's chest

to keep one's plans and strategies secret
refers to playing cards

to hold one's fire
to delay proposed action

to hold one's head high
to stay unruffled and to maintain one's dignity despite attempts by others to embarrass

to hold one's head just above water
to cope with problems but with little margin to spare or to stay solvent

to hold one's tongue
to keep quiet
John Donne (1571–1631), *The Canonization*, 'For God's sake hold your tongue, and let me love'

to hold out a fistful of dollars
to offer money by way of inducement

to hold out an olive branch
to make peace overtures
the olive branch was recognised as a symbol of peace and prosperity in many ancient civilisations; *Genesis* 8:11, 'And the dove came in to him in the evening; and lo, in her mouth was an olive leaf plucked off: so Noah knew that the waters were abated off the earth'

to hold someone at bay
successfully to resist an attacker
James Thomson (1700–48), *Autumn*, 'He stands at bay, and puts his last weak refuge in despair' — description of a stag

to hold someone on a short leash
to give a person very little freedom
refers to a lead used to restrain coursing hounds

to hold someone's hand
to give detailed on-the-job training and supervision

to hold the field
not to be superseded

to hold the floor
to dominate a conversation

to hold the fort
to be in charge during the temporary absence of a superior
Philip Paul Bliss (1838–76), *The Charm*, 'Hold the fort, for I am coming'

to hold the pen poised
to be ready to consummate a deal

to hold the power to do something in the hollow of one's hand
to have the right to make crucial decisions
Isaiah 40:12, ' ... who hath measured the waters in the hollow of his hand ... '

to hold the purse strings
to have control of expenditure
refers to a drawstring closing a purse

to hold the trump card
to be in an unbeatable position to defeat others
refers to playing cards

to hold the wrong end of the stick
to be completely mistaken about something

to hold water
(of an argument) to be soundly based

to put something on 'hold'
to put something aside for the time being with a view to resuming activity later on
refers to the telephone

holding

an argument holding water
a debating point of substance

to be left holding the baby
to be forced to accept responsibility for someone else's problems

holds

no holds barred
without any limitation
refers to wrestling

hole

a black hole
a place where things disappear without trace; OR an intermediate range of values producing anomalous results; OR a particularly obnoxious prison cell
the first and second definitions refer to an astronomical black hole — an area of extreme density from which even light cannot escape; the third definition refers to the infamous 'black hole of Calcutta'

a dry hole
an exercise that, after much effort, proves fruitless
refers to drilling for oil

a fox hole
a small space of refuge and shelter (especially in battle)
Matthew 8:20, 'the foxes have holes, and the birds of the air have nests; but

the son of man hath not where to lay his head'

a loophole
a means of getting around the intention of some regulation
refers, originally, to a small narrow space in a wall for shooting from, or for observation

a square peg in a round hole
obviously unsuited for the purpose'

to be in a hole
to experience some difficulties

to have money burning a hole in one's pocket
to be impatient to spend or invest available funds

to need something like a hole in the head
to be confronted with a completely undesired problem

to pigeon-hole
to put aside for further consideration in the distant future
refers to placing something in a small hole, like the small hole in a dovecot for the pigeons to walk in and out

to stop up one hole in a sieve
to do something quite useless

watch the doughnut — not the hole
look for the positive aspects

watering hole
hotel

holes

to expose holes
to expose weaknesses in an argument

holiday

a busman's holiday
leisure time spent in a way not significantly different from one's normal business activities

hollow

that has a hollow ring to it
that statement is insincere
refers to bell-ringing

to hold the power to do something in the hollow of one's hand
to have the right to make crucial decisions
Isaiah 40:12, ' ... who hath measured the waters in the hollow of his hand ... '

holy

an unholy alliance
a working relationship for a nefarious purpose between unlikely partners

search for the Holy Grail
work towards a difficult goal
refers to a vessel or platter supposedly used by Christ at the Last Supper and featuring in the Arthurian legends

holier

a holier-than-thou attitude
excessive righteousness

home

charity begins at home
a person's first responsibility should be to that person's family
John Fletcher (1579–1625), *The Wild-Goose Chase*, 'Charity and beating begins at home'

nothing to write home about
unimpressive

the chickens are coming home to roost
the consequences of a person's past actions are now being felt by that person
Robert Southey (1774–1843), *The Curse of Kehama* (1810), 'Curses are like young chickens, they always come home to roost'

till the cows come home
for a very long time, perhaps forever
Francis Beaumont (1584–1616) & John Fletcher (1579–1625), *The Scornful Lady*, 'Kiss till the cow comes home'

to be home and hosed
to be assured of victory or success in a task
refers to horse racing (a jocular reference to a horse leading in a race being already home and hosed down)

to be home on the sheep's back
to be doing well

to be too close to home
to be too near the truth to be welcome

to bring a fact home to someone
to make a person recognise a fact despite that person's inclination to the contrary

to bring home the bacon
to be successful
refers to bringing home a valued prize

to drive the lesson home

to take certain action that is unpleasant but that has the effect of registering a message

to eat someone out of house and home
to ruin a person by eating all that that person has
used in an exaggerated, humorous sense

to enter the home stretch
to commence the last stage
refers to horse racing

to keep the home fires burning
to maintain normal domestic activity during the temporary absence of the main provider of the household

to take one's bat and ball home
as a gesture of spite to remove an essential ingredient that one has contributed to a joint enterprise, and to refuse to take any further part in its activities
refers to cricket

homework

to do one's homework
to analyse an issue throughly

honest

to turn an honest penny
to earn money by hard work

honey

a land of milk and honey
a country in which everything is in abundant supply
Exodus 3:8, ' ... to bring them up out of that land unto a good land ... flowing with milk and honey'

honeymoon

a honeymoon
a short period enjoyed by a newcomer to some activity before that person's performance is criticised
refers to the holiday time (originally one 'moon' or month) immediately after a marriage ceremony

hook

by hook or by crook
by fair means or foul
perhaps refers to collection of firewood by different implements

hook, line, and sinker
wholly
refers to angling

to get someone off the hook
to rescue a person from a predicament
refers to angling

to let someone off the hook
to allow a person to escape the adverse consequences of that person's own actions
refers to angling

hooked

to be hooked on something
to be addicted to something
refers to angling

hoops

to jump through hoops
to be required to perform or undergo some ordeal
refers to circus performance

hoot

not to care a hoot
not to show the slightest concern or enthusiasm

hop

something is but a hop, skip, and jump away
something is nearby

to be on the hop
to be always bustling about

to catch someone on the hop
to take a person by surprise

to hop onto the bandwagon
to subscribe to an emerging majority opinion

horizon

the one bright spot on the horizon
the only hopeful aspect

there are black/storm clouds on the horizon
bad news is expected

to loom on the horizon
to be expected but not immediately

hornet

to stir up a hornet's nest
to take action that results in unpleasant side-effects

horns

the horns of a dilemma
two unpalatable alternatives between which a choice must be made
dilemma: Greek for 'two assumptions'

to lock horns with someone

to have an argument with another person

refers to fighting between male horned animals

to pull one's horns in

to retreat from previously stated views

refers to fighting between male horned animals

to take the bull by the horns

to come to grips with the realities of a difficult problem

horse

a dark horse

a person with unsuspected talents

Benjamin Disraeli (1804–81), *The Young Duke*, 'A dark horse, which had never been thought of, and which the careless St James had never even observed in the list, rushed past the grandstand in sweeping triumph'

a nod is the same as a wink to a blind horse

fine distinctions are not appropriate here

Captain Marryat (1792–1848), *Peter Simple*, 'But you're a dutiful son, so I'll say no more about it — a nod's as good as a wink to a blind horse'

a stalking horse

a pretext put forward to allow an attack to be made or an argument to be mounted

refers to a horse trained to allow a hunter to approach game (esp. fowl) without being seen; Shakespeare, *As You Like It* V:iv, 'He uses his folly like a stalking horse, and under the presentation of that he shoots his wit'

a Trojan horse

a surreptitious means of gaining entrance or breaching defences

refers to a large gift horse full of Greek soldiers used to bring about the fall of Troy, as described in Homer's *Iliad*; Virgil (70–19 BC), *Aeneid* II:49, *Timeo Danaos et dona ferentis* ('I fear the Greeks even when they bring gifts')

a two-horse race

a contest between only two serious contestants

a warhorse

an experienced and dependable campaigner in war, politics, sport, and other contests

a willing horse

a cheerful worker

horse sense

practical commonsense

horse trading

tough negotiations

I could eat a horse

I am very hungry

one can lead a horse to water, but one can't make it drink

one can give advice to a person but cannot ensure that it will be acted on

that is a horse of a very different colour

that is a different matter altogether

Shakespeare, *Twelfth Night*, 'My purpose is, indeed, a horse of that colour'

the horse-and-buggy days

long ago

to back the wrong horse

to have faith in, give support to, and/or invest in a project that proves to be unsuccessful

refers to betting on racehorses

to be on one's hobby horse

to dominate a conversation by insisting on talking about subjects in which one has an obsessive interest

refers to a person who dressed with a figure of a horse around the waist or on the head in Morris dancing — hence a figure of fun, a jester, a buffoon

to be on one's high horse

to be excessively pompous

refers to persons of high rank riding on tall horses; John Brown (1715–66), *Letter to Garrick*, 'Altogether upon the high horse'

to flog a dead horse

misguidedly to do something patently useless

to learn something from the horse's mouth

to get information from someone qualified to impart it

refers to the examination of a horse's teeth for an accurate assessment of its age

to look a gift horse in the mouth

to be suspicious about a benefit that has been volunteered

Samuel Butler (1612–80), *Hudibras*, 'He ne'er consider'd it, as loth to look a gift horse in the mouth'; refers to the examination of a horse's teeth for an accurate assessment of its age

to put the cart before the horse
to do things in the wrong order
Rudyard Kipling (1865–1936), *The Conundrum of the Workshops*, 'We know the tail must wag the dog, for the horse is drawn by the cart'

to shut the stable door after the horse has bolted
to take preventive action only after the relevant event

horses

hold your horses!
just wait a little!

horses are out of the barn
it is now too late

it is horses for courses
the correct means to an end needs to be chosen
refers to horse racing

to drive a coach and horses through something
to demonstrate the major errors or absurdities of something
Sir Stephen Rice (1673–1715), as quoted by W. King, *State of the Protestants of Ireland* (1672), 'I will drive a coach and six horses through the Act of Settlement'

to frighten the horses
to scare people off by one's ill-considered tactics
Mrs Patrick Campbell (1865–1940), quoting oral tradition, 'I don't mind where people make love, so long as they don't do it in the street and frighten the horses'

to swap/change horses in mid-stream
to alter that upon which one is reliant during the course of a project

wild horses would not cause me to do something
I refuse absolutely to do something
refers to a form of torture in which persons were dragged behind horses

wild horses would not drag that out of me
I refuse absolutely to reveal that
refers to a form of torture in which persons were dragged behind horses

horseplay

horseplay
boisterous and undignified behaviour
John Dryden (1631–1700), 'He [Collier] is too much given to horseplay in his raillery'

hosed

to be home and hosed
to be assured of victory or success in a task
refers to horse racing (a jocular reference to a horse leading in a race being already home and hosed down)

hot

a hot potato
a controversial issue that no one wants to handle, an embarrassing issue

a hothead
an impetuous person

hot-blooded
very passionate
Horace (65–8 BC), '*Non ego hoc ferrem calidus iuventa consule planco* (I shouldn't have put up with this when I was a hot-blooded youth, and Plancus was consul)'

I have had more of these than I have had hot dinners
I have had a very large number of these

red hot
urgent, and/or exciting, and/or dangerous

to be full of hot air
to make unsubstantiated empty statements; to be bombastic

to be hot off the press
to be the latest news
refers to old-style hot presses used in printing newspapers

to be hot on a subject
to be knowledgeable and enthusiastic about a subject

to be hot on the heels of something
to pursue something closely

to be hot stuff
to be skilful, or very passionate, or highly sexed

to be hot under the collar
to be very agitated

to be in hot water
to be in great difficulty

to be in the hot seat
to hold a position requiring one to answer criticism or accusations

to blow hot and cold
to vacillate
Revelations 3:15, 'I know thy works, that thou art neither cold nor hot'

to get hot
to get close to the solution; OR to get into good form; OR to become sexually excited; OR to become lucky, etc.
this metaphor has many shades of meaning, dependent on the context

to go hot foot
to do something fast

to make some place too hot for someone
to make a place unpleasant for someone

to run hot
(of equipment) to be subject to particularly high usage; (of persons) to be in good form

to strike while the iron is hot
to take advantage of a situation that cannot last
refers to the work of blacksmiths and farriers; John Dryden (1631–1700), *Aenis*, 'We must beat the iron while it is hot, but we may polish it at leisure'

hotbed

a hotbed of crime
a place where illegal activity flourishes
refers to a bed of earth, heated by fermenting manure, for artificially raising plants; hence, figuratively, a place that encourages the rapid growth of (usually undesirable) matter

hounds

to run with the hare and hunt with the hounds
to keep in with two opposing sides
refers to hunting

to set the hounds baying
to excite the gossips by providing material that they can use
Shakespeare, *Julius Caesar*, 'I had rather be a dog, and bay the moon, than such a Roman'

hour

at the eleventh hour
at the last moment
Matthew 20:9: 'And when they came that were hired about the eleventh hour, they received every man a penny'; refers to the last hour of the working day in biblical times, and therefore the last opportunity to secure work — hence the very last opportunity

house

a halfway house
an intermediate position
refers to an inn situated situated halfway between two towns on a journey

a house of cards
an organisation that gives a misleading impression of solidity

a madhouse
an organisation in great turmoil
John Clare (1793–1864) *The Exile*, 'madhouses, prisons, whoreshops'; and *Letter*, 'Dear Sir, I am in a madhouse and quite forget your name and who you are'

to be in the doghouse
to be in disgrace

to be on the house
to be free of cost

to bring the house down
to obtain rapturous applause
refers to the theatre

to eat someone out of house and home
to ruin a person by eating all that that person has
used in an exaggerated, humorous sense

to put one's house in order
to fix up the deficiencies in one's affairs
Isaiah 38:1, 'Set thine house in order; for thou shalt die and not live'

household

a household name
a very familiar name

houses

a plague on both your houses!
I am disgusted with both of you
Shakespeare, *Romeo and Juliet*, III:i, 'A plague o' both your houses!'

people in glass houses should not throw stones
those who are less than perfect are foolish to criticise others
John 8:7, 'He that is without sin among you, let him first cast a stone at her' (refers to ancient condemnation and punishment of people by stoning)

Hoyle

according to Hoyle

with authority

Edmond Hoyle (1671–1769) codified the laws of games — including card games (especially whist), backgammon, and chess — and wrote a number of treatises that were accepted as authoritative, leading to common use of the phrase 'according to Hoyle'; a book entitled *According to Hoyle* was published in 1965 containing the rules of 300 games

humble

to eat humble pie

to be prepared to humiliate oneself and apologise

a play on words — derived from the eating of 'umble pie' (entrails of a deer) by lowly persons

hungry

lean and hungry

efficient

Shakespeare, *Julius Caesar* I:ii, 'Yond' Cassius has a lean and hungry look; he thinks too much: such men are dangerous'

hunt

a witchhunt

an exercise seeking to find someone who can be blamed

refers to ancient practice of seeking out those who supposedly practised witchcraft

to run with the hare and hunt with the hounds

to keep in with two opposing sides

refers to hunting

hurdle

to jump/clear a hurdle

to overcome a problem or difficulty

to jump that hurdle when one comes to it

to deal with a particular problem only when it becomes necessary to do so

hurl

to hurl something in someone's face

to reproach a person in regard to something

hurt

someone wouldn't hurt a fly

someone is very gentle and kind-hearted

William Hazlitt (1778–1830). 'He would not hurt a fly'

Hyde

to do a Jekyll and Hyde

to have a split personality

Robert Louis Stevenson (1850–94), *The Strange Case of Dr Jekyll and Mr Hyde* (1886)

hydra

a hydra-headed monster

an evil that is not readily destroyable

refers to the hydra — in Greek legend, a multiple-headed monster that grew two more heads whenever one was cut off; it was killed by Heracles

hymnal

to all sing from the same hymnal

to act consistently with each other

refers to a book of hymns

I

i

to dot the i's and cross the t's

to be meticulous in completing documentation

ice

the ice is melting

friendly relations are being restored

to break the ice

to take the initiative in starting discussions

Francis Bacon (1561–1626), *Of Cunning*, 'In things that are tender and unpleasing, it is good to break the ice by some whose words are of less weight ...'

to cut no ice with someone

to have little effect on a person

perhaps refers to ice-skating

to put something on ice

to put something aside for the time being

to skate on thin ice

to act in disregard of obvious danger; to require tact in dealing with a sensitive subject in conversation

Ralph Waldo Emerson (1803–82), *Prudence*, 'In skating over thin ice, our safety is in our speed'

iceberg

to be the tip of the iceberg
to be only a very small portion of a much larger but less obvious whole

icing

to be icing on top of the cake
to be an additional benefit in an already satisfactory scenario

idea

the idea has legs
this notion seems a good one

to dust some idea off
to revive some proposal

to leap at an idea
to accept a suggestion enthusiastically

to pour cold water on some idea
to be unenthusiastic about some proposal or scornful of its apparent weaknesses

ideas

to be bankrupt of ideas
to be bereft of ideas

ill

it is an ill wind that blows no good
even a seeming misfortune leads to some blessings

image

to tarnish one's image
to become less highly regarded
refers to brass images

impetus

to have impetus
to move along forcefully

imprimatur

imprimatur
confirmation that something is in order
Latin, 'let it be printed'; refers to the formal ruling given by a Roman Catholic bishop authorising the publication of a book on religion or morals

inch

give someone an inch and that person will take an ell
make a small concession to a person and that person will abuse it by taking much more
derived from old measure of length (ell) originally based on the length of the forearm (the Old English word *eln* being cognate with the Latin *ulna*–a long bone of the forearm)

give someone an inch and that person will take a mile
make a small concession to a person and that person will abuse it by taking much more

not to give an inch
not to budge or concede to the slightest degree despite pressure to do so

to inch forward
to make slow progress
William Golding (1911–93), 'He inched along the path, with shuffling steps'

to resist something every inch of the way
to resist something utterly

Indians

more chiefs than Indians
a disproportionately large number of supervisors

inflame

to inflame a situation
to aggravate a situation
Shakespeare, *Julius Caesar* III:ii, 'It will inflame you, it will make you mad'

information

background information
(relating to some matter) supplementary information that enables the main information to be seen in context and understood better

ink

the ink is hardly dry
this involves indecent haste
refers to acting promptly, as soon as a document is signed

inn

no room at the inn
no available space
Luke 2:7, 'She [Mary] brought forth her firstborn son, and wrapped him in swaddling clothes, and laid him in a manger; because there was no room for them in the inn'

inner

a warm inner glow
satisfaction at some achievement
Joseph Conrad (1857–1924), *Youth*, 'the heat of life ... that glow in the heart that with every year grows dim, grows cold'

innings

to have had a good innings
to have enjoyed satisfactory time and success in an undertaking; to have had a successful life
refers to cricket

inside

to know something inside out
to know something very thoroughly

to turn something inside out
to examine something thoroughly

instructions

riding instructions
directions as to how to do something
refers to horse racing

interest

to pay something back with interest
to return a small favour with a bigger favour; or to extract retribution of greater value than the circumstances warrant

introduce

to introduce new blood
to recruit new members to some organisation

inundate

to inundate
to overload with replies, etc.

iron

ironclad
firm or rigorous
refers to armour-plated naval vessels

the iron curtain
the border between the communist nations and the rest of the world
used famously by Winston Churchill in a speech in 1946, but also attributed before this to Ethel Snowden (1920), Goebbels (1945), and by Churchill himself in 1945 (before his famous 1946 speech)

to give a cast-iron guarantee
to give a very secure undertaking to do something

to have a cast-iron case
to be assured absolutely of victory in a dispute, an argument, or in legal proceedings

to have something in an iron grip
to hold something very securely

to iron out something
to sort out a difficult problem

to rule with a rod of iron
to keep strict discipline
Psalms 2:9, 'Thou shalt break them with a rod of iron; thou shalt dash them in pieces like a potter's vessel'

to rule with an iron fist
to keep strict discipline

to rule with an iron hand
to keep strict discipline

to strike while the iron is hot
to take advantage of a situation that cannot last
refers to the work of blacksmiths and farriers; John Dryden (1631–1700), *Aenis*, 'We must beat the iron while it is hot, but we may polish it at leisure'

with an iron hand in a velvet glove
with a hard attitude made to seem soft

irons

to have other irons in the fire
to have the opportunity to do something else as an alternative
Francis Beaumont (1584–1616) & John Fletcher (1579–1625), *The Faithful Friends* I:ii, 'It is always good when a man has two irons in the fire'

issue

a bread-and-butter issue
a basic issue that is of importance to many people

to be a black-and-white issue
to involve very clear distinctions
Ben Jonson (1573–1637), *Every Man in his Honour*, 'I have it here in black and white'

to pre-empt some issue
deliberately to do something that has the effect of limiting the range of alternative approaches to a matter
refers to the right of certain persons (originally the Crown) to buy certain things before others have an opportunity issues

parish pump issues
issues of local importance lacking a wider perspective
refers to the local parish water pump

itching

to be itching to go
to be highly enthusiastic and keen to start

itchy

itchy feet
a desire to travel

to have itchy fingers
to be impatient

ivory

to be in an ivory tower
to be immersed in theoretical considerations and ignorant of the practical realities

Song of Solomon 7:4, 'Thy neck is as a tower of ivory'

J

Jack

a Jack of all trades
an amateur who can do many different tasks'

before one can say 'Jack Robinson'
very quickly

origin of phrase is disputed, but dates from at least the eighteenth century

jackals

to keep the jackals at bay
to pay one's creditors just sufficient to avoid repercussions

James Thomson (1700–48), *Autumn*, 'He stands at bay, and puts his last weak refuge in despair' — description of a stag

jacket

to keep someone in a strait jacket
to deny a person any discretionary powers at all

refers to a restraining 'jacket' used to control violent or insane persons

jackpot

to hit the jackpot
to be very lucky

refers to draw-poker, in which a pot or pool accumulates until one of the players can open the betting with a pair of jacks or better

jam

money for jam
remuneration easily earned

to be in a jam
to be in difficulties

to pick just the plums out of the jam
to take only the very best items

to put jam on someone's bread
to make a good situation even better

jaundiced

jaundiced
affected by jealousy

Alexander Pope (1688–1744), *An Essay on Criticism*, 'As all looks yellow to the jaundiced eye'

jaw

someone's jaw dropped
someone registered obvious astonishment and/or disappointment

Jekyll

to do a Jekyll and Hyde
to have a split personality

Robert Louis Stevenson (1850–94), *The Strange Case of Dr Jekyll and Mr Hyde* (1886)

jelly

to be set like a jelly
to be very well established

Jeremiah

Jeremiah
a person who looks on the gloomy side of everything

refers to the prophet Jeremiah in the Old Testament

Jericho

walls of Jericho
something seemingly solid but actually destructible

Joshua 6:20, 'When the priests blew with the trumpets … the wall fell down flat'

jerk

a knee-jerk reaction
a response made instantaneously and without any proper consideration

jetsam

flotsam and jetsam
persons or things in an unfixed and disordered state, and considered worthless

refers, respectively, to goods found floating, and to goods thrown overboard deliberately

jettison

to jettison some proposal

to abandon some proposal as worthless or impracticable

jewel

a jewel
any highly valued person or thing

the jewel in someone's crown
the most significant component

Jezebel

a Jezebel
a wicked shameless woman, especially one who wears heavy make-up
2 KIngs 9:30, 'Jezebel heard of it; and she painted her face, and tired her head'

jib

the cut of someone's jib
someone's personal appearance
Sir Walter Scott (1771–1832), 'If she disliked what the sailor calls the cut of their jib'; refers to the recognition of ships at sea by noting the appearance of their foresail

jigsaw

to be parts of a jigsaw
to be elements in the solution of something complex
refers to a jigsaw puzzle

to put the jigsaw together
to solve a problem by placing together a number of separate facts
refers to a jigsaw puzzle

Job

something would try the patience of Job
something is very vexatious
James 5:11, 'Ye have heard of the patience of Job'

job

a mansize job
a large task

someone's job is on the line
a person's career path is under consideration; AND/OR that person's present position is at risk

to do a hatchet job
to destroy some existing activity or to ruin a person's credibility

to have a job in front of one
to have all or much of a difficult task still to be completed

join

join the club!
you are only one of many people with similar problems

to join forces
to cooperate with one another in order to achieve a common objective

to join hands with someone
to cooperate with a person

joint

to put someone's nose out of joint
to upset another person

Joneses

to keep up with the Joneses
to maintain a lifestyle beyond one's means in order to match that of some neighbourhood role model
refers to keeping pace with Jones amid pomp, but whether this relates to the metaphor is problematical: William Wordsworth (1770–1850), *Jones! As from Calais* (1807), 'Jones! as from Calais southward you and I went pacing side by side, this public way streamed with the pomp of a too-credulous day'

jot

not a jot
not even a small amount
refers to the Greek letter *iota* (i)

jowl

cheek by jowl
close to each other

joy

to jump for joy
to express great satisfaction

Juan

to be a Don Juan
to be a libertine
refers to Don Juan Tenorio, legendary fourteenth-century libertine of Seville, who features in many plays and operas

Judas

to play Judas
to betray a person
Matthew 26:14, 16, 'Then one of the twelve, called Judas Iscariot ... sought opportunity to betray him'

judge

to judge a book by its cover
foolishly to go only by superficial appearances

juggernaut

juggernaut

large overpowering force
Sanskrit: 'world protector'; a title of Krishna in Hinduism

jugular

to go for the jugular
to attack a very vital and vulnerable point with a view to a decisive victory

juice

to stew in one's juice
to suffer the adverse consequences of one's acts or omissions
Shakespeare, *Hamlet* III:iv, 'But to live in the rank sweat of an enseamed bed, stew'd in corruption'

jumbo

mumbo jumbo
blatant nonsense
refers to a deity worshipped by primitive tribes

jump

something is but a hop, skip, and jump away
something is nearby

to be for the high jump
to face dismissal or the end of one's career
refers to death by hanging

to get the jump on someone
to get an advantage over a person

to jump a hurdle
to overcome a problem or difficulty

to jump at the opportunity
enthusiastically to take immediate advantage of a good chance

to jump down someone's throat
to react angrily to the remarks of the other party to a conversation

to jump for joy
to express great satisfaction

to jump in feet first
to take a calculated risk

to jump into bed with someone
to enter into a joint enterprise with another person

to jump into the ring
enthusiastically to join in a contest or challenge
refers to the practice of jumping into a boxing ring to make a challenge

to jump on the bus
to join an activity already well under way

to jump straight in at the deep end
to do something without proper preparation

to jump that hurdle when one comes to it
to deal with a particular problem only when it becomes necessary to do so

to jump the gun
to start before one is meant to
refers to a starting pistol in a race

to jump through hoops
to be required to perform or undergo some ordeal
refers to circus performance

to jump to a conclusion
to infer something without proper consideration

to jump to attention
to show respect

to jump up and down
to show excitement or anger or frustration

to nearly jump out of one's skin
to receive a fright

to see which way the cat jumps
to await developments

to want to jump all one's fences at once
unrealistically to want to solve all problems at once, rather than sequentially
refers to steeplechasing on horseback

you can jump in the lake
I intend to take no notice whatsoever of you or your views

jumper

stick it up your jumper
I have absolutely no interest in you and what you saying!
refers to the jumpers worn by members of football teams

jungle

a jungle
a place where everyone makes his or her own rules

the law of the jungle
the principle that those having power will use it at the expense of all others
Rudyard Kipling (1865–1936), *The Law of the Jungle*, 'Now this is the law of the jungle — as old and as true as the sky; and the wolf that shall keep it may

prosper, but the wolf that shall break it must die'

jury

the jury is still out
no decision has yet been made; OR there has not yet been an indication as to how the matter is viewed in the community

justice

the wheels of justice grind slowly
it takes a long time to get a decision from the courts of law
Friedrich von Logau (1604–55), *Sinngedichte* (translated by H. W. Longfellow), 'Though the mills of God grind slowly, yet they grind exceeding small; though with patience he stands waiting, with exactness grinds he all'

K

keel

to keep something on an even keel
to ensure that something is kept balanced and stable
nautical metaphor

keelhaul

to keelhaul someone
to rebuke or castigate harshly
refers to ancient nautical punishment of hauling an offender underneath a ship from one side to the other — the result often being fatal

keep

keep your shirt on!
relax!
refers to removing a shirt in preparation for a fight

to be unable to keep people away with a big stick
to be faced with a large crowd or much demand

to keep a civil tongue in one's head
to be polite, especially under provocation

to keep a cool head
to stay calm and rational in a crisis
Rudyard Kipling (1865–1936), *If*, 'If you can keep your head when all about you are losing theirs ... '

to keep a level head
to stay calm and rational in a crisis
Rudyard Kipling (1865–1936), *If*, 'If you can keep your head when all about you are losing theirs ... '

to keep a tally
to keep a record
from Latin *talea* (a rod or stick); refers to a stick with notches (made to indicate a count), the stick then being split lengthways and each party to a transaction receiving one half as a record of the transaction

to keep a weather eye out for something
to look out with particular care
nautical metaphor; refers to the eye that is turned towards the wind

to keep an ear to the ground
to be well informed as to current developments
refers to listening for distant sound by applying one's ear to the ground

to keep body and soul together
barely to stay alive

to keep off someone's patch
not to interfere with or compete against another person in that person's customary area of activity

to keep one's chin up
to maintain one's morale

to keep one's cotton-picking fingers off something
not to interfere (in a meddlesome fashion) with something

to keep one's distance
to avoid familiarity

to keep one's ears open
to be alert for useful information

to keep one's eye on someone
to supervise a person

to keep one's eye on something
to monitor a situation

to keep one's eyes open
to be on the lookout for useful information

to keep one's eyes peeled for something
to be on the constant lookout for something
refers to keeping the eyelids open

to keep one's fingers crossed
to hope for a good outcome
refers to making the sign of the Christian cross to protect against ill-fortune

to keep one's hair on
to remain calm in a crisis
Shakespeare, *Macbeth* I:iii, ' … whose horrid image doth unfix my hair'

to keep one's hand in
to engage in activities that reinforce skills that one has previously acquired

to keep one's head
to remain calm in a crisis or unexpectedly to retain an elected or appointed position
Rudyard Kipling (1865–1936), *If*, 'If you can keep your head when all about you are losing theirs … '

to keep one's head down
to stay out of trouble, AND/OR to work very diligently

to keep one's mouth shut
not to discuss some matter

to keep one's nose clean
to act with circumspection and honesty despite temptation to do otherwise

to keep one's nose out of something
not to meddle in something

to keep one's nose to the grindstone
to work with particular diligence
refers to having one's head down low while working on a grindstone sharpening tools

to keep one's pecker up
to stay cheerful
refers to keeping one's head up (with 'pecker' referring to mouth — as in a bird's mouth)

to keep one's powder dry
to retain key arguments or resources in reserve for use later
refers to gunpowder in battle

to keep out of someone's hair
to let someone get on with that person's work in his or her own way

to keep someone in a strait jacket
to deny a person any discretionary powers at all
refers to a restraining 'jacket' used to control violent or insane persons

to keep someone in the dark
deliberately to keep a person uninformed

to keep someone on that person's toes
to induce a person to be eager and alert

to keep someone posted
to keep a person informed

to keep someone's seat warm
to hold a position temporarily with a view to another person's taking it over permanently in the near future

to keep something dark
to keep something secret

to keep something for a rainy day
to keep something in reserve for bad times

to keep something on an even keel
to ensure that something is kept balanced and stable
nautical metaphor

to keep something under one's hat
to maintain a confidence

to keep something under wraps
to keep a matter confidential, especially pending an official announcement

to keep something up one's sleeve
secretly to retain something in reserve for use in the future or at a later stage of negotiations
refers to playing cards or magicians

to keep tabs on something
to monitor something

to keep the ball rolling
to take advantage of the existing momentum or to participate actively

to keep the home fires burning
to maintain normal domestic activity during the temporary absence of the main provider of the household

to keep the jackals at bay
to pay one's creditors just sufficient to avoid repercussions
James Thomson (1700–48), Autumn, 'He stands at bay, and puts his last weak refuge in despair' — description of a stag

to keep the lid on something
to keep a matter under control
refers to cooking

to keep the pot boiling
to ensure that an issue stays current

refers to cooking

to keep the wolf from the door
to struggle to survive (esp. with respect to hunger)

to keep track of something
to be completely aware of where something is and how it is functioning
refers to hunting

to keep up with the ball
to maintain awareness of a situation

to keep up with the Joneses
to maintain a lifestyle beyond one's means in order to match that of some neighbourhood role model
refers to keeping pace with Jones amid pomp, but whether this relates to the metaphor is problematical: William Wordsworth (1770–1850), *Jones! As from Calais* (1807), 'Jones! as from Calais southward you and I went pacing side by side, this public way streamed with the pomp of a too-credulous day'

why keep a dog and bark oneself?
it is silly to pay for assistance and then do things personally

keeper

to let something go to the keeper
to deliberately ignore a particular incident
refers to cricket

keepers

keepers of the flame
persons entrusted to maintain old traditions and keen to do so
refers to those entrusted with keeping a sacred flame of remembrance alight

kettle

the pot calling the kettle black
criticising another person without realising one's own even greater shortcomings

to be a different kettle of fish
to be something very dissimilar
refers to a riverside picnic where freshly caught fish is cooked and eaten

to be a fine kettle of fish
to be a terrible muddle
refers to a riverside picnic where freshly caught fish is cooked and eaten

key

to strike the right key
to make comments that set the appropriate tone in a speech or conversation
refers to music

keynote

keynote address
opening address, designed to set the theme of a conference
refers to music

kick

a free kick
an advantageous opportunity accorded to a person
refers to football

a kick in the pants
an admonition

a kick in the shins
an unexpected and undeserved setback

I could kick myself
I regret that I acted thus

to kick a man when he is down
to take unfair advantage of a person already in difficulty

to kick heads in
to demonstrate extreme annoyance at, or dislike of, certain persons

to kick in
to contribute financially

to kick off
to start some action
refers to football

to kick one's heels
to be kept waiting

to kick over the traces
to become insubordinate
refers to the straps designed to keep a horse restrained

to kick some proposal around
to examine a proposal from all angles
refers to football

to kick someone around
to abuse a person

to kick someone in the guts
to take action needlessly hurtful to another person

to kick someone in the teeth
to inflict a grave or humiliating setback, criticism, or punishment upon a person

to kick someone out
to expel a person

to kick someone upstairs
to promote a person to a purely ceremonial position
to kick the bucket
to die
to kick the cat
to take out one's anger on some innocent party
to kick the communist can
to take every opportunity to exacerbate fear of communism in others to kick up a fuss
to create a commotion

kicking

to be alive and kicking
to be in good form
to drag someone kicking and screaming to do something
to force a person into some action that the person is most reluctant to undertake

kid

to be the new kid on the block
to lack the experience of others
to treat someone with kid gloves
to handle a person with great discretion
refers to very soft leather gloves made from the skin of young goats

kill

to be dressed to kill
to be very smartly dressed with the intention of making a striking impression — usually with a view to a romantic or sexual conquest
to be in at the kill
to be present at the climatic finish to something
refers to hunting
to kill oneself laughing
to be greatly amused
to kill some proposal stone dead
to take action that stops a proposal completely
refers to death by stoning
to kill the fatted calf
to demonstrate welcome and complete acceptance of another person
Luke 15:23. 'And bring hither the fatted calf and let us eat, and be merry'
to kill the goose that lays the golden eggs
through excessive greed, to sacrifice future gains for a short-term advantage
based on a Greek fable about a man who killed the goose that laid golden eggs; his aim was to collect the whole stock of eggs at once but, in doing so, he ended his future supply
to kill two birds with one stone
to achieve a second objective in the course of achieving the first objective

killed

to be killed in the rush
to be the supplier of something extremely popular

killing

to make a killing
to be in a very successful business venture

kindred

kindred spirit
person with similar interests and eccentricities
John Keats (1795–1821), *O Solitude!*, 'Almost the highest bliss of human-kind, / when to thy haunts two kindred spirits flee'

king

a cat may look at a king
don't give yourself airs!
to pay a king's ransom
to pay a very large sum

kingmaker

kingmaker
person engaging in behind-the-scenes activities to promote another person to a particular leadership position

kiss

to be the kiss of death
to be something intended to be helpful but resulting in total destruction
to kiss and make up
to reconcile differences that one has with another person
to kiss something good-bye
to give something up as permanently lost
to kiss the ground
to revere or bless the land; OR to be overthrown
to kiss the rod

to accept punishment meekly
Shakespeare, *The Two Gentlemen of Verona* I:ii, 'and presently all humbled kiss the rod!'

kit

to have a field marshal's bâton in one's kit
to be ambitious
variously attributed:
Louis XVIII (1755–1824), 'There is not one of you who has not in his knapsack the field marshal's bâton; it is up to you to bring it out' (speech to the Saint-Cyr cadets, 9 Aug. 1819, *Moniteur*, 10 Aug. 1819);
Napoleon I (1769–1821), 'Every French soldier carries in his cartridge-pouch the bâton of a marshal of France'; Mark Pattison (1813–84), 'Every private in the French army carries in his haversack the bâton of a marshal'

kitchen

everything but the kitchen sink
virtually all things
if one can't stand the heat one should stay out of the kitchen
if one cannot put up with the pressure of a situation, one should get out of it
US President Harry S. Truman (1884–1972), *Mr Citizen*, ch. 15, 'If you can't stand the heat, get out of the kitchen'
to get the rounds of the kitchen
(of a husband) to be subject to personal abuse by his wife

kite

to fly a kite
to issue uncovered cheques in the hope that they will be covered before clearance; OR to test public reaction to a measure in contemplation by leaking broad details of it to the media

kittens

to have kittens
to be in a state of great dismay
refers to a superstition that certain acts would cause women to bear kittens instead of children

knee

a knee-jerk reaction
a response made instantaneously and without any proper consideration
since that person was knee-high to a grasshopper
since that person was a very young child

kneed

weak-kneed
unassertive or irresolute

knees

to be cut off at the knees
to have a pet project aborted
to beg on bended knees
to request in great earnestness
to force someone on to that person's knees
to inflict a humiliating defeat on a person
to go down on one's hands and knees to someone
with great humility to ask a favour of a person

knell

to sound the death knell of something
to indicate the impending end of something
refers to the knell (sound) of a bell rung at a funeral; Shakespeare, *Macbeth* II:i, 'The bell invites me ... it is a knell that summons thee to heaven or to hell'

knickers

to get one's knickers in a knot
to become unduly excited

knife

before one can say 'knife'
very quickly
one could have cut the atmosphere with a knife
those present were very tense
to be on a knife edge
to be in danger; OR to be a very close result
to hold a knife at someone's throat
to exert undue pressure on another person in an endeavour to achieve a result that would otherwise not be forthcoming
to stick a knife into someone
to act vindictively towards a person
to wield the knife
to terminate the services of one or more persons or to prune expenditure

knives

the knives are out
there is an active campaign against someone

to sharpen the knives
to get ready for a concerted attack on a person or principle

knight

a knight in shining armour
a person who comes to the rescue; a champion
derived from mediaeval tales of valiant knights rescuing those in distress

a white knight
a person voluntarily coming to the assistance of another person at considerable personal cost
derived from mediaeval tales of valiant knights rescuing those in distress, white being associated with purity and goodness

knit

to knit one's brows
to indicate one's displeasure

knitting

to stick to one's knitting
to confine oneself to what one is used to doing

knock

on the deathknock
at the last possible moment
refers to the mythical figure of 'Death' knocking on the door to claim a victim

that person couldn't knock the skin off a rice pudding
that person is weak or ineffective

to knock an idea on the head
utterly to reject a proposal

to knock on doors
to seek out opportunities

to knock someone off that person's perch
to displace a person from a leadership position in some competitive situation

to knock something into a cocked hat
to defeat easily in a game or contest of skill
refers to a game of nine-pins in which the pins were arranged in a triangle like a cocked hat

to knock the stuffing out of someone
to demoralise a person completely

to knock two heads together
to make two persons come to their senses and deal with each other

knot

to cut the Gordian knot
to solve, especially by force, a virtually insoluble problem
refers to a complicated knot tied by Gordius and eventually cut by Alexander the Great

to get into a knot
to get into state of confusion

to get one's knickers in a knot
to become unduly excited

to tie the knot
to marry
may refer to the knotted girdles worn by brides in ancient Greece

knots

at a rate of knots
very fast
nautical metaphor; refers to the original measure of a ships's speed by noting the rate at which the ship passed a regular series of knots tied in a rope which was maintained in position beside the ship

know

by their fruits ye shall know them
their true nature will be revealed by their results
Matthew 7:20, 'wherefore by their fruits ye shall know them'

I don't know whether I'm Arthur or Martha
I'm confused

not to know someone from Adam
to be unable to recognise a person
refers to the name of the first man as recorded in *Genesis* 2

the devil one knows is better than the devil one does not know
the status quo is more comfortable than change

the left hand does not know what the right hand is doing
a person or an organisation is not aware of inconsistencies in conduct
Matthew 6:3, 'But when you give alms, do not let your left hand know what your right hand is doing'

to know a thing or two about something
to have acquired a lifetime of cunning about a subject

to know how many beans make five
to have common sense
refers to an old riddle

to know on which side one's bread is buttered
to be aware of the important personally advantageous considerations

to know one's mind
to form and adhere to an opinion

to know one's onions
to be well informed in some area
refers to Dr C. T. Onions, editor of the *Shorter Oxford English Dictionary*

to know something in one's heart of hearts
to know something — although reluctant to admit it, even to oneself
Shakespeare, *Hamlet* III:ii, 'In my heart's core, ay, in my heart of heart'

to know something inside out
to know something very thoroughly

to know the ropes
to know how to do one's job
nautical metaphor

to know where one stands
to know what one supports or how one is affected

to know where the shoe pinches
to realise from personal experience what the cause of some problem really is

to know which way to turn
to know which strategy to adopt or where to seek assistance

knows

as every schoolboy knows
as is recognised by everyone
Jonathon Swift (1667–1745), *The Country Life*, 1:81,'How haughtily he cocks his nose, / To tell what every schoolboy knows'; Lord Macaulay (1800–59), *Lord Clive* (Jan. 1840), 'Every schooboy knows who imprisoned Montezuma, and who strangled Atahualpa'

father knows best
as an expert, I know better than you do what is most suitable for you

heaven only knows
it is not known to me or anyone else

the devil one knows is better than the devil one does not know
the status quo is more comfortable than change

knuckles

to rap someone over the knuckles
to admonish a person

kosher

to be kosher
to fulfil all requirements
refers to food complying with all aspects of Jewish religious law; Hebrew *kaser* ('fit, proper')

L

L-plates

to have L-plates
to be new to a task
refers to learner's plates on the vehicle of a novice driver

label

to give something a label
to classify something

labour

to labour mightily and bring forth a mouse
to be quite ineffective

lace

strait-laced
puritanical
refers to the wearing of a very tightly laced bodice or other garment

ladder

rungs up a ladder
gradual steps to an ultimate goal

to be at the bottom of the ladder
to be in the most junior position in some hierarchy

ladders

a game of snakes and ladders
a series of ups and downs
refers to a board game

lady

it's not over until the fat lady sings
it is not finished yet

probably refers to operatic performances, but during a radio broadcast made by the present author, a listener suggested that the metaphor refers to Kate Smith singing the US national anthem

laid

to be a laid-down misPre

to be very easily accomplished and/or to be certain of outcome

refers to card playing where one player undertakes not to win any tricks while playing with the disadvantage of having that player's cards exposed to observation by others

lake

you can jump in the lake

I intend to take no notice whatsoever of you or your views

lamb

a lamb led to slaughter

a naVve person allowing himself or herself to be exploited

Isaiah 53:5, 'He was oppressed, and he was afflicted, yet he opened not his mouth: he is brought as a lamb to the slaughter'

one might as well be hanged for a sheep as for a lamb

further action will not increase the adverse consequences already in train

refers to the stealing of either sheep or lambs being capital crimes under old English law

sacrificial lamb

somebody unfairly made to suffer for the mistakes of others

Exodus 29:41, 'Sacrifice the other lamb at twilight ... an offering made to the Lord by fire'

to be mutton dressed up as lamb

foolishly to pretend to be younger

to wait two shakes of a lamb's tail

to wait just a few moments

lame

a lame dog

a person under some disadvantage needing attention and assistance

a lame duck

a person unable to fend for himself or herself

a 'lame-duck president' is a president still in office but without influence because the commencement of the successor's term is imminent

land

a land of milk and honey

a country in which everything is in abundant supply

Exodus 3:8, ' ... to bring them up out of that land unto a good land ... flowing with milk and honey'

to ascertain the lie of the land

to establish the pertinent facts and opinions

to be in cloud-cuckoo land

to be mad or to have unrealistic expectations

'cloud-cuckoo land' was an imaginary city built in the air by the birds (according to the *Nephelococcygia* of *The Birds* by Aristophanes) — hence any utopian fantastic scheme

to be in the land of the living

to be alive

to land something

to achieve something

refers to angling

landmark

a landmark ruling

a decision marking an important change or development in the state of affairs'

landscape

to be part of the landscape

to be present and fully accepted without question

landslide

a landslide

an electoral result involving victory or defeat by a very large margin

lane

life in the fast lane

existence full of exciting, high-pressure activity

to go down memory lane

to reminisce

language

to speak the same language

to have a good understanding and similar ideas

lap

to be in the lap of the gods

to be a matter of apparent chance beyond human control
refers to wax tablets inscribed with requests and placed on the knees of statues of Greek gods

to drop into one's lap
to turn up fortuitously

to dump something in someone's lap
to impose an unwelcome responsibility on another person

to lap it up
to enjoy the attention

large

to be a small cog in a large wheel
to be a relatively unimportant person in a large organisation

larger

larger than life
exaggerated; more than normal

lark

to rise with the lark
to get up early

last

a cobbler should stick to his last
a person should confine himself or herself to activities for which that person has been trained

the last bastion
the only remaining defensive measure

the last of the Mohicans
to be the last of a group
refers to a near-extinct tribe of North American natives; title of a novel by James Fenimore Cooper (1789–1851)

the last (or final) straw
the latest step, which, when added to a large number of seemingly harmless previous steps, sets off a sudden significant event resulting from the cumulative effect
see 'the straw that broke the camel's back'

to be on one's last legs
to be nearly worn out

to have come down in the last shower
to be naVve
refers to someone having just arrived with the last shower of rain

to make a last-ditch stand
to make a brave effort to stave off final defeat
King William III (1650–1702), 'There is one way never to see it lost ... and that is to die in the last ditch' (quoted by Burnet, *History of His Own Times*,1715)

to play the last card in the pack
to be forced to use one's last expedient
refers to playing cards

to squeeze the last drop out of something
to get the maximum advantage out of some favourable situation

late

late in the day
when a project is well advanced

lather

to get a lather up/to whip oneself into a lather
to become unduly excited
refers to horses sweating profusely when excited

laugh

to laugh all the way to the bank
to appreciate one's good fortune

to laugh one's head off
to enjoy something greatly

to laugh something out of court
to ridicule a proposition as having no basis whatsoever
refers to courts of law

to laugh up one's sleeve
to laugh surreptitiously

you will laugh on the other side of your face
you will regret this

laughing

to kill oneself laughing
to be greatly amused

laundry

a laundry list
a large set of demands

laurels

to look to one's laurels
to be careful not to lose one's reputation for some skill
refers to laurel wreaths presented to winners of events at the ancient Olympics

to rest on one's laurels

to use a reputation for success earned in earlier times as a substitute for current endeavour

refers to laurel wreaths presented to winners of events at the ancient Olympics

law

Murphy's law

the principle that everything that can go wrong will go wrong

Parkinson's law

the principle that work expands to match the work capacity available

title of a book (1957) by Prof. C. Northcote Parkinson

the law of the jungle

the principle that those having power will use it at the expense of all others

Rudyard Kipling (1865–1936), *The Law of the Jungle*, 'Now this is the law of the jungle — as old and as true as the sky; and the wolf that shall keep it may prosper, but the wolf that shall break it must die'

to lay down the law

to be officious

lawyer

a bush lawyer

a person without legal qualifications who has a reasonable, although not perfect, knowledge of the law, and who likes to make technical points in arguments

lay

not to lay a finger on someone

to refrain from hurting a person

to be able to lay one's hands on something

to be able to locate something

to lay a proposal on the table

to make a proposal available for discussion or to adjourn discussion on a proposal for an indefinite period

to lay down the law

to be officious

to lay it on the line

to make clear what the accepted rules of behaviour are

to lay it on with a trowel

to flatter, eulogise, or otherwise make comment in an excessive manner

Shakespeare, *As You Like It* I:ii, 'Well said; that was laid on with a trowel'

to lay one's cards on the table

to be utterly frank and open or to honestly disclose one's position

refers to playing cards

to lay one's hands on something

to acquire or find something

to lay some theory to rest

to abandon some theory as being no longer appropriate

refers to death —as in 'laying out' (preparing a corpse for disposal), or as in 'laying someone to rest' (at a funeral)

lays

to kill the goose that lays the golden eggs

through excessive greed, to sacrifice future gains for a short-term advantage

based on a Greek fable about a man who killed the goose that laid golden eggs; his aim was to collect the whole stock of eggs at once but, in doing so, he ended his future supply

lead

all roads lead to Rome

all alternatives will have the same outcome

refers to roads radiating from the great imperial capital to all parts of the Roman empire

one can lead a horse to water, but one can't make it drink

one can give advice to a person but cannot ensure that it will be acted on

to go down like a lead balloon

to receive a very cool reception

to have lead in one's saddlebags

to work with a handicap

refers to horse-racing handicaps in which lead in the saddlebags makes winning more difficult

to lead a dog's life

to be ill-treated

to lead someone a merry dance

to mislead a person

refers to the complex dances of earlier centuries when one person led another through complex steps

to lead someone by the nose

to induce another person to comply with one's wishes

refers to leading animals (such as bulls) by a ring through the nose

to lead someone up the garden path

to mislead a person by deliberately fallacious arguments

to lead with one's chin

by one's brash behaviour to virtually invite one's opponents to take action against one

refers to boxing

to swing the lead

to cheat an employer by not working while being paid to do so or by malingering; to avoid work or some other task by concocting a plausible excuse for not doing it, or by pretending to be ill

originally referred to a leadsman lazily swinging the line, rather than getting on with taking soundings

leading

a leading edge

an advantage through possession of the latest technology or knowledge

refers to the foremost edge of an aircraft's wings

a leading question

a question phrased in such a way as to suggest the answer

a legal term, often misused by lay speakers who really mean merely 'a very pertinent question'

the blind leading the blind

persons without the necessary skills for a task purporting to impart those skills to others

Matthew 15:14, 'And if the blind lead the blind, both shall fall into the ditch'

to be the leading light

to be the most important person in a venture

Exodus 13:21, 'And the Lord went before them by day in a pillar of a cloud, to lead them the way; and by night in a pillar of fire, to give them light'

leaf

to take a leaf out of someone's book

to model oneself on another person

refers to taking a page from the 'Book of Life' — *Rev* 20: 12, 'and the books were opened ... and the dead were judged out of those things that were written in the books, according to their works'

to turn over a new leaf

to reform

refers to turning over a page in the 'Book of Life' — *Rev* 20: 12, 'and the books were opened ... and the dead were judged out of those things that were written in the books, according to their works'

league

to be in the same league

to have comparable skills

refers to sporting competitions

lean

a shoulder to lean on

sympathy

lean and hungry

efficient

Shakespeare, *Julius Caesar* I:ii, 'Yond' Cassius has a lean and hungry look; he thinks too much: such men are dangerous'

to lean on someone

to utilise the support of another person; OR to pressure another person to do something against that person's inclination

leap

a leap in the dark

a decisive move into the unknown

Thomas Hobbes (1588–1679), 'I am about to take my last voyage, a great leap in the dark' (quoted by Watkins, *Anecdotes of Men of Learning*)

a quantum leap

a gigantic step forward

a term derived from quantum mechanics

to leap at an idea

to accept a suggestion enthusiastically

to leap-frog something

to overtake something, with the likelihood of, in turn, being overtaken

refers to a game in which participants jump over each other in turn

to leap in

to commence an activity without considering the wisdom of doing so or the best way to proceed

leaps

by leaps and bounds

with surprisingly fast progress

learn

to learn a lesson

to benefit from one's experience

to learn something from the horse's mouth
to get information from someone qualified to impart it
refers to the examination of a horse's teeth for an accurate assessment of its age

to learn the ropes
to be taught the elementary features
nautical metaphor

lease

a new lease of life
the prospect of a better existence from now on, or of better functioning after repair

leash

to hold someone on a short leash
to give a person very little freedom
refers to a lead used to restrain coursing hounds

least

to take the line of least resistance
to follow the easiest course of action
refers to the route taken by the shockwaves of a buried explosive charge in reaching the surface of the earth

leave

to leave no stone unturned
to be very thorough
refers to an instruction from the oracle of Delphi regarding a search for Persian treasure (477 BC)

to leave one's mark on something
to be responsible for permanently altering the way something is operated
refers to the practice of illiterate persons making their 'mark' upon documents — usually signified by the sign of the cross preceded or followed by the person's name

to leave oneself wide open
to act in such a way that one's opponents will find much that can be easily criticised
refers to a bodily posture that is vulnerable to attack

to leave others for dead
to be vastly superior

to leave someone cold
to fail to impress a person

to leave someone high and dry
to isolate a person from a desired involvement; to withdraw all support from a person
nautical metaphor referring to a boat stranded out of water

to leave someone in the lurch
to desert a person who is in difficulties
refers to the score in certain games — especially cribbage

to leave someone out in the cold
to be excluded, ignored or neglected

to leave someone reeling
to leave a person in a state of shock

to leave something up in the air
to have an unresolved problem

to leave the door open
to provide an opportunity

leaving

a case of rats leaving a sinking ship
the desertion of an enterprise in anticipation of imminent failure

without leaving any footprints
without making any impression

led

a lamb led to slaughter
a naVve person allowing himself or herself to be exploited
Isaiah 53:5, 'He was oppressed, and he was afflicted, yet he opened not his mouth: he is brought as a lamb to the slaughter'

leech

leech
person taking undue advantage of others
refers to the blood-sucking activities of leeches

leeway

to make up leeway
to get back to a normal position or to get to the position held by one's competitors
refers to the drift of a ship to leeward of the desired course

left

a left-handed compliment
a thinly disguised insult

the left hand does not know what the right hand is doing

a person or an organisation is not aware of inconsistencies in conduct
Matthew 6:3, 'But when you give alms, do not let your left hand know what your right hand is doing'

to be left holding the baby
to be forced to accept responsibility for someone else's problems

to be left with a nasty taste in one's mouth
to be appalled or very disappointed at another person's unethical behaviour to one

to have two left feet
to be clumsy

leg

not to have a leg to stand on
to have one's arguments completely demolished; OR to be without acceptable excuse or explanation

to cost an arm and a leg
to be excessively expensive

to do the leg work
to carry out the part of a project that requires actually physically walking around and collecting information, etc.

to give someone a leg up
to give a person some assistance
refers to mounting a horse

to have a leg in
to have an opportunity which has the potential to lead to bigger things

to pull someone's leg
to tell a false but plausible story as an act of humour

to shake a leg
to hurry up

to talk the hind leg off a donkey
to talk excessively

legs

not to have any legs
(of an argument) to be unacceptable

the idea has legs
this notion seems a good one

to be on one's last legs
to be nearly worn out

to have one's tail between one's legs
to be dejected or humiliated
refers to dogs

to stand up on one's hind legs
to assert one's authority
refers to animals adopting aggressive posture

leg-rope

to put a leg-rope on someone
to give a person very little freedom
refers to a restraining rope on cattle on other animals

lemon

the answer is a lemon
there is no appropriate answer to that sort of proposition

to sell someone a lemon
to sell a person a grossly defective product on the basis that it represents quality

to squeeze the lemon dry
to get the maximum advantage out of some favourable situation
Sir Eric Geddes (1875–1937), 'The Germans ... are going to pay every penny; they are going to be squeezed, as a lemon is squeezed — until the pips squeak. My only doubt is not whether we can squeeze hard enough, but whether there is enough juice.' (10 December 1918)

lend

to lend a hand
to assist

to lend one's name to something
to endorse something

to lend someone an ear
to pay attention to a person
Shakespeare, *Julius Caesar* III:ii, 'Friends, Romans, countrymen, lend me your ears'

to lend weight to something
to use one's influence in support of some cause

length

at arm's length
between parties who are strangers bearing no special duty to each other and who have no financial or other relationship with each other
a legal term

lengths

to go to great lengths
to take much trouble

leopard

a leopard cannot change its spots

each person is born with certain unalterable characteristics

Jeremiah 13:23, 'Can the Ethiopian change his skin, or the leopard his spots?'

lesson

to drive the lesson home

to take certain action that is unpleasant but that has the effect of registering a message

to learn a lesson

to benefit from one's experience

to teach someone a lesson

to inflict something unpleasant on a person in the hope that it will lead to a change in that person's behaviour

let

not to let grass grow under one's feet

not to let inertia or delay spoil something

let the cards fall where they may

irrespective of what happens

refers to playing cards

to let blood

to allow some harm as the price for achieving some greater benefit

refers to surgical removal of a patient's blood

to let fly at someone

to launch a verbal or physical assault on a person

to let it all hang out

to be uninhibited; to unburden oneself

to let off steam

to engage in noisy or robust activity as a form of relaxation

refers to release of pressure from a boiler

to let one's hair down

to relax

to let one's head go

to do as one wants to

refers to letting a horse have its head (and run as it wishes to)

to let one's heart rule one's head

to act on emotion rather than on reason

George Colman the younger (1762–1836), *Who Wants a Guinea?*, 'His heart runs away with his head'

to let sleeping dogs lie

to refrain from raising an issue that is not obviously requiring attention

to let someone off the hook

to allow a person to escape the adverse consequences of that person's own actions

refers to angling

to let something go to the keeper

to deliberately ignore a particular incident

refers to cricket

to let something slip through one's fingers

to allow something to escape from one's ownership or control

to let the cat out of the bag

to reveal an embarrassing secret

refers to the practice of selling a person a cat (purported to be a pig) in a bag (or poke) — hence 'a pig in a poke'; if the person opened the bag and looked inside, that person 'let the cat out of the bag'

to let the genie out of the bottle

to cause something irreversible to take place

'genie' was adopted (to refer to a spirit released from a bottle) by the French translators of *Arabian Nights' Entertainments*

move over and let the greyhound see the rabbit

stand aside to allow things to get under way

refers to hunting with greyhounds

letter

a dead letter

a rule still in existence but no longer observed in practice

a red-letter day

an important occasion

refers to the colour used to indicate days of obligation in the Christian Church missal — as opposed to black-letter days, which are optional days

letting

bloodletting

removal (perhaps violent) of persons from office or employment

refers to surgical removal of a patient's blood

level

a level playing field

competition on equal terms

level best

making all possible effort

perhaps refers to railways

level-headed

rational

to be level pegging

(of contestants) to have little between them

refers to cribbage

to be on the level

to be honest

a term derived from freemasonry

to keep a level head

to stay calm and rational in a crisis

Rudyard Kipling (1865–1936), *If*, 'If you can keep your head when all about you are losing theirs ... '

water will find its own level

people will reach an appropriate position relative to others

level-headed

level-headed

rational

Liberty

Liberty Hall

a place where one is free to do as one wishes

Oliver Goldsmith (1730–74), *She Stoops to Conquer* ii, 'This is Liberty Hall gentlemen'

licence

a licence to print money

a lucrative government-conferred monopoly or privilege

Lord Thomson of Fleet (1894–1977), 'It's just like having a licence to print your own money' (after the opening of Scottish commercial television, as recorded in Braddon, *Roy Thomson of Fleet Street*)

lick

to lick one's chops

to look forward to something with pleasurable anticipation

refers to salivation in anticipation of food

to lick one's wounds

to adjust oneself to defeat

refers to a dog cleaning its own wounds

to lick someone's boots

to show humility

to lick something into shape

to make something presentable and effective

refers to mediaeval belief that bear cubs are born shapeless and have to be licked into shape by their mothers — a story related in the encyclopaedia of the Arab physician Avicenna (970–1037)

lid

to blow the lid off something

to expose something no matter how embarrassing this might be

to keep the lid on something

to keep a matter under control

refers to cooking

lie

a white lie

a false statement uttered in a good cause

one has made one's bed and one will now have to lie on it

one has to bear the consequences of one's actions

to ascertain the lie of the land

to establish the pertinent facts and opinions

to let sleeping dogs lie

to refrain from raising an issue that is not obviously requiring attention

to lie low

to stay inconspicuous

to nail a lie

to expose an untruth

lies

uneasy lies the head that wears a crown

leadership involves some risks and some burdens (esp. the risk of being deposed)

Shakespeare, *Henry IV*, Part 2, III:i, 'Uneasy lies the head that wears a crown'

life

a new lease of life

the prospect of a better existence from now on, or of better functioning after repair

I cannot for the life of me

I just cannot

larger than life

exaggerated; more than normal

life in the fast lane

existence full of exciting, high-pressure activity

life raft
financial assistance sufficient to avert insolvency

not on your life
definitely not

to be the life and soul of the party
to be the prime enthusiast for a cause
Shakespeare, *A Midsummer Night's Dream*, 'My love, my life, my soul, fair Helena!'

to breathe life into a corpse
to revive something moribund

to lead a dog's life
to be ill-treated

to save someone's life
to be of great help to a person

you can bet your life on something
something is certain to happen

lifeblood

the lifeblood
the main or essential ingredient; OR the person or factor instilling enthusiasm

lifeline

to throw someone a lifeline
to give significant assistance to a person

lift

not to lift a finger to help someone
to refuse to assist

to lift one's game
to raise the standard of one's performance

light

a highlight
a particularly important item
originally refers (1658) to a a term from art (painting)

a chink of light
a small hope of a solution or breakthrough

a light in the sky
a sign of great hope

guiding light
a principle or example to follow in any activity
Exodus 13:21, 'And the Lord went before them by day in a pillar of a cloud, to lead them the way; and by night in a pillar of fire, to give them light'

in the cold light of day
in an unemotional atmosphere at a later stage

light dawns
the point is understood

light on the hill
distant goal acting as an inspiration
usually attributed to Australian prime minister, Ben Chifley (1949)

light-fingered
habitually likely to steal
William Makepeace Thackeray (1811–63), 'The light-fingered gentry pick pockets furiously'

shining light
eminent or scholarly person
John 5:35, 'He [John the Baptist] was a burning and a shining light'

to be in the limelight
to be exposed to public attention
refers to an invention by Thomas Drummond (1797–1840) in 1826 by which a bright light was produced from combustion of hydrogen and oxygen on a surface of lime; came to be used in the theatre to beam a powerful light on one person to the exclusion of others

to be the leading light
to be the most important person in a venture
Exodus 13:21, 'And the Lord went before them by day in a pillar of a cloud, to lead them the way; and by night in a pillar of fire, to give them light'

to bring something to light
to draw to public attention

to get the red light
to be forbidden to do something
refers to the 'stop' signal on roads and rail

to give the green light
to grant permission
refers to the 'go' signal on roads and rail

to hide one's light under a bushel
to keep others in ignorance of one's skills and experience
Luke 11:33, 'No man, when he hath lighted a candle, putteth it in a secret place, neither under a bushel'

to light a fuse
to set in train processes that will cause a serious reaction
refers to explosives

to see someone in a good light
to regard a person favourably

to see the light
to understand the real situation
refers to the conversion of Saul (Paul) on the road to Damascus, *Acts* 9:3, 4 'And suddenly there shined round about him a light from heaven: and he fell to the earth'

to see the light at the end of the tunnel
to perceive relief at the imminent end of a period of prolonged difficulty

to see the light of day
to be made public

to shed light on something
to give explanations

to steal the spotlight
to become the centre of attention
refers to the theatre

to turn the spotlight on something
to draw public attention to something

lightly

to tread lightly
to be careful

lightning

a lightning rod
a person or thing used to attract trouble in order to divert that trouble away safely
refers to a metallic rod or wire fixed to the top of a building to divert lightning

lights

to see red lights flashing
to be conscious of the danger
refers to the 'stop' signal on roads and rail, or perhaps to lights on an emergency vehicle

lightweight

lightweight
uninfluential
refers to boxing

Lilliputian

Lilliputian
small
refers to a place in *Gulliver's Travels* (1726) by Jonathon Swift (1667–1745)

lily

lily-livered
cowardly
refers to a supersitition that the liver of a coward contained no blood

lily-white
honest and incorruptible
based on a belief that the lily sprang from the tears of Eve as she left the Garden of Eden; the lily is traditionally a symbol of purity and innocence in Christian art

to gild the lily
to add superfluous ornamentation to something already beautiful
Shakespeare *King John* IV:i, 'to gild refined gold, to paint the lily'

limb

to go out on a limb
to put oneself in an isolated or stranded position

limbo

to be in limbo
to have one's ultimate fate yet to be determined
refers to the region (in Christian belief) on the border of hell; neither heaven nor hell

to consign something to limbo
to consider something as being in a temporary state of inaction pending future developments
refers to the region (in Christian belief) on the border of hell; neither heaven nor hell

limelight

to be in the limelight
to be exposed to public attention
refers to an invention by Thomas Drummond (1797–1840) in 1826 by which a bright light was produced from combustion of hydrogen and oxygen on a surface of lime; came to be used in the theatre to beam a powerful light on one person to the exclusion of others

limit

the sky is the limit
there is no restriction upon what can be done

linchpin

linchpin
an essential person or feature central to a project
refers to a pin passed through an axle-end to keep a wheel in position

line

hook, line, and sinker
wholly
refers to angling

someone's job is on the line

a person's career path is under consideration; AND/OR that person's present position is at risk

the bottom line
the conclusion that matters or the net effect of a series of developments
refers to the last line is a series of calculations or accounts

the Plimsoll line
the standard
refers to the mark fixing the maximum load line of a merchant ship in water, and to Samuel Plimsoll MP (1824–98) who campaigned for safe shipping practices

to be further down the line
to have a low priority; OR to be further advanced in a project, at a later stage

to be in the firing line
to be among the first to be under attack

to be line ball
to be equal or to be a matter about which it is very difficult to make a definitive decision one way or the other
refers to sport (especially tennis)

to be out of line
to adopt a stance not held by others
military metaphor

to draw a line in the sand
to indicate clearly the limits of acceptability beyond which people should not go

to draw the line at that
to refuse to go any further

to fall into line
to conform with others
military metaphor

to lay it on the line
to make clear what the accepted rules of behaviour are

to line one's pockets
to make, improperly and secretly, a profit out of some transaction

to make a beeline for something
to go straight to something with great enthusiasm or to head for some goal by the most direct route

to put one's reputation on the line
to take a public stance in the realisation that there is a risk that one's reputation will suffer if one is proved wrong

to sign on the dotted line
to confirm one's agreement

to step out of line
to infringe accepted rules of behaviour
military metaphor

to swallow the line
to accept as truth the story being proffered
refers to angling

to take a hard line
to be uncompromising

to take the line of least resistance
to follow the easiest course of action
refers to the route taken by the shockwaves of a buried explosive charge in reaching the surface of the earth

to toe the line
to conform
refers to the starting line of a footrace

to tread a fine/thin line
cautiously to take action in circumstances where either too much or too little will cause difficulties

linen

to wash one's dirty linen in public
to expose one's embarrassing domestic affairs to the world at large'

lines

to read between the lines
to appreciate the true significance of something not put into words to sit on the sidelines
not to take part in the main action

lingers

the melody lingers on
the benefit of past actions remains

lining

every cloud has a silver lining
there are consolations and potential benefits even in seemingly adverse situations

link

the weakest link in the chain
the least efficient component in a project the overall efficiency of which is governed by the efficiency of the least efficient component

lion

the lion's share

the biggest portion

to beard the lion in his den

to tackle a daunting opponent in that person's own familiar surroundings

Sir Walter Scott (1771–1832), *Marmion*, 'And darest thou then to beard the lion in his den ... ' (probably a reference to the story of Daniel in the den of lions as related in *Daniel* 6:16)

to put one's head into the lion's mouth

recklessly to expose oneself to great danger

refers to circus performance

to throw someone to the lions

to sacrifice or condemn a person to that person's fate

refers to execution or bloodsport by throwing persons to be eaten by lions

lip

a stiff upper lip

obstinate courage in the face of pain or adversity

to bite one's lip

to control emotion such as anger or mirth

to pay lip service to some rules

to disregard some rules in practice while acknowledging them in words

lipped

to be tight-lipped

to keep confidences or to be uncommunicative

lips

to seal one's lips

to keep a confidence

list

a laundry list

a large set of demands

a shopping list

an itemised catalogue of things that one wishes to acquire or achieve

listening

a listening post

a place where information of strategic value can be collected

military metaphor

litmus

a litmus test

a simple examination that reveals the true state of affairs

refers to a test with litmus paper to establish whether a solution is acid or alkaline

little

a little bird told me

I heard from an informant who cannot be named

Ecclesiastes 10:20, 'Even in your thought do not curse the king ... for a bird of the air will carry your voice or some winged creature tell the matter'

a little tin god

a petty tyrant

I'll soon stop that person's little game

that person's activities are not tolerated and I will ensure that they cease

asses and little pitchers have long ears

children have a tendency to overhear things

tall oaks from little acorns grow

even major enterprises have to have small beginnings

David Everett (1769–1813), *Lines Written for a School Declamation*, 'Large streams from little fountains flow, / tall oaks from little acorns grow'

to be a big fish in a little pond

to be a person holding an important office but in an unimportant organisation

to twist someone around one's little finger

to exert easy control over a person

live

not to live in each other's pockets

to each follow his or her own lifestyle

those who live by the sword shall die by the sword

those that are rough with others must accept the likelihood of unfavourable treatment in return

Matthew 26:52, 'All they that take the sword shall perish by the sword'

to be a live wire

to be an enthusiast

refers to electrical wires

to live from hand to mouth

being in poor financial circumstances to survive (with little safety margin)

refers to immediate consumption of whatever one has in one's hand

to live in a fool's paradise
to delude oneself into a state of happy contentment when reality is quite different
to live on borrowed time
to live longer than expected

livered
lily-livered
cowardly
refers to a supersitition that the liver of a coward contained no blood

living
to be in the land of the living
to be alive

lizard
flat out like a lizard drinking
to be hard at work
a play on words, not strictly a simile

Lloyd's
to be A1 at Lloyd's
to be in perfect order
refers to the classification of ships in Lloyd's register in London

load
a load of rubbish
blatant nonsense
that has taken a load off my mind
I am relieved

loaded
the dice are loaded against someone
a person is unlikely to succeed in something
refers to cheating in gambling with dice
to be the throw of a loaded die
to be an act of deceit
refers to cheating in gambling with dice

loaf
half a loaf is better than none
it is more advantageous to accept less than is really desired than risk missing out completely
John Heywood (1546), 'Throw no gift at the giver's head;/better is half a loaf than no bread

lock
lock, stock and barrel
entirely
the lock, stock and barrel of a gun is the complete firearm
to lock antlers/horns with someone
to have an argument with another person
refers to fighting between male horned animals
to lock someone into some arrangement
to create an agreement which cannot be broken by one of the parties
to lock something up in the old oak chest
to put in a safe place and out of mind

loggerheads
to be at loggerheads
constantly to fight one another

logjam
a logjam
a stoppage of activity caused by input in greater volume than allowed for
refers to a crowded mass of cut logs in a river

loins
to gird up one's loins
to get ready for action
Job 38:3 'Gird up thy loins now like a man'

London
it is London to a brick on
it is virtually certain
a metaphor coined by the Australian horse-race caller, Ken Howard, to indicate that one could bet the whole of London against a single brick — in the confident expectation of winning

lone
a lone wolf
a person who prefers to act without involving others
to be a lone voice crying out in the wilderness
to be the only person stating unpopular views
John 1:23, 'I am the voice of one crying in the wilderness'

long
asses and little pitchers have long ears
children have a tendency to overhear things
for the long haul
as a long-term proposition
he must have a long spoon that sups with the devil

great care is needed when negotiating with disreputable parties

Shakespeare apparently alludes to an old proverb in *The Tempest* II:ii, 'Mercy! mercy! this is a devil ... I will leave him, I have no long spoon!'

it is a long time between drinks
activity is occurring only very spasmodically

it is as broad as it is long
it does not really matter

one's long suit
one's main skills

refers to playing cards

take a long walk on a short pier
go away, I want no dealings with you

that is a long shot
there is only a remote possibility

the long and the short of it
all that needs to be said about this

to be long in the tooth
to be old

to beat by a long shot
to defeat very convincingly

to draw a long bow
to state a conclusion that, although possible, is unlikely on the known facts

refers to archery

to enter a long road
to commence a task that will take a long time

to have a long arm
to have far-reaching power

to have a long face
to look miserable

to throw a long shadow
to have widespread ramifications

to win by a long chalk
to win very conclusively

refers to scoring in a contest by making chalk marks on a score board

look

a cat may look at a king
don't give yourself airs!

distant fields look greener
activities of which one has no experience seem more attractive than is really the case

Psalms 23:1, 'The Lord is my shepherd ... he shall feed me in a green pasture'

things look black
there is little hope of success or prosperity or a favourable outcome

to give someone a black look
to indicate one's displeasure with a person

to look a gift horse in the mouth
to be suspicious about a benefit that has been volunteered

Samuel Butler (1612–80), *Hudibras*, 'He ne'er consider'd it, as loth to look a gift horse in the mouth'; refers to the examination of a horse's teeth for an accurate assessment of its age

to look after number one
to act selfishly

to look at someone sideways
silently and politely to indicate one's disapproval

to look daggers at someone
to look at a person in a way that indicates great animosity

Shakespeare, *Hamlet* III:ii, 'I will speak daggers to her, but use none'

to look down the barrel of a gun
to be given little choice in a matter

to look down the nose at something
to treat a matter with obvious contempt

to look for a needle in a haystack
to attempt something with a very small chance of success

to look in the pink
to look well

Oliver Goldsmith (1730–74), *She Stoops to Conquer*, 'the very pink of perfection'

to look on the dark side
to be pessimistic

to look though the wrong end of the telescope
completely to miss the point

to look to one's laurels
to be careful not to lose one's reputation for some skill

refers to laurel wreaths presented to winners of events at the ancient Olympics

to need to look over one's shoulder
to be subject to attack which is not obvious

looks

one looks for elephants in elephant country

one needs to search in the right place
someone looks as if butter would not melt in his or her mouth
a person looks sweet and innocent

loom

to loom on the horizon
to be expected but not immediately

loop

a loophole
a means of getting around the intention of some regulation
refers, originally, to a small narrow space in a wall for shooting from, or for observation

loose

a loose cannon on the deck
a person or factor out of control and likely to cause trouble
nautical metaphor
all hell broke loose
great confusion erupted
John Milton (1608–74) *Paradise Lost*, 'Wherefore with thee came not all hell broke loose?'
footloose and fancyfree
unmarried and without any romantic attachments
to have a loose tongue
to speak foolishly or indiscreetly
to have a screw loose
to be mentally unbalanced
to play fast and loose
to ignore one's obligations, be unreliable
refers to old fairground game in which the player was cheated
to tie up the loose ends
to complete the minor outstanding items of some substantially finished project

lose

heads I win, tails you lose
whichever way this matter goes I will benefit at your expense
refers to the tossing of a coin
not to lose any sleep over something
not to worry about some matter
to lose face
to experience embarrassment by an affront to one's dignity
to lose heart
to be discouraged
to lose money hand over fist
to lose money very fast and comprehensively
to lose one's head
to become agitated or confused
Rudyard Kipling (1865–1936), *If*, 'If you can keep your head when all about you are losing theirs … '
to lose one's marbles
to become senile
to lose one's nerve
to abandon, out of fear, a decision to do something
to lose one's right arm
to lose some highly valued assistance
to lose one's shirt
to make heavy financial losses
Luke 6:29 (RSV), ' … and from him who takes away your coat do not withhold even your shirt'
to lose one's touch
to cease to be familiar with, or adept at, something
to lose steam
to slow down
refers to a steam engine or boiler

loses

what one loses on the swings one gains on the roundabouts
there are advantages and disadvantages that offset each other
Patrick Reginald Chalmers (1872–1942), *Green Days and Blue Days: Roundabouts and Swings*, 'what's lost upon the roundabouts we pulls up on the swings!'

losing

to be on the losing end of the stick
to be worse off while the other party to a transaction becomes correspondingly better off

lost

get lost!
just go away!
you can get lost
I intend to take no notice whatsoever of you or your views

loud

to come through loud and clear
to be well understood
refers to radio reception

love

I would love to be a fly on the wall
I would love to observe what goes on without those under observation being aware of my presence

love me, love my dog
if you accept me then you must also accept my associates
Latin proverb: *Qui me amat, amat et canem meam*, quoted by St Bernard of Clairvaux (1090–1153)

not for love or money
definitely not

to fall head-over-heels in love
to fall very much in love

to fall in love with something
to have lost detachment in assessing the merits of some matter

lovely

everything in the garden is lovely
everything is fine
Genesis 2:8–9, 'And the Lord God planted a garden ... to grow every tree that is pleasant to the sight'

low

low-down
confidential information relevant to something

to lie low
to stay inconspicuous

lower

to lower one's sights
to reduce one's ambition
military metaphor

to lower the boom
to bring to account and punish

lowest

the lowest common denominator
the highest level of taste found among all the members of some target audience
this mathematical phrase is used despite the fact that 'the highest common multiple' would be more logical

luck

the very best of British luck
you will have a hard time of it, but you carry my best wishes

to be the luck of the draw
to be a chance result
refers to card games or a raffle

to push one's luck
having already done well in something, then to take risks which can prejudice everything

to take pot luck
to take whatever happens by chance to be available
refers to a cooking pot of food

lucky

one can thank one's lucky stars
one was extremely fortunate
refers to astrology

lukewarm

lukewarm
unenthusiastic although not hostile

lump

to have a lump in one's throat
to feel emotional

lurch

to leave someone in the lurch
to desert a person who is in difficulties
refers to the score in certain games — especially cribbage

lurk

to lurk in the shadows
to have a low profile at the moment, but with the possibility of becoming much more conspicuous at any time

lying

to take something lying down
to accept a disadvantage without protest

lynx

lynx-eyed
having acute vision

M

macabre

danse macabre
gruesome final step
French, 'ghastly dance'; now used to describe a gruesome literary or theatrical production (refers to fourteenth-century religious art depicting persons being led to the grave by death)

machine

a sausage machine
the turning out of large volumes without particular thought

when the wash comes through the machine
in due course

to be a well-oiled piece of machinery
to be functioning very satisfactorily

mackerel

to throw a sprat to catch a mackerel
to risk a little in the hope of gaining much

mad

a madhouse
an organisation in great turmoil
John Clare (1793–1864) *The Exile*, 'madhouses, prisons, whoreshops'; and *Letter*, 'Dear Sir, I am in a madhouse and quite forget your name and who you are'

made

not to be made of money
not to be wealthy

ready-made
easily fabricated or available without difficulty

magic

a magic bullet
a highly effective guaranteed remedy

not to be a magic pudding
not to represent an everlasting supply of something
from the name of a book by Norman Lindsay

the magic moment
the perfect time

there is no magic in that
that is quite ordinary

to be black magic
to lack any scientific or logical basis
refers to witchcraft

to get a magic carpet ride to something
to be given an easy and fortunate passage to an objective
refers to the magic carpet (of Oriental legend) that transported its owners wherever they wished

to wave a magic wand
to direct affairs without the restraints of the real world

magnet

to be a magnet
to be an attractive person or thing to which other persons or things are drawn

maiden

the answer to a maiden's prayer
an unexpected but very welcome happening

main

to splice the main brace
to serve an extra ration of rum
nautical metaphor

mainstream

mainstream
orthodox

make

nothing to make a song or dance about
unexciting or unimportant

one can lead a horse to water, but one can't make it drink
one can give advice to a person but cannot ensure that it will be acted on

one can't make a silk purse out of a sow's ear
it is impossible to manufacture something of a high standard from inferior raw materials
Malcolm Bradbury (1932–), 'For the mass of men, you can't make a silk purse out of a sow's ear'

one cannot make an omelette without breaking eggs
the desired end dictates the means even if they cause harm to others

one cannot make bricks without straw
one cannot achieve results in the absence of adequate resources
Exodus 6:7 'Ye shall no more give the people straw to make bricks ... let them go and gather straw for themselves'

one swallow does not make a summer
much further evidence is desirable before any action taken
refers to an old English proverb, probably ultimately derived from the Greek proverb: 'One swallow does not make a

spring' (recorded in Aristotle's *Nicomachoean Ethics* I:vii:16)

the empty can makes the most noise
the least worthy arguments often attract the most publicity

to be unable to make head nor tail of something
to be unable to understand how something functions or what something means

to kiss and make up
to reconcile differences that one has with another person

to know how many beans make five
to have common sense
refers to an old riddle

to make a beeline for something
to go straight to something with great enthusiasm or to head for some goal by the most direct route

to make a clean breast of something
to confess

to make a federal case out of something
to attach far too much significance to a trivial issue

to make a good fist of something
to make a good attempt at, or to succeed in, a difficult task

to make a hero of oneself
to do something for personal glorification

to make a hog of oneself
to demonstrate greed
refers to gluttonous swine

to make a killing
to be in a very successful business venture

to make a last-ditch stand
to make a brave effort to stave off final defeat
King William III (1650–1702), 'There is one way never to see it lost ... and that is to die in the last ditch' (quoted by Burnet, *History of His Own Times*,1715)

to make a name for oneself
to earn a good reputation by virtue of some skill

to make a noise about something
to complain or express dissatisfaction about something

to make a rod for one's own back
to make a handicap for oneself

to make a scene
to create a fuss
refers to the theatre

to make a song and dance about something
to create a fuss

to make a splash
to create a sensation

to make a wigwam for a goose's bridle
to do something unspecified
nonsense said to children

to make a world of difference
to make a great deal of difference

to make an ass of oneself
to act stupidly in public

to make an exhibition of oneself
to behave in a way that invites ridicule

to make bad blood between two parties
to cause ill feeling between two parties

to make ends meet
to live within one's income
Thomas Fuller (1608–61), 'Worldly wealth he cared not for, desiring only to make both ends meet', referring to Edmund Grindall, in *The History of the Worthies of England* (1662), *Worthies of Cumberland*

to make eyes at someone
to look at a person amorously

to make feathers fly
to cause a flurry of consternation and vigorous activity
refers to the fighting of cock birds

to make hay while the sun shines
to utilise an opportunity before it disappears
John Betjeman (1906–84), *The Last Laugh*, 'I made hay while the sun shone'

to make headway
to make progress

to make heavy weather of something
to struggle excessively with a relatively simple task
nautical metaphor

to make mincemeat of something
to devastate something

to make mountains out of mole-hills
to treat a minor problem as though it were a major disaster

to make no bones about it
to be brutally frank

to make noise enough to wake the dead
to be excessively noisy

to make one's mark
to make an impression on people
refers to the practice of illiterate persons making their 'mark' upon documents — usually signified by the sign of the cross followed by the person's name

to make one's mouth water
to excite desire
refers to salivation

to make oneself scarce
to take oneself out of view

to make or break someone
to be a factor leading either to a person's success or to that person's failure, with no intermediate position

to make overtures to someone
to make suggestions to a person, inviting further negotiations

to make ripples
to disturb the status quo

to make some place too hot for someone
to make a place unpleasant for someone

to make someone's blood boil
to make a person very angry

to make someone's flesh creep
to frighten a person with something horrific

to make someone's hair curl
(of news) to give someone a shock
W. S. Gilbert, *Ruddigore* (1887), 'when he's excited he uses language that would make your hair curl'

to make someone's hair stand on end
to give a person shocking news
Job 4:15, 'Then a spirit passed before my face; the hair of my flesh stood up'; Shakespeare, *Hamlet* I:v, 'would harrow up thy soul … and each particular hair to stand an end'

to make something one's trade mark
to have a distinctive characteristic or way of doing things

to make sparks fly
to inflame or cause friction in a situation
Job 5:7, 'Man is born unto trouble, as the sparks fly upward'

to make the beast with two backs
to engage in sexual intercourse
Shakespeare, *Othello* I:i, 'Your daughter and the Moor are now making the beast with two backs'

to make the fur fly
to create a disturbance
refers to animals fighting

to make the grade
to succeed

to make the wheels go round
to cause something to happen

to make tracks
to leave

to make up leeway
to get back to a normal position or to get to the position held by one's competitors
refers to the drift of a ship to leeward of the desired course

to make up one's mind
to reach a conclusion after contemplating a matter

maker

matchmaker
intermediary facilitating or instigating some merger

makes

the empty can makes the most noise
the least worthy arguments often attract the most publicity

what makes someone tick
what causes a person to act as that person does
refers to the workings of a clock

man

a man of straw
a person of no substance, a counterfeit, a sham; OR a person invented in order to be triumphantly defeated; OR a person who has no assets while giving a contrary appearance

Exodus 6:7 'Ye shall no more give the people straw to make bricks ... let them go and gather straw for themselves'

a one-man band
a person performing many different roles singlehandedly

a poor man's something
a second-best version

every man and his dog
everybody

he is your man
he conforms to an ideal
Ev. S. Joann. 19:5 (Vulgate Bible): *Ecce Homo* ('Behold the man')

one man's meat is another man's poison
different people have different tastes

the man in the street
the average citizen

to be a man of steel
to be a person with moral courage

to be one's own man
to be free and independent, and able to act in accordance with one's own values

to kick a man when he is down
to take unfair advantage of a person already in difficulty

to see a man about a dog
to do something unspecified

to send a boy on a man's errand
to engage a person to do a task beyond that person's capabilities

manage

to stage manage something
to arrange how something happens
refers to the theatre

manger

to be a dog in the manger
spitefully to deny something to others, notwithstanding its uselessness to oneself
from *Aesop's Fables*

manna

manna from heaven
unexpected benefits
derived from Hebrew *man-hu* ('what is this?'); *Exodus* 16:15, 'It is manna: for they wist not what it was. And Moses said unto them: this is the bread which the Lord hath given you to eat'

mansize

a mansize job
a large task

mantle

to assume someone's mantle
to take over another person's role
refers to the passing of Elijah's mantle to Elisha: *2Kings* 2:13, 'He took up also the mantle of Elijah that fell from him ... '

map

to put something on the map
to make prominent or significant'

marathon

marathon
requiring great endurance
refers to the run to Athens made by a lone messenger to announce Athenian victory over the Persians at the battle of Marathon in 490 BC; according to tradition, the messenger fell dead on arrival

marble

to be carved in marble
to be virtually unalterable

marbles

to lose one's marbles
to become senile

march

in the course of a day's march
while carrying out one's normal activities
military metaphor

to march to a different drum
to show an independent approach
military metaphor

to steal a march on someone
to anticipate another person's actions and get in ahead
military metaphor

marching

to get one's marching orders
to be told to leave
military metaphor

mare

a mare's nest
a discovery with illusory benefits

margin

safety margin
allowance for miscalculations

marines

tell it to the marines

such nonsense is not believable

although now referring to a very unlikely tale, it originally applied to an unlikely tale that was, in fact, true — refers to King Charles II believing the unlikely (but true) tale of flying fish because the marines (the maritime regiment) testified that it was so

mark

a hallmark

a standard

refers to the official assay mark on gold and silver, originally put on at the Goldsmiths' Hall, London

a landmark ruling

a decision marking an important change or development in the state of affairs'

high-water mark

the best or highest level achieved by an enterprise

mark my words

you will find out that I am right

the mark of Cain

disgrace

refers (wrongly) to a supposed mark of disgrace placed upon Cain as punishment for the killing of his brother; the mark was, in fact, a sign of God's protection against anyone attempting to kill Cain; *Genesis* 4:15, 'And the Lord set a mark upon Cain, lest any finding him should kill him'

the river found its mark

equilibrium between two pressures has been achieved

to be first off the mark

to start ahead of all others

refers to the starting mark of a race

to be slow off the mark

to be slow to start something

refers to the starting mark of a race

to be up to the mark

to be of the right standard

refers to the official assay mark on gold and silver, originally put on at the Goldsmiths' Hall, London

to be wide of the mark

to have a belief that is far removed from the true position

refers to archery

to have a black mark against one's name

to have a tarnished reputation

to hit the mark

to achieve one's object or to make the correct decision

refers to archery

to leave one's mark on something

to be responsible for permanently altering the way something is operated

refers to the practice of illiterate persons making their 'mark' upon documents — usually signified by the sign of the cross preceded or followed by the person's name

to make one's mark

to make an impression on people

refers to the practice of illiterate persons making their 'mark' upon documents — usually signified by the sign of the cross followed by the person's name

to make something one's trade mark

to have a distinctive characteristic or way of doing things

to mark time

to do nothing while awaiting developments

refers to marching

to overstep the mark

to fail to observe the proprieties

refers to gaining an unfair advantage in a contest (originally the mark between two fighters)

marks

to get full marks for something

to receive the highest praise for something

market

to be a drug on the market

to be in overplentiful supply

Marquis

to play by Marquis of Queensberry rules

to act ethically

refers to regulations regarding boxing matches drawn up by John Sholto Douglas, Eighth Marquis of Queensberry (1843–83), in 1867

marriage

someone's marriage is on the rocks

someone's marriage has broken down

refers to ships wrecked on rocks

marshal

to have a field marshal's bâton in one's kit
to be ambitious
variously attributed:
Louis XVIII (1755–1824), 'There is not one of you who has not in his knapsack the field marshal's bâton; it is up to you to bring it out' (speech to the Saint-Cyr cadets, 9 Aug. 1819, *Moniteur*, 10 Aug. 1819);
Napoleon I (1769–1821), 'Every French soldier carries in his cartridge-pouch the bâton of a marshal of France'; Mark Pattison (1813–84), 'Every private in the French army carries in his haversack the bâton of a marshal'

Martha

I don't know whether I'm Arthur or Martha

I'm confused mask

to unmask someone
to reveal a person's true identity

mast

to nail one's colours to the mast
publicly to declare one's position and to maintain it in the face of criticism
nautical metaphor

master

a chessmaster
a clever strategist
a master stroke
particularly brilliant action
a past master
an expert with long experience
derived from freemasonry

match

game, set, and match
completion
refers to tennis
the whole shooting match
the whole lot
to put a match to petrol
to cause an actual disaster out of a potentially disastrous situation

matchmaker

matchmaker
intermediary facilitating or instigating some merger

matter

it is mind over matter
one's resolve to overcome suffering will succeed
not to matter a row of beans
to be utterly unimportant

maverick

maverick
a person who likes to do things differently from other persons
refers to Samuel A. Maverick (1803–70), Texas engineer, who owned but did not brand cattle

McCoy

to be the real McCoy
the genuine article
perhaps refers to an American boxer who became world welterweight champion in 1890

mealy

mealy-mouthed
afraid of giving offence, not outspoken, hypocritical

mean

golden mean
a moderate compromise between two extremes
from mathematics: the division of a straight line into two portions so that the ratio of the smaller to the larger equals the ratio of the larger to the whole
to mean business
to demonstrate a serious intent to do something

measure

to take someone's measure
to sum up a person's character or skills

meat

one man's meat is another man's poison
different people have different tastes
to be easy meat
to be an opponent who is readily outwitted
to be meat and drink
to be very pleasurable; or to be basic, familiar, and essential to one's experience of life'
Matthew 25:35, 'For I was an hungred, and ye gave me meat: I was thirsty and ye gave me drink'; Shakespeare, 'It is meat and drinke to me to see a clowne'
to be the meat in the sandwich

to be caught in the middle of a dispute between other parties

refers to the food snack popularised by the fourth Earl of Sandwich (1718–92)

to contain much meat

to contain much material worthy of consideration

to make mincemeat of something

to devastate something

Mecca

a Mecca for something

a place at which supporters of something congregate

refers to the birthplace of the prophet Muhammad

medicine

strong medicine

a tough remedy

to get a taste of one's own medicine

to suffer from an initiative intended to affect only other persons

to take one's medicine

to submit to something unpleasant but necessary

meet

to make ends meet

to live within one's income

Thomas Fuller (1608–61), 'Worldly wealth he cared not for, desiring only to make both ends meet', referring to Edmund Grindall, in *The History of the Worthies of England* (1662), *Worthies of Cumberland*

to meet one's Waterloo

to receive a decisive defeat

refers to Napoleon's fate at the Battle of Waterloo (1815)

melody

the melody lingers on

the benefit of past actions remains

melt

someone looks as if butter would not melt in his or her mouth

a person looks sweet and innocent

melting

a melting pot

a country where people with different ethnic backgrounds merge, over time, into one nation

refers to a vessel for melting and mixing metals

the ice is melting

friendly relations are being restored

to go back into the melting pot

to be up for reconsideration from the beginning

refers to a vessel for melting and mixing metals

memory

to go down memory lane

to reminisce

men

to separate the men from the boys

to distinguish between those with and without certain skills

two men and a dog

very few people

mend

to mend bridges

to restore a broken-up relationship

to mend fences

to achieve a reconciliation

mentioned

to be mentioned in dispatches

to be favourably mentioned

refers to military recognition for bravery

merrier

the more the merrier

everyone is welcome

merry

to be on a merry-go-round

to be a circular exercise ending in no definite result

to lead someone a merry dance

to mislead a person

refers to the complex dances of earlier centuries when one person led another through complex steps

to raise merry hell

to cause an uproar by outlandish, reckless, or larrikinish behaviour

in the eighteenth century there were clubs of reckless young men, known as 'hell-fire clubs', who were said to 'raise merry hell'

mess

to clean up a mess

to sort out mistakes or neglect

to sell one's birthright for a mess of pottage

through foolishness to exchange something of substance for something of little value

Genesis 25:34, 'Then Jacob gave Esau bread and pottage of lentils ... thus Esau despised his birthright'

message

to get the message

to understand the real import of what is being said

messenger

to shoot the messenger

to blame the person who brings news of an undesired happening instead of the person really responsible for that happening

meteoric

meteoric

brilliant, dazzling, rapid

Mexican

a Mexican standoff

a situation where neither of two parties is making a move

refers to poker

mice

mice have been here

intruders have entered this place

when the cat is away the mice will play

in the absence of supervision discipline will be lax

microscope

to be under the microscope

to be the subject of close examination

mid

to swap/change horses in mid-stream

to alter that upon which one is reliant during the course of a project

Midas

the Midas touch

attributes that cause a person's ventures to be extremely profitable

refers to King Midas of Phrygia who, in Greek mythology, had the power to turn everything he touched into gold

middle

a middle-of-the-road solution

a solution near the middle of a range of possibilities

midnight

at five minutes to midnight

almost at the last moment

to burn the midnight oil

to work late into the night

Francis Quarles (1592–1644), *Emblems*, 'We spend our midday sweat, our midnight oil; / we tire the night in thought, the day in toil'

milch

a milch cow

an easy and plentiful source of some desired benefit

mile

a milestone

a significant stage or achievement in a life or a history

refers to markers along a road indicating distance in miles

give someone an inch and that person will take a mile

make a small concession to a person and that person will abuse it by taking much more

someone would run a mile

a person would do anything to escape that person's responsibilities

to be able to spot trouble a mile away

to be able to perceive problems before they actually occur

to be ahead by a country mile

to be in a comfortable lead

in the long distances of certain rural areas, a 'country mile' is jocularly believed to be a very long mile

to go the extra mile

to work beyond the call of duty

Matthew 5:41, 'Whosoever shall compel thee to go a mile, go with him twain'

to miss something by a mile

to be nowhere near one's target

to stick out a mile

to be very apparent

mileage

to get some mileage out of something

to benefit from something

miles

to be miles apart

to have great philosophical differences

to be miles away
to have one's mind on other matters

milestone

a milestone
a significant stage or achievement in a life or a history
refers to markers along a road indicating distance in miles

milk

a land of milk and honey
a country in which everything is in abundant supply
Exodus 3:8, ' ... to bring them up out of that land unto a good land ... flowing with milk and honey'

it is no use crying over spilt milk
there is nothing to be gained by lamenting over an irredeemable error

to be cream on top of the milk
to be an additional benefit in an already satisfactory scenario

mill

it is all grist to the mill
this is all useful material for the task at hand

run of the mill
normal or average

to put someone through the mill
to make someone endure significant hardship through severe practical experience

mills

the mills of God grind slowly
retribution might be delayed but is inevitable
Friedrich von Logau (1604–55), *Sinngedichte* (translated by H. W. Longfellow), 'Though the mills of God grind slowly, yet they grind exceeding small; though with patience he stands waiting, with exactness grinds he all'

millstone

a millstone around someone's neck
a great burden

mince

not to mince words
to speak bluntly

mincemeat

to make mincemeat of something
to devastate something

mind

a thought in the back of one's mind
an undeveloped idea

in one's mind's eye
using a vivid imagination

it is mind over matter
one's resolve to overcome suffering will succeed

that has taken a load/weight off my mind
I am relieved

the mind boggles
this is astonishing

to be of one mind
(of several people) to be agreed

to be out of one's cotton-picking mind
to act irrationally

to broaden someone's mind
to expose a person to a greater variety of experiences and interests than that person had previously experienced

to change one's mind
to alter the views that one had previously formed

to cloud one's mind
to allow irrelevant or extraneous factors to affect one's impartiality or judgment

to cross one's mind
to think of something

to drive someone out of that person's mind
to produce insanity in a person
often used jocularly, with exaggeration

to give someone a piece of one's mind
to abuse another person

to have a butterfly mind
not to concentrate on the matter on hand

to have a mind of one's own
not to be easily influenced

to have a one-track mind
to keep coming back to one narrow topic of conversation

to have an open mind
to be willing to assess evidence on its merits and without prejudging it

to have half a mind to do something

to be tempted or mildly inclined to do something

to know one's mind
to form and adhere to an opinion

to make up one's mind
to reach a conclusion after contemplating a matter

to prey on one's mind
(of a problem) to keep worrying one

to put someone's mind at rest
to reassure a person

to slip one's mind
to be overlooked or forgotten

to speak one's mind
to express one's views frankly and forcefully

to spring to mind
to occur suddenly to a person

minds

to be in two minds
to be undecided between two alternatives

mine

a goldmine
a source of much wealth or of many facts

minefield

a minefield
a source of great hidden danger or of difficulties not obvious at first

minnows

to miss the sharks while netting the minnows
to succeed in minor aspects but fail in the ones that really matter

mint

to charge a mint
to impose very high prices

minutes

at five minutes to midnight
almost at the last moment

mirage

mirage
illusory benefit

mire

to sink deeper into the mire
to get into even greater difficulty

mirrors

it is all done with mirrors
this is achieved by magic or illusion

misPre

to be a laid-down misPre
to be very easily accomplished and/or to be certain of outcome
refers to card playing where one player undertakes not to win any tricks while playing with the disadvantage of having that player's cards exposed to observation by others

miss

not to miss a beat
to carry on without the slightest interruption

to miss something by a mile
to be nowhere near one's target

to miss the boat/bus/train
to fail to exploit an opportunity

to miss the sharks while netting the minnows
to succeed in minor aspects but fail in the ones that really matter

mite

not a mite
not at all
refers to a coin of small value — *Mark* 12:42, 'A certain poor widow ... threw in two mites, which make a farthing'

mixed

a mixed bag
some advantages and some disadvantages

to be a mixed blessing
to be an outcome with some desirable and some undesirable features

Mohicans

the last of the Mohicans
to be the last of a group
refers to a near-extinct tribe of North American natives; title of a novel by James Fenimore Cooper (1789–1851)

molehills

to make mountains out of molehills
to treat a minor problem as though it were a major disaster

moment

at the psychological moment
at the most appropriate instant of time
the phrase refers to the German, *das psychologische Momentum* ('psychological momentum') — thus confusing

the German word for 'momentum' or 'motive' with the term for an instant of time

the magic moment
the perfect time

momentum

to have momentum
to move along forcefully

money

a licence to print money
a lucrative government-conferred monopoly or privilege
Lord Thomson of Fleet (1894–1977), 'It's just like having a licence to print your own money' (after the opening of Scottish commercial television, as recorded in Braddon, *Roy Thomson of Fleet Street*)

money for jam
remuneration easily earned

not for love or money
definitely not

not to be made of money
not to be wealthy

pin money
an allowance to a wife for her personal use
probably refers to money for purchase of hair pins and other decorative pins

that is money down the drain
money has been wastefully lost on a failed project

the money is rolling in
the scheme is very profitable

to be a money spinner
to produce large profits easily and quickly

to be money for old rope
to be an easily made profit

to have a run for one's money
to at least get some enjoyment out of an otherwise abortive exercise
refers to betting on horse racing

to have money burning a hole in one's pocket
to be impatient to spend or invest available funds

to have money flowing out of one's ears
to be very rich

to lose money hand over fist
to lose money very fast and comprehensively

to put money on the table
to back one's judgment in a tangible way or to demonstrate one's sincerity

to put one's money where one's mouth is
to back one's boasting by putting assets at risk

to see the colour of someone's money
to get evidence of the sincerity of a person's proposal

to throw good money after bad
to waste further money in a vain attempt to recover money already lost

monkey

monkey business
mischievous or underhand activity

to play monkey tricks on someone
to engage in discreditable behaviour affecting a person

to want the organ-grinder, not the monkey
to wish to deal with the person in authority rather than an underling
refers to a street musician using a barrel-organ, often accompanied by a pet monkey

monster

a hydra-headed monster
an evil that is not readily destroyable
refers to the hydra — in Greek legend, a multiple-headed monster that grew two more heads whenever one was cut off; it was killed by Heracles

month

to be the flavour of the month
to be a person or commodity temporarily popular
refers to sales or marketing of foods of a particular flavour

moon

once in a blue moon
very rarely
refers to the volcanic eruption at Krakatoa in 1883 when volcanic dust caused the moon to appear blue

to be over the moon
to be very excited

moonlight

a moonlight flit
an escape from creditors

moonshine

moonshine
unrealistic ideas

more

I have had more of these than I have had hot dinners
I have had a very large number of these

more chiefs than Indians
a disproportionately large number of supervisors

more power to your elbow
may your praiseworthy efforts continue and be strengthened

once more unto the breach
let us get on and undertake the task again
Shakespeare, *Henry V* III:i, 'Once more unto the breach, dear friends, once more; / Or close the wall up with our English dead!'

the more the merrier
everyone is welcome

there is more than one way to skin a cat
this can be achieved in a variety of ways

to be more than flesh can stand
to be more than a person reasonably can be expected to endure

to be more than one bargained for
to be more than one expected

to be more than one can poke a stick at
to be more than can reasonably be handled

to bite off more than one can chew
to be over ambitious and thus unrealistic as to one's capabilities

to have more degrees than a thermometer
to be too academic
a play on the word 'degree'

to have more important fish to fry
to have more important things to do

to spread the net more widely
to become more comprehensive

mortem

to conduct a post mortem on something
to review past actions with a view to learning lessons for the future
Latin, *post mortem*, 'after the death'

mortgage

to have a mortgage on something
to have a moral claim in regard to a matter
refers to a charge over property recognised by the law

to mortgage the future
to get benefits now but at a cost in due course
refers to a charge over property recognised by the law

mosaic

a mosaic
something with a large number of different aspects to it

moss

a rolling stone gathers no moss
a person who keeps changing jobs will not have a successful career
Tusser, *Five Hundred Points of Good Husbandrie* (1573), 'The stone that is rolling can gather no moss. / For master and servant oft changing is loss'

mote

a mote in someone's eye
a fault in another person that is trifling in comparison with an unrecognised major fault in oneself
Matthew 7:3, 'Why beholdest thou the mote that is in thy brother's eye, but considerest not the beam that is in thine own eye?'

moth

moth-eaten
antiquated, shabby

mothball

to mothball equipment
to take out of active service and put in storage
refers to storing clothes protected by mothballs

mother

a mother hen
an over-protective person
Matthew 12:37, 'Even as a hen gathereth her chickens under her wings'

motherhood

a motherhood statement
a statement so obvious and uncontroversial as not to be worth making
such as 'motherhood is a good thing'

motion

to set the wheels in motion
to institute appropriate action

mould

to be cast in someone's mould
to take after another person

mountain

if the mountain will not come to Muhammad then Muhammad will go to the mountain
on recognising that one has insufficient power to effect one's most desired solution one decides to make do with the next best alternative
refers to the story of Muhammad humbly submitting to the greater power of God when Mt Safa did not obey the prophet's command to come to him

mountains

to make mountains out of mole-hills
to treat a minor problem as though it were a major disaster

mouse

a game of cat and mouse
negotiations between two parties of unequal bargaining power during which the stronger makes some temporary concessions to the weaker without, however, affecting the latter's eventual total defeat

to labour mightily and bring forth a mouse
to be quite ineffective

mouth

someone looks as if butter would not melt in his or her mouth
a person looks sweet and innocent

to be a big mouth
to lack discretion in one's conversation

to be born with a silver spoon in one's mouth
to be brought up by wealthy parents
refers to the traditional gift of a silver spoon (an 'apostle spoon') to a child at baptism — the child born of wealthy parents is assured of riches from the moment of birth and thus does not have to await baptism to receive a valuable gift

to be down in the mouth
to be depressed
refers to facial expression

to be left with a nasty taste in one's mouth
to be appalled or very disappointed at another person's unethical behaviour to one

to foam at the mouth
to show extreme uncontrollable anger
refers to a rabid animal; Washington Irving (1783–1859), 'Fall down in convulsions [and] foam at the mouth'

to have one's heart in one's mouth
to be very apprehensive

to keep one's mouth shut
not to discuss some matter

to learn something from the horse's mouth
to get information from someone qualified to impart it
refers to the examination of a horse's teeth for an accurate assessment of its age

to live from hand to mouth
being in poor financial circumstances to survive (with little safety margin)
refers to immediate consumption of whatever one has in one's hand

to look a gift horse in the mouth
to be suspicious about a benefit that has been volunteered
Samuel Butler (1612–80), *Hudibras*, 'He ne'er consider'd it, as loth to look a gift horse in the mouth'; refers to the examination of a horse's teeth for an accurate assessment of its age

to make one's mouth water
to excite desire
refers to salivation

to put one's foot in one's mouth
to say something foolish

to put one's head into the lion's mouth
recklessly to expose oneself to great danger
refers to circus performance

to put one's money where one's mouth is
to back one's boasting by putting assets at risk

to put words into someone's mouth
to attempt to get someone to say something in the particular terms drafted by another person

to shoot one's mouth off
to speak without thinking

you took the words right out of my mouth
you have just said what I was about to say

mouthed

hard-mouthed
uncontrollable
refers to horses that are 'hard' in the mouth or bite (and thus difficult to control)

mealy-mouthed
afraid of giving offence, not outspoken, hypocritical

mouths

out of the mouths of babes and sucklings
(as indiscreetly revealed) the truth
Psalms 8:2, 'Out of the mouths of babes and sucklings hast thou ordained strength ... '

to take food out of the mouths of children
cruelly to deprive the needy

movable

a movable feast
an event not customarily held on a set date
refers to the feast days of the Christian Church, some of which are held on fixed days ('immovable feasts') and some of which vary with the date of Easter ('movable feasts')

move

move over and let the greyhound see the rabbit
stand aside to allow things to get under way
refers to hunting with greyhounds

to move down a notch
to accept a lower position
refers to gradations of notches on a measuring stick

to move heaven and earth
to do everything possible
Revelation 21:1, 'And I saw a new heaven and a new earth, for the first heaven and the first earth had passed away'; a reference to the apocalyptic vision of the greatest possible change to all creation

to move on to greener pastures
to move to a better environment; to commence a new, better career
Psalms 23:1, 'The Lord is my shepherd: therefore can I lack nothing. he shall feed me in a green pasture: and lead me forth beside the waters of comfort'

to move the goal posts
unfairly to alter the rules after some action (that relied on the old rules) has already started
refers to sporting games

your move!
the next step is up to you
refers to chess and similar games

mover

prime mover
person initiating and promoting a cause

moving

a moving target
an objective subject to constant revision

muckraker

a muckraker
a person who sets out to publicise features harming another person's reputation

mud

a stick in the mud
an unenterprising person

a person's name is mud
a person is in disgrace, lacking in popularity, lacking in credibility
a play on the name of US physician Dr Samuel Mudd who, in 1865, was convicted of being a co-conspirator with John Wilkes Booth in the assassination of President Abraham Lincoln; since then a public and judicial campaign has been waged by family and supporters (extending even to some later US presidents) to assert Mudd's innocence; other people, just as vehemently, assert Mudd's guilt

some mud will stick
reputations will be hurt even after accusations are proved false

to sink deeper into the mud
to get into even greater difficulty

to sling mud
to make unfair imputations

muddy

to muddy the waters

deliberately to confuse an issue by creating a diversion

mug

a mug's game

an activity that wise persons eschew

perhaps refers to the practice of representing faces (often humorous) on drinking mugs

Muhammad

if the mountain will not come to Muhammad then Muhammad will go to the mountain

on recognising that one has insufficient power to effect one's most desired solution one decides to make do with the next best alternative

refers to the story of Muhammad humbly submitting to the greater power of God when Mt Safa did not obey the prophet's command to come to him

mullock

to poke mullock at someone

to ridicule a person, or to rubbish that person's arguments

refers to the heap of rubbish at the top of a mineshaft

mumbo

mumbo jumbo

blatant nonsense

refers to a deity worshipped by primitive tribes

murder

to be sheer murder

to be extremely unpleasant or difficult; OR to be an inglorious defeat

to get away with murder

to do something outrageous without penalty

to scream blue murder

to make serious allegations; OR to protest violently

perhaps refers to the French *morbleu* (altered version of *mort Dieu*, 'God's death'), a comic oath attributed to French speakers

Murphy

Murphy's law

the principle that everything that can go wrong will go wrong

muscles

to flex one's muscles

to assert one's personality or powers

museum

a museum piece

an old article the use of which is no longer efficient

mushroom

to mushroom

to expand rapidly

refers to the rapid (overnight) growth of mushrooms

music

music to one's ears

comments that one is very pleased to hear

Shakespeare, *Romeo and Juliet* II:i, 'How silver-sweet sound lovers' tongues by night, / like softest music to attending ears!'

to face the music

to accept responsibility when confronted by one's critics

refers to the theatre

when the music stops

suddenly and soon

refers to an imminent crisis leading to some resolution of a matter, as in a game of musical chairs

musical

to play musical chairs

to be a part of a general reshuffling (of duties or functions) that is not necessarily to everyone's liking

refers to a parlour game culminating in a sudden scrambling for positions

mutton

to be mutton dressed up as lamb

foolishly to pretend to be younger

myopia

myopia

an inability to see the longer term consequences of actions

refers to short-sightedness

myself

I could kick myself

I regret that I acted thus

N

n

to the nth degree

with great precision
refers to mathematics

nail

a thumbnail sketch
brief but pertinent details
refers to an artist assessing perspective by judging the object to be painted against a thumbnail held close to the eye

on the nail
immediately
origin obscure

to be another nail in someone's coffin
to represent a further step towards someone's downfall

to fight tooth and nail
to strive very hard to win

to hit the nail right on the head
astutely to come to the correct conclusion

to nail a lie
to expose an untruth

to nail one's colours to the mast
publicly to declare one's position and to maintain it in the face of criticism
nautical metaphor

to nail someone
to fix the blame on a person; to convict; to secure

to nail someone to the wall
to outmanoeuvre and trap someone

to nail something down
to define something precisely

nails

to bite one's fingernails
anxiously to await a decision

to hang on by one's nails
to have only a slender hold
also: 'to hang on by one's fingernails'

name

a household name
a very familiar name

a person's name is mud
a person is in disgrace, lacking in popularity, lacking in credibility
a play on the name of US physician Dr Samuel Mudd who, in 1865, was convicted of being a co-conspirator with John Wilkes Booth in the assassination of President Abraham Lincoln; since then a public and judicial campaign has been waged by family and supporters (extending even to some later US presidents) to assert Mudd's innocence; other people, just as vehemently, assert Mudd's guilt

a rose by any other name would smell as sweet
the form does not affect the substance
Shakespeare, *Romeo and Juliet* II:ii, 'What's in a name? That which we call a rose / By any other name would smell as sweet'

so-and-so is the name of the game
so-and-so is the essential element of the exercise

to give a dog a bad name
to malign a person

to have a black mark against one's name
to have a tarnished reputation

to lend one's name to something
to endorse something

to make a name for oneself
to earn a good reputation by virtue of some skill

names

no names, no packdrill
the identities of the parties will be kept confidential to protect them
military metaphor

to drop names
to slip names of celebrities allegedly known to the speaker into a conversation in an attempt to impress

narrow

to be on the straight and narrow
to be completely virtuous
Matthew 7:14, 'Strait is the gate, and narrow is the way, which leadeth unto life'

nasty

a nasty piece of work
an unpleasant person
perhaps a later pejorative reversal of Shakespeare's hymn of praise to humanity, *Hamlet* II:ii, 'What a piece of work is a man!'

to be left with a nasty taste in one's mouth
to be appalled or very disappointed at another person's unethical behaviour to one

natural

to die a natural death

by virtue of changed circumstances or the effluxion of time to be no longer relevant

nature

the nature of the beast
the reality of the situation
Revelation 13:17, ' ... he that had the mark, or the name of the beast, or the number of his name'

to be second nature to someone
to be learned behaviour that has now become intuitive

navel

to contemplate one's navel
to be introspective
refers to a contemplative posture (as in yoga)

neck

a bottleneck
a factor obstructing an even flow

a millstone around someone's neck
a great burden

at a break-neck pace
very fast
refers to horseriding at great speed

it is neck or nothing
a desperate effort is called for
refers to a winning margin in horse racing

neck and neck
(of contestants) with little between them
refers to a winning margin in horse racing

neck of the woods
localised area
refers to a narrow stretch of wooded country

to be a pain in the neck
to be an unpleasant person or to be a nuisance

to be an albatross around someone's neck
to be a great burden
refers to a mythical mariner who suffered terrible ordeals as a result of killing an albatross; Samuel Taylor Coleridge (1772–1834), *The Ancient Mariner*, 1798, 'Why look'st thou so? — with my cross-bow, I shot the albatross'

to be up to one's neck in something
to be very deeply involved in something

to break one's neck to do something
to be particularly keen
refers to reckless enthusiasm

to breathe down someone's neck
to cause annoyance to another person by remaining in that person's vicinity or by supervising that person too closely; OR to be narrowly behind another person in some competitive situation

to cop it in the neck
to be severely castigated or reprimanded
refers to death by decapitation

to save someone's neck
to come to the rescue of a person
refers to death by hanging

to send a chill down someone's neck
to be worrying news

to stick one's neck out
to have the courage of one's convictions or to take a calculated risk
refers to execution by decapitation

need

to need something like a hole in the head
to be confronted with a completely undesired problem

to need to have one's head read
to engage in behaviour so foolish that a psychiatric examination seems called for

to need to look over one's shoulder
to be subject to attack which is not obvious

to need to sharpen one's pencil
to be required to improve one's performance

to need the wisdom of Solomon
to require great sagacity when faced with a difficult decision
refers to King Solomon's ingenious solution to an apparently insoluble dilemma as described in *1 Kings* 3:16–28

to need to watch one's back
to find it necessary to take care in case others act against one's interests

you need your head read

your behaviour is so foolish that you require psychiatric examination

needle

to look for a needle in a haystack
to attempt something with a very small chance of success

needles

to be on pins and needles
to be very agitated

needs

one needs to crawl before one can walk
skills are best developed in logical stages

neither

neither fish flesh nor good red herring
unclassifiable by virtue of being neither one thing nor another
Miguel de Cervantes (1547–1616), *Don Quixote*

to be neither here nor there
to be irrelevant or unimportant

Nellies

nervous Nellies
persons unwilling to take any risks

nemesis

nemesis
an agent of retribution
refers to the goddess of retribution in Greek mythology

nerve

the hip-pocket nerve
the assessment of issues by their financial effects on one

to have a nerve
to be impudent

to lose one's nerve
to abandon, out of fear, a decision to do something

to touch a nerve
to mention a sensitive subject

nerves

to get on someone's nerves
by one's behaviour to cause annoyance to a person

to have nerves of steel
not to be easily frightened

nervous

nervous Nellies
persons unwilling to take any risks

nest

a mare's nest
a discovery with illusory benefits

a nest egg
a sum of money set aside in case of need; a nucleus of savings
derived from the custom of placing an egg in a hen's nest as an inducement for the hen to lay more

to be a cuckoo in the nest
to purport to be a member of a group of people although having no such right and, in the process, to usurp the rights of those entitled to be there
refers to a cuckoo depositing its eggs in the nests of other birds

to feather one's own nest
improperly to appropriate things for oneself (especially in financial transactions)

to foul one's own nest
to disparage or bring discredit on one's home or workplace

to stir up a hornet's nest
to take action that results in unpleasant side-effects

net

a safety-net scheme
a scheme for dealing with the exceptional cases not covered by normal arrangements

to catch someone in the net
unexpectedly to involve a particular person in the course of activity designed to involve many others

to slip through the net
to happen as an isolated case despite steps taken to prevent such events

to spread the net more widely
to become more comprehensive

nets

to draw the nets closer
to intensify one's efforts

netting

to miss the sharks while netting the minnows
to succeed in minor aspects but fail in the ones that really matter

nettle

to grasp the nettle

to deal with an unpleasant difficulty by decisive action

Aaron Hill (1685–1750), 'Tender-hearted stroke a nettle, / And it stings you for your pains; / Grasp it like a man of mettle, / And it soft as silk remains'

new

a new broom

a changed regime that is likely to alter the status quo

a new lease of life

the prospect of a better existence from now on, or of better functioning after repair

new guard

changed regime

one cannot teach an old dog new tricks

people become set in their ways irreversibly

to be a new ball game

to be subject to completely revised rules or very different conditions

to be the dawn of a new day

to be the start of a different regime

to be the new kid on the block

to lack the experience of others

to break new ground

to do something for which there is no precedent

refers to ploughing of ground

to introduce new blood

to recruit new members to some organisation

to plough new ground

to engage laboriously in an untried activity

to put a new face on something

to alter the way something should be regarded

to turn over a new leaf

to reform

refers to turning over a page in the 'Book of Life' — *Rev* 20: 12, 'and the books were opened … and the dead were judged out of those things that were written in the books, according to their works'

Newcastle

to carry coals to Newcastle

to do something ridiculously unnecessary

refers to the coal-mining district of Newcastle, UK

nice

that has a nice ring to it

that sounds attractive

refers to bell-ringing

niche

to carve out a niche for oneself

deliberately to create an opportunity to use one's talents effectively

to find one's niche

to find the opportunity to use one's talents

night

a fly-by-night operator

a person who disappears suddenly and without warning in an attempt to avoid the payment of debts or compensation or the obligations under some contract

ships that pass in the night

a fleeting, transitory acquaintance

Henry Wadsworth Longfellow (1807–82), *The Theologian's Tale (Tales of a Wayside Inn)*, 'Ships that pass in the night, and speak each other in passing … '

the night is young

the project is at a very early stage

to be a night owl

habitually to go to bed late

to spend a sleepless night

to worry about something

nightie

to be off like a bride's nightie

to act promptly

nightmare

a nightmare

an unpleasant experience

nimble

nimble-footed

quick to change the direction of one's activities when circumstances warrant

nine

a nine-day wonder

an exciting event, but one that will cease to arouse interest when the novelty has worn off

old English proverb: 'a wonder lasts nine days, and then the puppy's eyes are open'; Shakespeare was probably alluding to this proverb (or similar) in *Henry VI Pt III*, III:ii, 'That would be ten days' wonder, at the least / That's a day longer than a wonder lasts'

a stitch in time saves nine
preventive maintenance saves money in the long run

to be on cloud nine
to be very happy

nines

to be dressed up to the nines
to be attired in garments of the highest standard
perhaps a corruption of 'to then eyen' ('to the eyes'); Thomas Hardy (1840–1928), 'She's dressed up to the nines for some grand party'

nineteen

to talk nineteen to the dozen
to speak very quickly

nip

to nip something in the bud
to stop some activity in its early stages when stopping it is still relatively easy
refers to the first signs of growth in plants

nit

to nitpick
to criticise a person in respect of very minor matters
refers to the removal of lice eggs (nits) from the hair of an animal or person

no

a gun with no bullets
something incomplete and therefore useless for the desired purpose

a rolling stone gathers no moss
a person who keeps changing jobs will not have a successful career
Tusser, *Five Hundred Points of Good Husbandrie* (1573), 'The stone that is rolling can gather no moss. / For master and servant oft changing is loss'

it is an ill wind that blows no good
even a seeming misfortune leads to some blessings

it is no use crying over spilt milk
there is nothing to be gained by lamenting over an irredeemable error

no dice
the proposal is totally unacceptable

no holds barred
without any limitation
refers to wrestling

no names, no packdrill
the identities of the parties will be kept confidential to protect them
military metaphor

no room at the inn
no available space
Luke 2:7, 'She [Mary] brought forth her firstborn son, and wrapped him in swaddling clothes, and laid him in a manger; because there was no room for them in the inn'

no sweat
this presents no difficulty

no way!
definitely not!

something has no guts in it
something has no substance to it

there are no flies on someone
a person is alert and astute

there is no magic in that
that is quite ordinary

there is no room to swing a cat
this place is very small
refers to the swinging of a whip (a cat-o'-nine-tails) in the confined space of a ship's hull

there is no such animal
that does not exist

to be no angel
to have a great many serious faults

to be no bed of roses
to be difficult or uncomfortable
Robert Louis Stevenson (1850–94), *Virginibus Puerisque* I:i, 'Marriage is like life in this — that it is a field of battle, and not a bed of roses'

to be no fun
to be difficult; to be lacking in levity

to be no picnic
to be unpleasant

to be no skin off someone's nose
not to matter to a person

to cut no ice with someone
to have little effect on a person
perhaps refers to ice-skating

to have no stomach for something
to have no liking, inclination, or fortitude for something

to leave no stone unturned
to be very thorough

refers to an instruction from the oracle of Delphi regarding a search for Persian treasure (477 BC)

to make no bones about it
to be brutally frank

to take no prisoners
to be utterly ruthless
military metaphor

nobody

to be a nobody
to be unimportant

nod

a nod and a wink
a sign that understanding has been reached in a matter that, in the interests of discretion, has not been discussed aloud
Captain Marryat (1792–1848), *Peter Simple*, 'But you're a dutiful son, so I'll say no more about it — a nod's as good as a wink to a blind horse'

a nod is the same as a wink to a blind horse
fine distinctions are not appropriate here
Captain Marryat (1792–1848), *Peter Simple*, 'But you're a dutiful son, so I'll say no more about it — a nod's as good as a wink to a blind horse'

to get the nod
to receive approval

noire

to be someone's bLte noire
to be a person whose ideas and actions cause upset and loathing in another person
French, *bLte noire* ('black beast')

noise

the empty can makes the most noise
the least worthy arguments often attract the most publicity

to make a noise about something
to complain or express dissatisfaction about something

nook

in every nook and cranny
everywhere

noose

to put one's head in the noose
to expose oneself to great danger likely to lead to one's downfall
refers to death by hanging

to tighten the noose
to get closer to inflicting defeat
refers to death by hanging

north

to head north
(of prices, etc.) to go up

nose

to be no skin off someone's nose
not to matter to a person

to be on the nose
(of a proposal or scheme) not to be quite honest, not to be popular; OR to be smelly

to bite someone's nose off
to speak to a person with excessive aggression

to cut one's nose off to spite one's face
to act in pique in a way that harms only oneself

to follow one's nose
to act intuitively

to get a bloody nose
to suffer an undignified rebuff

to get up someone's nose
to irritate a person

to have a good nose for business
to be able to identify profitable business situations

to keep one's nose clean
to act with circumspection and honesty despite temptation to do otherwise

to keep one's nose out of something
not to meddle in something

to keep one's nose to the grindstone
to work with particular diligence
refers to having one's head down low while working on a grindstone sharpening tools

to lead someone by the nose
to induce another person to comply with one's wishes
refers to leading animals (such as bulls) by a ring through the nose

to look down the nose at something
to treat a matter with obvious contempt

to pay through the nose
to pay an excessive price
refers to an onerous tax imposed by the Danes in Ireland in the ninth century whereby those who refused to pay had their noses slit

to poke one's nose into something
to interfere

to poke one's nose outside
to venture outside

to put someone's nose out of joint
to upset another person

to rub someone's nose in it
to humiliate a person by highlighting something embarrassing to that person

to take a nose dive
to fall steeply, suddenly and unexpectedly

to take something on the nose
meekly to accept a rebuff

to thumb one's nose at someone
to show one's contempt for someone in authority and ostentatiously to disregard that person's orders

to turn up one's nose at something
to express one's disdain

under someone's nose
in a person's immediate area of responsibility or in circumstances where that person should have known something

nosed

hard-nosed
tough in negotiations

notch

to move down a notch
to accept a lower position
refers to gradations of notches on a measuring stick

note

to hit a sour note
to say or do something inappropriate to a situation
refers to music

to strike the right note
to say or do something appropriate to a situation
refers to music

notes

to compare notes
to exchange information about some subject of mutual interest

nothing

nothing is sacred
nothing is safe from interference

it is neck or nothing
a desperate effort is called for
refers to a winning margin in horse racing

notion

not to have the foggiest notion
to know nothing at all about the subject

nuclear

to have a nuclear ships policy
to neither confirm nor deny something
refers to the US policy of neither confirming nor denying whether a particular ship is carrying nuclear arms

nudge

to give something a nudge forward
to give modest encouragement to something

number

one's opposite number
a person with similar responsibilities in another organisation

someone's number is up
a person's period of activity or influence is about to expire; OR one is about to die

to look after number one
to act selfishly

numbered

one's days are numbered
one is about to be abolished
Daniel 5:26, 'God hath numbered thy kingdom, and finished it'

nurse

to nurse one's bruises/wounds
to adjust oneself to defeat

nut

a hard nut to crack
a difficult problem to be solved; OR someone not easily influenced

to use a sledgehammer to crack a nut

to devote vastly more resources to a project than is warranted by all the circumstances

nuts

nuts and bolts
basic ingredients

to be nuts
to be crazy

to be nuts about someone
to be infatuated with a person

nutshell

in a nutshell
by way of summary

O

oak

to have a heart of oak
to be brave
refers to a famous sea song and naval march from the pantomime, *Harlequin's Invasion* (1759), by Garrick and Boyce.

to lock something up in the old oak chest
to put in a safe place and out of mind

oaks

tall oaks from little acorns grow
even major enterprises have to have small beginnings
David Everett (1769–1813), *Lines Written for a School Declamation*, 'Large streams from little fountains flow, / tall oaks from little acorns grow'

oar

to stick one's oar in
to intervene without invitation in a dispute to which one is not a party
refers to rowing

oats

to feel one's oats
to be energetic and lively (UK and Australia); to be self-important (USA)
refers to an energetic horse fed on oats

to sow wild oats
to indulge in foolish behaviour while a young adult

ocean

an ocean full of fish
plenty of opportunity

to be only a drop in the ocean
to be quite insignificant in the total scene

odds

that is over the odds
that is unacceptable
refers to betting on horse races

to be at odds with someone
to disagree with a person

to beat the odds
to do better than could reasonably have been expected
refers to betting on horse races or similar

to have the odds stacked against one
to be faced with many difficulties frustrating a project
refers to betting

to pay over the odds
to pay too much
refers to betting on horse races

off

off one's own bat
on a person's own initiative and without outside help
refers to cricket

off the cuff
impromptu
perhaps refers to notes scribbled on the shirt cuff for use during a speech

off the peg
(of clothes) ready-made

off the top of one's head
impromptu, based on experience or intuition, but without detailed consideration

oil

not to be an oil painting
to be ugly

the squeaky wheel gets the oil
those complaining the most loudly will get their problems sorted out first

to burn the midnight oil
to work late into the night
Francis Quarles (1592–1644), *Emblems*, 'We spend our midday sweat, our midnight oil; / we tire the night in thought, the day in toil'

to get the good oil

to receive useful, reliable and timely information

to oil the wheels
to make things go smoothly

to pour oil on troubled waters
to calm down a situation

to run something on the smell of an oil rag
to run something very economically and efficiently

oiled

to be a well-oiled piece of machinery
to be functioning very satisfactorily

oily

to run something on the smell of an oily rag
to run something very economically and efficiently

ointment

a fly in the ointment
a minor flaw that spoils a thing
Ecclesiastes 10:1, 'Dead flies cause the ointment of the apothecary to send forth a stinking savour: so doth a little folly him that is in reputation for wisdom and honour'

old

an old flame
a former lover

an old head on young shoulders
experience, knowledge, and maturity in a young person

an old wives' tale
a traditionally held theory without any scientific backing

it is on for young and old
the excitement has started (esp. referring to fighting)

one cannot teach an old dog new tricks
people become set in their ways irreversibly

to be a chip off the old block
to resemble one's father in behaviour and/or appearance

to be a good old stick
to be a kind and thoughtful person

to be money for old rope
to be an easily made profit

to be old hat
to be old-fashioned; OR well known to the point of tedium

to lock something up in the old oak chest
to put in a safe place and out of mind

to open up an old wound
to take action which revives a long-standing grievance

to rekindle an old flame
to inspire the reinstatement of a former loving relationship
David Garrick (1717–79), 'Kitty, a fair, but frozen maid, kindled a flame I still deplore'

olive

to hold out an olive branch
to make peace overtures
the olive branch was recognised as a symbol of peace and prosperity in many ancient civilisations; *Genesis* 8:11, 'And the dove came in to him in the evening; and lo, in her mouth was an olive leaf plucked off: so Noah knew that the waters were abated off the earth'

omega

from alpha to omega
from start to finish
refers to the first and last letters of the Greek alphabet

omelette

one cannot make an omelette without breaking eggs
the desired end dictates the means even if they cause harm to others

to unscramble the omelette
to undo something that cannot be undone

on

on a cold day in hell
never

on a wing and a prayer
reliance on the merest chance in a desperate situation'
also applied to an emergency landing by an aircraft; originally a song (1943) by H. Adamson

on one's own doorstep
in one's own domain

on our side of the fence
in the group representing our vested interest

on the back of something
by virtue of something

on the deathknock
at the last possible moment
refers to the mythical figure of 'Death' knocking on the door to claim a victim
on the nail
immediately
origin obscure
on the one hand
putting one side of the proposition
on the other hand
putting the opposing side of the proposition
on the quiet
surreptitiously
on the radar screen
in someone's consciousness
on the surface
on the basis of a superficial first impression

once

if I've told you once I've told you a thousand times
I express resentment at the need constantly to repeat some statement

one

a one-way street
a flow of activity in only one direction
a one-man band
a person performing many different roles singlehandedly
a thousand and one
many
on the one hand
putting one side of the proposition
one for the road
a final drink before leaving
one-eyed
biased
to be of one mind
(of several people) to be agreed
to be one in the eye for someone
to represent an unexpected and unwelcome defeat
to be one out of the box
to be unexpectedly superb
refers to magician's trick
to be only round one
to be only the first of many stages
refers to boxing
to go back to square one
to start all over again
refers to board games
to have a one-track mind
to keep coming back to one narrow topic of conversation
to look after number one
to act selfishly

onions

to know one's onions
to be well informed in some area
refers to Dr C. T. Onions, editor of the *Shorter Oxford English Dictionary*

only

not to be the only pebble on the beach
not to be the only person available for some task, or affected by some set of circumstances

open

an open sesame
access to something normally inaccessible
refers to the password for the opening of the robbers' cave in the tale of *The Forty Thieves* in *Arabian Nights' Entertainments*
one's door is always open
people can take their problems to one at any time
open-hearted
cordial
Ecclesiasticus 8:19, 'Open not thine heart to every man'
open slather
freedom for people to do what they want
to be an open-and-shut case
to be an unarguable proposition
a phrase popular in detective novels and probably a play on the two meanings of the word 'case'
to be out in the open
(of information) to be publicly available
to come out into the open
to start being frank
to have an open mind
to be willing to assess evidence on its merits and without prejudging it
to keep one's ears open
to be alert for useful information
to keep one's eyes open

to be on the lookout for useful information

to keep one's eyes open for something
to be on the lookout for an opportunity to do something

to leave oneself wide open
to act in such a way that one's opponents will find much that can be easily criticised
refers to a bodily posture that is vulnerable to attack

to leave the door open
to provide an opportunity

to open doors
to create opportunities

to open a Pandora's box
to do something that produces all sorts of undesired and unexpected side-effects
refers to the woman in Greek mythology who brought misery to the world; Pandora's box contained all human ills and, when opened, it released uncontrollable misery on humanity

to open someone's eyes to something
to alert another person to the truth of something
Matthew 9:30, 'And their eyes were opened'

to open the batting
to be the first in a series of persons speaking or doing something
refers to cricket

to open the floodgates
to take action that will have massive consequences
Shakespeare, *Othello* I:iii, 'My particular grief is of so flood-gate and o'erbearing nature that it engluts and swallows other sorrows'

to open up an old wound
to take action which revives a long-standing grievance

with an open hand
generously

with one's eyes wide open
fully conscious of the ramifications

with open arms
enthusiastically

opener

to be an eye-opener
to be a surprise

opening

an opening wide enough to drive a coach and four through
an excellent opportunity to demonstrate the major errors or absurdities of something
the saying seems sometimes also to have referred to six horses: Sir Stephen Rice (1673–1715), as quoted by W. King, *State of the Protestants of Ireland* (1672), 'I will drive a coach and six horses through the Act of Settlement'

opening gambit
the first in a series of strategic moves
usually refers to chess (see also *gambit*); Italian *gambetto*, literally 'tripping up'

opening shot
first step in an activity expected to last a long time
military metaphor

opera

a soap opera
a low-quality radio or television serial
refers to the original sponsorship of such programs by soap companies

operator

a fly-by-night operator
a person who disappears suddenly and without warning in an attempt to avoid the payment of debts or compensation or the obligations under some contract

opportunity

a golden opportunity
an unparalleled chance or occasion

a window of opportunity
an opportunity temporarily available

to grab an opportunity with both hands
to seize an opportunity with great enthusiasm

to jump at the opportunity
enthusiastically to take immediate advantage of a good chance

opposite

one's opposite number
a person with similar responsibilities in another organisation

oranges

to add/compare apples with oranges
to lump unconnected things together quite illogically

orchestrate

to orchestrate something
to arrange for something to happen

order

in apple-pie order
in perfect order and condition

pecking order
order of seniority
refers to the activity of hens and other birds

the order of the day
the customary behaviour

to be a tall order
to be an unreasonable expectation

to put one's house in order
to fix up the deficiencies in one's affairs
Isaiah 38:1, 'Set thine house in order; for thou shalt die and not live'

ordered

just what the doctor ordered
exactly right

orders

to get one's marching orders
to be told to leave
military metaphor

organ-grinder

to want the organ-grinder, not the monkey
to wish to deal with the person in authority rather than an underling
refers to a street musician using a barrel-organ, often accompanied by a pet monkey

ostrich

to be an ostrich
to refuse to face up to an unpleasant truth
refers to the reputed habit of ostriches in danger

other

a rose by any other name would smell as sweet
the form does not affect the substance
Shakespeare, *Romeo and Juliet* II:ii, 'What's in a name? That which we call a rose / By any other name would smell as sweet'

it is six of one and half a dozen of the other
it does not matter either way
Captain Marryat (1792–1848), *The Pirate* ch. 4, 'I never knows the children. It's just six of one and halfa dozen of the other.'

not to live in each other's pockets
to each follow his or her own lifestyle

on the other hand
putting the opposing side of the proposition

the boot is on the other foot
the advantage is reversed

the other side of the coin
the arguments for the opposite point of view

to be at each other's throats
to be always fighting

to be on the other side of the fence
to have an opposing point of view or position

to beat each other over the head
to be always fighting

to go in one ear and out the other
to leave no impression

to have other irons in the fire
to have the opportunity to do something else as an alternative
Francis Beaumont (1584–1616) & John Fletcher (1579–1625), *The Faithful Friends* I:ii, 'It is always good when a man has two irons in the fire'

to turn the other cheek
to refuse, on moral grounds, to retaliate to provocation in like manner
Matthew 5:38, 39, 'Ye have heard that it hath been said an eye for an eye and a tooth for a tooth: but I say unto you ... whosoever shall smite thee on the right cheek, turn to him the other also'

to wait for the other shoe to drop
to await the seemingly imminent and inevitable
refers to a person being disturbed by a neighbour who drops one shoe on the floor, the listener then being frustrated when the sound of the other shoe being dropped is not heard

you will laugh on the other side of your face
you will regret this

ounce

not to have an ounce of sense
to be stupid

to drain every ounce out of something
to get the maximum use or pleasure out of something

out

out of the frying pan into the fire
from one bad situation to an even worse one

out of the mouths of babes and sucklings
(as indiscreetly revealed) the truth
Psalms 8:2, 'Out of the mouths of babes and sucklings hast thou ordained strength ... '

outcome

one shudders to think what the outcome might be
there is great concern as to the outcome

outfit

a twopenny-halfpenny outfit
a quite insignificant operation

outgun

to outgun someone
to assert superiority over another person by use of more powerful devices

outside

to poke one's nose outside
to venture outside

over

over my dead body
never

overboard

to go overboard
to act foolishly and in an excessive way

overkill

overkill
more action than really required for the purpose

overshadow

to overshadow
to cover or obscure with a greater power; to make less important
Luke 1:35, 'And the power of the highest shall overshadow thee'

overstep

to overstep the mark
to fail to observe the proprieties
refers to gaining an unfair advantage in a contest (originally the mark between two fighters)

overtime

to work overtime at something
to spend a lot of time and effort at doing something

overtones

overtones
subtle or implied themes

overtures

to make overtures to someone
to make suggestions to a person, inviting further negotiations

owl

to be a night owl
habitually to go to bed late

own

in one's own backyard
in one's own domain

off one's own bat
on a person's own initiative and without outside help
refers to cricket

on one's own doorstep
in one's own domain

one's own flesh and blood
one's own offspring, ancestors, or close relatives
Genesis 2:23, 'Bone of my bones, and flesh of my flesh'

to be hoist with one's own petard
to have one's own case used against one
refers to being blown up by one's own petard (bomb); Shakespeare, *Hamlet* III:iv, 'for 'tis sport to have the engineer hoist with his own petard'

to be on one's own turf
to engage in one's own customary area of activity

to be one's own man
to be free and independent, and able to act in accordance with one's own values

to be someone after one's own heart
to be a person who shares one's beliefs

1 Samuel 13:14 'A man after his own heart'

to beat someone at that person's own game
to outwit a person in that person's own specialisation

to blow one's own trumpet
immodestly to publicise one's own attributes .
refers to the trumpet as an instrument of triumph; *Joshua* 6:20, 'When the priests blew with the trumpets ... the wall fell down flat'

to cut one's own throat
to act in a way that damages one's own interests

to dig one's own grave
to take action that results in an unintended disaster for oneself

to fall over one's own feet
to be very clumsy

to feather one's own nest
improperly to appropriate things for oneself (especially in financial transactions)

to foul one's own nest
to disparage or bring discredit on one's home or workplace

to get a taste of one's own medicine
to suffer from an initiative intended to affect only other persons

to get one's own back on someone
to extract revenge

to have a mind of one's own
not to be easily influenced

to make a rod for one's own back
to make a handicap for oneself

to pay someone back in that person's own coin
to retaliate in kind

to pull oneself up by one's own shoelaces
to make a superhuman effort

to put one's own stamp on something
to effect something with one's own characteristic style

to run one's own ship
to do things and organise subordinates in one's own way

to score an own goal
to make a foolish mistake that counts against oneself
refers to soccer

to sign one's own death warrant
foolishly to do something that is inevitably bound to lead to utter disaster

to stand on one's own two feet
not to require the help of others

to write one's own ticket
to set one's own terms and conditions
refers to betting on a horse with a bookmaker where the chance of that horse winning is considered so unlikely that the punter is allowed to choose the odds

under one's own power
without external help

under one's own steam
without external help
refers to a steam engine (especially in a ship)

water will find its own level
people will reach an appropriate position relative to others

oyster

the world is one's oyster
one has enormous scope for activity
Shakespeare, *The Merry Wives of Windsor*, II:ii, 'Why, then the world's mine oyster'

P

p

to watch one's P's and Q's
to be very careful
perhaps refers to pints and quarts of beer on a hotel slate, or perhaps to easily confused printer's type

pace

at a break-neck pace
very fast
refers to horseriding at great speed

at a snail's pace
very slowly
Shakespeare, *As You Like It* II:vii, 'The whining schoolboy ... creeping like snail unwillingly to school'

to set the pace
to give a lead in regard to a rate of progression

refers to horse racing and foot racing

paces

to put someone through his or her paces
to test a person
refers to testing a horse

pack

to be at the head of the pack
to be the best of many, or the *de facto* leader

to bring someone back to the pack
to make a person conform

to pack one's bags
to signal one's intention to depart

to play every card in the pack
to try very hard and use every conceivable argument
refers to playing cards

to play the last card in the pack
to be forced to use one's last expedient
refers to playing cards

packing

to send someone packing
to dismiss a person ignominiously

packdrill

no names, no packdrill
the identities of the parties will be kept confidential to protect them
military metaphor

paddle

to be up the creek without a paddle
to be in trouble

to paddle one's canoe
to do something unaided and in one's own way
phrase first used by Captain Marryat (1792–1848) *Settlers in Canada*, ch. viii (1844)

paddock

to have a spell in the paddock
to have leave of absence
refers to resting of horses from racing or work

paid

that has put paid to it
the project can no longer proceed
refers to the counting house and an account being labelled as 'paid' (meaning 'settled'); thus, the matter is settled and finished

pain

to be a pain in the neck
to be an unpleasant person or to be a nuisance

pains

growing pains
problems encountered by virtue of expansion
refers to the pains sometimes felt in the limbs by children and adolescents

paint

to paint a black picture
to state a set of unfavourable factors

to paint oneself into a corner
foolishly to put oneself into a position from which escape is impossible

to paint someone black
to ruin a person's reputation

to paint the town red
to go on an exciting social outing

painter

to cut the painter
to become separated
nautical metaphor; refers to cutting a boat loose from its moorings

painting

not to be an oil painting
to be ugly

pair

a pigeon pair
one son and one daughter as the only offspring
refers to the old belief that pigeons always sat on two eggs that produced a male and a female, and that this pair remained together throughout life palace

a palace revolt
the overthrow of those in authority by their subordinates

pale

to be beyond the pale
to be socially unacceptable, especially for unacceptable standards or behaviour
'the Pale' originally (fourteenth century and later) referred to that part of Ireland under British rule (Latin *palus* 'a stake', marking a fence or boundary)

to be only a pale shadow of something
to be a weak imitation

palings

that person has some palings off the fence
that person is mentally disturbed

palms

to grease someone's palms
to bribe a person
Francis Quarles (1592–1644), English poet, *The Virgin Widow* IV:i, 'grease my fist with a tester or two, and you shall find it in your pennyworth'

palpable

palpable
readily understandable
literally 'touchable'; Shakespeare, *Hamlet* V:ii, 'a hit, a very palpable hit'

pan

a flash in the pan
something that begins promisingly but does not last
refers to the priming of old guns

out of the frying pan into the fire
from one bad situation to an even worse one

to pan out
to turn out, to happen
refers to a gold prospector's pan used to seek gold in gravel of streams

pancake

every Pancake Tuesday
only on occasions
refers to Shrove Tuesday, when pancakes are traditionally eaten

Pandora

to open a Pandora's box
to do something that produces all sorts of undesired and unexpected side-effects
refers to the woman in Greek mythology who brought misery to the world; Pandora's box contained all human ills and, when opened, it released uncontrollable misery on humanity

panic

to hit the panic button
to act hastily and irrationally

pants

a kick in the pants
an admonition

to bore the pants off someone
to weary a person by dull and uninteresting conversation

to catch someone with his pants down
to act when another person least expects it

to charm the pants off someone
to delight a person

to fly by the seat of one's pants
to act by instinct in the absence of specific knowledge or instructions

to scare the pants off someone
to frighten a person greatly

to wear the pants
to be the dominant party

paper

a paper tiger
an empty threat

only a cigarette paper between them
virtually equal or close together

paper warfare
an excessive amount of correspondence or excessive bureaucracy

to have shares in a paper company
to institute unnecessary clerical procedures

to paper over the cracks
to institute extremely superficial and basically ineffective remedies
refers to placing wallpaper over cracks in a wall

to put pen to paper
to set out one's ideas in written form

to start with a blank sheet of paper
to commence an exercise without being bound by any established practices

par

to be below par
to be less than the desired standard

to be par for the course
to be normal
refers to golf

parachute

golden parachute
(in a remuneration package) generous provisions that come into play in certain circumstances

paradise

to live in a fool's paradise
to delude oneself into a state of happy contentment when reality is quite different

parallel

parallel
similar or corresponding

paralyse

to paralyse something
to bring something to a standstill

parcel

to be part and parcel
to be the essential ingredients

pariah

pariah
social outcast
refers to members of a low caste in India

paring

cheese paring
miserly

parish

parish pump issues
issues of local importance lacking a wider perspective
refers to the local parish water pump

park

to be in the right ballpark
to be approximately correct
refers to baseball

Parkinson

Parkinson's law
the principle that work expands to match the work capacity available
title of a book (1957) by Prof. C. Northcote Parkinson

parochial

parochial
narrow-minded
refers to parish or local issues

parry

to parry some argument
to deflect some argument
refers to fencing

part

to be part and parcel
to be the essential ingredients

to be part of the furniture
to be so familiar that one's presence goes completely unnoticed

to be part of the landscape
to be present and fully accepted without question

to play one's part
to cooperate or carry out one's obligations under some arrangement
refers to the theatre; Shakespeare, *As You Like It*, I:vii, 'All the world's a stage ... and one man in his time plays many parts'

parting

to fire a parting shot/shaft
to make a defiant gesture on leaving
sometimes also referred to as a 'Parthian shot/shaft' — refers to missiles shot backwards by fleeing Parthian horsemen

Parthian

to fire a Parthian shot/shaft
to make a defiant or cutting gesture or remark on leaving
sometimes also referred to as 'a parting shot/shaft' — refers to missiles shot backwards by fleeing Parthian horsemen

parts

to be parts of a jigsaw
to be elements in the solution of something complex
refers to a jigsaw puzzle

party

the party is over
the previous pleasant arrangements have been discontinued

to be the life and soul of the party
to be the prime enthusiast for a cause
Shakespeare, *A Midsummer Night's Dream*, 'My love, my life, my soul, fair Helena!'

to come to the party
to agree to someone's terms

pas

faux pas
something indiscreet or offending social conventions
French: 'false step'

pass

ships that pass in the night
a fleeting, transitory acquaintance

Henry Wadsworth Longfellow (1807–82), *The Theologian's Tale (Tales of a Wayside Inn)*, 'Ships that pass in the night, and speak each other in passing … '

to pass on the bâton
to hand over to a successor

to pass the ball along
to cooperate with others

to pass the buck
to shift responsibility to someone else
refers to the buckhorn knife passed around the table to indicate the dealer while playing poker

to pass with flying colours
to be very successful in a test or contest
refers to ships returning to port with colours flying triumphantly

passport

to be a passport to success
to be a means of achieving success

past

a past master
an expert with long experience
derived from freemasonry

pastor

pastor
religious official in charge of a congregation
from Latin *pastor* (form of *pascere)* meaning 'to feed or graze'; an example of a metaphor applied originally to flocks of sheep, and now having become established in the English language in its metaphorical sense of caring for a religious flock

pastures

to move on to greener pastures
to move to a better environment; to commence a new, better career
Psalms 23:1, 'The Lord is my shepherd: therefore can I lack nothing. he shall feed me in a green pasture: and lead me forth beside the waters of comfort'

pat

to pat oneself on the back
immodestly to congratulate oneself

to pat someone on the back
to congratulate a person or to reassure a person

patch

a sticky patch
a period fraught with difficulties

not to be a patch on someone
not to be comparable to a person

to be on someone's cabbage patch
to engage in a competitive activity in a territory regarded by someone already there as rightfully belonging exclusively to that person

to keep off someone's patch
not to interfere with or compete against another person in that person's customary area of activity

to patch up some quarrel
to reconcile one's differences

patchwork

a patchwork quilt
a result arising from many uncoordinated inputs

path

slippery path
dangerous course of action

to be on a path strewn with roses
to lead a very pleasant life

to be on the war path
to be on the lookout for faults that can be criticised

to beat a path to someone's door
to seek a person out in great numbers
Ralph Waldo Emerson (1803–82), *Sarah S. B. Yule, Borrowings*, 'If a man write a better book, preach a better sermon, or make a better mouse-trap than his neighbour, tho' he build his house in the woods, the world will make a beaten path to his door'

to block someone's path
to interfere with a person's opportunity to advance

to cross someone's path
to meet another person by chance

to lead someone up the garden path
to mislead a person by deliberately fallacious arguments

to smooth the path for someone
to use one's influence to make arrangements so that a person's task will be easier or more readily accomplished
Isaiah 40:3, 'Prepare ye the way of the Lord; make smooth in the desert a highway for our God'

to tread a particular path

to follow a certain (perhaps new or lonely) course of action

patience

something would try the patience of Job
something is very vexatious
James 5:11, 'Ye have heard of the patience of Job'

to have the patience of a saint
to endure annoyances with particular calm

Paul

to rob Peter to pay Paul
to discharge one debt or responsibility by incurring another
John Wyclif (c.1380), *Select Works* III 174, 'How should God approve that you rob Peter, and give this robbery to Paul in the name of Christ?' (perhaps refers to an ecclestiastical property dispute between two churches)

pave

to pave the way
to prepare for something

paw

to be a cat's paw
to be a person who is being used as a tool by others
refers to the fable of the monkey who used the paw of his friend, the cat, to extract roasted chestnuts from the fire

pawn

a pawn
a person of small importance who is manipulated by others
from Old French *poön, peon* ('foot soldier'); now applied to the smallest piece on the chess board

pay

to pay a king's ransom
to pay a very large sum

to pay lip service to some rules
to disregard some rules in practice while acknowledging them in words

to pay off
to be successful; OR formally to complete a ship's period of active service

to pay over the odds
to pay too much
refers to betting on horse races

to pay someone back in that person's own coin
to retaliate in kind

to pay something back with interest
to return a small favour with a bigger favour; or to extract retribution of greater value than the circumstances warrant

to pay the price
to suffer the adverse consequences of one's acts or omissions

to pay through the nose
to pay an excessive price
refers to an onerous tax imposed by the Danes in Ireland in the ninth century whereby those who refused to pay had their noses slit

to rob Peter to pay Paul
to discharge one debt or responsibility by incurring another
John Wyclif (c.1380), *Select Works* III 174, 'How should God approve that you rob Peter, and give this robbery to Paul in the name of Christ?' (perhaps refers to an ecclesiastical property dispute between two churches)

to strike pay dirt
to become successful
refers to soil containing gold or other precious metal

pays

he who pays the piper calls the tune
a person contributing money or resources to a project is entitled to control it

pea

a pea-and-thimble trick
a clever fraud committed in the presence of its victim without this being obvious at the time
refers to a sleight-of-hand trick played with three thimbles and a pea, the thimbles being moved about and observers being asked to guess under which thimble the pea is

peanuts

to earn peanuts
to get a reward that is far too small in relation to the value of the services rendered

pearl

a pearl
a thing of great excellence

pearls

to cast pearls before swine
to confer valuable benefits on someone who neither recognises nor appreciates them
Matthew 7:6, 'Neither cast ye your pearls before swine'

pebble

not to be the only pebble on the beach
not to be the only person available for some task, or affected by some set of circumstances

to throw a pebble against the window
gently to draw attention to oneself

pecked

hen-pecked
subject to domination by one's wife
Lord Byron (1788–1824), *Don Juan*, But — Oh! ye lords of ladies intellectual, inform us truly, have they not hen-peck'd you all?

pecker

to keep one's pecker up
to stay cheerful
refers to keeping one's head up (with 'pecker' referring to mouth — as in a bird's mouth)

pecking

pecking order
order of seniority
refers to the activity of hens and other birds

pedal

to back pedal
to reverse to some extent previously applied policies
refers to riding a cycle

to soft pedal
to restrain oneself
refers to playing an organ or piano

pedestal

to put someone on a pedestal
to admire a person and regard that person as being more marvellous than is warranted

pedestrian

pedestrian
uninspired
refers to travelling by foot

peeled

to keep one's eyes peeled for something
to be on the constant lookout for something
refers to keeping the eyelids open

peg

a peg to hang a hat on
something that provides a convenient or plausible excuse for some particular action

a square peg in a round hole
obviously unsuited for the purpose'

off the peg
(of clothes) ready-made

to peg out
to die
refers to the final act in a game of cribbage

to take someone down a peg or two
to humble a person (especially a conceited person)
refers to scoring in backgammon or cribbage; Samuel Butler (1612–80), *Hudibras* II:ii, 'And took your grandees down a peg'

pegging

to be level pegging
(of contestants) to have little between them
refers to cribbage

pen

to hold the pen poised
to be ready to consummate a deal

to put pen to paper
to set out one's ideas in written form

with a stroke of the pen
by edict

pence

to be only ten pence in the shilling
to be slightly stupid
refers to 'old' shillings and pence when a shilling equalled twelve pence

pencil

to need to sharpen one's pencil
to be required to improve one's performance

pendulum

the swing of the pendulum

the alternation of prospects, fortune, or experience penetrate

to penetrate someone's thick skull
to make a person understand something difficult or acknowledge something unwelcome

pennies

to be unable to rub two pennies together
to be very poor

to throw in one's six pennies' worth
modestly to supply one's own facts or views

penny

a twopenny halfpenny outfit
a quite insignificant operation

if you gave that person a penny for that person's thoughts you would get change
that person is extremely stupid

in for a penny, in for a pound
once something is commenced it ought be finished; OR if one is willing to take a small risk then one might as well take a bigger one

penny-pinching
excessively mean

the penny dropped
a person has just realised a fact that should have been obvious
refers to old-fashioned pay toilets

to cost a pretty penny
to be very expensive

to turn an honest penny
to earn money by hard work

people

people in glass houses should not throw stones
those who are less than perfect are foolish to criticise others
John 8:7, 'He that is without sin among you, let him first cast a stone at her' (refers to ancient condemnation and punishment of people by stoning)

people stayed away in droves
few people came
refers to a moving group of cattle, sheep, or other animals

to be unable to keep people away with a big stick
to be faced with a large crowd or much demand

perch

to knock someone off that person's perch
to displace a person from a leadership position in some competitive situation

person

one's right-hand person
one's chief aide
Hebrews 1:1, 'His son ... by whom he also made the worlds ... sat down on the right hand of the majesty in heaven'

perspective

to put something into perspective
to explain the background of something so that its significance in relation to other things can be better appreciated

petard

to be hoist with one's own petard
to have one's own case used against one
refers to being blown up by one's own petard (bomb); Shakespeare, *Hamlet* III:iv, 'for 'tis sport to have the engineer hoist with his own petard'

Peter

to rob Peter to pay Paul
to discharge one debt or responsibility by incurring another
John Wyclif (c.1380), *Select Works* III 174, 'How should God approve that you rob Peter, and give this robbery to Paul in the name of Christ?' (perhaps refers to an ecclesiastical property dispute between two churches)

to tickle the peter
to rob one's employer
refers to slang term for cash box

petrel

to be a stormy petrel
a person who disturbs a pleasant state of affairs by agitating for change
refers to the bird (petrel) that flies low over water during a storm and appears to be alternately touching one foot and then the other to the surface of the water as though walking upon it; the bird is sometimes thought to be the harbinger of a storm, and is named after St Peter

who walked upon the stormy waters of Lake Gennesareth

petrified

to be petrified
to be made immobile with fear
refers to Greek *petros* (Latin: *petra*) = 'stone'; *Matthew* 16:18, 'Thou art Peter, and upon this rock I will build my church'

petrol

to pour petrol on the flames
to make a bad situation worse

to put a match to petrol
to cause an actual disaster out of a potentially disastrous situation

petshop

every galah in the petshop
everybody

petticoat

petticoat government
rule by women

phoenix

to rise from the ashes like a phoenix
to be the replacement for something destroyed in some disaster
refers to a mythical bird that was supposed to rise from the ashes of its funeral pile/pyre with renewed youth

photo

a photo finish
a close result in a contest
refers to horse racing

pick

not to just pick something out of a hat
to choose carefully, after weighing all the considerations
refers to choosing by lot by choosing things unseen from a hat

to hand-pick someone
to choose a person carefully for that person's individual attributes

to have a bone to pick
to have a grievance that requires discussion

to pick just the plums out of the jam
to take only the very best items

to nitpick
to criticise a person in respect of very minor matters
refers to the removal of lice eggs (nits) from the hair of an animal or person

to pick someone's brain
to get the benefit of another person's knowledge and experience

to pick up the pieces
to resume previous activities to the maximum extent possible after some setback

picking

to engage in cherry picking
(in business) to accept only the potentially most lucrative deals

to keep one's cotton-picking fingers off something
not to interfere (in a meddlesome fashion) with something

pickle

to be in a pickle
to be in difficulties
Shakespeare, *The Tempest* V:i, 'How cam'st thou in this pickle?'

picnic

to be no picnic
to be unpleasant

picture

to balance the picture
to quote facts or arguments in contradiction

to change the whole picture
to alter the major assumptions on which some assessment was based

to conjure up a picture
to use words to convey a vivid impression

to have a clear picture of something
to have a good understanding of something

to paint a black picture
to state a set of unfavourable factors

to present a rosy picture
to state a set of favourable factors

to put someone in the picture
to fill a person in with the background of a situation

to see the big picture
to have the vision and imagination enabling a project to be developed as part of a bigger whole

pie

in apple-pie order
in perfect order and condition

pie in the sky
a hoped for result unlikely to be achieved

to eat humble pie
to be prepared to humiliate oneself and apologise
a play on words — derived from the eating of 'umble pie' (entrails of a deer) by lowly persons

to have a finger in the pie
to have an interest in a project, especially an officious involvement

pies

to have one's fingers in many different pies
to be engaged in a variety of separate activities

piece

a museum piece
an old article the use of which is no longer efficient

a nasty piece of work
an unpleasant person
perhaps a later pejorative reversal of Shakespeare's hymn of praise to humanity, *Hamlet* II:ii, 'What a piece of work is a man!'

early in the piece
at an early stage of some activity

to be a piece of cake
to be very easy or greatly to one's liking

to be a well-oiled piece of machinery
to be functioning very satisfactorily

to give someone a piece of one's mind
to abuse another person

to have a piece of someone
to vent one's frustration on a person

to have a piece of the action
to be one of several parties to a project

pieces

to be cut to pieces
to be very upset; OR to be completely overrun and defeated

to be shot to pieces
to have one's case seriously damaged

to be thrilled to pieces
to be greatly thrilled

to fall to pieces
to collapse

to pick up the pieces
to resume previous activities to the maximum extent possible after some setback

pier

take a long walk on a short pier
go away, I want no dealings with you

pig

a guinea pig
a person on whom some new practice is tried out
refers to use of guinea pigs in medical experimentation

pig-headed
unduly obstinate

to buy a pig in a poke
to buy goods of unknown quality
refers to the practice of selling a person a cat (purported to be a pig) in a bag (or poke); if the person opened the bag and looked inside, that person 'let the cat out of the bag'

pigeon

a pigeon pair
one son and one daughter as the only offspring
refers to the old belief that pigeons always sat on two eggs that produced a male and a female, and that this pair remained together throughout life

to be one's pigeon
to be one's area of responsibility

to pigeon-hole
to put aside for further consideration in the distant future
refers to placing something in a small hole, like the small hole in a dovecot for the pigeons to walk in and out

pigeons

to throw a cat among the pigeons
to cause consternation and upset

pigheaded

pigheaded
unduly obstinate

pill

to be a bitter pill to swallow
to be a great humiliation or disappointment that has to be endured

to sugar the pill
to cause something to be more acceptable

pillar

a pillar of some organisation
a significant supporter of some organisation

to drive someone from pillar to post
to send a person to a series of places in a vain attempt to achieve something

originally a term from royal tennis, referring to the balls being struck and banging about structures in the (indoors) court

pillory

to put someone in the pillory
to hold a person up to ridicule for that person's beliefs

refers to a form of punishment involving public humiliation

pin

not to care a pin for something
not to have the slightest interest in something

pin money
an allowance to a wife for her personal use

probably refers to money for purchase of hair pins and other decorative pins

to be able to hear a pin drop
to experience silence

to pin someone down
to find a person willing to accept blame or responsibility; OR to force a person to announce a decision or concede a point

refers to wrestling

to pin the tail on the donkey
to put the blame on a person who has with some effort been identified as responsible

refers to children's parlour game

pinch

to feel the pinch
to be adversely affected by stringency (esp. financial)

to know where the shoe pinches
to realise from personal experience what the cause of some problem really is

pinching

penny-pinching
excessively mean

pineapple

to have hold of the wrong end of the pineapple
to be utterly mistaken

pink

to be tickled pink
to be very pleased

Oliver Goldsmith (1730–74), *She Stoops to Conquer*, 'the very pink of perfection'

to look in the pink
to look well

Oliver Goldsmith (1730–74), *She Stoops to Conquer*, 'the very pink of perfection'

pinned

with one's ears pinned back
chastened

refers to the aggressive attitude of horses

pinpoint

to pinpoint
to identify very precisely

pinprick

a pinprick
a trifling irritation

pins

for two pins I would do so-and-so
my tolerance is almost exhausted and I am very tempted to do so-and-so

to be on pins and needles
to be very agitated

pint

one can't get a quart into a pint pot
one cannot do the impossible

pintsize

pintsize
small

pip

to pip someone at the post
to achieve something only just ahead of a rival

refers to the winning post in horse racing

pipe

put that in your pipe and smoke it
contemplate that fact if you can!

a strong rebuke given to an adversary; R. H. Barham (1788–1845), *Lay of St*

Odille, 'So put that in your pipe, my Lord Otto, and smoke it!'

to pipe someone on board
to welcome a person
nautical metaphor

pipedream

a pipedream
a fanciful notion, wished for but unlikely
probably derived from smoking opium in pipes

pipeline

a pipeline to someone
an intermediary used as a means of communicating ideas to a person

in the pipeline
being dealt with

piper

he who pays the piper calls the tune
a person contributing money or resources to a project is entitled to control it

pirate

pirate
(of radio) unlicensed; (of recordings or computer software) published in breach of copyright law

pistol

to hold a pistol at someone's head
to put pressure on a person to make a particular decision regardless of that person's desires in the matter

pit

a pit of disaster
great and unexpected misfortune

pitch

to be at fever pitch
to be in a state of excited activity

to be up to concert pitch
to be ready

to cruel someone's pitch
to spoil a person's chances

to queer the pitch for someone
to spoil the opportunity a person has to do something

pitchers

asses and little pitchers have long ears
children have a tendency to overhear things

pitfall

pitfall
unsuspected danger
refers to capturing animals by inducing them to fall into a pit

place

a place in the sun
a favourable situation

to be between a rock and a hard place
to be faced with two equally difficult and uncomfortable choices

to have one's heart in the right place
to have good intentions, to mean well

to make some place too hot for someone
to make a place unpleasant for someone

to put someone back in his or her place
to require a person to act in accordance with that person's level of seniority

plague

a plague on both your houses!
I am disgusted with both of you
Shakespeare, *Romeo and Juliet*, III:i, 'A plague o' both your houses!'

to be of plague proportions
to be great in number
refers to the plagues of locusts, frogs, etc., as described in *Exodus* chs 8 and 10 (and elsewhere)

plain

to be plain sailing
to be quite straightforward and very easy
refers to navigation by means of a 'plane chart' on which meridians and parallels of latitude are represented by equidistant straight lines

planet

to be off the planet
to be extremely naVve or uninformed

plank

to walk the plank
to face certain doom
refers to execution of persons at sea

plate

to bring a plate
to take food to a party

to have too much on one's plate
to be unable to cope with one's workload

to serve something up to someone on a plate
to make something especially easy for a particular person

plates

to have L-plates
to be new to a task
refers to learner's plates on the vehicle of a novice driver

platter

to hand over something on a silver platter
to provide a valuable benefit for virtually nothing
refers to first-class service

play

don't play games with me!
do not insult my intelligence by that sort of conduct

foul play
treachery or murder
Shakespeare: *Hamlet* II:i, 'All is not well; I doubt some foul play'

horseplay
boisterous and undignified behaviour
John Dryden (1631–1700), 'He [Collier] is too much given to horseplay in his raillery'

to be child's play
to be easy or to require only elementary skills and knowledge

to be in full play
to be fully operational

to find out the state of play
to ascertain the current position of some project

to play a deep game
to show cunning

to play ball
to cooperate

to play by Marquis of Queensberry rules
to act ethically
refers to regulations regarding boxing matches drawn up by John Sholto Douglas, Eighth Marquis of Queensberry (1843–83), in 1867

to play by the book
to apply the rules strictly

to play down something
to seek to have less emphasis or attention given to something

to play ducks and drakes
not to treat the matter seriously
derived from the old name given to the game of throwing a stone such that it skips across the surface of water; hence: 'to throw away idly and carelessly

to play every card in the pack
to try very hard and use every conceivable argument
refers to playing cards

to play fast and loose
to ignore one's obligations, be unreliable
refers to old fairground game in which the player was cheated

to play gooseberry
to act as an unwelcome chaperon

to play it by ear
to develop one's strategy to always fit in with circumstances as they change from time to time
refers to playing music without the benefit of a written score

to play it cool
to take a low-key and rational approach

to play it safe
to take no risks

to play Judas
to betray a person
Matthew 26:14, 16, 'Then one of the twelve, called Judas Iscariot ... sought opportunity to betray him'

to play monkey tricks on someone
to engage in discreditable behaviour affecting a person

to play musical chairs
to be a part of a general reshuffling (of duties or functions) that is not necessarily to everyone's liking
refers to a parlour game culminating in a sudden scrambling for positions

to play one's cards right
to approach a matter sensibly
refers to playing cards

to play one's part

to cooperate or carry out one's obligations under some arrangement
refers to the theatre; Shakespeare, *As You Like It*, I:vii, 'All the world's a stage ... and one man in his time plays many parts'

to play possum
to lie low; to feign unconsciousness or death
refers to the possum's habit of attempting to evade capture by feigning death

to play right into someone's hands
to act so as to give a person an unintended advantage

to play Russian roulette
to engage in a dangerously unpredictable exercise
refers to an act of daring in which one squeezes the trigger of a revolver held to the head (after loading one chamber and spinning the cylinder — thus the one being fired is determined by chance)

to play second fiddle
to fulfil a subordinate role
refers to playing in an orchestra

to play the cards as they fall
to deal with problems as they arise
refers to playing cards

to play the game
to observe the letter and the spirit of the rules; to act honourably

to play the giddy goat
to act the fool
'giddy' derived from Old English *gidig* ('possessed by a god')

to play the last card in the pack
to be forced to use one's last expedient
refers to playing cards

to play the trump card
to make a final move, thereby defeating one's opponents
refers to playing cards

to play to the gallery
to do something that appeals to unrefined opinion rather than something that is right
refers to the theatre

to play with dynamite
to invite trouble by virtue of one's risky conduct

to play with fire
to invite trouble by meddling with dangerous matters

to underplay some situation
to make something seem less significant than it is

two can play at that game
it is possible to retaliate

when the cat is away the mice will play
in the absence of supervision discipline will be lax

without any cards to play
without the means to achieve something
refers to playing cards

players

a trap for young players
a significant likelihood of the inexperienced or naVve making mistakes

playing

a level playing field
competition on equal terms

plead

to plead the fifth amendment
to refuse to answer an unwelcome question
refers to the fifth amendment of the United States constitution, which provides protection against self-incrimination

Plimsoll

the Plimsoll line
the standard
refers to the mark fixing the maximum load line of a merchant ship in water, and to Samuel Plimsoll MP (1824–98) who campaigned for safe shipping practices

plot

to plot a safe course through troubled waters
to make a plan that overcomes certain difficulties
nautical metaphor

plough

speed the plough!
let us get on with this as fast as possible!
George Chapman (?1559–?1634), *Bussy d'Ambois*, I:i, 'speed his plough!'

to plough new ground
to engage laboriously in an untried activity

to plough on

methodically and painstakingly to continue with an activity

to plough profits back
to retain profits in a business

to put one's hand to the plough
voluntarily to undertake some task
Luke 9:62. 'No man, having put his hand to the plough, and looking back, is fit for the Kingdom of God'

pluck

to pluck figures out of the air
to make figures up arbitrarily

plug

to pull the plug
to terminate an activity suddenly
refers to electricity

plum

the plum
the best item in a collection

plums

to pick just the plums out of the jam
to take only the very best items

plunge

to take the plunge
to make an irreversible initial action; to commit oneself to a course of action
refers to leaping into water

poach

to poach on someone's preserves
to encroach uninvited on another person's territory

poacher

to appoint a poacher to be gamekeeper
to engage, perhaps foolishly, a formerly dishonest person to a position where that person's specialised knowledge can assist the prevention of similar dishonest activity by others

pocket

the hip-pocket nerve
the assessment of issues by their financial effects on one

to be in someone's pocket
to be subject to undue influence by another person

to be out of pocket
to have lost money in a transaction

to have money burning a hole in one's pocket
to be impatient to spend or invest available funds

to put one's hand in one's pocket
to provide money from one's own resources, especially for a charitable purpose

pockets

not to live in each other's pockets
to each follow his or her own lifestyle

to have deep pockets
to have large financial resources and to be willing to use them if the circumstances seem right

to line one's pockets
to make, improperly and secretly, a profit out of some transaction

point

not to put too fine a point on it
speaking bluntly
Charles Dickens (1812–70) *Bleak House* ch. 11, '"not to put too fine a point upon it" — a favourite apology for plain-speaking with Mr Snagsby'

the crowning point
the height of a person's achievement

to pinpoint
to identify very precisely

to point the bone at someone
to accuse a person
an Australian Aboriginal method of applying a curse

to point the finger at someone
to accuse a person or allege some indiscretion on that person's part

to reach boiling point
to reach a climax; OR to be close to losing one's temper

to refuse point blank
to refuse outright
refers to pointing at the white spot (blank, French blanc) in the centre of an archery target

to score a point
to make a clever contribution in the course of debate

to take the point
to understand and concede the truth of a proposition being advanced

pointing

it is pointing in the right direction

it is proceeding towards success

points

to get brownie points
to receive credit for being very well behaved, or for meritorious achievement
refers to junior girl guide members; the metaphor is often used jocularly or sarcastically with respect to adults

to score points
to make a good impression

to score top points
to achieve the outstanding score; to be considered the best

poised

to hold the pen poised
to be ready to consummate a deal

poison

one man's meat is another man's poison
different people have different tastes

to hand someone a poisoned chalice
to confer a seeming benefit on a person that will turn out to be a significant detriment

poke

to be better than a poke in the eye with a burnt stick
to be not particularly welcome, but better than other alternatives

to be more than one can poke a stick at
to be more than can reasonably be handled

to buy a pig in a poke
to buy goods of unknown quality
refers to the practice of selling a person a cat (purported to be a pig) in a bag (or poke); if the person opened the bag and looked inside, that person 'let the cat out of the bag'

to poke mullock at someone
to ridicule a person, or to rubbish that person's arguments
refers to the heap of rubbish at the top of a mineshaft

to poke one's nose into something
to interfere

to poke one's nose outside
to venture outside

poker

a game of poker
negotiations in which the parties try to bluff each other
refers to playing cards

a poker face
a facial expression that does not reveal one's thoughts during negotiations
refers to playing cards

polarise

to polarise
to cause people to identify themselves as belonging to groups holding opposing views
refers to electromagnetic poles

pole

not to touch something with a forty-foot barge pole
to go out of one's way to avoid something

to be at the bottom of the totem pole
to be in the most junior position in some hierarchy
refers to a pole with emblems or carvings having religious significance

poles

to be poles apart
to have ideas that are very different

policy

to have a nuclear ships policy
to neither confirm nor deny something
refers to the US policy of neither confirming nor denying whether a particular ship is carrying nuclear arms

political

a political football
a political issue that is being exploited for political point-scoring and gamesmanship, rather than being debated on its merits

to be a political animal
to be a person who thinks and acts politically in all aspects of life

pond

to be a big fish in a little pond
to be a person holding an important office but in an unimportant organisation

pontificate

to pontificate
to speak as if with great authority and with an assumed air of infallibility
refers to the pope (or pontiff)

pony

a show pony
a vain and ostentatious person

poor

a poor man's something
a second-best version

poor devil
person to be pitied

popped

someone's eyes popped
a person expressed great surprise

poppies

to cut tall poppies down to size
to diminish the self-importance of haughty persons

pork

to pork barrel
to spend taxpayers' money in one area in order to attract political support
refers to times of slavery in America when pork was provided to slaves gathered around the pork barrel

port

any port in a storm
anything that helps to avoid difficulties is welcome

port of call
one of a series of places being visited
nautical metaphor

position

to be in a commanding position
to have a strategic advantage

positively

positively purring
(of a person) very pleased; (of an engine) running very smoothly
refers to a cat's purring

possum

to play possum
to lie low; to feign unconsciousness or death
refers to the possum's habit of attempting to evade capture by feigning death

to stir the possum
to set out to raise controversial issues

post

a listening post
a place where information of strategic value can be collected
military metaphor

a staging post
a designated stopping or resting place on a journey
refers to the place at which the horses drawing a stagecoach were changed over

to conduct a post mortem on something
to review past actions with a view to learning lessons for the future
Latin, *post mortem*, 'after the death'

to drive someone from pillar to post
to send a person to a series of places in a vain attempt to achieve something
originally a term from royal tennis, referring to the balls being struck and banging about structures in the (indoors) court

to go post haste
to go very fast
refers to urgent postal messages (originally carried on horseback)

to pip someone at the post
to achieve something only just ahead of a rival
refers to the winning post in horse racing

to signpost something
to give an indication of the alternatives available

postage

only a postage stamp between them
virtually equal or close together

posted

to keep someone posted
to keep a person informed

posts

to move the goal posts
unfairly to alter the rules after some action (that relied on the old rules) has already started
refers to sporting games

pot

a melting pot

a country where people with different ethnic backgrounds merge, over time, into one nation
refers to a vessel for melting and mixing metals

a pot of gold
wealth, especially a reward long wished-for

one can't get a quart into a pint pot
one cannot do the impossible

the pot calling the kettle black
criticising another person without realising one's own even greater shortcomings

to go back into the melting pot
to be up for reconsideration from the beginning
refers to a vessel for melting and mixing metals

to keep the pot boiling
to ensure that an issue stays current
refers to cooking

to seek the pot of gold at the end of the rainbow
to have naVve expectations
refers to the proverbial belief in the existence of a pot of gold at the end of a rainbow

to stir the pot
to set out to raise controversial issues

to sweeten the pot
to provide a few additional inducements

to take pot luck
to take whatever happens by chance to be available
refers to a cooking pot of food

pots

fleshpots
sumptuous living
Exodus 16:3, ' ... in the land of Egypt, when we sat by the fleshpots and when we did eat bread to the full'

potato

a hot potato
a controversial issue that no one wants to handle, an embarrassing issue

potatoes

to be small potatoes
to be quite unimportant

potshot

to take a potshot at someone
to make an opportunistic disparaging remark about a person
refers to shooting game for food and not in accordance with the rules of the sport

pottage

to sell one's birthright for a mess of pottage
through foolishness to exchange something of substance for something of little value
Genesis 25:34, 'Then Jacob gave Esau bread and pottage of lentils ... thus Esau despised his birthright'

pound

in for a penny, in for a pound
once something is commenced it ought be finished; OR if one is willing to take a small risk then one might as well take a bigger one

one's pound of flesh
that which is strictly due to one, albeit excessive and lacking in compassion
Shakespeare, *Merchant of Venice* IV:i, 'The pound of flesh, which I demand of him, is dearly bought; 't is mine, and I will have it!'

pour

to pour cold water on some idea
to be unenthusiastic about some proposal or scornful of its apparent weaknesses

to pour oil on troubled waters
to calm down a situation

to pour one's heart out to someone
to reveal one's innermost hopes and fears to another person

to pour petrol on the flames
to make a bad situation worse

to pour vitriol on something
to criticise something sharply
refers to sulphuric acid or to the caustic sulphates of various elements

pours

it never rains but it pours
crises often occur together

powder

to keep one's powder dry
to retain key arguments or resources in reserve for use later
refers to gunpowder in battle

power

more power to your elbow
may your praiseworthy efforts continue and be strengthened

the power behind the throne
a person exercising the real authority but without having the official right to do so
William Pitt, Earl of Chatham (1708–78) ('Pitt the Elder'), 'There is something behind the throne greater than the king himself'

to hold the power to do something in the hollow of one's hand
to have the right to make crucial decisions
Isaiah 40:12, ' ... who hath measured the waters in the hollow of his hand ... '

under one's own power
without external help

praises

to sing someone's praises
to commend a person exuberantly

prayer

on a wing and a prayer
reliance on the merest chance in a desperate situation'
also applied to an emergency landing by an aircraft; originally a song (1943) by H. Adamson

the answer to a maiden's prayer
an unexpected but very welcome happening

pre-empt

to pre-empt some issue
deliberately to do something that has the effect of limiting the range of alternative approaches to a matter
refers to the right of certain persons (originally the Crown) to buy certain things before others have an opportunity
preach

to preach to the converted
to say something to those who already believe in it

prepare

to prepare one's ground
to get ready for a confrontation
refers to military battle

present

to present a rosy picture
to state a set of favourable factors

preserves

to poach on someone's preserves
to encroach uninvited on another person's territory

press

to be hot off the press
to be the latest news
refers to old-style hot presses used in printing newspapers

to press a button
to make something happen

pressure

to apply pressure on someone
to induce a person to do something that that person would otherwise not do by implying adverse consequences if the person does not cooperate

pretty

to cost a pretty penny
to be very expensive

to sit pretty
to be in an advantageous or comfortable position

prey

to prey on one's mind
(of a problem) to keep worrying one

price

that has nothing to do with the price of fish
that is quite irrelevant

to pay the price
to suffer the adverse consequences of one's acts or omissions

what has that to do with the price of fish?
what is the relevance of this?

prick

a pinprick
a trifling irritation

to prick up one's ears
suddenly to start paying attention to a conversation in progress as a result of a half-heard phrase
refers to horses and dogs

pride

to swallow one's pride
to take action despite the humiliating nature of this course

priest

the high priest of something

the leading advocate of something
refers to religious leaders

prima

a prima donna
a person with an exaggerated opinion of that person's own importance making relations with others needlessly difficult
Italian, 'first lady'

prime

prime mover
person initiating and promoting a cause

to engage in pump priming
to spend public money with the aim of attracting parochial electoral support
refers to priming a water pump

print

a licence to print money
a lucrative government-conferred monopoly or privilege
Lord Thomson of Fleet (1894–1977), 'It's just like having a licence to print your own money' (after the opening of Scottish commercial television, as recorded in Braddon, *Roy Thomson of Fleet Street*)

to fill in the fine print
to provide the precise details in respect of something presently existing in broad outline only

prisoners

to take no prisoners
to be utterly ruthless
military metaphor

prize

to win the booby prize
to do worse than all others

to win the prize in a canter
to win very easily
refers to horse racing

prizes

not to be here to win prizes
to be altruistic

problem

a problem child
a source of unnecessary difficulty

to come to grips with some problem
to be on the way to solving a problem

produce

to produce something out of thin air
to get hold of something in circumstances where this seemed impossible
Shakespeare, *The Tempest* IV:i, ' ... are melted into air, into thin air'

profile

profile
description
refers to a view of a person (esp. a person's face) from the side

profit

to walk away with a profit
to achieve a profit on concluding a project

profits

to plough profits back
to retain profits in a business

promise

to promise the earth
to give extravagant assurances
Matthew 5:5, 'Blessed are the meek, for they shall inherit the earth'

promote

to promote someone over the heads of others
to promote a person to a position more senior than that held by some persons previously outranking the promoted person

proof

the proof of the pudding is in the eating
the success of a venture will be measured by its results

proportions

to be of plague proportions
to be great in number
refers to the plagues of locusts, frogs, etc., as described in *Exodus* chs 8 and 10 (and elsewhere)

prudence

to cast prudence to the winds
to cease being careful or wise

prune

to prune
to remove the superfluous
refers to horticulture

psychological

at the psychological moment
at the most appropriate instant of time
the phrase refers to the German, *das psychologische Momentum* ('psychological momentum') — thus confusing the German word for 'momentum' or 'motive' with the term for an instant of time

public

to be in the public eye
to have one's every action subject to scrutiny by the community

to wash one's dirty linen in public
to expose one's embarrassing domestic affairs to the world at large'

pudding

that person couldn't knock the skin off a rice pudding
that person is weak or ineffective

not to be a magic pudding
not to represent an everlasting supply of something
from the name of a book by Norman Lindsay

the proof of the pudding is in the eating
the success of a venture will be measured by its results

pull

not to pull any punches
to be brutally frank
refers to boxing

pull your head in!
do not interfere in this! you are advised to withdraw from this situation

to have pull
to have influence

to pull a fast one
to gain an advantage by questionable means

to pull a rabbit out of the hat
to produce an unexpected and seemingly miraculous but highly desirable solution
refers to magician's trick

to pull at one's heart strings
to affect one emotionally

to pull one's fingers out
to cease indolence and get on with a job with alacrity

to pull one's head in
to retreat from a previously held stance
refers to habit of a tortoise in avoiding danger

to pull one's horns in
to retreat from previously stated views
refers to fighting between male horned animals

to pull one's socks up
to set out to improve or correct one's inadequate behaviour or performance

to pull one's weight
to do one's proper share of the work requiring to be done
refers to rowing

to pull oneself together
by gathering one's faculties and strength, to rouse oneself to a renewed effort

to pull oneself up by one's bootstraps
to make a praiseworthy effort to better oneself unaided

to pull oneself up by one's own shoelaces
to make a superhuman effort

to pull out all stops
to make maximum effort
refers to organ playing at maximum volume

to pull someone's chestnuts out of the fire
to retrieve a situation for someone else
refers to fable of a monkey getting roasting chestnuts out of a fire by using the cat's paw to achieve the desired result

to pull someone's leg
to tell a false but plausible story as an act of humour

to pull something off
to achieve success in some enterprise

to pull something out of the fire
to salvage something in a seemingly hopeless situation

to pull strings
to use one's special influence with those in a position to make favourable decisions which might otherwise not be forthcoming
refers to the actions of a puppeteer in directing the action

to pull the plug
to terminate an activity suddenly
refers to electricity

to pull the rug out from under someone
unexpectedly to withdraw support

to pull the wool over someone's eyes
to deceive or deliberately mislead another person
derived from the inability of some sheep to see clearly if wool is across their eyes

to pull together
to work in harmony
refers to rowing

to pull up the drawbridge
defensively to withdraw and refuse to cooperate'
refers to the drawbridge over a defensive moat around a castle

pulse

to have one's fingers on the pulse
to know what is going on
medical/nursing metaphor

pump

parish pump issues
issues of local importance lacking a wider perspective
refers to the local parish water pump

to engage in pump priming
to spend public money with the aim of attracting parochial electoral support
refers to priming a water pump

pumps

all hands to the pumps
everybody is requested to help out
nautical metaphor

punch

to be punch drunk
to be stupefied by repeated setbacks or bad news
refers to a form of brain damage suffered by boxers who have received repeated blows to the head

to beat someone to the punch
to get to some objective ahead of some keen rival
refers to boxing

punches

not to pull any punches
to be brutally frank
refers to boxing

to telegraph one's punches
by one's actions to give advance warning of one's future plans
refers to sending an advance message

punctuate

to punctuate something
to interrupt something
refers to punctuation marks used in writing

punishment

to be a glutton for punishment
a person who is eager to work very hard even without the prospect of commensurate reward
Rudyard Kipling (1865–1936), 'He's honest, and a glutton for work'

punt

to take a punt
to take a calculated risk
refers to gambling

pup

to sell someone a pup
to cheat a person in a transaction, especially by misrepresentation as to the true value of something

purple

to be purple with rage
to be very angry

purpose

the devil can cite scripture for his purpose
a person can quote a respectable or hostile authority while advocating a disreputable cause of that person's own
Shakespeare, *The Merchant of Venice* I:ii, 'The devil can cite scripture for his purpose'

purring

positively purring
(of a person) very pleased; (of an engine) running very smoothly
refers to a cat's purring

purse

one can't make a silk purse out of a sow's ear
it is impossible to manufacture something of a high standard from inferior raw materials

Malcolm Bradbury (1932–), 'For the mass of men, you can't make a silk purse out of a sow's ear'

to button up one's purse
to refuse to spend money

to hold the purse strings
to have control of expenditure
refers to a drawstring closing a purse

to tighten the purse strings
to reduce outlays
refers to a drawstring closing a purse

push

to push a barrow
to promote a particular cause

to push one's luck
having already done well in something, then to take risks which can prejudice everything

to push someone around
to exercise, in an obnoxious manner, one's superiority over another person

to push someone over the brink/edge
by a small action to cause the absolute ruin (financially or emotionally) of someone already in peril

to push water uphill
foolishly to attempt the impossible

pushing

to be pushing uphill
to face difficulties

pussyfoot

to pussyfoot around
to take stealthy, cautious, non-committal steps
refers to a cat prowling

put

not to put a foot wrong
to behave impeccably
refers to dancing steps

not to put all one's eggs in the one basket
to spread one's risks

not to put too fine a point on it
speaking bluntly
Charles Dickens (1812–70) *Bleak House* ch. 11, '"not to put too fine a point upon it" — a favourite apology for plain-speaking with Mr Snagsby'

put that in your pipe and smoke it
contemplate that fact if you can!
a strong rebuke given to an adversary; R. H. Barham (1788–1845), *Lay of St Odille*, 'So put that in your pipe, my Lord Otto, and smoke it!'

put your back into it!
work energetically!

that has put paid to it
the project can no longer proceed
refers to the counting house and an account being labelled as 'paid' (meaning 'settled'); thus, the matter is settled and finished

to put a bomb under someone
to induce a person to take some action

to put a brave face on it
to face adversity cheerfully

to put a burden on someone's shoulders
to impose responsibilities on a person

to put a leg-rope on someone
to give a person very little freedom
refers to a restraining rope on cattle on other animals

to put a match to petrol
to cause an actual disaster out of a potentially disastrous situation

to put a new face on something
to alter the way something should be regarded

to put a rocket under someone
to induce a person to take some action

to put a spoke in someone's wheel
to interfere with another person's activity, so preventing its continuance

to put a wall around someone
to stop a person associating with others

to put flesh and bone on something
to supply details of a proposal previously revealed only in outline

to put jam on someone's bread
to make a good situation even better

to put money on the table
to back one's judgment in a tangible way or to demonstrate one's sincerity

to put on airs and graces
to act in an affected manner

to put one's back into something
to work hard at achieving some goal

to put one's best face on something

to focus on the positive features surrounding a basically disastrous situation

to put one's best foot forward
to make a special effort

to put one's feet up
to relax

to put one's finger on something
to identify the essential features of something

to put one's foot down
to assert one's authority and insist on something

to put one's foot in it
to make a foolish mistake

to put one's foot in one's mouth
to say something foolish

to put one's hand in one's pocket
to provide money from one's own resources, especially for a charitable purpose

to put one's hand to the plough
voluntarily to undertake some task
Luke 9:62. 'No man, having put his hand to the plough, and looking back, is fit for the Kingdom of God'

to put one's hand up
to identify oneself or to volunteer

to put one's head in the noose
to expose oneself to great danger likely to lead to one's downfall
refers to death by hanging

to put one's head into the lion's mouth
recklessly to expose oneself to great danger
refers to circus performance

to put one's head on the block
to have the courage of one's convictions
refers to execution by decapitation

to put one's house in order
to fix up the deficiencies in one's affairs
Isaiah 38:1, 'Set thine house in order; for thou shalt die and not live'

to put one's money where one's mouth is
to back one's boasting by putting assets at risk

to put one's own stamp on something
to effect something with one's own characteristic style

to put one's reputation on the line
to take a public stance in the realisation that there is a risk that one's reputation will suffer if one is proved wrong

to put one's roots down
to settle in

to put one's shirt on something
to invest heavily in some speculative venture
Luke 6:29 (RSV), ' ... and from him who takes away your coat do not withhold even your shirt'

to put one's shoulder to the wheel
to make a strong effort

to put one's thinking cap on
to concentrate on finding a solution to a difficult problem

to put oneself out of court
to disqualify oneself from being considered for something
refers to royal courtiers

to put pen to paper
to set out one's ideas in written form

to put several heads together
to confer and pool ideas

to put someone back in his/her box/place
to make it clear to a person that that person's views are not welcome

to put someone back on his or her feet
to restore to a functioning condition

to put someone in the picture
to fill a person in with the background of a situation

to put someone in the pillory
to hold a person up to ridicule for that person's beliefs
refers to a form of punishment involving public humiliation

to put someone on a pedestal
to admire a person and regard that person as being more marvellous than is warranted

to put someone on the back foot
to make a person less confident of that person's position

to put someone on the spot
to embarrass a person

to put someone through his or her person's paces
to test a person
refers to testing a horse

to put someone through the mill
to make someone endure significant hardship through severe practical experience

to put someone's mind at rest
to reassure a person

to put someone's nose out of joint
to upset another person

to put something at someone's door
to blame a person

to put something back on its feet
to restore to a functioning condition

to put something into cold storage
to put something aside to be dealt with at some indeterminate future time

to put something into perspective
to explain the background of something so that its significance in relation to other things can be better appreciated

to put something into the 'too-hard' basket
to defer consideration of a difficult issue

to put something on 'hold'
to put something aside for the time being with a view to resuming activity later on
refers to the telephone

to put something on ice
to put something aside for the time being

to put something on the map
to make prominent or significant'

to put something to bed
finally to dispose of something

to put the acid on someone
to make demands on a person
refers to test for gold with *aqua fortis* (nitric acid)

to put the boot in
to issue a severe (possibly sadistic) reprimand to a person

to put the brake on someone
to stop or slow down a person

to put the cart before the horse
to do things in the wrong order
Rudyard Kipling (1865–1936), *The Conundrum of the Workshops*, 'We know the tail must wag the dog, for the horse is drawn by the cart'

to put the fear of God into someone
to frighten a person into behaving properly
Ecclesiastes 12:13, 'Fear God, and keep his commandments; for this is the whole duty of man'

to put the genie back in the bottle
to undo something that cannot be undone
'genie' was adopted (to refer to a spirit released from a bottle) by the French translators of *Arabian Nights' Entertainments*

to put the jigsaw together
to solve a problem by placing together a number of separate facts
refers to a jigsaw puzzle

to put the screws on someone
to assert pressure on a person

to put the skids under someone
to cause or hasten the ruin of someone

to put the wind up someone
to alarm a person

to put two and two together
to reach a conclusion (usually obvious) by combining isolated pieces of information

to put up the shutters
to cease an established activity

to put words into someone's mouth
to attempt to get someone to say something in the particular terms drafted by another person

putty

to be putty in someone's hands
to be far too easily influenced by another person
refers to material able to be fashioned into various shapes

puzzle

a Chinese puzzle
a perplexing enigma

pyjamas

to be the cat's pyjamas
to be the very best, to be superlatively good

American slang (origin obscure)

Pyrrhic

a Pyrrhic victory
a win that costs more than if there had been a loss
refers to the Battle at Asculum in 279 BC at which King Pyrrhus of Epirus defeated the Romans

Q

q

to watch one's P's and Q's
to be very careful
perhaps refers to pints and quarts of beer on a hotel slate, or perhaps to easily confused printer's type

quagmire

to be in a quagmire
to be in great difficulty

quake

to quake in one's boots
to be afraid

quantum

a quantum leap
a gigantic step forward
a term derived from quantum mechanics

quarrel

to patch up some quarrel
to reconcile one's differences

quart

one can't get a quart into a pint pot
one cannot do the impossible

Queensberry

to play by Marquis of Queensberry rules
to act ethically
refers to regulations regarding boxing matches drawn up by John Sholto Douglas, Eighth Marquis of Queensberry (1843–83), in 1867

Queer

to be in Queer street
to be in debt
origin obscure

queer

a queer fish
an unusual type of person

to queer the pitch for someone
to spoil the opportunity a person has to do something

question

a burning question
a much discussed question

a leading question
a question phrased in such a way as to suggest the answer
a legal term, often misused by lay speakers who really mean merely 'a very pertinent question'

a sixty-four thousand dollar question
a pertinent but very difficult question
refers to a radio quiz show in which an initial $1000 prize doubled with the successful answering of progressively more difficult questions

there is a big question mark hanging over someone's head
there are considerable doubts about a person's competence, integrity, or suitability
refers to Damocles who had the sword of Dionysius hanging, by a slender thread, over his head — as a symbol of perpetual risk in life; the story is told in Cicero, *Tusculanae Disputationes*

quick

to be quick on one's feet
cleverly to take advantage of a situation

to be quick on the draw
to act precipitately
refers to drawing a firearm

to be quick on the trigger
to respond to something very quickly with little aforethought
refers to firing guns

quid

not to be the full quid
not to be very intelligent

quiet

on the quiet
surreptitiously

to shed a quiet tear for something
privately to lament the death or loss of something

quietly

quietly to fold up one's tent

surreptitiously to abandon a previously cherished stance

Henry Wadsworth Longfellow (1807–82), *The Day is Done*, 'The cares that infest the day shall fold their tents, like the Arabs, and as silently steal away'

quilt

a patchwork quilt

a result arising from many uncoordinated inputs

quit

to quit the scene

to depart

refers to the theatre

quiver

another arrow in one's quiver

an additional reason

quote

to quote chapter and verse

to authenticate the information

refers to quoting the full details of a scriptural reference

R

rabbit

a rabbit warren

a building with a maze of rooms and passages

move over and let the greyhound see the rabbit

stand aside to allow things to get under way

refers to hunting with greyhounds

to pull a rabbit out of the hat

to produce an unexpected and seemingly miraculous but highly desirable solution

refers to magician's trick

race

a two-horse race

a contest between only two serious contestants

not to be in the race

to lack the required standard

rat race

relentless struggle in life to get ahead of one's working rivals

your race is run

you have had your opportunity

Hebrews 12:1, 'Let us run ... the race that is set before us'

rack

to go to rack and ruin

to face downfall or destruction

'rack' was originally spelt 'wrack' (a variant of wreck)

radar

on the radar screen

in someone's consciousness

Rafferty

Rafferty rules

the complete absence of rules

origin obscure

raft

life raft

financial assistance sufficient to avert insolvency

rag

to be a red rag to a bull

to be something that makes a person very angry and very excited

refers to the erroneous belief that the colour red, rather than the motion of waving, excites a bull

to run something on the smell of an oil/oily rag

to run something very economically and efficiently

rage

to be purple with rage

to be very angry

rags

rags to riches

the transition from poverty to wealth

railroad

to railroad something through

to rush people into accepting a proposal

rails

to run off the rails

to depart significantly from the intended course of action

railway

what a way to run a railway!

the way things are done is disgraceful

refers to a cartoon

rain

to rain cats and dogs
to rain heavily
derived from ancient northern mythology in which cats and dogs were symbolically linked to weather: the cat can be taken as a symbol of falling rain and the dog as a symbol of wind gusts

rainbow

to seek the pot of gold at the end of the rainbow
to have naVve expectations
refers to the proverbial belief in the existence of a pot of gold at the end of a rainbow

rainbows

to chase rainbows
to be quite unrealistic

rains

it never rains but it pours
crises often occur together

rainy

to keep something for a rainy day
to keep something in reserve for bad times

raise

to raise Cain
to create a disturbance
Genesis 4:5, 'And Cain was very wroth, and his countenance fell'

to raise merry hell
to cause an uproar by outlandish, reckless, or larrikinish behaviour
in the eighteenth century there were clubs of reckless young men, known as 'hell-fire clubs', who were said to 'raise merry hell'

to raise one's eyebrows
to show surprise or disbelief

to raise one's voice for some cause
publicly to advocate some cause

to raise someone's hackles
to make a person angry
refers to feathers raised in anger on the back of the neck of certain birds; also, by analogy, refers to hairs raised in anger on the neck of dogs

to raise something to a fine art form
to refine a thing or a process to the point where doing it is a highly skilled task

to raise the spectre of something
to draw attention to the expectation of something worrying
refers to a ghost or apparition

to raise the stake
to increase the amount of potential gain or loss in a project
refers to gambling

raiser

curtain raiser
introduction
refers to the theatre

raising

hair-raising
scary
Job 4:15, 'Then a spirit passed before my face; the hair of my flesh stood up'; Shakespeare, *Hamlet* I:v, 'would harrow up thy soul ... and each particular hair to stand an end'

rake

to rake over old coals
to seek to reopen a matter decided on long ago

raker

a muckraker
a person who sets out to publicise features harming another person's reputation

rally

to rally to the flag
to show support for a cause under attack
refers to military battle

ram

to ram something down someone's throat
to pressure another person into accepting an idea with which that person does not agree

rank

to be the first cab off the rank
to be the first chosen or tried out

ranks

to break ranks
to identify oneself as having separate interests or views from the rest of a group

military metaphor

to close ranks
to sink minor differences in order to present a unified front to a common enemy
military metaphor

ransom

to pay a king's ransom
to pay a very large sum

rap

to rap someone over the knuckles
to admonish a person

rapt

to be rapt in something
to be thoroughly involved with something and enjoying it immensely
shortened form of 'enraptured'

rare

to be a rare bird
to be an unusual type of individual

rarefied

in a rarefied atmosphere
in ignorance of the real world

rat

rat race
relentless struggle in life to get ahead of one's working rivals

to smell a rat
to become suspicious

rate

at a rate of knots
very fast
nautical metaphor; refers to the original measure of a ships's speed by noting the rate at which the ship passed a regular series of knots tied in a rope which was maintained in position beside the ship

rats

a case of rats leaving a sinking ship
the desertion of an enterprise in anticipation of imminent failure

rattling

sabre-rattling
threatening war or violence

raw

a raw deal
unfair treatment

razoo

not to have a brass razoo
to be very poor
refers to an imaginary coin of trivial value

razor

to be on the razor's edge
to be critically balanced; OR to be in danger

reaction

a knee-jerk reaction
a response made instantaneously and without any proper consideration

read

to need to have one's head read
to engage in behaviour so foolish that a psychiatric examination seems called for

to read between the lines
to appreciate the true significance of something not put into words

to read the riot act
to reprimand persons who are excessively noisy or otherwise misbehaving
refers to the police reading out to a rowdy crowd extracts from a law requiring the crowd's dispersement

you need your head read
your behaviour is so foolish that you require psychiatric examination

you wouldn't read about it!
that is unbelievable

ready

ready-made
easily fabricated or available without difficulty

real

to be a real trooper
to be a person willing to try anything

to be the real McCoy
the genuine article
perhaps refers to an American boxer who became world welterweight champion in 1890

reap

to reap as one has sown
to experience the consequences of one's own actions
Galatians 6:7, 'Whatsoever a man soweth, that shall he also reap'

to reap the whirlwind

to suffer the adverse consequences of a bad act

Hosea 8:7, 'They have sown the wind, and they shall reap the whirlwind'

to sow the wind and reap the whirlwind

to make bad mistakes and to suffer the even worse consequences

Hosea 8:7, 'They have sown the wind, and they shall reap the whirlwind'

rear

to rear its ugly head

to make an unwelcome appearance

rearrange

to rearrange the deckchairs on the Titanic

to take an initiative that is quite useless because it does not take much greater change into account

refers to the liner *Titanic* which struck an iceberg and sank in 1912

reason

without rhyme or reason

quite unaccountably

rebound

to rebound with a vengeance

to return to an issue with great enthusiasm

receive

to receive the coup de grâce

to be finished off by an opponent

French, 'mercy stroke'

recharge

to recharge one's batteries

to have a recuperative break

recipe

a recipe for disaster

a certain way of achieving disaster

record

track record

proven performance

red

a red-letter day

an important occasion

refers to the colour used to indicate days of obligation in the Christian Church missal — as opposed to black-letter days, which are optional days

neither fish flesh nor good red herring

unclassifiable by virtue of being neither one thing nor another

Miguel de Cervantes (1547–1616), *Don Quixote*

red hot

urgent, and/or exciting, and/or dangerous

red tape

excessively bureaucratic procedures

refers to bureaucrats and lawyers securing their briefs with red tape; the term is said to have been coined by Charles Dickens (1812–70), but popularised by Thomas Carlyle (1795–1881)

the red-carpet treatment

courtesies extended to a person to make that person feel important and welcome

refers to the welcome accorded a visiting dignitary

to be a red herring

to be something designed to divert attention away from the main question

refers to hunting with hounds — a red herring was dragged across the scent trail to train hounds to ignore distractions and follow the correct trail

to be a red rag to a bull

to be something that makes a person very angry and very excited

refers to the erroneous belief that the colour red, rather than the motion of waving, excites a bull

to be in the red

to owe money

refers to the red ink used to indicate a liability in a manuscript accounting ledger

to be left red-faced

to be embarrassed

to catch someone red-handed

to apprehend a person in the course of committing a wrongdoing

refers originally to being caught with blood on one's hands

to get the red light

to be forbidden to do something

refers to the 'stop' signal on roads and rail

to paint the town red

to go on an exciting social outing

to see red

to become very angry

to see red lights flashing

to be conscious of the danger

refers to the 'stop' signal on roads and rail, or perhaps to lights on an emergency vehicle

reed

to be a broken reed
to be a weak and unreliable person
Isaiah 36:6 and *2 Kings* 18:21, 'Lo, thou trustest in the staff of this broken reed, on Egypt; whereon if a man lean, it will go into his hand and pierce it'

reek

to reek to high heaven
to be patently unethical
Shakespeare, *Hamlet* III:iii, 'O! my offence is rank, it smells to heaven'

reeling

to leave someone reeling
to leave a person in a state of shock

refuse

to refuse point blank
to refuse outright
refers to pointing at the white spot (blank, French blanc) in the centre of an archery target

rehearsal

dress rehearsal
a preliminary practice or experience before the real thing

rein

a tight rein
strong controls
refers to riding or driving horses

to give rein to one's fancy
to let one's imagination have free scope
refers to riding or driving horses

to give someone free rein
to confer complete discretion on another person
refers to riding or driving horses

to rein in something
to keep better control over something
refers to riding or driving horses

to take over the reins
to assume control
refers to riding or driving horses

reinvent

to reinvent the wheel
to waste resources doing something already accomplished

rekindle

to rekindle an old flame
to inspire the reinstatement of a former loving relationship
David Garrick (1717–79), 'Kitty, a fair, but frozen maid, kindled a flame I still deplore'

relief

to heave a sigh of relief
to express satisfaction at the achievement of a solution to a difficult problem
John Keats (1795–1821), *I stood tip-toe upon a little hill*, 'born of the very sigh that silence heaves'

religiously

religiously
conscientiously

repel

to repel boarders
to keep out unwanted persons
refers to naval battles

republic

a banana republic
a country with a poor economy

reputation

to put one's reputation on the line
to take a public stance in the realisation that there is a risk that one's reputation will suffer if one is proved wrong

resist

to resist something every inch of the way
to resist something utterly

resistance

to take the line of least resistance
to follow the easiest course of action
refers to the route taken by the shockwaves of a buried explosive charge in reaching the surface of the earth

responsive

to strike a responsive chord
to get a favourable reaction to a proposal
refers to music

rest

to be head and shoulders above the rest

to be significantly more capable than others

to lay some theory to rest
to abandon some theory as being no longer appropriate
refers to death –as in 'laying out' (preparing a corpse for disposal), or as in 'laying someone to rest' (at a funeral)

to put someone's mind at rest
to reassure a person

to rest on one's laurels
to use a reputation for success earned in earlier times as a substitute for current endeavour
refers to laurel wreaths presented to winners of events at the ancient Olympics

retreat

to beat a retreat
to abandon some project
military metaphor

to retreat into one's shell
to become shy and introverted
refers to the action of tortoises and other animals when threatened

return

to return the compliment
to reciprocate; OR to extract revenge

revolt

a palace revolt
the overthrow of those in authority by their subordinates

rhinoceros

to have the hide of a rhinoceros
to be unaffected by, and unresponsive to, valid criticism

rhyme

without rhyme or reason
quite unaccountably

ribbon

blue ribbon
of superb quality
refers to the insignia of the Order of the Garter, or perhaps to the ribands used in agricultural shows and at race meetings

ribbons

to be shot to ribbons
(of an argument) to be utterly discredited

to tear something to ribbons
to damage something severely; to castigate severely

rice

that person couldn't knock the skin off a rice pudding
that person is weak or ineffective

rich

a rich vein of gold
much useful information; a good source of something desirable

that is a bit rich
that is very cheeky

riches

rags to riches
the transition from poverty to wealth

rid

to get rid of the dead wood
to terminate the services of unsatisfactory personnel
refers to pruning of bushes

ride

a roller-coaster ride
a series of successes followed by failures

to get a magic carpet ride to something
to be given an easy and fortunate passage to an objective
refers to the magic carpet (of Oriental legend) that transported its owners wherever they wished

to get an armchair ride
to be given a particularly easy time

to go along for the ride
to seek to benefit from a project in which others contribute the effort

to ride high
to be successful but vulnerable
refers to riding a horse while sitting high and upright — a posture likely to result in a fall

to ride on the back of someone
without effort to benefit from the prior efforts of others

to ride on the sheep's back
to benefit from the production of wool

to ride out the storm
to come safely through some dangerous situation
nautical metaphor

to ride roughshod over someone
to disregard the feelings and wishes of a person

refers to a horse that is roughshod — having shoes with nail-heads projecting to prevent slipping

to ride the wave
to be successful for the time being
refers to surfing

to take someone for a ride
to deceive a person

riding

to be riding for a fall
to act in a reckless manner
refers to riding horses in a dangerous manner likely to result in a fall

riding instructions
directions as to how to do something
refers to horse racing

right

a step in the right direction
the first in a series of measures designed to correct some problem

I would give my right arm for something
I am very keen to acquire something

it is pointing in the right direction
it is proceeding towards success

one's right-hand person
one's chief aide
Hebrews 1:1, 'His son ... by whom he also made the worlds ... sat down on the right hand of the majesty in heaven'

right on the bell
at the last possible moment
refers to boxing

the left hand does not know what the right hand is doing
a person or an organisation is not aware of inconsistencies in conduct
Matthew 6:3, 'But when you give alms, do not let your left hand know what your right hand is doing'

to be in the right ballpark
to be approximately correct
refers to baseball

to get on someone's right side
to make a good impression on a person

to have one's heart in the right place
to have good intentions, to mean well

to hit the nail right on the head
astutely to come to the correct conclusion

to hit someone right between the eyes
to be brutally frank
refers to fighting

to lose one's right arm
to lose some highly valued assistance

to play one's cards right
to approach a matter sensibly
refers to playing cards

to sell one's birthright for a mess of pottage
through foolishness to exchange something of substance for something of little value
Genesis 25:34, 'Then Jacob gave Esau bread and pottage of lentils ... thus Esau despised his birthright'

to set someone on the right road
to show a person how to go about doing something

to start off on the right foot
to commence an operation with great care to do it correctly
refers to marching

to strike the right chord
to appeal successfully to someone's emotions
refers to music

to strike the right key
to make comments that set the appropriate tone in a speech or conversation
refers to music

to strike the right note
to say or do something appropriate to a situation
refers to music

rights

to sleep on one's rights
to fail to exercise some entitlement within a reasonable period

ring

that has a hollow ring to it
that statement is insincere
refers to bell-ringing

that has a nice ring to it
that sounds attractive
refers to bell-ringing

to jump into the ring
enthusiastically to join in a contest or challenge
refers to the practice of jumping into a boxing ring to make a challenge

to ring a bell
to sound familiar or recall something to mind

to ring down the curtain on something
to treat something as concluded

to ring the changes
to exhaust the number of different ways of doing something
refers to the permutations used for ringing peals of church bells

to step into the ring
to enter a competitive environment
refers to a boxing ring

to throw one's hat into the ring
publicly to announce one's interest in some position
refers to custom of throwing one's hat into a ring to indicate a willingness to take part in a boxing challenge

ringing

the alarm bells are ringing
it is unwise to proceed

rings

to run rings around someone
to outwit another person easily

riot

to read the riot act
to reprimand persons who are excessively noisy or otherwise misbehaving
refers to the police reading out to a rowdy crowd extracts from a law requiring the crowd's dispersement

to run riot
to act impetuously and without restraint

Rip

to be a Rip Van Winkle
to be a person out of touch with current conditions
refers to the character of a story told by Washington Irving (1783–1859) in his book *Sketch Book* (1819); the character slept for about twenty years and awoke to find himself in a changed world

rip

to rip someone off
to exploit a person

to rip something to shreds
to damage something severely

ripples

to make ripples
to disturb the status quo

rise

to rise from the ashes like a phoenix
to be the replacement for something destroyed in some disaster
refers to a mythical bird that was supposed to rise from the ashes of its funeral pile/pyre with renewed youth

to rise with the lark
to get up early

rises

the curtain rises on something
something is about to start
refers to the theatre

rising

rising star
person making good progress in that person's career

Ritz

the doors of the Ritz are open to all
despite rhetoric to the contrary wealthy people have many advantages over poor people
refers to the Ritz Hotel, London, founded in 1906 by César Ritz

river

the river found its mark
equilibrium between two pressures has been achieved

to be a river of gold
to be a source of ongoing great profitability

to sell someone down the river
to betray a person who has placed trust in one
refers to selling slaves to owners further down the river

riveted

to be riveted to one's seat
to find the activity being watched very exciting and worthy of full attention

road

a middle-of-the-road solution
a solution near the middle of a range of possibilities

a road hog

an inconsiderate motorist
refers to gluttonous swine
fork in the road
time or place for decision
one for the road
a final drink before leaving
road blocks
difficulties
the royal road to success
the way of attaining success without effort
this is the end of the road for someone
a person will have no further opportunity to do something
a road to Damascus experience
a sudden, dramatic conversion
refers to the sudden conversion of Paul (Saul) — *Acts* 9:3, 'And as he journeyed, he came to Damascus: and suddenly there shined around him a light from heaven: And he fell to the earth'
to come to the end of the road
to come to the point where hope and endeavour are finished
to enter a long road
to commence a task that will take a long time
to face a rocky road ahead
to be likely to encounter difficulties
to get the show on the road
to commence a planned activity
refers to a travelling circus
to go down a particular road
to adopt a particular strategy
to happen down the road
to happen later
to road-test something
to try something out under real conditions
to set someone on the right road
to show a person how to go about doing something

roads
all roads lead to Rome
all alternatives will have the same outcome
refers to roads radiating from the great imperial capital to all parts of the Roman empire
to be at the cross-roads
to need to choose between several mutually exclusive alternatives

roar
to be within a bull's roar of something
to be very close to something

roasting
a roasting
a scolding

rob
to rob Peter to pay Paul
to discharge one debt or responsibility by incurring another
John Wyclif (c.1380), *Select Works* III 174, 'How should God approve that you rob Peter, and give this robbery to Paul in the name of Christ?' (perhaps refers to an ecclesiastical property dispute between two churches)

robbery
daylight robbery
the charging of grossly excessive prices
highway robbery
the charging of grossly excessive prices
refers to robbery by armed brigands on the highways

robin
a round robin
(1) a series of cheques from A to B, from B to C, from C to A, and so on, leaving all of them in the same net position as before; (2) a document signed by members of an organisation which has the same effect as a resolution of a meeting; (3) a petition arranged with the names in a circle such that no name appears at the top; (4) a sporting tournament in which each competitor competes once with each of the others
refers to corruption of French *rond* ('round') and *ruban* ('a ribbon')

Robinson
before one can say 'Jack Robinson'
very quickly
origin of phrase is disputed, but dates from at least the eighteenth century
not to be Robinson Crusoe
to be one of a large number of people with a common problem
refers to Daniel Defoe's *Robinson Crusoe*

rock

bedrock price
lowest possible price

rock bottom
very low

to be between a rock and a hard place
to be faced with two equally difficult and uncomfortable choices

to rock the boat
to disturb the comfortable status quo

rocks

to be on the rocks
to be bankrupt
refers to ships wrecked on rocks

to have rocks in the head
to be stupid or mentally unbalanced

someone's marriage is on the rocks
someone's marriage has broken down
refers to ships wrecked on rocks

rocket

to give someone a rocket
to reprimand a person severely

to put a rocket under someone
to induce a person to take some action

to skyrocket
(of a price or value) to increase greatly in a short time

rocky

to face a rocky road ahead
to be likely to encounter difficulties

rod

a lightning rod
a person or thing used to attract trouble in order to divert that trouble away safely
refers to a metallic rod or wire fixed to the top of a building to divert lightning

to kiss the rod
to accept punishment meekly
Shakespeare, *The Two Gentlemen of Verona* I:ii, 'and presently all humbled kiss the rod!'

to make a rod for one's own back
to make a handicap for oneself

to rule with a rod of iron
to keep strict discipline
Psalms 2:9, 'Thou shalt break them with a rod of iron; thou shalt dash them in pieces like a potter's vessel'

rogue

a rogue elephant
a person of vicious temper who does not function as part of the group and who acts in an undisciplined way

roll

heads will roll
transgressors will be punished
refers to execution by decapitation

the caravan will roll on
the activity will continue

to roll off the tongue
to be said very easily

to roll up one's sleeves
to get on with a job energetically

rolled

to get rolled
to be outvoted

roller

a roller-coaster ride
a series of successes followed by failures

rolling

a rolling stone gathers no moss
a person who keeps changing jobs will not have a successful career
Tusser, *Five Hundred Points of Good Husbandrie* (1573), 'The stone that is rolling can gather no moss. / For master and servant oft changing is loss'

the money is rolling in
the scheme is very profitable

to have an audience rolling in the aisles
to amuse an audience

to keep the ball rolling
to take advantage of the existing momentum or to participate actively

to start the ball rolling
to commence and advance enthusiastically an activity

Rolls-Royce

a Rolls-Royce solution
a high quality but excessively expensive way of doing something

Rome

all roads lead to Rome
all alternatives will have the same outcome

refers to roads radiating from the great imperial capital to all parts of the Roman empire

Rome was not built in a day
complicated things require time

to fiddle while Rome burns
to neglect important considerations while concentrating on trivial side-issues

refers to Nero's behaviour during the burning of Rome (AD 64) when he played a lyre and watched the spectacle from a height

when in Rome do as the Romans do
it is best to conform to the local customs

roof

the roof has fallen in
an enterprise has collapsed

to go through the roof
(of a person) to be very upset; OR (of prices) to escalate greatly

to hit the roof
to be very angry

to throw a few stones on the roof and see who comes out
to attempt to change a boring situation or resolve a stalemate

under one roof
under the same management; OR in the same building

rooftops

to scream something from the rooftops
to communicate a message to a wide audience

room

no room at the inn
no available space

Luke 2:7, 'She [Mary] brought forth her firstborn son, and wrapped him in swaddling clothes, and laid him in a manger; because there was no room for them in the inn'

there is no room to swing a cat
this place is very small

refers to the swinging of a whip (a cat-o'-nine-tails) in the confined space of a ship's hull

roost

the chickens are coming home to roost
the consequences of a person's past actions are now being felt by that person

Robert Southey (1774–1843), *The Curse of Kehama* (1810), 'Curses are like young chickens, they always come home to roost'

to rule the roost
to dominate

refers to the habit of roosters and hens to have an established order of dominance

rooster

today a rooster, tomorrow a feather duster
when circumstances change, an important person can, immediately, become unimportant

rooted

deep-rooted
firmly established, strongly felt

roots

grass roots
at the lowest level of a hierarchy

to put one's roots down
to settle in

to strike at the roots of something
to work towards the destruction of something

rope

to be money for old rope
to be an easily made profit

to give someone enough rope to hang himself or herself
to give a person the opportunity to do something that is likely to get that person into severe trouble

to give someone too much rope
to give a person too much latitude

refers to tethering of animals

to put a leg-rope on someone
to give a person very little freedom

refers to a restraining rope on cattle on other animals

ropes

to be on the ropes
to be facing defeat

refers to boxing

to know the ropes
to know how to do one's job

nautical metaphor

to learn the ropes

to be taught the elementary features
nautical metaphor

to show someone the ropes
to teach a beginner how to do something
nautical metaphor

rosa

sub rosa
in strict confidence
Latin *sub rosa* 'under the rose' — refers to being under the rose (as a symbol of secrecy)

rose

a rose between two thorns
something beautiful in the midst of ugliness

a rose by any other name would smell as sweet
the form does not affect the substance
Shakespeare, *Romeo and Juliet* II:ii, 'What's in a name? That which we call a rose / By any other name would smell as sweet'

to come up smelling like a rose
not to have a stain on one's character

to see something through rose-coloured glasses/spectacles
to appreciate only the advantages and to disregard completely the disadvantages

roses

to be on a path strewn with roses
to lead a very pleasant life

to be no bed of roses
to be difficult or uncomfortable
Robert Louis Stevenson (1850–94), *Virginibus Puerisque* I:i, 'Marriage is like life in this — that it is a field of battle, and not a bed of roses'

rosy

to present a rosy picture
to state a set of favourable factors

rot

the rot set in
conditions started to deteriorate

wouldn't it rot your socks!
what an unpleasant surprise!

rotten

a rotten apple
an isolated dishonest person in an otherwise honest group

rotten to the core
completely corrupt

something is rotten in the state of Denmark
the situation is corrupt and unacceptable
Shakespeare, *Hamlet* III:iv, 'Something is rotten in the state of Denmark'

rough

to be a rough diamond
to have many attributes, but an uncultivated manner lacking social polish

to feel the rough side of someone's tongue
to be verbally abused by a person

to take the rough with the smooth
to accept the hardships of life along with its pleasant features

roughshod

to ride roughshod over someone
to disregard the feelings and wishes of a person
refers to a horse that is roughshod — having shoes with nail-heads projecting to prevent slipping

roulette

to play Russian roulette
to engage in a dangerously unpredictable exercise
refers to an act of daring in which one squeezes the trigger of a revolver held to the head (after loading one chamber and spinning the cylinder — thus the one being fired is determined by chance)

round

a round robin
(1) a series of cheques from A to B, from B to C, from C to A, and so on, leaving all of them in the same net position as before; (2) a document signed by members of an organisation which has the same effect as a resolution of a meeting; (3) a petition arranged with the names in a circle such that no name appears at the top; (4) a sporting tournament in which each competitor competes once with each of the others
refers to corruption of French *rond* ('round') and *ruban* ('a ribbon')

a square peg in a round hole
obviously unsuited for the purpose'

to be only round one

to be only the first of many stages
refers to boxing

to be on a merry-go-round
to be a circular exercise ending in no definite result

to be round the bend
to be crazy
refers to the Kew Asylum in Victoria, Australia; the institution was built on the banks the River Yarra, on a curved part of the river originally known as the 'Old Bend'

to make the wheels go round
to cause something to happen

to turn round
to reverse one's policy

rounds

going the rounds
(of a rumour) being spread

to get the rounds of the kitchen
(of a husband) to be subject to personal abuse by his wife

to win some rounds
to be partly successful
refers to boxing

roundabouts

what one loses on the swings one gains on the roundabouts
there are advantages and disadvantages that offset each other
Patrick Reginald Chalmers (1872–1942), *Green Days and Blue Days: Roundabouts and Swings*, 'what's lost upon the roundabouts we pulls up on the swings!'

row

not to matter a row of beans
to be utterly unimportant

to be on skid row
to have no means
may refer to dissolute townships associated with logging timber (which used skidding rows of timber)

to have a hard row to hoe
to have a difficult assignment
refers to agriculture; James Russell Lowell (1819–91), *The Biglow Papers*, 'You've a darned long row to hoe'

royal

a battle royal
a fight or argument with many simultaneous participants
refers to cockfighting

the royal road to success
the way of attaining success without effort

rub

there's the rub
that is where a difficulty arises
Hamlet III:i, 'To sleep: perchance to dream: ay there's the rub'; the term is also used in bowls

not to have the wherewithal to rub two sticks together
to be very poor

to be unable to rub two pennies together
to be very poor

to rub it in
to humiliate another person by emphasising that person's defeat

to rub off on someone
to benefit a person through an association that increases that person's skills

to rub one's chin
to muse

to rub one's eyes
to express astonishment

to rub one's hands with glee
to express great satisfaction

to rub salt into someone's wound
deliberately to make damage even worse

to rub shoulders with someone
to mingle with a person

to rub someone up the wrong way
to annoy a person with actions that fail to recognise that person's current mood

to rub someone's nose in it
to humiliate a person by highlighting something embarrassing to that person

rubber

to rubber-stamp something
to endorse something without considering the merits

rubbish

a load of rubbish
blatant nonsense

Rubicon

to cross the Rubicon

to make an irreversible decision in regard to some commitment
refers to Caesar's crossing of the Rubicon River in Gaul in 49 BC thus declaring war on Pompey

rudderless

to be a rudderless ship
to be without direction

ruffle

to ruffle someone's feathers
to engage in behaviour that irritates another person

rug

to pull the rug out from under someone
unexpectedly to withdraw support

to sweep something under the rug
to pretend that some blemish does not exist

ruin

to go to rack and ruin
to face downfall or destruction
'rack' was originally spelt 'wrack' (a variant of wreck)

rule

a rule of thumb
a simple yet useful approximation
refers to the use of the thumb for making rough measurements

to fly in the face of some rule
blatantly to disregard some rule

to let one's heart rule one's head
to act on emotion rather than on reason
George Colman the younger (1762–1836), *Who Wants a Guinea?*, 'His heart runs away with his head'

to rule the roost
to dominate
refers to the habit of roosters and hens to have an established order of dominance

to rule with a rod of iron
to keep strict discipline
Psalms 2:9, 'Thou shalt break them with a rod of iron; thou shalt dash them in pieces like a potter's vessel'

to rule with an iron hand
to keep strict discipline

rules

ground rules
basic principles
refers to the rules observed at a particular playing ground

Rafferty rules
the complete absence of rules
origin obscure

to bend the rules
to overlook minor infractions of the rules

to pay lip service to some rules
to disregard some rules in practice while acknowledging them in words

to play by Marquis of Queensberry rules
to act ethically
refers to regulations regarding boxing matches drawn up by John Sholto Douglas, Eighth Marquis of Queensberry (1843–83), in 1867

ruling

a landmark ruling
a decision marking an important change or development in the state of affairs'

ruminate

to ruminate
to ponder over a matter
refers to the chewing of the cud by ruminant animals

run

a dry run
a trial exercise
refers to a creek bed that is dry until heavy rain causes it to become a stream

run of the mill
normal or average

someone would run a mile
a person would do anything to escape that person's responsibilities

still waters run deep
a person with a quiet manner might have many unrecognised characteristics — both good and bad
W. H. Auden (1907–73), *Twelve Songs VIII*, 'Still waters run deep, my dear, there's never smoke without fire'

to have a dream run
to encounter no difficulties

to have a run for one's money
to at least get some enjoyment out of an otherwise abortive exercise
refers to betting on horse racing

to have to run fast just to stand still

competition is such that merely to maintain one's relative position one needs to make positive progress

to run for cover
to seek to avoid blame

to run a tight ship
to manage an efficient organisation
refers to ropes that are tight or taut

to run around in circles
to engage in excited but useless activity

to run hot
(of equipment) to be subject to particularly high usage; (of persons) to be in good form

to run into a dead end
to get nowhere in an investigation

to run into a firestorm
to be faced with many protests

to run into heavy weather
to encounter difficulties
nautical metaphor

to run its course
to come to a natural end

to run off the rails
to depart significantly from the intended course of action

to run one's own ship
to do things and organise subordinates in one's own way

to run out of steam
to lose one's energy and enthusiasm
refers to steam engines

to run rings around someone
to outwit another person easily

to run riot
to act impetuously and without restraint

to run someone off that person's feet
to keep a person very busy on some physical task

to run someone to earth
to locate a person
refers to fox hunting

to run someone to ground
to discover the whereabouts of a person
refers to fox hunting

to run the gauntlet
to be subjected to criticism
from Swedish *gantlopp* ('laneway') in reference to a military punishment inflicted on delinquents made to run between two files of soldiers, as used in Thirty Years' War, Holy Roman Empire, 1618–48

to run to seed
to become shabby
refers to plants maturing past the glory of the flowering phase

to run with something
to take advantage of some current development
refers to rugby

to run with the ball
to make the most of the opportunity
refers to rugby

to run with the hare and hunt with the hounds
to keep in with two opposing sides
refers to hunting

your race is run
you have had your opportunity
Hebrews 12:1, 'Let us run ... the race that is set before us'

rungs

rungs up a ladder
gradual steps to an ultimate goal

runner

front runner
person expected to win; OR someone who performs well only when holding an advantage

running

the sands are running out
the time available for some action is nearly at an end
refers to an hour-glass of running sand

the tide is running in favour of some proposition
public opinion supports some proposition

to be up and running
to be operative

to set a hare running
to initiate an activity to achieve a related and desired effect
refers to hunting

runs

to have the runs on the board
to have a demonstrable record of achievement
refers to scoring in cricket

rush

fools rush in where angels fear to tread

unsophisticated persons take unwise risks in circumstances where more knowledgeable persons would exercise caution

Alexander Pope (1688–1744), *An Essay on Criticism* 1:625, 'For fools rush in where angels fear to tread'

to be killed in the rush

to be the supplier of something extremely popular

to rush one's fences

to act precipitately

refers to steeplechasing on horseback

rushed

to be rushed off one's feet

to be overwhelmed with tasks to perform and services to provide

Russian

to play Russian roulette

to engage in a dangerously unpredictable exercise

refers to an act of daring in which one squeezes the trigger of a revolver held to the head (after loading one chamber and spinning the cylinder — thus the one being fired is determined by chance)

rut

to be in a rut

to lead a dull life, with no change from long-established habits

S

sabre

sabre-rattling

threatening war or violence

sack

to get the sack

to be dismissed

refers to the bag of tradesmen's tools

sackcloth

to wear sackcloth and ashes

humbly to demonstrate repentance

Esther 4:3, 'There was great mourning ... and many lay in sackcloth and ashes'

sacred

a sacred cow

an institution, person, idea, custom, etc. treated as being immune from criticism and change

refers to Hindu veneration of the cow

a sacred trust

a moral obligation

nothing is sacred

nothing is safe from interference

sacrificial

sacrificial lamb

somebody unfairly made to suffer for the mistakes of others

Exodus 29:41, 'Sacrifice the other lamb at twilight ... an offering made to the Lord by fire'

saddle

to be in the saddle

to be in command

refers to horse riding

saddlebags

to have lead in one's saddlebags

to work with a handicap

refers to horse-racing handicaps in which lead in the saddlebags makes winning more difficult

safe

to play it safe

to take no risks

to plot a safe course through troubled waters

to make a plan that overcomes certain difficulties

nautical metaphor

safety

a safety-net scheme

a scheme for dealing with the exceptional cases not covered by normal arrangements

safety margin

allowance for miscalculations

to act as a safety valve

to be a procedure that allows persons with grievances to ventilate them in an orderly fashion

sail

to sail against the wind

to oppose the views currently being held by others

to sail close to the wind

to take a considered risk; to test the limits of what is possible or acceptable

refers to sailing in a manner such that sails remain filled while keeping the boat headed as near as possible into the wind

to sail under false colours

to pretend that one's real character or beliefs are different from what they really are

refers to a ship concealing its true identity

to set sail

to commence a voyage

to trim one's sails

to modify one's policy or opinion in accordance with changing circumstances

refers to adjusting sails to suit wind conditions

sailing

to be plain sailing

to be quite straightforward and very easy

refers to navigation by means of a 'plane chart' on which meridians and parallels of latitude are represented by equidistant straight lines

sails

to take the wind out of someone's sails

to upset a person by anticipating that person's actions or by using arguments which that person was proposing to use

refers to a tactical manoeuvre in sailing whereby one boat blocks or 'takes' the wind advantage of another

saint

a saint

a very good person

to have the patience of a saint

to endure annoyances with particular calm

sale

fire sale

a forced sale, realising bargain prices

refers to the sale of goods damaged by fire

garage sale

sale of miscellaneous assets at cheap prices

Sally

an Aunt Sally

a person who can readily be singled out and criticised as the proxy for a group

refers to an old game in which objects were thrown at the figure of the head of a woman

salt

below the salt

in a subordinate position

refers to the seating order at ancient Roman dining tables

not to be worth one's salt

not to be worth one's wages; to be inefficient or incapable

refers to Roman soldiers being paid in salt — a practice giving rise to the modern word 'salary'

the salt of the earth

special people who make a vital contribution to society

Matthew 5:13, 'Ye are the salt of the earth'

to rub salt into someone's wound

deliberately to make damage even worse

to take something with a grain of salt

to regard the facts in a statement with considerable scepticism

salvage

to salvage something out of the wreck

to achieve some minor benefits out of a disastrous situation

refers to shipwrecks

salvo

to fire a salvo at someone

to present a series of criticisms to a person

refers to simultaneous discharge of firearms in a battle or as a salute (Italian *salva*, 'salutation')

Samaritan

a good Samaritan

a person going out of that person's way to do a kindness to others

Luke 10:33, 'But a certain Samaritan, as he journeyed, came where he was: and when he saw him, he had compassion on him'

same

a nod is the same as a wink to a blind horse
fine distinctions are not appropriate here
Captain Marryat (1792–1848), *Peter Simple*, 'But you're a dutiful son, so I'll say no more about it — a nod's as good as a wink to a blind horse'

by the same token
by the same argument, in a similar way

not to be in the same street as someone
not to be of comparable quality

to all sing from the same hymnal
to act consistently with each other
refers to a book of hymns

to be able to chew gum and walk at the same time
to be able to do two relatively simple things simultaneously
used ironically to disparage a person of limited capacities

to be in the same boat
to share a common set of difficulties

to be in the same league
to have comparable skills
refers to sporting competitions

to be on the same wavelength
to think on similar lines
refers to radio reception

to be tarred with the same brush
to be damned merely because of one's association with another person
refers to treating cuts on sheep with a tarbrush

to speak the same language
to have a good understanding and similar ideas

sand

to bury one's head in the sand
to refuse to face up to an unpleasant truth
refers to the reputed habit of ostriches in danger

to draw a line in the sand
to indicate clearly the limits of acceptability beyond which people should not go

sands

the sands are running out
the time available for some action is nearly at an end
refers to an hour-glass of running sand

shifting sands
arguments that are constantly being changed

sandwich

to be the ham/meat in the sandwich
to be caught in the middle of a dispute between other parties
refers to the food snack popularised by the fourth Earl of Sandwich (1718–92)

sank

one's heart sank
one realised the extent of some disaster

sauce

what is sauce for the goose is sauce for the gander
arguments that apply in one case also apply in another

sausage

a sausage machine
the turning out of large volumes without particular thought

sausages

that person wouldn't give you the steam off his or her sausages
that person is very mean

save

to save a bundle
to save much money

to save face
to avoid humiliation or loss of reputation

to save one's bacon
to escape harm
refers to the value attached to bacon as a stored food

to save one's skin
to get off safely

to save someone's life
to be of great help to a person

to save someone's neck
to come to the rescue of a person
refers to death by hanging

saved

saved by the bell
rescued before disaster strikes

refers to boxing

say

before one can say 'Jack Robinson'

very quickly

origin of phrase is disputed, but dates from at least the eighteenth century

scales

to tip the scales

to be a factor that, in combination with other factors, results in a particular decision that would otherwise not have been reached

refers to balance scales

scalp

to be after someone's scalp

to be keen to penalise a person

refers to the savage practice of removing the scalp of a killed person as a trophy

scapegoat

a scapegoat

a person who is forced to take the blame for something not that person's fault

Leviticus 16:10, 'But the goat, on which the lot fell to be the scapegoat ... to make an atonement'

scar

to scar someone

to cause a lasting unpleasant effect on someone

scarce

to make oneself scarce

to take oneself out of view

to scare the pants off someone

to frighten a person greatly

scatter

a scatter-gun approach

an effort going here, there and everywhere, instead of being properly targeted

to scatter something to the four winds

permanently to get rid of something

refers to the north, south, east, and west winds

scenario

scenario

an imagined or postulated arrangement

refers to the theatre

scene

to make a scene

to create a fuss

refers to the theatre

to quit the scene

to depart

refers to the theatre

to set the scene for something

to get things ready for something

refers to the theatre

scenes

behind the scenes

out of public view or awareness

refers to the theatre

scent

to throw someone off the scent

to deceive a person by giving out misleading indications

refers to fox hunting

scheme

a safety-net scheme

a scheme for dealing with the exceptional cases not covered by normal arrangements

school

to tell tales out of school

to gossip mischievously and reveal secrets about others

schoolboy

as every schoolboy knows

as is recognised by everyone

Jonathon Swift (1667–1745), *The Country Life*, 1:81,'How haughtily he cocks his nose, / To tell what every schoolboy knows'; Lord Macaulay (1800–59), *Lord Clive* (Jan. 1840), 'Every schooboy knows who imprisoned Montezuma, and who strangled Atahualpa'

score

to even the score

to respond by way of retribution for some past action of another person

to score a goal

to achieve an objective

to score a hat trick

to have three successive favourable outcomes

refers to a bowler in cricket taking three wickets in three balls; such a feat being originally rewarded with the prize of a new hat

to score a point

to make a clever contribution in the course of debate

to score an own goal
to make a foolish mistake that counts against oneself
refers to soccer

to score points
to make a good impression

to score top points
to achieve the outstanding score; to be considered the best

to see the score
to appreciate the reality of a situation

to underscore something
to emphasise something
refers to typeface in printing and publishing

scot

to get off scot-free
to go unpunished
refers to an exemption from tax; scot (from old norse *skot*) means tax

scrape

to scrape the bottom of the barrel
to be forced to use the last available resources; to lower one's standards because one is short of resources

scrapheap

to be destined for the scrapheap
to face a future in which one will have no meaningful role

scratch

to be back to scratch
to have to start all over again
perhaps refers to the scratch mark in a boxing ring used to indicate an ability or willingness to fight, or perhaps refers to a starting line in a race from which competitors not receiving an advantage begin the race

to be up to scratch
to be of the required standard
perhaps refers to the scratch mark in a boxing ring used to indicate an ability or willingness to fight, or perhaps refers to a starting line in a race from which competitors not receiving an advantage begin the race

to scratch the surface
to deal with only a small portion of a much larger whole

to scratch one another's backs
to help each other

to scratch one's head
to be amazed or puzzled

to scratch something together
to improvise

to start from behind scratch
to be faced with a handicap
refers to the starting mark (with no handicap advantage) in a race

to start from scratch
to commence something without the benefit of any past activity
refers to the starting mark (with no handicap advantage) in a race

scream

to scream and yell
to protest violently

to scream blue murder
to make serious allegations; OR to protest violently
perhaps refers to the French *morbleu* (altered version of *mort Dieu*, 'God's death'), a comic oath attributed to French speakers

to scream one's head off
to utter loud and piercing cries as if in great pain

to scream something from the rooftops
to communicate a message to a wide audience

screaming

to drag someone kicking and screaming to do something
to force a person into some action that the person is most reluctant to undertake

screen

on the radar screen
in someone's consciousness

to set up a smokescreen
deliberately to confuse an issue by disguising its salient features

screw

to have a screw loose
to be mentally unbalanced

to tighten the screw
to increase the moral and psychological pressure

screwed

to have one's head screwed on
to be shrewd

screws

to put the screws on someone
to assert pressure on a person

scripture

the devil can cite scripture for his purpose
a person can quote a respectable or hostile authority while advocating a disreputable cause of that person's own
Shakespeare, *The Merchant of Venice* I:ii, 'The devil can cite scripture for his purpose'

Scrooge

to be a real Scrooge
to be mean and unmoved
refers to a character in Charles Dickens' *A Christmas Carol*

Scylla

to be between Scylla and Charybdis
to be faced with two equally unpalatable alternatives that cannot both be avoided
refers to the voyage of Ulysses

sea

a sea-change
a significant transformation
Shakespeare, *The Tempest* I:ii, 'Nothing of him that doth fade / but doth suffer a sea-change / into something rich and strange

a South Sea bubble
an unrealistic financial venture that is bound to result in total loss
refers to a notorious financial scandal involving the South Sea Company (UK) in 1720

to be all at sea
to be confused as to what is going on and what to do next

to be between the devil and the deep blue sea
to be faced with two equally unpalatable alternatives that cannot both be avoided

seal

a seal of approval
confirmation that something is satisfactory

to seal one's lips
to keep a confidence

to seal someone's fate
to cause a certain final outcome adversely affecting a person'

to set the seal on something
to confirm absolutely that something is agreed

seams

to be bursting at the seams
to be very crowded

to come apart at the seams
(of an arrangement) to break down

seamless

seamless
unified, continuous, uninterrupted, imperceptible
John 19: 23, ' ... and also his [Jesus'] coat; now the coat was seamless, woven from the top throughout'

search

search for the Holy Grail
work towards a difficult goal
refers to a vessel or platter supposedly used by Christ at the Last Supper and featuring in the Arthurian legends

to search one's heart
to seek after one's innermost feelings and motivations
Jeremiah 17:10, 'I, the Lord, search the heart ... to give every man according to his ways, and according to the fruit of his doings'

searching

a soul-searching exercise
a deep and penetrating examination of personal motives and conscience

season

the silly season
the holiday period, when hard news is scarce and journalistic standards are lowered

seat

a back-seat driver
a person seeking to exercise control when it is not that person's responsibility

to be in the box seat
to be in a very powerful position to control activity
refers to the driver's seat in a horse-drawn carriage

to be in the driver's seat
to be in charge

to be in the hot seat
to hold a position requiring one to answer criticism or accusations

to be on the edge of one's seat
to be very excited or anxious regarding what is currently happening

to be riveted to one's seat
to find the activity being watched very exciting and worthy of full attention

to fly by the seat of one's pants
to act by instinct in the absence of specific knowledge or instructions

to keep someone's seat warm
to hold a position temporarily with a view to another person's taking it over permanently in the near future

to take a back seat
not to involve oneself actively

second

a second-class citizen
a person not treated as an equal

second childhood
dotage
Shakespeare, *As You Like It* II:vii, 'Last scene of all, / that ends this strange eventful history, / is second childishness, and mere oblivion'

the second eleven
the second rank of persons who are performing a function less important than that performed by others
refers to a second-level sporting team, esp. cricket

to be second nature to someone
to be learned behaviour that has now become intuitive

to have a second string to one's bow
to have an additional qualification appropriate to the task
refers to archery

to play second fiddle
to fulfil a subordinate role
refers to playing in an orchestra

see

blind Freddy could see that something is such-and-such
it is very obvious that something is such-and-such

not to see the wood for the trees
to overlook the general picture because of undue concentration on the details

suck it and see
discover experimentally how something works

to see a man about a dog
to do something unspecified

to see blood
to be very angry
refers to a frenzy excited in some animals by the sight of blood

to see daylight
to discern the way ahead towards the right answer

to see eye to eye with someone
to agree
Isaiah 52:8, 'For they shall see eye to eye, when the Lord shall bring again Zion'

to see red
to become very angry

to see red lights flashing
to be conscious of the danger
refers to the 'stop' signal on roads and rail, or perhaps to lights on an emergency vehicle

to see someone in a good light
to regard a person favourably

to see someone in the flesh
to see someone in person

to see something with half an eye
to sum up a matter instantly
refers to taking note with a mere glance

to see the back of someone
to know that a person is no longer involved in something

to see the big picture
to have the vision and imagination enabling a project to be developed as part of a bigger whole

to see the colour of someone's eyes
to see how a person matches expectations or requirements

to see the colour of someone's money
to get evidence of the sincerity of a person's proposal

to see the light
to understand the real situation
refers to the conversion of Saul (Paul) on the road to Damascus, *Acts* 9:3, 4 'And

suddenly there shined round about him a light from heaven: and he fell to the earth'

to see the light at the end of the tunnel
to perceive relief at the imminent end of a period of prolonged difficulty

to see the light of day
to be made public

to see the score
to appreciate the reality of a situation

to see the writing on the wall
to appreciate the inevitability of some event

Daniel 5:5ff, 'A man's hand ... wrote ... upon the plaister of the wall of the king's palace ... thou art weighed in the balances and art found wanting'

to see which way the cat jumps
to await developments

to see which way the wind is blowing
to establish the factors relevant to a situation

John Seldon (1584–1654), 'Take a straw and throw it up into the air, you shall see by that which way the wind is'

seed

to run to seed
to become shabby

refers to plants maturing past the glory of the flowering phase

seeds

to sow seeds
to propagate ideas in the hope that they will be adopted

seek

to seek the pot of gold at the end of the rainbow
to have naVve expectations

refers to the proverbial belief in the existence of a pot of gold at the end of a rainbow

sell

to sell off the family silver
to sell off one's prized possessions

to sell one's birthright for a mess of pottage
through foolishness to exchange something of substance for something of little value

Genesis 25:34, 'Then Jacob gave Esau bread and pottage of lentils ... thus Esau despised his birthright'

to sell someone a lemon
to sell a person a grossly defective product on the basis that it represents quality

to sell someone a pup
to cheat a person in a transaction, especially by misrepresentation as to the true value of something

to sell someone down the river
to betray a person who has placed trust in one

refers to selling slaves to owners further down the river

send

to send a chill down someone's neck
to be worrying news

to send a cold shiver down someone's spine
to horrify a person

to send a smoke signal
to give an indication

refers to a means of communication used by North American indigenous peoples

to send someone away with a flea in the ear
to give a person frank, but unwelcome, facts

perhaps refers to fleas trapped in the armour of ancient knights, or perhaps from the discomfort felt by a dog with a flea in its ear; or perhaps, figuratively, to any lingering irritation in the ear

to send someone packing
to dismiss a person ignominiously

to send someone to Coventry
ostentatiously and collectively to ignore a person by way of punishment

refers to the refusal of the citizens of Coventry (UK) to have any social contact whatsoever with royalist soldiers in the English Civil War

sense

a sixth sense
intuition

refers to the five senses — sight, hearing, smell, taste, and touch

horse sense
practical commonsense

not to have an ounce of sense

to be stupid

sentenced

to be sentenced to some fate
to be condemned by circumstances to endure some fate

separate

to separate the men from the boys
to distinguish between those with and without certain skills

to separate the sheep from the goats
to distinguish between the worthy and the unworthy
Matthew 25:32, 'and he shall separate them one from one another, as a shepherd divideth his sheep from the goats'

to separate the wheat from the chaff
to separate the worthy from the unworthy
Matthew 3:12, 'His winnowing fork is in his hand, and he will clear his threshing floor and gather his wheat into the granary, but the chaff he will burn with unquenchable fire'

serve

to serve something up to someone on a plate
to make something especially easy for a particular person

service

to pay lip service to some rules
to disregard some rules in practice while acknowledging them in words

yeoman service
valuable assistance over a long time
refers to an officer in an official household or military establishment

sesame

an open sesame
access to something normally inaccessible
refers to the password for the opening of the robbers' cave in the tale of *The Forty Thieves* in *Arabian Nights' Entertainments*

set

game, set, and match
completion
refers to tennis

the rot set in
conditions started to deteriorate

the stage is set
something is about to happen
refers to the theatre

the sun has set on something
something has concluded

to be set like a jelly
to be very well established

to have one's heart set on something
to be very keen to achieve something

to set a hare running
to initiate an activity to achieve a related and desired effect
refers to hunting

to set one's cap at someone
(of females) to try to attract a person as a marriage partner

to set one's sights on something
to aim to achieve something
military metaphor

to set sail
to commence a voyage

to set someone on the right road
to show a person how to go about doing something

to set someone's teeth on edge
to cause a person intense irritation or discomfort
Ezekiel 18:2, 'The fathers have eaten sour grapes, and the children's teeth are set on edge'; Shakespeare, *Henry IV Pt 1* III:i, 'And that would set my teeth nothing on edge, nothing so much as mincing poetry'

to set something in concrete
to make something virtually unalterable

to set the hounds baying
to excite the gossips by providing material that they can use
Shakespeare, *Julius Caesar*, 'I had rather be a dog, and bay the moon, than such a Roman'

to set the pace
to give a lead in regard to a rate of progression
refers to horse racing and foot racing

to set the scene for something
to get things ready for something
refers to the theatre

to set the seal on something
to confirm absolutely that something is agreed

to set the Thames on fire
to do something noteworthy
similar sayings exist regarding setting fire to the Rivers Seine, Tiber, and Rhine

to set the wheels in motion
to institute appropriate action

to set the world on fire
to do something remarkable

to set tongues wagging
to behave in a way that encourages scandal mongers

to set up a smokescreen
deliberately to confuse an issue by disguising its salient features

settles

when the dust settles
when sufficient time has passed to allow matters to be perceived clearly

sevens

to be at sixes and sevens
to be confused, concerned and undecided
refers to a dispute between the Merchant Taylors and the Skinners over order of precedence in an annual London procession (who was to be sixth and who was to be seventh); in 1484 it was decided that henceforth the two guilds should alternate between 'sixes' and 'sevens' in consecutive years

seventh

to be in a seventh heaven
to be ecstatically happy in a state of bliss
refers to the highest state of heavenly bliss in Judaism, Christianity, and Islam

several

to put several heads together
to confer and pool ideas

severe

to be a severe blow
to be a great disappointment

sew

to sew something up
to negotiate a deal

sexy

sexy
highly marketable

shackles

golden shackles
financial arrangements designed to discourage employees changing from one employer to another

shade

to throw someone in the shade
to surpass a person

shadow

to be in someone's shadow
to be unable to assert one's personality because of association with a more important person

to be only a pale shadow of something
to be a weak imitation

to cast a shadow over something
to introduce a note of warning or sadness in regard to some matter

to overshadow
to cover or obscure with a greater power; to make less important
Luke 1:35, 'And the power of the highest shall overshadow thee'

to shadow box
to go through the motions without achieving or intending to achieve anything
refers to training for boxing by punching at one's own moving shadow

to throw a long shadow
to have widespread ramifications

shadows

to lurk in the shadows
to have a low profile at the moment, but with the possibility of becoming much more conspicuous at any time

shaft

to fire a parting shaft
to make a defiant or cutting gesture or remark on leaving
sometimes also referred to as a 'Parthian shot/shaft' — refers to missiles shot backwards by fleeing Parthian horsemen

shaggy

a shaggy dog story
a laborious, far-fetched, amusing story
refers to the shaggy dog that originally featured in many of these stories

shake

golden handshake

a large payment in connection with, or as an inducement to, retirement

to shake a leg
to hurry up

to shake a tree
to do something to see what will result

to shake down
to sleep on an improvised bed

to shake one's head
to indicate disbelief or wonder or disapproval
Shakespeare, *Macbeth* III:iv, 'Never shake thy gory locks at me'

shakes

in two shakes of a duck's tail
in an instant

to wait two shakes of a lamb's tail
to wait just a few moments

shaky

to be on shaky ground
not to have strong arguments

shambles

to throw something into a shambles
to make something messy and useless

shape

not to do something in any shape or form
not to do something in any way at all

shipshape
in excellent condition
nautical metaphor

to lick something into shape
to make something presentable and effective
refers to mediaeval belief that bear cubs are born shapeless and have to be licked into shape by their mothers — a story related in the encyclopaedia of the Arab physician Avicenna (970–1037)

share

a share of the cake
a portion of the total available for distribution

the lion's share
the biggest portion

shares

to have shares in a paper company
to institute unnecessary clerical procedures

sharks

to miss the sharks while netting the minnows
to succeed in minor aspects but fail in the ones that really matter

sharp

sharp dealer
person engaging in barely honest or mildly unethical practices
refers to poker

to have a sharp tongue
to speak in a cutting and abrasive fashion

sharpen

to need to sharpen one's pencil
to be required to improve one's performance

to sharpen one's axe
to get ready for a difficult task

to sharpen the knives
to get ready for a concerted attack on a person or principle

shattering

earth-shattering
very significant

shave

to be a close shave
to be a narrow escape

shed

to shed a quiet tear for something
privately to lament the death or loss of something

to shed crocodile tears
hypocritically to show concern or sympathy for a person in distress
refers to the reflex lacrimation of a crocodile while eating

to shed light on something
to give explanations

sheep

a black sheep
a disreputable member of an otherwise reputable group

one might as well be hanged for a sheep as for a lamb
further action will not increase the adverse consequences already in train
refers to the stealing of either sheep or lambs being capital crimes under old English law

to be a wolf in sheep's clothing

to be a hypocrite; to be dangerous although masquerading as something harmless

Matthew 7:15, 'Beware of false prophets, which come to you in sheep's clothing, but inwardly they are ravening wolves'

to be home on the sheep's back

to be doing well

to cast sheep's eyes at someone

to look at a person amorously

to ride on the sheep's back

to benefit from the production of wool

to separate the sheep from the goats

to distinguish between the worthy and the unworthy

Matthew 25:32, 'and he shall separate them one from one another, as a shepherd divideth his sheep from the goats'

to spoil the ship for a ha'p'orth of tar

to engage in a false economy

the current word 'ship' is actually a mistake for the original word 'sheep', and the tar refers to the treatment of wounds

sheepish

sheepish

embarrassed, as though guilty

sheer

to be sheer murder

to be extremely unpleasant or difficult; OR to be an inglorious defeat

sheet

the sheet anchor

the ultimate of one's confidence

refers to a large ship's anchor used in an emergency

to start with a blank sheet of paper

to commence an exercise without being bound by any established practices

shelf

to be on the shelf

to have been put aside and no longer in active use; OR to be a woman past the usual age of marriage

shell

in a nutshell

by way of summary

to be shell-shocked

to be stunned by unexpected bad news

refers to psychological disturbance following exposure to wartime bombardment (esp. refers to World War I)

to retreat into one's shell

to become shy and introverted

refers to the action of tortoises and other animals when threatened

shelve

to shelve some proposal

to abandon some proposal

shepherd

to shepherd some group

to marshal the members of some group

shibboleth

a shibboleth

a doctrine once held as essential but now abandoned as having outlived its usefulness

refers to a word used as a test to determine to which tribe an Israelite belonged; *Judges* 12:6, 'Say now 'shibboleth': and he said 'sibboleth', for he could not ... pronounce it right'

shifting

shifting sands

arguments that are constantly being changed

shilling

to be only ten pence in the shilling

to be slightly stupid

refers to 'old' shillings and pence when a shilling equalled twelve pence

to cut someone off with a shilling

to exclude a person as a beneficiary under one's will

refers to the mistaken belief that a will cannot be upset in favour of a person actually named in a will and clearly not overlooked

shin

a kick in the shins

an unexpected and undeserved setback

shine

he wouldn't give you the shine off his suit

he is very mean

to take a shine to someone

to be keen on a person

to take the shine off something
to spoil the performance of something

to take the shine out of something
demonstrably to surpass

shines

to make hay while the sun shines
to utilise an opportunity before it disappears

John Betjeman (1906–84), *The Last Laugh*, 'I made hay while the sun shone'

shining

a knight in shining armour
a person who comes to the rescue; a champion

derived from mediaeval tales of valiant knights rescuing those in distress

shining light
eminent or scholarly person

John 5:35, 'He [John the Baptist] was a burning and a shining light'

shingle

to hang up one's shingle
to go into business offering expert personal services

refers to an external notice advertising one's name and qualifications

ship

a case of rats leaving a sinking ship
the desertion of an enterprise in anticipation of imminent failure

enough to sink a battleship
much more than sufficient

shipshape
in excellent condition

nautical metaphor

to abandon ship
to abrogate one's responsibilities or to abandon a project

refers to the order given when a ship is about to sink

to be a happy ship
to have a contented workforce

to be a rudderless ship
to be without direction

to run a tight ship
to manage an efficient organisation

refers to ropes that are tight or taut

to run one's own ship
to do things and organise subordinates in one's own way

to spoil the ship for a ha'p'orth of tar
to engage in a false economy

the current word 'ship' is actually a mistake for the original word 'sheep', and the tar refers to the treatment of wounds

when one's ship comes in
when one's business venture is successfully completed; OR when luck arrives

ships

ships that pass in the night
a fleeting, transitory acquaintance

Henry Wadsworth Longfellow (1807–82), *The Theologian's Tale (Tales of a Wayside Inn)*, 'Ships that pass in the night, and speak each other in passing ... '

to have a nuclear ships policy
to neither confirm nor deny something

refers to the US policy of neither confirming nor denying whether a particular ship is carrying nuclear arms

shirt

keep your shirt on!
relax!

refers to removing a shirt in preparation for a fight

so-and-so would give you the shirt off his or her back
so-and-so is very generous

Luke 6:29 (RSV), ' ... and from him who takes away your coat do not withhold even your shirt'

to lose one's shirt
to make heavy financial losses

Luke 6:29 (RSV), ' ... and from him who takes away your coat do not withhold even your shirt'

to wear a hair shirt
to practise self-discipline

refers to a shirt worn next to the skin by ascetics and penitent persons

shiver

to send a cold shiver down someone's spine
to horrify a person

shoals

to founder on the shoals of something
to come to grief because of unexpected dangers

refers to a ship running aground in undetected shallow water

shocked

to be shell-shocked
to be stunned by unexpected bad news
refers to psychological disturbance following exposure to wartime bombardment (esp. refers to World War I)

shoe

if the shoe fits then wear it
if a general proposition describes your specific circumstances, then consider that it applies to you

to know where the shoe pinches
to realise from personal experience what the cause of some problem really is

to wait for the other shoe to drop
to await the seemingly imminent and inevitable
refers to a person being disturbed by a neighbour who drops one shoe on the floor, the listener then being frustrated when the sound of the other shoe being dropped is not heard

shoelaces

to pull oneself up by one's own shoelaces
to make a superhuman effort

shoes

to be in someone's shoes
to have another person's responsibility

to fill someone's shoes
to be a good successor

to tremble in one's shoes
to be afraid

shoestring

to do something on a shoestring
to do something with great economy

shoot

shoot!
go on, speak!

to be on a slippery shoot
to court disaster
refers to an opening in the side of a shearing shed known as the porthole or chute (spelling variations include shoot and shute); after a sheep is shorn it is pushed through the porthole and slides down

to shoot for the stars
to be unrealistic

to shoot from the hip
to speak without careful assessment of the situation

to shoot one's bolt
to waste one's only opportunity; to have expended all one's effort
refers to an arrow, especially one for a crossbow

to shoot one's mouth off
to speak without thinking

to shoot oneself in the foot
to act in a foolish way and thus harm one's own cause

to shoot someone down in flames
utterly to destroy another person's arguments
refers to loss of aircraft in battle

to shoot something out of the water
to destroy something

to shoot the messenger
to blame the person who brings news of an undesired happening instead of the person really responsible for that happening

shooter

a straight shooter
a person who is frank and outspoken

a trouble-shooter
a person good at finding and then rectifying faults

shooting

the whole shooting match
the whole lot

shop

a bull in a china shop
a careless person likely to cause great damage

to shop around
to explore alternatives

to shut up shop
to cease an established activity

to talk shop
to discuss business or professional matters on a social occasion

shopping

a shopping list
an itemised catalogue of things that one wishes to acquire or achieve

short

take a long walk on a short pier
go away, I want no dealings with you
the long and the short of it
all that needs to be said about this
to be a shorthand way of saying something
to be a way of saying something in summarised form
refers to a form of taking summarising notes
to be short and sweet
to be very brief and to the point
to be short-changed
to be given less than is due to one
to be short-sighted
not to recognise the likely consequences
to draw the short straw
to be chosen (perhaps by lot) to undertake an undesired task
to get someone by the short and curly hairs
to have domination over a person
to give someone short shrift
to be impatient with a person; to give a person little of one's time
'shrift' refers to prescribing penance and giving absolution after a confession; hence 'short shrift' refers to the brevity of the penance and absolution pronounced by a priest after a confession by a condemned person just before an execution
to have a short fuse
to lose one's temper very readily
refers to explosives
to hold someone on a short leash
to give a person very little freedom
refers to a lead used to restrain coursing hounds
to short-circuit something
to do something, eliminating various intermediate steps
refers to electrical circuits
to take short cuts
to do something by a faster but less thorough method

short-changed

to be short-changed
to be given less than is due to one

short-sighted

to be short-sighted
not to recognise the likely consequences

shorthand

to be a shorthand way of saying something
to be a way of saying something in summarised form
refers to a form of taking summarising notes

shot

a big shot
an important person
a shot in the arm
something to revive a person's enthusiasm
refers to medical injections
a shot in the dark
a hopeful attempt at the unknown; a sheer guess
a siting shot
an initial move designed to establish facts for use in a later action
military metaphor
opening shot
first step in an activity expected to last a long time
military metaphor
that is a long shot
there is only a remote possibility
to be a sitting shot
to be a person whose actions make one very vulnerable to criticism
to be shot to pieces
to have one's case seriously damaged
to be shot to ribbons
(of an argument) to be utterly discredited
to beat by a long shot
to defeat very convincingly
to fire a parting shot
to make a defiant or cutting gesture or remark on leaving
sometimes also referred to as a 'Parthian shot/shaft' — refers to missiles shot backwards by fleeing Parthian horsemen
to give one's best shot
to make the best attempt possible
to have a shot at someone
to use subtly chosen words implying friendly criticism but designed to embarrass another person

to have a shot at something
to attempt to achieve something

to take a potshot at someone
to make an opportunistic disparaging remark about a person
refers to shooting game for food and not in accordance with the rules of the sport

shotgun

a shotgun wedding
a wedding held to ensure that an impending birth will be legitimate
refers to threats by the bride's father to kill the bridegroom

shots

shots across the bow
warnings
nautical metaphor

to call the shots
to have the direction over a project

shoulder

a shoulder to cry on
sympathy

a shoulder to lean on
sympathy

shoulder to shoulder
in close proximity

straight from the shoulder
bluntly
refers to boxing

to give someone the cold shoulder
ostentatiously to ignore a person

to have a chip on one's shoulder
unreasonably to resent something

to need to look over one's shoulder
to be subject to attack which is not obvious

to put one's shoulder to the wheel
to make a strong effort

to shoulder the blame
to accept the responsibility for error

to take a weight off someone's shoulder
to assist a person by relieving that person of some responsibility

to work shoulder to shoulder
to work with united effort

shoulders

an old head on young shoulders
experience, knowledge, and maturity in a young person

to be head and shoulders above the rest
to be significantly more capable than others

to carry the world on one's shoulders
to perform a huge task alone
refers to Atlas, who was condemned to bear the heavens on his shoulders for leading the Titans against the gods

to have broad shoulders
to be able to cope well with responsibility

to put a burden on someone's shoulders
to impose responsibilities on a person

to rub shoulders with someone
to mingle with a person

to shrug one's shoulders
to indicate that one does not know or care, or that one is unable or unwilling to assist

to stand on someone's shoulders
to build up on another person's ideas

shouting

to be all over bar the shouting
to be virtually finished

show

a show pony
a vain and ostentatious person

a sideshow
an unimportant adjunct
refers to a carnival

the show must go on
despite difficulties the action in contemplation has to proceed
refers to the theatre

to get the show on the road
to commence a planned activity
refers to a travelling circus

to give the show away
indiscreetly to reveal sensitive information
perhaps refers to revealing the plot of a theatre play

to show dividends
to be successful

to show one's face
to appear

to show one's slip
to reveal details which one meant to keep private

refers to women's petticoats

to show one's true colours
to disclose one's real character or beliefs
nautical metaphor

to show someone the door
to ask a person to leave

to show someone the ropes
to teach a beginner how to do something
nautical metaphor

to show the flag
to visit a place in order to boost morale there
military metaphor

to show the white feather
to indicate cowardice
refers to cross-bred birds, not regarded as useful in cock fighting

to steal the show
to have the maximum appeal to those watching
refers to the theatre

showcase

to showcase something
to display something attractively with a view to getting attention

showdown

showdown
a final test or confrontation after declaring one's position
refers to poker

shower

to have come down in the last shower
to be naVve
refers to someone having just arrived with the last shower of rain

shreds

to rip something to shreds
to damage something severely

shrift

to give someone short shrift
to be impatient with a person; to give a person little of one's time
'shrift' refers to prescribing penance and giving absolution after a confession; hence 'short shrift' refers to the brevity of the penance and absolution pronounced by a priest after a confession by a condemned person just before an execution

shrinking

a shrinking violet
a shy person

shrug

to shrug one's shoulders
to indicate that one does not know or care, or that one is unable or unwilling to assist

to shrug something off
to indicate that one is unable or unwilling to do something; OR to dispose of something without further concern and get on with other activities

shudders

one shudders to think what the outcome might be
there is great concern as to the outcome

shut

to be an open-and-shut case
to be an unarguable proposition

to keep one's mouth shut
not to discuss some matter

to shut one's eyes to something
deliberately to take no notice of something, especially in dereliction of one's duty

to shut the door on someone
to deny another person a desired opportunity

to shut the stable door after the horse has bolted
to take preventive action only after the relevant event

to shut up shop
to cease an established activity

shutters

to put up the shutters
to cease an established activity

Shylock

a Shylock
a hard-hearted creditor who insists on his or her legal due
refers to a character from Shakespeare's *Merchant of Venice*

side

a broadside
a short verbal attack
refers to all the guns situated or able to fire on one side of a ship

flip side
the arguments for the other point of view
on our side of the fence
in the group representing our vested interest
the bright side
the favourable aspects
the other side of the coin
the arguments for the opposite point of view
to be a thorn in someone's side
to be a constant annoyance or affliction
2 Corinthians 12:7, 10: 'There was given to me a thorn in the flesh ... I will glory in my infirmities'
to be born on the wrong side of the blanket
to be illegitimate
to be on the other side of the fence
to have an opposing point of view or position
to be on the side of the angels
to be on the side of righteousness
Benjamin Disraeli (1804–81), 'Is man an ape or an angel? Now I am on the side of the angels' (speech debating theory of evolution, Diocese of Oxford, 25 November 1864)
to feel the rough side of someone's tongue
to be verbally abused by a person
to get on someone's right side
to make a good impression on a person
to get out of bed on the wrong side
to be grumpy
to know on which side one's bread is buttered
to be aware of the important personally advantageous considerations
to look on the dark side
to be pessimistic
to split one's side
to be convulsed with laughter
you will laugh on the other side of your face
you will regret this

sidelight
sidelight
incidental happening

sidelines
to sit on the sidelines
not to take part in the main action

sideshow
a sideshow
an unimportant adjunct
refers to a carnival

sidetracked
to be sidetracked
to be diverted from one's main task
refers to railways

sideways
to look at someone sideways
silently and politely to indicate one's disapproval

sieve
to stop up one hole in a sieve
to do something quite useless

sift
to sift
to examine closely and assess the components appropriately

sigh
to heave a sigh of relief
to express satisfaction at the achievement of a solution to a difficult problem
John Keats (1795–1821), *I stood tip-toe upon a little hill*, 'born of the very sigh that silence heaves'

sight
to be a sight for sore eyes
to be something welcome
with 20/20 hindsight
with the benefit of knowing what happened
refers to American system of expressing perfect visual acuity

sighted
to be short-sighted
not to recognise the likely consequences

sights
to lower one's sights
to reduce one's ambition
military metaphor
to set one's sights on something
to aim to achieve something
military metaphor

sign

a tell-tale sign
a visible indication revealing true facts despite efforts at concealment

to sign on the dotted line
to confirm one's agreement

to sign one's own death warrant
foolishly to do something that is inevitably bound to lead to utter disaster

signal

to send a smoke signal
to give an indication
refers to a means of communication used by North American indigenous peoples

signpost

to signpost something
to give an indication of the alternatives available

silence

deafening silence
great apathy and lack of enthusiasm

silence is golden
peace and quiet is valued; it is better to keep one's own counsel
Swiss proverb, 'speech is silvern; silence is golden' (quoted by Thomas Carlyle (1795–1881)

silk

one can't make a silk purse out of a sow's ear
it is impossible to manufacture something of a high standard from inferior raw materials
Malcolm Bradbury (1932–), 'For the mass of men, you can't make a silk purse out of a sow's ear'

silly

the silly season
the holiday period, when hard news is scarce and journalistic standards are lowered

silver

every cloud has a silver lining
there are consolations and potential benefits even in seemingly adverse situations

to be born with a silver spoon in one's mouth
to be brought up by wealthy parents
refers to the traditional gift of a silver spoon (an 'apostle spoon') to a child at baptism — the child born of wealthy parents is assured of riches from the moment of birth and thus does not have to await baptism to receive a valuable gift

to hand over something on a silver platter
to provide a valuable benefit for virtually nothing
refers to first-class service

to have a silver tongue
to be eloquent
Proverbs 10:20, 'The tongue of the just is as choice silver: the heart of the wicked is little worth'

to sell off the family silver
to sell off one's prized possessions

Simon

a simple Simon
a foolish, gullible, or halfwitted person
refers to a well-known nusery rhyme character (who met a pieman)

simple

a simple Simon
a foolish, gullible, or halfwitted person
refers to a well-known nusery rhyme character (who met a pieman)

sins

for one's sins
by way of punishment, as it were

sing

to all sing from the same hymnal
to act consistently with each other
refers to a book of hymns

to sing a particular song
to state particular views

to sing for one's supper
to carry out a task in order to receive a favour in return

to sing someone's praises
to commend a person exuberantly

single

single-handedly
without help from other persons

sings

it's not over until the fat lady sings
it is not finished yet
probably refers to operatic performances, but during a radio broadcast

made by the present author, a listener suggested that the metaphor refers to Kate Smith singing the US national anthem

sink

enough to sink a battleship
much more than sufficient

everything but the kitchen sink
virtually all things

it is a case of sink or swim
it is a case of success or failure with no other alternatives
refers to the 'testing' of so-called witches by throwing them into water to see if they would sink or swim

to sink deeper into the mud/mire
to get into even greater difficulty

to sink slowly in the west
to fail gradually
refers to the setting of the sun in the western sky

to sink without a trace
to disappear completely

sinking

a case of rats leaving a sinking ship
the desertion of an enterprise in anticipation of imminent failure

with a sinking heart
with growing despondency

sinker

hook, line, and sinker
wholly
refers to angling

sit

to sit on one's hands
deliberately to do nothing

to sit on someone
to repress a person

to sit on the fence
to refuse to choose between two alternatives

to sit on the sidelines
not to take part in the main action

to sit pretty
to be in an advantageous or comfortable position

to sit tight
to do nothing; to await developments
refers to poker

siting

a siting shot
an initial move designed to establish facts for use in a later action
military metaphor

sitting

to be a sitting duck
to be vulnerable to exploitation

to be a sitting shot
to be a person whose actions make one very vulnerable to criticism

to be sitting on a volcano
to be safe for the time being but exposed to the risk of a sudden great disaster

six

it is six of one and half a dozen of the other
it does not matter either way
Captain Marryat (1792–1848), *The Pirate* ch. 4, 'I never knows the children. It's just six of one and half a dozen of the other.'

to be six feet under
to be dead
refers to the depth of a grave

to hit someone for six
to damage a person's cause severely
refers to cricket

to throw in one's six pennies' worth
modestly to supply one's own facts or views

sixes

to be at sixes and sevens
to be confused, concerned and undecided
refers to a dispute between the Merchant Taylors and the Skinners over order of precedence in an annual London procession (who was to be sixth and who was to be seventh); in 1484 it was decided that henceforth the two guilds should alternate between 'sixes' and 'sevens' in consecutive years

sixth

a sixth sense
intuition
refers to the five senses — sight, hearing, smell, taste, and touch

sixty-four

a sixty-four thousand dollar question

a pertinent but very difficult question

refers to a radio quiz show in which an initial $1000 prize doubled with the successful answering of progressively more difficult questions

size

to cut tall poppies down to size

to diminish the self-importance of haughty persons

to try something on for size

cheekily to do something

skate

to skate around some subject

by diversionary tactics to avoid discussing some subject

to skate on thin ice

to act in disregard of obvious danger; to require tact in dealing with a sensitive subject in conversation

Ralph Waldo Emerson (1803–82), *Prudence*, 'In skating over thin ice, our safety is in our speed'

skates

to get one's skates on

to hurry up

skeleton

a skeleton in the closet/cupboard

an unpleasant truth the knowledge of which has been deliberately suppressed

William Makepeace Thackeray (1811–63), *The Newcomes* (1855), ' … they have a skelton or two in their closets as well as their neighbours'

to flesh out the skeleton

to supply the missing pertinent details

sketch

a thumbnail sketch

brief but pertinent details

refers to an artist assessing perspective by judging the object to be painted against a thumbnail held close to the eye

skid

to be on skid row

to have no means

may refer to dissolute townships associated with logging timber (which used skidding rows of timber)

skids

to put the skids under someone

to cause or hasten the ruin of someone

skin

a cleanskin

a person without a criminal record or other blemish on that person's reputation

probably refers to an unblemished animal skin

that person couldn't knock the skin off a rice pudding

that person is weak or ineffective

there is more than one way to skin a cat

this can be achieved in a variety of ways

to be no skin off someone's nose

not to matter to a person

to escape by the skin of one's teeth

to only just avoid some disaster

Job 19:20, 'I am escaped with the skin of my teeth'

to get under someone's skin

to cause intense annoyance to another person; OR to arouse interest in another person

may refer to the itching caused by certain parasitic creatures in or under the skin

to hang on by the skin of one's teeth

to be barely surviving

Job 19:20, 'I am escaped with the skin of my teeth'

to have a thick skin

to be impervious to criticism

to jump nearly out of one's skin

to receive a fright

to save one's skin

to get off safely

skip

something is but a hop, skip, and jump away

something is nearby

skirt

to skirt around the difficulties

to proceed with care and avoid problems

skirts

to hide under someone's skirts

to let someone else take the consequences of one's actions
refers to childish seeking for protection

skittles
not to be all beer and skittles
not to be all pleasant and easy

skull
to penetrate someone's thick skull
to make a person understand something difficult or acknowledge something unwelcome

sky
a light in the sky
a sign of great hope
blue sky
unrealistic optimism
pie in the sky
a hoped for result unlikely to be achieved
the sky fell in
a very serious problem arose
Matthew 24:29, 'Immediately after the distress of those days the sun will be darkened, and the moon will not give its light; the stars will fall from the sky, and the heavenly bodies will be shaken'
the sky is the limit
there is no restriction upon what can be done

skyrocket
to skyrocket
(of a price or value) to increase greatly in a short time

slack
to take up the slack
to take advantage of surplus capacity
refers to working with ropes

slam
to slam the door in someone's face
ostentatiously to refuse to have any dealings with a person

slap
a slap in the face
a calculated insult or action amounting to a rebuke
a slap on the wrist
a mild rebuke

slate
to wipe the slate clean
to forgive past indiscretions

slather
open slather
freedom for people to do what they want

slaughter
a lamb led to slaughter
a naVve person allowing himself or herself to be exploited
Isaiah 53:5, 'He was oppressed, and he was afflicted, yet he opened not his mouth: he is brought as a lamb to the slaughter'

sledgehammer
to use a sledgehammer to crack a nut
to devote vastly more resources to a project than is warranted by all the circumstances

sleep
not to get a wink of sleep
not to sleep at all
not to lose any sleep over something
not to worry about some matter
to go to sleep
to become inactive
to sleep on one's rights
to fail to exercise some entitlement within a reasonable period

sleeping
the choice is between eating well or sleeping well
one can invest for maximum yield or maximum security, but not both
to let sleeping dogs lie
to refrain from raising an issue that is not obviously requiring attention

sleepless
to spend a sleepless night
to worry about something

sleeve
to have a card up one's sleeve
secretly to have information relevant to a transaction
refers to card games
to have an ace up one's sleeve
to hold an impressive counter-argument in reserve
refers to card games; from Latin *as* ('unity', that is 'one' or 'a single point')
to keep something up one's sleeve

secretly to retain something in reserve for use in the future or at a later stage of negotiations

refers to playing cards or magicians

to laugh up one's sleeve

to laugh surreptitiously

to wear one's heart on one's sleeve

to lack the reserve expected of one

refers to the fashion of wearing a sign of romantic attachment on one's sleeve; Shakespeare *Othello* I:i, 'But I will wear my heart upon my sleeve'

sleeves

to roll up one's sleeves

to get on with a job energetically

sleight

sleight of hand

deceit by trickery

Daniel Defoe (1660–1731), 'All the artifice and sleight of hand they were masters of'

slender

to hang by a slender thread

to be in a precarious situation

refers to Damocles who had the sword of Dionysius hanging, by a slender thread, over his head — as a symbol of perpetual risk in life; the story is told in Cicero, *Tusculanae Disputationes*

slice

to have a slice of the action

to be one of several parties to a project

sliced

to claim that something is the best thing since sliced bread

to have a high opinion of the importance or novelty of an invention or practice

slide

to be on a slippery slide

to court disaster

refers to an opening in the side of a shearing shed known as the porthole or chute (spelling variations include shoot and shute); after a sheep is shorn it is pushed through the porthole and slides down

to slide under the bar

not to arouse suspicion

sling

to sling mud

to make unfair imputations

slings

slings and arrows

adverse fortunes in life; hurtful experiences

Shakespeare, *Hamlet* III:i, 'Whether 'tis nobler in the mind to suffer / the slings and arrows of outrageous fortune, / or to take arms against a sea of troubles, / and by opposing end them?'

slip

a slip of the tongue

incorrect words uttered accidentally

to let something slip through one's fingers

to allow something to escape from one's ownership or control

to show one's slip

to reveal details which one meant to keep private

refers to women's petticoats

to slip one's mind

to be overlooked or forgotten

to slip through the cracks

to be overlooked

to slip through the net

to happen as an isolated case despite steps taken to prevent such events

to slip under one's guard

to cause a mistake to be made despite care being taken to prevent this

refers to fencing

slippery

a slippery customer

a shifty person

slippery path

dangerous course of action

to be on a slippery chute/shoot/slide

to court disaster

refers to an opening in the side of a shearing shed known as the porthole or chute (spelling variations include shoot and shute); after a sheep is shorn it is pushed through the porthole and slides down

slipping

to be slipping

to be losing one's cunning or expertise

slog

to slog it out
(of two competing parties) to engage in an exchange of actions designed to harm each other, especially one with no finesse or style
refers to boxing or fighting

slough

a slough of despond
a feeling of hopelessness
refers to a swamp; John Bunyan (1628–88), *The Pilgrim's Progress* Pt I, 'The name of the slough was despond'

slow

to be slow off the mark
to be slow to start something
refers to the starting mark of a race

slowly

the mills of God grind slowly
retribution might be delayed but is inevitable
Friedrich von Logau (1604–55), *Sinngedichte* (translated by H. W. Longfellow), 'Though the mills of God grind slowly, yet they grind exceeding small; though with patience he stands waiting, with exactness grinds he all'

to bleed to death slowly
to be heading in gradual steps towards total ruin

to sink slowly in the west
to fail gradually
refers to the setting of the sun in the western sky

sly

a sly dog
a knowing, cunning, clever person (esp. one who discreet about that person's own personal weaknesses)

smack

a smack in the eye
a rebuff

small

by small steps
gradually

it's a small world
it is surprising to meet people one knows in unexpected places

to be a small cog in a large wheel
to be a relatively unimportant person in a large organisation

to be small beer
to be quite unimportant

to be small potatoes
to be quite unimportant

smart

to be a smart Alec
to give witty but cheeky responses to one's superiors or customers
origin obscure, but dates back to 1860s in USA

smell

a rose by any other name would smell as sweet
the form does not affect the substance
Shakespeare, *Romeo and Juliet* II:ii, 'What's in a name? That which we call a rose / By any other name would smell as sweet'

to run something on the smell of an oil/oily rag
to run something very economically and efficiently

to smell a rat
to become suspicious

to smell blood
to divine imminent victory

to smell out something
to discover something by careful investigation

to smell trouble
to perceive difficulties

smelling

to come up smelling like a rose
not to have a stain on one's character

smells

something smells
something is suspicious

smile

to wipe the smile off someone's face
to destroy a person's complacency

wipe that smile off your face!
treat this matter more seriously!

smoke

put that in your pipe and smoke it
contemplate that fact if you can!
a strong rebuke given to an adversary; R. H. Barham (1788–1845), *Lay of St Odille*, 'So put that in your pipe, my Lord Otto, and smoke it!'

the big smoke
the big city

to go up in smoke
to come to nothing

to send a smoke signal
to give an indication
refers to a means of communication used by North American indigenous peoples

when the smoke clears
when sufficient time has passed to see what is going on

where there is smoke there is fire
if there is a hint of trouble, then it is highly likely that there really is trouble
W. H. Auden (1907–73), *Twelve Songs* VIII, 'Still waters run deep, my dear, there's never smoke without fire'

smokescreen

to set up a smokescreen
deliberately to confuse an issue by disguising its salient features

smoking

smoking gun
damning evidence

smooth

to be in smooth water
to have no troubles
nautical metaphor

to smooth the path for someone
to use one's influence to make arrangements so that a person's task will be easier or more readily accomplished
Isaiah 40:3, 'Prepare ye the way of the Lord; make smooth in the desert a highway for our God'

to take the rough with the smooth
to accept the hardships of life along with its pleasant features

smorgasbord

smorgasbord
a series of different items from which a number can be chosen
from the Swedish words for 'butter', 'goose', and 'table'

snag

to strike a snag
to encounter a difficulty
refers to angling

snail

at a snail's pace
very slowly
Shakespeare, *As You Like It*, II:vii, 'The whining schoolboy ... creeping like snail unwillingly to school'

snake

a snake in the grass
a person of low character who manages to disguise that trait
Virgil, *Eclogue*, 'There's a snake hidden in the grass'

snakes

a game of snakes and ladders
a series of ups and downs
refers to a board game

snap

to snap at someone's heels
to be in very close pursuit
refers to hounds pursuing a fox

to snap one's fingers
to gesture contemptuously, especially in the expectation of immediate obedience

to snap someone's head off
to speak to a person with excessive aggression

sneezed

that is not to be sneezed at
that is so significant that it should not be rejected

snow

to snow someone under
to overload a person with work

snowball

to snowball
to grow rapidly in size or influence

snowflake

to have a snowflake's chance in hell
to have no hope or possibility at all

soap

a soap opera
a low-quality radio or television serial
refers to the original sponsorship of such programs by soap companies

to be on one's soap box
to hold forth on an issue about which one feels keenly
refers to orators standing on soap boxes (strong wooden boxes) as a platform

to soft soap someone
to flatter a person

socks

to chop someone off at the socks
to stop someone's proposals prematurely

to pull one's socks up
to set out to improve or correct one's inadequate behaviour or performance

wouldn't it rot your socks!
what an unpleasant surprise!

Sodom

a Sodom and Gomorrah
a place of vice
Genesis 18:20, 'Sodom and Gomorrah ... their sin is very great'

soft

to have a soft spot for someone
to be very fond of a person

to have a soft underbelly
to have a weakness that can be exploited

to soft pedal
to restrain oneself
refers to playing an organ or piano

to soft soap someone
to flatter a person

soften

to soften someone up
to make a person more favourably disposed to one's wishes

to soften the blow
to take action to reduce the trauma of bad news

softly

speak softly and carry a big stick
be polite to your potential enemies but maintain an active and visible defensive and offensive capability
from a speech by US President Theodore Roosevelt in 1901

sold

to be sold on something
to be utterly dedicated to a proposal

soldier

to be a brave soldier
courageously to do one's duty

to soldier on
to carry on despite difficulties

Solomon

to need the wisdom of Solomon
to require great sagacity when faced with a difficult decision
refers to King Solomon's ingenious solution to an apparently insoluble dilemma as described in *1 Kings* 3:16–28

solution

a middle-of-the-road solution
a solution near the middle of a range of possibilities

a Rolls-Royce solution
a high quality but excessively expensive way of doing something

somersault

to turn a complete somersault
to reverse one's established policy

son

favourite son
person preferred by many people for some office

song

nothing to make a song or dance about
unexciting or unimportant

swan song
last appearance before retirement
refers to the ancient (but erroneous) belief that the swan sings beautifully before it dies; such a belief is referred to by Plato, Aristotle, Shakespeare, Spenser, and Coleridge (among others)

to buy something for a song
to buy something very cheaply

to make a song and dance about something
to create a fuss

to sing a particular song
to state particular views

soothing

soothing syrup
insincere expressions of sympathy or flattery

sore

eyesore
extremely ugly object

to be a sight for sore eyes
to be something welcome

to open up a festering sore
to upset a person by drawing attention to a long-standing grievance apparently forgotten

sorrows

to drown one's sorrows
to drink by way of solace and in an attempt to forget some misfortune

soul

a soul brother
a person of similar ideals

a soul-searching exercise
a deep and penetrating examination of personal motives and conscience

heart and soul
with great energy
Matthew 22:36–40, 'Thou shalt love the Lord thy God with all thy heart and with all thy soul and with all thy mind'

soul-destroying
breaking the spirit or will to continue

to bare one's soul
talkatively to give a revealing insight into oneself

to be the life and soul of the party
to be the prime enthusiast for a cause
Shakespeare, *A Midsummer Night's Dream*, 'My love, my life, my soul, fair Helena!'

to keep body and soul together
barely to stay alive

sound

to sound alarm bells
to give warning

to sound the death knell of something
to indicate the impending end of something
refers to the knell (sound) of a bell rung at a funeral; Shakespeare, *Macbeth* II:i, 'The bell invites me ... it is a knell that summons thee to heaven or to hell'

sounding

to act as a sounding board
to give, on request, constructive criticisms of ideas tentatively held
refers, originally, to a board placed behind a speaker (esp. a preacher) to reflect the speaker's voice forwards to the congregation or audience

to take a sounding
to ascertain people's views
nautical metaphor referring to ascertaining the depth of water

soup

to be in the soup
to be in great difficulties

sour

that is just sour grapes
those are disparaging remarks made only because that person is peeved and resentful at someone else's better fortune
derived from Aesop's fable of 'the fox and the grapes' about expressing deliberate disparagement of a desired but unattainable object; 'sour grapes' also occurs in *Ezekiel* 18:2, 'the fathers have eaten sour grapes, and the children's teeth are set on edge'

to hit a sour note
to say or do something inappropriate to a situation
refers to music

to turn sour
to become unsatisfactory

south

a South Sea bubble
an unrealistic financial venture that is bound to result in total loss
refers to a notorious financial scandal involving the South Sea Company (UK) in 1720

to head south
(of prices, etc.) to go down

sow

one can't make a silk purse out of a sow's ear
it is impossible to manufacture something of a high standard from inferior raw materials
Malcolm Bradbury (1932–), 'For the mass of men, you can't make a silk purse out of a sow's ear'

to get the wrong sow by the ear
to reach an incorrect conclusion

to sow seeds
to propagate ideas in the hope that they will be adopted

to sow the wind and reap the whirlwind
to make bad mistakes and to suffer the even worse consequences
Hosea 8:7, 'They have sown the wind, and they shall reap the whirlwind'

to sow wild oats
to indulge in foolish behaviour while a young adult

sown

to reap as one has sown
to experience the consequences of one's own actions
Galatians 6:7, 'Whatsoever a man soweth, that shall he also reap'

space

to get some breathing space
to get more time in which to accomplish something

spade

to call a spade a spade
to speak bluntly; not to use euphemisms

spades

delivered in spades
to a considerable degree; in large numbers

spadework

to do the spadework
to do the hard or menial work in preparation for a project

Spain

a castle in Spain
a desirable imagining, but an impracticable proposition

spanner

to throw a spanner into the works
to cause an unexpected complication

spare

to carry a spare tyre
to be fat

spark

to spark on all cylinders
to work extremely well

sparks

to make sparks fly
to inflame or cause friction in a situation
Job 5:7, 'Man is born unto trouble, as the sparks fly upward'

Spartan

Spartan
tough and efficient, with a complete absence of the finer things of life

speak

speak of the devil
here is the person we were just discussing

speak softly and carry a big stick
be polite to your potential enemies but maintain an active and visible defensive and offensive capability
from a speech by US President Theodore Roosevelt in 1901

to speak one's mind
to express one's views frankly and forcefully

to speak the same language
to have a good understanding and similar ideas

to speak volumes for something
to be highly expressive; to exemplify extremely well

spearhead

to spearhead something
to lead a movement

spectacles

to see something through rose-coloured spectacles
to appreciate only the advantages and to disregard completely the disadvantages

spectre

to raise the spectre of something
to draw attention to the expectation of something worrying
refers to a ghost or apparition

spectrum

spectrum
wide range of different opinions or backgrounds

speed

speed the plough!
let us get on with this as fast as possible!
George Chapman (?1559–?1634), *Bussy d'Ambois*, I:i, 'speed his plough!'

spell

to break the spell
to spoil the effect

to have a spell in the paddock
to have leave of absence
refers to resting of horses from racing or work

to spell something out
to explain something in detail

spellbinding

spellbinding
fascinating to an audience

spend

to spend a sleepless night
to worry about something

spider

to be the centre of the spider's web
to control an operation that involves numerous and/or complex ingredients

spike

to spike someone's guns
to sabotage (or negate the effect of) an opponent's devices

spill

to spill the beans
indiscreetly to reveal sensitive information

spilt

it is no use crying over spilt milk
there is nothing to be gained by lamenting over an irredeemable error

spin

tailspin
a loss of control; a state of chaos
refers to a spin by an aircraft with the tail spiralling

to be in a flat spin
to be in a state of agitation or panic
refers to an aircraft that is falling while spinning in a horizontal plane

to spin a yarn
to tell an amusing or unlikely story
a play on words referring to spinning yarn for cloth

to spin something out
to prolong some matter

spine

to send a cold shiver down someone's spine
to horrify a person

spinner

to be a money spinner
to produce large profits easily and quickly

spirit

kindred spirit
person with similar interests and eccentricities
John Keats (1795–1821), *O Solitude!*, 'Almost the highest bliss of human-kind, / when to thy haunts two kindred spirits flee'

the spirit is willing but the flesh is weak
the body is not up to the demands made on it–physically or morally
Matthew 26:41: 'Watch and pray, that ye enter not into temptation: the spirit indeed is willing but the flesh is weak

spit

spit it out!
unburden yourself!

spite

to cut one's nose off to spite one's face
to act in pique in a way that harms only oneself

splash

to make a splash
to create a sensation

spleen

to vent one's spleen on someone
to demonstrate one's ill-temper to a person
refers to the belief that the spleen was the site of melancholy and moroseness

splice

to splice the main brace
to serve an extra ration of rum
nautical metaphor

split

to split hairs
to draw absurdly fine distinctions

to split one's side
to be convulsed with laughter

spoil

to spoil the ship for a ha'p'orth of tar
to engage in a false economy
the current word 'ship' is actually a mistake for the original word 'sheep', and the tar refers to the treatment of wounds

too many cooks spoil the broth
more than one leader can confuse and harm a project spoke

to put a spoke in someone's wheel
to interfere with another person's activity, so preventing its continuance

sponge

to throw in the sponge
to concede defeat

refers to boxing

spoon

he must have a long spoon that sups with the devil
great care is needed when negotiating with disreputable parties
Shakespeare apparently alludes to an old proverb in *The Tempest* II:ii, 'Mercy! mercy! this is a devil ... I will leave him, I have no long spoon!'

to be born with a silver spoon in one's mouth
to be brought up by wealthy parents
refers to the traditional gift of a silver spoon (an 'apostle spoon') to a child at baptism — the child born of wealthy parents is assured of riches from the moment of birth and thus does not have to await baptism to receive a valuable gift

to get the wooden spoon
to come ingloriously last
refers to the custom of awarding a silver cup to the winner and a wooden spoon to the loser

spot

the one bright spot on the horizon
the only hopeful aspect

to be a tender spot
to be a sensitive subject requiring tact

to have a blind spot about something
to have a lack of understanding and perception about something
refers to that part of the retina insensitive to light, at the point of entry of the optic nerve

to have a soft spot for someone
to be very fond of a person

to put someone on the spot
to embarrass a person

spotlight

to steal the spotlight
to become the centre of attention
refers to the theatre

to turn the spotlight on something
to draw public attention to something

spots

a leopard cannot change its spots
each person is born with certain unalterable characteristics
Jeremiah 13:23, 'Can the Ethiopian change his skin, or the leopard his spots?'

sprat

to throw a sprat to catch a mackerel
to risk a little in the hope of gaining much

spread

to spread one's wings
to test or develop one's abilities, to lead a life of greater scope than previously

to spread oneself thin
to attempt to do more than is feasible in the available time

to spread the gospel
to propagate principles or attitudes that one believes to be true
Mark 16:15, 'Go ye into the world and preach the gospel to every creature'

to spread the net more widely
to become more comprehensive

spring

a spring cleaning
a regular (usually annual) review with a view to discarding the obsolete and retaining that which is useful

to spring to mind
to occur suddenly to a person

springboard

a springboard
a situation from which one is able to make a rapid advance

spur

to spur someone on
to agitate a person into doing something
refers to riding horses

spurs

to win one's spurs
to gain recognition after a period of effort
refers to the earning of a knighthood in battle

square

a square peg in a round hole
obviously unsuited for the purpose'

four square
honest and reliable
refers to a solid building construction

to go back to square one
to start all over again
refers to board games

to try to square the circle
to attempt the impossible
refers to a classical problem in geometry, namely, to construct with a compass a square of the same area as a given circle

squeaky

the squeaky wheel gets the oil
those complaining the most loudly will get their problems sorted out first

squeeze

to squeeze someone out
to force a person to leave

to squeeze the last drop out of something
to get the maximum advantage out of some favourable situation

to squeeze the lemon dry
to get the maximum advantage out of some favourable situation
Sir Eric Geddes (1875–1937), 'The Germans ... are going to pay every penny; they are going to be squeezed, as a lemon is squeezed — until the pips squeak. My only doubt is not whether we can squeeze hard enough, but whether there is enough juice.' (10 December 1918)

squib

a damp squib
disappointingly ineffective action
refers to fireworks that fail to go off

stab

a stab in the dark
a sheer guess

to stab someone in the back
deliberately and surreptitiously to harm a person who regarded one as a friend

stable

to shut the stable door after the horse has bolted
to take preventive action only after the relevant event

stables

a Herculean cleaning of the stables
a thorough revision of operating procedure
refers to the labours of Hercules (Heracles in Greek) who had twelve labours imposed upon him by Eurystheus — one of which was the cleaning of the stables of King Augeas in a single day

stacked

to have the cards stacked against one
to be faced with many difficulties frustrating a project
refers to playing cards

to have the odds stacked against one
to be faced with many difficulties frustrating a project
refers to betting

stage

the stage is set
something is about to happen
refers to the theatre

to be centre stage
to have everyone's attention
refers to the theatre

to be on a world stage
to be prominent in international affairs
refers to the theatre

to stage manage something
to arrange how something happens
refers to the theatre

to upstage someone
to deprive someone of the glory that would otherwise have been enjoyed by that person
refers to the theatre

staging

a staging post
a designated stopping or resting place on a journey
refers to the place at which the horses drawing a stagecoach were changed over

stake

to raise the stake
to increase the amount of potential gain or loss in a project
refers to gambling

to stake a claim
to indicate one's desire to obtain something
refers to placing a series of stakes in the ground as a sign of claiming a place for gold mining

stalemate

stalemate

a final result in which neither party to a dispute is victorious

refers to chess

stalking

a stalking horse

a pretext put forward to allow an attack to be made or an argument to be mounted

refers to a horse trained to allow a hunter to approach game (esp. fowl) without being seen; Shakespeare, *As You Like It* V:iv, 'He uses his folly like a stalking horse, and under the presentation of that he shoots his wit'

stamp

only a postage stamp between them

virtually equal or close together

to get an elephant stamp

to receive praise

to put one's own stamp on something

to effect something with one's own characteristic style

to rubber-stamp something

to endorse something without considering the merits

stampede

to stampede someone into something

to pressure a person into taking some action

stamping

stamping ground

one's favourite place for certain activities

stand

if one can't stand the heat one should stay out of the kitchen

if one cannot put up with the pressure of a situation, one should get out of it

US President Harry S. Truman (1884–1972), *Mr Citizen*, ch. 15, 'If you can't stand the heat, get out of the kitchen'

not to have a leg to stand on

to have one's arguments completely demolished; OR to be without acceptable excuse or explanation

to be more than flesh can stand

to be more than a person reasonably can be expected to endure

to have to run fast just to stand still

competition is such that merely to maintain one's relative position one needs to make positive progress

to make a last-ditch stand

to make a brave effort to stave off final defeat

King William III (1650–1702), 'There is one way never to see it lost ... and that is to die in the last ditch' (quoted by Burnet, *History of His Own Times*,1715)

to make someone's hair stand on end

to give a person shocking news

Job 4:15, 'Then a spirit passed before my face; the hair of my flesh stood up'; Shakespeare, *Hamlet* I:v, 'would harrow up thy soul ... and each particular hair to stand an end'

to stand in someone's way

to prevent a person achieving that person's goal

to stand in the breach

to fill a gap in the defences and bear the brunt of an attack or criticism

Shakespeare, *Henry V* III:i, 'Once more unto the breach, dear friends, once more; / Or close the wall up with our English dead!'

to stand on one's own two feet

not to require the help of others

to stand on someone's shoulders

to build up on another person's ideas

to stand one's ground

to maintain a stance in the face of opposition

refers to military battle

to stand out from the crowd

to be noticeably better than one's competitors

to stand over someone with a big stick

to intimidate a person in order to get that person to act in a particular way

to stand up and be counted

publicly to announce one's position on some issue

to stand up on one's hind legs

to assert one's authority

refers to animals adopting aggressive posture

standard

a standard bearer

a highly visible activist for a cause
military metaphor

stands

to know where one stands
to know what one supports or how one is affected

standing

to be able to do something standing on one's head
to be able to do something very easily

standoff

a Mexican standoff
a situation where neither of two parties is making a move
refers to poker

standstill

a standstill
an inability to proceed

star

rising star
person making good progress in that person's career

stare

to stare someone in the face
to be obvious

stars

one can thank one's lucky stars
one was extremely fortunate
refers to astrology

to have stars in one's eyes
to receive a blow on the head that affects one's vision; OR to have unrealistic expectations of one's position and prospects

to shoot for the stars
to be unrealistic

start

to have a head start
to have an advantage over others
refers to horse racing

to start from behind scratch
to be faced with a handicap
refers to the starting mark (with no handicap advantage) in a race

to start from scratch
to commence something without the benefit of any past activity
refers to the starting mark (with no handicap advantage) in a race

to start from taws
to begin from the beginning

to start off on the right foot
to commence an operation with great care to do it correctly
refers to marching

to start the ball rolling
to commence and advance enthusiastically an activity

to start to bite
to start to be effective

to start with a blank sheet of paper
to commence an exercise without being bound by any established practices

state

to be in a state of flux
to be subject to continuous change

to find out the state of play
to ascertain the current position of some project

statement

a motherhood statement
a statement so obvious and uncontroversial as not to be worth making
such as 'motherhood is a good thing'

stay

if one can't stand the heat one should stay out of the kitchen
if one cannot put up with the pressure of a situation, one should get out of it
US President Harry S. Truman (1884–1972), *Mr Citizen*, ch. 15, 'If you can't stand the heat, get out of the kitchen'

to stay afloat
to remain solvent

to stay tuned
to keep in touch for further information as it becomes available
refers to radio reception

stayed

people stayed away in droves
few people came
refers to a moving group of cattle, sheep, or other animals

steal

to steal a march on someone
to anticipate another person's actions and get in ahead
military metaphor

to steal someone's clothes

to plagiarise another person's ideas

to steal someone's heart
to move someone's affections towards another person or cause
Shakespeare, *Julius Caesar* III:ii, 'I come not, friends. to steal away your hearts'

to steal someone's thunder
to take credit for another person's good work
refers to a dispute over the copying of a machine invented by dramatist John Dennis (1657–1734) to reproduce the sound of thunder during a play

to steal the show
to have the maximum appeal to those watching
refers to the theatre

to steal the spotlight
to become the centre of attention
refers to the theatre

steam

full-steam ahead!
get going as fast as possible!
refers to a steam engine (especially in a ship or train)

that person wouldn't give you the steam off his or her sausages
that person is very mean

to develop a head of steam
to gain momentum
refers to a steam engine or boiler

to let off steam
to engage in noisy or robust activity as a form of relaxation
refers to release of pressure from a boiler

to lose steam
to slow down
refers to a steam engine or boiler

to run out of steam
to lose one's energy and enthusiasm
refers to steam engines

under one's own steam
without external help
refers to a steam engine (especially in a ship)

steamroll

to steamroll something through
to use enormous force to achieve an objective
refers to a steamroller — a large earth-flattening machine

steel

to be a man of steel
to be a person with moral courage

to have nerves of steel
not to be easily frightened

to steel one's heart against something
to determine that, notwithstanding one's natural compassion, something shall not happen

stem

to stem the haemorrhage/bleeding
to put a stop to the financial losses of a project

to stem the tide
to make progress against something

step

a step in the right direction
the first in a series of measures designed to correct some problem

step by step
gradually

to get in step with someone
to do as another person does
refers to marching

to overstep the mark
to fail to observe the proprieties
refers to gaining an unfair advantage in a contest (originally the mark between two fighters)

to step down
to retire from some position

to step into the ring
to enter a competitive environment
refers to a boxing ring

to step on someone's corns/toes
to upset another person by interfering in that person's area of responsibility

to step out of line
to infringe accepted rules of behaviour
military metaphor

to take a giant step forward
to make a significant advance
Genesis 6:4, 'There were giants in the earth in those days'

to take a step backwards
to move further away from one's goal

to watch one's step
to be on the lookout for danger; OR to set out to improve one's behaviour

stepping

a stepping stone
a means to an end

steps

by small steps
gradually

to follow in someone's footsteps
to do as another person did

stereotype

a stereotype
(of a group) a general impression of the characteristics that is assumed to apply to all members of that group
refers to the plates formerly used in printing

stew

to be in a stew
to be in a difficult situation; OR to be in an anxious, agitated, or confused state

to stew in one's juice
to suffer the adverse consequences of one's acts or omissions
Shakespeare, *Hamlet* III:iv, 'But to live in the rank sweat of an enseamed bed, stew'd in corruption'

stick

a cobbler should stick to his last
a person should confine himself or herself to activities for which that person has been trained

a stick in the mud
an unenterprising person

any stick to beat a dog
any excuse will do if it serves one's purpose

some mud will stick
reputations will be hurt even after accusations are proved false

speak softly and carry a big stick
be polite to your potential enemies but maintain an active and visible defensive and offensive capability
from a speech by US President Theodore Roosevelt in 1901

stick it up your guernsey/jersey!
I have absolutely no interest in you and what you saying!
refers to the jumpers worn by members of football teams

to be a good old stick
to be a kind and thoughtful person

to be better than a poke in the eye with a burnt stick
to be not particularly welcome, but better than other alternatives

to be in a cleft stick
to be in a fix that allows for no alternatives

to be more than one can poke a stick at
to be more than can reasonably be handled

to be on the losing end of the stick
to be worse off while the other party to a transaction becomes correspondingly better off

to be unable to keep people away with a big stick
to be faced with a large crowd or much demand

to give someone a bit of stick
to criticise a person mildly

to hold the wrong end of the stick
to be completely mistaken about something

to stand over someone with a big stick
to intimidate a person in order to get that person to act in a particular way

to stick a knife into someone
to act vindictively towards a person

to stick one's neck out
to have the courage of one's convictions or to take a calculated risk
refers to execution by decapitation

to stick one's oar in
to intervene without invitation in a dispute to which one is not a party
refers to rowing

to stick out a mile
to be very apparent

to stick to one's game
to confine oneself to activities in areas in which one has knowledge and expertise

to stick to one's guns
to continue to hold certain beliefs notwithstanding opposition by others
refers to miltary battle

to stick to one's knitting
to confine oneself to what one is used to doing

to wield a big stick

to assert power

sticks

it sticks in my throat
I find it annoying and vexatious
Shakespeare, *Macbeth* II:ii, 'I had most need of blessing, and "Amen" / Stuck in my throat'

not to have the wherewithal to rub two sticks together
to be very poor

sticks and carrots
disincentives and incentives in combination
refers to the handling of donkeys

sticky

a sticky patch
a period fraught with difficulties

to be a sticky beak
to show excessive curiosity into matters not of one's concern

to be on a sticky wicket
to face some difficulties
refers to cricket

to come to a sticky end
to endure an unpleasant fate

to have sticky fingers
to be dishonest; OR to be very adept at catching a ball

stiff

a stiff upper lip
obstinate courage in the face of pain or adversity

stiff cheese!
circumstances that might be unwelcome but will not be altered, and in respect of which no great sympathy is felt

still

still waters run deep
a person with a quiet manner might have many unrecognised characteristics — both good and bad
W. H. Auden (1907–73), *Twelve Songs VIII*, 'Still waters run deep, my dear, there's never smoke without fire'

to have to run fast just to stand still
competition is such that merely to maintain one's relative position one needs to make positive progress

sting

to be the sting in the tail
to be the unexpected unpleasant conclusion

stir

to stir a finger
to make some minimum effort

to stir a hand
to volunteer assistance

to stir the possum
to set out to raise controversial issues

to stir the pot
to set out to raise controversial issues

to stir up a hornet's nest
to take action that results in unpleasant side-effects

stitch

a stitch in time saves nine
preventive maintenance saves money in the long run

to stitch up a deal
successfully to conclude a deal

stitches

to have someone in stitches
greatly to amuse a person

stock

lock, stock and barrel
entirely
the lock, stock and barrel of a gun is the complete firearm

to be a blue-chip stock
to be of excellent quality

to take stock
to contemplate the alternatives

stoke

to stoke the fires
to provoke a violent reaction

stomach

someone's eyes are bigger than that person's stomach
a person is unrealistic in regard to that person's ability to cope with something

to have butterflies in one's stomach
a feeling of anxiety

to have no stomach for something
to have no liking, inclination, or fortitude for something

stone

a milestone

a significant stage or achievement in a life or a history

refers to markers along a road indicating distance in miles

a rolling stone gathers no moss

a person who keeps changing jobs will not have a successful career

Tusser, *Five Hundred Points of Good Husbandrie* (1573), 'The stone that is rolling can gather no moss. / For master and servant oft changing is loss'

a stepping stone

a means to an end

cornerstone

key ingredient

the touchstone

the standard

refers to a dark flinty stone used to assess samples of gold by comparing streaks left on it with those streaks left by known gold-containing standards

to draw blood from a stone

to do the impossible

to have a heart of stone

to be unfeeling

Shakespeare, *Othello*, 'My heart is turned to stone'

to kill some proposal stone dead

to take action that stops a proposal completely

refers to death by stoning

to kill two birds with one stone

to achieve a second objective in the course of achieving the first objective

to leave no stone unturned

to be very thorough

refers to an instruction from the oracle of Delphi regarding a search for Persian treasure (477 BC)

within a stone's throw

very close

stones

people in glass houses should not throw stones

those who are less than perfect are foolish to criticise others

John 8:7, 'He that is without sin among you, let him first cast a stone at her' (refers to ancient condemnation and punishment of people by stoning)

to throw a few stones on the roof and see who comes out

to attempt to change a boring situation or resolve a stalemate

stonewalling

stonewalling

deliberate obstruction or delaying tactics

stools

to fall between two stools

not to fit neatly into either of two available alternatives, and to waver between them

stop

a whistlestop tour

a hurried (especially ceremonial) visit to many places

refers to a train journey

to come to a full stop

to cease activity completely

to stop up one hole in a sieve

to do something quite useless

stopped

to be stopped in one's tracks

suddenly and unexpectedly to be prevented from carrying on with a project

stopping

heart-stopping

exciting

stops

the buck stops here

I accept full responsibility

hand-lettered sign on desk of US President Harry S. Truman (Phillips, *The Truman Presidency*, Ch. 12)

to pull out all stops

to make maximum effort

refers to organ playing at maximum volume

when the music stops

suddenly and soon

refers to an imminent crisis leading to some resolution of a matter, as in a game of musical chairs

storage

to put something into cold storage

to put something aside to be dealt with at some indeterminate future time

store

to take over the store

to assume the management

storm

a storm in a teacup
a controversy about a minor matter but one that looms large in the minds of the parties

any port in a storm
anything that helps to avoid difficulties is welcome

the calm before the storm
the quiet period before an expected or inevitable crisis

there are storm clouds on the horizon
bad news is expected

to barnstorm
to travel around and actively promote one's cause or performance
refers to itinerant actors who performed in barns

to be in the eye of the storm
to be at the centre of a controversy

to brainstorm
to pool thoughts in the course of a session designed to generate fresh ideas and especially to build up on the ideas of others

to create a storm
to cause a fuss

to ride out the storm
to come safely through some dangerous situation
nautical metaphor

to run into a firestorm
to be faced with many protests

to take by storm
to captivate an audience

to weather the storm
to come safely through a crisis
nautical metaphor

stormy

to be a stormy petrel
a person who disturbs a pleasant state of affairs by agitating for change
refers to the bird (petrel) that flies low over water during a storm and appears to be alternately touching one foot and then the other to the surface of the water as though walking upon it; the bird is sometimes thought to be the harbinger of a storm, and is named after St Peter who walked upon the stormy waters of Lake Gennesareth

story

a cock-and-bull story
an explanation that is completely unbelievable and unacceptable
Laurence Sterne (1713–68), *Tristram Shandy*, 'Said my mother, "What is this story all about?" — "a cock and a bull," said Yorick.'

a shaggy dog story
a laborious, far-fetched, amusing story
refers to the shaggy dog that originally featured in many of these stories

a tall story
an interesting but untrue and unbelievable tale

to cap a story
to tell an even funnier story than the one just told

to dream up some story
to concoct a false story naVvely or maliciously

straight

a straight face
a facial expression that does not reveal one's thoughts in a humorous situation

a straight shooter
a person who is frank and outspoken

straight from the shoulder
bluntly
refers to boxing

to be on the straight and narrow
to be completely virtuous
Matthew 7:14, 'Strait is the gate, and narrow is the way, which leadeth unto life'

to jump straight in at the deep end
to do something without proper preparation

to maintain a straight bat
to operate in orthodox fashion, avoiding risk
refers to cricket

strain

to strain at a gnat
to be scrupulous about trifles
Matthew 23:23, ' … that strain at a gnat, and swallow a camel'

strait

strait-laced
puritanical

refers to the wearing of a very tightly laced bodice or other garment

to keep someone in a strait jacket
to deny a person any discretionary powers at all
refers to a restraining 'jacket' used to control violent or insane persons

straits

in dire straits
in great need

strangle

to strangle some discussion
to cut off some unfinished discussion

stranglehold

a stranglehold
exclusive and complete control
refers to wrestling or fighting

straps

to hit the straps
to really get going
refers to horses in harness

straw

a man of straw
a person of no substance, a counterfeit, a sham; OR a person invented in order to be triumphantly defeated; OR a person who has no assets while giving a contrary appearance one cannot make bricks without straw
one cannot achieve results in the absence of adequate resources
Exodus 6:7 'Ye shall no more give the people straw to make bricks ... let them go and gather straw for themselves'

the final (or last) straw
the latest step that, when added to a large number of seemingly harmless previous steps, sets off a significant event resulting from the cumulative effect
see 'the straw that broke the camel's back'

the straw that broke the camel's back
the latest step that, when added to a large number of seemingly harmless previous steps, sets off a sudden significant event resulting from the cumulative effect

to buy straw hats in winter
to buy in a depressed market when most other people are sellers

to draw the short straw
to be chosen (perhaps by lot) to undertake an undesired task

straws

straws in the wind
small but significant indicators of future events
John Seldon (1584–1654), 'Take a straw and throw it up into the air, you shall see by that which way the wind is'

to clasp/grasp at straws
desperately to resort to any expedient in a hopeless situation
refers to a drowning person

stream

mainstream
orthodox

to get on stream
to now operate successfully following the end of a settling-in period

to swap/change horses in mid-stream
to alter that upon which one is reliant during the course of a project

streamline

to streamline
to organise better by simplification

street

a one-way street
a flow of activity in only one direction

not to be in the same street as someone
not to be of comparable quality

the man in the street
the average citizen

to be in Queer street
to be in debt
origin obscure

to be up one's street
to be right within a person's expertise or area of interest

to walk in off the street
to come without prior arrangement or notification

streets

there is blood in the streets
much damage has been done to a cause

to be streets ahead
to outperform one's competitors by a wide margin

strength

to be a tower of strength
to be a person who supports and comforts another

strengthen

to strengthen someone's hand
to give a person additional authority or greater moral support or more facts to support that person's case

stretch

to enter the home stretch
to commence the last stage
refers to horse racing

strewn

to be on a path strewn with roses
to lead a very pleasant life

strictly

that is strictly for the birds
that is trivial nonsense appealing only to the naVve and the gullible

stride

to hit one's stride
to settle down to some task
refers to horses in harness

to take something in one's stride
to cope with something easily
refers to a horse jumping an obstacle

strike

to strike a blow
to begin or resume work

to strike a blow for some principle
to work towards the attainment of some principle

to strike a chord
to sound familiar or recall something to mind
refers to music

to strike a responsive chord
to get a favourable reaction to a proposal
refers to music

to strike a snag
to encounter a difficulty
refers to angling

to strike at the roots of something
to work towards the destruction of something

to strike gold
to have one's efforts suddenly rewarded by great success
refers to gold-mining

to strike pay dirt
to become successful
refers to soil containing gold or other precious metal

to strike the right chord
to appeal successfully to someone's emotions
refers to music

to strike the right key
to make comments that set the appropriate tone in a speech or conversation
refers to music

to strike the right note
to say or do something appropriate to a situation
refers to music

to strike while the iron is hot
to take advantage of a situation that cannot last
refers to the work of blacksmiths and farriers; John Dryden (1631–1700), *Aenis*, 'We must beat the iron while it is hot, but we may polish it at leisure'

strikes

it strikes me
it occurs to me

striking

to be within striking distance
to be fairly close

string

to have a second string to one's bow
to have an additional qualification appropriate to the task
refers to archery

strings

to be tied to someone's apron strings
to be excessively influenced by one's mother

to have strings attached
to be subject to conditions

to hold the purse strings
to have control of expenditure
refers to a drawstring closing a purse

to pull at one's heart strings
to affect one emotionally

to pull strings
to use one's special influence with those in a position to make favourable

decisions which might otherwise not be forthcoming
refers to the actions of a puppeteer in directing the action

to tighten the purse strings
to reduce outlays
refers to a drawstring closing a purse

stripes

to earn one's stripes
to deserve promotion
refers to military rank

stroke

a master stroke
particularly brilliant action

with a stroke of the pen
by edict

strong

strong medicine
a tough remedy

struck

to be thunder struck
to be amazed

to get stuck into some problem
to attempt to solve a problem with great vigour

to get stuck into someone
to castigate a person

the words stuck in my throat
I just could not get myself to say the intended words
Shakespeare, *Macbeth* II:ii, 'I had most need of blessing, and "Amen" / stuck in my throat'

stuff

to be hot stuff
to be skilful, or very passionate, or highly sexed

stuffing

to knock the stuffing out of someone
to demoralise a person completely

stumbling

stumbling block
an impediment or difficulty preventing the easy completion of some project; OR a dilemma involving a moral issue
1 Corinthians 8:9, 'But take heed lest by any means this liberty of yours become a stumbling block to them that are weak'

stumps

until stumps are drawn
until the end of the day's activities
refers to cricket

sub

sub rosa
in strict confidence
Latin *sub rosa* 'under the rose' — refers to being under the rose (as a symbol of secrecy)

subject

to be hot on a subject
to be knowledgeable and enthusiastic about a subject

success

the royal road to success
the way of attaining success without effort

to be a passport to success
to be a means of achieving success

suck

suck it and see
discover experimentally how something works

to suck someone in
to embroil an innocent party in an unethical enterprise

to teach one's grandmother how to suck eggs
to try to tell a much more experienced person something very obvious to that person

sucklings

out of the mouths of babes and sucklings
(as indiscreetly revealed) the truth
Psalms 8:2, 'Out of the mouths of babes and sucklings hast thou ordained strength … '

sudden

sudden death
instantaneously or without phasing in

sugar

to sugar the pill
to cause something to be more acceptable

suit

he wouldn't give you the shine off his suit
he is very mean

one's long suit
one's main skills
refers to playing cards

to follow suit
to do the same as others
refers to playing cards

summer

one swallow does not make a summer
much further evidence is desirable before any action taken
refers to an old English proverb, probably ultimately derived from the Greek proverb: 'One swallow does not make a spring' (recorded in Aristotle's *Nicomachoean Ethics* I:vii:16)

sun

a place in the sun
a favourable situation

everything under the sun
absolutely everything

the sun has set on something
something has concluded

to make hay while the sun shines
to utilise an opportunity before it disappears
John Betjeman (1906–84), *The Last Laugh*, 'I made hay while the sun shone'

supper

to sing for one's supper
to carry out a task in order to receive a favour in return

support

to drum-up support
actively to seek out support

sups

he must have a long spoon that sups with the devil
great care is needed when negotiating with disreputable parties
Shakespeare apparently alludes to an old proverb in *The Tempest* II:ii, 'Mercy! mercy! this is a devil … I will leave him, I have no long spoon!'

sure

sure-fire
guaranteed
refers to firearms

surface

on the surface
on the basis of a superficial first impression

to scratch the surface
to deal with only a small portion of a much larger whole

Svengali

to be a Svengali
to be a person who controls another
refers to George du Maurier's *Trilby*

swallow

one swallow does not make a summer
much further evidence is desirable before any action taken
refers to an old English proverb, probably ultimately derived from the Greek proverb: 'One swallow does not make a spring' (recorded in Aristotle's *Nicomachoean Ethics* I:vii:16)

to be a bitter pill to swallow
to be a great humiliation or disappointment that has to be endured

to be hard to swallow
not to be readily acceptable or believable
Matthew 23:23, ' … that strain at a gnat, and swallow a camel'

to swallow one's pride
to take action despite the humiliating nature of this course

to swallow the bait
to succumb to a temptation deliberately put in one's way
refers to angling

to swallow the line
to accept as truth the story being proffered
refers to angling

swallowed

someone has swallowed a dictionary
a person uses excessively long words

swamp

to swamp someone
to overload a person

swan

swan song
last appearance before retirement
refers to the ancient (but erroneous) belief that the swan sings beautifully before it dies; such a belief is referred to by

Plato, Aristotle, Shakespeare, Spenser, and Coleridge (among others)

swap

to swap horses in mid-stream
to change that upon which one is reliant during the course of a project

swarm

to swarm out
to appear in large numbers from within
refers to bees or wasps'

sweat

blood, sweat, and tears
hard work and much effort
Winston Churchill, House of Commons, 13 May 1940, 'I have nothing to offer but blood, toil, tears, and sweat'
no sweat
this presents no difficulty
to be in a cold sweat
to be afraid
to sweat it out
to await one's fate calmly

sweep

a clean sweep
a complete clearing out; OR winning all available prizes or awards
to sweep someone off that person's feet
to cause a person to lose all discernment (esp. with respect to romance)
to sweep something under the rug/carpet
to pretend that some blemish does not exist

sweet

a rose by any other name would smell as sweet
the form does not affect the substance
Shakespeare, *Romeo and Juliet* II:ii, 'What's in a name? That which we call a rose / By any other name would smell as sweet'
to be short and sweet
to be very brief and to the point
to have a sweet tooth
to be particularly fond of cakes and confectionery

sweeten

to sweeten a deal
to offer some concessions or incentives
to sweeten the pot
to provide a few additional inducements

sweetheart

a sweetheart deal
an agreement negotiated in private to the special benefit of those involved in the negotiations

swelled

a swelled head
an exaggerated idea of one's abilities or status

swim

it is a case of sink or swim
it is a case of success or failure with no other alternatives
refers to the 'testing' of so-called witches by throwing them into water to see if they would sink or swim
to be in the swim
to be a member of a group knowing what is going on
to swim against the tide
to take up a minority position

swine

to cast pearls before swine
to confer valuable benefits on someone who neither recognises nor appreciates them
Matthew 7:6, 'Neither cast ye your pearls before swine'

swing

the swing of the pendulum
the alternation of prospects, fortune, or experience
there is no room to swing a cat
this place is very small
refers to the swinging of a whip (a cat-o'-nine-tails) in the confined space of a ship's hull
to be in full swing
to be very active and going as well as possible
to swing the lead
to cheat an employer by not working while being paid to do so or by malingering; to avoid work or some other task by concocting a plausible excuse for not doing it, or by pretending to be ill

originally referred to a leadsman lazily swinging the line, rather than getting on with taking soundings

swings

what one loses on the swings one gains on the roundabouts
there are advantages and disadvantages that offset each other
Patrick Reginald Chalmers (1872–1942), *Green Days and Blue Days: Roundabouts and Swings*, 'what's lost upon the roundabouts we pulls up on the swings!'

swipe

to take a swipe at someone
to attempt to embarrass a person for something that person has done

swoop

in one fell swoop
all at the same time
Shakespeare, *Macbeth* IV:iii, 'What! all my pretty chickens and their dam, at one fell swoop?'

sword

those who live by the sword shall die by the sword
those that are rough with others must accept the likelihood of unfavourable treatment in return
Matthew 26:52, 'All they that take the sword shall perish by the sword'

to be a two-edged sword
to involve both advantages and disadvantages of similar significance
Psalms 149:6, 'Let the high praises of God be in their mouth, and a two-edged sword in their hand'

to fall on one's sword
voluntarily to sacrifice one's position as a result of a sense of responsibility for an error
refers to suicide of Roman soldiers

to have a sword of Damocles hanging over one
to be in imminent danger despite normal activity going on all around one
refers to Damocles who had the sword of Dionysius hanging, by a slender thread, over his head — as a symbol of perpetual risk in life; the story is told in Cicero, *Tusculanae Disputationes*

to hold a sword at someone's throat
to assert undue pressure on another person in an endeavour to achieve a result that would otherwise not be forthcoming

swords

to cross swords with someone
to have a disagreement with another person

syrup

soothing syrup
insincere expressions of sympathy or flattery

systems

to be all systems 'go'
to be ready to proceed as fast as possible

T

T

to a t
exactly

to dot the i's and cross the t's
to be meticulous in completing documentation

tabs

to keep tabs on something
to monitor something

table

the table groaned
the food was plentiful

to lay a proposal on the table
to make a proposal available for discussion or to adjourn discussion on a proposal for an indefinite period

to lay one's cards on the table
to be utterly frank and open or to honestly disclose one's position
refers to playing cards

to put money on the table
to back one's judgment in a tangible way or to demonstrate one's sincerity

tables

to turn the tables on someone
to cause the relative positions of oneself and another person to be reversed

refers to chess or draughts (and turning the table, or board, the other way around)

tack

to be on the wrong tack
to be using an inaccurate procedure or policy likely to lead to error
refers to sailing

to change tack
to alter one's direction
refers to sailing

tackle

to tackle someone head on
to confront a person directly

tacks

to get down to brass tacks
to discuss the aspects that really matter
perhaps refers to Cockney rhyming slang ('brass tacks' = 'facts')

tail

in two shakes of a duck's tail
in an instant

the tail end of something
the very end of something

the tail wagging the dog
a minor aspect with disproportionate effect on a major aspect

to be the sting in the tail
to be the unexpected unpleasant conclusion

to be unable to make head nor tail of something
to be unable to understand how something functions or what something means

to get off one's tail
to stir oneself from one's inertia

to grab the devil by the tail
to face up to difficulties

to have a tiger by the tail
to be involved in an activity that is much more dangerous than one had realised

to have one's tail between one's legs
to be dejected or humiliated
refers to dogs

to pin the tail on the donkey
to put the blame on a person who has with some effort been identified as responsible
refers to children's parlour game

to turn tail
to run away; OR to reverse oneself

to wait two shakes of a lamb's tail
to wait just a few moments

tailed

bright-eyed and bushy-tailed
naVve but enthusiastic

tails

heads I win, tails you lose
whichever way this matter goes I will benefit at your expense
refers to the tossing of a coin

to hang onto someone's coat-tails
to rely excessively on another's initiatives and achievements

to trail one's coat-tails
to invite a quarrel
refers to old Irish custom of trailing one's coat inviting a fight with anyone bold enough deliberately to tread on one's coat-tails

tailend

tailend Charlie
a person who habitually comes last
refers to the nickname given to the rear gunner in RAF aircraft during World War II

tailor

to tailor something
to do something in a way that has regard to the specific needs or preferences of a particular person

tailspin

tailspin
a loss of control; a state of chaos
refers to a spin by an aircraft with the tail spiralling

take

give someone an inch and that person will take an ell
make a small concession to a person and that person will abuse it by taking much more
derived from old measure of length (ell) originally based on the length of the forearm (the Old English word *eln* being cognate with the Latin *ulna*–a long bone of the forearm)

give someone an inch and that person will take a mile

make a small concession to a person and that person will abuse it by taking much more

take a long walk on a short pier
go away, I want no dealings with you

this is hard to take
it is difficult to face up to the reality of this

to be unable to take a trick
to be unable to achieve success in anything
refers to playing cards

to take a back seat
not to involve oneself actively

to take a bow
to receive recognition

to take a caning
to suffer the adverse consequences of one's acts or omissions

to take a dim view of something
not to regard something favourably

to take a giant step forward
to make a significant advance
Genesis 6:4, 'There were giants in the earth in those days'

to take a hard line
to be uncompromising

to take a leaf out of someone's book
to model oneself on another person
refers to taking a page from the 'Book of Life' — *Rev* 20: 12, 'and the books were opened … and the dead were judged out of those things that were written in the books, according to their works'

to take a nose dive
to fall steeply, suddenly and unexpectedly

to take a potshot at someone
to make an opportunistic disparaging remark about a person
refers to shooting game for food and not in accordance with the rules of the sport

to take a punt
to take a calculated risk
refers to gambling

to take a shine to someone
to be keen on a person

to take a sounding
to ascertain people's views
nautical metaphor referring to ascertaining the depth of water

to take a step backwards
to move further away from one's goal

to take a swipe at someone
to attempt to embarrass a person for something that person has done

to take a weight off someone's shoulder
to assist a person by relieving that person of some responsibility

to take by storm
to captivate an audience

to take food out of the mouths of children
cruelly to deprive the needy

to take heart from something
to be encouraged by something

to take it on the chin
to accept a misfortune cheerfully

to take no prisoners
to be utterly ruthless
military metaphor

to take off the gloves
to fight mercilessly or to debate with great ferocity
refers to bare-knuckle fighting before the introduction of the 'Marquis of Queensberry rules'

to take one's bat and ball home
as a gesture of spite to remove an essential ingredient that one has contributed to a joint enterprise, and to refuse to take any further part in its activities
refers to cricket

to take one's blinkers off
to face reality
refers to the use of leather screens on a bridle to prevent a horse seeing sideways

to take one's breath away
to surprise greatly, or astonish

to take one's hat off to someone
to be full of admiration for a person
refers to deferential gesture of removing one's hat

to take one's medicine
to submit to something unpleasant but necessary

to take over the reins
to assume control
refers to riding or driving horses

to take over the store
to assume the management

to take pot luck

to take whatever happens by chance to be available
refers to a cooking pot of food

to take short cuts
to do something by a faster but less thorough method

to take someone down a peg or two
to humble a person (especially a conceited person)
refers to scoring in backgammon or cribbage; Samuel Butler (1612–80), *Hudibras* II:ii, 'And took your grandees down a peg'

to take someone for a ride
to deceive a person

to take someone's measure
to sum up a person's character or skills

to take someone to the cleaners
to cheat a person financially

to take someone under one's wing
to protect a person
refers to birds protecting the young

to take something as gospel
to believe that something is true

to take something at face value
(of alleged facts) to accept something without question or challenge

to take something in hand
to assume control over something

to take something in one's stride
to cope with something easily
refers to a horse jumping an obstacle

to take something lying down
to accept a disadvantage without protest

to take something on board
to offer to give further consideration to a matter
nautical metaphor

to take something on the nose
meekly to accept a rebuff

to take something to heart
to learn to appreciate the significance of something; or to be much saddened by something

to take something with a grain of salt
to regard the facts in a statement with considerable scepticism

to take stock
to contemplate the alternatives

to take the bit between one's teeth
to face up to a problem
refers to riding or racing horses

to take the bull by the horns
to come to grips with the realities of a difficult problem

to take the edge off something
to weaken the force or impact of something

to take the gilt off the gingerbread
to strip something of its main attraction

to take the heat off someone
to remove pressure or harassment from someone

to take the line of least resistance
to follow the easiest course of action
refers to the route taken by the shockwaves of a buried explosive charge in reaching the surface of the earth

to take the plunge
to make an irreversible initial action; to commit oneself to a course of action
refers to leaping into water

to take the point
to understand and concede the truth of a proposition being advanced

to take the rough with the smooth
to accept the hardships of life along with its pleasant features

to take the shine off something
to spoil the performance of something

to take the shine out of something
demonstrably to surpass

to take the wind out of someone's sails
to upset a person by anticipating that person's actions or by using arguments which that person was proposing to use
refers to a tactical manoeuvre in sailing whereby one boat blocks or 'takes' the wind advantage of another

to take up the cudgels for someone
to defend a person
refers to a thick short stick used as a weapon

to take up the slack
to take advantage of surplus capacity
refers to working with ropes

takes

that takes the cake
that is quite absurd or outrageous or excessively cheeky

tale

a tell-tale sign
a visible indication revealing true facts despite efforts at concealment

an old wives' tale
a traditionally held theory without any scientific backing

tales

to tell tales out of school
to gossip mischievously and reveal secrets about others

talk

talk of the devil
here is the person we were just discussing

to have a heart-to-heart talk
to have a confidential discussion on a highly personal matter
John Henry Newman (1801–90), 'Heart speaks to heart' (*cor ad cor loquitur*), motto on coat-of-arms as cardinal

to talk nineteen to the dozen
to speak very quickly

to talk one's book
to present arguments that, although plausible, are really designed to foster one's vested interest

to talk shop
to discuss business or professional matters on a social occasion

to talk the hind leg off a donkey
to talk excessively

to talk through one's hat
to say things that demonstrate the speaker's ignorance of the subject

to talk turkey
to talk realistically
origin obscure; North American slang

tall

a tall poppy
a person with great power or responsibility and/or in receipt of high remuneration

a tall story
an interesting but untrue and unbelievable tale

tall oaks from little acorns grow
even major enterprises have to have small beginnings
David Everett (1769–1813), *Lines Written for a School Declamation*, 'Large streams from little fountains flow, / tall oaks from little acorns grow'

to be a tall order
to be an unreasonable expectation

to cut tall poppies down to size
to diminish the self-importance of haughty persons

tally

to keep a tally
to keep a record
from Latin *talea* (a rod or stick); refers to a stick with notches (made to indicate a count), the stick then being split lengthways and each party to a transaction receiving one half as a record of the transaction

tangent

to go off at a tangent
to depart from the main matter under consideration and follow instead some other matter only marginally related to it
refers to a line touching, but not intersecting, another geometrical figure

tangled

a tangled web
a series of lies, especially with inconsistencies leading to exposure
Sir Walter Scott (1771–1832), *Marmion* (1808), C. VI: vii, 'O what a tangled web we weave, when first we practise to deceive!'

tango

it takes two to tango
some activities cannot be carried out single-handedly
refers to a dance

tap

to be on tap
to be readily available on request
refers to serving beer from kegs

to turn off the tap
to deny further access to supplies or information

tape

red tape
excessively bureaucratic procedures

refers to bureaucrats and lawyers securing their briefs with red tape; the term is said to have been coined by Charles Dickens (1812–70), but popularised by Thomas Carlyle (1795–1881)

tar

to spoil the ship for a ha'p'orth of tar
to engage in a false economy
the current word 'ship' is actually a mistake for the original word 'sheep', and the tar refers to the treatment of wounds

target

a moving target
an objective subject to constant revision

target
objective
the literal target is the one aimed at with arrows, darts, bullets, etc.; figuratively it refers to intangible sales targets and the like

to zero in on a target
to move directly towards one's objective

tarnish

to tarnish one's image
to become less highly regarded
refers to brass images

tarred

to be tarred with the same brush
to be damned merely because of one's association with another person
refers to treating cuts on sheep with a tarbrush

task

to be a Herculean task
to be laborious
refers to the labours of Hercules (Heracles in Greek) who had twelve labours imposed upon him by Eurystheus — one of which was the cleaning of the stables of King Augeas in a single day

to break the back of a task
to complete the bulk of the work

taste

to be left with a nasty taste in one's mouth
to be appalled or very disappointed at another person's unethical behaviour to one

to get a taste of one's own medicine
to suffer from an initiative intended to affect only other persons

tat

tit for tat
reprisals
origin obscure; perhaps refers to Dutch *dit vor dat* ('this for that')

tatters

in tatters
utterly destroyed

taws

to get down to taws
to discuss the aspects that really matter

to start from taws
to begin from the beginning

tea

I would not do so-and-so for all the tea in China
I will never do so-and-so no matter how large the inducement

not to be someone's cup of tea
not to be to a person's liking; OR to be outside a person's expertise or area of interest

teach

one cannot teach an old dog new tricks
people become set in their ways irreversibly

to teach one's grandmother how to suck eggs
to try to tell a much more experienced person something very obvious to that person

to teach someone a lesson
to inflict something unpleasant on a person in the hope that it will lead to a change in that person's behaviour

teacup

a storm in a teacup
a controversy about a minor matter but one that looms large in the minds of the parties

team

a cricket team
eleven people

tear

to shed a quiet tear for something
privately to lament the death or loss of something

to tear one's hair out
to be frustrated and extremely agitated
refers to ancient demonstration of grief and mourning

to tear oneself away
to leave despite a great desire to stay

to tear someone apart
ruthlessly to destroy another person's case

to tear something to ribbons
to damage something severely; to castigate severely

tears

blood, sweat, and tears
hard work and much effort
Winston Churchill, House of Commons, 13 May 1940, 'I have nothing to offer but blood, toil, tears, and sweat'

to bore someone to tears
to weary a person by dull and uninteresting conversation or by lack of action

to drive someone almost to tears
to act in such a way as to cause someone significant distress

to shed crocodile tears
hypocritically to show concern or sympathy for a person in distress
refers to the reflex lacrimation of a crocodile while eating

teeth

one would give one's eye teeth for something
a person would very much like to achieve some objective
refers to the (valued) canine teeth directly under the eye

to bare one's teeth
to imply threats
refers to savage animals

to be armed to the teeth
to carry many weapons
perhaps refers to carrying a knife in the teeth

to be fed up to the back teeth
to be disgusted after prolonged provocation

to cut one's teeth on something
to get one's first experience by doing something

to escape by the skin of one's teeth
to only just avoid some disaster
Job 19:20, 'I am escaped with the skin of my teeth'

to get one's teeth into something
to tackle a task with enthusiasm

to gnash one's teeth
to express frustration
Matthew 8:12, 'There shall be weeping and gnashing of teeth'

to grit one's teeth
to get ready to suffer pain

to hang on by the skin of one's teeth
to be barely surviving *Job* 19:20, 'I am escaped with the skin of my teeth'

to have teeth
to be effective

to kick someone in the teeth
to inflict a grave or humiliating setback, criticism, or punishment upon a person

to lie through one's teeth
to tell blatant untruths

to set someone's teeth on edge
to cause a person intense irritation or discomfort
Ezekiel 18:2, 'The fathers have eaten sour grapes, and the children's teeth are set on edge'; Shakespeare, *Henry IV Pt 1* III:i, 'And that would set my teeth nothing on edge, nothing so much as mincing poetry'

to take the bit between one's teeth
to face up to a problem
refers to riding or racing horses

teething

teething trouble
problems in the early stages of a project
refers to a small child's discomfort when developing teeth

telegraph

to telegraph one's punches
by one's actions to give advance warning of one's future plans
refers to sending an advance message

telescope

to look though the wrong end of the telescope
completely to miss the point

tell

a tell-tale sign
a visible indication revealing true facts despite efforts at concealment
tell it to the marines
such nonsense is not believable
although now referring to a very unlikely tale, it originally applied to an unlikely tale that was, in fact, true — refers to King Charles II believing the unlikely (but true) tale of flying fish because the marines (the maritime regiment) testified that it was so
to tell tales out of school
to gossip mischievously and reveal secrets about others

ten

to be only ten pence in the shilling
to be slightly stupid
refers to 'old' shillings and pence when a shilling equalled twelve pence

tender

to be a tender spot
to be a sensitive subject requiring tact

tent

quietly to fold up one's tent
surreptitiously to abandon a previously cherished stance
Henry Wadsworth Longfellow (1807–82), *The Day is Done*, 'The cares that infest the day shall fold their tents, like the Arabs, and as silently steal away'

tentacles

tentacles
strong and unpleasant influence extending a long way from its base and in many directions

tenterhooks

to be on tenterhooks
anxiously to await some result
refers to cloth being stretched or 'tentered'; Latin: *tentus* ('stretched')

terrible

an enfant terrible
a person who causes embarrassment by inappropriate action, or by inappropriate speech about unpalatable issues'
French for 'terrible child'

test

a litmus test
a simple examination that reveals the true state of affairs
refers to a test with litmus paper to establish whether a solution is acid or alkaline
to be the acid test
to establish something beyond doubt
refers to test for gold with *aqua fortis* (nitric acid)
to road-test something
to try something out under real conditions
to test the water
to try out an idea in a small way

tether

to be at the end of one's tether
to be frustrated because one is at the very limit of one's resources of knowledge, authority, or patience
refers to tethering of animals with a rope

Thames

to set the Thames on fire
to do something noteworthy
similar sayings exist regarding setting fire to the Rivers Seine, Tiber, and Rhine

thank

one can thank one's lucky stars
one was extremely fortunate
refers to astrology

theme

variations on a theme
alternative approaches of a similar nature
refers to artistic themes

theory

to lay some theory to rest
to abandon some theory as being no longer appropriate
refers to death –as in 'laying out' (preparing a corpse for disposal), or as in 'laying someone to rest' (at a funeral)

there

to be neither here nor there
to be irrelevant or unimportant

thermometer

to have more degrees than a thermometer
to be too academic
a play on the word 'degree'

thick

through thick and thin

regardless of any obstacles

John Dryden (1631–1700), *Absolom and Achitophel*, 'Spurr'd boldly on, and dash'd through thick and thin'

to be in the thick of things

to get involved at the centre of some activity

to come in thick and fast

to arrive quickly and in great volume

to have a thick hide/skin

to be impervious to criticism

to penetrate someone's thick skull

to make a person understand something difficult or acknowledge something unwelcome

thimble

a pea-and-thimble trick

a clever fraud committed in the presence of its victim without this being obvious at the time

refers to a sleight-of-hand trick played with three thimbles and a pea, the thimbles being moved about and observers being asked to guess under which thimble the pea is

thin

*that **argument** is wearing a bit thin*

that case has been heard so often that it is losing its effect

refers to clothes or similar beginning to fail from continued use

through thick and thin

regardless of any obstacles

John Dryden (1631–1700), *Absolom and Achitophel*, 'Spurr'd boldly on, and dash'd through thick and thin'

to be the thin end of the wedge

to be a small action or thing that has the potential to cause much larger undesirable consequences

refers to wedges used for splitting wood

to be thin on the ground

to be scarce

to produce something out of thin air

to get hold of something in circumstances where this seemed impossible

Shakespeare, *The Tempest* IV:i, ' … are melted into air, into thin air'

to skate on thin ice

to act in disregard of obvious danger; to require tact in dealing with a sensitive subject in conversation

Ralph Waldo Emerson (1803–82), *Prudence*, 'In skating over thin ice, our safety is in our speed'

to spread oneself thin

to attempt to do more than is feasible in the available time

to tread a thin line

cautiously to take action in circumstances where either too much or too little will cause difficulties

to vanish into thin air

unexpectedly to disappear

Shakespeare, *The Tempest* IV:i, ' … are melted into air, into thin air'

things

to be in the thick of things

to get involved at the centre of some activity

think

one shudders to think what the outcome might be

there is great concern as to the outcome

to think twice before doing something

to consider with particular care

thinking

to put one's thinking cap on

to concentrate on finding a solution to a difficult problem

thinly

thinly veiled

barely concealed

third

to give someone the third degree

to apply pressure while questioning closely a person under suspicion

thirst

to thirst for blood

to be eager for revenge

Thomas

a doubting Thomas

a person who refuses to believe claims in the absence of proof

John 20:25, 'But he [Thomas] said … except I shall see in his hands the print of the nails … I will not believe'

thorn

to be a thorn in someone's flesh/side

to be a constant annoyance or affliction

2 *Corinthians* 12:7, 10: 'There was given to me a thorn in the flesh ... I will glory in my infirmities'

thorns

to wear one's crown of thorns

to have one's own difficulties

John 19:2, 'And the soldiers plaited a crown of thorns, and put it on his [Jesus'] head'

a rose between two thorns

something beautiful in the midst of ugliness

thought

a thought in the back of one's mind

an undeveloped idea

food for thought

material for examination in one's mind

Robert Southey (1774–1843), 'A lively tale, and fraught with ... food for thought'

thoughts

if you gave that person a penny for that person's thoughts you would get change

that person is extremely stupid

thousand

a sixty-four thousand dollar question

a pertinent but very difficult question

refers to a radio quiz show in which an initial $1000 prize doubled with the successful answering of progressively more difficult questions

a thousand and one

many

if I've told you once I've told you a thousand times

I express resentment at the need constantly to repeat some statement

thrash

to thrash with a feather

to impose only a minor punishment for a very serious offence

thread

the thread

the connecting link of a set of arguments

to hang by a slender thread

to be in a precarious situation

refers to Damocles who had the sword of Dionysius hanging, by a slender thread, over his head — as a symbol of perpetual risk in life; the story is told in Cicero, *Tusculanae Disputationes*

threat

to have a threat hanging over one's head

to fear some intimated unpleasant action

refers to Damocles who had the sword of Dionysius hanging, by a slender thread, over his head — as a symbol of perpetual risk in life; the story is told in Cicero, *Tusculanae Disputationes*

three

a three-card trick

an extremely simple yet effective ruse used by a dishonest person to induce victims to hand over some of their assets

yes sir, yes sir, three bags full!

(in servile response to some request) yes, very willingly!

refers to old nursery rhyme

thrilled

to be thrilled to pieces

to be greatly thrilled

throat

cut-throat

highly competitive

it sticks in my throat

I find it annoying and vexatious

Shakespeare, *Macbeth* II:ii, 'I had most need of blessing, and "Amen" / Stuck in my throat'

the words stuck in my throat

I just could not get myself to say the intended words

Shakespeare, *Macbeth* II:ii, 'I had most need of blessing, and "Amen" / Stuck in my throat'

to cut one's own throat

to act in a way that damages one's own interests

to have a frog in one's throat

to have a transient hoarseness, or a trivial throat obstruction

to have a lump in one's throat

to feel emotional

to have someone by the throat

to have a decisive advantage such that victory is assured

to hold a knife/sword at someone's throat
to exert undue pressure on another person in an endeavour to achieve a result that would otherwise not be forthcoming

to jump down someone's throat
to react angrily to the remarks of the other party to a conversation

to ram something down someone's throat
to pressure another person into accepting an idea with which that person does not agree

throats

to be at each other's throats
to be always fighting

throne

the power behind the throne
a person exercising the real authority but without having the official right to do so

William Pitt, Earl of Chatham (1708–78) ('Pitt the Elder'), 'There is something behind the throne greater than the king himself'

through

a breakthrough
major success in overcoming obstacles to knowledge or a proposal

an opening wide enough to drive a coach and four through
an excellent opportunity to demonstrate the major errors or absurdities of something

the saying seems sometimes also to have referred to six horses: Sir Stephen Rice (1673–1715), as quoted by W. King, *State of the Protestants of Ireland* (1672), 'I will drive a coach and six horses through the Act of Settlement'

through the back door
unofficially or surreptitiously

through thick and thin
regardless of any obstacles

John Dryden (1631–1700), *Absolom and Achitophel*, 'Spurr'd boldly on, and dash'd through thick and thin'

to bulldoze some proposal through
to ensure the passage of some measure in complete disregard of criticism or opposition

to come through loud and clear
to be well understood

refers to radio reception

to drive a coach and horses through something
to demonstrate the major errors or absurdities of something

Sir Stephen Rice (1673–1715), as quoted by W. King, *State of the Protestants of Ireland* (1672), 'I will drive a coach and six horses through the Act of Settlement'

to fall through
not to eventuate as expected

to filter through to someone
(of information) to reach a person eventually

to go through fire and water
to undertake all attendant risks

perhaps refers to ordeals of fire and water — ancient Anglo-Saxon ordeals of torture used to ascertain guilt or innocence

to go through something with a fine-tooth comb
to conduct an extremely thorough investigation

to go through the roof
(of a person) to be very upset; OR (of prices) to escalate greatly

to jump through hoops
to be required to perform or undergo some ordeal

refers to circus performance

to let something slip through one's fingers
to allow something to escape from one's ownership or control

to lie through one's teeth
to tell blatant untruths

to pay through the nose
to pay an excessive price

refers to an onerous tax imposed by the Danes in Ireland in the ninth century whereby those who refused to pay had their noses slit

to plot a safe course through troubled waters
to make a plan that overcomes certain difficulties

nautical metaphor

to put someone through his or her paces
to test a person

refers to testing a horse

to put someone through the mill
to make someone endure significant hardship through severe practical experience

to railroad something through
to rush people into accepting a proposal

to see something through rose-coloured glasses
to appreciate only the advantages and to disregard completely the disadvantages

to slip through the cracks
to be overlooked

to slip through the net
to happen as an isolated case despite steps taken to prevent such events

to steamroll something through
to use enormous force to achieve an objective
refers to a steamroller — a large earth-flattening machine

to talk through one's hat
to say things that demonstrate the speaker's ignorance of the subject

when the wash comes through the machine
in due course

throw

people in glass houses should not throw stones
those who are less than perfect are foolish to criticise others
John 8:7, 'He that is without sin among you, let him first cast a stone at her' (refers to ancient condemnation and punishment of people by stoning)

the final throw of the dice
one last, desperate gamble

to be the throw of a loaded die
to be an act of deceit
refers to cheating in gambling with dice

to throw a blanket over a proposal
to refuse to proceed with a proposal

to throw a cat among the pigeons
to cause consternation and upset

to throw a few stones on the roof and see who comes out
to attempt to change a boring situation or resolve a stalemate

to throw a long shadow
to have widespread ramifications

to throw a pebble against the window
gently to draw attention to oneself

to throw a spanner into the works
to cause an unexpected complication

to throw a sprat to catch a mackerel
to risk a little in the hope of gaining much

to throw brickbats at someone
to express displeasure with a person
refers to portions of brick, esp. ones used as missiles

to throw down the gauntlet
to issue a challenge
refers to the glove worn by a knight; OFr *gantelet* (diminutive of 'glove')

to throw dust into someone's eyes
to deceive a person by presenting inaccurate or misleading information
Koran: 'Neither didst thou, O Muhammad, cast dust into their eyes; but it was God who confounded them'

to throw good money after bad
to waste further money in a vain attempt to recover money already lost

to throw in one's hand
to give in or to give up
refers to playing cards

to throw in one's six pennies'/two cents' worth
modestly to supply one's own facts or views

to throw in the sponge/towel
to concede defeat
refers to boxing

to throw one's cap/hat into the air
to express joy; OR to celebrate some achievement

to throw one's hat into the ring
publicly to announce one's interest in some position
refers to custom of throwing one's hat into a ring to indicate a willingness to take part in a boxing challenge

to throw one's weight around
to assert one's real or assumed authority excessively

to throw out the baby with the bathwater
to discard a major benefit in the course of obtaining a comparatively minor advantage

to throw someone a bone
to fob a person off with a symbolic but unimportant gesture
refers to feeding a dog

to throw someone a few crumbs
to fob a person off with a few symbolic but unimportant concessions
Luke 16:21, 'a certain beggar ... desiring to be fed with the crumbs which fell from the rich man's table'

to throw someone a lifeline
to give significant assistance to a person

to throw someone in the shade
to surpass a person

to throw someone off the scent
to deceive a person by giving out misleading indications
refers to fox hunting

to throw someone to the lions
to sacrifice or condemn a person to that person's fate
refers to execution or bloodsport by throwing persons to be eaten by lions

to throw someone to the wolves
to expose a person to exploitation by more sophisticated persons

to throw something into a shambles
to make something messy and useless

to throw something out of the window
to reject completely an idea or proposal

to throw something to the dogs
to discard something as useless and worthless
Shakespeare, *Macbeth* v:iii, 'Throw physic to the dogs, I'll none of it'

to throw the ball back to someone
to return responsibility for something to another person

to throw the book at someone
to prosecute a person with all the vigour allowed by law

to throw up one's hands
to give up or quit (perhaps in frustration)

to throw in the sponge
to concede defeat
refers to boxing

within a stone's throw
very close

thud

to come down with a thud
to be suddenly disillusioned

thumb

a rule of thumb
a simple yet useful approximation
refers to the use of the thumb for making rough measurements

a thumbnail sketch
brief but pertinent details
refers to an artist assessing perspective by judging the object to be painted against a thumbnail held close to the eye

to be under someone's thumb
to be dominated by a person

to thumb one's nose at someone
to show one's contempt for someone in authority and ostentatiously to disregard that person's orders

thumbs

someone's fingers are all thumbs
a person is clumsy with his or her hands

to give a thumbs up
to approve or grant permission
refers to sign given by Roman emperor sparing a life

to twiddle one's thumbs
not to be involved in any worthwhile activity

thumper

a tub thumper
an orator who rants and raves
refers to the upturned tub once used as a platform at open-air meetings

thunder

to be thunder struck
to be amazed

to steal someone's thunder
to take credit for another person's good work
refers to a dispute over the copying of a machine invented by dramatist John Dennis (1657–1734) to reproduce the sound of thunder during a play

thunderbolt

a thunderbolt
a surprise
Shakespeare, *Julius Caesar* IV:iii, 'Be ready, gods, with all your thunderbolts; / dash him to pieces

tick

what makes someone tick
what causes a person to act as that person does
refers to the workings of a clock

ticket

just the ticket/that's the ticket
just what is needed
refers to tickets issued to the needy in nineteenth century England, to be exchanged for food, clothing, etc.

to write one's own ticket
to set one's own terms and conditions
refers to betting on a horse with a bookmaker where the chance of that horse winning is considered so unlikely that the punter is allowed to choose the odds

ticking

the clock is ticking
time is running out

tickle

to tickle the peter
to rob one's employer
refers to slang term for cash box

tickled

to be tickled pink
to be very pleased
Oliver Goldsmith (1730–74), *She Stoops to Conquer*, 'the very pink of perfection'

ticklish

ticklish
awkward; requiring delicate handling

tide

the tide has turned
conditions have changed

the tide is running in favour of some proposition
public opinion supports some proposition

to be caught by the tide
to be dealt with by something inevitable

to stem the tide
to make progress against something

to swim against the tide
to take up a minority position

to turn the tide
to reverse the direction of something

tie

to tie in with something
to be consistent with something

to tie someone's hands
to prevent a person from acting as that person sees fit

to tie someone's hands behind that person's back
to make it impossible for a person to act at all

to tie something up
to finalise the arrangements for something

to tie the knot
to marry
may refer to the knotted girdles worn by brides in ancient Greece

to tie up the loose ends
to complete the minor outstanding items of some substantially finished project

tied

to be tied down
to have responsibilities precluding alternative activities

to be tied to someone's apron strings
to be excessively influenced by one's mother

to be tied up
to be engaged

to have one hand tied behind one's back
to work with a handicap

tiger

a paper tiger
an empty threat

a toothless tiger
an authority that has been given powers totally inadequate for its task

to have a tiger by the tail
to be involved in an activity that is much more dangerous than one had realised

tight

a tight rein
strong controls
refers to riding or driving horses

a watertight contract
a contract without loopholes or escape clauses

tight-fisted
mean

to be in a tight corner

to have little or no chance of escape from a difficult situation

to be tight-lipped

to keep confidences or to be uncommunicative

to run a tight ship

to manage an efficient organisation

refers to ropes that are tight or taut

to sit tight

to do nothing; to await developments

refers to poker

tighten

to tighten one's belt

to lower one's rate of spending

to tighten the noose

to get closer to inflicting defeat

refers to death by hanging

to tighten the purse strings

to reduce outlays

refers to a drawstring closing a purse

to tighten the screw

to increase the moral and psychological pressure

tightrope

to walk a tightrope

to do something very dangerous in which one cannot afford to deviate from the required course of action

till

to have one's fingers in the till

to steal from one's employer

tilt

to tilt at windmills

to attack an imagined but non-existent enemy

refers to Cervantes' *Don Quixote* Pt I Ch VIII, in which the hero assumes that windmills are giants and gives battle

time

a stitch in time saves nine

preventive maintenance saves money in the long run

a time bomb

a source of serious problems that are certain to surface later on

it is a long time between drinks

activity is occurring only very spasmodically

that person would not give one the time of day

that person is unwilling to help anybody

time flies

time passes very quickly but, if wasted, can never be recovered

Virgil (70–19 BC) *Georgics* III:284, '*Fugit irreparabile tempus*' ('Time, which cannot be retrieved, is flying')

to be able to chew gum and walk at the same time

to be able to do two relatively simple things simultaneously

used ironically to disparage a person of limited capacities

to live on borrowed time

to live longer than expected

to mark time

to do nothing while awaiting developments

refers to marching

to work overtime at something

to spend a lot of time and effort at doing something

times

if I've told you once I've told you a thousand times

I express resentment at the need constantly to repeat some statement

tin

a little tin god

a petty tyrant

tinker

not worth a tinker's curse

worthless

from a tinker's custom of blocking up a hole with a pellet of bread before soldering, the pellet of bread being discarded as worthless after the soldering was completed

to tinker at the edges

to make minor or cosmetic changes without affecting the substance

refers to the common assumption that a tinker was an unreliable tradesman

tip

it is on the tip of my tongue

the right word has momentarily escaped me

to be the tip of the iceberg

to be only a very small portion of a much larger but less obvious whole

to tip a bucket on someone

to point out, in a humiliating way, another person's faults

to tip one's hand
to disclose details of one's position
refers to playing cards

to tip someone over the edge
to cause someone to exceed that person's limit of tolerance or endurance

to tip the balance/scales
to be further information or argument that results in an issue, that could have been decided either way, being determined in a particular way
refers to balance scales

to tip-toe around the difficulties
to act with discretion and care to conceal difficulties, or to prevent problems occurring

tips

to cling on by one's fingertips
to have only a slender hold

to have a subject at one's fingertips
to be very familiar with a subject

tired

dog-tired
tired out

tissue

only a tissue between them
virtually equal or close together

tit

tit for tat
reprisals
origin obscure; perhaps refers to Dutch *dit vor dat* ('this for that')

Titanic

to rearrange the deckchairs on the Titanic
to take an initiative that is quite useless because it does not take much greater change into account
refers to the liner *Titanic* which struck an iceberg and sank in 1912

toast

to have someone on toast
to have someone at a disadvantage, to be able to do what one wishes to a person

toe

a toehold
an opportunity small in itself but with the potential to lead to bigger things
refers to climbing trees, rockfaces, etc.

to dip one's toe in the water
gently to explore an opportunity

to tip-toe around the difficulties
to act with discretion and care to conceal difficulties, or to prevent problems occurring

to toe the line
to conform
refers to the starting line of a footrace

toes

to dig one's toes in
to become even more stubborn than at first

to keep someone on that person's toes
to induce a person to be eager and alert

to step/tread on someone's toes
to upset another person by interfering in that person's area of responsibility

together

birds of a feather flock together
persons of like interests gather in the same place
Samuel Rutherford (?1600–61), 'Fowls of a feather flock together'

to be unable to rub two pennies together
to be very poor

to knock two heads together
to make two persons come to their senses and deal with each other

to pull oneself together
by gathering one's faculties and strength, to rouse oneself to a renewed effort

to pull together
to work in harmony
refers to rowing

to put several heads together
to confer and pool ideas

to put two and two together
to reach a conclusion (usually obvious) by combining isolated pieces of information

to scratch something together
to improvise

token

by the same token

by the same argument, in a similar way

told

a little bird told me
I heard from an informant who cannot be named
Ecclesiastes 10:20, 'Even in your thought do not curse the king ... for a bird of the air will carry your voice or some winged creature tell the matter'

if I've told you once I've told you a thousand times
I express resentment at the need constantly to repeat some statement

Tom

every Tom, Dick, and Harry
virtually all ordinary people
appears to have been coined in Victorian times

tomorrow

today a rooster, tomorrow a feather duster
when circumstances change, an important person can, immediately, become unimportant

tones

overtones
subtle or implied themes

tongs

to go hammer and tongs
to do something with great energy
refers to energetic work of a blacksmith

tongue

a slip of the tongue
incorrect words uttered accidentally

I could have bitten my tongue off
I wish that I had not made such an inappropriate remark

it is on the tip of my tongue
the right word has momentarily escaped me

to bite one's tongue
to resist from criticising

to find one's tongue
to overcome one's shyness and speak

to have a loose tongue
to speak foolishly or indiscreetly

to have a sharp tongue
to speak in a cutting and abrasive fashion

to have a silver tongue
to be eloquent
Proverbs 10:20, 'The tongue of the just is as choice silver: the heart of the wicked is little worth'

to hold one's tongue
to keep quiet
John Donne (1571–1631), *The Canonization*, 'For God's sake hold your tongue, and let me love'

to keep a civil tongue in one's head
to be polite, especially under provocation

to roll off the tongue
to be said very easily

to speak with a forked tongue
to utter halftruths with the intention of misleading the listener

tongue in cheek
full of irony

tongues

to set tongues wagging
to behave in a way that encourages scandal mongers

tonic

to be a tonic
to cheer someone up

too-hard

to put something into the 'too-hard' basket
to defer consideration of a difficult issue

tools

tools
the means to do something
a metaphor in transition; used both literally and figuratively — a writer's tools, for example, include a pen (lit.) and a dictionary (fig.)

tooth

a tooth for a tooth
retaliation of equal magnitude to the original offence
Exodus 21:24, 'Eye for eye, tooth for tooth, hand for hand, foot for foot'; see also 'to turn the other cheek'

to be long in the tooth
to be old

to believe in the tooth fairy
to be particularly gullible

refers to the mythical figure who exchanges children's milk teeth for a small sum of money

to fight tooth and nail
to strive very hard to win

to go through something with a fine-tooth comb
to conduct an extremely thorough investigation

to have a sweet tooth
to be particularly fond of cakes and confectionery

toothless

a toothless tiger
an authority that has been given powers totally inadequate for its task

top

off the top of one's head
impromptu, based on experience or intuition, but without detailed consideration

the top dog
the person in the most powerful position
refers to the dominant dog in a pack

to be at the top of the tree
to be a leading member of one's profession

to be cream on top of the milk
to be an additional benefit in an already satisfactory scenario

to be icing on top of the cake
to be an additional benefit in an already satisfactory scenario

to be in top gear
to be making excellent progress
refers to mechanics

to be on top of the world
to be very happy

to be over the top
to be quite outrageous

to blow one's top
to show anger
refers to a volcano

to score top points
to achieve the outstanding score; to be considered the best

top drawer
first class

torch

to carry a torch for someone
to harbour (perhaps secret and unrequited) desires for love and marriage
refers to the torch of love

to hand on the torch
to pass on the traditions and aspirations of life
Lucretius (94?–55 BC), ' ... the generations of living creatures are changed and like the runners relay the torch of life'

torn

that's torn it
that has foiled the proposal

torpedo

to torpedo something
to make something suddenly ineffective
refers to genus of electric ray (fish), *Torpedo*, that has numbing effect on prey (Latin *torpere*, 'to be sluggish')

torrent

a torrent of words
a rapid and uninterrupted outpouring of words
refers to a fast-flowing stream of water

toss

it is a toss up
either alternative is equally acceptable
refers to the tossing of a coin

to argue the toss
to dispute a decision
refers to the tossing of a coin

to toss up
to decide on a fairly arbitrary basis
refers to the tossing of a coin

totem

to be at the bottom of the totem pole
to be in the most junior position in some hierarchy
refers to a pole with emblems or carvings having religious significance

touch

it was touch and go
there were considerable risks —- the objective was achieved, but only just
perhaps refers to the touching of the wheels of two moving vehicles

not to touch a hair on someone's head
not to harm a person

Matthew 10:30, 'the very hairs of your head are all numbered'

not to touch something with a forty-foot barge pole
to go out of one's way to avoid something

the Midas touch
attributes that cause a person's ventures to be extremely profitable
refers to King Midas of Phrygia who, in Greek mythology, had the power to turn everything he touched into gold

the touchstone
the standard
refers to a dark flinty stone used to assess samples of gold by comparing streaks left on it with those streaks left by known gold-containing standards

to lose one's touch
to cease to be familiar with, or adept at, something

to touch a nerve
to mention a sensitive subject

to touch base with someone
to make an initial contact
refers to baseball

to touch wood
to hope that our good luck will not go away
refers to ancient belief in sacred power of certain trees, especially oak, ash, hazel, hawthorn and willow

touché

touché
well said
French, 'touched'

tour

a Cook's tour
a guided tour of inspection
refers to Thomas Cook, who established the world's first travel/tourist company, and the first commercial guided tours

a whistlestop tour
a hurried (especially ceremonial) visit to many places
refers to a train journey

tour de force
feat of skill or strength
French, 'feat of strength'

towel

to throw in the towel
to concede defeat
refers to boxing

tower

a tower of Babel
a noisy and confused assembly
Genesis 11:9, 'Therefore is the name of it called Babel; because the Lord did there confound the language of all the earth' (from which the word 'babble' is also derived)

to be a tower of strength
to be a person who supports and comforts another

to be in an ivory tower
to be immersed in theoretical considerations and ignorant of the practical realities
Song of Solomon 7:4, 'Thy neck is as a tower of ivory'

town

the only game in town
the only event worthy of attention

to go to town
to do something enthusiastically, extravagantly, to the full

to paint the town red
to go on an exciting social outing

trace

to sink without a trace
to disappear completely

traces

to kick over the traces
to become insubordinate
refers to the straps designed to keep a horse restrained

track

to be down the track
to be making progress

to be off the beaten track
to do unconventional things; to be travelling along relatively unused routes

to be off the track
to be irrelevant

to be on the wrong track
to be heading towards an incorrect conclusion

to be on track
to be making the scheduled progress

to go down a particular track
to make decisions aimed at a particular goal

to have a one-track mind

to keep coming back to one narrow topic of conversation

to keep track of something
to be completely aware of where something is and how it is functioning
refers to hunting

track record
proven performance

tracks

to be stopped in one's tracks
suddenly and unexpectedly to be prevented from carrying on with a project

to cover one's tracks
to hide the evidence of one's involvement

to make tracks
to leave

trade

to make something one's trade mark
to have a distinctive characteristic or way of doing things

trading

horse trading
tough negotiations

trades

a Jack of all trades
an amateur who can do many different tasks'

trail

to blaze a trail
to be the first person to do something
refers to marking a course to be followed by making blazes on a tree

to trail one's coat-tails
to invite a quarrel
refers to old Irish custom of trailing one's coat inviting a fight with anyone bold enough deliberately to tread on one's coat-tails

train

to get on a gravy train
to take steps to become a recipient of benefits that are available but undeserved

to miss the train
to fail to exploit an opportunity

tram

to be on the wrong tram
to be completely mistaken as to the basic facts

trample

to trample someone under foot
by virtue of one's great power to treat a person's rights with contempt and not to give that person proper consideration

transfusion

to give something a blood transfusion
to give something new enthusiasm

transparent

transparent
(of behaviour, processes, etc.) to be easily discerned, to be obvious, to be evident

trap

a trap for young players
a significant likelihood of the inexperienced or naVve making mistakes

to walk into a trap
to be tricked into doing something

treacherous

to enter treacherous waters
to engage in an enterprise with risks that are not obvious
nautical metaphor

tread

fools rush in where angels fear to tread
unsophisticated persons take unwise risks in circumstances where more knowledgeable persons would exercise caution
Alexander Pope (1688–1744), *An Essay on Criticism* 1:625, 'For fools rush in where angels fear to tread'

to tread a fine/thin line
cautiously to take action in circumstances where either too much or too little will cause difficulties

to tread a particular path
to follow a certain (perhaps new or lonely) course of action

to tread lightly
to be careful

to tread on someone's corns/toes
to upset another person by interfering in that person's area of responsibility

to tread someone under foot

to oppress a person

treadmill

to be on a treadmill

to be involved in some unpleasant ongoing activity that cannot readily be stopped

treasure

a treasure trove

a valuable discovery

treat

to treat someone with kid gloves

to handle a person with great discretion

refers to very soft leather gloves made from the skin of young goats

treatment

the red-carpet treatment

courtesies extended to a person to make that person feel important and welcome

refers to the welcome accorded a visiting dignitary

tree

to bark up the wrong tree

to reach an incorrect conclusion and/or to pursue an erroneous course of action

to be at the top of the tree

to be a leading member of one's profession

to be up a gum tree

to be in difficulty; OR at the end of one's resources

to be up a tree

to be perplexed or cornered

to shake a tree

to do something to see what will result

trees

not to see the wood for the trees

to overlook the general picture because of undue concentration on the details

tremble

to tremble in one's shoes

to be afraid

trembling

in fear and trembling

in a state of apprehension

Philippians 2:12, 'Work out your own salvation with fear and trembling'

trenches

to be back in the trenches

to be made to carry out menial tasks

military metaphor

trick

a pea-and-thimble trick

a clever fraud committed in the presence of its victim without this being obvious at the time

refers to a sleight-of-hand trick played with three thimbles and a pea, the thimbles being moved about and observers being asked to guess under which thimble the pea is

a three-card trick

an extremely simple yet effective ruse used by a dishonest person to induce victims to hand over some of their assets

something has done the trick

something has achieved the desired purpose

refers to playing cards

to be unable to take a trick

to be unable to achieve success in anything

refers to playing cards

to score a hat trick

to have three successive favourable outcomes

refers to a bowler in cricket taking three wickets in three balls; such a feat being originally rewarded with the prize of a new hat

to use every trick in the book

to try very hard and use every conceivable argument

tricks

a whole bag of tricks

a series of articles or a series of artificial devices

one cannot teach an old dog new tricks

people become set in their ways irreversibly

to play monkey tricks on someone

to engage in discreditable behaviour affecting a person

trickle

a trickle

a small amount, in gradual stages

trigger

to be trigger-happy
to be impetuous
refers to firing guns

to be quick on the trigger
to respond to something very quickly with little aforethought
refers to firing guns

trigger
factor responsible for certain events occurring at that particular time

trim

to trim one's sails
to modify one's policy or opinion in accordance with changing circumstances
refers to adjusting sails to suit wind conditions

to trim the fat
to increase efficiency by reducing outlays

Trojan

a Trojan horse
a surreptitious means of gaining entrance or breaching defences
refers to a large gift horse full of Greek soldiers used to bring about the fall of Troy, as described in Homer's *Iliad*; Virgil (70–19 BC), *Aeneid* II:49, *Timeo Danaos et dona ferentis* ('I fear the Greeks even when they bring gifts')

trooper

to be a real trooper
to be a person willing to try anything

trouble

a trouble-shooter
a person good at finding and then rectifying faults

teething trouble
problems in the early stages of a project
refers to a small child's discomfort when developing teeth

to be able to spot trouble a mile away
to be able to perceive problems before they actually occur

to smell trouble
to perceive difficulties

troubled

to fish in troubled waters
to profit from a disturbed situation
refers to angling

to plot a safe course through troubled waters
to make a plan that overcomes certain difficulties
nautical metaphor

to pour oil on troubled waters
to calm down a situation

trousers

to catch someone with his trousers down
to act when another person least expects it

to wear the trousers
to be the dominant party

trove

a treasure trove
a valuable discovery

trowel

to lay it on with a trowel
to flatter, eulogise, or otherwise make comment in an excessive manner
Shakespeare, *As You Like It* I:ii, 'Well said; that was laid on with a trowel'

truck

it fell off the back of a truck
(of an item of goods) it was stolen; (of a politically sensitive document) it was leaked to me

true

to show one's true colours
to disclose one's real character or beliefs
nautical metaphor

true blue
superbly loyal
refers to the traditional blue colour of the Conservative Party in the UK

trump

to hold the trump card
to be in an unbeatable position to defeat others
refers to playing cards

to play the trump card
to make a final move, thereby defeating one's opponents
refers to playing cards

to trump someone
to defeat a person
refers to playing cards

trumps

to turn up trumps
to finish up better than expected or to experience unexpected good luck
refers to playing cards

trumpet

to blow one's own trumpet
immodestly to publicise one's own attributes
refers to the trumpet as an instrument of triumph; *Joshua* 6:20, 'When the priests blew with the trumpets ... the wall fell down flat'

trumpets

with a flourish of trumpets
triumphantly
refers to the trumpet as an instrument of triumph; *Joshua* 6:20, 'When the priests blew with the trumpets ... the wall fell down flat'

trust

a sacred trust
a moral obligation

try

something would try the patience of Job
something is very vexatious
James 5:11, 'Ye have heard of the patience of Job'

to try one's hand at something
to attempt a new activity, especially by way of experiment

to try something on for size
cheekily to do something

to try to square the circle
to attempt the impossible
refers to a classical problem in geometry, namely, to construct with a compass a square of the same area as a given circle

to try something out on the dog
to test the feasibility or safety of a dubious remedy or project

tsar

tsar
a person exercising excessive power over others

tub

a tub thumper
an orator who rants and raves
refers to the upturned tub once used as a platform at open-air meetings

tube

to go down the tube
to fail

tuck

to tuck something away in a drawer
to put something aside for the time being

Tuesday

every Pancake Tuesday
only on occasions
refers to Shrove Tuesday, when pancakes are traditionally eaten

tug

a tug of war
a dispute in which each protagonist desires a different course of action
refers to traditional fairground contest

to tug one's forelock
to pay obeisance to someone

tune

he who pays the piper calls the tune
a person contributing money or resources to a project is entitled to control it

to be in tune with someone
to think in a similar way to someone else

to change one's tune
to alter one's publicly expressed views

to fine-tune something
to adjust something in order to bring it to perfection or to make it fit the circumstances in a much more appropriate fashion

to tune in
to pay attention
refers to radio reception

tuned

to stay tuned
to keep in touch for further information as it becomes available
refers to radio reception

tunnel

to see the light at the end of the tunnel
to perceive relief at the imminent end of a period of prolonged difficulty

tunnel vision

an extremely narrow and inflexible way of considering issues

turf

to be on one's own turf
to engage in one's own customary area of activity

Turks

young Turks
members of an organisation who hold ideas regarded as too revolutionary
refers to an early twentieth-century revolutionary political party in what was to become Turkey

turkey

cold turkey
the sudden cessation of drugs to an addict and, by extension, the sudden cessation of any habitually pleasurable activity
probably refers to the appearance of the skin of drug addicts experiencing withdrawal symptoms (similarity to the skin of a plucked cold turkey)

to talk turkey
to talk realistically
origin obscure; North American slang

turn

someone would turn in his or her grave
someone would have been very surprised or displeased if he or she had known while still alive

not to turn a hair
to remain composed

to be a turn-up for the books
to be a surprising development
refers to bookmaking and gambling

to do a U-turn
to reverse one's thinking

to know which way to turn
to know which strategy to adopt or where to seek assistance

to turn a blind eye to something
to pretend that something obvious does not exist
refers to action by Horatio, Lord Nelson (1758–1805), when disregarding Admiralty signals: 'I have only one eye — I have a right to be blind sometimes — I really do not see the signal!' (at the Battle of Copenhagen, reported in Southey, *Life of Nelson*, ch. 7)

to turn a complete somersault
to reverse one's established policy

to turn an honest penny
to earn money by hard work

to turn around 180 degrees
completely to reverse a stance

to turn back the clock
to have another opportunity to do something that should have been done already; or to attempt to undo something that cannot be undone

to turn green
to become very envious
Shakespeare, *Othello* III:iii, 'O! beware, my Lord, of jealousy;/it is the green-ey'd monster ... '

to turn handstands
to express great joy

to turn off the tap
to deny further access to supplies or information

to turn one's back on someone
to decline to assist or deal with a person

to turn one's chips in
to convert one's assets or entitlements into cash

to turn one's guns on someone
to direct an attack or criticism at a person

to turn one's hand to something
to tackle some project (especially an unfamiliar project)

to turn over a new leaf
to reform
refers to turning over a page in the 'Book of Life' — *Rev* 20: 12, 'and the books were opened ... and the dead were judged out of those things that were written in the books, according to their works'

to turn round
to reverse one's policy

to turn someone on
to excite a person

to turn someone's head
to cause a person to get an exaggerated idea of that person's abilities or status

to turn something inside out
to examine something thoroughly

to turn something on its ear/head
to reverse something

to turn something upside down

to revolutionise something

to turn sour
to become unsatisfactory

to turn tail
to run away; OR to reverse oneself

to turn the corner
to commence being successful after initial failures

to turn the heat on something
to intensify the investigation of some matter

to turn the other cheek
to refuse, on moral grounds, to retaliate to provocation in like manner
Matthew 5:38, 39, 'Ye have heard that it hath been said an eye for an eye and a tooth for a tooth: but I say unto you ... whosoever shall smite thee on the right cheek, turn to him the other also'

to turn the spotlight on something
to draw public attention to something

to turn the tables on someone
to cause the relative positions of oneself and another person to be reversed
refers to chess or draughts (and turning the table, or board, the other way around)

to turn the tide
to reverse the direction of something

to turn turtle
to capsize

to turn up one's nose at something
to express one's disdain

to turn up the heat on someone
to increase the pressure on a person
Shakespeare, *Macbeth* II, i, 'Proceeding from the heat-oppressed brain'

to turn up trumps
to finish up better than expected or to experience unexpected good luck
refers to playing cards

to turn white
to express shock at unexpected news

turncoat

a turncoat
a person changing sides
refers to the practice of mercenary soldiers switching to the winning side and displaying that side's colours by turning their coats inside out

turned

as soon as someone's back was turned
at the moment it became possible to do something without a person's knowledge

the tide has turned
conditions have changed

the wheel has turned
circumstances have changed and another party is now enjoying good fortune

the wheel has turned the complete/full circle
things are now back to where they were before

the worm has turned
a previously compliant person is now asserting his or her personality

turning

the wheels have been turning
work has been going steadily on (contrast 'the wheel has turned')

turtle

to turn turtle
to capsize

twenty

with 20/20 hindsight
with the benefit of knowing what happened
refers to American system of expressing perfect visual acuity

twice

to think twice before doing something
to consider with particular care

twiddle

to twiddle one's thumbs
not to be involved in any worthwhile activity

twilight

twilight zone
state of imperfect understanding

twist

to twist someone around one's little finger
to exert easy control over a person

to twist someone's arm
to coerce another person to do something against that person's will or better judgment

two

a bird in the hand is worth two in the bush
a benefit currently available is more valuable than a seemingly much larger benefit that might or might not be achieved in the future

a two-horse race
a contest between only two serious contestants

a twopenny halfpenny outfit
a quite insignificant operation

for two pins I would do so-and-so
my tolerance is almost exhausted and I am very tempted to do so-and-so

in two shakes of a duck's tail
in an instant

it takes two to tango
some activities cannot be carried out single-handedly
refers to a dance

not to be the full two bob
not to be very intelligent
refers to slang term for two shillings

not to have the wherewithal to rub two sticks together
to be very poor

to be a two-edged sword
to involve both advantages and disadvantages of similar significance
Psalms 149:6, 'Let the high praises of God be in their mouth, and a two-edged sword in their hand'

to be in two minds
to be undecided between two alternatives

to drive a wedge between two persons
to set out to cause a division between two persons
refers to the use of wedges in timber work

to have two bob each way
to equivocate
refers to the slang term for two shillings, and to betting for a win or a place

to have two left feet
to be clumsy

to kill two birds with one stone
to achieve a second objective in the course of achieving the first objective

to knock two heads together
to make two persons come to their senses and deal with each other

to know a thing or two about something
to have acquired a lifetime of cunning about a subject

to put two and two together
to reach a conclusion (usually obvious) by combining isolated pieces of information

to take someone down a peg or two
to humble a person (especially a conceited person)
refers to scoring in backgammon or cribbage; Samuel Butler (1612–80), *Hudibras* II:ii, 'And took your grandees down a peg'

to throw in one's two cents' worth
modestly to supply one's own facts or views

to wait two shakes of a lamb's tail
to wait just a few moments

two can play at that game
it is possible to retaliate

two men and a dog
very few people

two-faced
insincere

twopenny

a twopenny-halfpenny outfit
a quite insignificant operation

tyre

to carry a spare tyre
to be fat

U

U-turn

to do a U-turn
to reverse one's thinking

ugly

an ugly duckling
an unprepossessing person or thing, the characteristics of which change in time to become attractive
refers to a cygnet in a brood of ducks in a children's story of that name by Hans Christian Andersen

to rear its ugly head
to make an unwelcome appearance

umbilical

to cut the umbilical cord
to free a person from the excessive influence of another; OR to separate a person from an essential source of supplies

umbrella

an umbrella
protection; or something all-embracing

under the umbrella of some organisation
under the auspices of some organisation

unable

to be unable to rub two pennies together
to be very poor

to be unable to take a trick
to be unable to achieve success in anything
refers to playing cards

uncharted

to be in uncharted waters
to be the first to experience something
nautical metaphor

uncle

Bob's your uncle!
that solves the problem!
refers to the many preferments given in the nineteenth century by UK Prime Minister (Robert) Lord Salisbury to his nephew A. J. Balfour (and to a number of other relatives of the prime minister)

under

a lot of water has flowed under the bridge since then
much has happened since then

everything under the sun
absolutely everything

not to let grass grow under one's feet
not to let inertia or delay spoil something

the wheels are back under the bus
normal activity has been resumed

to be hot under the collar
to be very agitated

to be six feet under
to be dead
refers to the depth of a grave

to be under someone's thumb
to be dominated by a person

to be under a cloud
to be under suspicion or to be out of favour

to be under someone's thumb
to be dominated by a person

to be under the microscope
to be the subject of close examination

to be under the weather
to be drunk or (less often) sick

to be water under the bridge
to matter no longer

to cut the ground from under someone's feet
to withdraw support unexpectedly and, in the process, to cause embarrassment; OR to demolish a person's case and cause defeat, especially by anticipating that person's arguments or plans

to get something under one's belt
to add to one's experience by achieving something worthwhile

to get under someone's skin
to cause intense annoyance to another person; OR to arouse interest in another person
may refer to the itching caused by certain parasitic creatures in or under the skin

to hide one's light under a bushel
to keep others in ignorance of one's skills and experience
Luke 11:33, 'No man, when he hath lighted a candle, putteth it in a secret place, neither under a bushel'

to hide under someone's skirts
to let someone else take the consequences of one's actions
refers to childish seeking for protection

to keep something under one's hat
to maintain a confidence

to keep something under wraps
to keep a matter confidential, especially pending an official announcement

to pull the rug out from under someone
unexpectedly to withdraw support

to put a bomb/rocket under someone
to induce a person to take some action
to put the skids under someone
to cause or hasten the ruin of someone
to sail under false colours
to pretend that one's real character or beliefs are different from what they really are
refers to a ship concealing its true identity
to slide under the bar
not to arouse suspicion
to slip under one's guard
to cause a mistake to be made despite care being taken to prevent this
refers to fencing
to snow someone under
to overload a person with work
to sweep something under the carpet/rug
to pretend that some blemish does not exist
to take someone under one's wing
to protect a person
refers to birds protecting the young
to trample someone under foot
by virtue of one's great power to treat a person's rights with contempt and not to give that person proper consideration
to tread someone under foot
to oppress a person
under one roof
under the same management; OR in the same building
under one's own power
without external help
under one's own steam
without external help
refers to a steam engine (especially in a ship)
under someone's nose
in a person's immediate area of responsibility or in circumstances where that person should have known something
under the umbrella of some organisation
under the auspices of some organisation
under the veil of something
on the pretext of something

underbelly
to have a soft underbelly
to have a weakness that can be exploited

undercurrent
an undercurrent
a barely noticeable feeling of dissent that is not being vocalised

underdog
underdog
a person or team that is likely to lose a contest and therefore likely to be the object of sympathy

undermine
to undermine someone's position
to injure another person's reputation and influence by unfair and secret tactics
to undermine something
to sabotage something

underplay
to underplay some situation
to make something seem less significant than it is
refers to playing cards

underscore
to underscore something
to emphasise something
refers to typeface in printing and publishing

unearth
to unearth something
to discover something after research

uneasy
uneasy lies the head that wears a crown
leadership involves some risks and some burdens (esp. the risk of being deposed)
Shakespeare, *Henry IV*, Part 2, III:i, 'Uneasy lies the head that wears a crown'

unholy
an unholy alliance
a working relationship for a nefarious purpose between unlikely partners

unmask
to unmask someone
to reveal a person's true identity

unscramble
to unscramble the omelette

to undo something that cannot be undone

unstuck

that person came unstuck
that person's plans did not work out

until

to go on until one is blue in the face
to do something difficult for a long time without being able to complete it

until stumps are drawn
until the end of the day's activities
refers to cricket

it's not over until the fat lady sings
it is not finished yet
probably refers to operatic performances, but during a radio broadcast made by the present author, a listener suggested that the metaphor refers to Kate Smith singing the US national anthem

unturned

to leave no stone unturned
to be very thorough
refers to an instruction from the oracle of Delphi regarding a search for Persian treasure (477 BC)

unveil

to unveil something
to give details not previously available

unwashed

the great unwashed
the general public

uphill

to be pushing uphill
to face difficulties

to fight an uphill battle
to face difficulties or to have formidable opposition
refers to military battle

to push water uphill
foolishly to attempt the impossible

upper

a stiff upper lip
obstinate courage in the face of pain or adversity

to gain the upper hand
to attain, after some effort, an advantage over another person

upset

to upset the applecart
to engage in conduct disturbing a peaceful state of affairs and thereby to cause discomfort

upside

the upside
the advantage

to turn something upside down
to revolutionise something

upstage

to upstage someone
to deprive someone of the glory that would otherwise have been enjoyed by that person
refers to the theatre

upstairs

to kick someone upstairs
to promote a person to a purely ceremonial position

use

it is no use crying over spilt milk
there is nothing to be gained by lamenting over an irredeemable error

to use every trick in the book
to try very hard and use every conceivable argument

Utopian

Utopian
ideally perfect
refers to the mythical island in Sir Thomas More's *Utopia* (Greek *ou topos*: 'no place')

V

vacuum

to fill a vacuum
to take advantage of an opportunity not acted on by others

value

to take something at face value
(of alleged facts) to accept something without question or challenge

valve

to act as a safety valve

to be a procedure that allows persons with grievances to ventilate them in an orderly fashion

vanguard

to be in the vanguard of something
to be among the first to do something
derived from French *avant-garde* ('forward guard')

vanish

to vanish into thin air
unexpectedly to disappear
Shakespeare, *The Tempest* IV:i, ' ... are melted into air, into thin air'

vapours

to have a fit of the vapours
to demonstrate exaggerated anxiety, hysteria, nervousness or similar

variations

variations on a theme
alternative approaches of a similar nature
refers to artistic themes

vegetable

to become a vegetable
to lose one's ability to respond to many external stimuli, especially those that normally contribute to the quality of life; to lead a monotonous life with no animation

veil

to draw a veil over something
pointedly to avoid discussing something

to unveil something
to give details not previously available

under the veil of something
on the pretext of something

veiled

thinly veiled
barely concealed

vein

a rich vein of gold
much useful information; a good source of something desirable

in another vein
as an alternative way of looking at things

velvet

with an iron hand in a velvet glove
with a hard attitude made to seem soft

vengeance

to attack with a vengeance
to attack strongly

to rebound with a vengeance
to return to an issue with great enthusiasm

venom

venom
virulent or malicious ill will
refers to the toxins of certain biting or stinging animals

vent

to vent one's spleen on someone
to demonstrate one's ill-temper to a person
refers to the belief that the spleen was the site of melancholy and moroseness

verse

to quote chapter and verse
to authenticate the information
refers to quoting the full details of a scriptural reference

victory

a Pyrrhic victory
a win that costs more than if there had been a loss
refers to the Battle at Asculum in 279 BC at which King Pyrrhus of Epirus defeated the Romans

view

a bird's-eye view
a general overview or summary of a subject, emphasising the major features

to take a dim view of something
not to regard something favourably

vine

to hear on the grapevine
to learn unofficially
the earlier form of the metaphor was a 'grapevine telegraph' as a means of communicating private information

to wither on the vine
by virtue of changed circumstances or the effluxion of time to be no longer relevant
John 15:5, 6, 'I am the vine, ye are the branches ... if a man abideth not in me, he is cast forth as a branch and is withered'

violet

a shrinking violet
a shy person

vision

tunnel vision
an extremely narrow and inflexible way of considering issues

visiting

a visiting fireman
an important person calling on business to whom certain courtesies need to be paid
US slang

vitriol

to pour vitriol on something
to criticise something sharply
refers to sulphuric acid or to the caustic sulphates of various elements

voice

to be a lone voice crying out in the wilderness
to be the only person stating unpopular views
John 1:23, 'I am the voice of one crying in the wilderness'

to raise one's voice for some cause
publicly to advocate some cause

volcano

to be sitting on a volcano
to be safe for the time being but exposed to the risk of a sudden great disaster

volley

to fire a volley at someone
to send a series of angry messages to someone
refers to a volley of missiles in battle; Alfred, Lord Tennyson (1809–92), *The Charge of the Light Brigade*, 'Cannon to right of them, cannon to left of them, cannon in front of them, volley'd and thunder'd'

volte

volte face
a reversal of previously held beliefs
French, 'a turning around'; the term 'volte' originally had use in both fencing and horsemanship

volumes

to speak volumes for something
to be highly expressive; to exemplify extremely well

vote

to vote with one's feet
to express one's attitude by one's physical movement towards or away from something

vulture

vulture
person benefiting from another's misfortune

W

wagging

the tail wagging the dog
a minor aspect with disproportionate effect on a major aspect

to set tongues wagging
to behave in a way that encourages scandal mongers

wagon

to be on the water wagon
to be teetotal

wait

to wait for the other shoe to drop
to await the seemingly imminent and inevitable
refers to a person being disturbed by a neighbour who drops one shoe on the floor, the listener then being frustrated when the sound of the other shoe being dropped is not heard

to wait hand and foot on someone
to serve a person's every real or imagined whim

to wait in the wings
to be prepared to stay unobtrusive till the appropriate time for action arrives
refers to the theatre

to wait two shakes of a lamb's tail
to wait just a few moments

to wait with bated breath
to be excited in anticipation of some event

wake

in the wake of someone
following a person's example
nautical metaphor

to make noise enough to wake the dead
to be excessively noisy

to wake up to something
to realise a fact or its significance

walk

one needs to crawl before one can walk
skills are best developed in logical stages

take a long walk on a short pier
go away, I want no dealings with you

to be able to chew gum and walk at the same time
to be able to do two relatively simple things simultaneously
used ironically to disparage a person of limited capacities

to walk a tightrope
to do something very dangerous in which one cannot afford to deviate from the required course of action

to walk all over someone
to act in a way that completely disregards another person's sensibility

to walk away from something
to abrogate one's responsibilities in regard to some matter

to walk away with a profit
to achieve a profit on concluding a project

to walk in off the street
to come without prior arrangement or notification

to walk into a trap
to be tricked into doing something

to walk on air
to be joyful

to walk the plank
to face certain doom
refers to execution of persons at sea

walkover

a walkover
an easy victory
refers to the winner walking over the finishing line for an unchallenged victory

wall

a chink in the wall
an opportunity to do something that otherwise could not be done

I would love to be a fly on the wall
I would love to observe what goes on without those under observation being aware of my presence

to bang one's head against a brick wall
to fight an unwinnable case

to be a crack in the wall
to represent a small opportunity that can be exploited

to be up against a brick wall
to be unable to achieve anything because of intractable opposition or apathy

to drive someone to the wall
to ruin a person

to drive someone up the wall
by one's actions, to cause extreme annoyance to the point of desperation

to go to the wall
to become bankrupt

to have one's back to the wall
to be hard-pressed by creditors or opponents

to nail someone to the wall
to outmanoeuvre and trap someone

to put a wall around someone
to stop a person associating with others

to see the writing on the wall
to appreciate the inevitability of some event
Daniel 5:5ff, 'A man's hand ... wrote ... upon the plaister of the wall of the king's palace ... thou art weighed in the balances and art found wanting'

walls

Chinese walls
a system to ensure that different parts of some organisation do not gain access to each other's confidential information

walls have ears
someone may be overhearing
words on wartime posters, reminding people of the existence of spies; might also refer to certain rooms in the Louvre, constructed so that conversations could be heard in other rooms

walls of Jericho
something seemingly solid but actually destructible

Joshua 6:20, 'When the priests blew with the trumpets ... the wall fell down flat'

wand

to wave a magic wand
to direct affairs without the restraints of the real world

want

to want someone's hide
to be keen to penalise a person

to want something both ways
to desire two mutually exclusive objectives

to want the best of both worlds
unreasonably to desire to get some advantage without incurring a corresponding disadvantage

to want the organ-grinder, not the monkey
to wish to deal with the person in authority rather than an underling
refers to a street musician using a barrel-organ, often accompanied by a pet monkey

to want to have one's cake and eat it too
to want two mutually exclusive alternatives

to want to jump all one's fences at once
unrealistically to want to solve all problems at once, rather than sequentially
refers to steeplechasing on horseback

war

a tug of war
a dispute in which each protagonist desires a different course of action
refers to traditional fairground contest

the cold war
the unfriendly relations between the communist nations and the rest of the world
phrase first used by Bernard M. Baruch (1870–1965) in a speech before the South Carolina legislature, although Baruch said that the phrase was suggested to him by H. B. Swope, former editor of the New York *World*; Baruch, 16 April 1947, 'Let us not be deceived — we are today in the midst of a cold war'

to be on the war path
to be on the lookout for faults that can be criticised

to build up a war chest
to accumulate cash in readiness for some move

warfare

paper warfare
an excessive amount of correspondence or excessive bureaucracy

warhorse

a warhorse
an experienced and dependable campaigner in war, politics, sport, and other contests

warm

a warm inner glow
satisfaction at some achievement
Joseph Conrad (1857–1924), *Youth*, 'the heat of life ... that glow in the heart that with every year grows dim, grows cold'

to keep someone's seat warm
to hold a position temporarily with a view to another person's taking it over permanently in the near future

to warm the cockles of someone's heart
to delight a person
refers to the cockle shell which looks like a heart; the formal name for bivalve molluscs (such as cockles) is *cardium* (Latin for 'heart')

to warm up
to get ready

warm-hearted
affectionate or generous

warning

to be a warning bell
to be a warning

warrant

to sign one's own death warrant
foolishly to do something that is inevitably bound to lead to utter disaster

warren

a rabbit warren
a building with a maze of rooms and passages

warts

warts and all
with the unfavourable features as well as the favourable ones

Oliver Cromwell's reported direction to the artist, Sir Peter Lely, painting his portrait

wash

backwash
consequence

hogwash
nonsense
refers to 'hog wash' — meaning kitchen swill for pigs (and therefore worthless)

in the wash-up
when everything is finalised

it will all come out in the wash
the facts will emerge as work proceeds

it won't wash
this explanation is not acceptable

the great unwashed
the general public

to be awash with something
to have plenty of something

to be chief cook and bottlewasher
to perform a range of duties single-handedly — ranging from important to menial

to be eye wash
to be nonsense

to brainwash someone
systematically and forcibly to instil certain attitudes in place of previous ideas in the mind of a person

to wash one's dirty linen in public
to expose one's embarrassing domestic affairs to the world at large'

to wash one's hands of something
emphatically to decline future responsibility
Matthew 27:24, 'He [Pilate] took water and washed his hands in full view of the crowd. "My hands are clean of this man's blood," he declared'

to whitewash
to attempt to conceal the guilt or mistakes of a person
refers to the use of whitewash on a wall to conceal blemishes

when the wash comes through the machine
in due course

washed

the great unwashed
the general public

to be all washed out
to feel feeble

washes

that washes with me
I agree

waste

to waste one's breath
to talk and request something without achieving anything

watch

a watchdog
a person or organisation monitoring behaviour

to need to watch one's back
to find it necessary to take care in case others act against one's interests

to watch one's P's and Q's
to be very careful
perhaps refers to pints and quarts of beer on a hotel slate, or perhaps to easily confused printer's type

to watch one's step
to be on the lookout for danger; OR to set out to improve one's behaviour

watch the doughnut — not the hole
look for the positive aspects

water

a backwater
a place of little activity

a lot of water has flowed under the bridge since then
much has happened since then

an argument holding water
a debating point of substance

come hell or high water
regardless of the difficulties or obstacles

high-water mark
the best or highest level achieved by an enterprise

one can lead a horse to water, but one can't make it drink
one can give advice to a person but cannot ensure that it will be acted on

there is blood in the water
something is likely to cause a person to go into a frenzy

to be a fish out of water
to be in difficulty by virtue of being in a strange environment

to be above water

(of securities) to have a market value in excess of the cost price

to be in deep/hot water
to be in great difficulty

to be in smooth water
to have no troubles
nautical metaphor

to be like water off a duck's back
(of advice or criticism) to be completely ignored

to be on the water wagon
to be teetotal

to be water under the bridge
to matter no longer

to blow/shoot something out of the water
to destroy something

to brave the water
to enter a venture with courage and determination

to dip one's toe in the water
gently to explore an opportunity

to go through fire and water
to undertake all attendant risks
perhaps refers to ordeals of fire and water — ancient Anglo-Saxon ordeals of torture used to ascertain guilt or innocence

to go to water
to succumb to pressure

to hold water
(of an argument) to be soundly based

to hold one's head just above water
to cope with problems but with little margin to spare or to stay solvent

to make one's mouth water
to excite desire
refers to salivation

to pour cold water on some idea
to be unenthusiastic about some proposal or scornful of its apparent weaknesses

to shoot/blow something out of the water
to destroy something

to test the water
to try out an idea in a small way

to water down something
to reduce the severe impact of something

water will find its own level
people will reach an appropriate position relative to others

watering

watering hole
hotel

Waterloo

to meet one's Waterloo
to receive a decisive defeat
refers to Napoleon's fate at the Battle of Waterloo (1815)

waters

still waters run deep
a person with a quiet manner might have many unrecognised characteristics — both good and bad
W. H. Auden (1907–73), *Twelve Songs VIII*, 'Still waters run deep, my dear, there's never smoke without fire'

to be in uncharted waters
to be the first to experience something
nautical metaphor

to cast one's bread upon the waters
to give generously because one will eventually be rewarded for one's generosity
Ecclesiastes 11:1, 'Cast thy bread upon the waters: for thou shalt find it after many days'

to enter treacherous waters
to engage in an enterprise with risks that are not obvious
nautical metaphor

to fish in troubled waters
to profit from a disturbed situation
refers to angling

to muddy the waters
deliberately to confuse an issue by creating a diversion

to plot a safe course through troubled waters
to make a plan that overcomes certain difficulties
nautical metaphor

to pour oil on troubled waters
to calm down a situation

watershed

a watershed
an occasion dividing two distinct phases of activity

refers to the geographical division between the headwaters of adjacent river systems

watertight

a watertight contract
a contract without loopholes or escape clauses

wave

a brainwave
a suddenly occurring bright idea

to be on the crest of a wave
to enjoy success that might not last

to ride the wave
to be successful for the time being
refers to surfing

to wave a finger at someone
to indicate mild displeasure at another person's actions

to wave a flag for someone
to promote a person's cause

to wave a magic wand
to direct affairs without the restraints of the real world

wavelength

to be on the same wavelength
to think on similar lines
refers to radio reception

to be on the wrong wavelength
to be incorrect in one's thinking
refers to radio reception

waves

to cause waves
to disturb the status quo

way

a halfway house
an intermediate position
refers to an inn situated situated halfway between two towns on a journey

a one-way street
a flow of activity in only one direction

no way!
definitely not!

that is the way the chips fall
that is the way that the benefits and detriments are distributed after an event

there is more than one way to skin a cat
this can be achieved in a variety of ways

to be a shorthand way of saying something
to be a way of saying something in summarised form
refers to a form of taking summarising notes

to go the way of all flesh
to die
Joshua 23:14, 'And, behold, this day I am going the way of all flesh'

to have fifty cents each way
to equivocate
refers to betting for a win or a place to have two bob each way
to equivocate
refers to the slang term for two shillings, and to betting for a win or a place to know which way to turn
to know which strategy to adopt or where to seek assistance

to laugh all the way to the bank
to appreciate one's good fortune

to make headway
to make progress

to pave the way
to prepare for something

to resist something every inch of the way
to resist something utterly

to rub someone up the wrong way
to annoy a person with actions that fail to recognise that person's current mood

to see which way the cat jumps
to await developments

to see which way the wind is blowing
to establish the factors relevant to a situation
John Seldon (1584–1654), 'Take a straw and throw it up into the air, you shall see by that which way the wind is'

to stand in someone's way
to prevent a person achieving that person's goal

to worm one's way in
subtly to insinuate oneself into a person's trust

what a way to run a railway!
the way things are done is disgraceful
refers to a cartoon

ways

to cut both ways
to involve both advantages and disadvantages of similar significance

to want something both ways
to desire two mutually exclusive objectives

wayside

to fall by the wayside
to be abandoned and to therefore drop out; to fail to stay the course
Matthew 13:4, 'And when he sowed, some seeds fell by the wayside, and the fowls came and gobbled them up'

weak

the spirit is willing but the flesh is weak
the body is not up to the demands made on it–physically or morally
Matthew 26:41: 'Watch and pray, that ye enter not into temptation: the spirit indeed is willing but the flesh is weak

weak-kneed
unassertive or irresolute

weakest

the weakest link in the chain
the least efficient component in a project the overall efficiency of which is governed by the efficiency of the least efficient component

wealth

a wealth of something
a great quantity of something

wean

to wean someone off something
to induce a person to abandon some entrenched practice

weapons

to use all the weapons at one's disposal
to utilise all available advantages

wear

if the cap fits then wear it
if that description corresponds with your characteristics, then you are in that category

if the shoe fits then wear it
if a general proposition describes your specific circumstances, then consider that it applies to you

to have to wear something
to have to put up with something

to wear a hair shirt
to practise self-discipline
refers to a shirt worn next to the skin by ascetics and penitent persons

to wear one's crown of thorns
to have one's own difficulties
John 19:2, 'And the soldiers plaited a crown of thorns, and put it on his [Jesus'] head'

to wear one's heart on one's sleeve
to lack the reserve expected of one
refers to the fashion of wearing a sign of romantic attachment on one's sleeve; Shakespeare *Othello* I:i, 'But I will wear my heart upon my sleeve'

to wear sackcloth and ashes
humbly to demonstrate repentance
Esther 4:3, 'There was great mourning ... and many lay in sackcloth and ashes'

to wear the pants/trousers
to be the dominant party

wearing

that argument is wearing a bit thin
that case has been heard so often that it is losing its effect
refers to clothes or similar beginning to fail from continued use

wears

uneasy lies the head that wears a crown
leadership involves some risks and some burdens (esp. the risk of being deposed)
Shakespeare, *Henry IV*, Part 2, III:i, 'Uneasy lies the head that wears a crown'

weather

a fair-weather friend
a person purporting to be a friend who offers no support in difficult times

to be under the weather
to be drunk or (less often) sick

to keep a weather eye out for something
to look out with particular care
nautical metaphor; refers to the eye that is turned towards the wind

to make heavy weather of something
to struggle excessively with a relatively simple task
nautical metaphor

to run into heavy weather
to encounter difficulties
nautical metaphor

to weather the storm
to come safely through a crisis
nautical metaphor

web

a tangled web
a series of lies, especially with inconsistencies leading to exposure
Sir Walter Scott (1771–1832), *Marmion* (1808), C. VI: vii, 'O what a tangled web we weave, when first we practise to deceive!'

to be the centre of the spider's web
to control an operation that involves numerous and/or complex ingredients

wed

to be wed to something
to be utterly dedicated to a proposal

wedding

a shotgun wedding
a wedding held to ensure that an impending birth will be legitimate
refers to threats by the bride's father to kill the bridegroom

wedding
amalgamation

wedge

to be the thin end of the wedge
to be a small action or thing that has the potential to cause much larger undesirable consequences
refers to wedges used for splitting wood

to drive a wedge between two persons
to set out to cause a division between two persons
refers to the use of wedges in timber work

weed

to weed some group out
to get rid of some elements not meeting a desired standard

weigh

to weigh anchor
to move to another address
nautical metaphor

to weigh in with a particular argument
to produce a strong argument

to weigh in with something
to bring something along
refers to jockeys (and equipment) being weighed after a horse race

to weigh two alternative propositions in the balance
to assess the relative significance of two alternative propositions
Daniel 5:27, 'Thou art weighed in the balances and art found wanting'

weight

a heavyweight
a person of importance or influence
refers originally to boxing

lightweight
uninfluential
refers to boxing

that has taken a weight off my mind
I am relieved

to be worth one's weight in gold
to be very valuable or useful

to carry weight
to be influential

to lend weight to something
to use one's influence in support of some cause

to pull one's weight
to do one's proper share of the work requiring to be done
refers to rowing

to take a weight off someone's shoulder
to assist a person by relieving that person of some responsibility

to throw one's weight around
to assert one's real or assumed authority excessively

well

one might as well be hanged for a sheep as for a lamb
further action will not increase the adverse consequences already in train
refers to the stealing of either sheep or lambs being capital crimes under old English law

the choice is between eating well or sleeping well

one can invest for maximum yield or maximum security, but not both

to be a well-oiled piece of machinery

to be functioning very satisfactorily

to go back to the well

to go to the original source

Genesis 24:20, 'And [Rebekah] ran again unto the well to draw water'

well-heeled

rich

west

to sink slowly in the west

to fail gradually

refers to the setting of the sun in the western sky

wet

to be a wet blanket

to be a spoil sport

to be wet behind the ears

to be excessively naVve and inexperienced

to get one's feet wet

to do the necessary initial parts of a task, despite their being unpleasant and menial

refers to nautical tasks

wether

bell-wether

first indication

refers to the leading sheep (wether) of a flock, this sheep having a bell hung around its neck

wheat

to separate the wheat from the chaff

to separate the worthy from the unworthy

Matthew 3:12, 'His winnowing fork is in his hand, and he will clear his threshing floor and gather his wheat into the granary, but the chaff he will burn with unquenchable fire'

wheel

a big wheel

an important person

fortune's wheel

the vicissitudes of life

refers to the traditional representation of the goddess Fortuna with a wheel in her hand, symbolising her fickleness

the squeaky wheel gets the oil

those complaining the most loudly will get their problems sorted out first

the wheel has turned

circumstances have changed and another party is now enjoying good fortune

the wheel has turned the complete/full circle

things are now back to where they were before

to be a fifth wheel

to be superfluous

to be a small cog in a large wheel

to be a relatively unimportant person in a large organisation

to put a spoke in someone's wheel

to interfere with another person's activity, so preventing its continuance

to put one's shoulder to the wheel

to make a strong effort

to reinvent the wheel

to waste resources doing something already accomplished

to wheel and deal

energetically to enter into commercial transactions of dubious propriety

refers to US slang: 'wheel' = important person or operator

to wheel someone in

to bring a person of interest into discussions, plans, etc.

wheels

the wheels are back under the bus

normal activity has been resumed

the wheels fell off

the plan failed

the wheels have been turning

work has been going steadily on (contrast 'the wheel has turned')

the wheels of justice grind slowly

it takes a long time to get a decision from the courts of law

Friedrich von Logau (1604–55), *Sinngedichte* (translated by H. W. Longfellow), 'Though the mills of God grind slowly, yet they grind exceeding small; though with patience he stands waiting, with exactness grinds he all'

to make the wheels go round

to cause something to happen

to oil the wheels

to make things go smoothly

to set the wheels in motion

to institute appropriate action

wheels within wheels

secret machinations

whet

to whet one's appetite

to arouse one's curiosity, interest, or desire

whip

to be a fair crack of the whip

to be just; to provide a fair opportunity

to crack the whip

to assert one's authority

refers to the use of a whip in riding or driving animals

to have the whip hand

to be in control of a situation

refers to the hand holding the whip in controlling horses, and perhaps slaves

to whip oneself into a lather

to become unduly excited

refers to horses sweating profusely when excited

whipping

a whipping boy

a person made to suffer for the faults of others

refers to a boy kept for whipping when a king or prince deserved punishment

whirlwind

to reap the whirlwind

to suffer the adverse consequences of a bad act

Hosea 8:7, 'They have sown the wind, and they shall reap the whirlwind'

to sow the wind and reap the whirlwind

to make bad mistakes and to suffer the even worse consequences

Hosea 8:7, 'They have sown the wind, and they shall reap the whirlwind'

whisker

by a whisker

only just

whisper

to hear a whisper

to learn of a rumoured fact

Shakespeare, *Macbeth*, V:i, 'Foul whisperings are abroad'; William Congreve (1670–1729), *Love for Love*, 'I know that's a secret, for it's whispered everywhere'

whistle

a whistlestop tour

a hurried (especially ceremonial) visit to many places

refers to a train journey

to blow the whistle on someone

to report a person's improper behaviour to the authorities or to publicise it

to whistle in the dark

to feign greater confidence than one really has

John Dryden (1631–1700), *Amphitryon* II:i, 'Whistling to keep myself from being afraid'

you can whistle for it

you wish in vain

refers to the superstition among sailors on a becalmed ship that a wind could be summoned up by whistling

whistles

bells and whistles

imaginative variations, or with ostentatious embellishments

white

a white elephant

an expensive and useless luxury

refers to gifts of sacred elephants by the King of Siam to persons then ruined by the expense of their upkeep

a white knight

a person voluntarily coming to the assistance of another person at considerable personal cost

derived from mediaeval tales of valiant knights rescuing those in distress, white being associated with purity and goodness

a white lie

a false statement uttered in a good cause

in black and white

in writing, spelling out all the details

Ben Jonson (1573–1637), *Every Man in hisHonour*, 'I have it here in black and white'

lily-white

honest and incorruptible

based on a belief that the lily sprang from the tears of Eve as she left the Garden of Eden; the lily is traditionally a symbol of purity and innocence in Christian art

to be a black-and-white issue

to involve very clear distinctions

Ben Jonson (1573–1637), *Every Man in his Honour*, 'I have it here in black and white'

to show the white feather
to indicate cowardice
refers to cross-bred birds, not regarded as useful in cock fighting

to turn white
to express shock at unexpected news

to white-ant someone
surreptitiously to seek to destroy a person
refers to the damage done to timber structures by white ants

whitewash

to whitewash
to attempt to conceal the guilt or mistakes of a person
refers to the use of whitewash on a wall to conceal blemishes

whoa

from go to whoa
from start to finish
refers to the commands given to horses

whole

a whole bag of tricks
a series of articles or a series of artificial devices

the whole box and dice
all relevant components

the whole gamut
the whole range of some activity
refers to the whole range of notes in music

the whole shooting match
the whole lot

to change the whole picture
to alter the major assumptions on which some assessment was based

to go the whole hog
to do something very thoroughly
origin uncertain; alternative explanations include: (i) Muslim divines attempting to ascertain how much of the whole hog could be eaten according to Islamic law (Cowper, 1779, 'but for one piece they thought it hard / from the whole hog to be debarred'); (ii) colloquial term for a shilling — that is, to spend the whole hog (or shilling) at one time; (iii) refers to the close shearing of lambs

wicket

to be on a sticky wicket
to face some difficulties
refers to cricket

wide

an opening wide enough to drive a coach and four through
an excellent opportunity to demonstrate the major errors or absurdities of something
the saying seems sometimes also to have referred to six horses: Sir Stephen Rice (1673–1715), as quoted by W. King, *State of the Protestants of Ireland* (1672), 'I will drive a coach and six horses through the Act of Settlement'

to be wide of the mark
to have a belief that is far removed from the true position
refers to archery

to give someone a wide berth
to go out of one's way to avoid contact with a person
nautical metaphor

to leave oneself wide open
to act in such a way that one's opponents will find much that can be easily criticised
refers to a bodily posture that is vulnerable to attack

with one's eyes wide open
fully conscious of the ramifications

wield

to wield a big stick
to assert power

to wield the knife
to terminate the services of one or more persons or to prune expenditure

wigwam

to make a wigwam for a goose's bridle
to do something unspecified
nonsense said to children

wild

a wild card
(in general) an unexpected unpredictable development; OR (in playing cards) a card of a value specified by the player holding it; OR (in sport) a player or a team given entrance to a competition by the organisers, even if the entry is not strictly merited; OR (in computing) a character that will

match any other character in a search string

a wild-goose chase
a futile chase or search
refers to old game of 'follow-the-leader' on horses in which the objective was to follow a winding and difficult course without ever catching up

to sow wild oats
to indulge in foolish behaviour while a young adult

wild cat
(of a strike) unofficial; OR (of an oil well) drilled as a pure prospect; OR (of a financial scheme) very hazardous

wild horses would not cause me to do something
I refuse absolutely to do something
refers to a form of torture in which persons were dragged behind horses

wild horses would not drag that out of me
I refuse absolutely to reveal that
refers to a form of torture in which persons were dragged behind horses

wilderness

to be a lone voice crying out in the wilderness
to be the only person stating unpopular views
John 1:23, 'I am the voice of one crying in the wilderness'

to be in the wilderness
to be out of office against one's will
Numbers 14:33, 'And your children shall wander in the wilderness forty years'

wildest

to be successful beyond one's wildest dreams
to be far more successful than one could have expected

willing

a willing horse
a cheerful worker

the spirit is willing but the flesh is weak
the body is not up to the demands made on it–physically or morally
Matthew 26:41: 'Watch and pray, that ye enter not into temptation: the spirit indeed is willing but the flesh is weak

willing bride
(commerce) keen partner

win

heads I win, tails you lose
whichever way this matter goes I will benefit at your expense
refers to the tossing of a coin

not to be here to win prizes
to be altruistic

to win by a long chalk
to win very conclusively
refers to scoring in a contest by making chalk marks on a score board

to win hands down
to win very convincingly
refers to a jockey riding confidently with hands low when a race is as good as won

to win one's spurs
to gain recognition after a period of effort
refers to the earning of a knighthood in battle

to win some rounds
to be partly successful
refers to boxing

to win the booby prize
to do worse than all others

to win the prize in a canter
to win very easily
refers to horse racing

wind

it is an ill wind that blows no good
even a seeming misfortune leads to some blessings

something is in the wind
something is going on secretly

straws in the wind
small but significant indicators of future events
John Seldon (1584–1654), 'Take a straw and throw it up into the air, you shall see by that which way the wind is'

the cold wind of change
the unpleasant realities of new circumstances

to get wind of something
to hear rumours giving advance information
refers to an animal sniffing the wind for the scent of another animal

to put the wind up someone
to alarm a person

to reap the whirlwind

to suffer the adverse consequences of a bad act

Hosea 8:7, 'They have sown the wind, and they shall reap the whirlwind'

to sail against the wind

to oppose the views currently being held by others

to sail close to the wind

to take a considered risk; to test the limits of what is possible or acceptable

refers to sailing in a manner such that sails remain filled while keeping the boat headed as near as possible into the wind

to see which way the wind is blowing

to establish the factors relevant to a situation

John Seldon (1584–1654), 'Take a straw and throw it up into the air, you shall see by that which way the wind is'

to sow the wind and reap the whirlwind

to make bad mistakes and to suffer the even worse consequences

Hosea 8:7, 'They have sown the wind, and they shall reap the whirlwind'

to take the wind out of someone's sails

to upset a person by anticipating that person's actions or by using arguments which that person was proposing to use

refers to a tactical manoeuvre in sailing whereby one boat blocks or 'takes' the wind advantage of another

winds

to cast prudence to the winds

to cease being careful or wise

to scatter something to the four winds

permanently to get rid of something

refers to the north, south, east, and west winds

windfall

windfall

unexpected good fortune

refers to fruit falling from a tree without having to be picked

windmills

to tilt at windmills

to attack an imagined but non-existent enemy

refers to Cervantes' *Don Quixote* Pt I Ch VIII, in which the hero assumes that windmills are giants and gives battle

window

a window of opportunity

an opportunity temporarily available

to engage in window dressing

to present someone or something in a falsely favourable light

refers to displays in shop windows

to fly out the window

to become irretrievably and wastefully lost

to throw a pebble against the window

gently to draw attention to oneself

to throw something out of the window

to reject completely an idea or proposal

wing

on a wing and a prayer

reliance on the merest chance in a desperate situation'

also applied to an emergency landing by an aircraft; originally a song (1943) by H. Adamson

to take someone under one's wing

to protect a person

refers to birds protecting the young

wings

to clip someone's wings

to reduce another person's freedom to act as that person thinks fit

refers to clipping the wings of birds, especially poultry

to spread one's wings

to test or develop one's abilities, to lead a life of greater scope than previously

to wait in the wings

to be prepared to stay unobtrusive till the appropriate time for action arrives

wink

a nod and a wink

a sign that understanding has been reached in a matter that, in the interests of discretion, has not been discussed aloud

Captain Marryat (1792–1848), *Peter Simple*, 'But you're a dutiful son, so I'll say no more about it — a nod's as good as a wink to a blind horse'

a nod is the same as a wink to a blind horse
fine distinctions are not appropriate here
Captain Marryat (1792–1848), *Peter Simple*, 'But you're a dutiful son, so I'll say no more about it — a nod's as good as a wink to a blind horse'

not to get a wink of sleep
not to sleep at all

Winkle

to be a Rip Van Winkle
to be a person out of touch with current conditions
refers to the character of a story told by Washington Irving (1783–1859) in his book *Sketch Book* (1819); the character slept for about twenty years and awoke to find himself in a changed world

winner

a bread-winner
a person earning by personal exertion the income of a household
Deuteronomy 8:3, 'Man doth not live by bread alone, but by every word that proceedeth out of the mouth of the Lord' (see also *Matthew* 5:4)

to be on a winner
to have faith in, give support to and/or invest in a project which proves to be successful
refers to betting on racing

winning

to hold a winning hand
to be in an unbeatable position to defeat others
refers to playing cards

winter

to buy straw hats in winter
to buy in a depressed market when most other people are sellers

wipe

to wipe the floor with someone
to inflict a humiliating defeat on a person

to wipe the slate clean
to forgive past indiscretions

to wipe the smile off someone's face
to destroy a person's complacency

wipe that smile off your face!
treat this matter more seriously!

wire

to be a live wire
to be an enthusiast
refers to electrical wires

to go haywire
to function in a disordered and strange fashion
refers to difficulty in handling coils of hay-binding wire

wires

to have one's wires crossed
to be mistaken about key facts
refers to a short-circuit in electrical wiring

wisdom

to need the wisdom of Solomon
to require great sagacity when faced with a difficult decision
refers to King Solomon's ingenious solution to an apparently insoluble dilemma as described in *1 Kings* 3:16–28

wish

a death wish
the contemplation or commission of action so foolish that it is likely to lead to utter disaster

witch

a witchhunt
an exercise seeking to find someone who can be blamed
refers to ancient practice of seeking out those who supposedly practised witchcraft

with

to be with it
to be fully informed and conversant with something, especially with modern trends, and to be part of such a movement

wither

to wither on the vine
by virtue of changed circumstances or the effluxion of time to be no longer relevant
John 15:5, 6, 'I am the vine, ye are the branches ... if a man abideth not in me, he is cast forth as a branch and is withered'

wives

an old wives' tale

a traditionally held theory without any scientific backing

wolf

a lone wolf

a person who prefers to act without involving others

to be a wolf in sheep's clothing

to be a hypocrite; to be dangerous although masquerading as something harmless

Matthew 7:15, 'Beware of false prophets, which come to you in sheep's clothing, but inwardly they are ravening wolves'

to cry 'wolf'

repeatedly to raise an unjustified concern with the result that one will be ignored when the circumstances change and a real threat emerges

refers to a story of a boy who cried 'wolf' (from *Aesop's Fables*)

to keep the wolf from the door

to struggle to survive (esp. with respect to hunger)

wolves

to throw someone to the wolves

to expose a person to exploitation by more sophisticated persons

wonder

a nine-day wonder

an exciting event, but one that will cease to arouse interest when the novelty has worn off

old English proverb: 'a wonder lasts nine days, and then the puppy's eyes are open'; Shakespeare was probably alluding to this proverb (or similar) in *Henry VI Pt III*, III:ii, 'That would be ten days' wonder, at the least / That's a day longer than a wonder lasts'

gutless wonder

coward

wood

not to see the wood for the trees

to overlook the general picture because of undue concentration on the details

to be babes in the wood

to be excessively naVve and inexperienced and thus ripe for exploitation

based on the folk legend of the babes in the wood of Wayland Hall, Norfolk

to get rid of the dead wood

to terminate the services of unsatisfactory personnel

refers to pruning of bushes

to touch wood

to hope that our good luck will not go away

refers to ancient belief in sacred power of certain trees, especially oak, ash, hazel, hawthorn and willow

wooden

to get the wooden spoon

to come ingloriously last

refers to the custom of awarding a silver cup to the winner and a wooden spoon to the loser

woods

neck of the woods

localised area

refers to a narrow stretch of wooded country

to be out of the woods

the previous difficulties have been overcome

woodwork

to crawl out of the woodwork

(referring to something unwelcome) to emerge from hiding or obscurity

wool

dyed in the wool

very loyal and partisan

refers to a garment in which the wool itself (from which the garment is woven) is dyed, rather than the completed garment being dyed as a piece (and thus less thoroughly)

to pull the wool over someone's eyes

to deceive or deliberately mislead another person

derived from the inability of some sheep to see clearly if wool is across their eyes

to wrap someone in cotton wool

to be overprotective towards a person

woolly

woolly-headed

slightly muddled

word

a word in someone's ear

a confidential discussion

from the word 'go'
from the beginning
John 1:1, 'In the beginning was the word'

the word is out
it is now known

words

a torrent of words
a rapid and uninterrupted outpouring of words
refers to a fast-flowing stream of water

mark my words
you will find out that I am right

not to mince words
to speak bluntly

the words stuck in my throat
I just could not get myself to say the intended words
Shakespeare, *Macbeth* II:ii, 'I had most need of blessing, and "Amen" / Stuck in my throat'

to eat one's words
to retract in a humiliated fashion

to echo someone's words
to repeat another person's views as though they were one's own

to get words in edgeways
to manage to interrupt a conversation or monologue in order to say something oneself

to put words into someone's mouth
to attempt to get someone to say something in the particular terms drafted by another person

you took the words right out of my mouth
you have just said what I was about to say

work

a nasty piece of work
an unpleasant person
perhaps a later pejorative reversal of Shakespeare's hymn of praise to humanity, *Hamlet* II:ii, 'What a piece of work is a man!'

donkey work
necessary but uninspiring routine work
refers to the laborious work done by a donkey

to do someone's dirty work
to do something unethical on behalf of another person

to do the leg work
to carry out the part of a project that requires actually physically walking around and collecting information, etc.

to do the spadework
to do the hard or menial work in preparation for a project

to have one's work cut out to do something
to have a difficult task to achieve something

to work hand in glove with someone
to work in close cooperation with a person or to be in collusion with a person to the detriment of others

to work overtime at something
to spend a lot of time and effort at doing something

to work shoulder to shoulder
to work with united effort

works

to be in the works
to be being dealt with

to get the works
to get the full treatment

to gum up the works
to cause an activity to cease by preventing normal functioning of the necessary processes

to throw a spanner into the works
to cause an unexpected complication

world

it's a small world
it is surprising to meet people one knows in unexpected places

the world is one's oyster
one has enormous scope for activity
Shakespeare, *The Merry Wives of Windsor*, II:ii, 'Why, then the world's mine oyster'

to be on a world stage
to be prominent in international affairs
refers to the theatre

to be on top of the world
to be very happy

to be out of this world
to be superb

to carry the world on one's shoulders

to perform a huge task alone
refers to Atlas, who was condemned to bear the heavens on his shoulders for leading the Titans against the gods to
make a world of difference
to make a great deal of difference
to present a happy face to the world
bravely to gloss over one's problems and to appear contented to others
to set the world on fire
to do something remarkable
why in the world?
what possible reason can there be for this?

worlds

to get the worst of all worlds
to get a series of disadvantages without achieving any corresponding advantages
to want the best of both worlds
unreasonably to desire to get some advantage without incurring a corresponding disadvantage

worm

a bookworm
a person who likes reading and study
the early bird gets the worm
a person who acts ahead of others gets an advantage over them
the worm has turned
a previously compliant person is now asserting his or her personality
to worm one's way in
subtly to insinuate oneself into a person's trust

worms

a can of worms
a collection of complex intertwined problems

worse

the bark is worse than the bite
the harsh words belie the reality of mild action
the cure is worse than the complaint/disease
the remedy involves more disadvantages than if it were not applied
Francis Bacon (1561–1626), *Of Seditions and Troubles*, 'The remedy is worse than the disease'

worst

to get the worst of all worlds
to get a series of disadvantages without achieving any corresponding advantages

worth

a bird in the hand is worth two in the bush
a benefit currently available is more valuable than a seemingly much larger benefit that might or might not be achieved in the future
not to be worth a continental
to have no value
refers to currency notes of early US issue which quickly depreciated in value
not to be worth one's salt
not to be worth one's wages; to be inefficient or incapable
refers to Roman soldiers being paid in salt — a practice giving rise to the modern word 'salary'
not to be worth the candle
to be too expensive in relation to the true value; AND/OR not to be worth the effort required
not worth a tinker's curse
worthless
from a tinker's custom of blocking up a hole with a pellet of bread before soldering, the pellet of bread being discarded as worthless after the soldering was completed
that person's blood is worth bottling
that person is very clever or competent
to be worth one's weight in gold
to be very valuable or useful
to throw in one's six pennies'/two cents' worth
modestly to supply one's own facts or views

wound

to open up an old wound
to take action which revives a long-standing grievance
to rub salt into someone's wound
deliberately to make damage even worse

wounded

to charge like a wounded bull

to impose excessive prices
a play on words; not a simile

wounds

to heal wounds
to effect a reconciliation
Shakespeare, *Two Gentlemen of Verona*, I:ii, 'Poor wounded name! my bosom, as a bed, shall lodge thee till thy wound be thoroughly healed'

to lick one's wounds
to adjust oneself to defeat
refers to a dog cleaning its own wounds

to nurse one's wounds
to adjust oneself to defeat

wrap

to wrap someone in cotton wool
to be overprotective towards a person

to wrap up a deal
to bring a deal to a successful conclusion

wraps

that wraps it up
that completes all the required tasks in this project

to keep something under wraps
to keep a matter confidential, especially pending an official announcement

wreck

to salvage something out of the wreck
to achieve some minor benefits out of a disastrous situation
refers to shipwrecks

wring

to wring one's hands
to express despair

wrist

a slap on the wrist
a mild rebuke

write

nothing to write home about
unimpressive

to write one's own ticket
to set one's own terms and conditions
refers to betting on a horse with a bookmaker where the chance of that horse winning is considered so unlikely that the punter is allowed to choose the odds

writing

to see the writing on the wall
to appreciate the inevitability of some event
Daniel 5:5ff, 'A man's hand ... wrote ... upon the plaister of the wall of the king's palace ... thou art weighed in the balances and art found wanting'

wrong

not to put a foot wrong
to behave impeccably
refers to dancing steps

to back the wrong horse
to have faith in, give support to, and/or invest in a project that proves to be unsuccessful
refers to betting on racehorses

to bark up the wrong tree
to reach an incorrect conclusion and/or to pursue an erroneous course of action

to be born on the wrong side of the blanket
to be illegitimate

to be on the wrong tack
to be using an inaccurate procedure or policy likely to lead to error
refers to sailing

to be on the wrong track
to be heading towards an incorrect conclusion

to be on the wrong tram
to be completely mistaken as to the basic facts

to be on the wrong wavelength
to be incorrect in one's thinking
refers to radio reception

to get off on the wrong foot with someone
to make an unfavourable initial impression on a person
refers to dancing

to get out of bed on the wrong side
to be grumpy

to get the wrong sow by the ear
to reach an incorrect conclusion

to have hold of the wrong end of the pineapple
to be utterly mistaken

to hold the wrong end of the stick
to be completely mistaken about something

to look though the wrong end of the telescope
completely to miss the point
to rub someone up the wrong way
to annoy a person with actions that fail to recognise that person's current mood

Y

yard
in one's own backyard
in one's own domain

yardstick
a yardstick
a standard by which something is measured
refers to a stick used for measuring a yard in distance

yarn
to spin a yarn
to tell an amusing or unlikely story
a play on words referring to spinning yarn for cloth

year
from the year dot
for a long time
refers to the year one — hence, colloquially, a time in the remote past

years
for donkey's years
for a long time

yell
to scream and yell
to protest violently

yeoman
yeoman service
valuable assistance over a long time
refers to an officer in an official household or military establishment

yesterday
not to have been born yesterday
not to be naVve

young
a trap for young players
a significant likelihood of the inexperienced or naVve making mistakes
an old head on young shoulders
experience, knowledge, and maturity in a young person
it is on for young and old
the excitement has started (esp. referring to fighting)
the night is young
the project is at a very early stage
young Turks
members of an organisation who hold ideas regarded as too revolutionary
refers to an early twentieth-century revolutionary political party in what was to become Turkey

your
your move!
the next step is up to you
refers to chess and similar games

Z

z
from a to z
from start to finish

zero
to zero in on a target
to move directly towards one's objective

zone
twilight zone
state of imperfect understanding

zugzwang
zugzwang
a disadvantageous action being forced on one
chess term: German, *Zug* move + *Zwang* 'compulsion, obligation' = a compulsory move

1

180
to turn around 180 degrees
completely to reverse a stance

Part II
Thematic Section

Animals

albatross

to be an albatross around someone's neck
to be a great burden
refers to a mythical mariner who suffered terrible ordeals as a result of killing an albatross; Samuel Taylor Coleridge (1772–1834), *The Ancient Mariner*, 1798, 'Why look'st thou so? — with my cross-bow, I shot the albatross'

animal

there is no such animal
that does not exist

to be a political animal
to be a person who thinks and acts politically in all aspects of life

ant

to white-ant someone
surreptitiously to seek to destroy a person
refers to the damage done to timber structures by white ants

antlers

to lock antlers with someone
to have an argument with another person
refers to fighting between male horned animals

ass

to make an ass of oneself
to act stupidly in public

bait

to swallow the bait
to succumb to a temptation deliberately put in one's way
refers to angling

bark

the bark is worse than the bite
the harsh words belie the reality of mild action

to bark up the wrong tree
to reach an incorrect conclusion and/or to pursue an erroneous course of action

bats

to have bats in the belfry
to be mad
literally refers to a tower or attic, or, figuratively, the head

bay

to hold someone at bay
successfully to resist an attacker
James Thomson (1700–48), *Autumn*, 'He stands at bay, and puts his last weak refuge in despair' — description of a stag

beak

to be a sticky beak
to show excessive curiosity into matters not of one's concern

bear

to be a bear of very little brain
to have little intelligence
refers to A. A. Milne's *Winnie-the-Pooh*

beast

the nature of the beast
the reality of the situation
Revelation 13:17, '... he that had the mark, or the name of the beast, or the number of his name'

to make the beast with two backs
to engage in sexual intercourse
Shakespeare, *Othello* I:i, 'Your daughter and the Moor are now making the beast with two backs'

beaver

an eager beaver
a person with great drive and enthusiasm even if this causes annoyance to others
refers to the industriousness of the beaver, and adapted as World War II US expression for a very keen person who habitually volunteered

to beaver away
to work diligently at some task
refers to the industriousness of the beaver

bee

to be a busy bee
to work with great diligence

to have a bee in one's bonnet
to have an obsession

beeline

to make a beeline for something
to go straight to something with great enthusiasm or to head for some goal by the most direct route

bLte

to be someone's bLte noire
to be a person whose ideas and actions cause upset and loathing in another person
French, *bLte noire* ('black beast')

bird

a bird in the hand is worth two in the bush
a benefit currently available is more valuable than a seemingly much larger benefit that might or might not be achieved in the future

a bird's-eye view
a general overview or summary of a subject, emphasising the major features

a little bird told me
I heard from an informant who cannot be named
Ecclesiastes 10:20, 'Even in your thought do not curse the king ... for a bird of the air will carry your voice or some winged creature tell the matter'

the bird has flown
the person sought is no longer about

the bird is carved
the necessary action has been taken

the early bird gets the worm
a person who acts ahead of others gets an advantage over them

to be a rare bird
to be an unusual type of individual

to have a bird brain
to be stupid

birds

birds of a feather flock together
persons of like interests gather in the same place
Samuel Rutherford (?1600–61), 'Fowls of a feather flock together'

that is strictly for the birds
that is trivial nonsense appealing only to the naVve and the gullible

to kill two birds with one stone
to achieve a second objective in the course of achieving the first objective

bit

to champ at the bit
to be impatient
refers to horses keen to begin

blood

to smell blood
to divine imminent victory

bone

a bone of contention
the subject matter of violent disagreement
probably refers to dogs fighting over a bone

to have a bone to pick
to have a grievance that requires discussion

to throw someone a bone
to fob a person off with a symbolic but unimportant gesture
refers to feeding a dog

bones

the bare bones
(of a story) nothing but the essential elements

bull

a bull in a china shop
a careless person likely to cause great damage

a cock-and-bull story
an explanation that is completely unbelievable and unacceptable
Laurence Sterne (1713–68), *Tristram Shandy*, 'Said my mother, "What is this story all about?" — "a cock and a bull," said Yorick.'

to be a red rag to a bull
to be something that makes a person very angry and very excited
refers to the erroneous belief that the colour red, rather than the motion of waving, excites a bull

to be within a bull's roar of something
to be very close to something

to charge like a wounded bull
to impose excessive prices
a play on words; not a simile

to hit the bull's eye
to be extremely accurate in an activity; to score
derived from archery

to take the bull by the horns
to come to grips with the realities of a difficult problem

butt

to butt in

to involve oneself, uninvited, in someone else's conversation

refers to the aggressive action of animals with the head

butterflies

to have butterflies in one's stomach

a feeling of anxiety

butterfly

to have a butterfly mind

not to concentrate on the matter on hand

buzz

to buzz off

to go away

calf

to kill the fatted calf

to demonstrate welcome and complete acceptance of another person

Luke 15:23. 'And bring hither the fatted calf and let us eat, and be merry'

camel

the straw that broke the camel's back

the latest step that, when added to a large number of seemingly harmless previous steps, sets off a sudden significant event resulting from the cumulative effect

cat

a cat-and-dog existence

a life full of frequent squabbles

a cat may look at a king

don't give yourself airs!

a copycat

a person who imitates another person's ideas

a fat cat

a well-remunerated politician, public servant, or businessperson

a game of cat and mouse

negotiations between two parties of unequal bargaining power during which the stronger makes some temporary concessions to the weaker without, however, affecting the latter's eventual total defeat

there is more than one way to skin a cat

this can be achieved in a variety of ways

to be a cat's paw

to be a person who is being used as a tool by others

refers to the fable of the monkey who used the paw of his friend, the cat, to extract roasted chestnuts from the fire

to be the cat's pyjamas

to be the very best, to be superlatively good

American slang (origin obscure)

to bell the cat

to do some dangerous but highly useful mission

refers to a fable in which none of the mice was willing to put a warning bell on a cat

to kick the cat

to take out one's anger on some innocent party

to let the cat out of the bag

to reveal an embarrassing secret

refers to the practice of selling a person a cat (purported to be a pig) in a bag (or poke) — hence 'a pig in a poke'; if the person opened the bag and looked inside, that person 'let the cat out of the bag'

to see which way the cat jumps

to await developments

to throw a cat among the pigeons

to cause consternation and upset

when the cat is away the mice will play

in the absence of supervision discipline will be lax

wild cat

(of a strike) unofficial; OR (of an oil well) drilled as a pure prospect; OR (of a financial scheme) very hazardous

cats

to rain cats and dogs

to rain heavily

derived from ancient northern mythology in which cats and dogs were symbolically linked to weather: the cat can be taken as a symbol of falling rain and the dog as a symbol of wind gusts

chameleon

a chameleon

a person without character who changes stance repeatedly to reflect the current circumstances

chicken

chicken and egg
a situation involving two factors each of which causes the other, making it impossible to decide which came first

chicken-hearted
showing little courage

to be chicken feed
to be small and unimportant

chickens

the chickens are coming home to roost
the consequences of a person's past actions are now being felt by that person

Robert Southey (1774–1843), *The Curse of Kehama* (1810), 'Curses are like young chickens, they always come home to roost'

to count one's chickens before they are hatched
to treat as fact the expected results of a future proposal

originally attributed to Erasmus (1466–1536) in slightly different form

chops

to lick one's chops
to look forward to something with pleasurable anticipation

refers to salivation in anticipation of food

cobwebs

to blow the cobwebs away
to revive an old issue

cock

a cock-and-bull story
an explanation that is completely unbelievable and unacceptable

Laurence Sterne (1713–68), *Tristram Shandy*, 'Said my mother, "What is this story all about?" — "a cock and a bull," said Yorick.'

cock-eyed
stupid

cocoon

in a cocoon
in a safe and isolated environment

cow

a cash cow
a source of ready money

a milch cow
an easy and plentiful source of some desired benefit

a sacred cow
an institution, person, idea, custom, etc. treated as being immune from criticism and change

refers to Hindu veneration of the cow

cows

till the cows come home
for a very long time, perhaps forever

Francis Beaumont (1584–1616) & John Fletcher (1579–1625), *The Scornful* Lady, 'Kiss till the cow comes home'

crawl

to crawl out of the woodwork
(referring to something unwelcome) to emerge from hiding or obscurity

crestfallen

crestfallen
dejected

refers to the crest of a fighting cock

crocodile

to shed crocodile tears
hypocritically to show concern or sympathy for a person in distress

refers to the reflex lacrimation of a crocodile while eating

crow

as the crow flies
by the shortest distance

to eat crow
to act in a humiliating fashion to achieve a desired outcome

from an incident in New England (North America) in the Anglo–American War of 1812–14

to have a crow's eye
to be cunning or alert

cuckoo

to be a cuckoo in the nest
to purport to be a member of a group of people although having no such right and, in the process, to usurp the rights of those entitled to be there

refers to a cuckoo depositing its eggs in the nests of other birds

to be in cloud-cuckoo land
to be mad or to have unrealistic expectations

'cloud-cuckoo land' was an imaginary city built in the air by the birds (according to the *Nephelococcygia* of *TheBirds* by

Aristophanes) — hence any utopian fantastic scheme

cud

to chew the cud
to reflect on something
refers to the chewing of the cud by ruminant animals

dinosaur

a dinosaur
someone or something with incredibly outmoded ideas

dog

a cat-and-dog existence
a life full of frequent squabbles

a dogfight
a confused fight, especially between aeroplanes

a lame dog
a person under some disadvantage needing attention and assistance

a shaggy dog story
a laborious, far-fetched, amusing story
refers to the shaggy dog that originally featured in many of these stories

a sly dog
a knowing, cunning, clever person (esp. one who discreet about that person's own personal weaknesses)

a watchdog
a person or organisation monitoring behaviour

any stick to beat a dog
any excuse will do if it serves one's purpose

dog-eared
(of pages) well-thumbed
refers to the turned-down appearance of the ears of many dogs

dog-tired
tired out

every dog has its day
persons being criticised or persecuted will have their opportunity to reverse the situation; good luck comes sooner or later
Charles Kingsley (1819–75). *Young and Old*, 'Young blood must have its course, lad, and every dog his day'

every man and his dog
everybody

love me, love my dog
if you accept me then you must also accept my associates
Latin proverb: *Qui me amat, amat et canem meam*, quoted by St Bernard of Clairvaux (1090–1153)

not a dog's chance
virtually no hope at all

one cannot teach an old dog new tricks
people become set in their ways irreversibly

the tail wagging the dog
a minor aspect with disproportionate effect on a major aspect

the top dog
the person in the most powerful position
refers to the dominant dog in a pack

to be a dog in the manger
spitefully to deny something to others, notwithstanding its uselessness to oneself
from *Aesop's Fables*

to be a dog's breakfast
to be a very messy arrangement

to be a gay dog
to lead an idle life while flaunting the symbols of wealth

to be in the doghouse
to be in disgrace

to give a dog a bad name
to malign a person

to have a hair of the dog that bit one
to drink more alcohol in an attempt to overcome the effects of alcohol already consumed
refers to the belief that the hair of the rabid dog that bit a person was a cure for the madness that can ensue

to lead a dog's life
to be ill-treated

to see a man about a dog
to do something unspecified

to try something out on the dog
to test the feasibility or safety of a dubious remedy or project

two men and a dog
very few people

underdog
a person or team that is likely to lose a contest and therefore likely to be the object of sympathy

why keep a dog and bark oneself?
it is silly to pay for assistance and then do things personally

dogs

all the dogs are barking
this news is being widely disseminated

to call off the dogs
to abandon a pursuit or inquiry
refers to hunt master calling off the dogs if they are on the wrong scent

to feed the dogs while they are barking
to do something while the opportunity is available

to go to the dogs
to be ruined

to let sleeping dogs lie
to refrain from raising an issue that is not obviously requiring attention

to rain cats and dogs
to rain heavily
derived from ancient northern mythology in which cats and dogs were symbolically linked to weather: the cat can be taken as a symbol of falling rain and the dog as a symbol of wind gusts

to throw something to the dogs
to discard something as useless and worthless
Shakespeare, *Macbeth* v:iii, 'Throw physic to the dogs, I'll none of it'

donkey

donkey work
necessary but uninspiring routine work
refers to the laborious work done by a donkey

for donkey's years
for a long time

to pin the tail on the donkey
to put the blame on a person who has with some effort been identified as responsible
refers to children's parlour game

to talk the hind leg off a donkey
to talk excessively

drakes

to play ducks and drakes
not to treat the matter seriously
derived from the old name given to the game of throwing a stone such that it skips across the surface of water; hence: 'to throw away idly and carelessly

drone

a drone
an idle person

droves

people stayed away in droves
few people came
refers to a moving group of cattle, sheep, or other animals

duck

a lame duck
a person unable to fend for himself or herself
a 'lame-duck president' is a president still in office but without influence because the commencement of the successor's term is imminent

in two shakes of a duck's tail
in an instant

to be a dead duck
to have failed; OR to be in a hopeless situation

to be a sitting duck
to be vulnerable to exploitation

to be like water off a duck's back
(of advice or criticism) to be completely ignored

to duck for cover
to seek to avoid blame

duckling

an ugly duckling
an unprepossessing person or thing, the characteristics of which change in time to become attractive
refers to a cygnet in a brood of ducks in a children's story of that name by Hans Christian Andersen

ducks

to play ducks and drakes
not to treat the matter seriously
derived from the old name given to the game of throwing a stone such that it skips across the surface of water; hence: 'to throw away idly and carelessly

eagle

to have an eagle eye
to be able very readily to notice small mistakes or fine details missed by others

ear

to turn something on its ear
to reverse something

earmark

to earmark
to allocate to a specific purpose
refers to marking animals

egg

to be a bad egg
to be a dishonest or disreputable person

elephant

a rogue elephant
a person of vicious temper who does not function as part of the group and who acts in an undisciplined way

a white elephant
an expensive and useless luxury
refers to gifts of sacred elephants by the King of Siam to persons then ruined by the expense of their upkeep

to get an elephant stamp
to receive praise

elephants

one looks for elephants in elephant country
one needs to search in the right place

eyed

bright-eyed and bushy-tailed
naVve but enthusiastic

feather

to feather one's own nest
improperly to appropriate things for oneself (especially in financial transactions)

to show the white feather
to indicate cowardice
refers to cross-bred birds, not regarded as useful in cock fighting

to thrash with a feather
to impose only a minor punishment for a very serious offence

feathers

to make feathers fly
to cause a flurry of consternation and vigorous activity
refers to the fighting of cock birds

to ruffle someone's feathers
to engage in behaviour that irritates another person

feet

to put something back on its feet
to restore to a functioning condition

ferret

to ferret something out
by diligent research to discover some secret
refers to a ferret pursuing rabbits in their burrows

fetter

to fetter someone
to stop a person acting on that person's own initiative

fish

a queer fish
an unusual type of person

an ocean full of fish
plenty of opportunity

neither fish flesh nor good red herring
unclassifiable by virtue of being neither one thing nor another
Miguel de Cervantes (1547–1616), *Don Quixote*

that has nothing to do with the price of fish
that is quite irrelevant

to be a big fish in a little pond
to be a person holding an important office but in an unimportant organisation

to be a cold fish
to be an unemotional person

to be a different kettle of fish
to be something very dissimilar
refers to a riverside picnic where freshly caught fish is cooked and eaten

to be a fine kettle of fish
to be a terrible muddle
refers to a riverside picnic where freshly caught fish is cooked and eaten

to be a fish out of water
to be in difficulty by virtue of being in a strange environment

to be in a goldfish bowl
to be very open to view

to fish for compliments
to drop hints in the hope that one will receive praise or recognition

to fish in troubled waters
to profit from a disturbed situation
refers to ang!'ng

to have more important fish to fry
to have more important things to do
what has that to do with the price of fish?
what is the relevance of this?

fishing

a fishing expedition
an exercise that sets out to gather incriminating information without knowing its exact nature or location

fishy

to be a fishy situation
to be a suspicious situation

flea

to send someone away with a flea in the ear
to give a person frank, but unwelcome, facts
perhaps refers to fleas trapped in the armour of ancient knights, or perhaps from the discomfort felt by a dog with a flea in its ear; or perhaps, figuratively, to any lingering irritation in the ear

flies

there are no flies on someone
a person is alert and astute

flock

flock
congregation in the charge of a religious official
numerous biblical references incl.: *Isaiah* 40:11, 'He shall feed his flock like a shepherd: he shall gather the lambs with his arm, and carry them in his bosom, and shall gently lead those that are with young'

fly

a fly in the ointment
a minor flaw that spoils a thing
Ecclesiastes 10:1, 'Dead flies cause the ointment of the apothecary to send forth a stinking savour: so doth a little folly him that is in reputation for wisdom and honour'
I would love to be a fly on the wall
I would love to observe what goes on without those under observation being aware of my presence
someone wouldn't hurt a fly
someone is very gentle and kind-hearted
William Hazlitt (1778–1830). 'He would not hurt a fly'
to fly the coop
to grow up and become independent
refers to a cage or pen for confining poultry and other birds
to make feathers fly
to cause a flurry of consternation and vigorous activity
refers to the fighting of cock birds
to make the fur fly
to create a disturbance
refers to animals fighting

fold

the fold
the body of believers
refers to an enclosure for sheep; *John* 10:16, 'Other sheep I have, which are not of this fold'

four

an opening wide enough to drive a coach and four through
an excellent opportunity to demonstrate the major errors or absurdities of something
the saying seems sometimes also to have referred to six horses: Sir Stephen Rice (1673–1715), as quoted by W. King, *State of the Protestants of Ireland* (1672), 'I will drive a coach and six horses through the Act of Settlement'

fox

a fox hole
a small space of refuge and shelter (especially in battle)
Matthew 8:20, 'the foxes have holes, and the birds of the air have nests; but the son of man hath not where to lay his head'

frog

to have a frog in one's throat
to have a transient hoarseness, or a trivial throat obstruction
to leap-frog something
to overtake something, with the likelihood of, in turn, being overtaken
refers to a game in which participants jump over each other in turn

fur

to make the fur fly
to create a disturbance
refers to animals fighting

galah

every galah in the petshop
everybody

game

to be fair game
to be someone who can be attacked legitimately
refers to hunting

gander

what is sauce for the goose is sauce for the gander
arguments that apply in one case also apply in another

gnat

to strain at a gnat
to be scrupulous about trifles
Matthew 23:23, '... that strain at a gnat, and swallow a camel'

go

from go to whoa
from start to finish
refers to the commands given to horses

goat

a scapegoat
a person who is forced to take the blame for something not that person's fault
Leviticus 16:10, 'But the goat, on which the lot fell to be the scapegoat ... to make an atonement'

to play the giddy goat
to act the fool
'giddy' derived from Old English *gidig* ('possessed by a god')

goats

to separate the sheep from the goats
to distinguish between the worthy and the unworthy
Matthew 25:32, 'and he shall separate them one from one another, as a shepherd divideth his sheep from the goats'

goldfish

to be in a goldfish bowl
to be very open to view

what is this — a bunch of grapes or a bowl of goldfish?
surely you know what this is?

goose

a wild-goose chase
a futile chase or search
refers to old game of 'follow-the-leader' on horses in which the objective was to follow a winding and difficult course without ever catching up

to be too frightened to say 'boo' to a goose
to be excessively shy

to cook one's goose
to make a fatal mistake; to ruin one's plans
nineteenth-century street ballad: 'If they come here we'll cook their geese'

to kill the goose that lays the golden eggs
through excessive greed, to sacrifice future gains for a short-term advantage
based on a Greek fable about a man who killed the goose that laid golden eggs; his aim was to collect the whole stock of eggs at once but, in doing so, he ended his future supply

to make a wigwam for a goose's bridle
to do something unspecified
nonsense said to children

what is sauce for the goose is sauce for the gander
arguments that apply in one case also apply in another

grasshopper

since that person was knee-high to a grasshopper
since that person was a very young child

hackles

to raise someone's hackles
to make a person angry
refers to feathers raised in anger on the back of the neck of certain birds; also, by analogy, refers to hairs raised in anger on the neck of dogs

halcyon

in halcyon days
in past happier times
Shakespeare, *Henry V, Part 1*, I:ii, 'Expect St Martin's summer, halcyon days'; refers to the fourteen days about the winter solstice when winds were calm, and to the mythical bird said to breed in a floating nest at that time

hamstrung

to be hamstrung

to have limited freedom to act as one would wish

refers to ancient practice of disabling a person or animal by cutting the hamstring muscles of the thigh

hard-mouthed

hard-mouthed

uncontrollable

refers to horses that are 'hard' in the mouth or bite (and thus difficult to control)

hare

first catch your hare

do things in logical order and after proper preparation

generally attributed to Hannah Gleese, habit-maker to the Prince of Wales and co-author of *The Art of Cookery Made Plain and Easy* (1747)

hare-brained

wildly stupid

Benjamin Disraeli (1804–81), speech 1878, 'The hare-brained chatter of irresponsible frivolity'

to chase every hare

to be easily sidetracked

to run with the hare and hunt with the hounds

to keep in with two opposing sides

refers to hunting

to set a hare running

to initiate an activity to achieve a related and desired effect

refers to hunting

harness

in harness

to be constrained and in work

head

to be unable to make head nor tail of something

to be unable to understand how something functions or what something means

to rear its ugly head

to make an unwelcome appearance

hen

a mother hen

an over-protective person

Matthew 12:37, 'Even as a hen gathereth her chickens under her wings'

hen-pecked

subject to domination by one's wife

Lord Byron (1788–1824), *Don Juan*, 'But — oh! ye lords of ladies intellectual, inform us truly, have they not hen-peck'd you all?'

herd

to follow the herd

to do what most other people are doing

herring

to be a red herring

to be something designed to divert attention away from the main question

refers to hunting with hounds — a red herring was dragged across the scent trail to train hounds to ignore distractions and follow the correct trail

hide

to cover one's hide

to provide excuses or take other evasive action in an attempt to avoid the adverse consequences of one's actions

hidebound

hidebound

narrow-minded

hog

a road hog

an inconsiderate motorist

refers to gluttonous swine

to go the whole hog

to do something very thoroughly

origin uncertain; alternative explanations include: (i) Muslim divines attempting to ascertain how much of the whole hog could be eaten according to Islamic law (Cowper, 1779, 'but for one piece they thought it hard/from the whole hog to be debarred'); (ii) colloquial term for a shilling — that is, to spend the whole hog (or shilling) at one time; (iii) refers to the close shearing of lambs

to make a hog of oneself

to demonstrate greed

refers to gluttonous swine

hogwash

hogwash

nonsense

refers to 'hog wash' — meaning kitchen swill for pigs (and therefore worthless)

hoot

not to care a hoot

not to show the slightest concern or enthusiasm

horns

the horns of a dilemma
two unpalatable alternatives between which a choice must be made
dilemma: Greek for 'two assumptions'

to lock horns with someone
to have an argument with another person
refers to fighting between male horned animals

to pull one's horns in
to retreat from previously stated views
refers to fighting between male horned animals

horse

a dark horse
a person with unsuspected talents
Benjamin Disraeli (1804–81), *The Young Duke*, 'A dark horse, which had never been thought of, and which the careless St James had never even observed in the list, rushed past the grandstand in sweeping triumph'

a nod is the same as a wink to a blind horse
fine distinctions are not appropriate here
Captain Marryat (1792–1848), *Peter Simple*, 'But you're a dutiful son, so I'll say no more about it — a nod's as good as a wink to a blind horse'

a stalking horse
a pretext put forward to allow an attack to be made or an argument to be mounted
refers to a horse trained to allow a hunter to approach game (esp. fowl) without being seen; Shakespeare, *As You Like It* V:iv, 'He uses his folly like a stalking horse, and under the presentation of that he shoots his wit'

a Trojan horse
a surreptitious means of gaining entrance or breaching defences
refers to a large gift horse full of Greek soldiers used to bring about the fall of Troy, as described in Homer's *Iliad*; Virgil (70–19 BC), *Aeneid* II:49, *Timeo Danaos et dona ferentis* ('I fear the Greeks even when they bring gifts')

a two-horse race
a contest between only two serious contestants

a warhorse
an experienced and dependable campaigner in war, politics, sport, and other contests

a willing horse
a cheerful worker

horse sense
practical commonsense

horse trading
tough negotiations

I could eat a horse
I am very hungry

one can lead a horse to water, but one can't make it drink
one can give advice to a person but cannot ensure that it will be acted on

that is a horse of a very different colour
that is a different matter altogether
Shakespeare, *Twelfth Night*, 'My purpose is, indeed, a horse of that colour'

the horse-and-buggy days
long ago

to back the wrong horse
to have faith in, give support to, and/or invest in a project that proves to be unsuccessful
refers to betting on racehorses

to be on one's hobby horse
to dominate a conversation by insisting on talking about subjects in which one has an obsessive interest
refers to a person who dressed with a figure of a horse around the waist or on the head in Morris dancing — hence a figure of fun, a jester, a buffoon

to be on one's high horse
to be excessively pompous
refers to persons of high rank riding on tall horses; John Brown (1715–66), *Letter to Garrick*, 'Altogether upon the high horse'

to flog a dead horse
misguidedly to do something patently useless

to learn something from the horse's mouth
to get information from someone qualified to impart it
refers to the examination of a horse's teeth for an accurate assessment of its age

to look a gift horse in the mouth
to be suspicious about a benefit that has been volunteered
Samuel Butler (1612–80), *Hudibras*, 'He ne'er consider'd it, as loth to look a gift horse in the mouth'; refers to the examination of a horse's teeth for an accurate assessment of its age

to put the cart before the horse
to do things in the wrong order
Rudyard Kipling (1865–1936), *The Conundrum of the Workshops*, 'We know the tail must wag the dog, for the horse is drawn by the cart'

to shut the stable door after the horse has bolted
to take preventive action only after the relevant event

horses

hold your horses!
just wait a little!

horses are out of the barn
it is now too late

it is horses for courses
the correct means to an end needs to be chosen
refers to horse racing

to drive a coach and horses through something
to demonstrate the major errors or absurdities of something
Sir Stephen Rice (1673–1715), as quoted by W. King, *State of the Protestants of Ireland* (1672), 'I will drive a coach and six horses through the Act of Settlement'

to frighten the horses
to scare people off by one's ill-considered tactics
Mrs Patrick Campbell (1865–1940), quoting oral tradition, 'I don't mind where people make love, so long as they don't do it in the street and frighten the horses'

to swap/change horses in mid-stream
to alter that upon which one is reliant during the course of a project

wild horses would not cause me to do something
I refuse absolutely to do something
refers to a form of torture in which persons were dragged behind horses

horseplay

horseplay
boisterous and undignified behaviour
John Dryden (1631–1700), 'He [Collier] is too much given to horseplay in his raillery'

hounds

to run with the hare and hunt with the hounds
to keep in with two opposing sides
refers to hunting

to set the hounds baying
to excite the gossips by providing material that they can use
Shakespeare, *Julius Caesar*, 'I had rather be a dog, and bay the moon, than such a Roman'

jackals

to keep the jackals at bay
to pay one's creditors just sufficient to avoid repercussions
James Thomson (1700–48), *Autumn*, 'He stands at bay, and puts his last weak refuge in despair' — description of a stag

kid

to treat someone with kid gloves
to handle a person with great discretion
refers to very soft leather gloves made from the skin of young goats

kittens

to have kittens
to be in a state of great dismay
refers to a superstition that certain acts would cause women to bear kittens instead of children

lamb

a lamb led to slaughter
a naVve person allowing himself or herself to be exploited
Isaiah 53:5, 'He was oppressed, and he was afflicted, yet he opened not his mouth: he is brought as a lamb to the slaughter'

one might as well be hanged for a sheep as for a lamb
further action will not increase the adverse consequences already in train
refers to the stealing of either sheep or lambs being capital crimes under old English law

sacrificial lamb
somebody unfairly made to suffer for the mistakes of others

Exodus 29:41, 'Sacrifice the other lamb at twilight ... an offering made to the Lord by fire'

to be mutton dressed up as lamb
foolishly to pretend to be younger

to wait two shakes of a lamb's tail
to wait just a few moments

lap

to lap it up
to enjoy the attention

lark

to rise with the lark
to get up early

leash

to hold someone on a short leash
to give a person very little freedom
refers to a lead used to restrain coursing hounds

leech

leech
person taking undue advantage of others
refers to the blood-sucking activities of leeches

leopard

a leopard cannot change its spots
each person is born with certain unalterable characteristics
Jeremiah 13:23, 'Can the Ethiopian change his skin, or the leopard his spots?'

lion

the lion's share
the biggest portion

to beard the lion in his den
to tackle a daunting opponent in that person's own familiar surroundings
Sir Walter Scott (1771–1832), *Marmion*, 'And darest thou then to beard the lion in his den ... ' (probably a reference to the story of Daniel in the den of lions as related in *Daniel* 6:16)

to put one's head into the lion's mouth
recklessly to expose oneself to great danger
refers to circus performance

to throw someone to the lions
to sacrifice or condemn a person to that person's fate
refers to execution or bloodsport by throwing persons to be eaten by lions

lizard

flat out like a lizard drinking
to be hard at work
a play on words, not strictly a simile

lynx

lynx-eyed
having acute vision

mackerel

to throw a sprat to catch a mackerel
to risk a little in the hope of gaining much

mare

a mare's nest
a discovery with illusory benefits

maverick

maverick
a person who likes to do things differently from other persons
refers to Samuel A. Maverick (1803–70), Texas engineer, who owned but did not brand cattle

mice

mice have been here
intruders have entered this place

when the cat is away the mice will play
in the absence of supervision discipline will be lax

minnows

to miss the sharks while netting the minnows
to succeed in minor aspects but fail in the ones that really matter

molehills

to make mountains out of molehills
to treat a minor problem as though it were a major disaster

monkey

monkey business
mischievous or underhand activity

to play monkey tricks on someone
to engage in discreditable behaviour affecting a person

to want the organ-grinder, not the monkey
to wish to deal with the person in authority rather than an underling

moth

moth-eaten
antiquated, shabby

mothball

to mothball equipment
to take out of active service and put in storage
refers to storing clothes protected by mothballs

mouse

a game of cat and mouse
negotiations between two parties of unequal bargaining power during which the stronger makes some temporary concessions to the weaker without, however, affecting the latter's eventual total defeat

to labour mightily and bring forth a mouse
to be quite ineffective

neck

at a break-neck pace
very fast
refers to horseriding at great speed

it is neck or nothing
a desperate effort is called for
refers to a winning margin in horse racing

neck and neck
(of contestants) with little between them
refers to a winning margin in horse racing

nest

a nest egg
a sum of money set aside in case of need; a nucleus of savings
derived from the custom of placing an egg in a hen's nest as an inducement for the hen to lay more

to feather one's own nest
improperly to appropriate things for oneself (especially in financial transactions)

to foul one's own nest
to disparage or bring discredit on one's home or workplace

nit

to nitpick
to criticise a person in respect of very minor matters
refers to the removal of lice eggs (nits) from the hair of an animal or person

organ-grinder

to want the organ-grinder, not the monkey
to wish to deal with the person in authority rather than an underling

ostrich

to be an ostrich
to refuse to face up to an unpleasant truth
refers to the reputed habit of ostriches in danger

owl

to be a night owl
habitually to go to bed late

oyster

the world is one's oyster
one has enormous scope for activity
Shakespeare, *The Merry Wives of Windsor*, II:ii, 'Why, then the world's mine oyster'

pack

to be at the head of the pack
to be the best of many, or the *de facto* leader

to bring someone back to the pack
to make a person conform

pearl

a pearl
a thing of great excellence

pecker

to keep one's pecker up
to stay cheerful
refers to keeping one's head up (with 'pecker' referring to mouth — as in a bird's mouth)

pecking

pecking order
order of seniority
refers to the activity of hens and other birds

perch

to knock someone off that person's perch
to displace a person from a leadership position in some competitive situation

petrel

to be a stormy petrel

a person who disturbs a pleasant state of affairs by agitating for change

refers to the bird (petrel) that flies low over water during a storm and appears to be alternately touching one foot and then the other to the surface of the water as though walking upon it; the bird is sometimes thought to be the harbinger of a storm, and is named after St Peter who walked upon the stormy waters of Lake Gennesareth

pig

a guinea pig

a person on whom some new practice is tried out

refers to use of guinea pigs in medical experimentation

pig-headed

unduly obstinate

to buy a pig in a poke

to buy goods of unknown quality

refers to the practice of selling a person a cat (purported to be a pig) in a bag (or poke); if the person opened the bag and looked inside, that person 'let the cat out of the bag'

pigeon

a pigeon pair

one son and one daughter as the only offspring

refers to the old belief that pigeons always sat on two eggs that produced a m[illegible] a female, and that this pair remained together throughout life

to be one's pigeon

to be one's area of responsibility

to pigeon-hole

to put aside for further consideration in the distant future

refers to placing something in a small hole, like the small hole in a dovecot for the pigeons to walk in and out

pigeons

to throw a cat among the pigeons

to cause consternation and upset

pitfall

pitfall

unsuspected danger

refers to capturing animals by inducing them to fall into a pit

plague

to be of plague proportions

to be great in number

refers to the plagues of locusts, frogs, etc., as described in *Exodus* chs 8 and 10 (and elsewhere)

pony

a show pony

a vain and ostentatious person

possum

to play possum

to lie low; to feign unconsciousness or death

refers to the possum's habit of attempting to evade capture by feigning death

to stir the possum

to set out to raise controversial issues

pup

to sell someone a pup

to cheat a person in a transaction, especially by misrepresentation as to the true value of something

purring

positively purring

(of a person) very pleased; (of an engine) running very smoothly

refers to a cat's purring

pussyfoot

to pussyfoot around

to take stealthy, cautious, non-committal steps

refers to a cat prowling

rabbit

a rabbit warren

a building with a maze of rooms and passages

move over and let the greyhound see the rabbit

stand aside to allow things to get under way

refers to hunting with greyhounds

to pull a rabbit out of the hat

to produce an unexpected and seemingly miraculous but highly desirable solution

refers to magician's trick

rat

rat race

relentless struggle in life to get ahead of one's working rivals

to smell a rat

to become suspicious

rats

a case of rats leaving a sinking ship
the desertion of an enterprise in anticipation of imminent failure

rein

a tight rein
strong controls
refers to riding or driving horses

to give rein to one's fancy
to let one's imagination have free scope
refers to riding or driving horses

to give someone free rein
to confer complete discretion on another person
refers to riding or driving horses

to rein in something
to keep better control over something
refers to riding or driving horses

to take over the reins
to assume control
refers to riding or driving horses

rhinoceros

to have the hide of a rhinoceros
to be unaffected by, and unresponsive to, valid criticism

roost

the chickens are coming home to roost
the consequences of a person's past actions are now being felt by that person
Robert Southey (1774–1843), *The Curse of Kehama* (1810), 'Curses are like young chickens, they always come home to roost'

to rule the roost
to dominate
refers to the habit of roosters and hens to have an established order of dominance

rooster

today a rooster, tomorrow a feather duster
when circumstances change, an important person can, immediately, become unimportant

ruminate

to ruminate
to ponder over a matter
refers to the chewing of the cud by ruminant animals

scapegoat

a scapegoat
a person who is forced to take the blame for something not that person's fault
Leviticus 16:10, 'But the goat, on which the lot fell to be the scapegoat ... to make an atonement'

sharks

to miss the sharks while netting the minnows
to succeed in minor aspects but fail in the ones that really matter

sheep

a black sheep
a disreputable member of an otherwise reputable group

one might as well be hanged for a sheep as for a lamb
further action will not increase the adverse consequences already in train
refers to the stealing of either sheep or lambs being capital crimes under old English law

to be a wolf in sheep's clothing
to be a hypocrite; to be dangerous although masquerading as something harmless
Matthew 7:15, 'Beware of false prophets, which come to you in sheep's clothing, but inwardly they are ravening wolves'

to be home on the sheep's back
to be doing well

to cast sheep's eyes at someone
to look at a person amorously

to ride on the sheep's back
to benefit from the production of wool

to separate the sheep from the goats
to distinguish between the worthy and the unworthy
Matthew 25:32, 'and he shall separate them one from one another, as a shepherd divideth his sheep from the goats'

to spoil the ship for a ha'p'orth of tar
to engage in a false economy

the current word 'ship' is actually a mistake for the original word 'sheep', and the tar refers to the treatment of wounds

sheepish

sheepish

embarrassed, as though guilty

shell

to retreat into one's shell

to become shy and introverted

refers to the action of tortoises and other animals when threatened

skin

a cleanskin

a person without a criminal record or other blemish on that person's reputation

probably refers to an unblemished animal skin

snail

at a snail's pace

very slowly

Shakespeare, *As You Like It*, II:vii, 'The whining schoolboy ... creeping like snail unwillingly to school'

snake

a snake in the grass

a person of low character who manages to disguise that trait

Virgil, *Eclogue*, 'There's a snake hidden in the grass'

snakes

a game of snakes and ladders

a series of ups and downs

refers to a board game

snap

to snap at someone's heels

to be in very close pursuit

refers to hounds pursuing a fox

sow

one can't make a silk purse out of a sow's ear

it is impossible to manufacture something of a high standard from inferior raw materials

Malcolm Bradbury (1932–), 'For the mass of men, you can't make a silk purse out of a sow's ear'

to get the wrong sow by the ear

to reach an incorrect conclusion

spider

to be the centre of the spider's web

to control an operation that involves numerous and/or complex ingredients

sprat

to throw a sprat to catch a mackerel

to risk a little in the hope of gaining much

spur

to spur someone on

to agitate a person into doing something

refers to riding horses

stampede

to stampede someone into something

to pressure a person into taking some action

stamping

stamping ground

one's favourite place for certain activities

sticks

sticks and carrots

disincentives and incentives in combination

refers to the handling of donkeys

sting

to be the sting in the tail

to be the unexpected unpleasant conclusion

stir

to stir up a hornet's nest

to take action that results in unpleasant side-effects

swallow

one swallow does not make a summer

much further evidence is desirable before any action taken

refers to an old English proverb, probably ultimately derived from the Greek proverb: 'One swallow does not make a spring' (recorded in Aristotle's *Nicomachoean Ethics* I:vii:16)

swarm

to swarm out

to appear in large numbers from within
refers to bees or wasps'

swine

to cast pearls before swine
to confer valuable benefits on someone who neither recognises nor appreciates them
Matthew 7:6, 'Neither cast ye your pearls before swine'

tail

the tail end of something
the very end of something
to be the sting in the tail
to be the unexpected unpleasant conclusion
to get off one's tail
to stir oneself from one's inertia
to have one's tail between one's legs
to be dejected or humiliated
refers to dogs
to turn tail
to run away; OR to reverse oneself

tailed

bright-eyed and bushy-tailed
naVve but enthusiastic

tarred

to be tarred with the same brush
to be damned merely because of one's association with another person
refers to treating cuts on sheep with a tarbrush

tentacles

tentacles
strong and unpleasant influence extending a long way from its base and in many directions

tiger

a paper tiger
an empty threat
a toothless tiger
an authority that has been given powers totally inadequate for its task
to have a tiger by the tail
to be involved in an activity that is much more dangerous than one had realised

teeth

to bare one's teeth
to imply threats
refers to savage animals
to take the bit between one's teeth
to face up to a problem
refers to riding or racing horses

torpedo

to torpedo something
to make something suddenly ineffective
refers to genus of electric ray (fish), *Torpedo*, that has numbing effect on prey (Latin *torpere*, 'to be sluggish')

traces

to kick over the traces
to become insubordinate
refers to the straps designed to keep a horse restrained

trample

to trample someone under foot
by virtue of one's great power to treat a person's rights with contempt and not to give that person proper consideration

turkey

cold turkey
the sudden cessation of drugs to an addict and, by extension, the sudden cessation of any habitually pleasurable activity
probably refers to the appearance of the skin of drug addicts experiencing withdrawal symptoms (similarity to the skin of a plucked cold turkey)
to talk turkey
to talk realistically
origin obscure; North American slang

turtle

to turn turtle
to capsize

underbelly

to have a soft underbelly
to have a weakness that can be exploited

venom

venom
virulent or malicious ill will
refers to the toxins of certain biting or stinging animals

vulture

vulture

person benefiting from another's misfortune

web

a tangled web
a series of lies, especially with inconsistencies leading to exposure
Sir Walter Scott (1771–1832), *Marmion* (1808), C. VI: vii, 'O what a tangled web we weave, when first we practise to deceive!'

wether

bell-wether
first indication
refers to the leading sheep (wether) of a flock, this sheep having a bell hung around its neck

whisker

by a whisker
only just

whoa

from go to whoa
from start to finish
refers to the commands given to horses

wing

to take someone under one's wing
to protect a person
refers to birds protecting the young

wings

to clip someone's wings
to reduce another person's freedom to act as that person thinks fit
refers to clipping the wings of birds, especially poultry

to spread one's wings
to test or develop one's abilities, to lead a life of greater scope than previously

wolf

a lone wolf
a person who prefers to act without involving others

to be a wolf in sheep's clothing
to be a hypocrite; to be dangerous although masquerading as something harmless
Matthew 7:15, 'Beware of false prophets, which come to you in sheep's clothing, but inwardly they are ravening wolves'

to cry 'wolf'
repeatedly to raise an unjustified concern with the result that one will be ignored when the circumstances change and a real threat emerges
refers to a story of a boy who cried 'wolf' (from *Aesop's Fables*)

to keep the wolf from the door
to struggle to survive (esp. with respect to hunger)

wolves

to throw someone to the wolves
to expose a person to exploitation by more sophisticated persons

wool

dyed in the wool
very loyal and partisan
refers to a garment in which the wool itself (from which the garment is woven) is dyed, rather than the completed garment being dyed as a piece (and thus less thoroughly)

worm

a bookworm
a person who likes reading and study

the early bird gets the worm
a person who acts ahead of others gets an advantage over them

the worm has turned
a previously compliant person is now asserting his or her personality

to worm one's way in
subtly to insinuate oneself into a person's trust

worms

a can of worms
a collection of complex intertwined problems

Art

art

to raise something to a fine art form
to refine a thing or a process to the point where doing it is a highly skilled task

canvas

to have a blank canvas
freedom to create anything
refers to an artist's canvas

exhibition

to make an exhibition of oneself

to behave in a way that invites ridicule

mosaic

a mosaic
something with a large number of different aspects to it

paint

to paint a black picture
to state a set of unfavourable factors

painting

not to be an oil painting
to be ugly

pedestal

to put someone on a pedestal
to admire a person and regard that person as being more marvellous than is warranted

perspective

to put something into perspective
to explain the background of something so that its significance in relation to other things can be better appreciated

picture

to balance the picture
to quote facts or arguments in contradiction

to change the whole picture
to alter the major assumptions on which some assessment was based

to conjure up a picture
to use words to convey a vivid impression

to have a clear picture of something
to have a good understanding of something

to present a rosy picture
to state a set of favourable factors

to put someone in the picture
to fill a person in with the background of a situation

to see the big picture
to have the vision and imagination enabling a project to be developed as part of a bigger whole

sketch

a thumbnail sketch
brief but pertinent details
refers to an artist assessing perspective by judging the object to be painted against a thumbnail held close to the eye

Aviation

baggage

to carry baggage
to handicap oneself

bale

to bale out of something
to abandon an enterprise in anticipation of disaster
refers to emergency parachute jump from an aeroplane

balloon

to go down like a lead balloon
to receive a very cool reception

when the balloon goes up
when the adverse facts come to light

blind

to fly blind
to do something in ignorance of the relevant facts
refers to pilots flying without visual guidance (and relying on instruments)

edge

a leading edge
an advantage through possession of the latest technology or knowledge
refers to the foremost edge of an aircraft's wings

fly

to fly by the seat of one's pants
to act by instinct in the absence of specific knowledge or instructions

to fly high
to be ambitious

to have to fly
to need to leave in order to reach the next destination quickly

to let fly at someone
to launch a verbal or physical assault on a person

flyer

a highflyer
an ambitious and/or successful person

flying

to achieve a flying start
to get operational very quickly

ground

to get something off the ground
to take a project beyond its initial stages and make it operational
refers to flying aircraft

parachute

golden parachute
(in a remuneration package) generous provisions that come into play in certain circumstances

radar

on the radar screen
in someone's consciousness

tailspin

tailspin
a loss of control; a state of chaos
refers to a spin by an aircraft with the tail spiralling

wing

on a wing and a prayer
reliance on the merest chance in a desperate situation
also applied to an emergency landing by an aircraft; originally a song (1943) by H. Adamson

zero

to zero in on a target
to move directly towards one's objective

Buildings

architect

to be the architect of something
to be the person devising something innovative

backyard

in one's own backyard
in one's own domain

belfry

to have bats in the belfry
to be mad
literally refers to a tower or attic, or, figuratively, the head

benchmark

a benchmark
a standard by which something is measured
refers to a mark (and associated bench) used in ancient building practices as a reference point for measuring and levelling

blowtorch

to apply the blowtorch to something
to apply very strong pressure to some person

blueprint

blueprint
a master plan for some activity or a model that others can copy
refers to a detailed architectural or engineering drawing — originally consisting of white lines on a blue background

bolts

nuts and bolts
basic ingredients

brick

it is London to a brick on
it is virtually certain
a metaphor coined by the Australian horse-race caller, Ken Howard, to indicate that one could bet the whole of London against a single brick — in the confident expectation of winning

to bang one's head against a brick wall
to fight an unwinnable case

to be up against a brick wall
to be unable to achieve anything because of intractable opposition or apathy

to drop a brick
to make a socially embarrassing or inappropriate announcement

brickbats

to throw brickbats at someone
to express displeasure with a person
refers to portions of brick, esp. ones used as missiles

bricks

one cannot make bricks without straw
one cannot achieve results in the absence of adequate resources

Exodus 6:7 'Ye shall no more give the people straw to make bricks ... let them go and gather straw for themselves'

bridge

a lot of water has flowed under the bridge since then
much has happened since then

to be water under the bridge
to matter no longer

to bridge a gap
to fill a need or make up a shortfall

to bridge a gulf
to overcome a wide divergence in views

Luke 16:26, 'Between us and you there is a great gulf fixed'

to cross a bridge only when one comes to it
to await the crystallisation of a situation before sorting it out

bridges

to build bridges
to work at improving relationships

to burn one's bridges
to do something irreversible

to mend bridges
to restore a broken-up relationship

brush

a broad-brush approach
the handling of a situation with a deliberate lack of attention to detail

carpet

to be on the carpet
to be lectured in regard to one's alleged misdeeds

castle

a castle in Spain
a desirable imagining, but an impracticable proposition

a castle in the air
a desirable imagining, but an impracticable proposition

ceiling

ceiling
upper permitted limit

cement

to cement a relationship
to do something in an endeavour to make a relationship permanent

chisel

to chisel away at something
to reduce the size of something in a series of small stages

circuit

a circuit-breaker
an event that breaks the tension in a dispute

refers to electrical circuits

closet

a skeleton in the closet
an unpleasant truth the knowledge of which has been deliberately suppressed

William Makepeace Thackeray (1811–63), *The Newcomes* (1855), ' ... they have a skelton or two in their closets as well as their neighbours'

to come out of the closet
to admit publicly one's homosexuality

corner

to back someone into a corner
to leave a person no option

to be around the corner
to be imminent

to be in a tight corner
to have little or no chance of escape from a difficult situation

to turn the corner
to commence being successful after initial failures

corners

to cut corners
to lower one's standards in order to complete something more quickly

cracks

to fall between the cracks
to be ineligible for something because one does not fit neatly into any of several relevant categories

to slip through the cracks
to be overlooked

door

a foot in the door
the opportunity to do business

never darken my door again
do not ever return

refers to the shadow cast by a person's presence in a doorway

not to break someone's door down

to be unenthusiastic about someone's goods or services

one's door is always open
people can take their problems to one at any time

through the back door
unofficially or surreptitiously

to be out the door
to have one's position terminated

to beat a path to someone's door
to seek a person out in great numbers
Ralph Waldo Emerson (1803–82), *Sarah S. B. Yule, Borrowings*, 'If a man write a better book, preach a better sermon, or make a better mouse-trap than his neighbour, tho' he build his house in the woods, the world will make a beaten path to his door'

to close the door on someone
to deny another person a desired opportunity

to keep the wolf from the door
to struggle to survive (esp. with respect to hunger)

to leave the door open
to provide an opportunity

to put something at someone's door
to blame a person

to show someone the door
to ask a person to leave

to shut the door on someone
to deny another person a desired opportunity

to shut the stable door after the horse has bolted
to take preventive action only after the relevant event

to slam the door in someone's face
ostentatiously to refuse to have any dealings with a person

doors

the doors of the Ritz are open to all
despite rhetoric to the contrary wealthy people have many advantages over poor people
refers to the Ritz Hotel, London, founded in 1906 by César Ritz

to knock on doors
to seek out opportunities

to open doors
to create opportunities

doorstep

on one's own doorstep
in one's own domain

drain

that is money down the drain
money has been wastefully lost on a failed project

drawbridge

to pull up the drawbridge
defensively to withdraw and refuse to cooperate'
refers to the drawbridge over a defensive moat around a castle

drawing

back to the drawing board
to start again from the very beginning

to be on the drawing board
to be being planned from the very beginning

dust

when the dust settles
when sufficient time has passed to allow matters to be perceived clearly

eavesdrop

to eavesdrop
deliberately to listen to conversations to which one is not a party
originally — by standing beneath the eaves of a house; James Shirley (1596–1666), 'It is not civil to eavesdrop him'

fence

that person has some palings off the fence
that person is mentally disturbed

on our side of the fence
in the group representing our vested interest

to be on the other side of the fence
to have an opposing point of view or position

to be over the fence
to be unreasonable

to sit on the fence
to refuse to choose between two alternatives

fences

to mend fences
to achieve a reconciliation

floor

to get in on the ground floor
to invest on very favourable terms

to hold the floor
to dominate a conversation

to wipe the floor with someone
to inflict a humiliating defeat on a person

framework

framework
outline of a proposal, upon which further details can be developed

garden

everything in the garden is lovely
everything is fine
Genesis 2:8–9, 'And the Lord God planted a garden ... to grow every tree that is pleasant to the sight'

gate

to close the gate
to deny an opportunity that was previously available

gatecrash

to gatecrash a gathering
to attend a gathering without any right to be there

gatepost

between you and me and the gatepost
confidentially

gateway

gateway to something
method of achieving something

glass

glass ceiling
an unstated but definite limit (resulting from prejudice) to promotion in employment

grain

something goes against the grain
something is completely and frustratingly against a person's inclination
refers to woodworking

Hall

Liberty Hall
a place where one is free to do as one wishes
Oliver Goldsmith (1730–74), *She Stoops to Conquer* ii, 'This is Liberty Hall gentlemen'

one can't beat City Hall
the ordinary citizen is powerless against bureaucracy

hammer

to go hammer and tongs
to do something with great energy
refers to energetic work of a blacksmith

hole

a square peg in a round hole
obviously unsuited for the purpose'

home

charity begins at home
a person's first responsibility should be to that person's family
John Fletcher (1579–1625), *The Wild-Goose Chase*, 'Charity and beating begins at home'

nothing to write home about
unimpressive

to be too close to home
to be too near the truth to be welcome

to bring a fact home to someone
to make a person recognise a fact despite that person's inclination to the contrary

to keep the home fires burning
to maintain normal domestic activity during the temporary absence of the main provider of the household

house

a halfway house
an intermediate position
refers to an inn situated situated halfway between two towns on a journey

a madhouse
an organisation in great turmoil
John Clare (1793–1864) *The Exile*, 'madhouses, prisons, whoreshops'; and *Letter*, 'Dear Sir, I am in a madhouse and quite forget your name and who you are'

to be on the house
to be free of cost

to bring the house down
to obtain rapturous applause
refers to the theatre

to eat someone out of house and home
to ruin a person by eating all that that person has
used in an exaggerated, humorous sense

to put one's house in order

to fix up the deficiencies in one's affairs
Isaiah 38:1, 'Set thine house in order; for thou shalt die and not live'

to eat someone out of house and home
to ruin a person by eating all that that person has
used in an exaggerated, humorous sense

household
a household name
a very familiar name

houses
people in glass houses should not throw stones
those who are less than perfect are foolish to criticise others
John 8:7, 'He that is without sin among you, let him first cast a stone at her' (refers to ancient condemnation and punishment of people by stoning)

inn
no room at the inn
no available space
Luke 2:7, 'She [Mary] brought forth her firstborn son, and wrapped him in swaddling clothes, and laid him in a manger; because there was no room for them in the inn'

kid
to be the new kid on the block
to lack the experience of others

kitchen
if one can't stand the heat one should stay out of the kitchen
if one cannot put up with the pressure of a situation, one should get out of it
US President Harry S. Truman (1884–1972), *Mr Citizen*, ch. 15, 'If you can't stand the heat, get out of the kitchen'

to get the rounds of the kitchen
(of a husband) to be subject to personal abuse by his wife

ladder
rungs up a ladder
gradual steps to an ultimate goal

to be at the bottom of the ladder
to be in the most junior position in some hierarchy

ladders
a game of snakes and ladders
a series of ups and downs
refers to a board game

laundry
a laundry list
a large set of demands

level
to be on the level
to be honest
a term derived from freemasonry

lock
to lock someone into some arrangement
to create an agreement which cannot be broken by one of the parties

marble
to be carved in marble
to be virtually unalterable

nail
on the nail
immediately
origin obscure

to hit the nail right on the head
astutely to come to the correct conclusion

to nail a lie
to expose an untruth

to nail someone
to fix the blame on a person; to convict; to secure

to nail something down
to define something precisely

niche
to carve out a niche for oneself
deliberately to create an opportunity to use one's talents effectively

to find one's niche
to find the opportunity to use one's talents

nook
in every nook and cranny
everywhere

nuts
nuts and bolts
basic ingredients

paint
to paint oneself into a corner

foolishly to put oneself into a position from which escape is impossible

paper

to paper over the cracks
to institute extremely superficial and basically ineffective remedies
refers to placing wallpaper over cracks in a wall

path

slippery path
dangerous course of action

to be on a path strewn with roses
to lead a very pleasant life

to beat a path to someone's door
to seek a person out in great numbers
Ralph Waldo Emerson (1803–82), *Sarah S. B. Yule, Borrowings*, 'If a man write a better book, preach a better sermon, or make a better mouse-trap than his neighbour, tho' he build his house in the woods, the world will make a beaten path to his door'

to block someone's path
to interfere with a person's opportunity to advance

to cross someone's path
to meet another person by chance

to lead someone up the garden path
to mislead a person by deliberately fallacious arguments

to smooth the path for someone
to use one's influence to make arrangements so that a person's task will be easier or more readily accomplished
Isaiah 40:3, 'Prepare ye the way of the Lord; make smooth in the desert a highway for our God'

to tread a particular path
to follow a certain (perhaps new or lonely) course of action

peg

a square peg in a round hole
obviously unsuited for the purpose'

penny

the penny dropped
a person has just realised a fact that should have been obvious
refers to old-fashioned pay toilets

pillar

a pillar of some organisation
a significant supporter of some organisation

putty

to be putty in someone's hands
to be far too easily influenced by another person
refers to material able to be fashioned into various shapes

riveted

to be riveted to one's seat
to find the activity being watched very exciting and worthy of full attention

rock

bedrock price
lowest possible price

roof

the roof has fallen in
an enterprise has collapsed

to go through the roof
(of a person) to be very upset; OR (of prices) to escalate greatly

to hit the roof
to be very angry

to throw a few stones on the roof and see who comes out
to attempt to change a boring situation or resolve a stalemate

under one roof
under the same management; OR in the same building

rooftops

to scream something from the rooftops
to communicate a message to a wide audience

screw

to have a screw loose
to be mentally unbalanced

to tighten the screw
to increase the moral and psychological pressure

shingle

to hang up one's shingle
to go into business offering expert personal services
refers to an external notice advertising one's name and qualifications

sink

everything but the kitchen sink

virtually all things

sledgehammer

to use a sledgehammer to crack a nut

to devote vastly more resources to a project than is warranted by all the circumstances

stables

a Herculean cleaning of the stables

a thorough revision of operating procedure

refers to the labours of Hercules (Heracles in Greek) who had twelve labours imposed upon him by Eurystheus — one of which was the cleaning of the stables of King Augeas in a single day

steamroll

to steamroll something through

to use enormous force to achieve an objective

refers to a steamroller — a large earth-flattening machine

stone

cornerstone

key ingredient

tacks

to get down to brass tacks

to discuss the aspects that really matter

perhaps refers to Cockney rhyming slang ('brass tacks' = 'facts')

tools

tools

the means to do something

a metaphor in transition; used both literally and figuratively — a writer's tools, for example, include a pen (lit.) and a dictionary (fig.)

tower

a tower of Babel

a noisy and confused assembly

Genesis 11:9, 'Therefore is the name of it called Babel; because the Lord did there confound the language of all the earth' (from which the word 'babble' is also derived)

to be a tower of strength

to be a person who supports and comforts another

to be in an ivory tower

to be immersed in theoretical considerations and ignorant of the practical realities

Song of Solomon 7:4, 'Thy neck is as a tower of ivory'

trowel

to lay it on with a trowel

to flatter, eulogise, or otherwise make comment in an excessive manner

Shakespeare, *As You Like It* I:ii, 'Well said; that was laid on with a trowel'

tunnel

tunnel vision

an extremely narrow and inflexible way of considering issues

wall

a chink in the wall

an opportunity to do something that otherwise could not be done

I would love to be a fly on the wall

I would love to observe what goes on without those under observation being aware of my presence

to bang one's head against a brick wall

to fight an unwinnable case

to be a crack in the wall

to represent a small opportunity that can be exploited

to be up against a brick wall

to be unable to achieve anything because of intractable opposition or apathy

to drive someone to the wall

to ruin a person

to drive someone up the wall

by one's actions, to cause extreme annoyance to the point of desperation

to go to the wall

to become bankrupt

to have one's back to the wall

to be hard-pressed by creditors or opponents

to nail someone to the wall

to outmanoeuvre and trap someone

to put a wall around someone

to stop a person associating with others

to see the writing on the wall

to appreciate the inevitability of some event

Daniel 5:5ff, 'A man's hand ... wrote ... upon the plaister of the wall of the king's palace ... thou art weighed in the balances and art found wanting'

walls

Chinese walls
a system to ensure that different parts of some organisation do not gain access to each other's confidential information

walls of Jericho
something seemingly solid but actually destructible
Joshua 6:20, 'When the priests blew with the trumpets ... the wall fell down flat'

walls have ears
someone may be overhearing
words on wartime posters, reminding people of the existence of spies; might also refer to certain rooms in the Louvre, constructed so that conversations could be heard in other rooms

way

to pave the way
to prepare for something

wedge

to be the thin end of the wedge
to be a small action or thing that has the potential to cause much larger undesirable consequences
refers to wedges used for splitting wood

to drive a wedge between two persons
to set out to cause a division between two persons
refers to the use of wedges in timber work

whitewash

to whitewash
to attempt to conceal the guilt or mistakes of a person
refers to the use of whitewash on a wall to conceal blemishes

windmills

to tilt at windmills
to attack an imagined but non-existent enemy
refers to Cervantes' *Don Quixote* Pt I Ch VIII, in which the hero assumes that windmills are giants and gives battle

window

a window of opportunity
an opportunity temporarily available

to engage in window dressing
to present someone or something in a falsely favourable light
refers to displays in shop windows

to fly out the window
to become irretrievably and wastefully lost

to throw a pebble against the window
gently to draw attention to oneself

to throw something out of the window
to reject completely an idea or proposal

yardstick

a yardstick
a standard by which something is measured
refers to a stick used for measuring a yard in distance

Cards

ace

to be within an ace of something
to be extremely close to something
from Latin *as* ('unity', that is 'one' or 'a single point')

to have an ace up one's sleeve
to hold an impressive counter-argument in reserve
refers to card games; from Latin *as* ('unity', that is 'one' or 'a single point')

aces

to hold all the aces
to be in an unbeatable position to defeat others
refers to playing cards; from Latin *as* ('unity', that is 'one' or 'a single point')

buck

the buck stops here
I accept full responsibility
hand-lettered sign on desk of US President Harry S. Truman (Phillips, *The Truman Presidency*, Ch. 12)

to pass the buck
to shift responsibility to someone else

refers to the buckhorn knife passed around the table to indicate the dealer while playing poker

card

a three-card trick
an extremely simple yet effective ruse used by a dishonest person to induce victims to hand over some of their assets

a wild card
(in general) an unexpected unpredictable development; OR (in playing cards) a card of a value specified by the player holding it; OR (in sport) a player or a team given entrance to a competition by the organisers, even if the entry is not strictly merited; OR (in computing) a character that will match any other character in a search string

to have a card up one's sleeve
secretly to have information relevant to a transaction
refers to card games

to hold the trump card
to be in an unbeatable position to defeat others
refers to playing cards

to play every card in the pack
to try very hard and use every conceivable argument
refers to playing cards

to play the last card in the pack
to be forced to use one's last expedient
refers to playing cards

to play the trump card
to make a final move, thereby defeating one's opponents
refers to playing cards

cards

a house of cards
an organisation that gives a misleading impression of solidity

let the cards fall where they may
irrespective of what happens
refers to playing cards

to be on the cards
to be likely

to have the cards stacked against one
to be faced with many difficulties frustrating a project
refers to playing cards

to hold all the cards
to be assured of victory
refers to playing cards

to hold one's cards close to one's chest
to keep one's plans and strategies secret
refers to playing cards

to lay one's cards on the table
to be utterly frank and open or to honestly disclose one's position
refers to playing cards

to play one's cards right
to approach a matter sensibly
refers to playing cards

to play the cards as they fall
to deal with problems as they arise
refers to playing cards

without any cards to play
without the means to achieve something
refers to playing cards

chip

to be a blue-chip stock
to be of excellent quality

to chip in
to contribute financially

chips

bargaining chips
benefits that can be conceded in negotiations to obtain some advantage

that is the way the chips fall
that is the way that the benefits and detriments are distributed after an event

to have had one's chips
to have received all that is going to be forthcoming

to turn one's chips in
to convert one's assets or entitlements into cash

when the chips are down
when all facts are known and taken into consideration

dealer

sharp dealer
person engaging in barely honest or mildly unethical practices
refers to poker

hand

to deal the final hand
to take steps that conclude a matter
refers to playing cards

to disclose one's hand
to give away information regarding one's intention
refers to playing cards

to force someone's hand
to take action causing another person to react
refers to playing cards

to hold a winning hand
to be in an unbeatable position to defeat others
refers to playing cards

to throw in one's hand
to give in or to give up
refers to playing cards

to tip one's hand
to disclose details of one's position
refers to playing cards

misPre

to be a laid-down misPre
to be very easily accomplished and/or to be certain of outcome
refers to card playing where one player undertakes not to win any tricks while playing with the disadvantage of having that player's cards exposed to observation by others

odds

to have the odds stacked against one
to be faced with many difficulties frustrating a project
refers to betting

pegging

to be level pegging
(of contestants) to have little between them
refers to cribbage

poker

a game of poker
negotiations in which the parties try to bluff each other
refers to playing cards

a poker face
a facial expression that does not reveal one's thoughts during negotiations
refers to playing cards

showdown

showdown
a final test or confrontation after declaring one's position
refers to poker

spades

delivered in spades
to a considerable degree; in large numbers

suit

one's long suit
one's main skills
refers to playing cards

to follow suit
to do the same as others
refers to playing cards

trick

something has done the trick
something has achieved the desired purpose
refers to playing cards

to be unable to take a trick
to be unable to achieve success in anything
refers to playing cards

trump

to hold the trump card
to be in an unbeatable position to defeat others
refers to playing cards

to play the trump card
to make a final move, thereby defeating one's opponents
refers to playing cards

to trump someone
to defeat a person
refers to playing cards

trumps

to turn up trumps
to finish up better than expected or to experience unexpected good luck
refers to playing cards

underplay

to underplay some situation
to make something seem less significant than it is
refers to playing cards

Chess

checkmate

checkmate

defeat

refers to chess

chess

to be a chess game

to be a complex, skilful exercise involving moves and countermoves

chessmaster

a chessmaster

a clever strategist

gambit

a gambit

(in a competitive situation) an opening move that involves short-term losses in the expectation of long-term gains

Italian *gambetto*, literally 'tripping up'

opening gambit

the first in a series of strategic moves

usually refers to chess (see also *gambit*); Italian *gambetto*, literally 'tripping up'

knight

a white knight

a person voluntarily coming to the assistance of another person at considerable personal cost

derived from mediaeval tales of valiant knights rescuing those in distress, white being associated with purity and goodness

move

your move!

the next step is up to you

refers to chess and similar games

pawn

a pawn

a person of small importance who is manipulated by others

from Old French *poön*, *peon* ('foot soldier'); now applied to the smallest piece on the chess board

stalemate

stalemate

a final result in which neither party to a dispute is victorious

refers to chess

zugzwang

zugzwang

a disadvantageous action being forced on one

chess term: German, *Zug* move + *Zwang* 'compulsion, obligation' = a compulsory move

Circuses

Aunt

an Aunt Sally

a person who can readily be singled out and criticised as the proxy for a group

refers to an old game in which objects were thrown at the figure of the head of a woman

balls

to have too many balls in the air

to attempt to do more than can be coped with

refers to juggling

card

to have a card up one's sleeve

secretly to have information relevant to a transaction

refers to card games

cards

to be on the cards

to be likely

circus

to be a real circus

to be a highly disorganised affair

conjure

to conjure up a picture

to use words to convey a vivid impression

to conjure up something

to produce something in circumstances where this seemed impossible

hoops

to jump through hoops

to be required to perform or undergo some ordeal

refers to circus performance

line

to tread a fine/thin line

cautiously to take action in circumstances where either too much or too little will cause difficulties

magic

the magic moment
the perfect time

there is no magic in that
that is quite ordinary

to wave a magic wand
to direct affairs without the restraints of the real world

merry

to be on a merry-go-round
to be a circular exercise ending in no definite result

to lead someone a merry dance
to mislead a person
refers to the complex dances of earlier centuries when one person led another through complex steps

net

a safety-net scheme
a scheme for dealing with the exceptional cases not covered by normal arrangements

pull

to pull a rabbit out of the hat
to produce an unexpected and seemingly miraculous but highly desirable solution
refers to magician's trick

roller

a roller-coaster ride
a series of successes followed by failures

sleight

sleight of hand
deceit by trickery
Daniel Defoe (1660–1731), 'All the artifice and sleight of hand they were masters of'

spotlight

to steal the spotlight
to become the centre of attention
refers to the theatre

to turn the spotlight on something
to draw public attention to something

swings

what one loses on the swings one gains on the roundabouts
there are advantages and disadvantages that offset each other
Patrick Reginald Chalmers (1872–1942), *Green Days and Blue Days: Roundabouts and Swings*, 'what's lost upon the roundabouts we pulls up on the swings!'

tightrope

to walk a tightrope
to do something very dangerous in which one cannot afford to deviate from the required course of action

trick

a pea-and-thimble trick
a clever fraud committed in the presence of its victim without this being obvious at the time
refers to a sleight-of-hand trick played with three thimbles and a pea, the thimbles being moved about and observers being asked to guess under which thimble the pea is

a three-card trick
an extremely simple yet effective ruse used by a dishonest person to induce victims to hand over some of their assets

to use every trick in the book
to try very hard and use every conceivable argument

tricks

a whole bag of tricks
a series of articles or a series of artificial devices

one cannot teach an old dog new tricks
people become set in their ways irreversibly

wand

to wave a magic wand
to direct affairs without the restraints of the real world

Clothes

apron

to be tied to someone's apron strings
to be excessively influenced by one's mother

belt

a belt-and-braces approach
action backing up other action by way of excessive caution
refers to wearing a belt as well as braces

to get something under one's belt
to add to one's experience by achieving something worthwhile

to hit someone below the belt
to act unfairly towards another person
refers to boxing

to tighten one's belt
to lower one's rate of spending

bonnet

to have a bee in one's bonnet
to have an obsession

boot

the boot is on the other foot
the advantage is reversed

to give someone the boot
to terminate a person's appointment

to put the boot in
to issue a severe (possibly sadistic) reprimand to a person

boots

to be too big for one's boots
to have an unwarranted belief in one's capabilities or status

to go in boots and all
to do something very roughly
refers to fighting violently

to hang up one's boots
to retire

to have one's heart in one's boots
to be afraid or dejected

to lick someone's boots
to show humility

to quake in one's boots
to be afraid

bootstraps

to be British to one's bootstraps
to be very demonstrative about one's Britishness

to pull oneself up by one's bootstraps
to make a praiseworthy effort to better oneself unaided

breeches

to be too big for one's breeches
to have an exaggerated idea of one's own importance

cap

a feather in one's cap
a meritorious personal achievement
refers to the practice in a number of cultures of adding a feather to the headgear of a person in recognition of a significant personal achievement

cap
upper permitted limit

if the cap fits then wear it
if that description corresponds with your characteristics, then you are in that category

to cap a story
to tell an even funnier story than the one just told

to earn a dunce's cap
to do something stupid
a 'dunce' being derived from the name of Duns Scotus (1265–1308) and his followers ('Dunsers') whose hair-splitting theology was later perceived to be opposed to learning and enlightenment; Thomas Fuller (1608–61), 'a dunce, void of learning but full of books'

to go cap in hand
to show humility while soliciting a favour

to put one's thinking cap on
to concentrate on finding a solution to a difficult problem

to set one's cap at someone
(of females) to try to attract a person as a marriage partner

to throw one's cap into the air
to express joy; OR to celebrate some achievement

cloak

cloak-and-dagger activity
secret activity
originally referred to as 'cloak-and-sword' comedies (Spanish: *comedias de capa y espada*) — plays by seventeenth-century Spanish dramatists involving swashbuckling adventure; later adapted to refer to intrigue and secrecy ('cloak and dagger')

to cloak something
to disguise the true nature of something

clothes

to steal someone's clothes
to plagiarise another person's ideas

clothing

to be a wolf in sheep's clothing
to be a hypocrite; to be dangerous although masquerading as something harmless

Matthew 7:15, 'Beware of false prophets, which come to you in sheep's clothing, but inwardly they are ravening wolves'

coat

to cut one's coat according to the cloth
to accommodate oneself to limitations beyond one's control and to do the best in the circumstances

coat-tails

to hang onto someone's coat-tails
to rely excessively on another's initiatives and achievements

to trail one's coat-tails
to invite a quarrel

refers to old Irish custom of trailing one's coat inviting a fight with anyone bold enough deliberately to tread on one's coat-tails

collar

to be hot under the collar
to be very agitated

cuff

off the cuff
impromptu

perhaps refers to notes scribbled on the shirt cuff for use during a speech

dress

dress rehearsal
a preliminary practice or experience before the real thing

to dress someone down
to scold a person

dressed

first in best dressed
persons acting early will do better than latecomers

to be dressed to kill
to be very smartly dressed with the intention of making a striking impression — usually with a view to a romantic or sexual conquest

to be dressed up to the nines
to be attired in garments of the highest standard

perhaps a corruption of 'to then eyen' ('to the eyes'); Thomas Hardy (1840–1928), 'She's dressed up to the nines for some grand party'

to be mutton dressed up as lamb
foolishly to pretend to be younger

garters

I will have that person's guts for garters
I am extremely angry and dissatisfied with that person

gauntlet

to throw down the gauntlet
to issue a challenge

refers to the glove worn by a knight; OFr *gantelet* (diminutive of 'glove')

glove

to work hand in glove with someone
to work in close cooperation with a person or to be in collusion with a person to the detriment of others

with an iron hand in a velvet glove
with a hard attitude made to seem soft

gloves

the gloves are off
there are now no restrictions on how we resolve our differences

refers to bare-knuckle fighting before the introduction of the 'Marquis of Queensberry rules'

to take off the gloves
to fight mercilessly or to debate with great ferocity

refers to bare-knuckle fighting before the introduction of the 'Marquis of Queensberry rules'

to treat someone with kid gloves
to handle a person with great discretion

refers to very soft leather gloves made from the skin of young goats

guernsey

stick it up your guernsey!
I have absolutely no interest in you and what you saying!

refers to the jumpers worn by members of football teams

to get a guernsey

to be given the opportunity to do something
refers to the jumpers worn by members of football teams

hat

a peg to hang a hat on
something that provides a convenient or plausible excuse for some particular action

at the drop of a hat
very readily
from the practice of signalling the beginning of a race or fight with the drop of a hat

I'll eat my hat if so-and-so happens
I do not believe that so-and-so will happen

not to just pick something out of a hat
to choose carefully, after weighing all the considerations
refers to choosing by lot by choosing things unseen from a hat

to be old hat
to be old-fashioned; OR well known to the point of tedium

to keep something under one's hat
to maintain a confidence

to knock something into a cocked hat
to defeat easily in a game or contest of skill
refers to a game of nine-pins in which the pins were arranged in a triangle like a cocked hat

to pull a rabbit out of the hat
to produce an unexpected and seemingly miraculous but highly desirable solution
refers to magician's trick

to score a hat trick
to have three successive favourable outcomes
refers to a bowler in cricket taking three wickets in three balls; such a feat being originally rewarded with the prize of a new hat

to take one's hat off to someone
to be full of admiration for a person
refers to deferential gesture of removing one's hat

to talk through one's hat
to say things that demonstrate the speaker's ignorance of the subject

to throw one's cap/hat into the air
to express joy; OR to celebrate some achievement

to throw one's hat into the ring
publicly to announce one's interest in some position
refers to custom of throwing one's hat into a ring to indicate a willingness to take part in a boxing challenge

to wear a particular hat
to act in a particular capacity or for a particular vested interest

hats

to buy straw hats in winter
to buy in a depressed market when most other people are sellers

iron

to iron out something
to sort out a difficult problem

jacket

to keep someone in a strait jacket
to deny a person any discretionary powers at all
refers to a restraining 'jacket' used to control violent or insane persons

knickers

to get one's knickers in a knot
to become unduly excited

lace

strait-laced
puritanical
refers to the wearing of a very tightly laced bodice or other garment

linen

to wash one's dirty linen in public
to expose one's embarrassing domestic affairs to the world at large'

mantle

to assume someone's mantle
to take over another person's role
refers to the passing of Elijah's mantle to Elisha: *2Kings* 2:13, 'He took up also the mantle of Elijah that fell from him … '

mask

to unmask someone
to reveal a person's true identity

nightie

to be off like a bride's nightie

to act promptly

pants

a kick in the pants
an admonition

to bore the pants off someone
to weary a person by dull and uninteresting conversation

to catch someone with his pants down
to act when another person least expects it

to charm the pants off someone
to delight a person

to fly by the seat of one's pants
to act by instinct in the absence of specific knowledge or instructions

to scare the pants off someone
to frighten a person greatly

to wear the pants
to be the dominant party

petticoat

petticoat government
rule by women

pin

not to care a pin for something
not to have the slightest interest in something

pin money
an allowance to a wife for her personal use
probably refers to money for purchase of hair pins and other decorative pins

to be able to hear a pin drop
to experience silence

pinpoint

to pinpoint
to identify very precisely

pins

for two pins I would do so-and-so
my tolerance is almost exhausted and I am very tempted to do so-and-so

to be on pins and needles
to be very agitated

pocket

the hip-pocket nerve
the assessment of issues by their financial effects on one

to be in someone's pocket
to be subject to undue influence by another person

to be out of pocket
to have lost money in a transaction

to have money burning a hole in one's pocket
to be impatient to spend or invest available funds

to put one's hand in one's pocket
to provide money from one's own resources, especially for a charitable purpose

pockets

not to live in each other's pockets
to each follow his or her own lifestyle

to have deep pockets
to have large financial resources and to be willing to use them if the circumstances seem right

to line one's pockets
to make, improperly and secretly, a profit out of some transaction

purse

one can't make a silk purse out of a sow's ear
it is impossible to manufacture something of a high standard from inferior raw materials
Malcolm Bradbury (1932–), 'For the mass of men, you can't make a silk purse out of a sow's ear'

to button up one's purse
to refuse to spend money

to hold the purse strings
to have control of expenditure
refers to a drawstring closing a purse

to tighten the purse strings
to reduce outlays
refers to a drawstring closing a purse

pyjamas

to be the cat's pyjamas
to be the very best, to be superlatively good
American slang (origin obscure)

sackcloth

to wear sackcloth and ashes
humbly to demonstrate repentance
Esther 4:3, 'There was great mourning ... and many lay in sackcloth and ashes'

seams

to be bursting at the seams
to be very crowded

to come apart at the seams

(of an arrangement) to break down

seamless

seamless
unified, continuous, uninterrupted, imperceptible
John 19: 23, ' ... and also his [Jesus'] coat; now the coat was seamless, woven from the top throughout'

sew

to sew something up
to negotiate a deal

shirt

keep your shirt on!
relax!
refers to removing a shirt in preparation for a fight

so-and-so would give you the shirt off his or her back
so-and-so is very generous
Luke 6:29 (RSV), ' ... and from him who takes away your coat do not withhold even your shirt'

to lose one's shirt
to make heavy financial losses
Luke 6:29 (RSV), ' ... and from him who takes away your coat do not withhold even your shirt'

to put one's shirt on something
to invest heavily in some speculative venture
Luke 6:29 (RSV), ' ... and from him who takes away your coat do not withhold even your shirt'

to wear a hair shirt
to practise self-discipline
refers to a shirt worn next to the skin by ascetics and penitent persons

shoe

if the shoe fits then wear it
if a general proposition describes your specific circumstances, then consider that it applies to you

to know where the shoe pinches
to realise from personal experience what the cause of some problem really is

to wait for the other shoe to drop
to await the seemingly imminent and inevitable
refers to a person being disturbed by a neighbour who drops one shoe on the floor, the listener then being frustrated when the sound of the other shoe being dropped is not heard

shoelaces

to pull oneself up by one's own shoelaces
to make a superhuman effort

shoes

to be in someone's shoes
to have another person's responsibility

to fill someone's shoes
to be a good successor

to tremble in one's shoes
to be afraid

shoestring

to do something on a shoestring
to do something with great economy

skirts

to hide under someone's skirts
to let someone else take the consequences of one's actions
refers to childish seeking for protection

sleeve

to have a card up one's sleeve
secretly to have information relevant to a transaction
refers to card games

to have an ace up one's sleeve
to hold an impressive counter-argument in reserve
refers to card games; from Latin *as* ('unity', that is 'one' or 'a single point')

to keep something up one's sleeve
secretly to retain something in reserve for use in the future or at a later stage of negotiations
refers to playing cards or magicians

to laugh up one's sleeve
to laugh surreptitiously

to wear one's heart on one's sleeve
to lack the reserve expected of one
refers to the fashion of wearing a sign of romantic attachment on one's sleeve; Shakespeare *Othello* I:i, 'But I will wear my heart upon my sleeve'

sleeves

to roll up one's sleeves
to get on with a job energetically

slip

to show one's slip

to reveal details which one meant to keep private
refers to women's petticoats

socks
to chop someone off at the socks
to stop someone's proposals prematurely
to pull one's socks up
to set out to improve or correct one's inadequate behaviour or performance
wouldn't it rot your socks!
what an unpleasant surprise!

stitch
a stitch in time saves nine
preventive maintenance saves money in the long run
to stitch up a deal
successfully to conclude a deal

suit
he wouldn't give you the shine off his suit
he is very mean

thread
the thread
the connecting link of a set of arguments
to hang by a slender thread
to be in a precarious situation
refers to Damocles who had the sword of Dionysius hanging, by a slender thread, over his head — as a symbol of perpetual risk in life; the story is told in Cicero, *Tusculanae Disputationes*

trousers
to catch someone with his trousers down
to act when another person least expects it
to wear the trousers
to be the dominant party

try
to try something on for size
cheekily to do something

turncoat
a turncoat
a person changing sides
refers to the practice of mercenary soldiers switching to the winning side and displaying that side's colours by turning their coats inside out

umbrella
an umbrella
protection; or something all-embracing
under the umbrella of some organisation
under the auspices of some organisation

unveil
to unveil something
to give details not previously available

veil
to draw a veil over something
pointedly to avoid discussing something
to unveil something
to give details not previously available
under the veil of something
on the pretext of something

veiled
thinly veiled
barely concealed

wash
it will all come out in the wash
the facts will emerge as work proceeds
it won't wash
this explanation is not acceptable
when the wash comes through the machine
in due course

wear
to have to wear something
to have to put up with something

wearing
that argument is wearing a bit thin
that case has been heard so often that it is losing its effect
refers to clothes or similar beginning to fail from continued use

wears
uneasy lies the head that wears a crown
leadership involves some risks and some burdens (esp. the risk of being deposed)
Shakespeare, *Henry IV*, Part 2, III:i, 'Uneasy lies the head that wears a crown'

Colours

black

a black hole

a place where things disappear without trace; OR an intermediate range of values producing anomalous results; OR a particularly obnoxious prison cell

the first and second definitions refer to an astronomical black hole — an area of extreme density from which even light cannot escape; the third definition refers to the infamous 'black hole of Calcutta'

a black sheep

a disreputable member of an otherwise reputable group

in black and white

in writing, spelling out all the details

Ben Jonson (1573–1637), *Every Man in his Honour*, 'I have it here in black and white'

the pot calling the kettle black

criticising another person without realising one's own even greater shortcomings

there are black clouds on the horizon

bad news is expected

things look black

there is little hope of success or prosperity or a favourable outcome

to be a black-and-white issue

to involve very clear distinctions

Ben Jonson (1573–1637), *Every Man in his Honour*, 'I have it here in black and white'

to be black magic

to lack any scientific or logical basis

refers to witchcraft

to be in someone's black books

to be out of favour with a person

biblical allusion: refers to God's judgment and the desirability of having one's name entered in the book of life; *Rev* 20: 12, 'and the books were opened ... and the dead were judged out of those things that were written in the books, according to their works'

to be in the black

to have money

refers to the black ink used to indicate a credit in a manuscript accounting ledger

to blackball someone

to reject a person as unsuitable

refers to a vote against someone by secretly placing a black ball in a box (as opposed to a white or red ball which indicated approval); the voting procedure was common in ancient Rome and Greece — hence 'ballot' (French, *ballotte*, 'a little ball')

to give someone a black look

to indicate one's displeasure with a person

to have a black mark against one's name

to have a tarnished reputation

to paint a black picture

to state a set of unfavourable factors

to paint someone black

to ruin a person's reputation

blue

a blueblood

a person of high birth

refers to the appearance of the blood of certain Spanish noble families — supposed to be more of a blue colour due to a lack of Moorish blood

blue ribbon

of superb quality

refers to the insignia of the Order of the Garter, or perhaps to the ribands used in agricultural shows and at race meetings

blue sky

unrealistic optimism

blue-eyed boy

person shown unjustified favouritism

once in a blue moon

very rarely

refers to the volcanic eruption at Krakatoa in 1883 when volcanic dust caused the moon to appear blue

to be a blue-chip stock

to be of excellent quality

to be a bolt from the blue

to be a totally unexpected event

to be between the devil and the deep blue sea

to be faced with two equally unpalatable alternatives that cannot both be avoided

to be in a blue funk

to be terrified

to come out of the blue

to be totally unexpected

to feel blue
to feel depressed
to go on until one is blue in the face
to do something difficult for a long time without being able to complete it
to have a blue fit
to be very agitated
to scream blue murder
to make serious allegations; OR to protest violently
perhaps refers to the French *morbleu* (altered version of *mort Dieu*, 'God's death'), a comic oath attributed to French speakers
true blue
superbly loyal
refers to the traditional blue colour of the Conservative Party in the UK

blueprint
blueprint
a master plan for some activity or a model that others can copy
refers to a detailed architectural or engineering drawing — originally consisting of white lines on a blue background

browned
to be browned off
to be fed up

colour
that is a horse of a very different colour
that is a different matter altogether
Shakespeare, *Twelfth Night*, 'My purpose is, indeed, a horse of that colour'
that takes on added colour
there are now further facts that alter the appearance of a matter
to see the colour of someone's eyes
to see how a person matches expectations or requirements
to see the colour of someone's money
to get evidence of the sincerity of a person's proposal

colours
to nail one's colours to the mast
publicly to declare one's position and to maintain it in the face of criticism
nautical metaphor
to pass with flying colours
to be very successful in a test or contest
refers to ships returning to port with colours flying triumphantly
to sail under false colours
to pretend that one's real character or beliefs are different from what they really are
refers to a ship concealing its true identity
to show one's true colours
to disclose one's real character or beliefs
naval metaphor

gild
to gild the lily
to add superfluous ornamentation to something already beautiful
Shakespeare *King John* IV:i, 'to gild refined gold, to paint the lily'

gilt
gilt-edged
very safe
nineteenth century; refers to certificates for government stock that were printed with a gold edging
to take the gilt off the gingerbread
to strip something of its main attraction

gold
a pot of gold
wealth, especially a reward long wished-for
a rich vein of gold
much useful information; a good source of something desirable
all that glisters/glitters is not gold
things are not always what they seem
Shakespeare, *Merchant of Venice*, II:vii, 'All that glisters is not gold'
to be a river of gold
to be a source of ongoing great profitability
to be worth one's weight in gold
to be very valuable or useful
to go for the gold
to aim for victory
refers to Olympic medals
to have a heart of gold
to have a generous disposition
Hilaire Belloc (1870–1953), 'With hearts of gold and lungs of bronze'

to seek the pot of gold at the end of the rainbow
to have naVve expectations
refers to the proverbial belief in the existence of a pot of gold at the end of a rainbow

to strike gold
to have one's efforts suddenly rewarded by great success
refers to gold-mining

golden

golden handshake
a large payment in connection with, or as an inducement to, retirement

golden mean
a moderate compromise between two extremes
from mathematics: the division of a straight line into two portions so that the ratio of the smaller to the larger equals the ratio of the larger to the whole

golden opportunity
an unparalleled chance or occasion

golden parachute
(in a remuneration package) generous provisions that come into play in certain circumstances

golden shackles
financial arrangements designed to discourage employees changing from one employer to another

silence is golden
peace and quiet is valued; it is better to keep one's own counsel
Swiss proverb, 'speech is silvern; silence is golden' (quoted by Thomas Carlyle (1795–1881)

to kill the goose that lays the golden eggs
through excessive greed, to sacrifice future gains for a short-term advantage
based on a Greek fable about a man who killed the goose that laid golden eggs; his aim was to collect the whole stock of eggs at once but, in doing so, he ended his future supply

green

a green chum
an inexperienced person
Shakespeare, *Antony & Cleopatra* I:v, 'my salad days, when I was green in judgment'

to be green
to be naVve
Shakespeare, *Antony & Cleopatra* I:v, 'my salad days, when I was green in judgment'

to give the green light
to grant permission
refers to the 'go' signal on roads and rail

to have green fingers
to be good at gardening

to turn green
to become very envious
Shakespeare, *Othello* III:iii, 'O! beware, my Lord, of jealousy;/it is the green-ey'd monster ... '

greener

distant fields look greener
activities of which one has no experience seem more attractive than is really the case
Psalms 23:1, 'The Lord is my shepherd ... he shall feed me in a green pasture'

to move on to greener pastures
to move to a better environment; to commence a new, better career
Psalms 23:1, 'The Lord is my shepherd: therefore can I lack nothing. he shall feed me in a green pasture: and lead me forth beside the waters of comfort'

grey

to be a grey area
to be in an undefined position straddling two or more possibilities
refers to something being neither black nor white

pink

to be tickled pink
to be very pleased
Oliver Goldsmith (1730–74), *She Stoops to Conquer*, 'the very pink of perfection'

to look in the pink
to look well
Oliver Goldsmith (1730–74), *She Stoops to Conquer*, 'the very pink of perfection'

purple

to be purple with rage
to be very angry

red

a red-letter day
an important occasion
refers to the colour used to indicate days of obligation in the Christian Church missal — as opposed to black-letter days, which are optional days

neither fish flesh nor good red herring
unclassifiable by virtue of being neither one thing nor another
Miguel de Cervantes (1547–1616), *Don Quixote*

red hot
urgent, and/or exciting, and/or dangerous

red tape
excessively bureaucratic procedures
refers to bureaucrats and lawyers securing their briefs with red tape; the term is said to have been coined by Charles Dickens (1812–70), but popularised by Thomas Carlyle (1795–1881)

the red-carpet treatment
courtesies extended to a person to make that person feel important and welcome
refers to the welcome accorded a visiting dignitary

to be a red herring
to be something designed to divert attention away from the main question
refers to hunting with hounds — a red herring was dragged across the scent trail to train hounds to ignore distractions and follow the correct trail

to be a red rag to a bull
to be something that makes a person very angry and very excited
refers to the erroneous belief that the colour red, rather than the motion of waving, excites a bull

to be in the red
to owe money
refers to the red ink used to indicate a liability in a manuscript accounting ledger

to be left red-faced
to be embarrassed

to catch someone red-handed
to apprehend a person in the course of committing a wrongdoing
refers originally to being caught with blood on one's hands

to get the red light
to be forbidden to do something
refers to the 'stop' signal on roads and rail

to paint the town red
to go on an exciting social outing

to see red
to become very angry

to see red lights flashing
to be conscious of the danger
refers to the 'stop' signal on roads and rail, or perhaps to lights on an emergency vehicle

rosy

to present a rosy picture
to state a set of favourable factors

silver

every cloud has a silver lining
there are consolations and potential benefits even in seemingly adverse situations

to be born with a silver spoon in one's mouth
to be brought up by wealthy parents
refers to the traditional gift of a silver spoon (an 'apostle spoon') to a child at baptism — the child born of wealthy parents is assured of riches from the moment of birth and thus does not have to await baptism to receive a valuable gift

to hand over something on a silver platter
to provide a valuable benefit for virtually nothing
refers to first-class service

to have a silver tongue
to be eloquent
Proverbs 10:20, 'The tongue of the just is as choice silver: the heart of the wicked is little worth'

to sell off the family silver
to sell off one's prized possessions

white

a white elephant
an expensive and useless luxury
refers to gifts of sacred elephants by the King of Siam to persons then ruined by the expense of their upkeep

a white knight
a person voluntarily coming to the assistance of another person at considerable personal cost
derived from mediaeval tales of valiant knights rescuing those in distress, white being associated with purity and goodness

a white lie
a false statement uttered in a good cause

in black and white
in writing, spelling out all the details

Ben Jonson (1573–1637), *Every Man in his Honour*, 'I have it here in black and white'

lily-white
honest and incorruptible
based on a belief that the lily sprang from the tears of Eve as she left the Garden of Eden; the lily is traditionally a symbol of purity and innocence in Christian art

to be a black-and-white issue
to involve very clear distinctions
Ben Jonson (1573–1637), *Every Man in his Honour*, 'I have it here in black and white'

to show the white feather
to indicate cowardice
refers to cross-bred birds, not regarded as useful in cock fighting

to turn white
to express shock at unexpected news

to white-ant someone
surreptitiously to seek to destroy a person
refers to the damage done to timber structures by white ants

whitewash

to whitewash
to attempt to conceal the guilt or mistakes of a person
refers to the use of whitewash on a wall to conceal blemishes

Commerce

A1

to be A1 at Lloyd's
to be in perfect order
refers to the classification of ships in Lloyd's register in London

adds

it adds up
it makes sense

bank

to laugh all the way to the bank
to appreciate one's good fortune

bankrupt

to be bankrupt of ideas
to be bereft of ideas

bargained

to be more than one bargained for
to be more than one expected

bargaining

bargaining chips
benefits that can be conceded in negotiations to obtain some advantage

basket

to put something into the 'too-hard' basket
to defer consideration of a difficult issue

cheque

to give someone a blank cheque
to give another person unlimited delegated authority

bob

not to be the full two bob
not to be very intelligent
refers to slang term for two shillings

to have two bob each way
to equivocate
refers to the slang term for two shillings, and to betting for a win or a place books

to balance the books
to get one's own back
refers to accountancy

to be on some organisation's books
to be a member or client of some organisation

to cook the books
fraudulently to maintain false records of financial transactions

buy

I buy that
I accept that idea

to buy a pig in a poke
to buy goods of unknown quality
refers to the practice of selling a person a cat (purported to be a pig) in a bag (or poke); if the person opened the bag and looked inside, that person 'let the cat out of the bag'

buy

I buy that
I accept that idea

to buy a pig in a poke
to buy goods of unknown quality
refers to the practice of selling a person a cat (purported to be a pig) in a bag (or poke); if the person opened the bag and looked inside, that person 'let the cat out of the bag'

to buy into some argument

to seek to participate in some discussion

to buy something for a song
to buy something very cheaply

to buy straw hats in winter
to buy in a depressed market when most other people are sellers

carbon

a carbon copy
an exact imitation
refers to the practice of producing a copy of a document by typing the original with carbon paper beneath, thus simultaneously making a copy

cents

to have fifty cents each way
to equivocate
refers to betting for a win or a place

to throw in one's two cents' worth
modestly to supply one's own facts or views

changed

to be short-changed
to be given less than is due to one

coal

to be at the coal face
to be in the place where the real work is done

coals

to carry coals to Newcastle
to do something ridiculously unnecessary
refers to the coal-mining district of Newcastle, UK

coin

the other side of the coin
the arguments for the opposite point of view

to pay someone back in that person's own coin
to retaliate in kind

customer

a slippery customer
a shifty person

dividends

to show dividends
to be successful

hedge

to hedge one's bets
to insure against a losing bet or investment by also investing on the opposite outcome

hedged

to be hedged around
(of a statement) to be surrounded by qualifications

horse

horse trading
tough negotiations

i

to dot the i's and cross the t's
to be meticulous in completing documentation

ink

the ink is hardly dry
this involves indecent haste
refers to acting promptly, as soon as a document is signed

iron

ironclad
firm or rigorous
refers to armour-plated naval vessels

to give a cast-iron guarantee
to give a very secure undertaking to do something

to have a cast-iron case
to be assured absolutely of victory in a dispute, an argument, or in legal proceedings

irons

to have other irons in the fire
to have the opportunity to do something else as an alternative
Francis Beaumont (1584–1616) & John Fletcher (1579–1625), *The Faithful Friends* I:ii, 'It is always good when a man has two irons in the fire'

line

the bottom line
the conclusion that matters or the net effect of a series of developments
refers to the last line is a series of calculations or accounts

to sign on the dotted line
to confirm one's agreement

list

a laundry list
a large set of demands

a shopping list

an itemised catalogue of things that one wishes to acquire or achieve

mark

a hallmark
a standard
refers to the official assay mark on gold and silver, originally put on at the Goldsmiths' Hall, London

to make something one's trade mark
to have a distinctive characteristic or way of doing things

message

to get the message
to understand the real import of what is being said

mite

not a mite
not at all
refers to a coin of small value — *Mark* 12:42, 'A certain poor widow ... threw in two mites, which make a farthing'

money

a licence to print money
a lucrative government-conferred monopoly or privilege
Lord Thomson of Fleet (1894–1977), 'It's just like having a licence to print your own money' (after the opening of Scottish commercial television, as recorded in Braddon, *Roy Thomson of Fleet Street*)

money for jam
remuneration easily earned

not for love or money
definitely not

not to be made of money
not to be wealthy

that is money down the drain
money has been wastefully lost on a failed project

the money is rolling in
the scheme is very profitable

to be a money spinner
to produce large profits easily and quickly

to be money for old rope
to be an easily made profit

to have a run for one's money
to at least get some enjoyment out of an otherwise abortive exercise
refers to betting on horse racing

to have money burning a hole in one's pocket
to be impatient to spend or invest available funds

to have money flowing out of one's ears
to be very rich

to lose money hand over fist
to lose money very fast and comprehensively

to put money on the table
to back one's judgment in a tangible way or to demonstrate one's sincerity

to put one's money where one's mouth is
to back one's boasting by putting assets at risk

to see the colour of someone's money
to get evidence of the sincerity of a person's proposal

to throw good money after bad
to waste further money in a vain attempt to recover money already lost

paid

that has put paid to it
the project can no longer proceed
refers to the counting house and an account being labelled as 'paid' (meaning 'settled'); thus, the matter is settled and finished

paper

to have shares in a paper company
to institute unnecessary clerical procedures

to start with a blank sheet of paper
to commence an exercise without being bound by any established practices

par

to be below par
to be less than the desired standard

to be par for the course
to be normal
refers to golf

pay

to pay a king's ransom
to pay a very large sum

to pay off
to be successful; OR formally to complete a ship's period of active service

to pay over the odds
to pay too much
refers to betting on horse races

to pay someone back in that person's own coin
to retaliate in kind

to pay something back with interest
to return a small favour with a bigger favour; or to extract retribution of greater value than the circumstances warrant

to pay the price
to suffer the adverse consequences of one's acts or omissions

to pay through the nose
to pay an excessive price
refers to an onerous tax imposed by the Danes in Ireland in the ninth century whereby those who refused to pay had their noses slit

to rob Peter to pay Paul
to discharge one debt or responsibility by incurring another
John Wyclif (c.1380), *Select Works* III 174, 'How should God approve that you rob Peter, and give this robbery to Paul in the name of Christ?' (perhaps refers to an ecclestiastical property dispute between two churches)

to strike pay dirt
to become successful
refers to soil containing gold or other precious metal

pays

he who pays the piper calls the tune
a person contributing money or resources to a project is entitled to control it

pen

to hold the pen poised
to be ready to consummate a deal

pennies

to be unable to rub two pennies together
to be very poor

to throw in one's six pennies' worth
modestly to supply one's own facts or views

penny

a twopenny halfpenny outfit
a quite insignificant operation

if you gave that person a penny for that person's thoughts you would get change
that person is extremely stupid

in for a penny, in for a pound
once something is commenced it ought be finished; OR if one is willing to take a small risk then one might as well take a bigger one

penny-pinching
excessively mean

the penny dropped
a person has just realised a fact that should have been obvious
refers to old-fashioned pay toilets

to cost a pretty penny
to be very expensive

to turn an honest penny
to earn money by hard work

pitch

to cruel someone's pitch
to spoil a person's chances

to queer the pitch for someone
to spoil the opportunity a person has to do something

pocket

the hip-pocket nerve
the assessment of issues by their financial effects on one

to be in someone's pocket
to be subject to undue influence by another person

to be out of pocket
to have lost money in a transaction

to have money burning a hole in one's pocket
to be impatient to spend or invest available funds

to put one's hand in one's pocket
to provide money from one's own resources, especially for a charitable purpose

pockets

to have deep pockets
to have large financial resources and to be willing to use them if the circumstances seem right

to line one's pockets

to make, improperly and secretly, a profit out of some transaction

pound

in for a penny, in for a pound
once something is commenced it ought be finished; OR if one is willing to take a small risk then one might as well take a bigger one

pre-empt

to pre-empt some issue
deliberately to do something that has the effect of limiting the range of alternative approaches to a matter
refers to the right of certain persons (originally the Crown) to buy certain things before others have an opportunity

price

that has nothing to do with the price of fish
that is quite irrelevant
to pay the price
to suffer the adverse consequences of one's acts or omissions
what has that to do with the price of fish?
what is the relevance of this?

quid

not to be the full quid
not to be very intelligent

razoo

not to have a brass razoo
to be very poor
refers to an imaginary coin of trivial value

sale

fire sale
a forced sale, realising bargain prices
refers to the sale of goods damaged by fire
garage sale
sale of miscellaneous assets at cheap prices

sell

to sell off the family silver
to sell off one's prized possessions
to sell one's birthright for a mess of pottage
through foolishness to exchange something of substance for something of little value
Genesis 25:34, 'Then Jacob gave Esau bread and pottage of lentils ... thus Esau despised his birthright'
to sell someone a lemon
to sell a person a grossly defective product on the basis that it represents quality
to sell someone a pup
to cheat a person in a transaction, especially by misrepresentation as to the true value of something
to sell someone down the river
to betray a person who has placed trust in one
refers to selling slaves to owners further down the river

shake

golden handshake
a large payment in connection with, or as an inducement to, retirement

share

a share of the cake
a portion of the total available for distribution
the lion's share
the biggest portion

shares

to have shares in a paper company
to institute unnecessary clerical procedures

shilling

to be only ten pence in the shilling
to be slightly stupid
refers to 'old' shillings and pence when a shilling equalled twelve pence
to cut someone off with a shilling
to exclude a person as a beneficiary under one's will
refers to the mistaken belief that a will cannot be upset in favour of a person actually named in a will and clearly not overlooked

shoot

to shoot the messenger
to blame the person who brings news of an undesired happening instead of the person really responsible for that happening

shop

a bull in a china shop
a careless person likely to cause great damage

to shop around
to explore alternatives
to shut up shop
to cease an established activity
to talk shop
to discuss business or professional matters on a social occasion

shopping
a shopping list
an itemised catalogue of things that one wishes to acquire or achieve

short-changed
to be short-changed
to be given less than is due to one

showcase
to showcase something
to display something attractively with a view to getting attention

shutters
to put up the shutters
to cease an established activity

slate
to wipe the slate clean
to forgive past indiscretions

sold
to be sold on something
to be utterly dedicated to a proposal

stamp
to rubber-stamp something
to endorse something without considering the merits

stock
to be a blue-chip stock
to be of excellent quality
to take stock
to contemplate the alternatives

store
to take over the store
to assume the management

trades
a Jack of all trades
an amateur who can do many different tasks'

value
to take something at face value
(of alleged facts) to accept something without question or challenge

wealth
a wealth of something
a great quantity of something

Crime

felony
to compound the felony
having already acted improperly, to make matters worse

hijack
to hijack a debate
to involve oneself in discussion on some matter and turn that discussion to one's advantage

murder
to be sheer murder
to be extremely unpleasant or difficult; OR to be an inglorious defeat
to get away with murder
to do something outrageous without penalty
to scream blue murder
to make serious allegations; OR to protest violently
perhaps refers to the French *morbleu* (altered version of *mort Dieu*, 'God's death'), a comic oath attributed to French speakers

pinching
penny-pinching
excessively mean

poach
to poach on someone's preserves
to encroach uninvited on another person's territory

rob
to rob Peter to pay Paul
to discharge one debt or responsibility by incurring another
John Wyclif (c.1380), *Select Works* III 174, 'How should God approve that you rob Peter, and give this robbery to Paul in the name of Christ?' (perhaps refers to an ecclesiasticald property dispute between two churches)

robbery
daylight robbery
the charging of grossly excessive prices

highway robbery
the charging of grossly excessive prices
refers to robbery by armed brigands on the highways

shotgun

a shotgun wedding
a wedding held to ensure that an impending birth will be legitimate
refers to threats by the bride's father to kill the bridegroom

throat

cut-throat
highly competitive

Death

block

someone's head is on the block
a person is in danger of being condemned; OR a person is in danger of having an appointment terminated
refers to execution by decapitation

blow

death blow
incident that results in the destruction of something

body

over my dead body
never

bucket

to kick the bucket
to die

coffin

to be another nail in someone's coffin
to represent a further step towards someone's downfall

corpse

to breathe life into a corpse
to revive something moribund

to chase a corpse
to harp on something long ago resolved or a lost cause

dead

a dead-end position
a job with no prospects of advancement

a dead letter
a rule still in existence but no longer observed in practice

dead and buried
(of some issue) definitely concluded, especially so long ago as to be nearly forgotten

drop dead!
go away, I want no dealings with you

I wouldn't be caught dead without some object
I regard some object as very important

over my dead body
never

to be a dead duck
to have failed; OR or to be in a hopeless situation

to cut someone dead
to snub a person

to flog a dead horse
misguidedly to do something patently useless

to get rid of the dead wood
to terminate the services of unsatisfactory personnel
refers to pruning of bushes

to kill some proposal stone dead
to take action that stops a proposal completely
refers to death by stoning

to leave others for dead
to be vastly superior

to make noise enough to wake the dead
to be excessively noisy

to run into a dead end
to get nowhere in an investigation

deadline

deadline
time by which something must be completed
refers to a line drawn around a military prison, beyond which a prisoner might be shot dead — hence, an absolute limit

death

a death wish
the contemplation or commission of action so foolish that it is likely to lead to utter disaster

death blow

incident that results in the destruction of something

death of a thousand cuts
a slow, unpleasant ending

sudden death
instantaneously or without phasing in

to be in at the death
to be present at the conclusion of something
refers to fox hunting — when the fox is caught and killed

to be on one's death bed
(of a person, organisation or piece of equipment) to be about to cease effectiveness

to be the kiss of death
to be something intended to be helpful but resulting in total destruction

to bore someone to death
to weary a person greatly by dull and uninteresting conversation or by lack of action

to die a natural death
by virtue of changed circumstances or the effluxion of time to be no longer relevant

to sign one's own death warrant
foolishly to do something that is inevitably bound to lead to utter disaster

to bleed to death slowly
to be heading in gradual steps towards total ruin

to sound the death knell of something
to indicate the impending end of something
refers to the knell (sound) of a bell rung at a funeral; Shakespeare, *Macbeth* II:i, 'The bell invites me ... it is a knell that summons thee to heaven or to hell'

deathknock

on the deathknock
at the last possible moment
refers to the mythical figure of 'Death' knocking on the door to claim a victim

die

those who live by the sword shall die by the sword
those that are rough with others must accept the likelihood of unfavourable treatment in return
Matthew 26:52, 'All they that take the sword shall perish by the sword'

to be the throw of a loaded die
to be an act of deceit
refers to cheating in gambling with dice

to die a natural death
by virtue of changed circumstances or the effluxion of time to be no longer relevant

to die hard
stubbornly to refuse to give up a belief or theory; not to give up easily

diehard

to be a diehard
to be a person who refuses to change, an obdurate person

dying

to be dying to do something
to be extremely keen to do something

fatal

to be fatal
to be sufficient to destroy some proposal

funeral

that is your funeral!
that is the fate that you will have to suffer

grave

someone would turn in his or her grave
someone would have been very surprised or displeased if he or she had known while still alive

to dig one's own grave
to take action that results in an unintended disaster for oneself

to have one foot in the grave
to be very old or dying
W. S. Gilbert 1836–1911, HMS *Pinafore* (1878), 'A greenery-yallery, Grosvenor Gallery/ Foot-in-the-grave young man!'

hang

to give someone enough rope to hang himself or herself
to give a person the opportunity to do something that is likely to get that person into severe trouble

hanged

one might as well be hanged for a sheep as for a lamb
further action will not increase the adverse consequences already in train

refers to the stealing of either sheep or lambs being capital crimes under old English law

hanging

not to be a hanging matter
to be only a minor mistake

kill

to be dressed to kill
to be very smartly dressed with the intention of making a striking impression — usually with a view to a romantic or sexual conquest

to be in at the kill
to be present at the climatic finish to something
refers to hunting

to kill oneself laughing
to be greatly amused

to kill some proposal stone dead
to take action that stops a proposal completely
refers to death by stoning

to kill the fatted calf
to demonstrate welcome and complete acceptance of another person
Luke 15:23. 'And bring hither the fatted calf and let us eat, and be merry'

to kill the goose that lays the golden eggs
through excessive greed, to sacrifice future gains for a short-term advantage
based on a Greek fable about a man who killed the goose that laid golden eggs; his aim was to collect the whole stock of eggs at once but, in doing so, he ended his future supply

to kill two birds with one stone
to achieve a second objective in the course of achieving the first objective

killed

to be killed in the rush
to be the supplier of something extremely popular

killing

to make a killing
to be in a very successful business venture

mortem

to conduct a post mortem on something
to review past actions with a view to learning lessons for the future
Latin, *post mortem*, 'after the death'

noose

to put one's head in the noose
to expose oneself to great danger likely to lead to one's downfall
refers to death by hanging

to tighten the noose
to get closer to inflicting defeat
refers to death by hanging

slaughter

a lamb led to slaughter
a naVve person allowing himself or herself to be exploited
Isaiah 53:5, 'He was oppressed, and he was afflicted, yet he opened not his mouth: he is brought as a lamb to the slaughter'

Education

book

to be a closed book
to be a secret

to close the book on something
to terminate an activity

to judge a book by its cover
foolishly to go only by superficial appearances

to play by the book
to apply the rules strictly

to take a leaf out of someone's book
to model oneself on another person
refers to taking a page from the 'Book of Life' — *Rev* 20: 12, 'and the books were opened … and the dead were judged out of those things that were written in the books, according to their works'

to talk one's book
to present arguments that, although plausible, are really designed to foster one's vested interest

to throw the book at someone
to prosecute a person with all the vigour allowed by law

to use every trick in the book
to try very hard and use every conceivable argument

books

to balance the books
to get one's own back
refers to accountancy

to be a turn-up for the books
to be a surprising development

to be in someone's black books
to be out of favour with a person
biblical allusion: refers to God's judgment and the desirability of having one's name entered in the book of life; *Rev* 20: 12, 'and the books were opened ... and the dead were judged out of those things that were written in the books, according to their works'

to be in someone's good books
to be well regarded by another person
biblical allusion: refers to God's judgment and the desirability of having one's name entered in the book of life; *Rev* 20: 12, 'and the books were opened ... and the dead were judged out of those things that were written in the books, according to their works'

to be on some organisation's books
to be a member or client of some organisation

to cook the books
fraudulently to maintain false records of financial transactions

bookworm

a bookworm
a person who likes reading and study

caning

to take a caning
to suffer the adverse consequences of one's acts or omissions

copybook

to blot one's copybook
to spoil one's previously good reputation or record

dictionary

someone has swallowed a dictionary
a person uses excessively long words

dunce

to earn a dunce's cap
to do something stupid
a 'dunce' being derived from the name of Duns Scotus (1265–1308) and his followers ('Dunsers') whose hair-splitting theology was later perceived to be opposed to learning and enlightenment; Thomas Fuller (1608–61), 'a dunce, void of learning but full of books'

golden mean
a moderate compromise between two extremes
from mathematics: the division of a straight line into two portions so that the ratio of the smaller to the larger equals the ratio of the larger to the whole

homework

to do one's homework
to analyse an issue throughly

lesson

to drive the lesson home
to take certain action that is unpleasant but that has the effect of registering a message

to learn a lesson
to benefit from one's experience

to teach someone a lesson
to inflict something unpleasant on a person in the hope that it will lead to a change in that person's behaviour

school

to tell tales out of school
to gossip mischievously and reveal secrets about others

schoolboy

as every schoolboy knows
as is recognised by everyone
Jonathon Swift (1667–1745), *The Country Life*, 1:81,'How haughtily he cocks his nose, / To tell what every schoolboy knows'; Lord Macaulay (1800–59), *Lord Clive* (Jan. 1840), 'Every schooboy knows who imprisoned Montezuma, and who strangled Atahualpa'

spell

to spell something out
to explain something in detail

Farming

apple

a rotten apple
an isolated dishonest person in an otherwise honest group

to be the apple of someone's eye
to be a much cherished person

refers to the pupil of the eye — 'the apple of the eye' as being the centre of visual perception and therefore especially cherished and much-valued

apples

to add/compare apples with oranges
to lump unconnected things together quite illogically

to compare apples with apples
to make a valid comparison

applecart

to upset the applecart
to engage in conduct disturbing a peaceful state of affairs and thereby to cause discomfort

ass

to make an ass of oneself
to act stupidly in public

asses

asses and little pitchers have long ears
children have a tendency to overhear things

axe

the axe has fallen
it is now too late
refers to execution by decapitation

to axe
to cancel

to have an axe to grind
to have a vested interest; to pursue a personal objective

to sharpen one's axe
to get ready for a difficult task

where the axe falls
who suffers the consequences

bag

it is in the bag
the enterprise has succeeded or surely will succeed

bait

to swallow the bait
to succumb to a temptation deliberately put in one's way
refers to angling

barn

horses are out of the barn
it is now too late

barnstorm

to barnstorm
to travel around and actively promote one's cause or performance
refers to itinerant actors who performed in barns

bean

not to have a bean
to have no money

beans

not to matter a row of beans
to be utterly unimportant

to be full of beans
to be very cheerful

to know how many beans make five
to have common sense
refers to an old riddle

to spill the beans
indiscreetly to reveal sensitive information

beast

the nature of the beast
the reality of the situation
Revelation 13:17, ' ... he that had the mark, or the name of the beast, or the number of his name'

bee

to be a busy bee
to work with great diligence

to have a bee in one's bonnet
to have an obsession

beeline

to make a beeline for something
to go straight to something with great enthusiasm or to head for some goal by the most direct route

bell

bell-wether
first indication
refers to the leading sheep (wether) of a flock, this sheep having a bell hung around its neck

bLte

to be someone's bLte noire
to be a person whose ideas and actions cause upset and loathing in another person
French, *bLte noire* ('black beast')

block

to be a chip off the old block
to resemble one's father in behaviour and/or appearance

bone

a bone of contention
the subject matter of violent disagreement
probably refers to dogs fighting over a bone

to get close to the bone
to cause discomfort by being accurate

to have a bone to pick
to have a grievance that requires discussion

to throw someone a bone
to fob a person off with a symbolic but unimportant gesture
refers to feeding a dog

to work one's fingers to the bone
to work very hard

bones

to make no bones about it
to be brutally frank

the bare bones
(of a story) nothing but the essential elements

bucket

to be only a drop in the bucket
to be quite insignificant in the total scene

to kick the bucket
to die

to tip a bucket on someone
to point out, in a humiliating way, another person's faults

bull

a bull in a china shop
a careless person likely to cause great damage

a cock-and-bull story
an explanation that is completely unbelievable and unacceptable
Laurence Sterne (1713–68), *Tristram Shandy*, 'Said my mother, "What is this story all about?" — "a cock and a bull," said Yorick.'

to be a red rag to a bull
to be something that makes a person very angry and very excited
refers to the erroneous belief that the colour red, rather than the motion of waving, excites a bull

to be within a bull's roar of something
to be very close to something

to charge like a wounded bull
to impose excessive prices
a play on words; not a simile

to hit the bull's eye
to be extremely accurate in an activity; to score
derived from archery

to take the bull by the horns
to come to grips with the realities of a difficult problem

bulldoze

to bulldoze some proposal through
to ensure the passage of some measure in complete disregard of criticism or opposition

bushel

to hide one's light under a bushel
to keep others in ignorance of one's skills and experience
Luke 11:33, 'No man, when he hath lighted a candle, putteth it in a secret place, neither under a bushel'

cabbage

to be on someone's cabbage patch
to engage in a competitive activity in a territory regarded by someone already there as rightfully belonging exclusively to that person

calf

to kill the fatted calf
to demonstrate welcome and complete acceptance of another person
Luke 15:23. 'And bring hither the fatted calf and let us eat, and be merry'

carrots

sticks and carrots
disincentives and incentives in combination
refers to the handling of donkeys

chaff

to separate the wheat from the chaff
to separate the worthy from the unworthy
Matthew 3:12, 'His winnowing fork is in his hand, and he will clear his threshing

floor and gather his wheat into the granary, but the chaff he will burn with unquenchable fire'

cherry

to engage in cherry picking
(in business) to accept only the potentially most lucrative deals

to get only one bite at the cherry
to receive no further opportunity

chicken

chicken and egg
a situation involving two factors each of which causes the other, making it impossible to decide which came first

chicken-hearted
showing little courage

to be chicken feed
to be small and unimportant

chickens

the chickens are coming home to roost
the consequences of a person's past actions are now being felt by that person

Robert Southey (1774–1843), *The Curse of Kehama* (1810), 'Curses are like young chickens, they always come home to roost'

to count one's chickens before they are hatched
to treat as fact the expected results of a future proposal

originally attributed to Erasmus (1466–1536) in slightly different form

chip

to be a chip off the old block
to resemble one's father in behaviour and/or appearance

chips

that is the way the chips fall
that is the way that the benefits and detriments are distributed after an event

when the chips are down
when all facts are known and taken into consideration

chops

to lick one's chops
to look forward to something with pleasurable anticipation

refers to salivation in anticipation of food

clover

to be in clover
to enjoy a life of ease and luxury

refers to grazing animals in rich pasture

cock

a cock-and-bull story
an explanation that is completely unbelievable and unacceptable

Laurence Sterne (1713–68), *Tristram Shandy*, 'Said my mother, "What is this story all about?" — "a cock and a bull," said Yorick.'

cock-eyed
stupid

to cock one's eye at someone
to glance knowingly at a person

core

rotten to the core
completely corrupt

to be the hard core
to be the central and most difficult problem

cotton

to be out of one's cotton-picking mind
to act irrationally

to keep one's cotton-picking fingers off something
not to interfere (in a meddlesome fashion) with something

to wrap someone in cotton wool
to be overprotective towards a person

cow

a cash cow
a source of ready money

a milch cow
an easy and plentiful source of some desired benefit

a sacred cow
an institution, person, idea, custom, etc. treated as being immune from criticism and change

refers to Hindu veneration of the cow

cows

till the cows come home
for a very long time, perhaps forever

Francis Beaumont (1584–1616) & John Fletcher (1579–1625), *The Scornful Lady*, 'Kiss till the cow comes home'

crocodile

to shed crocodile tears

hypocritically to show concern or sympathy for a person in distress

refers to the reflex lacrimation of a crocodile while eating

cud

to chew the cud

to reflect on something

refers to the chewing of the cud by ruminant animals

deflower

to deflower

to deprive of virginity

disseminate

to disseminate ideas

to spread ideas to a wide audience

literally, 'to scatter seeds in various places'

donkey

donkey work

necessary but uninspiring routine work

refers to the laborious work done by a donkey

for donkey's years

for a long time

to talk the hind leg off a donkey

to talk excessively

drakes

to play ducks and drakes

not to treat the matter seriously

derived from the old name given to the game of throwing a stone such that it skips across the surface of water; hence: 'to throw away idly and carelessly

drone

a drone

an idle person

droves

people stayed away in droves

few people came

refers to a moving group of cattle, sheep, or other animals

duck

a lame duck

a person unable to fend for himself or herself

a 'lame-duck president' is a president still in office but without influence because the commencement of the successor's term is imminent

in two shakes of a duck's tail

in an instant

to be a dead duck

to have failed; OR or to be in a hopeless situation

to be a sitting duck

to be vulnerable to exploitation

to be like water off a duck's back

(of advice or criticism) to be completely ignored

to duck for cover

to seek to avoid blame

refers to duck's habit of putting its head under water when threatened

duckling

an ugly duckling

an unprepossessing person or thing, the characteristics of which change in time to become attractive

refers to a cygnet in a brood of ducks in a children's story of that name by Hans Christian Andersen

ducks

to play ducks and drakes

not to treat the matter seriously

derived from the old name given to the game of throwing a stone such that it skips across the surface of water; hence: 'to throw away idly and carelessly

earmark

to earmark

to allocate to a specific purpose

refers to marking animals

earth

a down-to-earth solution

a realistic solution

egg

a nest egg

a sum of money set aside in case of need; a nucleus of savings

derived from the custom of placing an egg in a hen's nest as an inducement for the hen to lay more

chicken and egg

a situation involving two factors each of which causes the other, making it impossible to decide which came first

to be a bad egg

to be a dishonest or disreputable person

eggs

as sure as eggs is eggs

with great certainty

perhaps a corruption of the logician's formula: 'x is x'

not to put all one's eggs in the one basket
to spread one's risks

to kill the goose that lays the golden eggs
through excessive greed, to sacrifice future gains for a short-term advantage
based on a Greek fable about a man who killed the goose that laid golden eggs; his aim was to collect the whole stock of eggs at once but, in doing so, he ended his future supply

to teach one's grandmother how to suck eggs
to try to tell a much more experienced person something very obvious to that person

feather

birds of a feather flock together
persons of like interests gather in the same place
Samuel Rutherford (?1600–61), 'Fowls of a feather flock together'

to feather one's own nest
improperly to appropriate things for oneself (especially in financial transactions)

to show the white feather
to indicate cowardice
refers to cross-bred birds, not regarded as useful in cock fighting

to thrash with a feather
to impose only a minor punishment for a very serious offence

today a rooster, tomorrow a feather duster
when circumstances change, an important person can, immediately, become unimportant

feathers

to make feathers fly
to cause a flurry of consternation and vigorous activity
refers to the fighting of cock birds

to ruffle someone's feathers
to engage in behaviour that irritates another person

ferret

to ferret something out
by diligent research to discover some secret
refers to a ferret pursuing rabbits in their burrows

fetter

to fetter someone
to stop a person acting on that person's own initiative

field

a field day
a very enjoyable and successful occasion

to be in the field
to be out in the working environment as opposed to headquarters, a laboratory, etc.

to cover the field
to be comprehensive

to exhaust the field
to use up all the possibilities

to hold the field
not to be superseded

to play the field
to distribute one's favours among more than one person

fields

distant fields look greener
activities of which one has no experience seem more attractive than is really the case
Psalms 23:1, 'The Lord is my shepherd ... he shall feed me in a green pasture'

fig

one would not give a fig for something
one regards something as worthless

fish

a queer fish
an unusual type of person

an ocean full of fish
plenty of opportunity

neither fish flesh nor good red herring
unclassifiable by virtue of being neither one thing nor another
Miguel de Cervantes (1547–1616), *Don Quixote*

that has nothing to do with the price of fish
that is quite irrelevant

to be a big fish in a little pond

to be a person holding an important office but in an unimportant organisation

to be a cold fish
to be an unemotional person

to be a different kettle of fish
to be something very dissimilar
refers to a riverside picnic where freshly caught fish is cooked and eaten

to be a fine kettle of fish
to be a terrible muddle
refers to a riverside picnic where freshly caught fish is cooked and eaten

to be a fish out of water
to be in difficulty by virtue of being in a strange environment

to fish for compliments
to drop hints in the hope that one will receive praise or recognition

to fish in troubled waters
to profit from a disturbed situation
refers to angling

what has that to do with the price of fish?
what is the relevance of this?

fishing

a fishing expedition
an exercise that sets out to gather incriminating information without knowing its exact nature or location

fishy

fleece

to fleece someone
to cheat a person out of some asset
Thomas Carlyle (1795–1881), 'To divide what they fleeced from these poor drudges'

flock

flock
congregation in the charge of a religious official
numerous biblical references incl.: *Isaiah* 40:11, 'He shall feed his flock like a shepherd: he shall gather the lambs with his arm, and carry them in his bosom, and shall gently lead those that are with young'

fold

the fold
the body of believers
refers to an enclosure for sheep; *John* 10:16, 'Other sheep I have, which are not of this fold'

fruit

forbidden fruit
something particularly desired because it is not allowed
Genesis 2:17, 'but of the tree of the knowledge of good and evil, thou shalt not eat of it'

to bear fruit
to result in success

fruitless

fruitless
yielding no benefit

fruits

by their fruits ye shall know them
their true nature will be revealed by their results
Matthew 7:20, 'wherefore by their fruits ye shall know them'

fur

to make the fur fly
to create a disturbance
refers to animals fighting

game

to be fair game
to be someone who can be attacked legitimately
refers to hunting

gander

what is sauce for the goose is sauce for the gander
arguments that apply in one case also apply in another

goat

a scapegoat
a person who is forced to take the blame for something not their fault
Leviticus 16:10, 'But the goat, on which the lot fell to be the scapegoat ... to make an atonement'

to play the giddy goat
to act the fool
'giddy' derived from Old English *gidig* ('possessed by a god')

goats

to separate the sheep from the goats
to distinguish between the worthy and the unworthy

Matthew 25:32, 'and he shall separate them one from one another, as a shepherd divideth his sheep from the goats'

goose

a wild-goose chase
a futile chase or search
refers to old game of 'follow-the-leader' on horses in which the objective was to follow a winding and difficult course without ever catching up

to be too frightened to say 'boo' to a goose
to be excessively shy

to cook one's goose
to make a fatal mistake; to ruin one's plans
nineteenth-century street ballad: 'If they come here we'll cook their geese'

to kill the goose that lays the golden eggs
through excessive greed, to sacrifice future gains for a short-term advantage
based on a Greek fable about a man who killed the goose that laid golden eggs; his aim was to collect the whole stock of eggs at once but, in doing so, he ended his future supply

what is sauce for the goose is sauce for the gander
arguments that apply in one case also apply in another

gooseberry

to play gooseberry
to act as an unwelcome chaperon

grapes

that is just sour grapes
those are disparaging remarks made only because that person is peeved and resentful at someone else's better fortune
derived from Aesop's fable of 'the fox and the grapes' about expressing deliberate disparagement of a desired but unattainable object; 'sour grapes' also occurs in *Ezekiel* 18:2, 'the fathers have eaten sour grapes, and the children's teeth are set on edge'

what is this — a bunch of grapes or a bowl of goldfish?
surely you know what this is?

grapevine

to hear on the grapevine
to learn unofficially
the earlier form of the metaphor was a 'grapevine telegraph' as a means of communicating private information

grass

a snake in the grass
a person of low character who manages to disguise that trait
Virgil, *Eclogue*, 'There's a snake hidden in the grass'

grass roots
at the lowest level of a hierarchy

not to let grass grow under one's feet
not to let inertia or delay spoil something

grasshopper

since that person was knee-high to a grasshopper
since that person was a very young child

ground

to be thin on the ground
to be scarce

to break new ground
to do something for which there is no precedent
refers to ploughing of ground

to clear the ground
to dispose of the preliminaries
refers to clearing of ground in preparation for ploughing

to have one's feet firmly on the ground
to be very practical

to plough new ground
to engage laboriously in an untried activity

hamstrung

to be hamstrung
to have limited freedom to act as one would wish
refers to ancient practice of disabling a person or animal by cutting the hamstring muscles of the thigh

hare

first catch your hare
do things in logical order and after proper preparation
generally attributed to Hannah Gleese, habit-maker to the Prince of Wales and

co-author of *The Art of Cookery Made Plain and Easy* (1747)

hare-brained
wildly stupid
Benjamin Disraeli (1804–81), speech 1878, 'The hare-brained chatter of irresponsible frivolity'

to chase every hare
to be easily sidetracked

to run with the hare and hunt with the hounds
to keep in with two opposing sides
refers to hunting

to set a hare running
to initiate an activity to achieve a related and desired effect
refers to hunting

harness

in harness
to be constrained and in work

harvest

harvest
end result of labour
Matthew 8:37, 'The harvest truly is plenteous, but the labourers are few'

hay

to hit the hay
to go to sleep
refers to sleeping on beds of hay

to look for a needle in a haystack
to attempt something with a very small chance of success

to make hay while the sun shines
to utilise an opportunity before it disappears
John Betjeman (1906–84), *The Last Laugh*, 'I made hay while the sun shone'

haystack

to look for a needle in a haystack
to attempt something with a very small chance of success

hen

a mother hen
an over-protective person
Matthew 12:37, 'Even as a hen gathereth her chickens under her wings'

hen-pecked
subject to domination by one's wife
Lord Byron (1788–1824), *Don Juan*, 'But — oh! ye lords of ladies intellectual, inform us truly, have they not hen-peck'd you all?'

herd

to follow the herd
to do what most other people are doing

herring

neither fish flesh nor good red herring
unclassifiable by virtue of being neither one thing nor another
Miguel de Cervantes (1547–1616), *Don Quixote*

to be a red herring
to be something designed to divert attention away from the main question
refers to hunting with hounds — a red herring was dragged across the scent trail to train hounds to ignore distractions and follow the correct trail

hide

to cover one's hide
to provide excuses or take other evasive action in an attempt to avoid the adverse consequences of one's actions

to have a thick hide
to be impervious to criticism

to want someone's hide
to be keen to penalise a person

hidebound

hidebound
narrow-minded

hoe

to have a hard row to hoe
to have a difficult assignment
refers to agriculture; James Russell Lowell (1819–91), *The Biglow Papers*, 'You've a darned long row to hoe'

hog

a road hog
an inconsiderate motorist
refers to gluttonous swine

to go the whole hog
to do something very thoroughly
origin uncertain; alternative explanations include: (i) Muslim divines attempting to ascertain how much of the whole hog could be eaten according to Islamic law (Cowper, 1779, 'but for one piece they thought it hard/from the whole hog to be debarred'); (ii) colloquial term for a shilling — that is, to spend the whole hog (or shilling) at one time; (iii) refers to the close shearing of lambs

to make a hog of oneself
to demonstrate greed
refers to gluttonous swine

hogwash

hogwash
nonsense
refers to 'hog wash' — meaning kitchen swill for pigs (and therefore worthless)

hook

by hook or by crook
by fair means or foul
perhaps refers to collection of firewood by different implements

hook, line, and sinker
wholly
refers to angling

to get someone off the hook
to rescue a person from a predicament
refers to angling

to let someone off the hook
to allow a person to escape the adverse consequences of that person's own actions
refers to angling

hooked

to be hooked on something
to be addicted to something
refers to angling

horns

the horns of a dilemma
two unpalatable alternatives between which a choice must be made
dilemma: Greek for 'two assumptions'

to lock horns with someone
to have an argument with another person
refers to fighting between male horned animals

to pull one's horns in
to retreat from previously stated views
refers to fighting between male horned animals

to take the bull by the horns
to come to grips with the realities of a difficult problem

horse

a dark horse
a person with unsuspected talents
Benjamin Disraeli (1804–81), *The Young Duke*, 'A dark horse, which had never been thought of, and which the careless St James had never even observed in the list, rushed past the grandstand in sweeping triumph'

a nod is the same as a wink to a blind horse
fine distinctions are not appropriate here
Captain Marryat (1792–1848), *Peter Simple*, 'But you're a dutiful son, so I'll say no more about it — a nod's as good as a wink to a blind horse'

a stalking horse
a pretext put forward to allow an attack to be made or an argument to be mounted
refers to a horse trained to allow a hunter to approach game (esp. fowl) without being seen; Shakespeare, *As You Like It* V:iv, 'He uses his folly like a stalking horse, and under the presentation of that he shoots his wit'

a two-horse race
a contest between only two serious contestants

a willing horse
a cheerful worker

horse sense
practical commonsense

horse trading
tough negotiations

I could eat a horse
I am very hungry

one can lead a horse to water, but one can't make it drink
one can give advice to a person but cannot ensure that it will be acted on

that is a horse of a very different colour
that is a different matter altogether
Shakespeare, *Twelfth Night*, 'My purpose is, indeed, a horse of that colour'

the horse-and-buggy days
long ago

to back the wrong horse
to have faith in, give support to, and/or invest in a project that proves to be unsuccessful
refers to betting on racehorses

to be on one's hobby horse
to dominate a conversation by insisting on talking about subjects in which one has an obsessive interest
refers to a person who dressed with a figure of a horse around the waist or on

the head in Morris dancing — hence a figure of fun, a jester, a buffoon

to be on one's high horse
to be excessively pompous
refers to persons of high rank riding on tall horses; John Brown (1715–66), *Letter to Garrick*, 'Altogether upon the high horse'

to flog a dead horse
misguidedly to do something patently useless

to learn something from the horse's mouth
to get information from someone qualified to impart it
refers to the examination of a horse's teeth for an accurate assessment of its age

to look a gift horse in the mouth
to be suspicious about a benefit that has been volunteered
Samuel Butler (1612–80), *Hudibras*, 'He ne'er consider'd it, as loth to look a gift horse in the mouth'; refers to the examination of a horse's teeth for an accurate assessment of its age

to put the cart before the horse
to do things in the wrong order
Rudyard Kipling (1865–1936), *The Conundrum of the Workshops*, 'We know the tail must wag the dog, for the horse is drawn by the cart'

to shut the stable door after the horse has bolted
to take preventive action only after the relevant event

horses

hold your horses!
just wait a little!

horses are out of the barn
it is now too late

it is horses for courses
the correct means to an end needs to be chosen
refers to horse racing

to drive a coach and horses through something
to demonstrate the major errors or absurdities of something
Sir Stephen Rice (1673–1715), as quoted by W. King, *State of the Protestants of Ireland* (1672), 'I will drive a coach and six horses through the Act of Settlement'

to frighten the horses
to scare people off by one's ill-considered tactics
Mrs Patrick Campbell (1865–1940), quoting oral tradition, 'I don't mind where people make love, so long as they don't do it in the street and frighten the horses'

to swap/change horses in mid-stream
to alter that upon which one is reliant during the course of a project

wild horses would not cause me to do something
I refuse absolutely to do something
refers to a form of torture in which persons were dragged behind horses

wild horses would not drag that out of me
I refuse absolutely to reveal that
refers to a form of torture in which persons were dragged behind horses

horseplay

horseplay
boisterous and undignified behaviour
John Dryden (1631–1700), 'He [Collier] is too much given to horseplay in his raillery'

kid

to treat someone with kid gloves
to handle a person with great discretion
refers to very soft leather gloves made from the skin of young goats

lamb

a lamb led to slaughter
a naVve person allowing himself or herself to be exploited
Isaiah 53:5, 'He was oppressed, and he was afflicted, yet he opened not his mouth: he is brought as a lamb to the slaughter'

one might as well be hanged for a sheep as for a lamb
further action will not increase the adverse consequences already in train
refers to the stealing of either sheep or lambs being capital crimes under old English law

sacrificial lamb
somebody unfairly made to suffer for the mistakes of others
Exodus 29:41, 'Sacrifice the other lamb at twilight ... an offering made to the Lord by fire'

to be mutton dressed up as lamb
foolishly to pretend to be younger
to wait two shakes of a lamb's tail
to wait just a few moments

lemon

the answer is a lemon
there is no appropriate answer to that sort of proposition
to sell someone a lemon
to sell a person a grossly defective product on the basis that it represents quality
to squeeze the lemon dry
to get the maximum advantage out of some favourable situation
Sir Eric Geddes (1875–1937), 'The Germans ... are going to pay every penny; they are going to be squeezed, as a lemon is squeezed — until the pips squeak. My only doubt is not whether we can squeeze hard enough, but whether there is enough juice.' (10 December 1918)

mackerel

to throw a sprat to catch a mackerel
to risk a little in the hope of gaining much

mare

a mare's nest
a discovery with illusory benefits

maverick

maverick
a person who likes to do things differently from other persons
refers to Samuel A. Maverick (1803–70), Texas engineer, who owned but did not brand cattle

milk

a land of milk and honey
a country in which everything is in abundant supply
Exodus 3:8, '... to bring them up out of that land unto a good land ... flowing with milk and honey'
it is no use crying over spilt milk
there is nothing to be gained by lamenting over an irredeemable error
to be cream on top of the milk
to be an additional benefit in an already satisfactory scenario

mill

it is all grist to the mill
this is all useful material for the task at hand
run of the mill
normal or average
to put someone through the mill
to make someone endure significant hardship through severe practical experience

mills

the mills of God grind slowly
retribution might be delayed but is inevitable
Friedrich von Logau (1604–55), *Sinngedichte* (translated by H. W. Longfellow), 'Though the mills of God grind slowly, yet they grind exceeding small; though with patience he stands waiting, with exactness grinds he all'

millstone

a millstone around someone's neck
a great burden

minnows

to miss the sharks while netting the minnows
to succeed in minor aspects but fail in the ones that really matter

moth

moth-eaten
antiquated, shabby

move

move over and let the greyhound see the rabbit
stand aside to allow things to get under way
refers to hunting with greyhounds
to move on to greener pastures
to move to a better environment; to commence a new, better career
Psalms 23:1, 'The Lord is my shepherd: therefore can I lack nothing. he shall feed me in a green pasture: and lead me forth beside the waters of comfort'

mover

prime mover
person initiating and promoting a cause

mushroom

to mushroom

to expand rapidly

refers to the rapid (overnight) growth of mushrooms

nut

a hard nut to crack

a difficult problem to be solved; OR someone not easily influenced

to use a sledgehammer to crack a nut

to devote vastly more resources to a project than is warranted by all the circumstances

nuts

to be nuts

to be crazy

to be nuts about someone

to be infatuated with a person

nutshell

in a nutshell

by way of summary

oak

to have a heart of oak

to be brave

refers to a famous sea song and naval march from the pantomime, *Harlequin's Invasion* (1759), by Garrick and Boyce.

oats

to feel one's oats

to be energetic and lively (UK and Australia); to be self-important (USA)

refers to an energetic horse fed on oats

to sow wild oats

to indulge in foolish behaviour while a young adult

olive

to hold out an olive branch

to make peace overtures

the olive branch was recognised as a symbol of peace and prosperity in many ancient civilisations; *Genesis* 8:11, 'And the dove came in to him in the evening; and lo, in her mouth was an olive leaf plucked off: so Noah knew that the waters were abated off the earth'

onions

to know one's onions

to be well informed in some area

refers to Dr C. T. Onions, editor of the *Shorter Oxford English Dictionary*

oranges

to add/compare apples with oranges

to lump unconnected things together quite illogically

ostrich

to be an ostrich

to refuse to face up to an unpleasant truth

refers to the reputed habit of ostriches in danger

oyster

the world is one's oyster

one has enormous scope for activity

Shakespeare, *The Merry Wives of Windsor*, II:ii, 'Why, then the world's mine oyster'

pack

to be at the head of the pack

to be the best of many, or the *de facto* leader

to bring someone back to the pack

to make a person conform

paddock

to have a spell in the paddock

to have leave of absence

refers to resting of horses from racing or work

pastor

pastor

religious official in charge of a congregation

from Latin *pastor* (form of *pascere)* meaning 'to feed or graze'; an example of a metaphor applied originally to flocks of sheep, and now having become established in the English language in its metaphorical sense of caring for a religious flock

pastures

to move on to greener pastures

to move to a better environment; to commence a new, better career

Psalms 23:1, 'The Lord is my shepherd: therefore can I lack nothing. he shall feed me in a green pasture: and lead me forth beside the waters of comfort'

pea

a pea-and-thimble trick

a clever fraud committed in the presence of its victim without this being obvious at the time refers to a sleight-of-hand trick played with three thimbles and a pea, the thimbles being moved about and observers being asked to guess under which thimble the pea is

pearl

a pearl
a thing of great excellence

pearls

to cast pearls before swine
to confer valuable benefits on someone who neither recognises nor appreciates them

Matthew 7:6, 'Neither cast ye your pearls before swine'

pecker

to keep one's pecker up
to stay cheerful

refers to keeping one's head up (with 'pecker' referring to mouth — as in a bird's mouth)

pecking

pecking order
order of seniority

refers to the activity of hens and other birds

perch

to knock someone off that person's perch
to displace a person from a leadership position in some competitive situation

pig

a guinea pig
a person on whom some new practice is tried out

refers to use of guinea pigs in medical experimentation

pig-headed
unduly obstinate

to buy a pig in a poke
to buy goods of unknown quality

refers to the practice of selling a person a cat (purported to be a pig) in a bag (or poke); if the person opened the bag and looked inside, that person 'let the cat out of the bag'

pigeon

a pigeon pair
one son and one daughter as the only offspring

refers to the old belief that pigeons always sat on two eggs that produced a male and a female, and that this pair remained together throughout life

to be one's pigeon
to be one's area of responsibility

to pigeon-hole
to put aside for further consideration in the distant future

refers to placing something in a small hole, like the small hole in a dovecot for the pigeons to walk in and out

pigeons

to throw a cat among the pigeons
to cause consternation and upset

pineapple

to have hold of the wrong end of the pineapple
to be utterly mistaken

plough

speed the plough!
let us get on with this as fast as possible!

George Chapman (?1559–?1634), *Bussy d'Ambois*, I:i, 'speed his plough!'

to plough new ground
to engage laboriously in an untried activity

to plough on
methodically and painstakingly to continue with an activity

to plough profits back
to retain profits in a business

to put one's hand to the plough
voluntarily to undertake some task

Luke 9:62. 'No man, having put his hand to the plough, and looking back, is fit for the Kingdom of God'

plum

the plum
the best item in a collection

plums

to pick just the plums out of the jam
to take only the very best items

poach

to poach on someone's preserves
to encroach uninvited on another person's territory

poacher

to appoint a poacher to be gamekeeper
to engage, perhaps foolishly, a formerly dishonest person to a position where that person's specialised knowledge can assist the prevention of similar dishonest activity by others

pony

a show pony
a vain and ostentatious person

poppy

a tall poppy
a person with great power or responsibility and/or in receipt of high remuneration

poppies

to cut tall poppies down to size
to diminish the self-importance of haughty persons

potato

a hot potato
a controversial issue that no one wants to handle, an embarrassing issue

potatoes

to be small potatoes
to be quite unimportant

prune

to prune
to remove the superfluous
refers to horticulture

pump

parish pump issues
issues of local importance lacking a wider perspective
refers to the local parish water pump

to engage in pump priming
to spend public money with the aim of attracting parochial electoral support
refers to priming a water pump

rabbit

a rabbit warren
a building with a maze of rooms and passages

move over and let the greyhound see the rabbit
stand aside to allow things to get under way
refers to hunting with greyhounds

to pull a rabbit out of the hat
to produce an unexpected and seemingly miraculous but highly desirable solution
refers to magician's trick

reap

to reap as one has sown
to experience the consequences of one's own actions
Galatians 6:7, 'Whatsoever a man soweth, that shall he also reap'

to reap the whirlwind
to suffer the adverse consequences of a bad act
Hosea 8:7, 'They have sown the wind, and they shall reap the whirlwind'

to sow the wind and reap the whirlwind
to make bad mistakes and to suffer the even worse consequences
Hosea 8:7, 'They have sown the wind, and they shall reap the whirlwind'

rein

a tight rein
strong controls
refers to riding or driving horses

to give rein to one's fancy
to let one's imagination have free scope
refers to riding or driving horses

to give someone free rein
to confer complete discretion on another person
refers to riding or driving horses

to rein in something
to keep better control over something
refers to riding or driving horses

to take over the reins
to assume control
refers to riding or driving horses

roost

the chickens are coming home to roost
the consequences of a person's past actions are now being felt by that person
Robert Southey (1774–1843), *The Curse of Kehama* (1810), 'Curses are like young chickens, they always come home to roost'

to rule the roost
to dominate

refers to the habit of roosters and hens to have an established order of dominance

rooster

today a rooster, tomorrow a feather duster
when circumstances change, an important person can, immediately, become unimportant

rose

a rose between two thorns
something beautiful in the midst of ugliness

a rose by any other name would smell as sweet
the form does not affect the substance
Shakespeare, *Romeo and Juliet* II:ii, 'What's in a name? That which we call a rose / By any other name would smell as sweet'

to come up smelling like a rose
not to have a stain on one's character

to see something through rose-coloured glasses/spectacles
to appreciate only the advantages and to disregard completely the disadvantages

roses

to be on a path strewn with roses
to lead a very pleasant life

to be no bed of roses
to be difficult or uncomfortable
Robert Louis Stevenson (1850–94), *Virginibus Puerisque* I:i, 'Marriage is like life in this — that it is a field of battle, and not a bed of roses'

row

not to matter a row of beans
to be utterly unimportant

to have a hard row to hoe
to have a difficult assignment
refers to agriculture; James Russell Lowell (1819–91), *The Biglow Papers*, 'You've a darned long row to hoe'

ruminate

to ruminate
to ponder over a matter
refers to the chewing of the cud by ruminant animals

seed

to run to seed
to become shabby
refers to plants maturing past the glory of the flowering phase

seeds

to sow seeds
to propagate ideas in the hope that they will be adopted

sharks

to miss the sharks while netting the minnows
to succeed in minor aspects but fail in the ones that really matter

sheep

a black sheep
a disreputable member of an otherwise reputable group

one might as well be hanged for a sheep as for a lamb
further action will not increase the adverse consequences already in train
refers to the stealing of either sheep or lambs being capital crimes under old English law

to be a wolf in sheep's clothing
to be a hypocrite; to be dangerous although masquerading as something harmless
Matthew 7:15, 'Beware of false prophets, which come to you in sheep's clothing, but inwardly they are ravening wolves'

to be home on the sheep's back
to be doing well

to cast sheep's eyes at someone
to look at a person amorously

to ride on the sheep's back
to benefit from the production of wool

to separate the sheep from the goats
to distinguish between the worthy and the unworthy
Matthew 25:32, 'and he shall separate them one from one another, as a shepherd divideth his sheep from the goats'

to spoil the ship for a ha'p'orth of tar
to engage in a false economy
the current word 'ship' is actually a mistake for the original word 'sheep', and the tar refers to the treatment of wounds

sheepish

sheepish
embarrassed, as though guilty

shepherd

to shepherd some group

to marshal the members of some group

skin

a cleanskin

a person without a criminal record or other blemish on that person's reputation

probably refers to an unblemished animal skin

slippery

to be on a slippery chute/shoot

to court disaster

refers to an opening in the side of a shearing shed known as the porthole or chute (spelling variations include shoot and shute); after a sheep is shorn it is pushed through the porthole and slides down

sow

one can't make a silk purse out of a sow's ear

it is impossible to manufacture something of a high standard from inferior raw materials

Malcolm Bradbury (1932–), 'For the mass of men, you can't make a silk purse out of a sow's ear'

to get the wrong sow by the ear

to reach an incorrect conclusion

to sow seeds

to propagate ideas in the hope that they will be adopted

to sow the wind and reap the whirlwind

to make bad mistakes and to suffer the even worse consequences

Hosea 8:7, 'They have sown the wind, and they shall reap the whirlwind'

to sow wild oats

to indulge in foolish behaviour while a young adult

sown

to reap as one has sown

to experience the consequences of one's own actions

Galatians 6:7, 'Whatsoever a man soweth, that shall he also reap'

spade

to call a spade a spade

to speak bluntly; not to use euphemisms

spadework

to do the spadework

to do the hard or menial work in preparation for a project

sprat

to throw a sprat to catch a mackerel

to risk a little in the hope of gaining much

spur

to spur someone on

to agitate a person into doing something

refers to riding horses

spurs

to win one's spurs

to gain recognition after a period of effort

refers to the earning of a knighthood in battle

stampede

to stampede someone into something

to pressure a person into taking some action

sticks

sticks and carrots

disincentives and incentives in combination

refers to the handling of donkeys

straw

a man of straw

a person of no substance, a counterfeit, a sham; OR a person invented in order to be triumphantly defeated; OR a person who has no assets while giving a contrary appearance

Exodus 6:7 'Ye shall no more give the people straw to make bricks ... let them go and gather straw for themselves'

one cannot make bricks without straw

one cannot achieve results in the absence of adequate resources

Exodus 6:7 'Ye shall no more give the people straw to make bricks ... let them go and gather straw for themselves'

the final (or last) straw

the latest step that, when added to a large number of seemingly harmless previous steps, sets off a significant event resulting from the cumulative effect

see 'the straw that broke the camel's back'

the straw that broke the camel's back

the latest step that, when added to a large number of seemingly harmless previous steps, sets off a sudden significant event resulting from the cumulative effect

to draw the short straw

to be chosen (perhaps by lot) to undertake an undesired task

straws

straws in the wind

small but significant indicators of future events

John Seldon (1584–1654), 'Take a straw and throw it up into the air, you shall see by that which way the wind is'

to clasp/grasp at straws

desperately to resort to any expedient in a hopeless situation

refers to a drowning person

swarm

to swarm out

to appear in large numbers from within

refers to bees or wasps'

swine

to cast pearls before swine

to confer valuable benefits on someone who neither recognises nor appreciates them

Matthew 7:6, 'Neither cast ye your pearls before swine'

tally

to keep a tally

to keep a record

from Latin *talea* (a rod or stick); refers to a stick with notches (made to indicate a count), the stick then being split lengthways and each party to a transaction receiving one half as a record of the transaction

tarred

to be tarred with the same brush

to be damned merely because of one's association with another person

refers to treating cuts on sheep with a tarbrush

tether

to be at the end of one's tether

to be frustrated because one is at the very limit of one's resources of knowledge, authority, or patience

refers to tethering of animals with a rope

thorn

to be a thorn in someone's flesh/side

to be a constant annoyance or affliction

2 Corinthians 12:7, 10: 'There was given to me a thorn in the flesh ... I will glory in my infirmities'

thorns

to wear one's crown of thorns

to have one's own difficulties

John 19:2, 'And the soldiers plaited a crown of thorns, and put it on his [Jesus'] head'

a rose between two thorns

something beautiful in the midst of ugliness

traces

to kick over the traces

to become insubordinate

refers to the straps designed to keep a horse restrained

trample

to trample someone under foot

by virtue of one's great power to treat a person's rights with contempt and not to give that person proper consideration

trap

to walk into a trap

to be tricked into doing something

turkey

cold turkey

the sudden cessation of drugs to an addict and, by extension, the sudden cessation of any habitually pleasurable activity

probably refers to the appearance of the skin of drug addicts experiencing withdrawal symptoms (similarity to the skin of a plucked cold turkey)

to talk turkey

to talk realistically

origin obscure; North American slang

vegetable

to become a vegetable

to lose one's ability to respond to many external stimuli, especially those that normally contribute to the quality of life; to lead a monotonous life with no animation

vine

to hear on the grapevine

to learn unofficially

the earlier form of the metaphor was a 'grapevine telegraph' as a means of communicating private information

to wither on the vine

by virtue of changed circumstances or the effluxion of time to be no longer relevant

John 15:5, 6, 'I am the vine, ye are the branches ... if a man abideth not in me, he is cast forth as a branch and is withered'

weed

to weed some group out

to get rid of some elements not meeting a desired standard

wether

bell-wether

first indication

refers to the leading sheep (wether) of a flock, this sheep having a bell hung around its neck

wheat

to separate the wheat from the chaff

to separate the worthy from the unworthy

Matthew 3:12, 'His winnowing fork is in his hand, and he will clear his threshing floor and gather his wheat into the granary, but the chaff he will burn with unquenchable fire'

whip

to be a fair crack of the whip

to be just; to provide a fair opportunity

to crack the whip

to assert one's authority

refers to the use of a whip in riding or driving animals

to have the whip hand

to be in control of a situation

refers to the hand holding the whip in controlling horses, and perhaps slaves

to whip oneself into a lather

to become unduly excited

refers to horses sweating profusely when excited

whoa

from go to whoa

from start to finish

refers to the commands given to horses

wool

dyed in the wool

very loyal and partisan

refers to a garment in which the wool itself (from which the garment is woven) is dyed, rather than the completed garment being dyed as a piece (and thus less thoroughly)

to pull the wool over someone's eyes

to deceive or deliberately mislead another person

derived from the inability of some sheep to see clearly if wool is across their eyes

worm

a bookworm

a person who likes reading and study

the early bird gets the worm

a person who acts ahead of others gets an advantage over them

the worm has turned

a previously compliant person is now asserting his or her personality

to worm one's way in

subtly to insinuate oneself into a person's trust

Food and Drink

apple

a rotten apple

an isolated dishonest person in an otherwise honest group

in apple-pie order

in perfect order and condition

to be the apple of someone's eye

to be a much cherished person

refers to the pupil of the eye — 'the apple of the eye' as being the centre of visual perception and therefore especially cherished and much-valued

apples

to add/compare apples with oranges
to lump unconnected things together quite illogically

to compare apples with apples
to make a valid comparison

applecart

to upset the applecart
to engage in conduct disturbing a peaceful state of affairs and thereby to cause discomfort

bacon

to bring home the bacon
to be successful
refers to bringing home a valued prize

to save one's bacon
to escape harm
refers to the value attached to bacon as a stored food

bait

to swallow the bait
to succumb to a temptation deliberately put in one's way
refers to angling

baked

halfbaked
not well thought out

banana

a banana republic
a country with a poor economy

barrel

to pork barrel
to spend taxpayers' money in one area in order to attract political support
refers to times of slavery in America when pork was provided to slaves gathered around the pork barrel

to scrape the bottom of the barrel
to be forced to use the last available resources; to lower one's standards because one is short of resources

bean

not to have a bean
to have no money

beans

not to matter a row of beans
to be utterly unimportant

to be full of beans
to be very cheerful

to know how many beans make five
to have common sense
refers to an old riddle

to spill the beans
indiscreetly to reveal sensitive information

beer

not to be all beer and skittles
not to be all pleasant and easy

to be small beer
to be quite unimportant

to cry in one's beer
to show remorse

bird

the bird is carved
the necessary action has been taken

boil

to bring something to the boil
to bring something to a climax

to come off the boil
to require urgent attention no longer

boiled

hard-boiled
toughened by experience
refers to cooking (esp. eggs)

boiling

to keep the pot boiling
to ensure that an issue stays current
refers to cooking

to reach boiling point
to reach a climax; OR to be close to losing one's temper bone

a bone of contention
the subject matter of violent disagreement
probably refers to dogs fighting over a bone

to cut costs to the bone
to economise strictly

to get close to the bone
to cause discomfort by being accurate

to have a bone to pick
to have a grievance that requires discussion

to put flesh and bone on something
to supply details of a proposal previously revealed only in outline

to throw someone a bone

to fob a person off with a symbolic but unimportant gesture
refers to feeding a dog

bones

to make no bones about it
to be brutally frank
the bare bones
(of a story) nothing but the essential elements

bottle

a bottleneck
a factor obstructing an even flow
to be a full bottle on something
to be very knowledgeable about a subject
to bottle-up some feeling
to keep some feeling entirely to oneself

bread

a bread-and-butter issue
a basic issue that is of importance to many people
a bread-winner
a person earning by personal exertion the income of a household
Deuteronomy 8:3, 'Man doth not live by bread alone, but by every word that proceedeth out of the mouth of the Lord' (see also *Matthew* 5:4)
to be someone's bread and butter
to be a person's livelihood or to be a person's everyday experience
to cast one's bread upon the waters
to give generously because one will eventually be rewarded for one's generosity
Ecclesiastes 11:1, 'Cast thy bread upon the waters: for thou shalt find it after many days'
to claim that something is the best thing since sliced bread
to have a high opinion of the importance or novelty of an invention or practice
to know on which side one's bread is buttered
to be aware of the important personally advantageous considerations
to put jam on someone's bread
to make a good situation even better

breakfast

to be a dog's breakfast
to be a very messy arrangement
to be able to eat someone for breakfast
to be able to outwit a person very easily

broth

too many cooks spoil the broth

more than one leader can confuse and harm a project bull

a bull in a china shop
a careless person likely to cause great damage
a cock-and-bull story
an explanation that is completely unbelievable and unacceptable
Laurence Sterne (1713–68), *Tristram Shandy*, 'Said my mother, "What is this story all about?" — "a cock and a bull," said Yorick.'
to be a red rag to a bull
to be something that makes a person very angry and very excited
refers to the erroneous belief that the colour red, rather than the motion of waving, excites a bull
to be within a bull's roar of something
to be very close to something
to charge like a wounded bull
to impose excessive prices
a play on words; not a simile
to hit the bull's eye
to be extremely accurate in an activity; to score
derived from archery
to take the bull by the horns
to come to grips with the realities of a difficult problem

bunfight

a bunfight
a social gathering; a tea party

butter

a bread-and-butter issue
a basic issue that is of importance to many people
a butter fingers
a person unable to catch and/or hold on to an object
someone looks as if butter would not melt in his or her mouth

a person looks sweet and innocent

to be someone's bread and butter
to be a person's livelihood or to be a person's everyday experience

buttered

to know on which side one's bread is buttered
to be aware of the important personally advantageous considerations

cabbage

to be on someone's cabbage patch
to engage in a competitive activity in a territory regarded by someone already there as rightfully belonging exclusively to that person

cake

a share of the cake
a portion of the total available for distribution

that takes the cake
that is quite absurd or outrageous or excessively cheeky

to be a piece of cake
to be very easy or greatly to one's liking

to be icing on top of the cake
to be an additional benefit in an already satisfactory scenario

to want to have one's cake and eat it too
to want two mutually exclusive alternatives

calf

to kill the fatted calf
to demonstrate welcome and complete acceptance of another person

Luke 15:23. 'And bring hither the fatted calf and let us eat, and be merry'

can

a can of worms
a collection of complex intertwined problems

the empty can makes the most noise
the least worthy arguments often attract the most publicity

carrots

sticks and carrots
disincentives and incentives in combination

refers to the handling of donkeys

chalice

to hand someone a poisoned chalice
to confer a seeming benefit on a person that will turn out to be a significant detriment

cheese

cheese paring
miserly

stiff cheese!
circumstances that might be unwelcome but will not be altered, and in respect of which no great sympathy is felt

cheesed

to be cheesed off
to be disgusted

cherry

to engage in cherry picking
(in business) to accept only the potentially most lucrative deals

to get only one bite at the cherry
to receive no further opportunity

chestnuts

to pull someone's chestnuts out of the fire
to retrieve a situation for someone else

refers to fable of a monkey getting roasting chestnuts out of a fire by using the cat's paw to achieve the desired result

chew

to be able to chew gum and walk at the same time
to be able to do two relatively simple things simultaneously

used ironically to disparage a person of limited capacities

to bite off more than one can chew
to be over ambitious and thus unrealistic as to one's capabilities

to chew fat
to discuss a matter, often with grumbling and unhappiness

to chew someone's ear
to force one's conversation on an unwilling listener

to chew the cud
to reflect on something

refers to the chewing of the cud by ruminant animals

to have something to chew on
to have firm facts on which to base a decision

chicken

chicken and egg
a situation involving two factors each of which causes the other, making it impossible to decide which came first

chicken-hearted
showing little courage

to be chicken feed
to be small and unimportant

chickens

the chickens are coming home to roost
the consequences of a person's past actions are now being felt by that person

Robert Southey (1774–1843), *The Curse of Kehama* (1810), 'Curses are like young chickens, they always come home to roost'

to count one's chickens before they are hatched
to treat as fact the expected results of a future proposal

originally attributed to Erasmus (1466–1536) in slightly different form

chops

to lick one's chops
to look forward to something with pleasurable anticipation

refers to salivation in anticipation of food

clover

to be in clover
to enjoy a life of ease and luxury

refers to grazing animals in rich pasture

cock

a cock-and-bull story
an explanation that is completely unbelievable and unacceptable

Laurence Sterne (1713–68), *Tristram Shandy*, 'Said my mother, "What is this story all about?" — "a cock and a bull," said Yorick.'

cock-eyed
stupid

cocktail

a cocktail
a mixture of several components contributing to a result

refers to an aperitif; origin of name obscure

cook

there are many ways to cook eggs
there are many ways to achieve an objective

to be chief cook and bottlewasher
to perform a range of duties single-handedly — ranging from important to menial

to cook one's goose
to make a fatal mistake; to ruin one's plans

nineteenth-century street ballad: 'If they come here we'll cook their geese'

to cook the books
fraudulently to maintain false records of financial transactions

cookie

that is the way the cookie crumbles
that is the actual situation

core

rotten to the core
completely corrupt

to be the hard core
to be the central and most difficult problem

cow

a cash cow
a source of ready money

a milch cow
an easy and plentiful source of some desired benefit

cows

till the cows come home
for a very long time, perhaps forever

Francis Beaumont (1584–1616) & John Fletcher (1579–1625), *The Scornful* Lady, 'Kiss till the cow comes home'

cream

to be cream on top of the milk
to be an additional benefit in an already satisfactory scenario

crPme

crPme de la crPme
something quite superlative

French, 'the cream of the cream'

crumbs

to throw someone a few crumbs

to fob a person off with a few symbolic but unimportant concessions
Luke 16:21, 'a certain beggar ... desiring to be fed with the crumbs which fell from the rich man's table'

cud
to chew the cud
to reflect on something
refers to the chewing of the cud by ruminant animals

dinner
to be done like a dinner
to be defeated and humiliated

dinners
I have had more of these than I have had hot dinners
I have had a very large number of these

doughnut
watch the doughnut — not the hole
look for the positive aspects

drakes
to play ducks and drakes
not to treat the matter seriously
derived from the old name given to the game of throwing a stone such that it skips across the surface of water; hence: 'to throw away idly and carelessly

drink
one can lead a horse to water, but one can't make it drink
one can give advice to a person but cannot ensure that it will be acted on
to be meat and drink
to be very pleasurable; or to be basic, familiar, and essential to one's experience of life'
Matthew 25:35, 'For I was an hungred, and ye gave me meat: I was thirsty and ye gave me drink'; Shakespeare, 'It is meat and drinke to me to see a clowne'

drinks
it is a long time between drinks
activity is occurring only very spasmodically

drone
a drone
an idle person

drop
to squeeze the last drop out of something
to get the maximum advantage out of some favourable situation

droves
people stayed away in droves
few people came
refers to a moving group of cattle, sheep, or other animals

duck
a lame duck
a person unable to fend for himself or herself
a 'lame-duck president' is a president still in office but without influence because the commencement of the successor's term is imminent
in two shakes of a duck's tail
in an instant
to be a dead duck
to have failed; OR to be in a hopeless situation
to be a sitting duck
to be vulnerable to exploitation
to be like water off a duck's back
(of advice or criticism) to be completely ignored
to duck for cover
to seek to avoid blame

duckling
an ugly duckling
an unprepossessing person or thing, the characteristics of which change in time to become attractive
refers to a cygnet in a brood of ducks in a children's story of that name by Hans Christian Andersen

ducks
to play ducks and drakes
not to treat the matter seriously
derived from the old name given to the game of throwing a stone such that it skips across the surface of water; hence: 'to throw away idly and carelessly

eat
I could eat a horse
I am very hungry
I'll eat my hat if so-and-so happens
I do not believe that so-and-so will happen
to be able to eat someone for breakfast

to be able to outwit a person very easily

to eat crow
to act in a humiliating fashion to achieve a desired outcome
from an incident in New England (North America) in the Anglo–American War of 1812–14

to eat humble pie
to be prepared to humiliate oneself and apologise
a play on words — derived from the eating of 'umble pie' (entrails of a deer) by lowly persons

to eat one's head off
to eat excessively

to eat one's heart out
to suffer bitterly
Shakespeare, *Othello* IV:i, 'O God! That I were a man! I would eat his heart in the market place'

to eat one's words
to retract in a humiliated fashion

to eat out of someone's hands
to be very compliant and submissive

to eat someone alive
to defeat a person soundly

to eat someone out of house and home
to ruin a person by eating all that that person has
used in an exaggerated, humorous sense

to want to have one's cake and eat it too
to want two mutually exclusive alternatives

you can eat your heart out
I don't care if you are intensely aggrieved or jealous

eaten

moth-eaten
antiquated, shabby

eating

the choice is between eating well or sleeping well
one can invest for maximum yield or maximum security, but not both

the proof of the pudding is in the eating
the success of a venture will be measured by its results

egg

a nest egg
a sum of money set aside in case of need; a nucleus of savings
derived from the custom of placing an egg in a hen's nest as an inducement for the hen to lay more

chicken and egg
a situation involving two factors each of which causes the other, making it impossible to decide which came first

to be a bad egg
to be a dishonest or disreputable person

to be a curate's egg
to be good only in parts
refers to a cartoon (1895) showing the nervous young curate (Jones) in conversation with the Lord Bishop:
'I'm afraid you've got a bad egg, Mr Jones.'
'Oh no, my Lord, I assure you! Parts of it are excellent!'
Punch, vol. cix, p. 222, 1895

to have egg on one's face
to be embarrassed by the results of one's own stupidity

eggs

as sure as eggs is eggs
with great certainty
perhaps a corruption of the logician's formula: 'x is x'

not to put all one's eggs in the one basket
to spread one's risks

one cannot make an omelette without breaking eggs
the desired end dictates the means even if they cause harm to others

there are many ways to cook eggs
there are many ways to achieve an objective

to kill the goose that lays the golden eggs
through excessive greed, to sacrifice future gains for a short-term advantage
based on a Greek fable about a man who killed the goose that laid golden eggs; his aim was to collect the whole stock of eggs at once but, in doing so, he ended his future supply

to teach one's grandmother how to suck eggs

to try to tell a much more experienced person something very obvious to that person

fat

the fat is in the fire
action with certain unstoppable consequences has now been initiated

to chew fat
to discuss a matter, often with grumbling and unhappiness

to trim the fat
to increase efficiency by reducing outlays

fatted

to kill the fatted calf
to demonstrate welcome and complete acceptance of another person
Luke 15:23. 'And bring hither the fatted calf and let us eat, and be merry'

feast

a movable feast
an event not customarily held on a set date
refers to the feast days of the Christian Church, some of which are held on fixed days ('immovable feasts') and some of which vary with the date of Easter ('movable feasts')

to be either feast or famine
to go from one extreme to the other

fig

one would not give a fig for something
one regards something as worthless

fish

a queer fish
an unusual type of person

an ocean full of fish
plenty of opportunity

neither fish flesh nor good red herring
unclassifiable by virtue of being neither one thing nor another
Miguel de Cervantes (1547–1616), *Don Quixote*

that has nothing to do with the price of fish
that is quite irrelevant

to be a big fish in a little pond
to be a person holding an important office but in an unimportant organisation

to be a cold fish
to be an unemotional person

to be a different kettle of fish
to be something very dissimilar
refers to a riverside picnic where freshly caught fish is cooked and eaten

to be a fine kettle of fish
to be a terrible muddle
refers to a riverside picnic where freshly caught fish is cooked and eaten

to be a fish out of water
to be in difficulty by virtue of being in a strange environment

to be in a goldfish bowl
to be very open to view

to fish for compliments
to drop hints in the hope that one will receive praise or recognition

to fish in troubled waters
to profit from a disturbed situation
refers to angling

to have more important fish to fry
to have more important things to do

what has that to do with the price of fish?
what is the relevance of this?

fishing

a fishing expedition
an exercise that sets out to gather incriminating information without knowing its exact nature or location

fishy

to be a fishy situation
to be a suspicious situation

flavour

to be the flavour of the month
to be a person or commodity temporarily popular
refers to sales or marketing of foods of a particular flavour

flesh

neither fish flesh nor good red herring
unclassifiable by virtue of being neither one thing nor another
Miguel de Cervantes (1547–1616), *Don Quixote*

one's pound of flesh
that which is strictly due to one, albeit excessive and lacking in compassion
Shakespeare, *Merchant of Venice* IV:i, 'The pound of flesh, which I demand of

him, is dearly bought; 't is mine, and I will have it!'

fleshpots

fleshpots

sumptuous living

Exodus 16:3, ' ... in the land of Egypt, when we sat by the fleshpots and when we did eat bread to the full'

flock

flock

congregation in the charge of a religious official

numerous biblical references incl.: *Isaiah* 40:11, 'He shall feed his flock like a shepherd: he shall gather the lambs with his arm, and carry them in his bosom, and shall gently lead those that are with young'

fold

the fold

the body of believers

refers to an enclosure for sheep; *John* 10:16, 'Other sheep I have, which are not of this fold'

food

food for thought

material for examination in one's mind

Robert Southey (1774–1843), 'A lively tale, and fraught with ... food for thought'

to be at the bottom of the food chain

to be at the lowest level in a hierarchy

to take food out of the mouths of children

cruelly to deprive the needy

froth

froth and bubble

superficially attractive but really insignificant items

'Life is mainly froth and bubble ... ' (folk rhyme)

fruit

forbidden fruit

something particularly desired because it is not allowed

Genesis 2:17, 'but of the tree of the knowledge of good and evil, thou shalt not eat of it'

to bear fruit

to result in success

fruitless

fruitless

yielding no benefit

fruits

by their fruits ye shall know them

their true nature will be revealed by their results

Matthew 7:20, 'wherefore by their fruits ye shall know them'

fry

to have more important fish to fry

to have more important things to do

frying

out of the frying pan into the fire

from one bad situation to an even worse one

game

to be fair game

to be someone who can be attacked legitimately

refers to hunting

gander

what is sauce for the goose is sauce for the gander

arguments that apply in one case also apply in another

gel

to gel

to settle into a coherent state and thus make sense

gingerbread

to take the gilt off the gingerbread

to strip something of its main attraction

goat

a scapegoat

a person who is forced to take the blame for something not their fault

Leviticus 16:10, 'But the goat, on which the lot fell to be the scapegoat ... to make an atonement'

to play the giddy goat

to act the fool

'giddy' derived from Old English *gidig* ('possessed by a god')

goats

to separate the sheep from the goats

to distinguish between the worthy and the unworthy

Matthew 25:32, 'and he shall separate them one from one another, as a shepherd divideth his sheep from the goats'

goose

a wild-goose chase
a futile chase or search
refers to old game of 'follow-the-leader' on horses in which the objective was to follow a winding and difficult course without ever catching up

to be too frightened to say 'boo' to a goose
to be excessively shy

to cook one's goose
to make a fatal mistake; to ruin one's plans
nineteenth-century street ballad: 'If they come here we'll cook their geese'

to kill the goose that lays the golden eggs
through excessive greed, to sacrifice future gains for a short-term advantage
based on a Greek fable about a man who killed the goose that laid golden eggs; his aim was to collect the whole stock of eggs at once but, in doing so, he ended his future supply

what is sauce for the goose is sauce for the gander
arguments that apply in one case also apply in another

gooseberry

to play gooseberry
to act as an unwelcome chaperon

grain

to take something with a grain of salt
to regard the facts in a statement with considerable scepticism

grapes

that is just sour grapes
those are disparaging remarks made only because that person is peeved and resentful at someone else's better fortune
derived from Aesop's fable of 'the fox and the grapes' about expressing deliberate disparagement of a desired but unattainable object; 'sour grapes' also occurs in *Ezekiel* 18:2, 'the fathers have eaten sour grapes, and the children's teeth are set on edge'

what is this — a bunch of grapes or a bowl of goldfish?
surely you know what this is?

grapevine

to hear on the grapevine
to learn unofficially
the earlier form of the metaphor was a 'grapevine telegraph' as a means of communicating private information

grass

a snake in the grass
a person of low character who manages to disguise that trait
Virgil, *Eclogue*, 'There's a snake hidden in the grass'

grass roots
at the lowest level of a hierarchy

not to let grass grow under one's feet
not to let inertia or delay spoil something

gravy

to get on a gravy train
to take steps to become a recipient of benefits that are available but undeserved

gum

to be able to chew gum and walk at the same time
to be able to do two relatively simple things simultaneously
used ironically to disparage a person of limited capacities

ham

to be the ham in the sandwich
to be caught in the middle of a dispute between other parties

hamstrung

to be hamstrung
to have limited freedom to act as one would wish
refers to ancient practice of disabling a person or animal by cutting the hamstring muscles of the thigh

hard-boiled

hard-boiled
toughened by experience
refers to cooking (esp. eggs)

hare

first catch your hare

do things in logical order and after proper preparation

generally attributed to Hannah Gleese, habit-maker to the Prince of Wales and co-author of *The Art of Cookery Made Plain and Easy* (1747)

hare-brained

wildly stupid

Benjamin Disraeli (1804–81), speech 1878, 'The hare-brained chatter of irresponsible frivolity'

to chase every hare

to be easily sidetracked

to run with the hare and hunt with the hounds

to keep in with two opposing sides

refers to hunting

to set a hare running

to initiate an activity to achieve a related and desired effect

refers to hunting

hay

to look for a needle in a haystack

to attempt something with a very small chance of success

to make hay while the sun shines

to utilise an opportunity before it disappears

John Betjeman (1906–84), *The Last Laugh*, 'I made hay while the sun shone'

hen

a mother hen

an over-protective person

Matthew 12:37, 'Even as a hen gathereth her chickens under her wings'

hen-pecked

subject to domination by one's wife

Lord Byron (1788–1824), *Don Juan*, 'But — oh! ye lords of ladies intellectual, inform us truly, have they not hen-peck'd you all?'

herd

to follow the herd

to do what most other people are doing

herring

neither fish flesh nor good red herring

unclassifiable by virtue of being neither one thing nor another

Miguel de Cervantes (1547–1616), *Don Quixote*

to be a red herring

to be something designed to divert attention away from the main question

refers to hunting with hounds — a red herring was dragged across the scent trail to train hounds to ignore distractions and follow the correct trail

hog

a road hog

an inconsiderate motorist

refers to gluttonous swine

to go the whole hog

to do something very thoroughly

origin uncertain; alternative explanations include: (i) Muslim divines attempting to ascertain how much of the whole hog could be eaten according to Islamic law (Cowper, 1779, 'but for one piece they thought it hard/from the whole hog to be debarred'); (ii) colloquial term for a shilling — that is, to spend the whole hog (or shilling) at one time; (iii) refers to the close shearing of lambs

to make a hog of oneself

to demonstrate greed

refers to gluttonous swine

hogwash

hogwash

nonsense

refers to 'hog wash' — meaning kitchen swill for pigs (and therefore worthless)

honey

a land of milk and honey

a country in which everything is in abundant supply

Exodus 3:8, ' ... to bring them up out of that land unto a good land ... flowing with milk and honey'

horse

I could eat a horse

I am very hungry

one can lead a horse to water, but one can't make it drink

one can give advice to a person but cannot ensure that it will be acted on

hungry

lean and hungry

efficient

Shakespeare, *Julius Caesar* I:ii, 'Yond' Cassius has a lean and hungry look; he thinks too much: such men are dangerous'

ice

to put something on ice

to put something aside for the time being

icing

to be icing on top of the cake
to be an additional benefit in an already satisfactory scenario

jam

money for jam
remuneration easily earned

to be in a jam
to be in difficulties

to pick just the plums out of the jam
to take only the very best items

to put jam on someone's bread
to make a good situation even better

jelly

to be set like a jelly
to be very well established

kitchen

if one can't stand the heat one should stay out of the kitchen
if one cannot put up with the pressure of a situation, one should get out of it
US President Harry S. Truman (1884–1972), *Mr Citizen*, ch. 15, 'If you can't stand the heat, get out of the kitchen'

knife

before one can say 'knife'
very quickly

one could have cut the atmosphere with a knife
those present were very tense

to be on a knife edge
to be in danger; OR to be a very close result

to wield the knife
to terminate the services of one or more persons or to prune expenditure

knives

the knives are out
there is an active campaign against someone

to sharpen the knives
to get ready for a concerted attack on a person or principle

kosher

to be kosher
to fulfil all requirements
refers to food complying with all aspects of Jewish religious law; Hebrew *kaser* ('fit, proper')

lamb

a lamb led to slaughter
a naVve person allowing himself or herself to be exploited
Isaiah 53:5, 'He was oppressed, and he was afflicted, yet he opened not his mouth: he is brought as a lamb to the slaughter'

one might as well be hanged for a sheep as for a lamb
further action will not increase the adverse consequences already in train
refers to the stealing of either sheep or lambs being capital crimes under old English law

sacrificial lamb
somebody unfairly made to suffer for the mistakes of others
Exodus 29:41, 'Sacrifice the other lamb at twilight ... an offering made to the Lord by fire'

to be mutton dressed up as lamb
foolishly to pretend to be younger

to wait two shakes of a lamb's tail
to wait just a few moments

lemon

the answer is a lemon
there is no appropriate answer to that sort of proposition

to sell someone a lemon
to sell a person a grossly defective product on the basis that it represents quality

to squeeze the lemon dry
to get the maximum advantage out of some favourable situation
Sir Eric Geddes (1875–1937), 'The Germans ... are going to pay every penny; they are going to be squeezed, as a lemon is squeezed — until the pips squeak. My only doubt is not whether we can squeeze hard enough, but whether there is enough juice.' (10 December 1918)

loaf

half a loaf is better than none
it is more advantageous to accept less than is really desired than risk missing out completely

John Heywood (1546), 'Throw no gift at the giver's head;/better is half a loaf than no bread

mackerel

to throw a sprat to catch a mackerel
to risk a little in the hope of gaining much

manna

manna from heaven
unexpected benefits
derived from Hebrew *man-hu* ('what is this?'); *Exodus* 16:15, 'It is manna: for they wist not what it was. And Moses said unto them: this is the bread which the Lord hath given you to eat'

meat

one man's meat is another man's poison
different people have different tastes

to be easy meat
to be an opponent who is readily outwitted

to be meat and drink
to be very pleasurable; or to be basic, familiar, and essential to one's experience of life'
Matthew 25:35, 'For I was an hungred, and ye gave me meat: I was thirsty and ye gave me drink'; Shakespeare, 'It is meat and drinke to me to see a clowne'

to be the meat in the sandwich
to be caught in the middle of a dispute between other parties

to contain much meat
to contain much material worthy of consideration

to make mincemeat of something
to devastate something

milk

a land of milk and honey
a country in which everything is in abundant supply
Exodus 3:8, ' ... to bring them up out of that land unto a good land ... flowing with milk and honey'

it is no use crying over spilt milk
there is nothing to be gained by lamenting over an irredeemable error

to be cream on top of the milk
to be an additional benefit in an already satisfactory scenario

mince

not to mince words
to speak bluntly

mincemeat

to make mincemeat of something
to devastate something

minnows

to miss the sharks while netting the minnows
to succeed in minor aspects but fail in the ones that really matter

mug

a mug's game
an activity that wise persons eschew
perhaps refers to the practice of representing faces (often humorous) on drinking mugs

mushroom

to mushroom
to expand rapidly
refers to the rapid (overnight) growth of mushrooms

mutton

to be mutton dressed up as lamb
foolishly to pretend to be younger

nut

a hard nut to crack
a difficult problem to be solved; OR someone not easily influenced

to use a sledgehammer to crack a nut
to devote vastly more resources to a project than is warranted by all the circumstances

nuts

to be nuts
to be crazy

to be nuts about someone
to be infatuated with a person

nutshell

in a nutshell
by way of summary

oats

to feel one's oats
to be energetic and lively (UK and Australia); to be self-important (USA)
refers to an energetic horse fed on oats

to sow wild oats

to indulge in foolish behaviour while a young adult

olive

to hold out an olive branch

to make peace overtures

the olive branch was recognised as a symbol of peace and prosperity in many ancient civilisations; *Genesis* 8:11, 'And the dove came in to him in the evening; and lo, in her mouth was an olive leaf plucked off: so Noah knew that the waters were abated off the earth'

omelette

one cannot make an omelette without breaking eggs

the desired end dictates the means even if they cause harm to others

to unscramble the omelette

to undo something that cannot be undone

onions

to know one's onions

to be well informed in some area

refers to Dr C. T. Onions, editor of the *Shorter Oxford English Dictionary*

oranges

to add/compare apples with oranges

to lump unconnected things together quite illogically

oyster

the world is one's oyster

one has enormous scope for activity

Shakespeare, *The Merry Wives of Windsor*, II:ii, 'Why, then the world's mine oyster'

p

to watch one's P's and Q's

to be very careful

perhaps refers to pints and quarts of beer on a hotel slate, or perhaps to easily confused printer's type

pancake

every Pancake Tuesday

only on occasions

refers to Shrove Tuesday, when pancakes are traditionally eaten

pea

a pea-and-thimble trick

a clever fraud committed in the presence of its victim without this being obvious at the time

refers to a sleight-of-hand trick played with three thimbles and a pea, the thimbles being moved about and observers being asked to guess under which thimble the pea is

peanuts

to earn peanuts

to get a reward that is far too small in relation to the value of the services rendered

pickle

to be in a pickle

to be in difficulties

Shakespeare, *The Tempest* V:i, 'How cam'st thou in this pickle?'

picnic

to be no picnic

to be unpleasant

pie

in apple-pie order

in perfect order and condition

pie in the sky

a hoped for result unlikely to be achieved

to eat humble pie

to be prepared to humiliate oneself and apologise

a play on words — derived from the eating of 'umble pie' (entrails of a deer) by lowly persons

to have a finger in the pie

to have an interest in a project, especially an officious involvement

pies

to have one's fingers in many different pies

to be engaged in a variety of separate activities

pig

to buy a pig in a poke

to buy goods of unknown quality

refers to the practice of selling a person a cat (purported to be a pig) in a bag (or poke); if the person opened the bag and looked inside, that person 'let the cat out of the bag'

pigeon

a pigeon pair

one son and one daughter as the only offspring

refers to the old belief that pigeons always sat on two eggs that produced a male and a female, and that this pair remained together throughout life

to be one's pigeon
to be one's area of responsibility

to pigeon-hole
to put aside for further consideration in the distant future
refers to placing something in a small hole, like the small hole in a dovecot for the pigeons to walk in and out

pigeons

to throw a cat among the pigeons
to cause consternation and upset

pigheaded

pigheaded
unduly obstinate

pineapple

to have hold of the wrong end of the pineapple
to be utterly mistaken

plate

to bring a plate
to take food to a party

to have too much on one's plate
to be unable to cope with one's workload

to serve something up to someone on a plate
to make something especially easy for a particular person

platter

to hand over something on a silver platter
to provide a valuable benefit for virtually nothing
refers to first-class service

plum

the plum
the best item in a collection

plums

to pick just the plums out of the jam
to take only the very best items

poppy

a tall poppy
a person with great power or responsibility and/or in receipt of high remuneration

poppies

to cut tall poppies down to size
to diminish the self-importance of haughty persons

pork

to pork barrel
to spend taxpayers' money in one area in order to attract political support
refers to times of slavery in America when pork was provided to slaves gathered around the pork barrel

pot

one can't get a quart into a pint pot
one cannot do the impossible

the pot calling the kettle black
criticising another person without realising one's own even greater shortcomings

to keep the pot boiling
to ensure that an issue stays current
refers to cooking

to stir the pot
to set out to raise controversial issues

to sweeten the pot
to provide a few additional inducements

to take pot luck
to take whatever happens by chance to be available
refers to a cooking pot of food

pots

fleshpots
sumptuous living
Exodus 16:3, ' ... in the land of Egypt, when we sat by the fleshpots and when we did eat bread to the full'

potato

a hot potato
a controversial issue that no one wants to handle, an embarrassing issue

potatoes

to be small potatoes
to be quite unimportant

pottage

to sell one's birthright for a mess of pottage
through foolishness to exchange something of substance for something of little value

Genesis 25:34, 'Then Jacob gave Esau bread and pottage of lentils ... thus Esau despised his birthright'

pudding

that person couldn't knock the skin off a rice pudding
that person is weak or ineffective

not to be a magic pudding
not to represent an everlasting supply of something
from the name of a book by Norman Lindsay

the proof of the pudding is in the eating
the success of a venture will be measured by its results

rabbit

a rabbit warren
a building with a maze of rooms and passages

move over and let the greyhound see the rabbit
stand aside to allow things to get under way
refers to hunting with greyhounds

recipe

a recipe for disaster
a certain way of achieving disaster

roasting

a roasting
a scolding

roost

the chickens are coming home to roost
the consequences of a person's past actions are now being felt by that person
Robert Southey (1774–1843), *The Curse of Kehama* (1810), 'Curses are like young chickens, they always come home to roost'

to rule the roost
to dominate
refers to the habit of roosters and hens to have an established order of dominance

ruminate

to ruminate
to ponder over a matter
refers to the chewing of the cud by ruminant animals

salt

below the salt
in a subordinate position
refers to the seating order at ancient Roman dining tables

not to be worth one's salt
not to be worth one's wages; to be inefficient or incapable
refers to Roman soldiers being paid in salt — a practice giving rise to the modern word 'salary'

the salt of the earth
special people who make a vital contribution to society
Matthew 5:13, 'Ye are the salt of the earth'

to take something with a grain of salt
to regard the facts in a statement with considerable scepticism

sands

the sands are running out
the time available for some action is nearly at an end
refers to an hour-glass of running sand

sandwich

to be the ham/meat in the sandwich
to be caught in the middle of a dispute between other parties
refers to the food snack popularised by the fourth Earl of Sandwich (1718–92)

sauce

what is sauce for the goose is sauce for the gander
arguments that apply in one case also apply in another

sausage

a sausage machine
the turning out of large volumes without particular thought

sausages

that person wouldn't give you the steam off his or her sausages
that person is very mean

sharks

to miss the sharks while netting the minnows
to succeed in minor aspects but fail in the ones that really matter

sheep

a black sheep
a disreputable member of an otherwise reputable group

one might as well be hanged for a sheep as for a lamb
further action will not increase the adverse consequences already in train
refers to the stealing of either sheep or lambs being capital crimes under old English law

to be a wolf in sheep's clothing
to be a hypocrite; to be dangerous although masquerading as something harmless
Matthew 7:15, 'Beware of false prophets, which come to you in sheep's clothing, but inwardly they are ravening wolves'

to be home on the sheep's back
to be doing well

to separate the sheep from the goats
to distinguish between the worthy and the unworthy
Matthew 25:32, 'and he shall separate them one from one another, as a shepherd divideth his sheep from the goats'

silver

to be born with a silver spoon in one's mouth
to be brought up by wealthy parents
refers to the traditional gift of a silver spoon (an 'apostle spoon') to a child at baptism — the child born of wealthy parents is assured of riches from the moment of birth and thus does not have to await baptism to receive a valuable gift

to hand over something on a silver platter
to provide a valuable benefit for virtually nothing
refers to first-class service

to sell off the family silver
to sell off one's prized possessions

smorgasbord

smorgasbord
a series of different items from which a number can be chosen
from the Swedish words for 'butter', 'goose', and 'table'

soup

to be in the soup
to be in great difficulties

sour

that is just sour grapes
those are disparaging remarks made only because that person is peeved and resentful at someone else's better fortune
derived from Aesop's fable of 'the fox and the grapes' about expressing deliberate disparagement of a desired but unattainable object; 'sour grapes' also occurs in *Ezekiel* 18:2, 'the fathers have eaten sour grapes, and the children's teeth are set on edge'

spoon

he must have a long spoon that sups with the devil
great care is needed when negotiating with disreputable parties
Shakespeare apparently alludes to an old proverb in *The Tempest* II:ii, 'Mercy! mercy! this is a devil ... I will leave him, I have no long spoon!'

to be born with a silver spoon in one's mouth
to be brought up by wealthy parents
refers to the traditional gift of a silver spoon (an 'apostle spoon') to a child at baptism — the child born of wealthy parents is assured of riches from the moment of birth and thus does not have to await baptism to receive a valuable gift

to get the wooden spoon
to come ingloriously last
refers to the custom of awarding a silver cup to the winner and a wooden spoon to the loser

sprat

to throw a sprat to catch a mackerel
to risk a little in the hope of gaining much

stampede

to stampede someone into something
to pressure a person into taking some action

stew

to be in a stew
to be in a difficult situation; OR to be in an anxious, agitated, or confused state

to stew in one's juice

to suffer the adverse consequences of one's acts or omissions

Shakespeare, *Hamlet* III:iv, 'But to live in the rank sweat of an enseamed bed, stew'd in corruption'

sticks

sticks and carrots

disincentives and incentives in combination

refers to the handling of donkeys

storage

to put something into cold storage

to put something aside to be dealt with at some indeterminate future time

suck

suck it and see

discover experimentally how something works

to teach one's grandmother how to suck eggs

to try to tell a much more experienced person something very obvious to that person

sups

he must have a long spoon that sups with the devil

great care is needed when negotiating with disreputable parties

Shakespeare apparently alludes to an old proverb in *The Tempest* II:ii, 'Mercy! mercy! this is a devil … I will leave him, I have no long spoon!'

supper

to sing for one's supper

to carry out a task in order to receive a favour in return

swarm

to swarm out

to appear in large numbers from within

refers to bees or wasps'

sweet

to be short and sweet

to be very brief and to the point

to have a sweet tooth

to be particularly fond of cakes and confectionery

sweeten

to sweeten a deal

to offer some concessions or incentives

to sweeten the pot

to provide a few additional inducements

swine

to cast pearls before swine

to confer valuable benefits on someone who neither recognises nor appreciates them

Matthew 7:6, 'Neither cast ye your pearls before swine'

syrup

soothing syrup

insincere expressions of sympathy or flattery

tea

I would not do so-and-so for all the tea in China

I will never do so-and-so no matter how large the inducement

not to be someone's cup of tea

not to be to a person's liking; OR to be outside a person's expertise or area of interest

teacup

a storm in a teacup

a controversy about a minor matter but one that looms large in the minds of the parties

toast

to have someone on toast

to have someone at a disadvantage, to be able to do what one wishes to a person

turkey

cold turkey

the sudden cessation of drugs to an addict and, by extension, the sudden cessation of any habitually pleasurable activity

probably refers to the appearance of the skin of drug addicts experiencing withdrawal symptoms (similarity to the skin of a plucked cold turkey)

to talk turkey

to talk realistically

origin obscure; North American slang

vegetable

to become a vegetable

to lose one's ability to respond to many external stimuli, especially those that normally contribute to the quality of life; to lead a monotonous life with no animation

vine

to hear on the grapevine
to learn unofficially
the earlier form of the metaphor was a 'grapevine telegraph' as a means of communicating private information

to wither on the vine
by virtue of changed circumstances or the effluxion of time to be no longer relevant
John 15:5, 6, 'I am the vine, ye are the branches ... if a man abideth not in me, he is cast forth as a branch and is withered'

wether

bell-wether
first indication
refers to the leading sheep (wether) of a flock, this sheep having a bell hung around its neck

wheat

to separate the wheat from the chaff
to separate the worthy from the unworthy
Matthew 3:12, 'His winnowing fork is in his hand, and he will clear his threshing floor and gather his wheat into the granary, but the chaff he will burn with unquenchable fire'

Furniture

bed

one has made one's bed and one will now have to lie on it
one has to bear the consequences of one's actions

to be no bed of roses
to be difficult or uncomfortable
Robert Louis Stevenson (1850–94), *Virginibus Puerisque* I:i, 'Marriage is like life in this — that it is a field of battle, and not a bed of roses'

to be on one's death bed
(of a person, organisation or piece of equipment) to be about to cease effectiveness

to get out of bed on the wrong side
to be grumpy

to jump into bed with someone
to enter into a joint enterprise with another person

to put something to bed
finally to dispose of something

bedding

feather bedding
(in industrial relations) creating unnecessary jobs solely to increase employment; OR (in economics) assisting an inefficient industry by government grants or excessive tariff protection

bedfellow

bedfellow
collaborator

blanket

to be a wet blanket
to be a spoil sport

to be born on the wrong side of the blanket
to be illegitimate

to throw a blanket over a proposal
to refuse to proceed with a proposal

bowl

to be in a goldfish bowl
to be very open to view

carpet

the red-carpet treatment
courtesies extended to a person to make that person feel important and welcome
refers to the welcome accorded a visiting dignitary

to be on the carpet
to be lectured in regard to one's alleged misdeeds

to get a magic carpet ride to something
to be given an easy and fortunate passage to an objective
refers to the magic carpet (of Oriental legend) that transported its owners wherever they wished

to sweep something under the carpet

to pretend that some blemish does not exist

centrepiece

the centrepiece
(of a proposal) the highlight or the main ingredient

chair

to get an armchair ride
to be given a particularly easy time

chairs

to play musical chairs
to be a part of a general reshuffling (of duties or functions) that is not necessarily to everyone's liking
refers to a parlour game culminating in a sudden scrambling for positions

chest

to build up a war chest
to accumulate cash in readiness for some move

to lock something up in the old oak chest
to put in a safe place and out of mind

clock

the clock is ticking
time is running out

to turn back the clock
to have another opportunity to do something that should have been done already; or to attempt to undo something that cannot be undone

cupboard

a skeleton in the cupboard
an unpleasant truth the knowledge of which has been deliberately suppressed
William Makepeace Thackeray (1811–63), *The Newcomes* (1855), ' … they have a skelton or two in their closets as well as their neighbours'

the cupboard is bare
the wished-for resources are not available

curtain

curtain raiser
introduction
refers to the theatre

the curtain rises on something
something is about to start
refers to the theatre

the iron curtain
the border between the communist nations and the rest of the world
used famously by Winston Churchill in a speech in 1946, but also attributed before this to Ethel Snowden (1920), Goebbels (1945), and by Churchill himself in 1945 (before his famous 1946 speech)

to ring down the curtain on something
to treat something as concluded

curtains

it's curtains!
this is the end!

deckchairs

to rearrange the deckchairs on the Titanic
to take an initiative that is quite useless because it does not take much greater change into account
refers to the liner *Titanic* which struck an iceberg and sank in 1912

drawer

to tuck something away in a drawer
to put something aside for the time being

top drawer
first class

furniture

to be part of the furniture
to be so familiar that one's presence goes completely unnoticed

light

a chink of light
a small hope of a solution or breakthrough

to bring something to light
to draw to public attention

to hide one's light under a bushel
to keep others in ignorance of one's skills and experience
Luke 11:33, 'No man, when he hath lighted a candle, putteth it in a secret place, neither under a bushel'

to see someone in a good light
to regard a person favourably

to see the light
to understand the real situation
refers to the conversion of Saul (Paul) on the road to Damascus, *Acts* 9:3, 4 'And suddenly there shined round about him a

light from heaven: and he fell to the earth'

to shed light on something
to give explanations

mirrors

it is all done with mirrors
this is achieved by magic or illusion

peg

a peg to hang a hat on
something that provides a convenient or plausible excuse for some particular action

off the peg
(of clothes) ready-made

picture

to balance the picture
to quote facts or arguments in contradiction

to change the whole picture
to alter the major assumptions on which some assessment was based

to conjure up a picture
to use words to convey a vivid impression

to have a clear picture of something
to have a good understanding of something

to paint a black picture
to state a set of unfavourable factors

to present a rosy picture
to state a set of favourable factors

to put someone in the picture
to fill a person in with the background of a situation

to see the big picture
to have the vision and imagination enabling a project to be developed as part of a bigger whole

quilt

a patchwork quilt
a result arising from many uncoordinated inputs

rug

to pull the rug out from under someone
unexpectedly to withdraw support

to sweep something under the rug
to pretend that some blemish does not exist

seat

to be in the hot seat
to hold a position requiring one to answer criticism or accusations

to be on the edge of one's seat
to be very excited or anxious regarding what is currently happening

to be riveted to one's seat
to find the activity being watched very exciting and worthy of full attention

to keep someone's seat warm
to hold a position temporarily with a view to another person's taking it over permanently in the near future

shelf

to be on the shelf
to have been put aside and no longer in active use; OR to be a woman past the usual age of marriage

shelve

to shelve some proposal
to abandon some proposal

spring

a spring cleaning
a regular (usually annual) review with a view to discarding the obsolete and retaining that which is useful

stools

to fall between two stools
not to fit neatly into either of two available alternatives, and to waver between them

table

the table groaned
the food was plentiful

to lay a proposal on the table
to make a proposal available for discussion or to adjourn discussion on a proposal for an indefinite period

to lay one's cards on the table
to be utterly frank and open or to honestly disclose one's position
refers to playing cards

to put money on the table
to back one's judgment in a tangible way or to demonstrate one's sincerity

tables

to turn the tables on someone
to cause the relative positions of oneself and another person to be reversed

refers to chess or draughts (and turning the table, or board, the other way around)

Gambling

back

to back the wrong horse
to have faith in, give support to, and/or invest in a project that proves to be unsuccessful
refers to betting on racehorses

bet

a good bet
a good proposition
you bet!
definitely!
you can bet your life on something
something is certain to happen

bets

to hedge one's bets
to insure against a losing bet or investment by also investing on the opposite outcome

blank

to draw a blank
to be unsuccessful
refers to playing cards

board

to be above board
to be quite legitimate
refers to gambling

bob

to have two bob each way
to equivocate
refers to the slang term for two shillings, and to betting for a win or a place

books

to be a turn-up for the books
to be a surprising development
refers to bookmaking and gambling

canter

to win the prize in a canter
to win very easily
refers to horse racing

cents

to have fifty cents each way
to equivocate
refers to betting for a win or a place

chip

to be a blue-chip stock
to be of excellent quality
to chip in
to contribute financially

chips

bargaining chips
benefits that can be conceded in negotiations to obtain some advantage
that is the way the chips fall
that is the way that the benefits and detriments are distributed after an event
to have had one's chips
to have received all that is going to be forthcoming
to turn one's chips in
to convert one's assets or entitlements into cash
when the chips are down
when all facts are known and taken into consideration

dice

no dice
the proposal is totally unacceptable
the dice are loaded against someone
a person is unlikely to succeed in something
refers to cheating in gambling with dice
the final throw of the dice
one last, desperate gamble
the whole box and dice
all relevant components

die

the die is cast
the course of action is irreversible
to be the throw of a loaded die
to be an act of deceit
refers to cheating in gambling with dice

draw

to be the luck of the draw
to be a chance result
refers to card games or a raffle
to draw the short straw
to be chosen (perhaps by lot) to undertake an undesired task

hands

to win hands down
to win very convincingly

refers to a jockey riding confidently with hands low when a race is as good as won

head

to have a head start

to have an advantage over others

refers to horse racing

heads

heads I win, tails you lose

whichever way this matter goes I will benefit at your expense

refers to the tossing of a coin

home

to be home and hosed

to be assured of victory or success in a task

refers to horse racing (a jocular reference to a horse leading in a race being already home and hosed down)

to enter the home stretch

to commence the last stage

refers to horse racing

horse

a dark horse

a person with unsuspected talents

Benjamin Disraeli (1804–81), *The Young Duke*, 'A dark horse, which had never been thought of, and which the careless St James had never even observed in the list, rushed past the grandstand in sweeping triumph'

a two-horse race

a contest between only two serious contestants

it is horses for courses

the correct means to an end needs to be chosen

refers to horse racing

jackpot

to hit the jackpot

to be very lucky

refers to draw-poker, in which a pot or pool accumulates until one of the players can open the betting with a pair of jacks or better

London

it is London to a brick on

it is virtually certain

a metaphor coined by the Australian horse-race caller, Ken Howard, to indicate that one could bet the whole of London against a single brick — in the confident expectation of winning

luck

to be the luck of the draw

to be a chance result

refers to card games or a raffle

to push one's luck

having already done well in something, then to take risks which can prejudice everything

to take pot luck

to take whatever happens by chance to be available

refers to a cooking pot of food

Mexican

a Mexican standoff

a situation where neither of two parties is making a move

refers to poker

neck

neck and neck

(of contestants) with little between them

refers to a winning margin in horse racing

it is neck or nothing

a desperate effort is called for

refers to a winning margin in horse racing

odds

that is over the odds

that is unacceptable

refers to betting on horse races

to beat the odds

to do better than could reasonably have been expected

refers to betting on horse races or similar

to have the odds stacked against one

to be faced with many difficulties frustrating a project

refers to betting

to pay over the odds

to pay too much

refers to betting on horse races

photo

a photo finish

a close result in a contest

refers to horse racing

post

to pip someone at the post

to achieve something only just ahead of a rival

refers to the winning post in horse racing

punt

to take a punt

to take a calculated risk

refers to gambling

riding

riding instructions

directions as to how to do something

refers to horse racing

roulette

to play Russian roulette

to engage in a dangerously unpredictable exercise

refers to an act of daring in which one squeezes the trigger of a revolver held to the head (after loading one chamber and spinning the cylinder — thus the one being fired is determined by chance)

run

to have a run for one's money

to at least get some enjoyment out of an otherwise abortive exercise

refers to betting on horse racing

stake

to raise the stake

to increase the amount of potential gain or loss in a project

refers to gambling

tails

heads I win, tails you lose

whichever way this matter goes I will benefit at your expense

refers to the tossing of a coin

ticket

to write one's own ticket

to set one's own terms and conditions

refers to betting on a horse with a bookmaker where the chance of that horse winning is considered so unlikely that the punter is allowed to choose the odds

toss

it is a toss up

either alternative is equally acceptable

refers to the tossing of a coin

to argue the toss

to dispute a decision

refers to the tossing of a coin

to toss up

to decide on a fairly arbitrary basis

refers to the tossing of a coin

weigh

to weigh in with something

to bring something along

refers to jockeys (and equipment) being weighed after a horse race

wheel

fortune's wheel

the vicissitudes of life

refers to the traditional representation of the goddess Fortuna with a wheel in her hand, symbolising her fickleness

winner

to be on a winner

to have faith in, give support to and/or invest in a project which proves to be successful

refers to betting on racing

Geography

abyss

to be close to the abyss

to face imminent total destruction

avalanche

avalanche

a great volume manifesting itself in a short time

beach

not to be the only pebble on the beach

not to be the only person available for some task, or affected by some set of circumstances

brink

to push someone over the brink

by a small action to cause the absolute ruin (financially or emotionally) of someone already in peril

bush

a bird in the hand is worth two in the bush

a benefit currently available is more valuable than a seemingly much larger benefit that might or might not be achieved in the future

a bush lawyer

a person without legal qualifications who has a reasonable, although not perfect, knowledge of the law, and who likes to make technical points in arguments

to beat about the bush
to fail to come to the point
refers to hunters flushing game from cover by beating of the vegetation in which animals are hidden

bushed

to be bushed
to be lost or exhausted or puzzled or confused

cave

an Aladdin's cave
a place full of unexpected treasure
refers to a character and events in *Arabian Nights' Entertainments*

to cave-in
to yield to pressure

China

I would not do so-and-so for all the tea in China
I will never do so-and-so no matter how large the inducement

Chinese

Chinese walls
a system to ensure that different parts of some organisation do not gain access to each other's confidential information

a Chinese puzzle
a perplexing enigma

cliff

to be a cliff-hanger
to be very exciting with the result in doubt
refers to episodes of early serial films that ended with the hero in a hazardous plight to attract cinema-goers to the next episode

coast

the coast is clear
there are no observers to one's activity around

corners

from the four corners of the globe
from everywhere

country

one looks for elephants in elephant country
one needs to search in the right place

to be ahead by a country mile
to be in a comfortable lead
in the long distances of certain rural areas, a 'country mile' is jocularly believed to be a very long mile

course

to be on a collision course
to be headed for a clash with an opponent

to be on course
to be progressing satisfactorily towards one's goal

to run its course
to come to a natural end

creek

to be up the creek
to be mistaken completely

to be up the creek without a paddle
to be in trouble

current

an undercurrent
a barely noticeable feeling of dissent that is not being vocalised

dam

the dam burst
the cumulative effect of many things caused a disaster

Damascus

a road to Damascus experience
a sudden, dramatic conversion
refers to the sudden conversion of Paul (Saul) — *Acts* 9:3, 'And as he journeyed, he came to Damascus: and suddenly there shined around him a light from heaven: And he fell to the earth'

distance

to be within striking distance
to be fairly close

to keep one's distance
to avoid familiarity

distant

distant fields look greener
activities of which one has no experience seem more attractive than is really the case
Psalms 23:1, 'The Lord is my shepherd ... he shall feed me in a green pasture'

ditch

to make a last-ditch stand
to make a brave effort to stave off final defeat

King William III (1650–1702), 'There is one way never to see it lost ... and that is to die in the last ditch' (quoted by Burnet, *History of His Own Times*,1715)

downhill

to go downhill
to deteriorate

a dry run
a trial exercise
refers to a creek bed that is dry until heavy rain causes it to become a stream

to dry up
to cease

earth

a down-to-earth solution
a realistic solution

earth-shattering
very significant

how on earth?
just how?

the salt of the earth
special people who make a vital contribution to society
Matthew 5:13, 'Ye are the salt of the earth'

to bring someone down to earth
to disillusion a person

to charge the earth
to impose very high prices

to move heaven and earth
to do everything possible
Revelation 21:1, 'And I saw a new heaven and a new earth, for the first heaven and the first earth had passed away'; a reference to the apocalyptic vision of the greatest possible change to all creation

to promise the earth
to give extravagant assurances

to run someone to earth
to locate a person
refers to fox hunting

echo

to echo someone's words
to repeat another person's views as though they were one's own

eclipse

to eclipse someone
to make dim in comparison (in effect, to outshine a person)

fountainhead

fountainhead
chief or prime source of something (wisdom, knowledge, etc.)

Greek

something is all Greek to someone
something is incomprehensible to a person
Shakespeare, *Julius Caesar*, I:ii, 'but, for mine own part, it was Greek to me'

Greeks

I fear the Greeks even when they bear gifts
I am suspicious of generous behaviour from traditional opponents
Virgil (70–19 BC), *Aeneid* II:49, *Timeo Danaos et dona ferentis* ('I fear the Greeks even when they bring gifts'), in reference to the Trojan horse

ground

stamping ground
one's favourite place for certain activities

to be on shaky ground
not to have strong arguments

to be thin on the ground
to be scarce

to break new ground
to do something for which there is no precedent
refers to ploughing of ground

to clear the ground
to dispose of the preliminaries
refers to clearing of ground in preparation for ploughing

to cut the ground from under someone's feet
to withdraw support unexpectedly and, in the process, to cause embarrassment; OR to demolish a person's case and cause defeat, especially by anticipating that person's arguments or plans

to fall to the ground
to fail
Matthew 10:29, 'Are not two sparrows sold for a farthing? And one of them shall not fall on the ground without your Father ... '

to gain ground
to advance one's position relative to others
originally military; Shakespeare *Hamlet* IV:iv, 'we go to gain a little patch of ground'

to give ground
to make some concessions or to retreat or to concede some arguments
refers to military battle

to go to ground
to become unavailable to those seeking a person
refers to fox hunting

to have one's feet firmly on the ground
to be very practical

to have the high ground
to have an advantage in moral terms
refers to military battle

to keep an ear to the ground
to be well informed as to current developments
refers to listening for distant sound by applying one's ear to the ground

to kiss the ground
to revere or bless the land; OR to be overthrown

to plough new ground
to engage laboriously in an untried activity

to prepare one's ground
to get ready for a confrontation
refers to military battle

to run someone to ground
to discover the whereabouts of a person
refers to fox hunting

to stand one's ground
to maintain a stance in the face of opposition
refers to military battle

gulf

to bridge a gulf
to overcome a wide divergence in views
Luke 16:26, 'Between us and you there is a great gulf fixed'

here

to be neither here nor there
to be irrelevant or unimportant

hill

light on the hill
distant goal acting as an inspiration
usually attributed to Australian prime minister, Ben Chifley (1949)

to be over the hill
to be old, or past one's prime

to be pushing uphill
to face difficulties

to fight an uphill battle
to face difficulties or to have formidable opposition
refers to military battle

to go downhill
to deteriorate

to push water uphill
foolishly to attempt the impossible

hills

to head for the hills
to seek to escape one's commitments

Himalayan

of Himalayan proportions
huge
refers to Himalayan mountains (Sanskrit: 'snow abode')

horizon

the one bright spot on the horizon
the only hopeful aspect

there are black/storm clouds on the horizon
bad news is expected

to loom on the horizon
to be expected but not immediately

ice

the ice is melting
friendly relations are being restored

to break the ice
to take the initiative in starting discussions
Francis Bacon (1561–1626), *Of Cunning*, 'In things that are tender and unpleasing, it is good to break the ice by some whose words are of less weight ...'

to cut no ice with someone
to have little effect on a person
perhaps refers to ice-skating

to skate on thin ice
to act in disregard of obvious danger; to require tact in dealing with a sensitive subject in conversation
Ralph Waldo Emerson (1803–82), *Prudence*, 'In skating over thin ice, our safety is in our speed'

iceberg

to be the tip of the iceberg
to be only a very small portion of a much larger but less obvious whole

inundate

to inundate
to overload with replies, etc.

jungle

a jungle
a place where everyone makes his or her own rules

the law of the jungle
the principle that those having power will use it at the expense of all others
Rudyard Kipling (1865–1936), *The Law of the Jungle*, 'Now this is the law of the jungle — as old and as true as the sky; and the wolf that shall keep it may prosper, but the wolf that shall break it must die'

lake

you can jump in the lake
I intend to take no notice whatsoever of you or your views

land

a land of milk and honey
a country in which everything is in abundant supply
Exodus 3:8, ' ... to bring them up out of that land unto a good land ... flowing with milk and honey'

to ascertain the lie of the land
to establish the pertinent facts and opinions

to be in cloud-cuckoo land
to be mad or to have unrealistic expectations
'cloud-cuckoo land' was an imaginary city built in the air by the birds (according to the *Nephelococcygia* of *The Birds* by Aristophanes) — hence any utopian fantastic scheme

to be in the land of the living
to be alive

landmark

a landmark ruling
a decision marking an important change or development in the state of affairs'

landscape

to be part of the landscape
to be present and fully accepted without question

landslide

a landslide
an electoral result involving victory or defeat by a very large margin

lane

to go down memory lane
to reminisce

language

to speak the same language
to have a good understanding and similar ideas

level

a level playing field
competition on equal terms

level best
making all possible effort
perhaps refers to railways

to be on the level
to be honest
a term derived from freemasonry

to keep a level head
to stay calm and rational in a crisis
Rudyard Kipling (1865–1936), *If*, 'If you can keep your head when all about you are losing theirs ... '

water will find its own level
people will reach an appropriate position relative to others

line

to draw a line in the sand
to indicate clearly the limits of acceptability beyond which people should not go

lost

get lost!
just go away!

you can get lost
I intend to take no notice whatsoever of you or your views

mainstream

mainstream
orthodox

map

to put something on the map
to make prominent or significant'

marathon

marathon
requiring great endurance
refers to the run to Athens made by a lone messenger to announce Athenian victory over the Persians at the battle of Marathon in 490 BC; according to tradition, the messenger fell dead on arrival

Mecca

a Mecca for something
a place at which supporters of something congregate
refers to the birthplace of the prophet Muhammad

Mexican

a Mexican standoff
a situation where neither of two parties is making a move
refers to poker

mile

a milestone
a significant stage or achievement in a life or a history
refers to markers along a road indicating distance in miles

give someone an inch and that person will take a mile
make a small concession to a person and that person will abuse it by taking much more

someone would run a mile
a person would do anything to escape that person's responsibilities

to be able to spot trouble a mile away
to be able to perceive problems before they actually occur

to be ahead by a country mile
to be in a comfortable lead
in the long distances of certain rural areas, a 'country mile' is jocularly believed to be a very long mile

to go the extra mile
to work beyond the call of duty
Matthew 5:41, 'Whosoever shall compel thee to go a mile, go with him twain'

to miss something by a mile
to be nowhere near one's target

to stick out a mile
to be very apparent

mileage

to get some mileage out of something
to benefit from something

miles

to be miles apart
to have great philosophical differences

to be miles away
to have one's mind on other matters

milestone

a milestone
a significant stage or achievement in a life or a history
refers to markers along a road indicating distance in miles

mirage

mirage
illusory benefit

mire

to sink deeper into the mire
to get into even greater difficulty

molehills

to make mountains out of molehills
to treat a minor problem as though it were a major disaster

mountain

if the mountain will not come to Muhammad then Muhammad will go to the mountain
on recognising that one has insufficient power to effect one's most desired solution one decides to make do with the next best alternative
refers to the story of Muhammad humbly submitting to the greater power of God when Mt Safa did not obey the prophet's command to come to him

mud

a stick in the mud
an unenterprising person

a person's name is mud
a person is in disgrace, lacking in popularity, lacking in credibility
a play on the name of US physician Dr Samuel Mudd who, in 1865, was convicted of being a co-conspirator with John Wilkes Booth in the assassination of President Abraham Lincoln; since then a public and judicial campaign has been waged by family and supporters (extending even to some later US presidents) to assert Mudd's innocence; other people, just as vehemently, assert Mudd's guilt

some mud will stick
reputations will be hurt even after accusations are proved false

to sink deeper into the mud
to get into even greater difficulty

to sling mud
to make unfair imputations

muddy

to muddy the waters
deliberately to confuse an issue by creating a diversion

north

to head north
(of prices, etc.) to go up

patch

a sticky patch
a period fraught with difficulties

to keep off someone's patch
not to interfere with or compete against another person in that person's customary area of activity

place

a place in the sun
a favourable situation

to be between a rock and a hard place
to be faced with two equally difficult and uncomfortable choices

to make some place too hot for someone
to make a place unpleasant for someone

to put someone back in his or her place
to require a person to act in accordance with that person's level of seniority

pond

to be a big fish in a little pond
to be a person holding an important office but in an unimportant organisation

quagmire

to be in a quagmire
to be in great difficulty

river

the river found its mark
equilibrium between two pressures has been achieved

to be a river of gold
to be a source of ongoing great profitability

to sell someone down the river
to betray a person who has placed trust in one
refers to selling slaves to owners further down the river

roads

all roads lead to Rome
all alternatives will have the same outcome
refers to roads radiating from the great imperial capital to all parts of the Roman empire

to be at the cross-roads
to need to choose between several mutually exclusive alternatives

Rome

all roads lead to Rome
all alternatives will have the same outcome
refers to roads radiating from the great imperial capital to all parts of the Roman empire

Rome was not built in a day
complicated things require time

to fiddle while Rome burns
to neglect important considerations while concentrating on trivial side-issues
refers to Nero's behaviour during the burning of Rome (AD 64) when he played a lyre and watched the spectacle from a height

when in Rome do as the Romans do
it is best to conform to the local customs

Samaritan

a good Samaritan
a person going out of that person's way to do a kindness to others
Luke 10:33, 'But a certain Samaritan, as he journeyed, came where he was: and when he saw him, he had compassion on him'

sands

shifting sands
arguments that are constantly being changed

sea

a sea-change
a significant transformation
Shakespeare, *The Tempest* I:ii, 'Nothing of him that doth fade / but doth suffer a sea-change / into something rich and strange

a South Sea bubble
an unrealistic financial venture that is bound to result in total loss

refers to a notorious financial scandal involving the South Sea Company (UK) in 1720

to be all at sea
to be confused as to what is going on and what to do next

to be between the devil and the deep blue sea
to be faced with two equally unpalatable alternatives that cannot both be avoided

Sodom

a Sodom and Gomorrah
a place of vice
Genesis 18:20, 'Sodom and Gomorrah ... their sin is very great'

south

a South Sea bubble
an unrealistic financial venture that is bound to result in total loss
refers to a notorious financial scandal involving the South Sea Company (UK) in 1720

to head south
(of prices, etc.) to go down

Spain

a castle in Spain
a desirable imagining, but an impracticable proposition

stone

a rolling stone gathers no moss
a person who keeps changing jobs will not have a successful career
Tusser, *Five Hundred Points of Good Husbandrie* (1573), 'The stone that is rolling can gather no moss. / For master and servant oft changing is loss'

a stepping stone
a means to an end

to leave no stone unturned
to be very thorough
refers to an instruction from the oracle of Delphi regarding a search for Persian treasure (477 BC)

within a stone's throw
very close

straits

in dire straits
in great need

stream

mainstream
orthodox

to get on stream
to now operate successfully following the end of a settling-in period

to swap/change horses in mid-stream
to alter that upon which one is reliant during the course of a project

street

a one-way street
a flow of activity in only one direction

not to be in the same street as someone
not to be of comparable quality

the man in the street
the average citizen

to be in Queer street
to be in debt
origin obscure

to be up one's street
to be right within a person's expertise or area of interest

to walk in off the street
to come without prior arrangement or notification

streets

there is blood in the streets
much damage has been done to a cause

to be streets ahead
to outperform one's competitors by a wide margin

swamp

to swamp someone
to overload a person

Thames

to set the Thames on fire
to do something noteworthy
similar sayings exist regarding setting fire to the Rivers Seine, Tiber, and Rhine

top

to blow one's top
to show anger
refers to a volcano

town

the only game in town
the only event worthy of attention

to go to town
to do something enthusiastically, extravagantly, to the full

to paint the town red

to go on an exciting social outing

track

to be down the track
to be making progress

to be off the beaten track
to do unconventional things; to be travelling along relatively unused routes

to be off the track
to be irrelevant

to be on the wrong track
to be heading towards an incorrect conclusion

to be on track
to be making the scheduled progress

to go down a particular track
to make decisions aimed at a particular goal

to have a one-track mind
to keep coming back to one narrow topic of conversation

to keep track of something
to be completely aware of where something is and how it is functioning
refers to hunting

tracks

to be stopped in one's tracks
suddenly and unexpectedly to be prevented from carrying on with a project

to cover one's tracks
to hide the evidence of one's involvement

to make tracks
to leave

trickle

a trickle
a small amount, in gradual stages

Turks

young Turks
members of an organisation who hold ideas regarded as too revolutionary
refers to an early twentieth-century revolutionary political party in what was to become Turkey

uphill

to be pushing uphill
to face difficulties

to fight an uphill battle
to face difficulties or to have formidable opposition
refers to military battle

to push water uphill
foolishly to attempt the impossible

Utopian

Utopian
ideally perfect
refers to the mythical island in Sir Thomas More's *Utopia* (Greek *ou topos*: 'no place')

volcano

to be sitting on a volcano
to be safe for the time being but exposed to the risk of a sudden great disaster

water

a backwater
a place of little activity

a lot of water has flowed under the bridge since then
much has happened since then

an argument holding water
a debating point of substance

come hell or high water
regardless of the difficulties or obstacles

high-water mark
the best or highest level achieved by an enterprise

one can lead a horse to water, but one can't make it drink
one can give advice to a person but cannot ensure that it will be acted on

there is blood in the water
something is likely to cause a person to go into a frenzy

to be a fish out of water
to be in difficulty by virtue of being in a strange environment

to be above water
(of securities) to have a market value in excess of the cost price

to be in deep/hot water
to be in great difficulty

to be in smooth water
to have no troubles
nautical metaphor

to be like water off a duck's back
(of advice or criticism) to be completely ignored

to be on the water wagon
to be teetotal

to be water under the bridge
to matter no longer
to blow/shoot something out of the water
to destroy something
to brave the water
to enter a venture with courage and determination
to dip one's toe in the water
gently to explore an opportunity
to go through fire and water
to undertake all attendant risks
perhaps refers to ordeals of fire and water — ancient Anglo-Saxon ordeals of torture used to ascertain guilt or innocence
to go to water
to succumb to pressure
to hold water
(of an argument) to be soundly based
to hold one's head just above water
to cope with problems but with little margin to spare or to stay solvent
to make one's mouth water
to excite desire
refers to salivation
to pour cold water on some idea
to be unenthusiastic about some proposal or scornful of its apparent weaknesses
to shoot/blow something out of the water
to destroy something
to test the water
to try out an idea in a small way
to water down something
to reduce the severe impact of something
water will find its own level
people will reach an appropriate position relative to others

watering

watering hole
hotel

Waterloo

to meet one's Waterloo
to receive a decisive defeat
refers to Napoleon's fate at the Battle of Waterloo (1815)

waters

still waters run deep
a person with a quiet manner might have many unrecognised characteristics — both good and bad
W. H. Auden (1907–73), *Twelve Songs VIII*, 'Still waters run deep, my dear, there's never smoke without fire'
to be in uncharted waters
to be the first to experience something
nautical metaphor
to cast one's bread upon the waters
to give generously because one will eventually be rewarded for one's generosity
Ecclesiastes 11:1, 'Cast thy bread upon the waters: for thou shalt find it after many days'
to enter treacherous waters
to engage in an enterprise with risks that are not obvious
nautical metaphor
to fish in troubled waters
to profit from a disturbed situation
refers to angling
to muddy the waters
deliberately to confuse an issue by creating a diversion
to plot a safe course through troubled waters
to make a plan that overcomes certain difficulties
nautical metaphor
to pour oil on troubled waters
to calm down a situation

watershed

a watershed
an occasion dividing two distinct phases of activity
refers to the geographical division between the headwaters of adjacent river systems

watertight

a watertight contract
a contract without loopholes or escape clauses

wave

to be on the crest of a wave
to enjoy success that might not last
to ride the wave
to be successful for the time being
refers to surfing

way

a one-way street
a flow of activity in only one direction
no way!
definitely not!
to know which way to turn
to know which strategy to adopt or where to seek assistance
to pave the way
to prepare for something
to resist something every inch of the way
to resist something utterly
to see which way the wind is blowing
to establish the factors relevant to a situation
John Seldon (1584–1654), 'Take a straw and throw it up into the air, you shall see by that which way the wind is'
to stand in someone's way
to prevent a person achieving that person's goal

ways

to cut both ways
to involve both advantages and disadvantages of similar significance
to want something both ways
to desire two mutually exclusive objectives

wayside

to fall by the wayside
to be abandoned and to therefore drop out; to fail to stay the course
Matthew 13:4, 'And when he sowed, some seeds fell by the wayside, and the fowls came and gobbled them up'

wilderness

to be a lone voice crying out in the wilderness
to be the only person stating unpopular views
John 1:23, 'I am the voice of one crying in the wilderness'
to be in the wilderness
to be out of office against one's will
Numbers 14:33, 'And your children shall wander in the wilderness forty years'

wind

it is an ill wind that blows no good
even a seeming misfortune leads to some blessings
something is in the wind
something is going on secretly
straws in the wind
small but significant indicators of future events
John Seldon (1584–1654), 'Take a straw and throw it up into the air, you shall see by that which way the wind is'
the cold wind of change
the unpleasant realities of new circumstances
to get wind of something
to hear rumours giving advance information
refers to an animal sniffing the wind for the scent of another animal
to reap the whirlwind
to suffer the adverse consequences of a bad act
Hosea 8:7, 'They have sown the wind, and they shall reap the whirlwind'
to see which way the wind is blowing
to establish the factors relevant to a situation
John Seldon (1584–1654), 'Take a straw and throw it up into the air, you shall see by that which way the wind is'
to sow the wind and reap the whirlwind
to make bad mistakes and to suffer the even worse consequences
Hosea 8:7, 'They have sown the wind, and they shall reap the whirlwind'

winds

to cast prudence to the winds
to cease being careful or wise
to scatter something to the four winds
permanently to get rid of something
refers to the north, south, east, and west winds

windfall

windfall
unexpected good fortune
refers to fruit falling from a tree without having to be picked

wood

not to see the wood for the trees
to overlook the general picture because of undue concentration on the details
to be babes in the wood

to be excessively naVve and inexperienced and thus ripe for exploitation
based on the folk legend of the babes in the wood of Wayland Hall, Norfolk

woods

neck of the woods
localised area
refers to a narrow stretch of wooded country

to be out of the woods
the previous difficulties have been overcome

world

it's a small world
it is surprising to meet people one knows in unexpected places

the world is one's oyster
one has enormous scope for activity
Shakespeare, *The Merry Wives of Windsor*, II:ii, 'Why, then the world's mine oyster'

to be on a world stage
to be prominent in international affairs
refers to the theatre

to be on top of the world
to be very happy

to be out of this world
to be superb

to carry the world on one's shoulders
to perform a huge task alone
refers to Atlas, who was condemned to bear the heavens on his shoulders for leading the Titans against the gods to make a world of difference
to make a great deal of difference

to present a happy face to the world
bravely to gloss over one's problems and to appear contented to others

to set the world on fire
to do something remarkable

why in the world?
what possible reason can there be for this?

worlds

to get the worst of all worlds
to get a series of disadvantages without achieving any corresponding advantages

to want the best of both worlds
unreasonably to desire to get some advantage without incurring a corresponding disadvantage

Government

amendment

to plead the fifth amendment
to refuse to answer an unwelcome question
refers to the fifth amendment of the United States constitution, which provides protection against self-incrimination

bailiwick

to be in someone's bailiwick
to be some other person's responsibility
refers to a region under the jurisdiction of a particular bailiff

to defend one's bailiwick
to protect one's power, influence, or authority in regard to a particular activity
refers to a region under the jurisdiction of a particular bailiff

a friend at court
a person with influence who is willing to use it on one's behalf
refers to royal courtiers

crown

the jewel in someone's crown
the most significant component

uneasy lies the head that wears a crown
leadership involves some risks and some burdens (esp. the risk of being deposed)
Shakespeare, *Henry IV*, Part 2, III:i, 'Uneasy lies the head that wears a crown'

crowning

the crowning point
the height of a person's achievement

Denmark

something is rotten in the state of Denmark
the situation is corrupt and unacceptable
Shakespeare, *Hamlet* III:iv, 'Something is rotten in the state of Denmark'

empire

to engage in empire building
to set out to expand the size of the business or bureaucratic unit for which one is responsible, especially as a means of increasing one's own importance

estate

the fourth estate
the press
refers to the fourth 'power' in the realm (after the Lords Temporal, the Lords Spiritual, and the Commons); variously attributed to Edmund Burke (1729–97), Thomas Carlyle (1795–1881), and Lord Macaulay (1800–59)

flag

to rally to the flag
to show support for a cause under attack
refers to military battle

to show the flag
to visit a place in order to boost morale there
military metaphor

Hall

one can't beat City Hall
the ordinary citizen is powerless against bureaucracy

hard

to put something into the 'too-hard' basket
to defer consideration of a difficult issue

king

a cat may look at a king
don't give yourself airs!

to pay a king's ransom
to pay a very large sum

kingmaker

kingmaker
person engaging in behind-the-scenes activities to promote another person to a particular leadership position

landslide

a landslide
an electoral result involving victory or defeat by a very large margin

licence

a licence to print money
a lucrative government-conferred monopoly or privilege
Lord Thomson of Fleet (1894–1977), 'It's just like having a licence to print your own money' (after the opening of Scottish commercial television, as recorded in Braddon, *Roy Thomson of Fleet Street*)

mint

to charge a mint
to impose very high prices

palace

a palace revolt
the overthrow of those in authority by their subordinates

party

to come to the party
to agree to someone's terms

royal

the royal road to success
the way of attaining success without effort

rule

to rule the roost
to dominate
refers to the habit of roosters and hens to have an established order of dominance

to rule with a rod of iron
to keep strict discipline
Psalms 2:9, 'Thou shalt break them with a rod of iron; thou shalt dash them in pieces like a potter's vessel'

to rule with an iron hand
to keep strict discipline

scot

to get off scot-free
to go unpunished
refers to an exemption from tax; scot (from old norse *skot*) means tax

stonewalling

stonewalling
deliberate obstruction or delaying tactics

throne

the power behind the throne
a person exercising the real authority but without having the official right to do so
William Pitt, Earl of Chatham (1708–78) ('Pitt the Elder'), 'There is something behind the throne greater than the king himself'

tsar

tsar

a person exercising excessive power over others

Heraldry

escutcheon

to be a blot on someone's escutcheon

to be a blemish on a person's character

refers to the shield on which a coat of arms is depicted; hence, a sign of dishonour on the symbol of one's name and honour

heart

to have a heart-to-heart talk

to have a confidential discussion on a highly personal matter

John Henry Newman (1801–90), 'Heart speaks to heart' (*cor ad cor loquitur*), motto on coat-of-arms as cardinal

left-handed

a left-handed compliment

a thinly disguised insult

ribbon

blue ribbon

of superb quality

refers to the insignia of the Order of the Garter, or perhaps to the ribands used in agricultural shows and at race meetings

standard

a standard bearer

a highly visible activist for a cause

military metaphor

History

barrel

to have someone over a barrel

to take advantage of someone's weakened position in relation to oneself

bedlam

bedlam

a scene of uproar

refers to the Hospital of St Mary of Bethlehem ('Bedlam'), which was used as a lunatic asylum from 1547 onwards

Buckley

to have Buckley's chance

to have no expectation at all

a pun, a reference to what follows 'Buckley' in 'Buckley & Nunn', the name of a well-known former Melbourne retailer

candle

not fit to hold a candle to someone

greatly inferior to another person

refers to a servant holding a candle to assist a more senior person

not to be worth the candle

to be too expensive in relation to the true value; AND/OR not to be worth the effort required

to burn the candle at both ends

to exhaust one's resources through working excessive hours'

continental

not to be worth a continental

to have no value

refers to currency notes of early US issue which quickly depreciated in value

cross

to be a cross that one has to bear

to be a difficulty that one has to endure

Luke 14:27, 'And whosoever doth not bear his cross, and come after me, cannot be my disciple'

crusade

a crusade

an aggressive campaign to achieve some political or social objective

refers to the wars undertaken in the Middle Ages in an attempt to secure the rights of Christians to visit the Holy Land (from Latin *crus*, 'cross')

D-Day

D-Day

the long-awaited time at which some action commences

refers to the Allied invasion of Europe in World War II

feather

a feather in one's cap

a meritorious personal achievement

refers to the practice in a number of cultures of adding a feather to the headgear of a person in recognition of a significant personal achievement

fiefdom

fiefdom

a sphere of operation in which a person exercises absolute control regardless of the wishes of others

heir

heir apparent

the person likely to succeed another

Hobson

Hobson's choice

no right at all to select

refers to Thomas Hobson, a Cambridge horsekeeper, who offered customers seeking a change of horses a single beast on a 'take it or leave it' basis

Indians

more chiefs than Indians

a disproportionately large number of supervisors

knight

a knight in shining armour

a person who comes to the rescue; a champion

derived from mediaeval tales of valiant knights rescuing those in distress

a white knight

a person voluntarily coming to the assistance of another person at considerable personal cost

derived from mediaeval tales of valiant knights rescuing those in distress, white being associated with purity and goodness

mud

a person's name is mud

a person is in disgrace, lacking in popularity, lacking in credibility

a play on the name of US physician Dr Samuel Mudd who, in 1865, was convicted of being a co-conspirator with John Wilkes Booth in the assassination of President Abraham Lincoln; since then a public and judicial campaign has been waged by family and supporters (extending even to some later US presidents) to assert Mudd's innocence; other people, just as vehemently, assert Mudd's guilt

oil

to burn the midnight oil

to work late into the night

Francis Quarles (1592–1644), *Emblems*, 'We spend our midday sweat, our midnight oil; / we tire the night in thought, the day in toil'

pale

to be beyond the pale

to be socially unacceptable, especially for unacceptable standards or behaviour

'the Pale' originally (fourteenth century and later) referred to that part of Ireland under British rule (Latin *palus* 'a stake', marking a fence or boundary)

Parthian

to fire a Parthian shot/shaft

to make a defiant or cutting gesture or remark on leaving

sometimes also referred to as 'a parting shot/shaft' — refers to missiles shot backwards by fleeing Parthian horsemen

pillory

to put someone in the pillory

to hold a person up to ridicule for that person's beliefs

refers to a form of punishment involving public humiliation

Pyrrhic

a Pyrrhic victory

a win that costs more than if there had been a loss

refers to the Battle at Asculum in 279 BC at which King Pyrrhus of Epirus defeated the Romans

riot

to read the riot act

to reprimand persons who are excessively noisy or otherwise misbehaving

refers to the police reading out to a rowdy crowd extracts from a law requiring the crowd's dispersement

Rubicon

to cross the Rubicon

to make an irreversible decision in regard to some commitment

refers to Caesar's crossing of the Rubicon River in Gaul in 49 BC thus declaring war on Pompey

salt

below the salt

in a subordinate position

refers to the seating order at ancient Roman dining tables

Spartan

Spartan
tough and efficient, with a complete absence of the finer things of life

Titanic

to rearrange the deckchairs on the Titanic
to take an initiative that is quite useless because it does not take much greater change into account
refers to the liner *Titanic* which struck an iceberg and sank in 1912

treadmill

to be on a treadmill
to be involved in some unpleasant ongoing activity that cannot readily be stopped

tsar

tsar
a person exercising excessive power over others

turncoat

a turncoat
a person changing sides
refers to the practice of mercenary soldiers switching to the winning side and displaying that side's colours by turning their coats inside out

warts

warts and all
with the unfavourable features as well as the favourable ones
Oliver Cromwell's reported direction to the artist, Sir Peter Lely, painting his portrait

Waterloo

to meet one's Waterloo
to receive a decisive defeat
refers to Napoleon's fate at the Battle of Waterloo (1815)

whipping

a whipping boy
a person made to suffer for the faults of others
refers to a boy kept for whipping when a king or prince deserved punishment

witch

a witchhunt
an exercise seeking to find someone who can be blamed
refers to ancient practice of seeking out those who supposedly practised witchcraft

Human Body

appetite

to whet one's appetite
to arouse one's curiosity, interest, or desire

arm

a shot in the arm
something to revive a person's enthusiasm
refers to medical injections

at arm's length
between parties who are strangers bearing no special duty to each other and who have no financial or other relationship with each other
a legal term

I would give my right arm for something
I am very keen to acquire something

to chance one's arm
to take a great risk
refers to the stripes on the uniforms of non-commissioned officers

to cost an arm and a leg
to be excessively expensive

to have a long arm
to have far-reaching power

to lose one's right arm
to lose some highly valued assistance

to twist someone's arm
to coerce another person to do something against that person's will or better judgment

armpits

to be in something up to one's armpits
to be involved very deeply in something

babes

out of the mouths of babes and sucklings
(as indiscreetly revealed) the truth

Psalms 8:2, 'Out of the mouths of babes and sucklings hast thou ordained strength ... '

to be babes in the wood
to be excessively naVve and inexperienced and thus ripe for exploitation
based on the folk legend of the babes in the wood of Wayland Hall, Norfolk

baby

to be left holding the baby
to be forced to accept responsibility for someone else's problems

to be one's baby
to be one's area of responsibility; to be one's special object of devotion or doting

to throw out the baby with the bathwater
to discard a major benefit in the course of obtaining a comparatively minor advantage

back

as soon as someone's back was turned
at the moment it became possible to do something without a person's knowledge

back-breaking
overburdening

behind someone's back
in a way that deliberately conceals an activity from a person

put your back into it!
work energetically!

so-and-so would give you the shirt off his or her back
so-and-so is very generous
Luke 6:29 (RSV), ' ... and from him who takes away your coat do not withhold even your shirt'

to back someone into a corner
to leave a person no option

to be able to do something with one hand behind one's back
to be able to do something very easily

to cover one's back
to take precautions

to engage in back-biting
to criticise in a trivial, annoying unfriendly manner

to get off someone's back
to leave a person alone to carry on without constant criticism

to get someone's back up
to annoy or antagonise a person

to have one's back to the wall
to be hard-pressed by creditors or opponents

to make a rod for one's own back
to make a handicap for oneself

to make the beast with two backs
to engage in sexual intercourse
Shakespeare, *Othello* I:i, 'Your daughter and the Moor are now making the beast with two backs'

to need to watch one's back
to find it necessary to take care in case others act against one's interests

to pat oneself on the back
immodestly to congratulate oneself

to pat someone on the back
to congratulate a person or to reassure a person

to put one's back into something
to work hard at achieving some goal

to ride on the back of someone
without effort to benefit from the prior efforts of others

to see the back of someone
to know that a person is no longer involved in something

to stab someone in the back
deliberately and surreptitiously to harm a person who regarded one as a friend

to tie someone's hands behind that person's back
to make it impossible for a person to act at all

to turn one's back on someone
to decline to assist or deal with a person

backbone

backbone
chief strength or character

barefaced

barefaced
shameless

bedfellow

bedfellow
collaborator

belly

a fire in someone's belly
ambition or driving force producing great enthusiasm

I've had a belly full
I have had enough of this

bend

to bend over backwards to do something
to go to great trouble to accommodate another person's wishes

bite

to bite
to respond predictably to a remark designed to provoke

to bite off more than one can chew
to be over ambitious and thus unrealistic as to one's capabilities

to bite one's fingernails
anxiously to await a decision

to bite one's lip
to control emotion such as anger or mirth

to bite one's tongue
to resist from criticising

to bite someone's head off
rudely and excessively to express displeasure at a person

to bite someone's nose off
to speak to a person with excessive aggression

to bite the bullet
to face up to the difficulties of a situation

refers to the use of biting on a bullet as a means of controlling one's reaction to pain in a surgical procedure without anaesthetic (for example, following a military battle)

to bite the dust
to fall, to fail, to die

to bite the hand that feeds one
to show ingratitude

Edmund Burke (1729–97), *Thoughts and Details on Scarcity* (1797), 'And having looked to government for bread, on the very first scarcity they will turn and bite the hand that fed them'

to get only one bite at the cherry
to receive no further opportunity

to start to bite
to start to be effective

blind

blind Freddy could see that something is such-and-such
it is very obvious that something is such-and-such

the blind leading the blind
persons without the necessary skills for a task purporting to impart those skills to others

Matthew 15:14, 'And if the blind lead the blind, both shall fall into the ditch'

to be blind to something
to be unaware of some matter and its significance

to fly blind
to do something in ignorance of the relevant facts

refers to pilots flying without visual guidance (and relying on instruments)

to have a blind spot about something
to have a lack of understanding and perception about something

refers to that part of the retina insensitive to light, at the point of entry of the optic nerve

to turn a blind eye to something
to pretend that something obvious does not exist

refers to action by Horatio, Lord Nelson (1758–1805), when disregarding Admiralty signals: 'I have only one eye — I have a right to be blind sometimes — I really do not see the signal!' (at the Battle of Copenhagen, reported in Southey, *Life of Nelson*, ch. 7)

blindly

to follow someone blindly
to follow a person unquestioningly

blinkers

to take one's blinkers off
to face reality

refers to the use of leather screens on a bridle to prevent a horse seeing sideways

blood

a blueblood
a person of high birth

refers to the appearance of the blood of certain Spanish noble families — supposed to be more of a blue colour due to a lack of Moorish blood

bad blood
animosity

blood, sweat, and tears
hard work and much effort
Winston Churchill, House of Commons, 13 May 1940, 'I have nothing to offer but blood, toil, tears, and sweat'
bloodshed
serious harm that is deliberately caused
fresh blood
newly joined members of some organisation
one's own flesh and blood
one's own offspring, ancestors, or close relatives
Genesis 2:23, 'Bone of my bones, and flesh of my flesh'
that person's blood is worth bottling
that person is very clever or competent
the lifeblood
the main or essential ingredient; OR the person or factor instilling enthusiasm
there is blood in the streets
much damage has been done to a cause
there is blood in the water
something is likely to cause a person to go into a frenzy
there is blood on the floor
this has caused great anguish
to be after someone's blood
to be keen to make a person the victim of an angry confrontation
to be in someone's blood
to be something about which a person is inherently very knowledgeable or keen
to curdle one's blood
to be horrific
to do something in cold blood
to be cruel without feeling any emotion about it
to draw blood from a stone
to do the impossible
to draw first blood
to get an early advantage
to give something a blood transfusion
to give something new enthusiasm
to have blood on one's hands
to be the person responsible for someone else's predicament
Matthew 27:24, 'He [Pilate] took water and washed his hands in full view of the crowd. "My hands are clean of this man's blood," he declared'
to introduce new blood
to recruit new members to some organisation
to let blood
to allow some harm as the price for achieving some greater benefit
refers to surgical removal of a patient's blood
to make bad blood between two parties
to cause ill feeling between two parties
to make someone's blood boil
to make a person very angry
to see blood
to be very angry
refers to a frenzy excited in some animals by the sight of blood
to smell blood
to divine imminent victory
to thirst for blood
to be eager for revenge

bloodbath

a bloodbath
catastrophic losses

blooded

full-blooded
vigorous, with every effort
hot-blooded
very passionate
Horace (65–8 BC), '*Non ego hoc ferrem calidus iuventa consule planco* (I shouldn't have put up with this when I was a hot-blooded youth, and Plancus was consul'

bloodletting

bloodletting
removal (perhaps violent) of persons from office or employment
refers to surgical removal of a patient's blood

bloody

to get a bloody nose
to suffer an undignified rebuff

blush

at first blush

at first sight
refers to Middle English term *blusche*, 'a gleam, a glimpse'

body

a body blow
a very damaging event

over my dead body
never

to keep body and soul together
barely to stay alive

bone

backbone
chief strength or character

to cut costs to the bone
to economise strictly

to get close to the bone
to cause discomfort by being accurate

to gnaw one's fingers to the bone
to fret

to point the bone at someone
to accuse a person
an Australian Aboriginal method of applying a curse

to put flesh and bone on something
to supply details of a proposal previously revealed only in outline

to work one's fingers to the bone
to work very hard

boneheaded

boneheaded
stupid

bones

to feel something in one's bones
to suspect something without having any real evidence for it

to make no bones about it
to be brutally frank

the bare bones
(of a story) nothing but the essential elements

bounce

to bounce back
to resume a cheerful existence after some setback

bow

to bow down
to succumb to pressure

to bow out
to retire from some activity

to take a bow
to receive recognition

boy

a whipping boy
a person made to suffer for the faults of others
refers to a boy kept for whipping when a king or prince deserved punishment

as every schoolboy knows
as is recognised by everyone
Jonathon Swift (1667–1745), *The Country Life*, 1:81,'How haughtily he cocks his nose, / To tell what every schoolboy knows'; Lord Macaulay (1800–59), *Lord Clive* (Jan. 1840), 'Every schooboy knows who imprisoned Montezuma, and who strangled Atahualpa'

blue-eyed boy
person shown unjustified favouritism

since Adam was a boy
for a very long time
refers to the name of the first man as recorded in *Genesis* 2

to be a good boy
to be cooperative

to send a boy on a man's errand
to engage a person to do a task beyond that person's capabilities

boys

to separate the men from the boys
to distinguish between those with and without certain skills

brain

anyone with even half a brain
anyone with any degree of common sense or knowledge

to be a bear of very little brain
to have little intelligence
refers to A. A. Milne's *Winnie-the-Pooh*

to have a bird brain
to be stupid

to have something on one's brain
to be obsessed with some notion

to pick someone's brain
to get the benefit of another person's knowledge and experience

brainchild

brainchild
inspired original idea

brained

hare-brained
wildly stupid

Benjamin Disraeli (1804–81), speech 1878, 'The hare-brained chatter of irresponsible frivolity'

brainstorm

to brainstorm
to pool thoughts in the course of a session designed to generate fresh ideas and especially to build up on the ideas of others

brainwash

to brainwash someone
systematically and forcibly to instil certain attitudes in place of previous ideas in the mind of a person

brainwave

a brainwave
a suddenly occurring bright idea

breast

to beat one's breast
to express sorrow
refers to traditional expression of grief

to make a clean breast of something
to confess

breath

not to hold one's breath for something
to give up all expectation

to be a breath of fresh air
to be a pleasant change from the past

to draw a deep breath
to get ready for exertion or for emotional news

to take one's breath away
to surprise greatly, or astonish

to wait with bated breath
to be excited in anticipation of some event

to waste one's breath
to talk and request something without achieving anything

breathe

to breathe down someone's neck
to cause annoyance to another person by remaining in that person's vicinity or by supervising that person too closely; OR to be narrowly behind another person in some competitive situation

to breathe easy
(following some crisis) to relax

to breathe life into a corpse
to revive something moribund

breathing

to get some breathing space
to get more time in which to accomplish something

bride

to be off like a bride's nightie
to act promptly

willing bride
(commerce) keen partner

brow

highbrow
intellectual or cultural

brows

to knit one's brows
to indicate one's displeasure

bruises

to nurse one's bruises
to adjust oneself to defeat

bump

to bump into someone
to meet a person accidentally

butt

to butt in
to involve oneself, uninvited, in someone else's conversation
refers to the aggressive action of animals with the head

to get up off one's butt
to cease being apathetic
refers to US slang for the buttocks

cheek

cheek by jowl
close to each other

to turn the other cheek
to refuse, on moral grounds, to retaliate to provocation in like manner
Matthew 5:38, 39, 'Ye have heard that it hath been said an eye for an eye and a tooth for a tooth: but I say unto you ... whosoever shall smite thee on the right cheek, turn to him the other also'

tongue in cheek
full of irony

cheering

the cheering could be heard a block away
there was great rejoicing

chest

to build up a war chest
to accumulate cash in readiness for some move

to get something off one's chest
to confess

to hold one's cards close to one's chest
to keep one's plans and strategies secret
refers to playing cards

child

a problem child
a source of unnecessary difficulty

brainchild
inspired original idea

to be child's play
to be easy or to require only elementary skills and knowledge

chin

to keep one's chin up
to maintain one's morale

to lead with one's chin
by one's brash behaviour to virtually invite one's opponents to take action against one
refers to boxing

to rub one's chin
to muse

to take it on the chin
to accept a misfortune cheerfully

cold

to be in a cold sweat
to be afraid

to get cold feet
to become scared

to give someone the cold shoulder
ostentatiously to ignore a person

to leave someone cold
to fail to impress a person

to leave someone out in the cold
to be excluded, ignored or neglected

to send a cold shiver down someone's spine
to horrify a person

cold-hearted

cold-hearted
cruel or mean or unmoved
Edmund Burke (1729–97), *Reflections on the Revolution in France*, 'This barbarous philosophy, which is the offspring of cold hearts ... '

cord

to cut the cord
to sever a connection
refers to the umbilical cord

to cut the umbilical cord
to free a person from the excessive influence of another; OR to separate a person from an essential source of supplies

corns

to step/tread on someone's corns
to upset another person by interfering in that person's area of responsibility

cradle

to be the cradle of something
to be the place where some idea was first nurtured

crawl

one needs to crawl before one can walk
skills are best developed in logical stages

to crawl out of the woodwork
(referring to something unwelcome) to emerge from hiding or obscurity

crucify

to crucify someone
to do severe damage unfairly to a person's reputation or credibility
Mark 15:13, 'And they cried out again, Crucify him'

Crusoe

not to be Robinson Crusoe
to be one of a large number of people with a common problem
refers to Daniel Defoe's *Robinson Crusoe*

crutch

a crutch
an artificial non-permanent support

cry

a cry for help
a subconscious or indirect indication that a person is in need of psychological counselling

a shoulder to cry on
sympathy

to be a far cry from something

to be a long way from something; to be quite dissimilar

to cry in one's beer
to show remorse

to cry one's eyes out
to express great sadness at a situation

to cry 'wolf'
repeatedly to raise an unjustified concern with the result that one will be ignored when the circumstances change and a real threat emerges
refers to a story of a boy who cried 'wolf' (from *Aesop's Fables*)

crying

it is no use crying over spilt milk
there is nothing to be gained by lamenting over an irredeemable error

daddy

the daddy of them all
the biggest and/or best example of something

dream

a pipedream
a fanciful notion, wished for but unlikely
probably derived from smoking opium in pipes

to dream up some story
to concoct a false story naVvely or maliciously

to have a dream run
to encounter no difficulties

dreams

to be successful beyond one's wildest dreams
to be far more successful than one could have expected

ear

a word in someone's ear
a confidential discussion

to be out on one's ear
to be ejected from a situation or place or to have one's services abruptly terminated

to chew someone's ear
to force one's conversation on an unwilling listener

to go in one ear and out the other
to leave no impression

to have someone's ear
to have a person's attention
Shakespeare, *Julius Caesar* III:ii, 'Friends, Romans, countrymen, lend me your ears'; *Hamlet* I: iii, 'Give every man thine ear, but few thy voice'

to keep an ear to the ground
to be well informed as to current developments
refers to listening for distant sound by applying one's ear to the ground

to lend someone an ear
to pay attention to a person
Shakespeare, *Julius Caesar* III:ii, 'Friends, Romans, countrymen, lend me your ears'

to play it by ear
to develop one's strategy to always fit in with circumstances as they change from time to time
refers to playing music without the benefit of a written score

to send someone away with a flea in the ear
to give a person frank, but unwelcome, facts
perhaps refers to fleas trapped in the armour of ancient knights, or perhaps from the discomfort felt by a dog with a flea in its ear; or perhaps, figuratively, to any lingering irritation in the ear

to turn something on its ear
to reverse something

ears

asses and little pitchers have long ears
children have a tendency to overhear things

music to one's ears
comments that one is very pleased to hear
Shakespeare, *Romeo and Juliet* II:i, 'How silver-sweet sound lovers' tongues by night, / like softest music to attending ears!'

to be all ears
to be very attentive

to be up to one's ears in something
to be involved very deeply in something

to be wet behind the ears
to be excessively naVve and inexperienced

to come out of one's ears
to be plentiful

to come to someone's ears
to come to someone's attention
to drag someone by the head and ears
to force a person to reveal the true facts
to fall around someone's ears
to collapse utterly around someone
to fall on deaf ears
to be totally disregarded
to have money flowing out of one's ears
to be very rich
to keep one's ears open
to be alert for useful information
to prick up one's ears
suddenly to start paying attention to a conversation in progress as a result of a halfheard phrase
refers to horses and dogs
walls have ears
someone may be overhearing
words on wartime posters, reminding people of the existence of spies; might also refer to certain rooms in the Louvre, constructed so that conversations could be heard in other rooms
were your ears burning?
we were discussing you
Pliny: 'When our ears do glow and tingle, some do talk of us in our absence'
with one's ears pinned back
chastened
refers to the aggressive attitude of horses

elbow

elbow grease
hard manual work
old jocular saying, in existence for several centuries, referring to the vigorous use of the elbow in rubbing, polishing, scrubbing, etc.
more power to your elbow
may your praiseworthy efforts continue and be strengthened
to elbow someone out
to force a person to move aside and thus enable oneself to assume that person's position

elbows

to be up to one's elbows in something
to be very busy and involved with something

enfant

an enfant terrible
a person who causes embarrassment by inappropriate action, or by inappropriate speech about unpalatable issues'
French for 'terrible child'

eye

a mote in someone's eye
a fault in another person that is trifling in comparison with an unrecognised major fault in oneself
Matthew 7:3, 'Why beholdest thou the mote that is in thy brother's eye, but considerest not the beam that is in thine own eye?'
a smack in the eye
a rebuff
an eye for an eye
retaliation of equal magnitude to the original offence
Exodus 21:24, 'Eye for eye, tooth for tooth, hand for hand, foot for foot'; see also 'to turn the other cheek'
beauty is in the eye of the beholder
some things are matters for subjective judgments
Shakespeare *Love's Labour Lost* II:i, 'Beauty is bought by judgment of the eye'
in one's mind's eye
using a vivid imagination
one would give one's eye teeth for something
a person would very much like to achieve some objective
refers to the (valued) canine teeth directly under the eye
to be an eye-opener
to be a surprise
to be better than a poke in the eye with a burnt stick
to be not particularly welcome, but better than other alternatives
to be easy on the eye
to be visually attractive
to be eye wash
to be nonsense
to be in the eye of the storm
to be at the centre of a controversy
to be in the public eye

to have one's every action subject to scrutiny by the community

to be one in the eye for someone
to represent an unexpected and unwelcome defeat

to be only a gleam in someone's eyes
not yet conceived, let alone achieved

to be the apple of someone's eye
to be a much cherished person

refers to the pupil of the eye — 'the apple of the eye' as being the centre of visual perception and therefore especially cherished and much-valued

to cast an eye over something
to look at something critically

to catch someone's eye
to attract the attention of another person, or to seek permission to address that person

to cock one's eye at someone
to glance knowingly at a person

to do someone in the eye
to cheat a person

to have an eye for something
to have particular expertise in assessing something

to keep a weather eye out for something
to look out with particular care

nautical metaphor; refers to the eye that is turned towards the wind

to keep an eye on the ball
to monitor a fast-changing situation

to keep one's eye on someone
to supervise a person

to keep one's eye on something
to monitor a situation

to see eye to eye with someone
to agree

Isaiah 52:8, 'For they shall see eye to eye, when the Lord shall bring again Zion'

to see something out of the corner of one's eye
only just to see something

to see something with half an eye
to sum up a matter instantly

refers to taking note with a mere glance

to turn a blind eye to something
to pretend that something obvious does not exist

refers to action by Horatio, Lord Nelson (1758–1805), when disregarding Admiralty signals: 'I have only one eye — I have a right to be blind sometimes — I really do not see the signal!' (at the Battle of Copenhagen, reported in Southey, *Life of Nelson*, ch. 7)

with an eye towards doing something
with the intention that something particular be done

eyeball

eyeball to eyeball
confronting each other and taking account of each other's reactions

eyeballs

to be up to the eyeballs in something
to be involved very deeply in something

eyebrows

to raise one's eyebrows
to show surprise or disbelief

eyed

blue-eyed boy
person shown unjustified favouritism

bright-eyed and bushy-tailed
naVve but enthusiastic

one-eyed
biased

eyeful

to get an eyeful of something
to obtain a very good view of something

eyelid

not to bat an eyelid
to fail to express any surprise

eyelids

to hang on by the eyelids
to have only a slender hold

eyes

all eyes are on something
everyone's attention is focused on something

in someone's eyes
in a person's judgment

someone's eyes are bigger than that person's stomach

a person is unrealistic in regard to that person's ability to cope with something

someone's eyes popped
a person expressed great surprise

to be a sight for sore eyes
to be something welcome

to be all eyes
to observe very closely

to clap eyes on something
to catch sight of something

to cry one's eyes out
to express great sadness at a situation

to have eyes at/in the back of one's head
to know more of what is going on than is generally realised

to have one's beady eyes on something
to await the chance to acquire something to which one is not properly entitled

to have one's eyes glued to something
to concentrate on looking at something to the exclusion of other competing calls for attention

to have stars in one's eyes
to receive a blow on the head that affects one's vision; OR to have unrealistic expectations of one's position and prospects

to hit someone right between the eyes
to be brutally frank
refers to fighting

to keep one's eyes open
to be on the lookout for useful information

to keep one's eyes open for something
to be on the lookout for an opportunity to do something

to keep one's eyes peeled for something
to be on the constant lookout for something
refers to keeping the eyelids open

to make eyes at someone
to look at a person amorously

to open someone's eyes to something
to alert another person to the truth of something
Matthew 9:30, 'And their eyes were opened'

to pick the eyes out of something
to choose the most valuable items from among a large number

to pull the wool over someone's eyes
to deceive or deliberately mislead another person
derived from the inability of some sheep to see clearly if wool is across their eyes

to rub one's eyes
to express astonishment

to see the colour of someone's eyes
to see how a person matches expectations or requirements

to shut one's eyes to something
deliberately to take no notice of something, especially in dereliction of one's duty

to throw dust into someone's eyes
to deceive a person by presenting inaccurate or misleading information
Koran: 'Neither didst thou, O Muhammad, cast dust into their eyes; but it was God who confounded them'

with one's eyes wide open
fully conscious of the ramifications

eyesore

eyesore
extremely ugly object

face

a poker face
a facial expression that does not reveal one's thoughts during negotiations
refers to playing cards

a slap in the face
a calculated insult or action amounting to a rebuke

a straight face
a facial expression that does not reveal one's thoughts in a humorous situation

someone's face fell
someone registered obvious disappointment

to blow up in someone's face
to rebound on a person

to cut one's nose off to spite one's face
to act in pique in a way that harms only oneself
to do an about face
to reverse a previously enunciated policy
to face a rocky road ahead
to be likely to encounter difficulties
to face the music
to accept responsibility when confronted by one's critics
refers to the theatre
to fall flat on one's face
to fail or to be seriously embarrassed by a bad error of judgment
to go on until one is blue in the face
to do something difficult for a long time without being able to complete it
to have a long face
to look miserable
to have egg on one's face
to be embarrassed by the results of one's own stupidity
to hurl something in someone's face
to reproach a person in regard to something
to lose face
to experience embarrassment by an affront to one's dignity
to present a happy face to the world
bravely to gloss over one's problems and to appear contented to others
to put a brave face on it
to face adversity cheerfully
to put a new face on something
to alter the way something should be regarded
to put one's best face on something
to focus on the positive features surrounding a basically disastrous situation
to save face
to avoid humiliation or loss of reputation
to set one's face against something
to oppose some matter
to show one's face
to appear
to slam the door in someone's face
ostentatiously to refuse to have any dealings with a person
to stare someone in the face
to be obvious
to take something at face value
(of alleged facts) to accept something without question or challenge
to wipe the smile off someone's face
to destroy a person's complacency
volte face
a reversal of previously held beliefs
French, 'a turning around'
wipe that smile off your face!
treat this matter more seriously!
you will laugh on the other side of your face
you will regret this

faced

to be left red-faced
to be embarrassed
two-faced
insincere

fell

someone's face fell
someone registered obvious disappointment
they fell over themselves to do something
they showed great keenness while doing something

finger

not to lay a finger on someone
to refrain from hurting a person
not to lift a finger to help someone
to refuse to assist
to have a finger in something
to be involved in something
to have a finger in the pie
to have an interest in a project, especially an officious involvement
to point the finger at someone
to accuse a person or allege some indiscretion on that person's part
to put one's finger on something
to identify the essential features of something
to stir a finger

to make some minimum effort

to twist someone around one's little finger
to exert easy control over a person

to wave a finger at someone
to indicate mild displeasure at another person's actions

fingered

light-fingered
habitually likely to steal
William Makepeace Thackeray (1811–63), 'The light-fingered gentry pick pockets furiously'

fingernails

to bite one's fingernails
anxiously to await a decision

to hang on by one's fingernails
to have only a slender hold

fingerprints

someone's fingerprints are all over this
it is obvious that a particular person was solely responsible for this

fingers

a butter fingers
a person unable to catch and/or hold on to an object

someone's fingers are all thumbs
a person is clumsy with his or her hands

to burn one's fingers
to suffer (esp. loss of money) through foolishness or meddling
refers to taking chestnuts from a fire

to gnaw one's fingers to the bone
to fret

to have green fingers
to be good at gardening

to have itchy fingers
to be impatient

to have one's fingers in many different pies
to be engaged in a variety of separate activities

to have one's fingers in the till
to steal from one's employer

to have one's fingers on the pulse
to know what is going on
medical/nursing metaphor

to have sticky fingers
to be dishonest; OR to be very adept at catching a ball

to keep one's cotton-picking fingers off something
not to interfere (in a meddlesome fashion) with something

to keep one's fingers crossed
to hope for a good outcome
refers to making the sign of the Christian cross to protect against ill-fortune

to let something slip through one's fingers
to allow something to escape from one's ownership or control

to pull one's fingers out
to cease indolence and get on with a job with alacrity

to snap one's fingers
to gesture contemptuously, especially in the expectation of immediate obedience

to work one's fingers to the bone
to work very hard

fingertips

to cling on by one's fingertips
to have only a slender hold

to have a subject at one's fingertips
to be very familiar with a subject

fist

hand over fist
rapidly overtaking each other during progress towards a common goal
refers to movement of the hands in climbing a rope or similar

fist

to lose money hand over fist
to lose money very fast and comprehensively

to make a good fist of something
to make a good attempt at, or to succeed in, a difficult task

to rule with an iron fist
to keep strict discipline

fisted

ham-fisted
undiplomatic and clumsy
refers to having large and clumsy hands

hard-fisted
mean

tight-fisted

mean

fistful

to hold out a fistful of dollars
to offer money by way of inducement

fit

not to get along with someone in a fit
not to get along with a person in any circumstances

to have a blue fit
to be very agitated

to have a fit
to be in a state of great agitation

to have a fit of the vapours
to demonstrate exaggerated anxiety, hysteria, nervousness or similar

flank

to expose one's flank
to leave oneself open to the possibility of having advantage taken

flesh

one's own flesh and blood
one's own offspring, ancestors, or close relatives
Genesis 2:23, 'Bone of my bones, and flesh of my flesh'

the spirit is willing but the flesh is weak
the body is not up to the demands made on it–physically or morally
Matthew 26:41: 'Watch and pray, that ye enter not into temptation: the spirit indeed is willing but the flesh is weak

to be a thorn in someone's flesh
to be a constant annoyance or affliction
2 Corinthians 12:7, 10: 'There was given to me a thorn in the flesh ... I will glory in my infirmities'

to be more than flesh can stand
to be more than a person reasonably can be expected to endure

to flesh out the skeleton
to supply the missing pertinent details

to go the way of all flesh
to die
Joshua 23:14, 'And, behold, this day I am going the way of all flesh'

to make someone's flesh creep
to frighten a person with something horrific

to put flesh and bone on something
to supply details of a proposal previously revealed only in outline

to see someone in the flesh
to see someone in person

foot

a foot in the door
the opportunity to do business

not to put a foot wrong
to behave impeccably
refers to dancing steps

the boot is on the other foot
the advantage is reversed

to bind someone hand and foot
completely to limit a person's freedom to act

to get off on the wrong foot with someone
to make an unfavourable initial impression on a person
refers to dancing

to go hot foot
to do something fast

to have one foot in the grave
to be very old or dying
W. S. Gilbert 1836–1911, HMS *Pinafore* (1878), 'A greenery-yallery, Grosvenor Gallery/ Foot-in-the-grave young man!'

to have one's foot on something
to be about to acquire something or to be able to acquire something
perhaps refers to limbering-up exercises before Roman footraces in which competitors were said to 'have their foot in (or on)' — meaning that they were ready to begin the task

to pussyfoot around
to take stealthy, cautious, non-committal steps
refers to a cat prowling

to put one's best foot forward
to make a special effort

to put one's foot down
to assert one's authority and insist on something

to put one's foot in it
to make a foolish mistake

to put one's foot in one's mouth
to say something foolish

to put someone on the back foot
to make a person less confident of that person's position

to shoot oneself in the foot

to act in a foolish way and thus harm one's own cause

to start off on the right foot
to commence an operation with great care to do it correctly
refers to marching

to tread someone under foot
to oppress a person

to wait hand and foot on someone
to serve a person's every real or imagined whim

footed

nimble-footed
quick to change the direction of one's activities when circumstances warrant

to catch someone flat-footed
to take someone unawares or making mistakes

foothold

to gain a foothold
to achieve a position from which further advances can readily be made

footloose

footloose and fancyfree
unmarried and without any romantic attachments

footnote

a footnote
a passing comment by way of elaboration

footprints

without leaving any footprints
without making any impression

footsteps

to follow in someone's footsteps
to do as another person did

forelock

to tug one's forelock
to pay obeisance to someone

freckles

to be up to one's freckles in something
to be very deeply involved in something

frown

to frown on something
to disapprove of some matter

gall

gall
impudence

giant

a giant
a person whose ability and achievements exceed that of most other people
Genesis 6:4, 'There were giants in the earth in those days'

to take a giant step forward
to make a significant advance
Genesis 6:4, 'There were giants in the earth in those days'

grin

to grin and bear it
to suffer adversity cheerfully

grips

to come to grips with some problem
to be on the way to solving a problem

gut

a gut feeling
a belief based purely on intuition and unsupported by facts or evidence

gutful

to have had a gutful
to have experienced something to the point of utter intolerance to any more

gutless

gutless wonder
coward

guts

I will have that person's guts for garters
I am extremely angry and dissatisfied with that person

something has no guts in it
something has no substance to it

to kick someone in the guts
to take action needlessly hurtful to another person

haemorrhage

to stem the haemorrhage
to put a stop to the financial losses of a project

hair

hair-raising
scary

Job 4:15, 'Then a spirit passed before my face; the hair of my flesh stood up'; Shakespeare, *Hamlet* I:v, 'would harrow up thy soul ... and each particular hair to stand an end'

not to touch a hair on someone's head
not to harm a person
Matthew 10:30, 'the very hairs of your head are all numbered'

not to turn a hair
to remain composed

to a hair
exactly
Matthew 10:30, 'the very hairs of your head are all numbered'

to be within a hair's breadth of something
to be extremely close to something

to keep one's hair on
to remain calm in a crisis
Shakespeare, *Macbeth* I:iii, ' ... whose horrid image doth unfix my hair'

to keep out of someone's hair
to let someone get on with that person's work in his or her own way

to let one's hair down
to relax

to make someone's hair curl
(of news) to give someone a shock
W. S. Gilbert, *Ruddigore* (1887), 'when he's excited he uses language that would make your hair curl'

to make someone's hair stand on end
to give a person shocking news
Job 4:15, 'Then a spirit passed before my face; the hair of my flesh stood up'; Shakespeare, *Hamlet* I:v, 'would harrow up thy soul ... and each particular hair to stand an end'

to tear one's hair out
to be frustrated and extremely agitated
refers to ancient demonstration of grief and mourning

hairs

to get someone by the short and curly hairs
to have domination over a person

to split hairs
to draw absurdly fine distinctions

hand

a bird in the hand is worth two in the bush
a benefit currently available is more valuable than a seemingly much larger benefit that might or might not be achieved in the future

at first hand
personally

hand over fist
rapidly overtaking each other during progress towards a common goal
refers to movement of the hands in climbing a rope or similar

on the one hand
putting one side of the proposition

on the other hand
putting the opposing side of the proposition

one's right-hand person
one's chief aide
Hebrews 1:1, 'His son ... by whom he also made the worlds ... sat down on the right hand of the majesty in heaven'

sleight of hand
deceit by trickery
Daniel Defoe (1660–1731), 'All the artifice and sleight of hand they were masters of'

the hand of fate
chance

the left hand does not know what the right hand is doing
a person or an organisation is not aware of inconsistencies in conduct
Matthew 6:3, 'But when you give alms, do not let your left hand know what your right hand is doing'

to be able to do something with one hand behind one's back
to be able to do something very easily

to be at hand
to be in the vicinity, ready to help

to be in hand
to be under control

to bind someone hand and foot
completely to limit a person's freedom to act

to bite the hand that feeds one
to show ingratitude
Edmund Burke (1729–97), *Thoughts and Details on Scarcity* (1797), 'And having looked to government for bread,

on the very first scarcity they will turn and bite the hand that fed them'

to gain the upper hand
to attain, after some effort, an advantage over another person

to get out of hand
to get out of control

to give someone a free hand
to authorise a person to act as that person sees fit

to give someone a hand
to assist a person

to go cap in hand
to show humility while soliciting a favour

to hand on the torch
to pass on the traditions and aspirations of life
Lucretius (94?–55 BC), ' … the generations of living creatures are changed and like the runners relay the torch of life'

to hand over something on a silver platter
to provide a valuable benefit for virtually nothing
refers to first-class service

to hand someone a poisoned chalice
to confer a seeming benefit on a person that will turn out to be a significant detriment

to hand-pick someone
to choose a person carefully for that person's individual attributes

to have a hand in something
to be one of the participants in some project

to have one hand tied behind one's back
to work with a handicap

to have the whip hand
to be in control of a situation
refers to the hand holding the whip in controlling horses, and perhaps slaves

to hold someone's hand
to give detailed on-the-job training and supervision

to hold the power to do something in the hollow of one's hand
to have the right to make crucial decisions
Isaiah 40:12, ' … who hath measured the waters in the hollow of his hand … '

to keep one's hand in
to engage in activities that reinforce skills that one has previously acquired

to lend a hand
to assist

to live from hand to mouth
being in poor financial circumstances to survive (with little safety margin)
refers to immediate consumption of whatever one has in one's hand

to lose money hand over fist
to lose money very fast and comprehensively

to put one's hand to the plough
voluntarily to undertake some task
Luke 9:62. 'No man, having put his hand to the plough, and looking back, is fit for the Kingdom of God'

to put one's hand up
to identify oneself or to volunteer

to put one's hand in one's pocket
to provide money from one's own resources, especially for a charitable purpose

to rule with an iron hand
to keep strict discipline

to stir a hand
to volunteer assistance

to strengthen someone's hand
to give a person additional authority or greater moral support or more facts to support that person's case

to take something in hand
to assume control over something

to try one's hand at something
to attempt a new activity, especially by way of experiment

to turn one's hand to something
to tackle some project (especially an unfamiliar project)

to wait hand and foot on someone
to serve a person's every real or imagined whim

to work hand in glove with someone
to work in close cooperation with a person or to be in collusion with a person to the detriment of others

with a heavy hand
in an oppressive fashion

with a high hand
arrogantly

Exodus 14: 8 'And the children of Israel went out with an high hand'

with an iron hand in a velvet glove
with a hard attitude made to seem soft

with an open hand
generously

hand-pick

to hand-pick someone
to choose a person carefully for that person's individual attributes

handed

a back-handed compliment
a polite expression seemingly of praise but really intended as an insult

a left-handed compliment
a thinly disguised insult

high-handed
overbearing

to catch someone red-handed
to apprehend a person in the course of committing a wrongdoing

refers originally to being caught with blood on one's hands

handedly

single-handedly
without help from other persons

handful

a handful
a small number or amount

to be a handful
to be difficult to manage

P. G. Wodehouse (1881–1975), 'Bailey will find her rather a handful. Does she ever sit still, by the way?'

hands

all hands on deck
everybody is requested to help out

nautical metaphor

all hands to the pumps
everybody is requested to help out

nautical metaphor

to accept something with both hands
to accept something eagerly

to be able to lay one's hands on something
to be able to locate something

to be in someone's hands
to be being dealt with by someone with the necessary authority

Ecclesiasticus 2:11, 'We will fall into the hands of the Lord, and not into the hands of men: for as his majesty is, so is his mercy'

to be out of someone's hands
to be up for decision by a different person

Ecclesiasticus 2:11, 'We will fall into the hands of the Lord, and not into the hands of men: for as his majesty is, so is his mercy'

to be putty in someone's hands
to be far too easily influenced by another person

refers to material able to be fashioned into various shapes

to eat out of someone's hands
to be very compliant and submissive

to get one's hands dirty
to do the necessary but unpleasant or menial parts of a task

to go down on one's hands and knees to someone
with great humility to ask a favour of a person

to grab an opportunity with both hands
to seize an opportunity with great enthusiasm

to have a fight on one's hands
to encounter resistance or opposition to a proposal

to have blood on one's hands
to be the person responsible for someone else's predicament

Matthew 27:24, 'He [Pilate] took water and washed his hands in full view of the crowd. "My hands are clean of this man's blood," he declared'

to have clean hands
to be innocent or to act ethically

Matthew 27:24, 'He [Pilate] took water and washed his hands in full view of the crowd. "My hands are clean of this man's blood," he declared'

to have one's hands full
to be fully occupied

to join hands with someone
to cooperate with a person

to lay one's hands on something
to acquire or find something

to play right into someone's hands
to act so as to give a person an unintended advantage

to rub one's hands with glee
to express great satisfaction

to sit on one's hands
deliberately to do nothing

to throw up one's hands
to give up or quit (perhaps in frustration)

to tie someone's hands
to prevent a person from acting as that person sees fit

to tie someone's hands behind that person's back
to make it impossible for a person to act at all

to wash one's hands of something
emphatically to decline future responsibility
Matthew 27:24, 'He [Pilate] took water and washed his hands in full view of the crowd. "My hands are clean of this man's blood," he declared'

to win hands down
to win very convincingly
refers to a jockey riding confidently with hands low when a race is as good as won

to wring one's hands
to express despair

handshake

golden handshake
a large payment in connection with, or as an inducement to, retirement

handstands

to turn handstands
to express great joy

hang

to give someone enough rope to hang himself or herself
to give a person the opportunity to do something that is likely to get that person into severe trouble

to hang on by one's fingernails [or nails]
to have only a slender hold

to hang on by the eyelids
to have only a slender hold

to hang on by the skin of one's teeth
to be barely surviving
Job 19:20, 'I am escaped with the skin of my teeth'

to hang one's head
to be ashamed of oneself; OR to be disappointed and lacking in morale
Shakespeare, *Henry VIII* III:i, 'Even the billows of the sea, / hung their heads and then lay by'

hanging

not to be a hanging matter
to be only a minor mistake

there is a big question mark hanging over someone's head
there are considerable doubts about a person's competence, integrity, or suitability
refers to Damocles who had the sword of Dionysius hanging, by a slender thread, over his head — as a symbol of perpetual risk in life; the story is told in Cicero, *Tusculanae Disputationes*

to have a cloud hanging over one's head
there is doubt as to one's future
refers to the pillar of cloud (God) passing judgment on the Hebrews; the pillar of cloud is described in *Exodus* 13:21 *et seq.*

to have a sword of Damocles hanging over one
to be in imminent danger despite normal activity going on all around one
refers to Damocles who had the sword of Dionysius hanging, by a slender thread, over his head — as a symbol of perpetual risk in life; the story is told in Cicero, *Tusculanae Disputationes*

to have a threat hanging over one's head
to fear some intimated unpleasant action
refers to Damocles who had the sword of Dionysius hanging, by a slender thread, over his head — as a symbol of perpetual risk in life; the story is told in Cicero, *Tusculanae Disputationes*

hanged

one might as well be hanged for a sheep as for a lamb
further action will not increase the adverse consequences already in train
refers to the stealing of either sheep or lambs being capital crimes under old English law

hard-headed

hard-headed
realistic

hard-hearted

hard-hearted
unsympathetic
Exodus 7:3, ' ... and I will harden Pharaoh's heart'

hard-mouthed

hard-mouthed
uncontrollable
refers to horses that are 'hard' in the mouth or bite (and thus difficult to control)

hard-nosed

hard-nosed
tough in negotiations

head

a hothead
an impetuous person

a swelled head
an exaggerated idea of one's abilities or status

an old head on young shoulders
experience, knowledge, and maturity in a young person

head first
precipitately

head over heels
to be turned upside down; OR to be very excited

not to touch a hair on someone's head
not to harm a person
Matthew 10:30, 'the very hairs of your head are all numbered'

off the top of one's head
impromptu, based on experience or intuition, but without detailed consideration

pull your head in!
do not interfere in this! you are advised to withdraw from this situation

someone's head is on the block
a person is in danger of being condemned; OR a person is in danger of having an appointment terminated
refers to execution by decapitation

that is on your head
you will have to accept responsibility for that
Shakespeare, *Merchant of Venice*, IV:i, 'My deeds upon my head'

there is a big question mark hanging over someone's head
there are considerable doubts about a person's competence, integrity, or suitability
refers to Damocles who had the sword of Dionysius hanging, by a slender thread, over his head — as a symbol of perpetual risk in life; the story is told in Cicero, *Tusculanae Disputationes*

to bang one's head against a brick wall
to fight an unwinnable case

to be able to do something standing on one's head
to be able to do something very easily

to be head and shoulders above the rest
to be significantly more capable than others

to be off one's head
to be crazy

to be over someone's head
to be beyond a person's ability to understand

to beat each other over the head
to be always fighting

to belt someone over the head
to override someone's views or arguments, often involving the use of heavy pressure

to bite someone's head off
rudely and excessively to express displeasure at a person

to bury one's head in the sand
to refuse to face up to an unpleasant truth
refers to the reputed habit of ostriches in danger

to come to a head
to reach culmination
medical metaphor; refers to abscess formation

to confront someone head on
to meet and face up to someone in a hostile and direct fashion

to drag someone by the head and ears
to force a person to reveal the true facts

to eat one's head off
to eat excessively

to fall head-over-heels in love
to fall very much in love

to get one's head blown off

to be abused very soundly

to give someone his or her head
to let a person do as that person wishes

to go off one's head
to lose one's temper

to go over someone's head
to bypass lower levels of authority and approach someone more senior instead; OR to be beyond a person's ability to understand

to go to someone's head
to cause a person to get an exaggerated idea of that person's abilities or status

to hang one's head
to be ashamed of oneself; OR to be disappointed and lacking in morale
Shakespeare, *Henry VIII* III:i, 'Even the billows of the sea, / hung their heads and then lay by'

to have a cloud hanging over one's head
there is doubt as to one's future
refers to the pillar of cloud (God) passing judgment on the Hebrews; the pillar of cloud is described in *Exodus* 13:21 *et seq.*

to have a threat hanging over one's head
to fear some intimated unpleasant action
refers to Damocles who had the sword of Dionysius hanging, by a slender thread, over his head — as a symbol of perpetual risk in life; the story is told in Cicero, *Tusculanae Disputationes*

to have eyes at/in the back of one's head
to know more of what is going on than is generally realised

to have one's head in the clouds
to be unrealistic

to have one's head screwed on
to be shrewd

to have rocks in the head
to be stupid or mentally unbalanced

to head someone in the right direction
to assist a person to achieve something

to hold a gun/pistol at someone's head
to put pressure on a person to make a particular decision regardless of that person's desires in the matter

to hold one's head high
to stay unruffled and to maintain one's dignity despite attempts by others to embarrass

to hold one's head just above water
to cope with problems but with little margin to spare or to stay solvent

to keep a civil tongue in one's head
to be polite, especially under provocation

to keep a cool head
to stay calm and rational in a crisis
Rudyard Kipling (1865–1936), *If*, 'If you can keep your head when all about you are losing theirs ... '

to keep a level head
to stay calm and rational in a crisis
Rudyard Kipling (1865–1936), *If*, 'If you can keep your head when all about you are losing theirs ... '

to keep one's head
to remain calm in a crisis or unexpectedly to retain an elected or appointed position
Rudyard Kipling (1865–1936), *If*, 'If you can keep your head when all about you are losing theirs ... '

to keep one's head down
to stay out of trouble, AND/OR to work very diligently

to knock an idea on the head
utterly to reject a proposal

to laugh one's head off
to enjoy something greatly

to let one's head go
to do as one wants to
refers to letting a horse have its head (and run as it wishes to)

to let one's heart rule one's head
to act on emotion rather than on reason
George Colman the younger (1762–1836), *Who Wants a Guinea?*, 'His heart runs away with his head'

to lose one's head
to become agitated or confused
Rudyard Kipling (1865–1936), *If*, 'If you can keep your head when all about you are losing theirs ... '

to need something like a hole in the head
to be confronted with a completely undesired problem

to need to have one's head read
to engage in behaviour so foolish that a psychiatric examination seems called for

to pull one's head in
to retreat from a previously held stance
refers to habit of a tortoise in avoiding danger

to put one's head in the noose
to expose oneself to great danger likely to lead to one's downfall
refers to death by hanging

to put one's head into the lion's mouth
recklessly to expose oneself to great danger
refers to circus performance

to put one's head on the block
to have the courage of one's convictions
refers to execution by decapitation

to scratch one's head
to be amazed or puzzled

to scream one's head off
to utter loud and piercing cries as if in great pain

to shake one's head
to indicate disbelief or wonder or disapproval
Shakespeare, *Macbeth* III:iv, 'Never shake thy gory locks at me'

to snap someone's head off
to speak to a person with excessive aggression

to tackle someone head on
to confront a person directly

to turn someone's head
to cause a person to get an exaggerated idea of that person's abilities or status

to turn something on its head
to reverse something

uneasy lies the head that wears a crown
leadership involves some risks and some burdens (esp. the risk of being deposed)
Shakespeare, *Henry IV*, Part 2, III:i, 'Uneasy lies the head that wears a crown'

you need your head read
your behaviour is so foolish that you require psychiatric examination

headache

a headache
a cause for worry

headed

hard-headed
realistic

level-headed
rational

pig-headed
unduly obstinate

woolly-headed
slightly muddled

heads

heads will roll
transgressors will be punished
refers to execution by decapitation

to kick heads in
to demonstrate extreme annoyance at, or dislike of, certain persons

to knock two heads together
to make two persons come to their senses and deal with each other

to promote someone over the heads of others
to promote a person to a position more senior than that held by some persons previously outranking the promoted person

to put several heads together
to confer and pool ideas

headway

to make headway
to make progress

heal

to heal wounds
to effect a reconciliation
Shakespeare, *Two Gentlemen of Verona*, I:ii, 'Poor wounded name! my bosom, as a bed, shall lodge thee till thy wound be thoroughly healed'

health

to get a clean bill of health
after proper investigation to be found not wanting

hear

to hear a whisper
to learn of a rumoured fact
Shakespeare, *Macbeth*, V:i, 'Foul whisperings are abroad'; William Congreve (1670–1729), *Love for Love*, 'I know that's a secret, for it's whispered everywhere'

to hear on the grapevine
to learn unofficially
the earlier form of the metaphor was a 'grapevine telegraph' as a means of communicating private information

heard

the cheering could be heard a block away
there was great rejoicing

heart

from the bottom of one's heart
very sincerely

heart and soul
with great energy
Matthew 22:36–40, 'Thou shalt love the Lord thy God with all thy heart and with all thy soul and with all thy mind'

heart failure
a shock

heart-stopping
exciting

one's heart bleeds for someone
one feels truly sad for a person's fate
derived from the Christian Church's veneration of the sacred heart of Jesus (*sacré couer*) which was symbolised by a bleeding heart — sacrificed for the sake of humanity

one's heart is not in some cause
one has little enthusiasm for some cause

one's heart sank
one realised the extent of some disaster

this does my heart good
I rejoice at this
Shakespeare, *A Midsummer Night's Dream* I:ii, ' ... will do any man's heart good to hear'

to be close to one's heart
to be a project about which one is very keen

to be in [or of] good heart
to be cheerful, especially in adversity

to be someone after one's own heart
to be a person who shares one's beliefs
1 Samuel 13:14 'A man after his own heart'

to break someone's heart
to act in a way causing great upset to another person
Psalms 69:21, 'Thy rebuke hath broken my heart; I am full of heaviness'; Shakespeare *Hamlet* I:ii, 'But break my heart ... ')

to eat one's heart out
to suffer bitterly
Shakespeare, *Othello* IV:i, 'O God! That I were a man! I would eat his heart in the market place'

to give someone heart
to cause a person to cheer up

to have a change of heart
to form a new view in place of a strongly held prior view

to have a heart
to have compassion

to have a heart of gold
to have a generous disposition
Hilaire Belloc (1870–1953), 'With hearts of gold and lungs of bronze'

to have a heart of oak
to be brave
refers to a famous sea song and naval march from the pantomime, *Harlequin's Invasion* (1759), by Garrick and Boyce.

to have a heart of stone
to be unfeeling
Shakespeare, *Othello*, 'My heart is turned to stone'

to have a heart-to-heart talk
to have a confidential discussion on a highly personal matter
John Henry Newman (1801–90), 'Heart speaks to heart' (*cor ad cor loquitur*), motto on coat-of-arms as cardinal

to have one's heart in one's boots
to be afraid or dejected

to have one's heart in one's mouth
to be very apprehensive

to have one's heart in something
to be enthusiastic about and committed to a cause

to have one's heart in the right place
to have good intentions, to mean well

to have one's heart set on something
to be very keen to achieve something

to know something in one's heart of hearts
to know something — although reluctant to admit it, even to oneself
Shakespeare, *Hamlet* III:ii, 'In my heart's core, ay, in my heart of heart'

to let one's heart rule one's head
to act on emotion rather than on reason
George Colman the younger (1762–1836), *Who Wants a Guinea?*, 'His heart runs away with his head'

to lose heart
to be discouraged

to pour one's heart out to someone
to reveal one's innermost hopes and fears to another person

to pull at one's heart strings
to affect one emotionally

to search one's heart
to seek after one's innermost feelings and motivations
Jeremiah 17:10, 'I, the Lord, search the heart … to give every man according to his ways, and according to the fruit of his doings'

to steal someone's heart
to move someone's affections towards another person or cause
Shakespeare, *Julius Caesar* III:ii, 'I come not, friends. to steal away your hearts'

to steel one's heart against something
to determine that, notwithstanding one's natural compassion, something shall not happen

to take heart from something
to be encouraged by something

to take something to heart
to learn to appreciate the significance of something; or to be much saddened by something

to warm the cockles of someone's heart
to delight a person
refers to the cockle shell which looks like a heart; the formal name for bivalve molluscs (such as cockles) is *cardium* (Latin for 'heart')

to wear one's heart on one's sleeve
to lack the reserve expected of one
refers to the fashion of wearing a sign of romantic attachment on one's sleeve; Shakespeare *Othello* I:i, 'But I will wear my heart upon my sleeve'

with a heavy heart
in sorrow
Johann Wolfgang von Goethe (1749–1832), *Gretchen am Spinnrad*, 'My peace is gone, my heart is heavy'

with a sinking heart
with growing despondency

you can eat your heart out
I don't care if you are intensely aggrieved or jealous

heartache

heartache
sadness
William Blake (1757–1827), *To Hayley*, 'Thy friendship oft has made my heart to ache'

heartbreak

heartbreak
despair
Psalms 69:21, 'Thy rebuke hath broken my heart; I am full of heaviness'; Shakespeare *Hamlet* I:ii, 'But break my heart … '

heartburn

heartburn
distress or regret at some disappointment
originally referred to passion, as in *Luke* 24:32, 'Did not our hearts burn within us, while he talked with us by the way?'

hearted

chicken-hearted
showing little courage

cold-hearted
cruel or mean or unmoved
Edmund Burke (1729–97), *Reflections on the Revolution in France*, 'This barbarous philosophy, which is the offspring of cold hearts … '

half-hearted
unenthusiastic

hard-hearted
unsympathetic
Exodus 7:3, ' … and I will harden Pharaoh's heart'

open-hearted

cordial
Ecclesiasticus 8:19, 'Open not thine heart to every man'
warm-hearted
affectionate or generous

heat

if one can't stand the heat one should stay out of the kitchen
if one cannot put up with the pressure of a situation, one should get out of it
US President Harry S. Truman (1884–1972), *Mr Citizen*, ch. 15, 'If you can't stand the heat, get out of the kitchen'
to take the heat off someone
to remove pressure or harassment from someone
to turn the heat on something
to intensify the investigation of some matter
to turn up the heat on someone
to increase the pressure on a person
Shakespeare, *Macbeth* II, i, 'Proceeding from the heat-oppressed brain'

heave

to heave a sigh a relief
to express satisfaction at the achievement of a solution to a difficult problem
John Keats (1795–1821), *I stood tip-toe upon a little hill*, 'born of the very sigh that silence heaves'

heavyweight

a heavyweight
a person of importance or influence
refers originally to boxing

heel

to be someone's Achilles' heel
to represent a weakness in an otherwise strong position
refers to Achilles, Greek warrior and hero of Homer's *Iliad*, who was invulnerable except for his heel
to bring someone to heel
to make a person conform
refers to the training of dogs

heeled

well-heeled
rich

heels

head over heels
to be turned upside down; OR to be very excited
to be hard/hot on the heels of something
to pursue something closely
to fall head-over-heels in love
to fall very much in love
to cool one's heels
to be kept waiting
to dig one's heels in
to become even more stubborn than at first
to drag one's heels
to perform unduly slowly
to kick one's heels
to be kept waiting
to snap at someone's heels
to be in very close pursuit
refers to hounds pursuing a fox

heir

heir apparent
the person likely to succeed another

hero

to make a hero of oneself
to do something for personal glorification

hiccup

a hiccup
a temporary minor holdup

hide

to cover one's hide
to provide excuses or take other evasive action in an attempt to avoid the adverse consequences of one's actions
to have a thick hide
to be impervious to criticism
to have the hide of a rhinoceros
to be unaffected by, and unresponsive to, valid criticism
to hide under someone's skirts
to let someone else take the consequences of one's actions
refers to childish seeking for protection
to want someone's hide
to be keen to penalise a person

hidebound

hidebound
narrow-minded

high

high-handed
overbearing

since that person was knee-high to a grasshopper
since that person was a very young child

to hold one's head high
to stay unruffled and to maintain one's dignity despite attempts by others to embarrass

with a high hand
arrogantly
Exodus 14: 8 'And the children of Israel went out with an high hand'

highbrow

highbrow
intellectual or cultural

hind

to stand up on one's hind legs
to assert one's authority
refers to animals adopting aggressive posture

hindsight

with 20/20 hindsight
with the benefit of knowing what happened
refers to American system of expressing perfect visual acuity

hip

the hip-pocket nerve
the assessment of issues by their financial effects on one

to shoot from the hip
to speak without careful assessment of the situation

hit

to hit one's stride
to settle down to some task
refers to horses in harness

to hit someone below the belt
to act unfairly towards another person
refers to boxing

to hit someone hard
greatly to affect a person emotionally; OR to cost a person a lot of money

to hit someone right between the eyes
to be brutally frank
refers to fighting

hold

not to hold one's breath for something
to give up all expectation

to hold one's head high
to stay unruffled and to maintain one's dignity despite attempts by others to embarrass

to hold one's head just above water
to cope with problems but with little margin to spare or to stay solvent

to hold one's tongue
to keep quiet
John Donne (1571–1631), *The Canonization*, 'For God's sake hold your tongue, and let me love'

to hold someone's hand
to give detailed on-the-job training and supervision

to hold the power to do something in the hollow of one's hand
to have the right to make crucial decisions
Isaiah 40:12, ' ... who hath measured the waters in the hollow of his hand ... '

holding

to be left holding the baby
to be forced to accept responsibility for someone else's problems

holds

no holds barred
without any limitation
refers to wrestling

hole

to need something like a hole in the head
to be confronted with a completely undesired problem

hop

something is but a hop, skip, and jump away
something is nearby

to be on the hop
to be always bustling about

to catch someone on the hop
to take a person by surprise

to hop onto the bandwagon
to subscribe to an emerging majority opinion

hot

a hothead
an impetuous person
hot-blooded
very passionate
Horace (65–8 BC), '*Non ego hoc ferrem calidus iuventa consule planco* (I shouldn't have put up with this when I was a hot-blooded youth, and Plancus was consul)'

hungry

lean and hungry
efficient
Shakespeare, *Julius Caesar* I:ii, 'Yond' Cassius has a lean and hungry look; he thinks too much: such men are dangerous'

hurl

to hurl something in someone's face
to reproach a person in regard to something

itching

to be itching to go
to be highly enthusiastic and keen to start

itchy

itchy feet
a desire to travel
to have itchy fingers
to be impatient

jaundiced

jaundiced
affected by jealousy
Alexander Pope (1688–1744), *An Essay on Criticism*, 'As all looks yellow to the jaundiced eye'

jaw

someone's jaw dropped
someone registered obvious astonishment and/or disappointment

Joneses

to keep up with the Joneses
to maintain a lifestyle beyond one's means in order to match that of some neighbourhood role model
Wordsworth refers to keeping pace with Jones amid pomp, but whether this relates to the metaphor is problematical: William Wordsworth (1770–1850), *Jones! As from Calais* (1807), 'Jones! as from Calais southward you and I went pacing side by side, this public way streamed with the pomp of a too-credulous day'

jowl

cheek by jowl
close to each other

jugular

to go for the jugular
to attack a very vital and vulnerable point with a view to a decisive victory

jump

something is but a hop, skip, and jump away
something is nearby
to be for the high jump
to face dismissal or the end of one's career
refers to death by hanging
to get the jump on someone
to get an advantage over a person
to jump a hurdle
to overcome a problem or difficulty
to jump at the opportunity
enthusiastically to take immediate advantage of a good chance
to jump down someone's throat
to react angrily to the remarks of the other party to a conversation
to jump for joy
to express great satisfaction
to jump in feet first
to take a calculated risk
to jump into bed with someone
to enter into a joint enterprise with another person
to jump into the ring
enthusiastically to join in a contest or challenge
refers to the practice of jumping into a boxing ring to make a challenge
to jump on the bus
to join an activity already well under way
to jump straight in at the deep end
to do something without proper preparation
to jump that hurdle when one comes to it
to deal with a particular problem only when it becomes necessary to do so
to jump the gun
to start before one is meant to

refers to a starting pistol in a race

to jump through hoops
to be required to perform or undergo some ordeal
refers to circus performance

to jump to a conclusion
to infer something without proper consideration

to jump to attention
to show respect

to jump up and down
to show excitement or anger or frustration

to nearly jump out of one's skin
to receive a fright

you can jump in the lake
I intend to take no notice whatsoever of you or your views

kick

a free kick
an advantageous opportunity accorded to a person
refers to football

a kick in the pants
an admonition

a kick in the shins
an unexpected and undeserved setback

I could kick myself
I regret that I acted thus

to kick a man when he is down
to take unfair advantage of a person already in difficulty

to kick heads in
to demonstrate extreme annoyance at, or dislike of, certain persons

to kick in
to contribute financially

to kick off
to start some action
refers to football

to kick one's heels
to be kept waiting

to kick some proposal around
to examine a proposal from all angles
refers to football

to kick someone around
to abuse a person

to kick someone in the guts
to take action needlessly hurtful to another person

to kick someone in the teeth
to inflict a grave or humiliating setback, criticism, or punishment upon a person

to kick someone out
to expel a person

to kick someone upstairs
to promote a person to a purely ceremonial position

to kick the bucket
to die

to kick the cat
to take out one's anger on some innocent party

to kick the communist can
to take every opportunity to exacerbate fear of communism in others

to kick up a fuss
to create a commotion

kicking

to be alive and kicking
to be in good form

to drag someone kicking and screaming to do something
to force a person into some action that the person is most reluctant to undertake

knee

a knee-jerk reaction
a response made instantaneously and without any proper consideration

since that person was knee-high to a grasshopper
since that person was a very young child

kneed

weak-kneed
unassertive or irresolute

knees

to be cut off at the knees
to have a pet project aborted

to beg on bended knees
to request in great earnestness

to force someone on to that person's knees
to inflict a humiliating defeat on a person

to go down on one's hands and knees to someone
with great humility to ask a favour of a person

knitting

to stick to one's knitting
to confine oneself to what one is used to doing

knuckles

to rap someone over the knuckles
to admonish a person

lap

to drop into one's lap
to turn up fortuitously

to dump something in someone's lap
to impose an unwelcome responsibility on another person

lather

to get a lather up/to whip oneself into a lather
to become unduly excited
refers to horses sweating profusely when excited

lean

a shoulder to lean on
sympathy

lean and hungry
efficient
Shakespeare, *Julius Caesar* I:ii, 'Yond' Cassius has a lean and hungry look; he thinks too much: such men are dangerous'

to lean on someone
to utilise the support of another person; OR to pressure another person to do something against that person's inclination

leap

a leap in the dark
a decisive move into the unknown
Thomas Hobbes (1588–1679), 'I am about to take my last voyage, a great leap in the dark' (quoted by Watkins, *Anecdotes of Men of Learning*)

a quantum leap
a gigantic step forward
a term derived from quantum mechanics

to leap at an idea
to accept a suggestion enthusiastically

to leap-frog something
to overtake something, with the likelihood of, in turn, being overtaken
refers to a game in which participants jump over each other in turn

to leap in
to commence an activity without considering the wisdom of doing so or the best way to proceed

leaps

by leaps and bounds
with surprisingly fast progress

leg

not to have a leg to stand on
to have one's arguments completely demolished; OR to be without acceptable excuse or explanation

to cost an arm and a leg
to be excessively expensive

to do the leg work
to carry out the part of a project that requires actually physically walking around and collecting information, etc.

to give someone a leg up
to give a person some assistance
refers to mounting a horse

to have a leg in
to have an opportunity which has the potential to lead to bigger things

to pull someone's leg
to tell a false but plausible story as an act of humour

to shake a leg
to hurry up

legs

not to have any legs
(of an argument) to be unacceptable

the idea has legs
this notion seems a good one

to be on one's last legs
to be nearly worn out

to have one's tail between one's legs
to be dejected or humiliated
refers to dogs

to stand up on one's hind legs
to assert one's authority
refers to animals adopting aggressive posture

lick

to lick one's chops
to look forward to something with pleasurable anticipation
refers to salivation in anticipation of food

to lick one's wounds

to adjust oneself to defeat
refers to a dog cleaning its own wounds

to lick someone's boots
to show humility

to lick something into shape
to make something presentable and effective
refers to mediaeval belief that bear cubs are born shapeless and have to be licked into shape by their mothers — a story related in the encyclopaedia of the Arab physician Avicenna (970–1037)

lie

one has made one's bed and one will now have to lie on it
one has to bear the consequences of one's actions

to lie low
to stay inconspicuous

lies

uneasy lies the head that wears a crown
leadership involves some risks and some burdens (esp. the risk of being deposed)
Shakespeare, *Henry IV*, Part 2, III:i, 'Uneasy lies the head that wears a crown'

life

a new lease of life
the prospect of a better existence from now on, or of better functioning after repair

I cannot for the life of me
I just cannot

larger than life
exaggerated; more than normal

life in the fast lane
existence full of exciting, high-pressure activity

life raft
financial assistance sufficient to avert insolvency

not on your life
definitely not

to be the life and soul of the party
to be the prime enthusiast for a cause
Shakespeare, *A Midsummer Night's Dream*, 'My love, my life, my soul, fair Helena!'

to breathe life into a corpse
to revive something moribund

to save someone's life
to be of great help to a person

you can bet your life on something
something is certain to happen

lifeblood

the lifeblood
the main or essential ingredient; OR the person or factor instilling enthusiasm

lifeline

to throw someone a lifeline
to give significant assistance to a person

lift

not to lift a finger to help someone
to refuse to assist

lip

a stiff upper lip
obstinate courage in the face of pain or adversity

to bite one's lip
to control emotion such as anger or mirth

to pay lip service to some rules
to disregard some rules in practice while acknowledging them in words

lipped

to be tight-lipped
to keep confidences or to be uncommunicative

lips

to seal one's lips
to keep a confidence

listening

a listening post
a place where information of strategic value can be collected
military metaphor

livered

lily-livered
cowardly
refers to a supersitition that the liver of a coward contained no blood

loins

to gird up one's loins
to get ready for action
Job 38:3 'Gird up thy loins now like a man'

look

distant fields look greener

activities of which one has no experience seem more attractive than is really the case

Psalms 23:1, 'The Lord is my shepherd ... he shall feed me in a green pasture'

things look black
there is little hope of success or prosperity or a favourable outcome

to give someone a black look
to indicate one's displeasure with a person

to look a gift horse in the mouth
to be suspicious about a benefit that has been volunteered

Samuel Butler (1612–80), *Hudibras*, 'He ne'er consider'd it, as loth to look a gift horse in the mouth'; refers to the examination of a horse's teeth for an accurate assessment of its age

to look after number one
to act selfishly

to look at someone sideways
silently and politely to indicate one's disapproval

to look daggers at someone
to look at a person in a way that indicates great animosity

Shakespeare, *Hamlet* III:ii, 'I will speak daggers to her, but use none'

to look down the barrel of a gun
to be given little choice in a matter

to look down the nose at something
to treat a matter with obvious contempt

to look for a needle in a haystack
to attempt something with a very small chance of success

to look in the pink
to look well

Oliver Goldsmith (1730–74), *She Stoops to Conquer*, 'the very pink of perfection'

to look on the dark side
to be pessimistic

to look though the wrong end of the telescope
completely to miss the point

to look to one's laurels
to be careful not to lose one's reputation for some skill

refers to laurel wreaths presented to winners of events at the ancient Olympics

to need to look over one's shoulder
to be subject to attack which is not obvious

looks

one looks for elephants in elephant country
one needs to search in the right place

someone looks as if butter would not melt in his or her mouth
a person looks sweet and innocent

lying

to take something lying down
to accept a disadvantage without protest

man

a man of straw
a person of no substance, a counterfeit, a sham; OR a person invented in order to be triumphantly defeated; OR a person who has no assets while giving a contrary appearance

Exodus 6:7 'Ye shall no more give the people straw to make bricks ... let them go and gather straw for themselves'

a one-man band
a person performing many different roles singlehandedly

a poor man's something
a second-best version

every man and his dog
everybody

he is your man
he conforms to an ideal

one man's meat is another man's poison
different people have different tastes

the man in the street
the average citizen

to be a man of steel
to be a person with moral courage

to be one's own man
to be free and independent, and able to act in accordance with one's own values

to kick a man when he is down
to take unfair advantage of a person already in difficulty

to see a man about a dog
to do something unspecified

to send a boy on a man's errand

to engage a person to do a task beyond that person's capabilities

mind

a thought in the back of one's mind
an undeveloped idea

in one's mind's eye
using a vivid imagination

it is mind over matter
one's resolve to overcome suffering will succeed

that has taken a load/weight off my mind
I am relieved

the mind boggles
this is astonishing

to be of one mind
(of several people) to be agreed

to be out of one's cotton-picking mind
to act irrationally

to broaden someone's mind
to expose a person to a greater variety of experiences and interests than that person had previously experienced

to change one's mind
to alter the views that one had previously formed

to cloud one's mind
to allow irrelevant or extraneous factors to affect one's impartiality or judgment

to cross one's mind
to think of something

to drive someone out of that person's mind
to produce insanity in a person
often used jocularly, with exaggeration

to give someone a piece of one's mind
to abuse another person

to have a butterfly mind
not to concentrate on the matter on hand

to have a mind of one's own
not to be easily influenced

to have a one-track mind
to keep coming back to one narrow topic of conversation

to have an open mind
to be willing to assess evidence on its merits and without prejudging it

to have half a mind to do something
to be tempted or mildly inclined to do something

to know one's mind
to form and adhere to an opinion

to make up one's mind
to reach a conclusion after contemplating a matter

to prey on one's mind
(of a problem) to keep worrying one

to put someone's mind at rest
to reassure a person

to slip one's mind
to be overlooked or forgotten

to speak one's mind
to express one's views frankly and forcefully

to spring to mind
to occur suddenly to a person

minds

to be in two minds
to be undecided between two alternatives

Mohicans

the last of the Mohicans
to be the last of a group
refers to a near-extinct tribe of North American natives; title of a novel by James Fenimore Cooper (1789–1851)

motherhood

a motherhood statement
a statement so obvious and uncontroversial as not to be worth making
such as 'motherhood is a good thing'

mouth

someone looks as if butter would not melt in his or her mouth
a person looks sweet and innocent

to be a big mouth
to lack discretion in one's conversation

to be born with a silver spoon in one's mouth
to be brought up by wealthy parents
refers to the traditional gift of a silver spoon (an 'apostle spoon') to a child at baptism — the child born of wealthy parents is assured of riches from the moment of birth and thus does not have to await baptism to receive a valuable gift

to be down in the mouth

to be depressed
refers to facial expression

to be left with a nasty taste in one's mouth
to be appalled or very disappointed at another person's unethical behaviour to one

to foam at the mouth
to show extreme uncontrollable anger
refers to a rabid animal; Washington Irving (1783–1859), 'Fall down in convulsions [and] foam at the mouth'

to have one's heart in one's mouth
to be very apprehensive

to keep one's mouth shut
not to discuss some matter

to live from hand to mouth
being in poor financial circumstances to survive (with little safety margin)
refers to immediate consumption of whatever one has in one's hand

to make one's mouth water
to excite desire
refers to salivation

to put one's foot in one's mouth
to say something foolish

to put one's money where one's mouth is
to back one's boasting by putting assets at risk

to put words into someone's mouth
to attempt to get someone to say something in the particular terms drafted by another person

to shoot one's mouth off
to speak without thinking

you took the words right out of my mouth
you have just said what I was about to say

mouthed

mealy-mouthed
afraid of giving offence, not outspoken, hypocritical

mouths

out of the mouths of babes and sucklings
(as indiscreetly revealed) the truth
Psalms 8:2, 'Out of the mouths of babes and sucklings hast thou ordained strength ... '

to take food out of the mouths of children
cruelly to deprive the needy

muscles

to flex one's muscles
to assert one's personality or powers

myopia

myopia
an inability to see the longer term consequences of actions
refers to short-sightedness

nail

a thumbnail sketch
brief but pertinent details
refers to an artist assessing perspective by judging the object to be painted against a thumbnail held close to the eye

to fight tooth and nail
to strive very hard to win

to nail someone to the wall
to outmanoeuvre and trap someone

nails

to bite one's fingernails
anxiously to await a decision

to hang on by one's nails
to have only a slender hold
also: 'to hang on by one's fingernails'

navel

to contemplate one's navel
to be introspective
refers to a contemplative posture (as in yoga)

neck

a millstone around someone's neck
a great burden

at a break-neck pace
very fast
refers to horseriding at great speed

to be a pain in the neck
to be an unpleasant person or to be a nuisance

to be an albatross around someone's neck
to be a great burden
refers to a mythical mariner who suffered terrible ordeals as a result of killing an albatross; Samuel Taylor Coleridge (1772–1834), *The Ancient Mariner*, 1798, 'Why look'st thou so? — with my cross-bow, I shot the albatross'

to be up to one's neck in something
to be very deeply involved in something

to break one's neck to do something
to be particularly keen
refers to reckless enthusiasm

to breathe down someone's neck
to cause annoyance to another person by remaining in that person's vicinity or by supervising that person too closely; OR to be narrowly behind another person in some competitive situation

to cop it in the neck
to be severely castigated or reprimanded
refers to death by decapitation

to save someone's neck
to come to the rescue of a person
refers to death by hanging

to send a chill down someone's neck
to be worrying news

to stick one's neck out
to have the courage of one's convictions or to take a calculated risk
refers to execution by decapitation

nerve

the hip-pocket nerve
the assessment of issues by their financial effects on one

to have a nerve
to be impudent

to lose one's nerve
to abandon, out of fear, a decision to do something

to touch a nerve
to mention a sensitive subject

nerves

to get on someone's nerves
by one's behaviour to cause annoyance to a person

to have nerves of steel
not to be easily frightened

nervous

nervous Nellies
persons unwilling to take any risks

nightmare

a nightmare
an unpleasant experience

nod

a nod and a wink
a sign that understanding has been reached in a matter that, in the interests of discretion, has not been discussed aloud
Captain Marryat (1792–1848), *Peter Simple*, 'But you're a dutiful son, so I'll say no more about it — a nod's as good as a wink to a blind horse'

to get the nod
to receive approval

nose

to be no skin off someone's nose
not to matter to a person

to be on the nose
(of a proposal or scheme) not to be quite honest, not to be popular; OR to be smelly

to bite someone's nose off
to speak to a person with excessive aggression

to cut one's nose off to spite one's face
to act in pique in a way that harms only oneself

to follow one's nose
to act intuitively

to get a bloody nose
to suffer an undignified rebuff

to get up someone's nose
to irritate a person

to have a good nose for business
to be able to identify profitable business situations

to keep one's nose clean
to act with circumspection and honesty despite temptation to do otherwise

to keep one's nose out of something
not to meddle in something

to keep one's nose to the grindstone
to work with particular diligence
refers to having one's head down low while working on a grindstone sharpening tools

to lead someone by the nose
to induce another person to comply with one's wishes

refers to leading animals (such as bulls) by a ring through the nose

to look down the nose at something
to treat a matter with obvious contempt

to pay through the nose
to pay an excessive price
refers to an onerous tax imposed by the Danes in Ireland in the ninth century whereby those who refused to pay had their noses slit

to poke one's nose into something
to interfere

to poke one's nose outside
to venture outside

to put someone's nose out of joint
to upset another person

to rub someone's nose in it
to humiliate a person by highlighting something embarrassing to that person

to take a nose dive
to fall steeply, suddenly and unexpectedly

to take something on the nose
meekly to accept a rebuff

to thumb one's nose at someone
to show one's contempt for someone in authority and ostentatiously to disregard that person's orders

to turn up one's nose at something
to express one's disdain

under someone's nose
in a person's immediate area of responsibility or in circumstances where that person should have known something

nosed

hard-nosed
tough in negotiations

nudge

to give something a nudge forward
to give modest encouragement to something

old

an old head on young shoulders
experience, knowledge, and maturity in a young person

it is on for young and old
the excitement has started (esp. referring to fighting)

to open up an old wound
to take action which revives a long-standing grievance

palms

to grease someone's palms
to bribe a person
Francis Quarles (1592–1644), English poet, *The Virgin Widow* IV:i, 'grease my fist with a tester or two, and you shall find it in your pennyworth'

palpable

palpable
readily understandable
literally 'touchable'; Shakespeare, *Hamlet* V:ii, 'a hit, a very palpable hit'

paralyse

to paralyse something
to bring something to a standstill

pas

faux pas
something indiscreet or offending social conventions
French: 'false step'

people

people in glass houses should not throw stones
those who are less than perfect are foolish to criticise others
John 8:7, 'He that is without sin among you, let him first cast a stone at her' (refers to ancient condemnation and punishment of people by stoning)

people stayed away in droves
few people came
refers to a moving group of cattle, sheep, or other animals

to be unable to keep people away with a big stick
to be faced with a large crowd or much demand

person

one's right-hand person
one's chief aide
Hebrews 1:1, 'His son ... by whom he also made the worlds ... sat down on the right hand of the majesty in heaven'

piece

to give someone a piece of one's mind
to abuse another person

to have a piece of someone
to vent one's frustration on a person

profile

profile
description
refers to a view of a person (esp. a person's face) from the side

pull

not to pull any punches
to be brutally frank
refers to boxing

pull your head in!
do not interfere in this! you are advised to withdraw from this situation

to have pull
to have influence

to pull a fast one
to gain an advantage by questionable means

to pull at one's heart strings
to affect one emotionally

to pull one's fingers out
to cease indolence and get on with a job with alacrity

to pull one's head in
to retreat from a previously held stance
refers to habit of a tortoise in avoiding danger

to pull one's horns in
to retreat from previously stated views
refers to fighting between male horned animals

to pull one's socks up
to set out to improve or correct one's inadequate behaviour or performance

to pull one's weight
to do one's proper share of the work requiring to be done
refers to rowing

to pull oneself together
by gathering one's faculties and strength, to rouse oneself to a renewed effort

to pull oneself up by one's bootstraps
to make a praiseworthy effort to better oneself unaided

to pull oneself up by one's own shoelaces
to make a superhuman effort

to pull someone's leg
to tell a false but plausible story as an act of humour

to pull the wool over someone's eyes
to deceive or deliberately mislead another person
derived from the inability of some sheep to see clearly if wool is across their eyes

to pull together
to work in harmony
refers to rowing

pulse

to have one's fingers on the pulse
to know what is going on
medical/nursing metaphor

punches

not to pull any punches
to be brutally frank
refers to boxing

to telegraph one's punches
by one's actions to give advance warning of one's future plans
refers to sending an advance message

push

to push someone around
to exercise, in an obnoxious manner, one's superiority over another person

to push someone over the brink/edge
by a small action to cause the absolute ruin (financially or emotionally) of someone already in peril

reeling

to leave someone reeling
to leave a person in a state of shock

rub

to rub one's chin
to muse

to rub one's eyes
to express astonishment

to rub one's hands with glee
to express great satisfaction

to rub shoulders with someone
to mingle with a person

to rub someone up the wrong way
to annoy a person with actions that fail to recognise that person's current mood

to rub someone's nose in it

to humiliate a person by highlighting something embarrassing to that person

run

someone would run a mile
a person would do anything to escape that person's responsibilities

to have a dream run
to encounter no difficulties

to have to run fast just to stand still
competition is such that merely to maintain one's relative position one needs to make positive progress

to run for cover
to seek to avoid blame

to run around in circles
to engage in excited but useless activity

to run rings around someone
to outwit another person easily

to run someone off that person's feet
to keep a person very busy on some physical task

to run someone to earth
to locate a person
refers to fox hunting

to run someone to ground
to discover the whereabouts of a person
refers to fox hunting

to run the gauntlet
to be subjected to criticism
from Swedish *gantlopp* ('laneway') in reference to a military punishment inflicted on delinquents made to run between two files of soldiers, as used in Thirty Years' War, Holy Roman Empire, 1618–48

to run with something
to take advantage of some current development
refers to rugby

to run with the ball
to make the most of the opportunity
refers to rugby

your race is run
you have had your opportunity
Hebrews 12:1, 'Let us run ... the race that is set before us'

running

to be up and running
to be operative

scalp

to be after someone's scalp
to be keen to penalise a person
refers to the savage practice of removing the scalp of a killed person as a trophy

scar

to scar someone
to cause a lasting unpleasant effect on someone

scent

to throw someone off the scent
to deceive a person by giving out misleading indications
refers to fox hunting

scratch

to scratch one another's backs
to help each other

to scratch one's head
to be amazed or puzzled

scream

to scream and yell
to protest violently

to scream blue murder
to make serious allegations; OR to protest violently
perhaps refers to the French *morbleu* (altered version of *mort Dieu*, 'God's death'), a comic oath attributed to French speakers

to scream one's head off
to utter loud and piercing cries as if in great pain

to scream something from the rooftops
to communicate a message to a wide audience

screaming

to drag someone kicking and screaming to do something
to force a person into some action that the person is most reluctant to undertake

sense

a sixth sense
intuition
refers to the five senses — sight, hearing, smell, taste, and touch

shadow

to be in someone's shadow

to be unable to assert one's personality because of association with a more important person

to be only a pale shadow of something
to be a weak imitation

to cast a shadow over something
to introduce a note of warning or sadness in regard to some matter

to overshadow
to cover or obscure with a greater power; to make less important
Luke 1:35, 'And the power of the highest shall overshadow thee'

to shadow box
to go through the motions without achieving or intending to achieve anything
refers to training for boxing by punching at one's own moving shadow

to throw a long shadow
to have widespread ramifications

shadows

to lurk in the shadows
to have a low profile at the moment, but with the possibility of becoming much more conspicuous at any time

shave

to be a close shave
to be a narrow escape

short-sighted

to be short-sighted
not to recognise the likely consequences

shoulder

a shoulder to cry on
sympathy

a shoulder to lean on
sympathy

shoulder to shoulder
in close proximity

straight from the shoulder
bluntly
refers to boxing

to give someone the cold shoulder
ostentatiously to ignore a person

to have a chip on one's shoulder
unreasonably to resent something

to need to look over one's shoulder
to be subject to attack which is not obvious

to put one's shoulder to the wheel
to make a strong effort

to shoulder the blame
to accept the responsibility for error

to take a weight off someone's shoulder
to assist a person by relieving that person of some responsibility

to work shoulder to shoulder
to work with united effort

shoulders

an old head on young shoulders
experience, knowledge, and maturity in a young person

to be head and shoulders above the rest
to be significantly more capable than others

to carry the world on one's shoulders
to perform a huge task alone
refers to Atlas, who was condemned to bear the heavens on his shoulders for leading the Titans against the gods to have broad shoulders
to be able to cope well with responsibility

to put a burden on someone's shoulders
to impose responsibilities on a person

to rub shoulders with someone
to mingle with a person

to shrug one's shoulders
to indicate that one does not know or care, or that one is unable or unwilling to assist

to stand on someone's shoulders
to build up on another person's ideas

shouting

to be all over bar the shouting
to be virtually finished

shrug

to shrug one's shoulders
to indicate that one does not know or care, or that one is unable or unwilling to assist

to shrug something off
to indicate that one is unable or unwilling to do something; OR to dispose of something without further

concern and get on with other activities

shudders

one shudders to think what the outcome might be
there is great concern as to the outcome

side

to be a thorn in someone's side
to be a constant annoyance or affliction
2 Corinthians 12:7, 10: 'There was given to me a thorn in the flesh ... I will glory in my infirmities'

to feel the rough side of someone's tongue
to be verbally abused by a person

to get on someone's right side
to make a good impression on a person

to get out of bed on the wrong side
to be grumpy

to split one's side
to be convulsed with laughter

you will laugh on the other side of your face
you will regret this

sigh

to heave a sigh a relief
to express satisfaction at the achievement of a solution to a difficult problem
John Keats (1795–1821), *I stood tip-toe upon a little hill*, 'born of the very sigh that silence heaves'

sight

to be a sight for sore eyes
to be something welcome

with 20/20 hindsight
with the benefit of knowing what happened
refers to American system of expressing perfect visual acuity

sighted

to be short-sighted
not to recognise the likely consequences

sights

to lower one's sights
to reduce one's ambition
military metaphor

to set one's sights on something
to aim to achieve something
military metaphor

sit

to sit on one's hands
deliberately to do nothing

to sit on someone
to repress a person

to sit on the fence
to refuse to choose between two alternatives

to sit on the sidelines
not to take part in the main action

to sit pretty
to be in an advantageous or comfortable position

to sit tight
to do nothing; to await developments
refers to poker

sitting

to be sitting on a volcano
to be safe for the time being but exposed to the risk of a sudden great disaster

skate

to skate around some subject
by diversionary tactics to avoid discussing some subject

to skate on thin ice
to act in disregard of obvious danger; to require tact in dealing with a sensitive subject in conversation
Ralph Waldo Emerson (1803–82), *Prudence*, 'In skating over thin ice, our safety is in our speed'

skates

to get one's skates on
to hurry up

skeleton

a skeleton in the closet/cupboard
an unpleasant truth the knowledge of which has been deliberately suppressed
William Makepeace Thackeray (1811–63), *The Newcomes* (1855), ' ... they have a skelton or two in their closets as well as their neighbours'

to flesh out the skeleton
to supply the missing pertinent details

skin

a cleanskin

a person without a criminal record or other blemish on that person's reputation

probably refers to an unblemished animal skin

to be no skin off someone's nose
not to matter to a person

to escape by the skin of one's teeth
to only just avoid some disaster

Job 19:20, 'I am escaped with the skin of my teeth'

to get under someone's skin
to cause intense annoyance to another person; OR to arouse interest in another person

may refer to the itching caused by certain parasitic creatures in or under the skin

to hang on by the skin of one's teeth
to be barely surviving

Job 19:20, 'I am escaped with the skin of my teeth'

to have a thick skin
to be impervious to criticism

to jump nearly out of one's skin
to receive a fright

to save one's skin
to get off safely

skip

something is but a hop, skip, and jump away
something is nearby

skull

to penetrate someone's thick skull
to make a person understand something difficult or acknowledge something unwelcome

sleep

not to get a wink of sleep
not to sleep at all

not to lose any sleep over something
not to worry about some matter

to go to sleep
to become inactive

to sleep on one's rights
to fail to exercise some entitlement within a reasonable period

sleeping

the choice is between eating well or sleeping well
one can invest for maximum yield or maximum security, but not both

sleepless

to spend a sleepless night
to worry about something

smell

to smell a rat
to become suspicious

to smell blood
to divine imminent victory

to smell out something
to discover something by careful investigation

to smell trouble
to perceive difficulties

smelling

to come up smelling like a rose
not to have a stain on one's character

smells

something smells
something is suspicious

smile

to wipe the smile off someone's face
to destroy a person's complacency

wipe that smile off your face!
treat this matter more seriously!

sneezed

that is not to be sneezed at
that is so significant that it should not be rejected

sore

eyesore
extremely ugly object

to be a sight for sore eyes
to be something welcome

to open up a festering sore
to upset a person by drawing attention to a long-standing grievance apparently forgotten

spine

to send a cold shiver down someone's spine
to horrify a person

spit

spit it out!
unburden yourself!

spleen

to vent one's spleen on someone

to demonstrate one's ill-temper to a person

refers to the belief that the spleen was the site of melancholy and moroseness

spot

to be a tender spot

to be a sensitive subject requiring tact

to have a blind spot about something

to have a lack of understanding and perception about something

refers to that part of the retina insensitive to light, at the point of entry of the optic nerve

to have a soft spot for someone

to be very fond of a person

spread

to spread oneself thin

to attempt to do more than is feasible in the available time

stand

not to have a leg to stand on

to have one's arguments completely demolished; OR to be without acceptable excuse or explanation

to be more than flesh can stand

to be more than a person reasonably can be expected to endure

to have to run fast just to stand still

competition is such that merely to maintain one's relative position one needs to make positive progress

to make someone's hair stand on end

to give a person shocking news

Job 4:15, 'Then a spirit passed before my face; the hair of my flesh stood up'; Shakespeare, *Hamlet* I:v, 'would harrow up thy soul ... and each particular hair to stand an end'

to stand in someone's way

to prevent a person achieving that person's goal

to stand on one's own two feet

not to require the help of others

to stand on someone's shoulders

to build up on another person's ideas

to stand one's ground

to maintain a stance in the face of opposition

refers to military battle

to stand out from the crowd

to be noticeably better than one's competitors

to stand over someone with a big stick

to intimidate a person in order to get that person to act in a particular way

to stand up and be counted

publicly to announce one's position on some issue

to stand up on one's hind legs

to assert one's authority

refers to animals adopting aggressive posture

step

a step in the right direction

the first in a series of measures designed to correct some problem

step by step

gradually

to get in step with someone

to do as another person does

refers to marching

to overstep the mark

to fail to observe the proprieties

refers to gaining an unfair advantage in a contest (originally the mark between two fighters)

to step down

to retire from some position

to step into the ring

to enter a competitive environment

refers to a boxing ring

to step on someone's corns/toes

to upset another person by interfering in that person's area of responsibility

to step out of line

to infringe accepted rules of behaviour

military metaphor

to take a giant step forward

to make a significant advance

Genesis 6:4, 'There were giants in the earth in those days'

to take a step backwards

to move further away from one's goal

to watch one's step

to be on the lookout for danger; OR to set out to improve one's behaviour

stepping

a stepping stone

a means to an end

steps

by small steps
gradually

to follow in someone's footsteps
to do as another person did

stick

to be better than a poke in the eye with a burnt stick
to be not particularly welcome, but better than other alternatives

to be unable to keep people away with a big stick
to be faced with a large crowd or much demand

to give someone a bit of stick
to criticise a person mildly

to hold the wrong end of the stick
to be completely mistaken about something

to stand over someone with a big stick
to intimidate a person in order to get that person to act in a particular way

to stick one's neck out
to have the courage of one's convictions or to take a calculated risk
refers to execution by decapitation

sticks

it sticks in my throat
I find it annoying and vexatious
Shakespeare, *Macbeth* II:ii, 'I had most need of blessing, and "Amen" / Stuck in my throat'

stitches

to have someone in stitches
greatly to amuse a person

stomach

someone's eyes are bigger than that person's stomach
a person is unrealistic in regard to that person's ability to cope with something

to have butterflies in one's stomach
a feeling of anxiety

to have no stomach for something
to have no liking, inclination, or fortitude for something

strangle

to strangle some discussion
to cut off some unfinished discussion

stranglehold

a stranglehold
exclusive and complete control
refers to wrestling or fighting

stride

to hit one's stride
to settle down to some task
refers to horses in harness

to take something in one's stride
to cope with something easily
refers to a horse jumping an obstacle

suck

suck it and see
discover experimentally how something works

to suck someone in
to embroil an innocent party in an unethical enterprise

to teach one's grandmother how to suck eggs
to try to tell a much more experienced person something very obvious to that person

swallow

to be a bitter pill to swallow
to be a great humiliation or disappointment that has to be endured

to be hard to swallow
not to be readily acceptable or believable
Matthew 23:23, ' … that strain at a gnat, and swallow a camel'

to swallow one's pride
to take action despite the humiliating nature of this course

to swallow the bait
to succumb to a temptation deliberately put in one's way
refers to angling

to swallow the line
to accept as truth the story being proffered
refers to angling

swallowed

someone has swallowed a dictionary
a person uses excessively long words

sweat

blood, sweat, and tears
hard work and much effort

Winston Churchill, House of Commons, 13 May 1940, 'I have nothing to offer but blood, toil, tears, and sweat'

no sweat
this presents no difficulty

to be in a cold sweat
to be afraid

to sweat it out
to await one's fate calmly

taste

to be left with a nasty taste in one's mouth
to be appalled or very disappointed at another person's unethical behaviour to one

to get a taste of one's own medicine
to suffer from an initiative intended to affect only other persons

tear

to shed a quiet tear for something
privately to lament the death or loss of something

to tear one's hair out
to be frustrated and extremely agitated
refers to ancient demonstration of grief and mourning

to tear oneself away
to leave despite a great desire to stay

to tear someone apart
ruthlessly to destroy another person's case

to tear something to ribbons
to damage something severely; to castigate severely

tears

blood, sweat, and tears
hard work and much effort
Winston Churchill, House of Commons, 13 May 1940, 'I have nothing to offer but blood, toil, tears, and sweat'

to bore someone to tears
to weary a person by dull and uninteresting conversation or by lack of action

to drive someone almost to tears
to act in such a way as to cause someone significant distress

to shed crocodile tears
hypocritically to show concern or sympathy for a person in distress
refers to the reflex lacrimation of a crocodile while eating

teeth

one would give one's eye teeth for something
a person would very much like to achieve some objective
refers to the (valued) canine teeth directly under the eye

to bare one's teeth
to imply threats
refers to savage animals

to be armed to the teeth
to carry many weapons
perhaps refers to carrying a knife in the teeth

to be fed up to the back teeth
to be disgusted after prolonged provocation

to cut one's teeth on something
to get one's first experience by doing something

to escape by the skin of one's teeth
to only just avoid some disaster
Job 19:20, 'I am escaped with the skin of my teeth'

to get one's teeth into something
to tackle a task with enthusiasm

to gnash one's teeth
to express frustration
Matthew 8:12, 'There shall be weeping and gnashing of teeth'

to grit one's teeth
to get ready to suffer pain

to hang on by the skin of one's teeth
to be barely surviving
Job 19:20, 'I am escaped with the skin of my teeth'

to have teeth
to be effective

to kick someone in the teeth
to inflict a grave or humiliating setback, criticism, or punishment upon a person

to lie through one's teeth
to tell blatant untruths

to set someone's teeth on edge
to cause a person intense irritation or discomfort
Ezekiel 18:2, 'The fathers have eaten sour grapes, and the children's teeth are set on edge'; Shakespeare, *Henry IV Pt*

1 III:i, 'And that would set my teeth nothing on edge, nothing so much as mincing poetry'

to take the bit between one's teeth
to face up to a problem
refers to riding or racing horses

teething

teething trouble
problems in the early stages of a project
refers to a small child's discomfort when developing teeth

think

one shudders to think what the outcome might be
there is great concern as to the outcome

to think twice before doing something
to consider with particular care

thinking

to put one's thinking cap on
to concentrate on finding a solution to a difficult problem

throat

cut-throat
highly competitive

it sticks in my throat
I find it annoying and vexatious
Shakespeare, *Macbeth* II:ii, 'I had most need of blessing, and "Amen" / Stuck in my throat'

the words stuck in my throat
I just could not get myself to say the intended words
Shakespeare, *Macbeth* II:ii, 'I had most need of blessing, and "Amen" / Stuck in my throat'

to cut one's own throat
to act in a way that damages one's own interests

to have a frog in one's throat
to have a transient hoarseness, or a trivial throat obstruction

to have a lump in one's throat
to feel emotional

to have someone by the throat
to have a decisive advantage such that victory is assured

to hold a knife/sword at someone's throat
to exert undue pressure on another person in an endeavour to achieve a result that would otherwise not be forthcoming

to jump down someone's throat
to react angrily to the remarks of the other party to a conversation

to ram something down someone's throat
to pressure another person into accepting an idea with which that person does not agree

throats

to be at each other's throats
to be always fighting

thumb

a rule of thumb
a simple yet useful approximation
refers to the use of the thumb for making rough measurements

a thumbnail sketch
brief but pertinent details
refers to an artist assessing perspective by judging the object to be painted against a thumbnail held close to the eye

to be under someone's thumb
to be dominated by a person

to thumb one's nose at someone
to show one's contempt for someone in authority and ostentatiously to disregard that person's orders

thumbs

someone's fingers are all thumbs
a person is clumsy with his or her hands

to give a thumbs up
to approve or grant permission
refers to sign given by Roman emperor sparing a life

to twiddle one's thumbs
not to be involved in any worthwhile activity

tickle

to tickle the peter
to rob one's employer
refers to slang term for cash box

tickled

to be tickled pink
to be very pleased
Oliver Goldsmith (1730–74), *She Stoops to Conquer*, 'the very pink of perfection'

ticklish

ticklish
awkward; requiring delicate handling

toe

a toehold
an opportunity small in itself but with the potential to lead to bigger things
refers to climbing trees, rockfaces, etc.

to dip one's toe in the water
gently to explore an opportunity

to tip-toe around the difficulties
to act with discretion and care to conceal difficulties, or to prevent problems occurring

to toe the line
to conform
refers to the starting line of a footrace

toes

to dig one's toes in
to become even more stubborn than at first

to keep someone on that person's toes
to induce a person to be eager and alert

to step/tread on someone's toes
to upset another person by interfering in that person's area of responsibility

tongue

a slip of the tongue
incorrect words uttered accidentally

I could have bitten my tongue off
I wish that I had not made such an inappropriate remark

it is on the tip of my tongue
the right word has momentarily escaped me

to bite one's tongue
to resist from criticising

to feel the rough side of someone's tongue
to be verbally abused by a person

to find one's tongue
to overcome one's shyness and speak

to have a loose tongue
to speak foolishly or indiscreetly

to have a sharp tongue
to speak in a cutting and abrasive fashion

to have a silver tongue
to be eloquent
Proverbs 10:20, 'The tongue of the just is as choice silver: the heart of the wicked is little worth'

to hold one's tongue
to keep quiet
John Donne (1571–1631), *The Canonization*, 'For God's sake hold your tongue, and let me love'

to keep a civil tongue in one's head
to be polite, especially under provocation

to roll off the tongue
to be said very easily

to speak with a forked tongue
to utter halftruths with the intention of misleading the listener

tongue in cheek
full of irony

tongues

to set tongues wagging
to behave in a way that encourages scandal mongers

tooth

a tooth for a tooth
retaliation of equal magnitude to the original offence
Exodus 21:24, 'Eye for eye, tooth for tooth, hand for hand, foot for foot'; see also 'to turn the other cheek'

to be long in the tooth
to be old

to believe in the tooth fairy
to be particularly gullible
refers to the mythical figure who exchanges children's milk teeth for a small sum of money

to fight tooth and nail
to strive very hard to win

to go through something with a fine-tooth comb
to conduct an extremely thorough investigation

to have a sweet tooth
to be particularly fond of cakes and confectionery

toothless

a toothless tiger
an authority that has been given powers totally inadequate for its task

touch

it was touch and go

there were considerable risks — - the objective was achieved, but only just
perhaps refers to the touching of the wheels of two moving vehicles

not to touch a hair on someone's head
not to harm a person
Matthew 10:30, 'the very hairs of your head are all numbered'

not to touch something with a forty-foot barge pole
to go out of one's way to avoid something

the Midas touch
attributes that cause a person's ventures to be extremely profitable
refers to King Midas of Phrygia who, in Greek mythology, had the power to turn everything he touched into gold

the touchstone
the standard
refers to a dark flinty stone used to assess samples of gold by comparing streaks left on it with those streaks left by known gold-containing standards

to lose one's touch
to cease to be familiar with, or adept at, something

to touch a nerve
to mention a sensitive subject

to touch base with someone
to make an initial contact
refers to baseball

to touch wood
to hope that our good luck will not go away
refers to ancient belief in sacred power of certain trees, especially oak, ash, hazel, hawthorn and willow

touché

touché
well said
French, 'touched'

tread

fools rush in where angels fear to tread
unsophisticated persons take unwise risks in circumstances where more knowledgeable persons would exercise caution
Alexander Pope (1688–1744), *An Essay on Criticism* 1:625, 'For fools rush in where angels fear to tread'

to tread a fine/thin line
cautiously to take action in circumstances where either too much or too little will cause difficulties

to tread a particular path
to follow a certain (perhaps new or lonely) course of action

to tread lightly
to be careful

to tread on someone's corns/toes
to upset another person by interfering in that person's area of responsibility

to tread someone under foot
to oppress a person

turn

someone would turn in his or her grave
someone would have been very surprised or displeased if he or she had known while still alive

not to turn a hair
to remain composed

to do a U-turn
to reverse one's thinking

to know which way to turn
to know which strategy to adopt or where to seek assistance

to turn a blind eye to something
to pretend that something obvious does not exist
refers to action by Horatio, Lord Nelson (1758–1805), when disregarding Admiralty signals: 'I have only one eye — I have a right to be blind sometimes — I really do not see the signal!' (at the Battle of Copenhagen, reported in Southey, *Life of Nelson*, ch. 7)

to turn a complete somersault
to reverse one's established policy

to turn around 180 degrees
completely to reverse a stance

to turn green
to become very envious
Shakespeare, *Othello* III:iii, 'O! beware, my Lord, of jealousy;/it is the green-ey'd monster ... '

to turn handstands
to express great joy

to turn one's back on someone
to decline to assist or deal with a person

to turn one's hand to something

to tackle some project (especially an unfamiliar project)

to turn round
to reverse one's policy

to turn someone's head
to cause a person to get an exaggerated idea of that person's abilities or status

to turn something inside out
to examine something thoroughly

to turn something on its ear/head
to reverse something

to turn something upside down
to revolutionise something

to turn tail
to run away; OR to reverse oneself

to turn the other cheek
to refuse, on moral grounds, to retaliate to provocation in like manner

Matthew 5:38, 39, 'Ye have heard that it hath been said an eye for an eye and a tooth for a tooth: but I say unto you ... whosoever shall smite thee on the right cheek, turn to him the other also'

to turn up one's nose at something
to express one's disdain

to turn white
to express shock at unexpected news

umbilical

to cut the umbilical cord
to free a person from the excessive influence of another; OR to separate a person from an essential source of supplies

unwashed

the great unwashed
the general public

in another vein
as an alternative way of looking at things

vision

tunnel vision
an extremely narrow and inflexible way of considering issues

voice

to be a lone voice crying out in the wilderness
to be the only person stating unpopular views

John 1:23, 'I am the voice of one crying in the wilderness'

to raise one's voice for some cause
publicly to advocate some cause

wake

to make noise enough to wake the dead
to be excessively noisy

to wake up to something
to realise a fact or its significance

walk

one needs to crawl before one can walk
skills are best developed in logical stages

take a long walk on a short pier
go away, I want no dealings with you

to be able to chew gum and walk at the same time
to be able to do two relatively simple things simultaneously

used ironically to disparage a person of limited capacities

to walk a tightrope
to do something very dangerous in which one cannot afford to deviate from the required course of action

to walk all over someone
to act in a way that completely disregards another person's sensibility

to walk away from something
to abrogate one's responsibilities in regard to some matter

to walk away with a profit
to achieve a profit on concluding a project

to walk in off the street
to come without prior arrangement or notification

to walk into a trap
to be tricked into doing something

to walk on air
to be joyful

to walk the plank
to face certain doom

refers to execution of persons at sea

walkover

a walkover
an easy victory

refers to the winner walking over the finishing line for an unchallenged victory

warts

warts and all
with the unfavourable features as well as the favourable ones
Oliver Cromwell's reported direction to the artist, Sir Peter Lely, painting his portrait

wean

to wean someone off something
to induce a person to abandon some entrenched practice

weight

a heavyweight
a person of importance or influence
refers originally to boxing

lightweight
uninfluential
refers to boxing

that has taken a weight off my mind
I am relieved

to be worth one's weight in gold
to be very valuable or useful

to carry weight
to be influential

to lend weight to something
to use one's influence in support of some cause

to pull one's weight
to do one's proper share of the work requiring to be done
refers to rowing

to take a weight off someone's shoulder
to assist a person by relieving that person of some responsibility

to throw one's weight around
to assert one's real or assumed authority excessively

wink

a nod and a wink
a sign that understanding has been reached in a matter that, in the interests of discretion, has not been discussed aloud
Captain Marryat (1792–1848), *Peter Simple*, 'But you're a dutiful son, so I'll say no more about it — a nod's as good as a wink to a blind horse'

a nod is the same as a wink to a blind horse
fine distinctions are not appropriate here
Captain Marryat (1792–1848), *Peter Simple*, 'But you're a dutiful son, so I'll say no more about it — a nod's as good as a wink to a blind horse'

not to get a wink of sleep
not to sleep at all

wound

to open up an old wound
to take action which revives a long-standing grievance

to rub salt into someone's wound
deliberately to make damage even worse

wounded

to charge like a wounded bull
to impose excessive prices
a play on words; not a simile

wounds

to heal wounds
to effect a reconciliation
Shakespeare, *Two Gentlemen of Verona*, I:ii, 'Poor wounded name! my bosom, as a bed, shall lodge thee till thy wound be thoroughly healed'

to lick one's wounds
to adjust oneself to defeat
refers to a dog cleaning its own wounds

to nurse one's wounds
to adjust oneself to defeat

wrist

a slap on the wrist
a mild rebuke

young

a trap for young players
a significant likelihood of the inexperienced or naVve making mistakes

an old head on young shoulders
experience, knowledge, and maturity in a young person

it is on for young and old
the excitement has started (esp. referring to fighting)

Law

act

to read the riot act

to reprimand persons who are excessively noisy or otherwise misbehaving

refers to the police reading out to a rowdy crowd extracts from a law requiring the crowd's dispersement

bail

to bail someone out

to render assistance to someone unable to help himself or herself

bailiwick

to be in someone's bailiwick

to be some other person's responsibility

refers to a region under the jurisdiction of a particular bailiff

to defend one's bailiwick

to protect one's power, influence, or authority in regard to a particular activity

refers to a region under the jurisdiction of a particular bailiff

to make a federal case out of something

to attach far too much significance to a trivial issue

compound

to compound the felony

having already acted improperly to make matters worse

court

to laugh something out of court

to ridicule a proposition as having no basis whatsoever

refers to courts of law

to put oneself out of court

to disqualify oneself from being considered for something

refers to royal courtiers

dock

to be in the dock

to need to defend one's stance

refers to a courtroom

draconian

draconian

excessively severe

refers to an especially harsh code of laws drawn up by the Athenian legislator, Drako (620 BC)

fingerprints

someone's fingerprints are all over this

it is obvious that a particular person was solely responsible for this

hang

to give someone enough rope to hang himself or herself

to give a person the opportunity to do something that is likely to get that person into severe trouble

hanging

not to be a hanging matter

to be only a minor mistake

hanged

one might as well be hanged for a sheep as for a lamb

further action will not increase the adverse consequences already in train

refers to the stealing of either sheep or lambs being capital crimes under old English law

jury

the jury is still out

no decision has yet been made; OR there has not yet been an indication as to how the matter is viewed in the community

justice

the wheels of justice grind slowly

it takes a long time to get a decision from the courts of law

Friedrich von Logau (1604–55), *Sinngedichte* (translated by H. W. Longfellow), 'Though the mills of God grind slowly, yet they grind exceeding small; though with patience he stands waiting, with exactness grinds he all'

kosher

to be kosher

to fulfil all requirements

refers to food complying with all aspects of Jewish religious law; Hebrew *kaser* ('fit, proper')

law

Murphy's law

the principle that everything that can go wrong will go wrong

Parkinson's law

the principle that work expands to match the work capacity available title of a book (1957) by Prof. C. Northcote Parkinson

the law of the jungle
the principle that those having power will use it at the expense of all others
Rudyard Kipling (1865–1936), *The Law of the Jungle*, 'Now this is the law of the jungle — as old and as true as the sky; and the wolf that shall keep it may prosper, but the wolf that shall break it must die'

to lay down the law
to be officious

lawyer

a bush lawyer
a person without legal qualifications who has a reasonable, although not perfect, knowledge of the law, and who likes to make technical points in arguments

leading

a leading question
a question phrased in such a way as to suggest the answer
a legal term, often misused by lay speakers who really mean merely 'a very pertinent question'

mortgage

to have a mortgage on something
to have a moral claim in regard to a matter
refers to a charge over property recognised by the law

to mortgage the future
to get benefits now but at a cost in due course
refers to a charge over property recognised by the law

scot

to get off scot-free
to go unpunished refers to an exemption from tax; scot (from old norse *skot*) means tax

sentenced

to be sentenced to some fate
to be condemned by circumstances to endure some fate

thumb

a rule of thumb
a simple yet useful approximation
refers to the use of the thumb for making rough measurements

Manufacture

balance

to tip the balance
to be further information or argument that results in an issue, that could have been decided either way, being determined in a particular way

boiler

not to bust one's boiler
not to exert oneself unduly
refers to a steam boiler

bronze

to be cast in bronze
to be virtually unalterable

button

to hit the panic button
to act hastily and irrationally

to press a button
to make something happen

can

the empty can makes the most noise
the least worthy arguments often attract the most publicity

chain

the weakest link in the chain
the least efficient component in a project the overall efficiency of which is governed by the efficiency of the least efficient component

to drag the chain
to perform unduly slowly
refers to a horse or bullock that is not pulling its weight, thus causing its chains to drag on the ground

cobbler

a cobbler should stick to his last
a person should confine himself or herself to activities for which that person has been trained

cog

to be a small cog in a large wheel
to be a relatively unimportant person in a large organisation

comb

to go through something with a fine-tooth comb

to conduct an extremely thorough investigation

cut

to be cut and dried

to be well settled or long established

refers to timber cut and dried, and ready for use

to cut one's coat according to the cloth

to accommodate oneself to limitations beyond one's control and to do the best in the circumstances

cutting

to be at the cutting edge of something

to be in a position where important decisions are made

fuel

to add fuel to the fire

to make a bad situation worse

goods

to deliver the goods

to achieve the objective; to supply what is required

grindstone

to keep one's nose to the grindstone

to work with particular diligence

refers to having one's head down low while working on a grindstone sharpening tools

hallmark

a hallmark

a standard

refers to the official assay mark on gold and silver, originally put on at the Goldsmiths' Hall, London

hammer

to go hammer and tongs

to do something with great energy

refers to energetic work of a blacksmith

iron

ironclad

firm or rigorous

refers to armour-plated naval vessels

to give a cast-iron guarantee

to give a very secure undertaking to do something

to have a cast-iron case

to be assured absolutely of victory in a dispute, an argument, or in legal proceedings

to strike while the iron is hot

to take advantage of a situation that cannot last

refers to the work of blacksmiths and farriers; John Dryden (1631–1700), *Aenis*, 'We must beat the iron while it is hot, but we may polish it at leisure'

irons

to have other irons in the fire

to have the opportunity to do something else as an alternative

Francis Beaumont (1584–1616) & John Fletcher (1579–1625), *The Faithful Friends* I:ii, 'It is always good when a man has two irons in the fire'

linchpin

linchpin

an essential person or feature central to a project

refers to a pin passed through an axle-end to keep a wheel in position

logjam

a logjam

a stoppage of activity caused by input in greater volume than allowed for

refers to a crowded mass of cut logs in a river

machine

a sausage machine

the turning out of large volumes without particular thought

to be a well-oiled piece of machinery

to be functioning very satisfactorily

made

ready-made

easily fabricated or available without difficulty

mould

to be cast in someone's mould

to take after another person

p

to watch one's P's and Q's

to be very careful

perhaps refers to pints and quarts of beer on a hotel slate, or perhaps to easily confused printer's type

pipeline

a pipeline to someone
an intermediary used as a means of communicating ideas to a person

in the pipeline
being dealt with

pot

a melting pot
a country where people with different ethnic backgrounds merge, over time, into one nation
refers to a vessel for melting and mixing metals

to go back into the melting pot
to be up for reconsideration from the beginning
refers to a vessel for melting and mixing metals

press

to be hot off the press
to be the latest news
refers to old-style hot presses used in printing newspapers

to press a button
to make something happen

pressure

to apply pressure on someone
to induce a person to do something that that person would otherwise not do by implying adverse consequences if the person does not cooperate

print

a licence to print money
a lucrative government-conferred monopoly or privilege
Lord Thomson of Fleet (1894–1977), 'It's just like having a licence to print your own money' (after the opening of Scottish commercial television, as recorded in Braddon, *Roy Thomson of Fleet Street*)

to fill in the fine print
to provide the precise details in respect of something presently existing in broad outline only

Rolls-Royce

a Rolls-Royce solution
a high quality but excessively expensive way of doing something

rope

to be money for old rope
to be an easily made profit

sack

to get the sack
to be dismissed
refers to the bag of tradesmen's tools

safety

safety margin
allowance for miscalculations

to act as a safety valve
to be a procedure that allows persons with grievances to ventilate them in an orderly fashion

seal

a seal of approval
confirmation that something is satisfactory

sift

to sift
to examine closely and assess the components appropriately

sparks

to make sparks fly
to inflame or cause friction in a situation
Job 5:7, 'Man is born unto trouble, as the sparks fly upward'

spin

to spin a yarn
to tell an amusing or unlikely story
a play on words referring to spinning yarn for cloth

to spin something out
to prolong some matter

spinner

to be a money spinner
to produce large profits easily and quickly

steel

to be a man of steel
to be a person with moral courage

to have nerves of steel
not to be easily frightened

to steel one's heart against something
to determine that, notwithstanding one's natural compassion, something shall not happen

stereotype

a stereotype

(of a group) a general impression of the characteristics that is assumed to apply to all members of that group
refers to the plates formerly used in printing

streamline
to streamline
to organise better by simplification

systems
to be all systems 'go'
to be ready to proceed as fast as possible

tailor
to tailor something
to do something in a way that has regard to the specific needs or preferences of a particular person

tenterhooks
to be on tenterhooks
anxiously to await some result
refers to cloth being stretched or 'tentered'; Latin: *tentus* ('stretched')

thread
the thread
the connecting link of a set of arguments

tinker
not worth a tinker's curse
worthless
from a tinker's custom of blocking up a hole with a pellet of bread before soldering, the pellet of bread being discarded as worthless after the soldering was completed
to tinker at the edges
to make minor or cosmetic changes without affecting the substance
refers to the common assumption that a tinker was an unreliable tradesman

tune
to fine-tune something
to adjust something in order to bring it to perfection or to make it fit the circumstances in a much more appropriate fashion

valve
to act as a safety valve
to be a procedure that allows persons with grievances to ventilate them in an orderly fashion

wheel
a big wheel
an important person
the squeaky wheel gets the oil
those complaining the most loudly will get their problems sorted out first
the wheel has turned
circumstances have changed and another party is now enjoying good fortune
the wheel has turned the complete/full circle
things are now back to where they were before
to be a fifth wheel
to be superfluous
to be a small cog in a large wheel
to be a relatively unimportant person in a large organisation
to put a spoke in someone's wheel
to interfere with another person's activity, so preventing its continuance
to put one's shoulder to the wheel
to make a strong effort
to reinvent the wheel
to waste resources doing something already accomplished

wheels
the wheels fell off
the plan failed
the wheels have been turning
work has been going steadily on (contrast 'the wheel has turned')
the wheels of justice grind slowly
it takes a long time to get a decision from the courts of law
Friedrich von Logau (1604–55), *Sinngedichte* (translated by H. W. Longfellow), 'Though the mills of God grind slowly, yet they grind exceeding small; though with patience he stands waiting, with exactness grinds he all'
to make the wheels go round
to cause something to happen
to oil the wheels
to make things go smoothly
to set the wheels in motion
to institute appropriate action
wheels within wheels
secret machinations

wire
to be a live wire

to be an enthusiast
refers to electrical wires

to go haywire
to function in a disordered and strange fashion
refers to difficulty in handling coils of hay-binding wire

wool

dyed in the wool
very loyal and partisan
refers to a garment in which the wool itself (from which the garment is woven) is dyed, rather than the completed garment being dyed as a piece (and thus less thoroughly)

works

to be in the works
to be being dealt with

to get the works
to get the full treatment

to gum up the works
to cause an activity to cease by preventing normal functioning of the necessary processes

to throw a spanner into the works
to cause an unexpected complication

yarn

to spin a yarn
to tell an amusing or unlikely story
a play on words referring to spinning yarn for cloth

Meteorology

air

a feeling in the air
a premonition held by many people

to be a breath of fresh air
to be a pleasant change from the past

to clear the air
to remove any possible misunderstandings

to pluck figures out of the air
to make figures up arbitrarily

to produce something out of thin air
to get hold of something in circumstances where this seemed impossible
Shakespeare, *The Tempest* IV:i, ' ... are melted into air, into thin air'

to vanish into thin air
unexpectedly to disappear
Shakespeare, *The Tempest* IV:i, ' ... are melted into air, into thin air'

atmosphere

atmosphere
psychological environment

in a rarefied atmosphere
in ignorance of the real world

one could have cut the atmosphere with a knife
those present were very tense

blue

to be a bolt from the blue
to be a totally unexpected event

breeze

it's a breeze
it is easy

climate

climate
commercial, political, or other environment

cloud

every cloud has a silver lining
there are consolations and potential benefits even in seemingly adverse situations

to be in cloud-cuckoo land
to be mad or to have unrealistic expectations
'cloud-cuckoo land' was an imaginary city built in the air by the birds (according to the *Nephelococcygia* of *The Birds* by Aristophanes) — hence any utopian fantastic scheme

to be on cloud nine
to be very happy

to be under a cloud
to be under suspicion or to be out of favour

to cast a cloud over something
to spoil the pleasure of an occasion

to cloud one's mind
to allow irrelevant or extraneous factors to affect one's impartiality or judgment

to have a cloud hanging over one's head
there is doubt as to one's future
refers to the pillar of cloud (God) passing judgment on the Hebrews; the pillar of cloud is described in *Exodus* 13:21 *et seq*.

clouds

there are black/storm clouds on the horizon
bad news is expected

to have one's head in the clouds
to be unrealistic

cold

in the cold light of day
in an unemotional atmosphere at a later stage

on a cold day in hell
never

the cold wind of change
the unpleasant realities of new circumstances

to blow hot and cold
to vacillate
Revelations 3:15, 'I know thy works, that thou art neither cold nor hot'

to come in out of the cold
to be welcomed into a group

to leave someone out in the cold
to be excluded, ignored or neglected

dark

to be in the dark
to be uninformed

to whistle in the dark
to feign greater confidence than one really has
John Dryden (1631–1700), *Amphitryon* II:i, 'Whistling to keep myself from being afraid'

dawn

a false dawn
an incident giving rise to unjustified hope
refers to a transient light that precedes the true dawn by about an hour

the crack of dawn
at the exact moment of sunrise

to be the dawn of a new day
to be the start of a different regime

dawns

light dawns
the point is understood

day

at the end of the day
in due course, or at the conclusion of a project

in the cold light of day
in an unemotional atmosphere at a later stage

late in the day
when a project is well advanced

on a cold day in hell
never

to be the dawn of a new day
to be the start of a different regime

to call it a day
to cease involvement with some activity

to keep something for a rainy day
to keep something in reserve for bad times

to see the light of day
to be made public

daylight

daylight robbery
the charging of grossly excessive prices

to see daylight
to discern the way ahead towards the right answer

draught

to feel the draught
to experience unfavourable conditions

drought

to break a drought
to resume supplies after an interval

eve

to be on the eve of something
to occur just before some event
refers to the evening of the day before

flash

in a flash
in an instant

floodgates

to open the floodgates
to take action that will have massive consequences
Shakespeare, *Othello* I:iii, 'My particular grief is of so flood-gate and o'erbearing nature that it engluts and swallows other sorrows'

fog

to be in a fog
to be in a state of confusion

foggiest

not to have the foggiest notion

to know nothing at all about the subject

ice

the ice is melting
friendly relations are being restored

to break the ice
to take the initiative in starting discussions

Francis Bacon (1561–1626), *Of Cunning*, 'In things that are tender and unpleasing, it is good to break the ice by some whose words are of less weight ...'

to cut no ice with someone
to have little effect on a person

perhaps refers to ice-skating

to skate on thin ice
to act in disregard of obvious danger; to require tact in dealing with a sensitive subject in conversation

Ralph Waldo Emerson (1803–82), *Prudence*, 'In skating over thin ice, our safety is in our speed'

iceberg

to be the tip of the iceberg
to be only a very small portion of a much larger but less obvious whole

lightning

a lightning rod
a person or thing used to attract trouble in order to divert that trouble away safely

refers to a metallic rod or wire fixed to the top of a building to divert lightning

moon

once in a blue moon
very rarely

refers to the volcanic eruption at Krakatoa in 1883 when volcanic dust caused the moon to appear blue

to be over the moon
to be very excited

moonlight

a moonlight flit
an escape from creditors

moonshine

moonshine
unrealistic ideas

rain

to rain cats and dogs
to rain heavily

derived from ancient northern mythology in which cats and dogs were symbolically linked to weather: the cat can be taken as a symbol of falling rain and the dog as a symbol of wind gusts

rainbow

to seek the pot of gold at the end of the rainbow
to have naVve expectations

refers to the proverbial belief in the existence of a pot of gold at the end of a rainbow

rainbows

to chase rainbows
to be quite unrealistic

rains

it never rains but it pours
crises often occur together

rainy

to keep something for a rainy day
to keep something in reserve for bad times

season

the silly season
the holiday period, when hard news is scarce and journalistic standards are lowered

shower

to have come down in the last shower
to be naVve

refers to someone having just arrived with the last shower of rain

sky

a light in the sky
a sign of great hope

blue sky
unrealistic optimism

pie in the sky
a hoped for result unlikely to be achieved

the sky fell in
a very serious problem arose

Matthew 24:29, 'Immediately after the distress of those days the sun will be darkened, and the moon will not give its light; the stars will fall from the sky, and the heavenly bodies will be shaken'

the sky is the limit
there is no restriction upon what can be done

to take up the slack

to take advantage of surplus capacity
refers to working with ropes

snow

to snow someone under
to overload a person with work

snowflake

to have a snowflake's chance in hell
to have no hope or possibility at all

star

rising star
person making good progress in that person's career

storm

a storm in a teacup
a controversy about a minor matter but one that looms large in the minds of the parties

any port in a storm
anything that helps to avoid difficulties is welcome

the calm before the storm
the quiet period before an expected or inevitable crisis

there are storm clouds on the horizon
bad news is expected

to barnstorm
to travel around and actively promote one's cause or performance
refers to itinerant actors who performed in barns

to be in the eye of the storm
to be at the centre of a controversy

to create a storm
to cause a fuss

to ride out the storm
to come safely through some dangerous situation
nautical metaphor

to take by storm
to captivate an audience

to weather the storm
to come safely through a crisis
nautical metaphor

stormy

to be a stormy petrel
a person who disturbs a pleasant state of affairs by agitating for change
refers to the bird (petrel) that flies low over water during a storm and appears to be alternately touching one foot and then the other to the surface of the water as though walking upon it; the bird is sometimes thought to be the harbinger of a storm, and is named after St Peter who walked upon the stormy waters of Lake Gennesareth

summer

one swallow does not make a summer
much further evidence is desirable before any action taken
refers to an old English proverb, probably ultimately derived from the Greek proverb: 'One swallow does not make a spring' (recorded in Aristotle's *Nicomachoean Ethics* I:vii:16)

sun

a place in the sun
a favourable situation

everything under the sun
absolutely everything

the sun has set on something
something has concluded

to make hay while the sun shines
to utilise an opportunity before it disappears
John Betjeman (1906–84), *The Last Laugh*, 'I made hay while the sun shone'

thunder

to be thunder struck
to be amazed

to steal someone's thunder
to take credit for another person's good work
refers to a dispute over the copying of a machine invented by dramatist John Dennis (1657–1734) to reproduce the sound of thunder during a play

thunderbolt

a thunderbolt
a surprise
Shakespeare, *Julius Caesar* IV:iii, 'Be ready, gods, with all your thunderbolts; / dash him to pieces

torrent

a torrent of words
a rapid and uninterrupted outpouring of words
refers to a fast-flowing stream of water

weather

a fair-weather friend

a person purporting to be a friend who offers no support in difficult times

to be under the weather
to be drunk or (less often) sick

to keep a weather eye out for something
to look out with particular care
nautical metaphor; refers to the eye that is turned towards the wind

to make heavy weather of something
to struggle excessively with a relatively simple task
nautical metaphor

to run into heavy weather
to encounter difficulties
nautical metaphor

to weather the storm
to come safely through a crisis
nautical metaphor

whirlwind

to reap the whirlwind
to suffer the adverse consequences of a bad act
Hosea 8:7, 'They have sown the wind, and they shall reap the whirlwind'

to sow the wind and reap the whirlwind
to make bad mistakes and to suffer the even worse consequences
Hosea 8:7, 'They have sown the wind, and they shall reap the whirlwind'

wind

it is an ill wind that blows no good
even a seeming misfortune leads to some blessings

something is in the wind
something is going on secretly

straws in the wind
small but significant indicators of future events
John Seldon (1584–1654), 'Take a straw and throw it up into the air, you shall see by that which way the wind is'

the cold wind of change
the unpleasant realities of new circumstances

to get wind of something
to hear rumours giving advance information
refers to an animal sniffing the wind for the scent of another animal

to put the wind up someone
to alarm a person

to reap the whirlwind
to suffer the adverse consequences of a bad act
Hosea 8:7, 'They have sown the wind, and they shall reap the whirlwind'

to sail against the wind
to oppose the views currently being held by others

to sail close to the wind
to take a considered risk; to test the limits of what is possible or acceptable
refers to sailing in a manner such that sails remain filled while keeping the boat headed as near as possible into the wind

to see which way the wind is blowing
to establish the factors relevant to a situation
John Seldon (1584–1654), 'Take a straw and throw it up into the air, you shall see by that which way the wind is'

to sow the wind and reap the whirlwind
to make bad mistakes and to suffer the even worse consequences
Hosea 8:7, 'They have sown the wind, and they shall reap the whirlwind'

to take the wind out of someone's sails
to upset a person by anticipating that person's actions or by using arguments which that person was proposing to use
refers to a tactical manoeuvre in sailing whereby one boat blocks or 'takes' the wind advantage of another

winds

to cast prudence to the winds
to cease being careful or wise

to scatter something to the four winds
permanently to get rid of something
refers to the north, south, east, and west winds

windfall

windfall
unexpected good fortune
refers to fruit falling from a tree without having to be picked

windmills

to tilt at windmills

to attack an imagined but non-existent enemy
refers to Cervantes' *Don Quixote* Pt I Ch VIII, in which the hero assumes that windmills are giants and gives battle

Mining and Oil

claim

to stake a claim
to indicate one's desire to obtain something
refers to placing a series of stakes in the ground as a sign of claiming a place for gold mining

coal

to be at the coal face
to be in the place where the real work is done

coals

to carry coals to Newcastle
to do something ridiculously unnecessary
refers to the coal-mining district of Newcastle, UK

to haul someone over the coals
to reprimand a person
refers to church punishment of heretics

to rake over old coals
to seek to reopen a matter decided on long ago

diamond

to be a rough diamond
to have many attributes, but an uncultivated manner lacking social polish

dirt

to strike pay dirt
to become successful
refers to soil containing gold or other precious metal

dry

a dry hole
an exercise that, after much effort, proves fruitless
refers to drilling for oil

fuse

to have a short fuse
to lose one's temper very readily
refers to explosives

to light a fuse
to set in train processes that will cause a serious reaction
refers to explosives

gold

a pot of gold
wealth, especially a reward long wished-for

a rich vein of gold
much useful information; a good source of something desirable

all that glisters/glitters is not gold
things are not always what they seem
Shakespeare, *Merchant of Venice*, II:vii, 'All that glisters is not gold'

to be a river of gold
to be a source of ongoing great profitability

to be worth one's weight in gold
to be very valuable or useful

to have a heart of gold
to have a generous disposition
Hilaire Belloc (1870–1953), 'With hearts of gold and lungs of bronze'

to seek the pot of gold at the end of the rainbow
to have naVve expectations
refers to the proverbial belief in the existence of a pot of gold at the end of a rainbow

to strike gold
to have one's efforts suddenly rewarded by great success
refers to gold-mining

golden

golden handshake
a large payment in connection with, or as an inducement to, retirement

golden opportunity
an unparalleled chance or occasion

golden parachute
(in a remuneration package) generous provisions that come into play in certain circumstances

golden shackles
financial arrangements designed to discourage employees changing from one employer to another

to kill the goose that lays the golden eggs
through excessive greed, to sacrifice future gains for a short-term advantage

based on a Greek fable about a man who killed the goose that laid golden eggs; his aim was to collect the whole stock of eggs at once but, in doing so, he ended his future supply

goldmine

a goldmine

a source of much wealth or of many facts

iron

ironclad

firm or rigorous

refers to armour-plated naval vessels

the iron curtain

the border between the communist nations and the rest of the world

used famously by Winston Churchill in a speech in 1946, but also attributed before this to Ethel Snowden (1920), Goebbels (1945), and by Churchill himself in 1945 (before his famous 1946 speech)

to give a cast-iron guarantee

to give a very secure undertaking to do something

to have a cast-iron case

to be assured absolutely of victory in a dispute, an argument, or in legal proceedings

to have something in an iron grip

to hold something very securely

to rule with a rod of iron

to keep strict discipline

Psalms 2:9, 'Thou shalt break them with a rod of iron; thou shalt dash them in pieces like a potter's vessel'

to rule with an iron fist

to keep strict discipline

to rule with an iron hand

to keep strict discipline

to strike while the iron is hot

to take advantage of a situation that cannot last

refers to the work of blacksmiths and farriers; John Dryden (1631–1700), *Aenis*, 'We must beat the iron while it is hot, but we may polish it at leisure'

with an iron hand in a velvet glove

with a hard attitude made to seem soft

irons

to have other irons in the fire

to have the opportunity to do something else as an alternative

Francis Beaumont (1584–1616) & John Fletcher (1579–1625), *The Faithful Friends* I:ii, 'It is always good when a man has two irons in the fire'

jewel

a jewel

any highly valued person or thing

the jewel in someone's crown

the most significant component

mark

to be up to the mark

to be of the right standard

refers to the official assay mark on gold and silver, originally put on at the Goldsmiths' Hall, London

mullock

to poke mullock at someone

to ridicule a person, or to rubbish that person's arguments

refers to the heap of rubbish at the top of a mineshaft

oil

to get the good oil

to receive useful, reliable and timely information

pan

to pan out

to turn out, to happen

refers to a gold prospector's pan used to seek gold in gravel of streams

petrified

to be petrified

to be made immobile with fear

refers to Greek *petros* (Latin: *petra*) = 'stone'; *Matthew* 16:18, 'Thou art Peter, and upon this rock I will build my church'

rock

bedrock price

lowest possible price

rock bottom

very low

to be between a rock and a hard place

to be faced with two equally difficult and uncomfortable choices

rocks

to have rocks in the head

to be stupid or mentally unbalanced

silver

to be born with a silver spoon in one's mouth

to be brought up by wealthy parents
refers to the traditional gift of a silver spoon (an 'apostle spoon') to a child at baptism — the child born of wealthy parents is assured of riches from the moment of birth and thus does not have to await baptism to receive a valuable gift

to hand over something on a silver platter
to provide a valuable benefit for virtually nothing
refers to first-class service

to have a silver tongue
to be eloquent
Proverbs 10:20, 'The tongue of the just is as choice silver: the heart of the wicked is little worth'

to sell off the family silver
to sell off one's prized possessions

stone

the touchstone
the standard
refers to a dark flinty stone used to assess samples of gold by comparing streaks left on it with those streaks left by known gold-containing standards

to draw blood from a stone
to do the impossible

to have a heart of stone
to be unfeeling
Shakespeare, *Othello*, 'My heart is turned to stone'

to kill two birds with one stone
to achieve a second objective in the course of achieving the first objective

to leave no stone unturned
to be very thorough
refers to an instruction from the oracle of Delphi regarding a search for Persian treasure (477 BC)

within a stone's throw
very close

stonewalling

stonewalling
deliberate obstruction or delaying tactics

tin

a little tin god
a petty tyrant

touchstone

the touchstone
the standard
refers to a dark flinty stone used to assess samples of gold by comparing streaks left on it with those streaks left by known gold-containing standards

treasure

a treasure trove
a valuable discovery

undermine

to undermine someone's position
to injure another person's reputation and influence by unfair and secret tactics

to undermine something
to sabotage something

Music

band

a one-man band
a person performing many different roles singlehandedly

bandwagon

to hop onto the bandwagon
to subscribe to an emerging majority opinion

beat

not to miss a beat
to carry on without the slightest interruption

to beat a drum for someone
to propagate another person's cause

to beat a retreat
to abandon some project
military metaphor

to beat one's drum
to publicise immodestly one's own attributes

board

to act as a sounding board
to give, on request, constructive criticisms of ideas tentatively held
refers, originally, to a board placed behind a speaker (esp. a preacher) to reflect the speaker's voice forwards to the congregation or audience

chord

to strike a chord
to sound familiar or recall something to mind
refers to music

to strike a responsive chord
to get a favourable reaction to a proposal
refers to music
to strike the right chord
to appeal successfully to someone's emotions
refers to music

clarion
a clarion call
a strong signal that is an unmistakable invitation to do something

donna
a prima donna
a person with an exaggerated opinion of that person's own importance making relations with others needlessly difficult
Italian, 'first lady'

drum
to beat a drum for someone
to propagate another person's cause
to beat one's drum
to publicise immodestly one's own attributes
to drum someone out of some organisation
to terminate in ignominy a person's employment or membership
refers to the ceremonial cashiering in the army to the beating of parade drums
to drum-up support
actively to seek out support
to march to a different drum
to show an independent approach
military metaphor

fanfare
with much fanfare
with great enthusiasm and public acclaim

fiddle
to fiddle while Rome burns
to neglect important considerations while concentrating on trivial side-issues
refers to Nero's behaviour during the burning of Rome (AD 64) when he played a lyre and watched the spectacle from a height
to play second fiddle
to fulfil a subordinate role
refers to playing in an orchestra

flip
flip side
the arguments for the other point of view

gamut
the whole gamut
the whole range of some activity
refers to the whole range of notes in music

harmonise
to harmonise several things
to make several things function cooperatively and effectively together

harmony
to be in harmony with someone
to work cooperatively and effectively together

key
to strike the right key
to make comments that set the appropriate tone in a speech or conversation
refers to music

keynote
keynote address
opening address, designed to set the theme of a conference
refers to music

melody
the melody lingers on
the benefit of past actions remains

music
music to one's ears
comments that one is very pleased to hear
Shakespeare, *Romeo and Juliet* II:i, 'How silver-sweet sound lovers' tongues by night, / like softest music to attending ears!'
to face the music
to accept responsibility when confronted by one's critics
refers to the theatre
when the music stops
suddenly and soon
refers to an imminent crisis leading to some resolution of a matter, as in a game of musical chairs

musical
to play musical chairs

to be a part of a general reshuffling (of duties or functions) that is not necessarily to everyone's liking
refers to a parlour game culminating in a sudden scrambling for positions

note

to hit a sour note
to say or do something inappropriate to a situation
refers to music

to strike the right note
to say or do something appropriate to a situation
refers to music

opera

a soap opera
a low-quality radio or television serial
refers to the original sponsorship of such programs by soap companies

orchestrate

to orchestrate something
to arrange for something to happen

organ-grinder

to want the organ-grinder, not the monkey
to wish to deal with the person in authority rather than an underling
refers to a street musician using a barrel-organ, often accompanied by a pet monkey

overtones

overtones
subtle or implied themes

overtures

to make overtures to someone
to make suggestions to a person, inviting further negotiations

pedal

to soft pedal
to restrain oneself
refers to playing an organ or piano

pipe

to pipe someone on board
to welcome a person
nautical metaphor

piper

he who pays the piper calls the tune
a person contributing money or resources to a project is entitled to control it

pitch

to be up to concert pitch
to be ready

play

to play it by ear
to develop one's strategy to always fit in with circumstances as they change from time to time
refers to playing music without the benefit of a written score

to play musical chairs
to be a part of a general reshuffling (of duties or functions) that is not necessarily to everyone's liking
refers to a parlour game culminating in a sudden scrambling for positions

sing

to all sing from the same hymnal
to act consistently with each other
refers to a book of hymns

to sing a particular song
to state particular views

to sing for one's supper
to carry out a task in order to receive a favour in return

to sing someone's praises
to commend a person exuberantly

sings

it's not over until the fat lady sings
it is not finished yet
probably refers to operatic performances, but during a radio broadcast made by the present author, a listener suggested that the metaphor refers to Kate Smith singing the US national anthem

song

nothing to make a song or dance about
unexciting or unimportant

swan song
last appearance before retirement
refers to the ancient (but erroneous) belief that the swan sings beautifully before it dies; such a belief is referred to by Plato, Aristotle, Shakespeare, Spenser, and Coleridge (among others)

to buy something for a song
to buy something very cheaply

to make a song and dance about something
to create a fuss

to sing a particular song
to state particular views

stops

to pull out all stops
to make maximum effort
refers to organ playing at maximum volume

tango

it takes two to tango
some activities cannot be carried out single-handedly
refers to a dance

theme

variations on a theme
alternative approaches of a similar nature
refers to artistic themes

time

to mark time
to do nothing while awaiting developments
refers to marching

trumpet

to blow one's own trumpet
immodestly to publicise one's own attributes
refers to the trumpet as an instrument of triumph; *Joshua* 6:20, 'When the priests blew with the trumpets ... the wall fell down flat'

trumpets

with a flourish of trumpets
triumphantly
refers to the trumpet as an instrument of triumph; *Joshua* 6:20, 'When the priests blew with the trumpets ... the wall fell down flat'

tune

he who pays the piper calls the tune
a person contributing money or resources to a project is entitled to control it

to be in tune with someone
to think in a similar way to someone else

to change one's tune
to alter one's publicly expressed views

to fine-tune something
to adjust something in order to bring it to perfection or to make it fit the circumstances in a much more appropriate fashion

whistle

you can whistle for it
you wish in vain
refers to the superstition among sailors on a becalmed ship that a wind could be summoned up by whistling

Mythology

Achilles

to be someone's Achilles' heel
to represent a weakness in an otherwise strong position
refers to Achilles, Greek warrior and hero of Homer's *Iliad*, who was invulnerable except for his heel

Aladdin

an Aladdin's cave
a place full of unexpected treasure
refers to a character and events in *Arabian Nights' Entertainments*

albatross

to be an albatross around someone's neck
to be a great burden
refers to a mythical mariner who suffered terrible ordeals as a result of killing an albatross; Samuel Taylor Coleridge (1772–1834), *The Ancient Mariner*, 1798, 'Why look'st thou so? — with my cross-bow, I shot the albatross'

carry

to carry the world on one's shoulders
to perform a huge task alone
refers to Atlas, who was condemned to bear the heavens on his shoulders for leading the Titans against the gods

crystal

a crystal ball
accurate knowledge of the future
refers to ancient means of divining the future

Damocles

to have a sword of Damocles hanging over one
to be in imminent danger despite normal activity going on all around one
refers to Damocles who had the sword of Dionysius hanging, by a slender thread, over his head — as a symbol of perpetual risk in life; the story is told in Cicero, *Tusculanae Disputationes*

days

in halcyon days
in past happier times
Shakespeare, *Henry V, Part 1*, I:ii, 'Expect St Martin's summer, halcyon days'
refers to the fourteen days about the winter solstice when winds were calm, and to the mythical bird said to breed in a floating nest at that time

Delphic

Delphic
deliberately obscure
refers to the Oracle at Delphi

fairy

a fairy godmother
a person who provides for one's needs
based on the mythical magical figure

to believe in the tooth fairy
to be particularly gullible
refers to the mythical figure who exchanges children's milk teeth for a small sum of money

genie

to let the genie out of the bottle
to cause something irreversible to take place
'genie' was adopted (to refer to a spirit released from a bottle) by the French translators of *Arabian Nights' Entertainments*

to put the genie back in the bottle
to undo something that cannot be undone
'genie' was adopted (to refer to a spirit released from a bottle) by the French translators of *Arabian Nights' Entertainments*

ghost

not the ghost of a chance
no hope at all
Katherine Mansfield (1888–1923), 'he hadn't a ghost of a chance, he hadn't an earthly'

to give up the ghost
to die
Mark 15:39, 'He so cried out and gave up the ghost' (refers to the use of 'ghost' to indicate one's spirit)

gifts

I fear the Greeks even when they bear gifts
I am suspicious of generous behaviour from traditional opponents
Virgil (70–19 BC), *Aeneid* II:49, *Timeo Danaos et dona ferentis* ('I fear the Greeks even when they bring gifts'), in reference to the Trojan horse

gods

to be in the lap of the gods
to be a matter of apparent chance beyond human control
refers to wax tablets inscribed with requests and placed on the knees of statues of Greek gods

Gordian

to cut the Gordian knot
to solve, especially by force, a virtually insoluble problem
refers to a complicated knot tied by Gordius and eventually cut by Alexander the Great

hang

to hang by a slender thread
to be in a precarious situation
refers to Damocles who had the sword of Dionysius hanging, by a slender thread, over his head — as a symbol of perpetual risk in life; the story is told in Cicero, *Tusculanae Disputationes*

hanging

there is a big question mark hanging over someone's head
there are considerable doubts about a person's competence, integrity, or suitability
refers to Damocles who had the sword of Dionysius hanging, by a slender thread, over his head — as a symbol of perpetual risk in life; the story is told in Cicero, *Tusculanae Disputationes*

to have a threat hanging over one's head
to fear some intimated unpleasant action

refers to Damocles who had the sword of Dionysius hanging, by a slender thread, over his head — as a symbol of perpetual risk in life; the story is told in Cicero, *Tusculanae Disputationes*

Herculean

a Herculean cleaning of the stables

a thorough revision of operating procedure

refers to the labours of Hercules (Heracles in Greek) who had twelve labours imposed upon him by Eurystheus — one of which was the cleaning of the stables of King Augeas in a single day

to be a Herculean task

to be laborious

refers to the labours of Hercules (Heracles in Greek) who had twelve labours imposed upon him by Eurystheus — one of which was the cleaning of the stables of King Augeas in a single day

hydra

a hydra-headed monster

an evil that is not readily destroyable

refers to the hydra — in Greek legend, a multiple-headed monster that grew two more heads whenever one was cut off; it was killed by Heracles

keepers

keepers of the flame

persons entrusted to maintain old traditions and keen to do so

refers to those entrusted with keeping a sacred flame of remembrance alight

magic

a magic bullet

a highly effective guaranteed remedy

not to be a magic pudding

not to represent an everlasting supply of something

from the name of a book by Norman Lindsay

the magic moment

the perfect time

there is no magic in that

that is quite ordinary

to be black magic

to lack any scientific or logical basis

refers to witchcraft

to get a magic carpet ride to something

to be given an easy and fortunate passage to an objective

refers to the magic carpet (of Oriental legend) that transported its owners wherever they wished

to wave a magic wand

to direct affairs without the restraints of the real world

Midas

the Midas touch

attributes that cause a person's ventures to be extremely profitable

refers to King Midas of Phrygia who, in Greek mythology, had the power to turn everything he touched into gold

nemesis

nemesis

an agent of retribution

refers to the goddess of retribution in Greek mythology

Pandora

to open a Pandora's box

to do something that produces all sorts of undesired and unexpected side-effects

refers to the woman in Greek mythology who brought misery to the world; Pandora's box contained all human ills and, when opened, it released uncontrollable misery on humanity

phoenix

to rise from the ashes like a phoenix

to be the replacement for something destroyed in some disaster

refers to a mythical bird that was supposed to rise from the ashes of its funeral pile/pyre with renewed youth

Scylla

to be between Scylla and Charybdis

to be faced with two equally unpalatable alternatives that cannot both be avoided

refers to the voyage of Ulysses

spell

to break the spell

to spoil the effect

spellbinding

spellbinding

fascinating to an audience

spirit

kindred spirit
person with similar interests and eccentricities
John Keats (1795–1821), *O Solitude!*, 'Almost the highest bliss of human-kind, / when to thy haunts two kindred spirits flee'

Trojan

a Trojan horse
a surreptitious means of gaining entrance or breaching defences
refers to a large gift horse full of Greek soldiers used to bring about the fall of Troy, as described in Homer's *Iliad*; Virgil (70–19 BC), *Aeneid* II:49, *Timeo Danaos et dona ferentis* ('I fear the Greeks even when they bring gifts')

Nautical

adrift

to come adrift
(of a plan) not to work out as intended

afloat

to stay afloat
to remain solvent

ahead

full-bore ahead!
proceed forward at full power!

anchor

the sheet anchor
the ultimate of one's confidence
refers to a large ship's anchor used in an emergency

to anchor
to fix firmly

to weigh anchor
to move to another address
nautical metaphor

backwash

backwash
consequence

berth

to give someone a wide berth
to go out of one's way to avoid contact with a person
nautical metaphor

board

to go overboard
to act foolishly and in an excessive way

to pipe someone on board
to welcome a person
nautical metaphor

to take something on board
to offer to give further consideration to a matter
nautical metaphor

boarders

to repel boarders
to keep out unwanted persons
refers to naval battles

boat

to be in the same boat
to share a common set of difficulties

to get off the boat
to dissociate oneself from some project

to miss the boat
to fail to exploit an opportunity

to rock the boat
to disturb the comfortable status quo

bow

shots across the bow
warnings
nautical metaphor

brace

to splice the main brace
to serve an extra ration of rum
nautical metaphor

canoe

to paddle one's canoe
to do something unaided and in one's own way
phrase first used by Captain Marryat (1792–1848) *Settlers in Canada*, ch. viii (1844)

cat

there is no room to swing a cat
this place is very small
refers to the swinging of a whip (a cat-o'-nine-tails) in the confined space of a ship's hull

colours

to nail one's colours to the mast
publicly to declare one's position and to maintain it in the face of criticism
nautical metaphor

to pass with flying colours

to be very successful in a test or contest
refers to ships returning to port with colours flying triumphantly

to sail under false colours
to pretend that one's real character or beliefs are different from what they really are
refers to a ship concealing its true identity

to show one's true colours
to disclose one's real character or beliefs
nautical metaphor

course

to be on a collision course
to be headed for a clash with an opponent

to be on course
to be progressing satisfactorily towards one's goal

to plot a safe course through troubled waters
to make a plan that overcomes certain difficulties
nautical metaphor

deck

a loose cannon on the deck
a person or factor out of control and likely to cause trouble
nautical metaphor

all hands on deck
everybody is requested to help out
nautical metaphor

to be back on deck
to have returned after an absence
nautical metaphor

decks

to clear the decks
to get ready for action
nautical metaphor

deckchairs

to rearrange the deckchairs on the Titanic
to take an initiative that is quite useless because it does not take much greater change into account
refers to the liner *Titanic* which struck an iceberg and sank in 1912

dock

to be in the dry dock
to be out of action while undergoing repairs
refers to ship repairs

doldrums

to be in the doldrums
to be depressed or to show no activity
refers to a region of little wind near the equator, becalming sailing ships

ebb

ebb and flow
fluctuations

to ebb away
to decline gradually

feet

to get one's feet wet
to do the necessary initial parts of a task, despite their being unpleasant and menial
refers to nautical tasks

figurehead

a figurehead
the ceremonial chief officer of some organisation without any real power
refers to the ornamental carving at the front of a ship

fish

an ocean full of fish
plenty of opportunity

fishing

a fishing expedition
an exercise that sets out to gather incriminating information without knowing its exact nature or location

flagship

flagship
most important member of a group of related entities
refers to the ship carrying an admiral's flag

flotsam

flotsam and jetsam
persons or things in an unfixed and disordered state, and considered worthless
refers, respectively, to goods found floating, and to goods thrown overboard deliberately

flow

ebb and flow
fluctuations

hatches

to batten down the hatches
to get ready for expected difficulties
nautical metaphor

helm

to be at the helm
to be in charge
nautical metaphor

high

to leave someone high and dry
to isolate a person from a desired involvement; to withdraw all support from a person
nautical metaphor referring to a boat stranded out of water

iceberg

to be the tip of the iceberg
to be only a very small portion of a much larger but less obvious whole

jetsam

flotsam and jetsam
persons or things in an unfixed and disordered state, and considered worthless
refers, respectively, to goods found floating, and to goods thrown overboard deliberately

jettison

to jettison some proposal
to abandon some proposal as worthless or impracticable

jib

the cut of someone's jib
someone's personal appearance
Sir Walter Scott (1771–1832), 'If she disliked what the sailor calls the cut of their jib'; refers to the recognition of ships at sea by noting the appearance of their foresail

keel

to keep something on an even keel
to ensure that something is kept balanced and stable
nautical metaphor

keelhaul

to keelhaul someone
to rebuke or castigate harshly
refers to ancient nautical punishment of hauling an offender underneath a ship from one side to the other — the result often being fatal

keep

to keep a weather eye out for something
to look out with particular care
nautical metaphor; refers to the eye that is turned towards the wind

knots

at a rate of knots
very fast
nautical metaphor; refers to the original measure of a ship's speed by noting the rate at which the ship passed a regular series of knots tied in a rope which was maintained in position beside the ship

lead

to swing the lead
to cheat an employer by not working while being paid to do so or by malingering; to avoid work or some other task by concocting a plausible excuse for not doing it, or by pretending to be ill
originally referred to a leadsman lazily swinging the line, rather than getting on with taking soundings

leeway

to make up leeway
to get back to a normal position or to get to the position held by one's competitors
refers to the drift of a ship to leeward of the desired course

lifeline

to throw someone a lifeline
to give significant assistance to a person

Lloyd's

to be A1 at Lloyd's
to be in perfect order
refers to the classification of ships in Lloyd's register in London

mast

to nail one's colours to the mast
publicly to declare one's position and to maintain it in the face of criticism
nautical metaphor

net

to catch someone in the net
unexpectedly to involve a particular person in the course of activity designed to involve many others
to slip through the net

to happen as an isolated case despite steps taken to prevent such events

to spread the net more widely
to become more comprehensive

nets

to draw the nets closer
to intensify one's efforts

netting

to miss the sharks while netting the minnows
to succeed in minor aspects but fail in the ones that really matter

ocean

an ocean full of fish
plenty of opportunity

to be only a drop in the ocean
to be quite insignificant in the total scene

oil

to pour oil on troubled waters
to calm down a situation

overboard

to go overboard
to act foolishly and in an excessive way

painter

to cut the painter
to become separated
nautical metaphor; refers to cutting a boat loose from its moorings

pebble

not to be the only pebble on the beach
not to be the only person available for some task, or affected by some set of circumstances

pier

take a long walk on a short pier
go away, I want no dealings with you

pirate

pirate
(of radio) unlicensed; (of recordings or computer software) published in breach of copyright law

plank

to walk the plank
to face certain doom
refers to execution of persons at sea

Plimsoll

the Plimsoll line
the standard
refers to the mark fixing the maximum load line of a merchant ship in water, and to Samuel Plimsoll MP (1824–98) who campaigned for safe shipping practices

pole

not to touch something with a forty-foot barge pole
to go out of one's way to avoid something

port

any port in a storm
anything that helps to avoid difficulties is welcome

port of call
one of a series of places being visited
nautical metaphor

pumps

all hands to the pumps
everybody is requested to help out
nautical metaphor

raft

life raft
financial assistance sufficient to avert insolvency

ripples

to make ripples
to disturb the status quo

ropes

to know the ropes
to know how to do one's job
nautical metaphor

to learn the ropes
to be taught the elementary features
nautical metaphor

to show someone the ropes
to teach a beginner how to do something
nautical metaphor

sail

to sail against the wind
to oppose the views currently being held by others

to sail close to the wind
to take a considered risk; to test the limits of what is possible or acceptable

refers to sailing in a manner such that sails remain filled while keeping the boat headed as near as possible into the wind

to sail under false colours
to pretend that one's real character or beliefs are different from what they really are

refers to a ship concealing its true identity

to set sail
to commence a voyage

to trim one's sails
to modify one's policy or opinion in accordance with changing circumstances

refers to adjusting sails to suit wind conditions

sailing

to be plain sailing
to be quite straightforward and very easy

refers to navigation by means of a 'plane chart' on which meridians and parallels of latitude are represented by equidistant straight lines

sails

to take the wind out of someone's sails
to upset a person by anticipating that person's actions or by using arguments which that person was proposing to use

refers to a tactical manoeuvre in sailing whereby one boat blocks or 'takes' the wind advantage of another

sea

a sea-change
a significant transformation

Shakespeare, *The Tempest* I:ii, 'Nothing of him that doth fade / but doth suffer a sea-change / into something rich and strange

a South Sea bubble
an unrealistic financial venture that is bound to result in total loss

refers to a notorious financial scandal involving the South Sea Company (UK) in 1720

to be all at sea
to be confused as to what is going on and what to do next

to be between the devil and the deep blue sea
to be faced with two equally unpalatable alternatives that cannot both be avoided

ship

a case of rats leaving a sinking ship
the desertion of an enterprise in anticipation of imminent failure

enough to sink a battleship
much more than sufficient

shipshape
in excellent condition

nautical metaphor

to abandon ship
to abrogate one's responsibilities or to abandon a project

refers to the order given when a ship is about to sink

to be a happy ship
to have a contented workforce

to be a rudderless ship
to be without direction

to run a tight ship
to manage an efficient organisation

refers to ropes that are tight or taut

to run one's own ship
to do things and organise subordinates in one's own way

to spoil the ship for a ha'p'orth of tar
to engage in a false economy

the current word 'ship' is actually a mistake for the original word 'sheep', and the tar refers to the treatment of wounds

when one's ship comes in
when one's business venture is successfully completed; OR when luck arrives

ships

ships that pass in the night
a fleeting, transitory acquaintance

Henry Wadsworth Longfellow (1807–82), *The Theologian's Tale (Tales of a Wayside Inn)*, 'Ships that pass in the night, and speak each other in passing ... '

to have a nuclear ships policy
to neither confirm nor deny something

refers to the US policy of neither confirming nor denying whether a particular ship is carrying nuclear arms

shoals

to founder on the shoals of something
to come to grief because of unexpected dangers
refers to a ship running aground in undetected shallow water

side

a broadside
a short verbal attack
refers to all the guns situated or able to fire on one side of a ship

sink

enough to sink a battleship
much more than sufficient
it is a case of sink or swim
it is a case of success or failure with no other alternatives
refers to the 'testing' of so-called witches by throwing them into water to see if they would sink or swim
to sink without a trace
to disappear completely

sinking

a case of rats leaving a sinking ship
the desertion of an enterprise in anticipation of imminent failure

slack

to take up the slack
to take advantage of surplus capacity
refers to working with ropes

snag

to strike a snag
to encounter a difficulty
refers to angling

sounding

to take a sounding
to ascertain people's views
nautical metaphor referring to ascertaining the depth of water

storm

a storm in a teacup
a controversy about a minor matter but one that looms large in the minds of the parties
any port in a storm
anything that helps to avoid difficulties is welcome
the calm before the storm
the quiet period before an expected or inevitable crisis
there are storm clouds on the horizon
bad news is expected
to be in the eye of the storm
to be at the centre of a controversy
to create a storm
to cause a fuss
to ride out the storm
to come safely through some dangerous situation
nautical metaphor
to weather the storm
to come safely through a crisis
nautical metaphor

stormy

to be a stormy petrel
a person who disturbs a pleasant state of affairs by agitating for change
refers to the bird (petrel) that flies low over water during a storm and appears to be alternately touching one foot and then the other to the surface of the water as though walking upon it; the bird is sometimes thought to be the harbinger of a storm, and is named after St Peter who walked upon the stormy waters of Lake Gennesareth

tack

to be on the wrong tack
to be using an inaccurate procedure or policy likely to lead to error
refers to sailing
to change tack
to alter one's direction
refers to sailing

tide

the tide has turned
conditions have changed
the tide is running in favour of some proposition
public opinion supports some proposition
to be caught by the tide
to be dealt with by something inevitable
to stem the tide
to make progress against something
to swim against the tide
to take up a minority position
to turn the tide

to reverse the direction of something

Titanic

to rearrange the deckchairs on the Titanic
to take an initiative that is quite useless because it does not take much greater change into account
refers to the liner *Titanic* which struck an iceberg and sank in 1912

wake

in the wake of someone
following a person's example
nautical metaphor

water

come hell or high water
regardless of the difficulties or obstacles

to be in smooth water
to have no troubles
nautical metaphor

waters

to be in uncharted waters
to be the first to experience something
nautical metaphor

to enter treacherous waters
to engage in an enterprise with risks that are not obvious
nautical metaphor

to fish in troubled waters
to profit from a disturbed situation
refers to angling

to plot a safe course through troubled waters
to make a plan that overcomes certain difficulties
nautical metaphor

to pour oil on troubled waters
to calm down a situation

wave

to be on the crest of a wave
to enjoy success that might not last

to ride the wave
to be successful for the time being
refers to surfing

waves

to cause waves
to disturb the status quo

wreck

to salvage something out of the wreck
to achieve some minor benefits out of a disastrous situation
refers to shipwrecks

Plants

acorns

tall oaks from little acorns grow
even major enterprises have to have small beginnings
David Everett (1769–1813), *Lines Written for a School Declamation*, 'Large streams from little fountains flow, / tall oaks from little acorns grow'

apple

a rotten apple
an isolated dishonest person in an otherwise honest group

in apple-pie order
in perfect order and condition

to be the apple of someone's eye
to be a much cherished person
refers to the pupil of the eye — 'the apple of the eye' as being the centre of visual perception and therefore especially cherished and much-valued

apples

to add/compare apples with oranges
to lump unconnected things together quite illogically

to compare apples with apples
to make a valid comparison

applecart

to upset the applecart
to engage in conduct disturbing a peaceful state of affairs and thereby to cause discomfort

bean

not to have a bean
to have no money

beans

not to matter a row of beans
to be utterly unimportant

to be full of beans
to be very cheerful

to know how many beans make five
to have common sense
refers to an old riddle

to spill the beans
indiscreetly to reveal sensitive information

blossom

to blossom
(of a person's attributes) to develop

bud

to nip something in the bud
to stop some activity in its early stages when stopping it is still relatively easy
refers to the first signs of growth in plants

bush

a bird in the hand is worth two in the bush
a benefit currently available is more valuable than a seemingly much larger benefit that might or might not be achieved in the future

a bush lawyer
a person without legal qualifications who has a reasonable, although not perfect, knowledge of the law, and who likes to make technical points in arguments

to beat about the bush
to fail to come to the point
refers to hunters flushing game from cover by beating of the vegetation in which animals are hidden

bushed

to be bushed
to be lost or exhausted or puzzled or confused

bushel

to hide one's light under a bushel
to keep others in ignorance of one's skills and experience
Luke 11:33, 'No man, when he hath lighted a candle, putteth it in a secret place, neither under a bushel'

bushfires

to fight bushfires
to deal with crises as they arise rather than take preventive action

cabbage

to be on someone's cabbage patch
to engage in a competitive activity in a territory regarded by someone already there as rightfully belonging exclusively to that person

carrots

sticks and carrots
disincentives and incentives in combination
refers to the handling of donkeys

chaff

to separate the wheat from the chaff
to separate the worthy from the unworthy
Matthew 3:12, 'His winnowing fork is in his hand, and he will clear his threshing floor and gather his wheat into the granary, but the chaff he will burn with unquenchable fire'

cherry

to engage in cherry picking
(in business) to accept only the potentially most lucrative deals

to get only one bite at the cherry
to receive no further opportunity

clover

to be in clover
to enjoy a life of ease and luxury
refers to grazing animals in rich pasture

core

rotten to the core
completely corrupt

to be the hard core
to be the central and most difficult problem

deflower

to deflower
to deprive of virginity

disseminate

to disseminate ideas
to spread ideas to a wide audience
literally, 'to scatter seeds in various places'

fall

windfall
unexpected good fortune
refers to fruit falling from a tree without having to be picked

fig

one would not give a fig for something
one regards something as worthless

fruit

forbidden fruit

something particularly desired because it is not allowed

Genesis 2:17, 'but of the tree of the knowledge of good and evil, thou shalt not eat of it'

to bear fruit
to result in success

fruitless

fruitless
yielding no benefit

fruits

by their fruits ye shall know them
their true nature will be revealed by their results

Matthew 7:20, 'wherefore by their fruits ye shall know them'

gooseberry

to play gooseberry
to act as an unwelcome chaperon

grain

something goes against the grain
something is completely and frustratingly against a person's inclination

refers to woodworking

grapes

that is just sour grapes
those are disparaging remarks made only because that person is peeved and resentful at someone else's better fortune

derived from Aesop's fable of 'the fox and the grapes' about expressing deliberate disparagement of a desired but unattainable object; 'sour grapes' also occurs in *Ezekiel* 18:2, 'the fathers have eaten sour grapes, and the children's teeth are set on edge'

what is this — a bunch of grapes or a bowl of goldfish?
surely you know what this is?

grapevine

to hear on the grapevine
to learn unofficially

the earlier form of the metaphor was a 'grapevine telegraph' as a means of communicating private information

grass

a snake in the grass
a person of low character who manages to disguise that trait

Virgil, *Eclogue*, 'There's a snake hidden in the grass'

grass roots
at the lowest level of a hierarchy

not to let grass grow under one's feet
not to let inertia or delay spoil something

hay

to hit the hay
to go to sleep

refers to sleeping on beds of hay

to look for a needle in a haystack
to attempt something with a very small chance of success

to make hay while the sun shines
to utilise an opportunity before it disappears

John Betjeman (1906–84), *The Last Laugh*, 'I made hay while the sun shone'

haystack

to look for a needle in a haystack
to attempt something with a very small chance of success

jungle

a jungle
a place where everyone makes his or her own rules

the law of the jungle
the principle that those having power will use it at the expense of all others

Rudyard Kipling (1865–1936), *The Law of the Jungle*, 'Now this is the law of the jungle — as old and as true as the sky; and the wolf that shall keep it may prosper, but the wolf that shall break it must die'

lemon

the answer is a lemon
there is no appropriate answer to that sort of proposition

to sell someone a lemon
to sell a person a grossly defective product on the basis that it represents quality

to squeeze the lemon dry
to get the maximum advantage out of some favourable situation

Sir Eric Geddes (1875–1937), 'The Germans ... are going to pay every penny; they are going to be squeezed, as a lemon is squeezed — until the pips squeak. My only doubt is not whether we can squeeze hard enough, but whether there is enough juice.' (10 December 1918)

lily

lily-livered

cowardly

refers to a supersitition that the liver of a coward contained no blood

lily-white

honest and incorruptible

based on a belief that the lily sprang from the tears of Eve as she left the Garden of Eden; the lily is traditionally a symbol of purity and innocence in Christian art

to gild the lily

to add superfluous ornamentation to something already beautiful

Shakespeare *King John* IV:i, 'to gild refined gold, to paint the lily'

limb

to go out on a limb

to put oneself in an isolated or stranded position

mushroom

to mushroom

to expand rapidly

refers to the rapid (overnight) growth of mushrooms

nettle

to grasp the nettle

to deal with an unpleasant difficulty by decisive action

Aaron Hill (1685–1750), 'Tender-hearted stroke a nettle, / And it stings you for your pains; / Grasp it like a man of mettle, / And it soft as silk remains'

nuts

to be nuts

to be crazy

to be nuts about someone

to be infatuated with a person

nutshell

in a nutshell

by way of summary

oak

to have a heart of oak

to be brave

refers to a famous sea song and naval march from the pantomime, *Harlequin's Invasion* (1759), by Garrick and Boyce.

to lock something up in the old oak chest

to put in a safe place and out of mind

oaks

tall oaks from little acorns grow

even major enterprises have to have small beginnings

David Everett (1769–1813), *Lines Written for a School Declamation*, 'Large streams from little fountains flow, / tall oaks from little acorns grow'

oats

to feel one's oats

to be energetic and lively (UK and Australia); to be self-important (USA)

refers to an energetic horse fed on oats

to sow wild oats

to indulge in foolish behaviour while a young adult

olive

to hold out an olive branch

to make peace overtures

the olive branch was recognised as a symbol of peace and prosperity in many ancient civilisations; *Genesis* 8:11, 'And the dove came in to him in the evening; and lo, in her mouth was an olive leaf plucked off: so Noah knew that the waters were abated off the earth'

onions

to know one's onions

to be well informed in some area

refers to Dr C. T. Onions, editor of the *Shorter Oxford English Dictionary*

oranges

to add/compare apples with oranges

to lump unconnected things together quite illogically

pea

a pea-and-thimble trick

a clever fraud committed in the presence of its victim without this being obvious at the time

refers to a sleight-of-hand trick played with three thimbles and a pea, the thimbles being moved about and observers being asked to guess under which thimble the pea is

peanuts

to earn peanuts

to get a reward that is far too small in relation to the value of the services rendered

pineapple

to have hold of the wrong end of the pineapple
to be utterly mistaken

plum

the plum
the best item in a collection

plums

to pick just the plums out of the jam
to take only the very best items

poppy

a tall poppy
a person with great power or responsibility and/or in receipt of high remuneration

poppies

to cut tall poppies down to size
to diminish the self-importance of haughty persons

potato

a hot potato
a controversial issue that no one wants to handle, an embarrassing issue

potatoes

to be small potatoes
to be quite unimportant

prune

to prune
to remove the superfluous
refers to horticulture

reed

to be a broken reed
to be a weak and unreliable person
Isaiah 36:6 and *2 Kings* 18:21, 'Lo, thou trustest in the staff of this broken reed, on Egypt; whereon if a man lean, it will go into his hand and pierce it'

rooted

deep-rooted
firmly established, strongly felt

roots

grass roots
at the lowest level of a hierarchy
to put one's roots down
to settle in
to strike at the roots of something
to work towards the destruction of something

rosa

sub rosa
in strict confidence
Latin *sub rosa* 'under the rose' — refers to being under the rose (as a symbol of secrecy)

rose

a rose between two thorns
something beautiful in the midst of ugliness
a rose by any other name would smell as sweet
the form does not affect the substance
Shakespeare, *Romeo and Juliet* II:ii, 'What's in a name? That which we call a rose / By any other name would smell as sweet'
to come up smelling like a rose
not to have a stain on one's character
to see something through rose-coloured glasses/spectacles
to appreciate only the advantages and to disregard completely the disadvantages

roses

to be on a path strewn with roses
to lead a very pleasant life
to be no bed of roses
to be difficult or uncomfortable
Robert Louis Stevenson (1850–94), *Virginibus Puerisque* I:i, 'Marriage is like life in this — that it is a field of battle, and not a bed of roses'

rosy

to present a rosy picture
to state a set of favourable factors

seed

to run to seed
to become shabby
refers to plants maturing past the glory of the flowering phase

seeds

to sow seeds
to propagate ideas in the hope that they will be adopted

straw

a man of straw

a person of no substance, a counterfeit, a sham; OR a person invented in order to be triumphantly defeated; OR a person who has no assets while giving a contrary appearance

Exodus 6:7 'Ye shall no more give the people straw to make bricks ... let them go and gather straw for themselves'

one cannot make bricks without straw

one cannot achieve results in the absence of adequate resources

Exodus 6:7 'Ye shall no more give the people straw to make bricks ... let them go and gather straw for themselves'

the final (or last) straw

the latest step that, when added to a large number of seemingly harmless previous steps, sets off a significant event resulting from the cumulative effect

see 'the straw that broke the camel's back'

the straw that broke the camel's back

the latest step that, when added to a large number of seemingly harmless previous steps, sets off a sudden significant event resulting from the cumulative effect

to buy straw hats in winter

to buy in a depressed market when most other people are sellers

to draw the short straw

to be chosen (perhaps by lot) to undertake an undesired task

straws

straws in the wind

small but significant indicators of future events

John Seldon (1584–1654), 'Take a straw and throw it up into the air, you shall see by that which way the wind is'

to clasp/grasp at straws

desperately to resort to any expedient in a hopeless situation

refers to a drowning person

thorn

to be a thorn in someone's flesh/side

to be a constant annoyance or affliction

2 Corinthians 12:7, 10: 'There was given to me a thorn in the flesh ... I will glory in my infirmities'

thorns

to wear one's crown of thorns

to have one's own difficulties

John 19:2, 'And the soldiers plaited a crown of thorns, and put it on his [Jesus'] head'

a rose between two thorns

something beautiful in the midst of ugliness

tree

to bark up the wrong tree

to reach an incorrect conclusion and/or to pursue an erroneous course of action

to be at the top of the tree

to be a leading member of one's profession

to be up a gum tree

to be in difficulty; OR at the end of one's resources

to be up a tree

to be perplexed or cornered

to shake a tree

to do something to see what will result

trees

not to see the wood for the trees

to overlook the general picture because of undue concentration on the details

vegetable

to become a vegetable

to lose one's ability to respond to many external stimuli, especially those that normally contribute to the quality of life; to lead a monotonous life with no animation

vine

to hear on the grapevine

to learn unofficially

the earlier form of the metaphor was a 'grapevine telegraph' as a means of communicating private information

to wither on the vine

by virtue of changed circumstances or the effluxion of time to be no longer relevant

John 15:5, 6, 'I am the vine, ye are the branches ... if a man abideth not in me, he is cast forth as a branch and is withered'

violet

a shrinking violet
a shy person

weed

to weed some group out
to get rid of some elements not meeting a desired standard

wheat

to separate the wheat from the chaff
to separate the worthy from the unworthy
Matthew 3:12, 'His winnowing fork is in his hand, and he will clear his threshing floor and gather his wheat into the granary, but the chaff he will burn with unquenchable fire'

wood

not to see the wood for the trees
to overlook the general picture because of undue concentration on the details

to be babes in the wood
to be excessively naVve and inexperienced and thus ripe for exploitation
based on the folk legend of the babes in the wood of Wayland Hall, Norfolk

to get rid of the dead wood
to terminate the services of unsatisfactory personnel
refers to pruning of bushes

to touch wood
to hope that our good luck will not go away
refers to ancient belief in sacred power of certain trees, especially oak, ash, hazel, hawthorn and willow

wooden

to get the wooden spoon
to come ingloriously last
refers to the custom of awarding a silver cup to the winner and a wooden spoon to the loser

woods

neck of the woods
localised area
refers to a narrow stretch of wooded country

to be out of the woods
the previous difficulties have been overcome

woodwork

to crawl out of the woodwork
(referring to something unwelcome) to emerge from hiding or obscurity

Religion and Biblical

Adam

not to know someone from Adam
to be unable to recognise a person
refers to the name of the first man as recorded in *Genesis* 2

since Adam was a boy
for a very long time
refers to the name of the first man as recorded in *Genesis* 2

after

to be someone after one's own heart
to be a person who shares one's beliefs
1 Samuel 13:14 'A man after his own heart'

altar

to sacrifice something on the altar of some belief
to give up some benefit as a matter of principle

angel

a fallen angel
a previously trusted person who has transgressed
refers to the fallen spirits who rebelled against God (Milton *Paradise Lost* Bk I, 392)

someone's guardian angel
someone's friend, watching over them and advancing their interests
Shakespeare, *Hamlet* IV:i, 'Angels and ministers of grace defend us!'

to be an angel
to be very helpful

to be no angel
to have a great many serious faults

angels

fools rush in where angels fear to tread

unsophisticated persons take unwise risks in circumstances where more knowledgeable persons would exercise caution

Alexander Pope (1688–1744), *An Essay on Criticism* 1:625, 'For fools rush in where angels fear to tread'

to be on the side of the angels

to be on the side of righteousness

Benjamin Disraeli (1804–81), 'Is man an ape or an angel? Now I am on the side of the angels' (speech debating theory of evolution, Diocese of Oxford, 25 November 1864)

anointed

the anointed one

the desired successor

refers to use of anointing oil to indicate and sanctify a chosen perso; *Exodus* 28:41, 'and shalt anoint them, and consecrate them, and sanctify them, that they may minister unto me in the priest's office'

antediluvian

antediluvian

very outmoded

literally 'before the flood' — refers to the time before the flood described in *Genesis* Chapter 6ff

apocryphal

apocryphal

fictitious but resembling truth and illustrating a point

Greek: *apocrypha*, 'hidden'

ashes

to wear sackcloth and ashes

humbly to demonstrate repentance

Esther 4:3, 'There was great mourning ... and many lay in sackcloth and ashes'

Babel

a tower of Babel

a noisy and confused assembly

Genesis 11:9, 'Therefore is the name of it called Babel; because the Lord did there confound the language of all the earth' (from which the word 'babble' is also derived)

babes

out of the mouths of babes and sucklings

(as indiscreetly revealed) the truth

Psalms 8:2, 'Out of the mouths of babes and sucklings hast thou ordained strength ... '

baptism

a baptism of fire

the commencement of an operation that presents great difficulty

refers to religious ceremonial washing as an initiation ceremony; metaphorical use (as here) attributed to Napoleon III in referring to to a soldier's first battle

beadledom

beadledom

stupid officiousness

refers to a church official (a beadle) appointed to deal with petty offenders

beard

to beard the lion in his den

to tackle a daunting opponent in that person's own familiar surroundings

Sir Walter Scott (1771–1832), *Marmion*, 'And darest thou then to beard the lion in his den ... ' (probably a reference to the story of Daniel in the den of lions as related in *Daniel* 6:16)

beast

the nature of the beast

the reality of the situation

Revelation 13:17, ' ... he that had the mark, or the name of the beast, or the number of his name'

beatify

to beatify someone

to describe a person as worthy of honour

refers to a step in the process towards canonisation as a saint

bible

a bible basher

a person who makes unwelcome attempts to force religious beliefs on others

to be the bible

to be the authority

bird

a little bird told me

I heard from an informant who cannot be named .

Ecclesiastes 10:20, 'Even in your thought do not curse the king ... for a bird of the air will carry your voice or some winged creature tell the matter'

birthright

to sell one's birthright for a mess of pottage

through foolishness to exchange something of substance for something of little value

Genesis 25:34, 'Then Jacob gave Esau bread and pottage of lentils ... thus Esau despised his birthright'

blessing

a blessing in disguise

an unwelcome but salutary experience

James Hervey (1696–1743), *Reflections on a Flower Garden*, 'Ee'en crosses from his sov'reign hand are blessings in disguise'

to be a mixed blessing

to be an outcome with some desirable and some undesirable features

to give one's blessing to something

to indicate one's approval of something

blind

the blind leading the blind

persons without the necessary skills for a task purporting to impart those skills to others

Matthew 15:14, 'And if the blind lead the blind, both shall fall into the ditch'

blood

to have blood on one's hands

to be the person responsible for someone else's predicament

Matthew 27:24, 'He [Pilate] took water and washed his hands in full view of the crowd. "My hands are clean of this man's blood," he declared'

blow

to blow hot and cold

to vacillate

Revelations 3:15, 'I know thy works, that thou art neither cold nor hot'

to blow one's own trumpet

immodestly to publicise one's own attributes

refers to the trumpet as an instrument of triumph; *Joshua* 6:20, 'When the priests blew with the trumpets ... the wall fell down flat'

book

to take a leaf out of someone's book

to model oneself on another person

refers to taking a page from the 'Book of Life' — *Rev* 20: 12, 'and the books were opened ... and the dead were judged out of those things that were written in the books, according to their works'

books

to be in someone's black books

to be out of favour with a person

biblical allusion: refers to God's judgment and the desirability of having one's name entered in the book of life; *Rev* 20: 12, 'and the books were opened ... and the dead were judged out of those things that were written in the books, according to their works'

to be in someone's good books

to be well regarded by another person

biblical allusion: refers to God's judgment and the desirability of having one's name entered in the book of life; *Rev* 20: 12, 'and the books were opened ... and the dead were judged out of those things that were written in the books, according to their works'

branch

to hold out an olive branch

to make peace overtures

the olive branch was recognised as a symbol of peace and prosperity in many ancient civilisations; *Genesis* 8:11, 'And the dove came in to him in the evening; and lo, in her mouth was an olive leaf plucked off: so Noah knew that the waters were abated off the earth'

bread

a bread-winner

a person earning by personal exertion the income of a household

Deuteronomy 8:3, 'Man doth not live by bread alone, but by every word that proceedeth out of the mouth of the Lord' (see also *Matthew* 5:4)

to cast one's bread upon the waters

to give generously because one will eventually be rewarded for one's generosity

Ecclesiastes 11:1, 'Cast thy bread upon the waters: for thou shalt find it after many days'

break

to break someone's heart

to act in a way causing great upset to another person

Psalms 69:21, 'Thy rebuke hath broken my heart; I am full of heaviness'; Shakespeare *Hamlet* I:ii, 'But break my heart … ')

bricks

one cannot make bricks without straw

one cannot achieve results in the absence of adequate resources

Exodus 6:7 'Ye shall no more give the people straw to make bricks … let them go and gather straw for themselves'

bushel

to hide one's light under a bushel

to keep others in ignorance of one's skills and experience

Luke 11:33, 'No man, when he hath lighted a candle, putteth it in a secret place, neither under a bushel'

Cain

the mark of Cain

disgrace

refers (wrongly) to a supposed mark of disgrace placed upon Cain as punishment for the killing of his brother; the mark was, in fact, a sign of God's protection against anyone attempting to kill Cain; *Genesis* 4:15, 'And the Lord set a mark upon Cain, lest any finding him should kill him'

to raise Cain

to create a disturbance

Genesis 4:5, 'And Cain was very wroth, and his countenance fell'

calf

to kill the fatted calf

to demonstrate welcome and complete acceptance of another person

Luke 15:23. 'And bring hither the fatted calf and let us eat, and be merry'

cast

to cast one's bread upon the waters

to give generously because one will eventually be rewarded for one's generosity

Ecclesiastes 11:1, 'Cast thy bread upon the waters: for thou shalt find it after many days'

to cast pearls before swine

to confer valuable benefits on someone who neither recognises nor appreciates them

Matthew 7:6, 'Neither cast ye your pearls before swine'

chaff

to separate the wheat from the chaff

to separate the worthy from the unworthy

Matthew 3:12, 'His winnowing fork is in his hand, and he will clear his threshing floor and gather his wheat into the granary, but the chaff he will burn with unquenchable fire'

changes

to ring the changes

to exhaust the number of different ways of doing something

refers to the permutations used for ringing peals of church bells

cheek

to turn the other cheek

to refuse, on moral grounds, to retaliate to provocation in like manner

Matthew 5:38, 39, 'Ye have heard that it hath been said an eye for an eye and a tooth for a tooth: but I say unto you … whosoever shall smite thee on the right cheek, turn to him the other also'

Christmases

all their Christmases came at once

they were overjoyed

church

a broad church

an organisation willing to accept members with a wide variety of different views

clay

to have feet of clay

to be vulnerable or not as good as thought

Daniel 2:42, 'And as the toes of the feet were part of iron and part of clay, so the kingdom shall be partly strong and partly broken'

clean

to have clean hands

to be innocent or to act ethically

Matthew 27:24, 'He [Pilate] took water and washed his hands in full view of the crowd. "My hands are clean of this man's blood," he declared'

cloud

to have a cloud hanging over one's head

there is doubt as to one's future

refers to the pillar of cloud (God) passing judgment on the Hebrews; the pillar of cloud is described in *Exodus* 13:21 *et seq.*

commandment

eleventh commandment

unwritten rule

refers to the ten commandments (*Exodus* 20:1–17)

cross

to be a cross that one has to bear

to be a difficulty that one has to endure

Luke 14:27, 'And whosoever doth not bear his cross, and come after me, cannot be my disciple'

crown

to wear one's crown of thorns

to have one's own difficulties

John 19:2, 'And the soldiers plaited a crown of thorns, and put it on his [Jesus'] head'

crucify

to crucify someone

to do severe damage unfairly to a person's reputation or credibility

Mark 15:13, 'And they cried out again, Crucify him'

crumbs

to throw someone a few crumbs

to fob a person off with a few symbolic but unimportant concessions

Luke 16:21, 'a certain beggar ... desiring to be fed with the crumbs which fell from the rich man's table'

curate

to be a curate's egg

to be good only in parts

refers to a cartoon (*Punch*, vol. cix, p. 222, 1895) showing the nervous young curate (Jones) in conversation with the Lord Bishop:

'I'm afraid you've got a bad egg, Mr Jones.'

'Oh no, my Lord, I assure you! Parts of it are excellent!'

Damascus

a road to Damascus experience

a sudden, dramatic conversion

refers to the sudden conversion of Paul (Saul) — *Acts* 9:3, 'And as he journeyed, he came to Damascus: and suddenly there shined around him a light from heaven: And he fell to the earth'

David

a David and Goliath battle

a struggle between two parties who are not evenly matched

refers to *1 Samuel* 17:23 ff

day

a red-letter day

an important occasion

refers to the colour used to indicate days of obligation in the Christian Church missal — as opposed to black-letter days, which are optional days

days

one's days are numbered

one is about to be abolished

Daniel 5:26, 'God hath numbered thy kingdom, and finished it'

devil

a devil-may-care attitude

a reckless attitude

be a devil!

take a chance!

he must have a long spoon that sups with the devil

great care is needed when negotiating with disreputable parties

Shakespeare apparently alludes to an old proverb in *The Tempest* II:ii, 'Mercy! mercy! this is a devil ... I will leave him, I have no long spoon!'

poor devil

person to be pitied

speak/talk of the devil

here is the person we were just discussing

the devil can cite scripture for his purpose

a person can quote a respectable or hostile authority while advocating a disreputable cause of that person's own

Shakespeare, *The Merchant of Venice* I:ii, 'The devil can cite scripture for his purpose'

the devil one knows is better than the devil one does not know
the status quo is more comfortable than change

to act as a devil's advocate
to put a point of view that one does not hold in order to draw out the best arguments regarding a proposition
refers to a church official vetting a candidate for sainthood (and ultimately to the testing of Job by Satan, *Job* 1:9 ff)

to be between the devil and the deep blue sea
to be faced with two equally unpalatable alternatives that cannot both be avoided

to give the devil his due
to be fair

to grab the devil by the tail
to face up to difficulties

doubting

a doubting Thomas
a person who refuses to believe claims in the absence of proof
John 20:25, 'But he [Thomas] said ... except I shall see in his hands the print of the nails ... I will not believe'

dust

to throw dust into someone's eyes
to deceive a person by presenting inaccurate or misleading information
Koran: 'Neither didst thou, O Muhammad, cast dust into their eyes; but it was God who confounded them'

earth

to promise the earth
to give extravagant assurances
Matthew 5:5, 'Blessed are the meek, for they shall inherit the earth'

eleventh

at the eleventh hour
at the last moment
Matthew 20:9: 'And when they came that were hired about the eleventh hour, they received every man a penny'; refers to the last hour of the working day in biblical times, and therefore the last opportunity to secure work — hence the very last opportunity

eleventh commandment
unwritten rule
refers to the ten commandments (*Exodus* 20:1–17)

enshrine

to enshrine
to incorporate as an important part of something

extra

to go the extra mile
to work beyond the call of duty
Matthew 5:41, 'Whosoever shall compel thee to go a mile, go with him twain'

eye

an eye for an eye
retaliation of equal magnitude to the original offence
Exodus 21:24, 'Eye for eye, tooth for tooth, hand for hand, foot for foot'; see also 'to turn the other cheek'

to see eye to eye with someone
to agree
Isaiah 52:8, 'For they shall see eye to eye, when the Lord shall bring again Zion'

eyes

to open someone's eyes to something
to alert another person to the truth of something
Matthew 9:30, 'And their eyes were opened'

faith

an article of faith
a fundamental belief on which certain behaviour is based

faithful

the old faithful
a greatly loved article

fall

to fall to the ground
to fail
Matthew 10:29, 'Are not two sparrows sold for a farthing? And one of them shall not fall on the ground without your Father ... '

fear

in fear and trembling
in a state of apprehension
Philippians 2:12, 'Work out your own salvation with fear and trembling'

to put the fear of God into someone
to frighten a person into behaving properly

Ecclesiastes 12:13, 'Fear God, and keep his commandments; for this is the whole duty of man'

flesh

one's own flesh and blood
one's own offspring, ancestors, or close relatives
Genesis 2:23, 'Bone of my bones, and flesh of my flesh'

to be a thorn in someone's flesh
to be a constant annoyance or affliction
2 Corinthians 12:7, 10: 'There was given to me a thorn in the flesh ... I will glory in my infirmities'

to go the way of all flesh
to die
Joshua 23:14, 'And, behold, this day I am going the way of all flesh'

fleshpots

fleshpots
sumptuous living
Exodus 16:3, ' ... in the land of Egypt, when we sat by the fleshpots and when we did eat bread to the full'

flock

flock
congregation in the charge of a religious official
numerous biblical references incl.: *Isaiah* 40:11, 'He shall feed his flock like a shepherd: he shall gather the lambs with his arm, and carry them in his bosom, and shall gently lead those that are with young'

fly

a fly in the ointment
a minor flaw that spoils a thing
Ecclesiastes 10:1, 'Dead flies cause the ointment of the apothecary to send forth a stinking savour: so doth a little folly him that is in reputation for wisdom and honour'

fold

the fold
the body of believers
refers to an enclosure for sheep; *John* 10:16, 'Other sheep I have, which are not of this fold'

forbidden

forbidden fruit
something particularly desired because it is not allowed
Genesis 2:17, 'but of the tree of the knowledge of good and evil, thou shalt not eat of it'

fox

a fox hole
a small space of refuge and shelter (especially in battle)
Matthew 8:20, 'the foxes have holes, and the birds of the air have nests; but the son of man hath not where to lay his head'

fruits

by their fruits ye shall know them
their true nature will be revealed by their results
Matthew 7:20, 'wherefore by their fruits ye shall know them'

garden

everything in the garden is lovely
everything is fine
Genesis 2:8–9, 'And the Lord God planted a garden ... to grow every tree that is pleasant to the sight'

ghost

to give up the ghost
to die
Mark 15:39, 'He so cried out and gave up the ghost' (refers to the use of 'ghost' to indicate one's spirit)

giant

a giant
a person whose ability and achievements exceed that of most other people
Genesis 6:4, 'There were giants in the earth in those days'

to take a giant step forward
to make a significant advance
Genesis 6:4, 'There were giants in the earth in those days'

gird

to gird up one's loins
to get ready for action
Job 38:3 'Gird up thy loins now like a man'

gnash

to gnash one's teeth
to express frustration
Matthew 8:12, 'There shall be weeping and gnashing of teeth'

gnat

to strain at a gnat

to be scrupulous about trifles

Matthew 23:23, '… that strain at a gnat, and swallow a camel'

God

the mills of God grind slowly

retribution might be delayed but is inevitable

Friedrich von Logau (1604–55), *Sinngedichte* (translated by H. W. Longfellow), 'Though the mills of God grind slowly, yet they grind exceeding small; though with patience he stands waiting, with exactness grinds he all'

to put the fear of God into someone

to frighten a person into behaving properly

Ecclesiastes 12:13, 'Fear God, and keep his commandments; for this is the whole duty of man'

god

a little tin god

a petty tyrant

godforsaken

godforsaken

dismal and without any redeeming feature

gods

to be in the lap of the gods

to be a matter of apparent chance beyond human control

refers to wax tablets inscribed with requests and placed on the knees of statues of Greek gods

Goliath

a David and Goliath battle

a struggle between two parties who are not evenly matched

refers to *1 Samuel* 17:23 ff

a Goliath

a giant or a person whose ability and achievements exceed that of most other people

refers to *1 Samuel* 17:23 ff

Gomorrah

a Sodom and Gomorrah

a place of vice

Genesis 18:20, 'Sodom and Gomorrah … their sin is very great'

gospel

to spread the gospel

to propagate principles or attitudes that one believes to be true

Mark 16:15, 'Go ye into the world and preach the gospel to every creature'

to take something as gospel

to believe that something is true

grapes

that is just sour grapes

those are disparaging remarks made only because that person is peeved and resentful at someone else's better fortune

derived from Aesop's fable of 'the fox and the grapes' about expressing deliberate disparagement of a desired but unattainable object; 'sour grapes' also occurs in *Ezekiel* 18:2, 'the fathers have eaten sour grapes, and the children's teeth are set on edge'

greener

distant fields look greener

activities of which one has no experience seem more attractive than is really the case

Psalms 23:1, 'The Lord is my shepherd … he shall feed me in a green pasture'

to move on to greener pastures

to move to a better environment; to commence a new, better career

Psalms 23:1, 'The Lord is my shepherd: therefore can I lack nothing. he shall feed me in a green pasture: and lead me forth beside the waters of comfort'

guiding

guiding light

a principle or example to follow in any activity

Exodus 13:21, 'And the Lord went before them by day in a pillar of a cloud, to lead them the way; and by night in a pillar of fire, to give them light'

gulf

to bridge a gulf

to overcome a wide divergence in views

Luke 16:26, 'Between us and you there is a great gulf fixed'

hair

to make someone's hair stand on end

to give a person shocking news

Job 4:15, 'Then a spirit passed before my face; the hair of my flesh stood up';

Shakespeare, *Hamlet* I:v, 'would harrow up thy soul ... and each particular hair to stand an end'

hair

hair-raising
scary
Job 4:15, 'Then a spirit passed before my face; the hair of my flesh stood up'; Shakespeare, *Hamlet* I:v, 'would harrow up thy soul ... and each particular hair to stand an end'

not to touch a hair on someone's head
not to harm a person
Matthew 10:30, 'the very hairs of your head are all numbered'

not to turn a hair
to remain composed

to a hair
exactly
Matthew 10:30, 'the very hairs of your head are all numbered'

to make someone's hair stand on end
to give a person shocking news
Job 4:15, 'Then a spirit passed before my face; the hair of my flesh stood up'; Shakespeare, *Hamlet* I:v, 'would harrow up thy soul ... and each particular hair to stand an end'

to wear a hair shirt
to practise self-discipline
refers to a shirt worn next to the skin by ascetics and penitent persons

hand

one's right-hand person
one's chief aide
Hebrews 1:1, 'His son ... by whom he also made the worlds ... sat down on the right hand of the majesty in heaven'

the left hand does not know what the right hand is doing
a person or an organisation is not aware of inconsistencies in conduct
Matthew 6:3, 'But when you give alms, do not let your left hand know what your right hand is doing'

to hold the power to do something in the hollow of one's hand
to have the right to make crucial decisions
Isaiah 40:12, ' ... who hath measured the waters in the hollow of his hand ... '

to put one's hand to the plough
voluntarily to undertake some task
Luke 9:62. 'No man, having put his hand to the plough, and looking back, is fit for the Kingdom of God'

with a high hand
arrogantly
Exodus 14: 8 'And the children of Israel went out with an high hand'

hands

to be in someone's hands
to be being dealt with by someone with the necessary authority
Ecclesiasticus 2:11, 'We will fall into the hands of the Lord, and not into the hands of men: for as his majesty is, so is his mercy'

to be out of someone's hands
to be up for decision by a different person
Ecclesiasticus 2:11, 'We will fall into the hands of the Lord, and not into the hands of men: for as his majesty is, so is his mercy'

to have blood on one's hands
to be the person responsible for someone else's predicament
Matthew 27:24, 'He [Pilate] took water and washed his hands in full view of the crowd. "My hands are clean of this man's blood," he declared'

to have clean hands
to be innocent or to act ethically
Matthew 27:24, 'He [Pilate] took water and washed his hands in full view of the crowd. "My hands are clean of this man's blood," he declared'

to wash one's hands of something
emphatically to decline future responsibility
Matthew 27:24, 'He [Pilate] took water and washed his hands in full view of the crowd. "My hands are clean of this man's blood," he declared'

hard-hearted

hard-hearted
unsympathetic
Exodus 7:3, ' ... and I will harden Pharaoh's heart'

harvest

harvest
end result of labour
Matthew 8:37, 'The harvest truly is plenteous, but the labourers are few'

heart

heart and soul
with great energy
Matthew 22:36–40, 'Thou shalt love the Lord thy God with all thy heart and with all thy soul and with all thy mind'

to be someone after one's own heart
to be a person who shares one's beliefs
1 Samuel 13:14 'A man after his own heart'

to break someone's heart
to act in a way causing great upset to another person
Psalms 69:21, 'Thy rebuke hath broken my heart; I am full of heaviness'; Shakespeare *Hamlet* I:ii, 'But break my heart … ')

to search one's heart
to seek after one's innermost feelings and motivations
Jeremiah 17:10, 'I, the Lord, search the heart … to give every man according to his ways, and according to the fruit of his doings'

heartbreak

heartbreak
despair
Psalms 69:21, 'Thy rebuke hath broken my heart; I am full of heaviness'; Shakespeare *Hamlet* I:ii, 'But break my heart … '

heartburn

heartburn
distress or regret at some disappointment
originally referred to passion, as in *Luke* 24:32, 'Did not our hearts burn within us, while he talked with us by the way?'

hearted

hard-hearted
unsympathetic
Exodus 7:3, ' … and I will harden Pharaoh's heart'

open-hearted
cordial
Ecclesiasticus 8:19, 'Open not thine heart to every man'

heaven

heaven help you!
you are in trouble
Psalms 121:1, 'My help cometh even from the Lord: who hath made heaven and earth'

heaven only knows
it is not known to me or anyone else

manna from heaven
unexpected benefits
derived from Hebrew *man-hu* ('what is this?'); *Exodus* 16:15, 'It is manna: for they wist not what it was. And Moses said unto them: this is the bread which the Lord hath given you to eat'

to be in a seventh heaven
to be ecstatically happy in a state of bliss
refers to the highest state of heavenly bliss in Judaism, Christianity, and Islam

to move heaven and earth
to do everything possible
Revelation 21:1, 'And I saw a new heaven and a new earth, for the first heaven and the first earth had passed away'; a reference to the apocalyptic vision of the greatest possible change to all creation

to reek to high heaven
to be patently unethical
Shakespeare, *Hamlet* III:iii, 'O! my offence is rank, it smells to heaven'

hell

all hell broke loose
great confusion erupted
John Milton (1608–74) *Paradise Lost*, 'Wherefore with thee came not all hell broke loose?'

come hell or high water
regardless of the difficulties or obstacles

on a cold day in hell
never

to be hell bent on something
to be very determined to achieve something, regardless of the adverse consequences

to frighten hell out of someone
to cause great alarm to a person

to give someone hell
to make life extremely difficult for a person

to have a snowflake's chance in hell
to have no hope or possibility at all

to raise merry hell

to cause an uproar by outlandish, reckless, or larrikinish behaviour

in the eighteenth century there were clubs of reckless young men, known as 'hell-fire clubs', who were said to 'raise merry hell'

hen

a mother hen

an over-protective person

Matthew 12:37, 'Even as a hen gathereth her chickens under her wings'

heresy

heresy

views different from those held by the majority

originally referred only to church orthodoxy, but now generalised metaphorical use

hog

to go the whole hog

to do something very thoroughly

origin uncertain; alternative explanations include: (i) Muslim divines attempting to ascertain how much of the whole hog could be eaten according to Islamic law (Cowper, 1779, 'but for one piece they thought it hard/from the whole hog to be debarred'); (ii) colloquial term for a shilling — that is, to spend the whole hog (or shilling) at one time; (iii) refers to the close shearing of lambs

holy

an unholy alliance

a working relationship for a nefarious purpose between unlikely partners

search for the Holy Grail

work towards a difficult goal

refers to a vessel or platter supposedly used by Christ at the Last Supper and featuring in the Arthurian legends

holier

a holier-than-thou attitude

excessive righteousness

honey

a land of milk and honey

a country in which everything is in abundant supply

Exodus 3:8, ' … to bring them up out of that land unto a good land … flowing with milk and honey'

house

to put one's house in order

to fix up the deficiencies in one's affairs

Isaiah 38:1, 'Set thine house in order; for thou shalt die and not live'

hymnal

to all sing from the same hymnal

to act consistently with each other

refers to a book of hymns

imprimatur

imprimatur

confirmation that something is in order

Latin, 'let it be printed'; refers to the formal ruling given by a Roman Catholic bishop authorising the publication of a book on religion or morals

inn

no room at the inn

no available space

Luke 2:7, 'She [Mary] brought forth her firstborn son, and wrapped him in swaddling clothes, and laid him in a manger; because there was no room for them in the inn'

ivory

to be in an ivory tower

to be immersed in theoretical considerations and ignorant of the practical realities

Song of Solomon 7:4, 'Thy neck is as a tower of ivory'

Jeremiah

Jeremiah

a person who looks on the gloomy side of everything

refers to the prophet Jeremiah in the Old Testament

Jericho

walls of Jericho

something seemingly solid but actually destructible

Joshua 6:20, 'When the priests blew with the trumpets … the wall fell down flat'

Jezebel

a Jezebel

a wicked shameless woman, especially one who wears heavy make-up

2 Kings 9:30, 'Jezebel heard of it; and she painted her face, and tired her head'

Job

something would try the patience of Job

something is very vexatious

James 5:11, 'Ye have heard of the patience of Job'

Judas

to play Judas

to betray a person

Matthew 26:14, 16, 'Then one of the twelve, called Judas Iscariot ... sought opportunity to betray him'

juggernaut

juggernaut

large overpowering force

Sanskrit: 'world protector'; a title of Krishna in Hinduism

keepers

keepers of the flame

persons entrusted to maintain old traditions and keen to do so

refers to those entrusted with keeping a sacred flame of remembrance alight

kosher

to be kosher

to fulfil all requirements

refers to food complying with all aspects of Jewish religious law; Hebrew *kaser* ('fit, proper')

lamb

a lamb led to slaughter

a naVve person allowing himself or herself to be exploited

Isaiah 53:5, 'He was oppressed, and he was afflicted, yet he opened not his mouth: he is brought as a lamb to the slaughter'

sacrificial lamb

somebody unfairly made to suffer for the mistakes of others

Exodus 29:41, 'Sacrifice the other lamb at twilight ... an offering made to the Lord by fire'

leaf

to take a leaf out of someone's book

to model oneself on another person

refers to taking a page from the 'Book of Life' — *Rev* 20: 12, 'and the books were opened ... and the dead were judged out of those things that were written in the books, according to their works'

to turn over a new leaf

to reform

refers to turning over a page in the 'Book of Life' — *Rev* 20: 12, 'and the books were opened ... and the dead were judged out of those things that were written in the books, according to their works'

leopard

a leopard cannot change its spots

each person is born with certain unalterable characteristics

Jeremiah 13:23, 'Can the Ethiopian change his skin, or the leopard his spots?'

light

guiding light

a principle or example to follow in any activity

Exodus 13:21, 'And the Lord went before them by day in a pillar of a cloud, to lead them the way; and by night in a pillar of fire, to give them light'

to hide one's light under a bushel

to keep others in ignorance of one's skills and experience

Luke 11:33, 'No man, when he hath lighted a candle, putteth it in a secret place, neither under a bushel'

shining light

eminent or scholarly person

John 5:35, 'He [John the Baptist] was a burning and a shining light'

to be the leading light

to be the most important person in a venture

Exodus 13:21, 'And the Lord went before them by day in a pillar of a cloud, to lead them the way; and by night in a pillar of fire, to give them light'

to see the light

to understand the real situation

refers to the conversion of Saul (Paul) on the road to Damascus, *Acts* 9:3, 4 'And suddenly there shined round about him a light from heaven: and he fell to the earth'

limbo

to be in limbo

to have one's ultimate fate yet to be determined

refers to the region (in Christian belief) on the border of hell; neither heaven nor hell

to consign something to limbo

to consider something as being in a temporary state of inaction pending future developments

refers to the region (in Christian belief) on the border of hell; neither heaven nor hell

lion

to beard the lion in his den

to tackle a daunting opponent in that person's own familiar surroundings

Sir Walter Scott (1771–1832), *Marmion*, 'And darest thou then to beard the lion in his den ... ' (probably a reference to the story of Daniel in the den of lions as related in *Daniel* 6:16)

man

he is your man

he conforms to an ideal

Ev. S. Joann. 19:5 (Vulgate Bible): *Ecce Homo* ('Behold the man')

mantle

to assume someone's mantle

to take over another person's role

refers to the passing of Elijah's mantle to Elisha: *2Kings* 2:13, 'He took up also the mantle of Elijah that fell from him ... '

meat

to be meat and drink

to be very pleasurable; or to be basic, familiar, and essential to one's experience of life'

Matthew 25:35, 'For I was an hungred, and ye gave me meat: I was thirsty and ye gave me drink'; Shakespeare, 'It is meat and drinke to me to see a clowne'

Mecca

a Mecca for something

a place at which supporters of something congregate

refers to the birthplace of the prophet Muhammad

mite

not a mite

not at all

refers to a coin of small value — *Mark* 12:42, 'A certain poor widow ... threw in two mites, which make a farthing'

mote

a mote in someone's eye

a fault in another person that is trifling in comparison with an unrecognised major fault in oneself

Matthew 7:3, 'Why beholdest thou the mote that is in thy brother's eye, but considerest not the beam that is in thine own eye?'

Muhammad

if the mountain will not come to Muhammad then Muhammad will go to the mountain

on recognising that one has insufficient power to effect one's most desired solution one decides to make do with the next best alternative

refers to the story of Muhammad humbly submitting to the greater power of God when Mt Safa did not obey the prophet's command to come to him

mumbo

mumbo jumbo

blatant nonsense

refers to a deity worshipped by primitive tribes

narrow

to be on the straight and narrow

to be completely virtuous

Matthew 7:14, 'Strait is the gate, and narrow is the way, which leadeth unto life'

numbered

one's days are numbered

one is about to be abolished

Daniel 5:26, 'God hath numbered thy kingdom, and finished it'

olive

to hold out an olive branch

to make peace overtures

the olive branch was recognised as a symbol of peace and prosperity in many ancient civilisations; *Genesis* 8:11, 'And the dove came in to him in the evening; and lo, in her mouth was an olive leaf plucked off: so Noah knew that the waters were abated off the earth'

overshadow

to overshadow

to cover or obscure with a greater power; to make less important

Luke 1:35, 'And the power of the highest shall overshadow thee'

pancake

every Pancake Tuesday

only on occasions

refers to Shrove Tuesday, when pancakes are traditionally eaten

paradise

to live in a fool's paradise
to delude oneself into a state of happy contentment when reality is quite different

parish

parish pump issues
issues of local importance lacking a wider perspective
refers to the local parish water pump

parochial

parochial
narrow-minded
refers to parish or local issues

Peter

to rob Peter to pay Paul
to discharge one debt or responsibility by incurring another
John Wyclif (c.1380), *Select Works* III 174, 'How should God approve that you rob Peter, and give this robbery to Paul in the name of Christ?' (perhaps refers to an ecclestiastical property dispute between two churches)

petrified

to be petrified
to be made immobile with fear
refers to Greek *petros* (Latin: *petra*) = 'stone'; *Matthew* 16:18, 'Thou art Peter, and upon this rock I will build my church'

plough

to put one's hand to the plough
voluntarily to undertake some task
Luke 9:62. 'No man, having put his hand to the plough, and looking back, is fit for the Kingdom of God'

point

to point the bone at someone
to accuse a person
an Australian Aboriginal method of applying a curse

pontificate

to pontificate
to speak as if with great authority and with an assumed air of infallibility
refers to the pope (or pontiff)

pottage

to sell one's birthright for a mess of pottage
through foolishness to exchange something of substance for something of little value
Genesis 25:34, 'Then Jacob gave Esau bread and pottage of lentils ... thus Esau despised his birthright'

prayer

on a wing and a prayer
reliance on the merest chance in a desperate situation'
also applied to an emergency landing by an aircraft; originally a song (1943) by H. Adamson

the answer to a maiden's prayer
an unexpected but very welcome happening

preach

to preach to the converted
to say something to those who already believe in it

priest

the high priest of something
the leading advocate of something
refers to religious leaders

race

your race is run
you have had your opportunity
Hebrews 12:1, 'Let us run ... the race that is set before us'

reap

to reap as one has sown
to experience the consequences of one's own actions
Galatians 6:7, 'Whatsoever a man soweth, that shall he also reap'

to reap the whirlwind
to suffer the adverse consequences of a bad act
Hosea 8:7, 'They have sown the wind, and they shall reap the whirlwind'

to sow the wind and reap the whirlwind
to make bad mistakes and to suffer the even worse consequences
Hosea 8:7, 'They have sown the wind, and they shall reap the whirlwind'

reed

to be a broken reed
to be a weak and unreliable person
Isaiah 36:6 and *2 Kings* 18:21, 'Lo, thou trustest in the staff of this broken reed,

on Egypt; whereon if a man lean, it will go into his hand and pierce it'

religiously

religiously
conscientiously

right

one's right-hand person
one's chief aide
Hebrews 1:1, 'His son … by whom he also made the worlds … sat down on the right hand of the majesty in heaven'

rule

to rule with a rod of iron
to keep strict discipline
Psalms 2:9, 'Thou shalt break them with a rod of iron; thou shalt dash them in pieces like a potter's vessel'

sackcloth

to wear sackcloth and ashes
humbly to demonstrate repentance
Esther 4:3, 'There was great mourning … and many lay in sackcloth and ashes'

sacred

a sacred cow
an institution, person, idea, custom, etc. treated as being immune from criticism and change
refers to Hindu veneration of the cow

a sacred trust
a moral obligation

nothing is sacred
nothing is safe from interference

sacrificial

sacrificial lamb
somebody unfairly made to suffer for the mistakes of others
Exodus 29:41, 'Sacrifice the other lamb at twilight … an offering made to the Lord by fire'

saint

a saint
a very good person

to have the patience of a saint
to endure annoyances with particular calm

salt

the salt of the earth
special people who make a vital contribution to society
Matthew 5:13, 'Ye are the salt of the earth'

Samaritan

a good Samaritan
a person going out of that person's way to do a kindness to others
Luke 10:33, 'But a certain Samaritan, as he journeyed, came where he was: and when he saw him, he had compassion on him'

scapegoat

a scapegoat
a person who is forced to take the blame for something not that person's fault
Leviticus 16:10, 'But the goat, on which the lot fell to be the scapegoat … to make an atonement'

scripture

the devil can cite scripture for his purpose
a person can quote a respectable or hostile authority while advocating a disreputable cause of that person's own
Shakespeare, *The Merchant of Venice* I:ii, 'The devil can cite scripture for his purpose'

seamless

seamless
unified, continuous, uninterrupted, imperceptible
John 19: 23, ' … and also his [Jesus'] coat; now the coat was seamless, woven from the top throughout'

search

search for the Holy Grail
work towards a difficult goal
refers to a vessel or platter supposedly used by Christ at the Last Supper and featuring in the Arthurian legends

to search one's heart
to seek after one's innermost feelings and motivations
Jeremiah 17:10, 'I, the Lord, search the heart … to give every man according to his ways, and according to the fruit of his doings'

separate

to separate the sheep from the goats
to distinguish between the worthy and the unworthy

Matthew 25:32, 'and he shall separate them one from one another, as a shepherd divideth his sheep from the goats'

to separate the wheat from the chaff

to separate the worthy from the unworthy

Matthew 3:12, 'His winnowing fork is in his hand, and he will clear his threshing floor and gather his wheat into the granary, but the chaff he will burn with unquenchable fire'

sheep

to be a wolf in sheep's clothing

to be a hypocrite; to be dangerous although masquerading as something harmless

Matthew 7:15, 'Beware of false prophets, which come to you in sheep's clothing, but inwardly they are ravening wolves'

to separate the sheep from the goats

to distinguish between the worthy and the unworthy

Matthew 25:32, 'and he shall separate them one from one another, as a shepherd divideth his sheep from the goats'

shibboleth

a shibboleth

a doctrine once held as essential but now abandoned as having outlived its usefulness

refers to a word used as a test to determine to which tribe an Israelite belonged; *Judges* 12:6, 'Say now 'shibboleth': and he said 'sibboleth', for he could not ... pronounce it right'

shirt

so-and-so would give you the shirt off his or her back

so-and-so is very generous

Luke 6:29 (RSV), '... and from him who takes away your coat do not withhold even your shirt'

to put one's shirt on something

to invest heavily in some speculative venture

Luke 6:29 (RSV), '... and from him who takes away your coat do not withhold even your shirt'

shrift

to give someone short shrift

to be impatient with a person; to give a person little of one's time

'shrift' refers to prescribing penance and giving absolution after a confession; hence 'short shrift' refers to the brevity of the penance and absolution pronounced by a priest after a confession by a condemned person just before an execution

silver

to have a silver tongue

to be eloquent

Proverbs 10:20, 'The tongue of the just is as choice silver: the heart of the wicked is little worth'

sins

for one's sins

by way of punishment, as it were

sky

the sky fell in

a very serious problem arose

Matthew 24:29, 'Immediately after the distress of those days the sun will be darkened, and the moon will not give its light; the stars will fall from the sky, and the heavenly bodies will be shaken'

smooth

to smooth the path for someone

to use one's influence to make arrangements so that a person's task will be easier or more readily accomplished

Isaiah 40:3, 'Prepare ye the way of the Lord; make smooth in the desert a highway for our God'

Sodom

a Sodom and Gomorrah

a place of vice

Genesis 18:20, 'Sodom and Gomorrah ... their sin is very great'

Solomon

to need the wisdom of Solomon

to require great sagacity when faced with a difficult decision

refers to King Solomon's ingenious solution to an apparently insoluble dilemma as described in *1 Kings* 3:16–28

soul

a soul brother

a person of similar ideals

a soul-searching exercise

a deep and penetrating examination of personal motives and conscience

heart and soul
with great energy
Matthew 22:36–40, 'Thou shalt love the Lord thy God with all thy heart and with all thy soul and with all thy mind'

soul-destroying
breaking the spirit or will to continue

to bare one's soul
talkatively to give a revealing insight into oneself

to be the life and soul of the party
to be the prime enthusiast for a cause
Shakespeare, *A Midsummer Night's Dream*, 'My love, my life, my soul, fair Helena!'

to keep body and soul together
barely to stay alive

sour

that is just sour grapes
those are disparaging remarks made only because that person is peeved and resentful at someone else's better fortune
derived from Aesop's fable of 'the fox and the grapes' about expressing deliberate disparagement of a desired but unattainable object; 'sour grapes' also occurs in *Ezekiel* 18:2, 'the fathers have eaten sour grapes, and the children's teeth are set on edge'

sow

to sow the wind and reap the whirlwind
to make bad mistakes and to suffer the even worse consequences
Hosea 8:7, 'They have sown the wind, and they shall reap the whirlwind'

sown

to reap as one has sown
to experience the consequences of one's own actions
Galatians 6:7, 'Whatsoever a man soweth, that shall he also reap'

sparks

to make sparks fly
to inflame or cause friction in a situation
Job 5:7, 'Man is born unto trouble, as the sparks fly upward'

spirit

kindred spirit
person with similar interests and eccentricities
John Keats (1795–1821), *O Solitude!*, 'Almost the highest bliss of human-kind, / when to thy haunts two kindred spirits flee'

the spirit is willing but the flesh is weak
the body is not up to the demands made on it–physically or morally
Matthew 26:41: 'Watch and pray, that ye enter not into temptation: the spirit indeed is willing but the flesh is weak

stones

people in glass houses should not throw stones
those who are less than perfect are foolish to criticise others
John 8:7, 'He that is without sin among you, let him first cast a stone at her' (refers to ancient condemnation and punishment of people by stoning)

straight

to be on the straight and narrow
to be completely virtuous
Matthew 7:14, 'Strait is the gate, and narrow is the way, which leadeth unto life'

stumbling

stumbling block
an impediment or difficulty preventing the easy completion of some project; OR a dilemma involving a moral issue
1 Corinthians 8:9, 'But take heed lest by any means this liberty of yours become a stumbling block to them that are weak'

sucklings

out of the mouths of babes and sucklings
(as indiscreetly revealed) the truth
Psalms 8:2, 'Out of the mouths of babes and sucklings hast thou ordained strength ... '

swallow

to be hard to swallow
not to be readily acceptable or believable
Matthew 23:23, ' ... that strain at a gnat, and swallow a camel'

sword

those who live by the sword shall die by the sword

those that are rough with others must accept the likelihood of unfavourable treatment in return

Matthew 26:52, 'All they that take the sword shall perish by the sword'

to be a two-edged sword

to involve both advantages and disadvantages of similar significance

Psalms 149:6, 'Let the high praises of God be in their mouth, and a two-edged sword in their hand'

teeth

to gnash one's teeth

to express frustration

Matthew 8:12, 'There shall be weeping and gnashing of teeth'

to escape by the skin of one's teeth

to only just avoid some disaster

Job 19:20, 'I am escaped with the skin of my teeth'

to hang on by the skin of one's teeth

to be barely surviving

Job 19:20, 'I am escaped with the skin of my teeth'

to set someone's teeth on edge

to cause a person intense irritation or discomfort

Ezekiel 18:2, 'The fathers have eaten sour grapes, and the children's teeth are set on edge'; Shakespeare, *Henry IV Pt 1* III:i, 'And that would set my teeth nothing on edge, nothing so much as mincing poetry'

Thomas

a doubting Thomas

a person who refuses to believe claims in the absence of proof

John 20:25, 'But he [Thomas] said ... except I shall see in his hands the print of the nails ... I will not believe'

thorn

to be a thorn in someone's side

to be a constant annoyance or affliction

2 Corinthians 12:7, 10: 'There was given to me a thorn in the flesh ... I will glory in my infirmities'

thorns

to wear one's crown of thorns

to have one's own difficulties

John 19:2, 'And the soldiers plaited a crown of thorns, and put it on his [Jesus'] head'

tooth

a tooth for a tooth

retaliation of equal magnitude to the original offence

Exodus 21:24, 'Eye for eye, tooth for tooth, hand for hand, foot for foot'; see also 'to turn the other cheek'

totem

to be at the bottom of the totem pole

to be in the most junior position in some hierarchy

refers to a pole with emblems or carvings having religious significance

tower

a tower of Babel

a noisy and confused assembly

Genesis 11:9, 'Therefore is the name of it called Babel; because the Lord did there confound the language of all the earth' (from which the word 'babble' is also derived)

to be in an ivory tower

to be immersed in theoretical considerations and ignorant of the practical realities

Song of Solomon 7:4, 'Thy neck is as a tower of ivory'

trembling

in fear and trembling

in a state of apprehension

Philippians 2:12, 'Work out your own salvation with fear and trembling'

trumpet

to blow one's own trumpet

immodestly to publicise one's own attributes

refers to the trumpet as an instrument of triumph; *Joshua* 6:20, 'When the priests blew with the trumpets ... the wall fell down flat'

trumpets

with a flourish of trumpets

triumphantly

refers to the trumpet as an instrument of triumph; *Joshua* 6:20, 'When the priests blew with the trumpets ... the wall fell down flat'

unholy

an unholy alliance

a working relationship for a nefarious purpose between unlikely partners

verse

to quote chapter and verse
to authenticate the information
refers to quoting the full details of a scriptural reference

vine

to wither on the vine
by virtue of changed circumstances or the effluxion of time to be no longer relevant
John 15:5, 6, 'I am the vine, ye are the branches ... if a man abideth not in me, he is cast forth as a branch and is withered'

wash

to wash one's hands of something
emphatically to decline future responsibility
Matthew 27:24, 'He [Pilate] took water and washed his hands in full view of the crowd. "My hands are clean of this man's blood," he declared'

wayside

to fall by the wayside
to be abandoned and to therefore drop out; to fail to stay the course
Matthew 13:4, 'And when he sowed, some seeds fell by the wayside, and the fowls came and gobbled them up'

weigh

to weigh two alternative propositions in the balance
to assess the relative significance of two alternative propositions
Daniel 5:27, 'Thou art weighed in the balances and art found wanting'

well

to go back to the well
to go to the original source
Genesis 24:20, 'And [Rebekah] ran again unto the well to draw water'

wheat

to separate the wheat from the chaff
to separate the worthy from the unworthy
Matthew 3:12, 'His winnowing fork is in his hand, and he will clear his threshing floor and gather his wheat into the granary, but the chaff he will burn with unquenchable fire'

whirlwind

to reap the whirlwind
to suffer the adverse consequences of a bad act
Hosea 8:7, 'They have sown the wind, and they shall reap the whirlwind'

to sow the wind and reap the whirlwind
to make bad mistakes and to suffer the even worse consequences
Hosea 8:7, 'They have sown the wind, and they shall reap the whirlwind'

wilderness

to be a lone voice crying out in the wilderness
to be the only person stating unpopular views
John 1:23, 'I am the voice of one crying in the wilderness'

word

from the word 'go'
from the beginning
John 1:1, 'In the beginning was the word'

wolf

to be a wolf in sheep's clothing
to be a hypocrite; to be dangerous although masquerading as something harmless
Matthew 7:15, 'Beware of false prophets, which come to you in sheep's clothing, but inwardly they are ravening wolves'

writing

to see the writing on the wall
to appreciate the inevitability of some event
Daniel 5:5ff, 'A man's hand ... wrote ... upon the plaister of the wall of the king's palace ... thou art weighed in the balances and art found wanting'

Science and Medicine

acid

to be the acid test
to establish something beyond doubt
refers to test for gold with *aqua fortis* (nitric acid)

to put the acid on someone

to make demands on a person
refers to test for gold with *aqua fortis* (nitric acid)

balance

to weigh two alternative propositions in the balance
to assess the relative significance of two alternative propositions
Daniel 5:27, 'Thou art weighed in the balances and art found wanting'

blow

to blow the lid off something
to expose something no matter how embarrassing this might be
to blow up
(of a person) to express rage

bread

to claim that something is the best thing since sliced bread
to have a high opinion of the importance or novelty of an invention or practice

bubble

a South Sea bubble
an unrealistic financial venture that is bound to result in total loss
refers to a notorious financial scandal involving the South Sea Company (UK) in 1720
the bubble has burst
the inevitable has occurred, or the scheme has come to ruination

burner

something is on the back burner
consideration is postponed pending further research

catalyst

a catalyst
a factor causing something to happen
in chemistry, a catalyst is strictly, a factor that facilitates (but does not initiate) a chemical reaction

chemistry

good chemistry
an ability to work closely together

circle

to try to square the circle
to attempt the impossible
refers to a classical problem in geometry, namely, to construct with a compass a square of the same area as a given circle

circuit

a circuit-breaker
an event that breaks the tension in a dispute
refers to electrical circuits
to short-circuit something
to do something, eliminating various intermediate steps
refers to electrical circuits

concrete

to set something in concrete
to make something virtually unalterable

count

the final countdown
the last stages of something
refers to the launch of space vehicles

crystallise

to crystallise
to emerge in its final form

cure

the cure is worse than the complaint/disease
the remedy involves more disadvantages than if it were not applied
Francis Bacon (1561–1626), *Of Seditions and Troubles*, 'The remedy is worse than the disease'

degree

to the nth degree
with great precision
refers to mathematics

degrees

to have more degrees than a thermometer
to be too academic
a play on the word 'degree'

denominator

the lowest common denominator
the highest level of taste found among all the members of some target audience
this mathematical phrase is used despite the fact that 'the highest common multiple' would be more logical

doctor

just what the doctor ordered
exactly right

to go for the doctor
to go all out or to make a desperate bid for something

eclipse

to eclipse someone
to make dim in comparison (in effect, to outshine a person)

element

to be in one's element
to be very comfortable in familiar surroundings or in an environment in which one can cope very readily

emollient

to be an emollient
to be a measure designed to make people more favourably disposed to one's wishes

encapsulate

to encapsulate some idea
to reduce the essential points of a complicated proposal to a small number of words

feedback

feedback
response from a target audience to those seeking to influence it
refers (originally) to the interaction between amplifiers and speakers fever

to be at fever pitch
to be in a state of excited activity

filter

to filter through to someone
(of information) to reach a person eventually

fireworks

fireworks
a spectacular display or effect (including anger, panic, confusion, etc.)

flame

an old flame
a former lover

to inflame a situation
to aggravate a situation
Shakespeare, *Julius Caesar* III:ii, 'It will inflame you, it will make you mad'

to rekindle an old flame
to inspire the reinstatement of a former loving relationship
David Garrick (1717–79), 'Kitty, a fair, but frozen maid, kindled a flame I still deplore'

flames

to fan the flames
to increase unrest

to pour petrol on the flames
to make a bad situation worse

flux

to be in a state of flux
to be subject to continuous change

focus

to bring something into focus
to put some matter into its proper context and explain its true significance

to focus on something
to concentrate attention on something

freeze

to freeze someone out
deliberately to exclude a person

galvanise

to galvanise someone into action
forcefully to shock or rouse someone into action
refers to Luigi Galvani (1737–98), Italian physiologist, whose name was applied to the shock received from a direct electric current

gravity

the centre of gravity
the natural point of importance to which things are attracted
refers to physics

to defy gravity
to go up when the expectation is to go down

hiccup

a hiccup
a temporary minor holdup

hot

red hot
urgent, and/or exciting, and/or dangerous

impetus

to have impetus
to move along forcefully

line

to take the line of least resistance
to follow the easiest course of action
refers to the route taken by the shockwaves of a buried explosive charge in reaching the surface of the earth

litmus

a litmus test

a simple examination that reveals the true state of affairs

refers to a test with litmus paper to establish whether a solution is acid or alkaline

loud

to come through loud and clear

to be well understood

refers to radio reception

magic

to be black magic

to lack any scientific or logical basis

refers to witchcraft

magnet

to be a magnet

to be an attractive person or thing to which other persons or things are drawn

medicine

strong medicine

a tough remedy

to get a taste of one's own medicine

to suffer from an initiative intended to affect only other persons

to take one's medicine

to submit to something unpleasant but necessary

meteoric

meteoric

brilliant, dazzling, rapid

microscope

to be under the microscope

to be the subject of close examination

momentum

to have momentum

to move along forcefully

pendulum

the swing of the pendulum

the alternation of prospects, fortune, or experience

pill

to be a bitter pill to swallow

to be a great humiliation or disappointment that has to be endured

to sugar the pill

to cause something to be more acceptable

planet

to be off the planet

to be extremely naVve or uninformed

polarise

to polarise

to cause people to identify themselves as belonging to groups holding opposing views

refers to electromagnetic poles

psychological

at the psychological moment

at the most appropriate instant of time

the phrase refers to the German, *das psychologische Momentum* ('psychological momentum') — thus confusing the German word for 'momentum' or 'motive' with the term for an instant of time

quantum

a quantum leap

a gigantic step forward

a term derived from quantum mechanics

scales

to tip the scales

to be a factor that, in combination with other factors, results in a particular decision that would otherwise not have been reached

refers to balance scales

shot

a shot in the arm

something to revive a person's enthusiasm

refers to medical injections

skyrocket

to skyrocket

(of a price or value) to increase greatly in a short time

spectacles

to see something through rose-coloured spectacles

to appreciate only the advantages and to disregard completely the disadvantages

spectrum

spectrum

wide range of different opinions or backgrounds

star

rising star

person making good progress in that person's career

stars

one can thank one's lucky stars
one was extremely fortunate
refers to astrology

to have stars in one's eyes
to receive a blow on the head that affects one's vision; OR to have unrealistic expectations of one's position and prospects

to shoot for the stars
to be unrealistic

Svengali

to be a Svengali
to be a person who controls another
refers to George du Maurier's *Trilby*

tangent

to go off at a tangent
to depart from the main matter under consideration and follow instead some other matter only marginally related to it
refers to a line touching, but not intersecting, another geometrical figure

telescope

to look though the wrong end of the telescope
completely to miss the point

tonic

to be a tonic
to cheer someone up

tune

to tune in
to pay attention
refers to radio reception

tuned

to stay tuned
to keep in touch for further information as it becomes available
refers to radio reception

umbilical

to cut the umbilical cord
to free a person from the excessive influence of another; OR to separate a person from an essential source of supplies

vacuum

to fill a vacuum
to take advantage of an opportunity not acted on by others

vitriol

to pour vitriol on something
to criticise something sharply
refers to sulphuric acid or to the caustic sulphates of various elements

water

to water down something
to reduce the severe impact of something

wavelength

to be on the same wavelength
to think on similar lines
refers to radio reception

to be on the wrong wavelength
to be incorrect in one's thinking
refers to radio reception

wheel

to reinvent the wheel
to waste resources doing something already accomplished

wires

to have one's wires crossed
to be mistaken about key facts
refers to a short-circuit in electrical wiring

Sex

bastard

a bastard
(by itself, or in expressions such as 'you bastard', or when qualified by pejorative adjectives) an unpleasant person; OR (in other contexts, especially when preceded by adjectives such as 'poor' or 'stupid') a person to be pitied or held in ridicule (often with elements of sympathy or endearment)

born

not to have been born yesterday
not to be naVve

to be born on the wrong side of the blanket
to be illegitimate

to be born with a silver spoon in one's mouth

to be brought up by wealthy parents

refers to the traditional gift of a silver spoon (an 'apostle spoon') to a child at baptism — the child born of wealthy parents is assured of riches from the moment of birth and thus does not have to await baptism to receive a valuable gift

birth

to give birth to something

to create or invent something

birthright

to sell one's birthright for a mess of pottage

through foolishness to exchange something of substance for something of little value

Genesis 25:34, 'Then Jacob gave Esau bread and pottage of lentils ... thus Esau despised his birthright'

emasculate

to emasculate something

to delete the essential features of something

jump

to jump into bed with someone

to enter into a joint enterprise with another person

love

to fall head-over-heels in love

to fall very much in love

to fall in love with something

to have lost detachment in assessing the merits of some matter

pull

to pull one's fingers out

to cease indolence and get on with a job with alacrity

sexy

sexy

highly marketable

Sports

back

to back the wrong horse

to have faith in, give support to, and/or invest in a project that proves to be unsuccessful

refers to betting on racehorses

ball

the ball is in someone's court

it is some other person's responsibility

refers to tennis

to be a new ball game

to be subject to completely revised rules or very different conditions

to be in the right ballpark

to be approximately correct

refers to baseball

to be line ball

to be equal or to be a matter about which it is very difficult to make a definitive decision one way or the other

refers to sport (especially tennis)

to be on the ball

to be fully informed

to be right behind the eight ball

to be in a position of extreme disadvantage

refers to US game of pool in which the ultimate objective is to pot the black ball (which is numbered 8)

to blackball someone

to reject a person as unsuitable

refers to a vote against someone by secretly placing a black ball in a box (as opposed to a white or red ball which indicated approval); the voting procedure was common in ancient Rome and Greece — hence 'ballot' (French, *ballotte*, 'a little ball')

to have the ball at one's feet

to have unlimited opportunity

refers to football games

to keep an eye on the ball

to monitor a fast-changing situation

to keep the ball rolling

to take advantage of the existing momentum or to participate actively

to keep up with the ball

to maintain awareness of a situation

to pass the ball along

to cooperate with others

to play ball

to cooperate

to run with the ball

to make the most of the opportunity

refers to rugby

to start the ball rolling

to commence and advance enthusiastically an activity

to take one's bat and ball home
as a gesture of spite to remove an essential ingredient that one has contributed to a joint enterprise, and to refuse to take any further part in its activities
refers to cricket

to throw the ball back to someone
to return responsibility for something to another person

bandy

to bandy something about
to discuss something in a light-hearted manner
perhaps from French *bander*, 'to take sides at tennis'

bar

to slide under the bar
not to arouse suspicion

base

to get to first base
to succeed in achieving the first stage in any undertaking
refers to baseball

to touch base with someone
to make an initial contact
refers to baseball

bat

off one's own bat
on a person's own initiative and without outside help
refers to cricket

to bat on
to continue an activity
refers to cricket

to go in to bat for someone
to carry out a task on another person's behalf
refers to cricket

to maintain a straight bat
to operate in orthodox fashion, avoiding risk
refers to cricket

to take one's bat and ball home
as a gesture of spite to remove an essential ingredient that one has contributed to a joint enterprise, and to refuse to take any further part in its activities
refers to cricket

bâton

to pass on the bâton
to hand over to a successor

bell

saved by the bell
rescued before disaster strikes
refers to boxing

blow

a blow-by-blow description
a very detailed word picture of some event
refers to boxing

to soften the blow
to take action to reduce the trauma of bad news

to strike a blow
to begin or resume work

bow

to draw a long bow
to state a conclusion that, although possible, is unlikely on the known facts
refers to archery

to have a second string to one's bow
to have an additional qualification appropriate to the task
refers to archery

box

to shadow box
to go through the motions without achieving or intending to achieve anything
refers to training for boxing by punching at one's own moving shadow

canter

to win the prize in a canter
to win very easily
refers to horse racing

canvas

to get off the canvas
to recover after near defeat
refers to boxing

chalk

chalk it up!
the success was unexpected
refers to scoring in a contest by making chalk marks on a score board

to win by a long chalk
to win very conclusively

refers to scoring in a contest by making chalk marks on a score board

compete

to compete on all fours with someone
to strive on equal terms
refers to the four limbs of the body

coup

to receive the coup de grâce
to be finished off by an opponent
French, 'mercy stroke'

course

to be par for the course
to be normal
refers to golf

courses

it is horses for courses
the correct means to an end needs to be chosen
refers to horse racing

court

the ball is in someone's court
it is some other person's responsibility
refers to tennis

cricket

a cricket team
eleven people

not to be cricket
to be unfair

draw

to draw first blood
to get an early advantage

duck

to break one's duck
to end a spell that had no results
refers to cricket in which a 'duck' represents no score

eleven

the second eleven
the second rank of persons who are performing a function less important than that performed by others
refers to a second-level sporting team, esp. cricket

end

to go off the deep end
to lose one's temper

to jump straight in at the deep end
to do something without proper preparation

fences

to rush one's fences
to act precipitately
refers to steeplechasing on horseback

to want to jump all one's fences at once
unrealistically to want to solve all problems at once, rather than sequentially
refers to steeplechasing on horseback

field

a field day
a very enjoyable and successful occasion

a level playing field
competition on equal terms

to be ahead of the field
to be better than one's competitors

to be in the field
to be out in the working environment as opposed to headquarters, a laboratory, etc.

to cover the field
to be comprehensive

to exhaust the field
to use up all the possibilities

to hold the field
not to be superseded

to play the field
to distribute one's favours among more than one person

finish

a photo finish
a close result in a contest
refers to horse racing

football

a political football
a political issue that is being exploited for political point-scoring and gamesmanship, rather than being debated on its merits

game

a game of poker
negotiations in which the parties try to bluff each other
refers to playing cards

a game of snakes and ladders
a series of ups and downs
refers to a board game

a mug's game
an activity that wise persons eschew
perhaps refers to the practice of representing faces (often humorous) on drinking mugs

game, set, and match
completion
refers to tennis

I'll soon stop that person's little game
that person's activities are not tolerated and I will ensure that they cease

it is just a game to someone
it is an exercise that a person does not take seriously

so-and-so is the name of the game
so-and-so is the essential element of the exercise

the game is up
the plan is no longer able to succeed

the only game in town
the only event worthy of attention

to be a new ball game
to be subject to completely revised rules or very different conditions

to beat someone at that person's own game
to outwit a person in that person's own specialisation

to give the game away
to cease involvement with some activity; OR to reveal the nature of a hidden activity or plan

to lift one's game
to raise the standard of one's performance

to play a deep game
to show cunning

to play the game
to observe the letter and the spirit of the rules; to act honourably

to stick to one's game
to confine oneself to activities in areas in which one has knowledge and expertise

two can play at that game
it is possible to retaliate

what is that person's game?
what is the significance of that person's actions?

games

don't play games with me!
do not insult my intelligence by that sort of conduct

fun and games
light-hearted amusement and games (esp. flirtatious and/or naughty)

gloves

the gloves are off
there are now no restrictions on how we resolve our differences
refers to bare-knuckle fighting before the introduction of the 'Marquis of Queensberry rules'

to take off the gloves
to fight mercilessly or to debate with great ferocity
refers to bare-knuckle fighting before the introduction of the 'Marquis of Queensberry rules'

go

from the word 'go'
from the beginning
John 1:1, 'In the beginning was the word'

goal

to move the goal posts
unfairly to alter the rules after some action (that relied on the old rules) has already started
refers to sporting games

to score a goal
to achieve an objective

to score an own goal
to make a foolish mistake that counts against oneself
refers to soccer

gold

to go for the gold
to aim for victory
refers to Olympic medals

grandstand

to grandstand
to put on an ostentatious performance designed to draw attention to oneself

greyhound

move over and let the greyhound see the rabbit
stand aside to allow things to get under way
refers to hunting with greyhounds

ground

to kiss the ground

to revere or bless the land; OR to be overthrown

guard

to catch someone off guard
to surprise a person
refers to fencing

to slip under one's guard
to cause a mistake to be made despite care being taken to prevent this
refers to fencing

guernsey

to get a guernsey
to be given the opportunity to do something
refers to the jumpers worn by members of football teams

gun

to jump the gun
to start before one is meant to
refers to a starting pistol in a race

harness

in harness
to be constrained and in work

heavyweight

a heavyweight
a person of importance or influence
refers originally to boxing

hit

to hit someone below the belt
to act unfairly towards another person
refers to boxing

to hit someone for six
to damage a person's cause severely
refers to cricket

hold

to hold someone at bay
successfully to resist an attacker
James Thomson (1700–48), *Autumn*, 'He stands at bay, and puts his last weak refuge in despair' — description of a stag

holds

no holds barred
without any limitation
refers to wrestling

hook

hook, line, and sinker
wholly
refers to angling

to get someone off the hook
to rescue a person from a predicament
refers to angling

to let someone off the hook
to allow a person to escape the adverse consequences of that person's own actions
refers to angling

hop

something is but a hop, skip, and jump away
something is nearby

horse

a dark horse
a person with unsuspected talents
Benjamin Disraeli (1804–81), *The Young Duke*, 'A dark horse, which had never been thought of, and which the careless St James had never even observed in the list, rushed past the grandstand in sweeping triumph'

a stalking horse
a pretext put forward to allow an attack to be made or an argument to be mounted
refers to a horse trained to allow a hunter to approach game (esp. fowl) without being seen; Shakespeare, *As You Like It* V:iv, 'He uses his folly like a stalking horse, and under the presentation of that he shoots his wit'

a two-horse race
a contest between only two serious contestants

a willing horse
a cheerful worker

horse sense
practical commonsense

that is a horse of a very different colour
that is a different matter altogether
Shakespeare, *Twelfth Night*, 'My purpose is, indeed, a horse of that colour'

to back the wrong horse
to have faith in, give support to, and/or invest in a project that proves to be unsuccessful
refers to betting on racehorses

to flog a dead horse
misguidedly to do something patently useless

to learn something from the horse's mouth
to get information from someone qualified to impart it

refers to the examination of a horse's teeth for an accurate assessment of its age

to look a gift horse in the mouth

to be suspicious about a benefit that has been volunteered

Samuel Butler (1612–80), *Hudibras*, 'He ne'er consider'd it, as loth to look a gift horse in the mouth'; refers to the examination of a horse's teeth for an accurate assessment of its age

horses

hold your horses!

just wait a little!

it is horses for courses

the correct means to an end needs to be chosen

refers to horse racing

to frighten the horses

to scare people off by one's ill-considered tactics

Mrs Patrick Campbell (1865–1940), quoting oral tradition, 'I don't mind where people make love, so long as they don't do it in the street and frighten the horses'

hurdle

to jump/clear a hurdle

to overcome a problem or difficulty

to jump that hurdle when one comes to it

to deal with a particular problem only when it becomes necessary to do so

innings

to have had a good innings

to have enjoyed satisfactory time and success in an undertaking; to have had a successful life

refers to cricket

jigsaw

to be parts of a jigsaw

to be elements in the solution of something complex

refers to a jigsaw puzzle

to put the jigsaw together

to solve a problem by placing together a number of separate facts

refers to a jigsaw puzzle

keeper

to let something go to the keeper

to deliberately ignore a particular incident

refers to cricket

kick

a free kick

an advantageous opportunity accorded to a person

refers to football

to kick off

to start some action

refers to football

laurels

to look to one's laurels

to be careful not to lose one's reputation for some skill

refers to laurel wreaths presented to winners of events at the ancient Olympics

to rest on one's laurels

to use a reputation for success earned in earlier times as a substitute for current endeavour

refers to laurel wreaths presented to winners of events at the ancient Olympics

to have lead in one's saddlebags

to work with a handicap

refers to horse-racing handicaps in which lead in the saddlebags makes winning more difficult

league

to be in the same league

to have comparable skills

refers to sporting competitions

leap

to leap-frog something

to overtake something, with the likelihood of, in turn, being overtaken

refers to a game in which participants jump over each other in turn

lightweight

lightweight

uninfluential

refers to boxing

to be line ball

to be equal or to be a matter about which it is very difficult to make a definitive decision one way or the other

refers to sport (especially tennis)

lurch

to leave someone in the lurch

to desert a person who is in difficulties

refers to the score in certain games — especially cribbage

mark

to be first off the mark

to start ahead of all others
refers to the starting mark of a race

to be slow off the mark
to be slow to start something
refers to the starting mark of a race

to be wide of the mark
to have a belief that is far removed from the true position
refers to archery

to hit the mark
to achieve one's object or to make the correct decision
refers to archery

to overstep the mark
to fail to observe the proprieties
refers to gaining an unfair advantage in a contest (originally the mark between two fighters)

McCoy

to be the real McCoy
the genuine article
perhaps refers to an American boxer who became world welterweight champion in 1890

neck

it is neck or nothing
a desperate effort is called for
refers to a winning margin in horse racing

neck and neck
(of contestants) with little between them
refers to a winning margin in horse racing

oar

to stick one's oar in
to intervene without invitation in a dispute to which one is not a party
refers to rowing

pace

at a break-neck pace
very fast
refers to horseriding at great speed

to set the pace
to give a lead in regard to a rate of progression
refers to horse racing and foot racing

paddle

to paddle one's canoe
to do something unaided and in one's own way
phrase first used by Captain Marryat (1792–1848) *Settlers in Canada*, ch. viii (1844)

parry

to parry some argument
to deflect some argument
refers to fencing

pedal

to back pedal
to reverse to some extent previously applied policies
refers to riding a cycle

peg

to peg out
to die
refers to the final act in a game of cribbage

to take someone down a peg or two
to humble a person (especially a conceited person)
refers to scoring in backgammon or cribbage; Samuel Butler (1612–80), *Hudibras* II:ii, 'And took your grandees down a peg'

pillar

to drive someone from pillar to post
to send a person to a series of places in a vain attempt to achieve something
originally a term from royal tennis, referring to the balls being struck and banging about structures in the (indoors) court

pin

to pin someone down
to find a person willing to accept blame or responsibility; OR to force a person to announce a decision or concede a point
refers to wrestling

play

don't play games with me!
do not insult my intelligence by that sort of conduct

foul play
treachery or murder
Shakespeare: *Hamlet* II:i, 'All is not well; I doubt some foul play'

to be in full play
to be fully operational

to find out the state of play
to ascertain the current position of some project
to play a deep game
to show cunning
to play ball
to cooperate
to play by Marquis of Queensberry rules
to act ethically
refers to regulations regarding boxing matches drawn up by John Sholto Douglas, Eighth Marquis of Queensberry (1843–83), in 1867
to play by the book
to apply the rules strictly
to play fast and loose
to ignore one's obligations, be unreliable
refers to old fairground game in which the player was cheated
to play it safe
to take no risks
to play the game
to observe the letter and the spirit of the rules; to act honourably
two can play at that game
it is possible to retaliate

players
a trap for young players
a significant likelihood of the inexperienced or naVve making mistakes

plunge
to take the plunge
to make an irreversible initial action; to commit oneself to a course of action
refers to leaping into water

points
to score points
to make a good impression
to score top points
to achieve the outstanding score; to be considered the best

pony
a show pony
a vain and ostentatious person

post
to pip someone at the post
to achieve something only just ahead of a rival
refers to the winning post in horse racing

prize
to win the booby prize
to do worse than all others
to win the prize in a canter
to win very easily
refers to horse racing

prizes
not to be here to win prizes
to be altruistic

punch
to be punch drunk
to be stupefied by repeated setbacks or bad news
refers to a form of brain damage suffered by boxers who have received repeated blows to the head
to beat someone to the punch
to get to some objective ahead of some keen rival
refers to boxing

punches
not to pull any punches
to be brutally frank
refers to boxing
to telegraph one's punches
by one's actions to give advance warning of one's future plans
refers to sending an advance message

race
a two-horse race
a contest between only two serious contestants
not to be in the race
to lack the required standard
your race is run
you have had your opportunity
Hebrews 12:1, 'Let us run ... the race that is set before us'

rein
a tight rein
strong controls
refers to riding or driving horses
to give rein to one's fancy
to let one's imagination have free scope
refers to riding or driving horses
to give someone free rein
to confer complete discretion on another person
refers to riding or driving horses

to rein in something
to keep better control over something
refers to riding or driving horses

to take over the reins
to assume control
refers to riding or driving horses

ride

to ride high
to be successful but vulnerable
refers to riding a horse while sitting high and upright — a posture likely to result in a fall

riding

to be riding for a fall
to act in a reckless manner
refers to riding horses in a dangerous manner likely to result in a fall

riding instructions
directions as to how to do something
refers to horse racing

ring

to jump into the ring
enthusiastically to join in a contest or challenge
refers to the practice of jumping into a boxing ring to make a challenge

to step into the ring
to enter a competitive environment
refers to a boxing ring

to throw one's hat into the ring
publicly to announce one's interest in some position
refers to custom of throwing one's hat into a ring to indicate a willingness to take part in a boxing challenge

ropes

to be on the ropes
to be facing defeat
refers to boxing

round

to be only round one
to be only the first of many stages
refers to boxing

rounds

to win some rounds
to be partly successful
refers to boxing

rub

there's the rub
that is where a difficulty arises
Hamlet III:i, 'To sleep: perchance to dream: ay there's the rub'; the term is also used in bowls

rules

Rafferty rules
the complete absence of rules
origin obscure

to play by Marquis of Queensberry rules
to act ethically
refers to regulations regarding boxing matches drawn up by John Sholto Douglas, Eighth Marquis of Queensberry (1843–83), in 1867

run

someone would run a mile
a person would do anything to escape that person's responsibilities

to have a dream run
to encounter no difficulties

to have a run for one's money
to at least get some enjoyment out of an otherwise abortive exercise
refers to betting on horse racing

to have to run fast just to stand still
competition is such that merely to maintain one's relative position one needs to make positive progress

to run rings around someone
to outwit another person easily

to run with something
to take advantage of some current development
refers to rugby

to run with the ball
to make the most of the opportunity
refers to rugby

your race is run
you have had your opportunity
Hebrews 12:1, 'Let us run ... the race that is set before us'

runner

front runner
person expected to win; OR someone who performs well only when holding an advantage

running

to set a hare running
to initiate an activity to achieve a related and desired effect
refers to hunting

runs

to have the runs on the board
to have a demonstrable record of achievement
refers to scoring in cricket

saddle

to be in the saddle
to be in command
refers to horse riding

saddlebags

to have lead in one's saddlebags
to work with a handicap
refers to horse-racing handicaps in which lead in the saddlebags makes winning more difficult

score

to even the score
to respond by way of retribution for some past action of another person

to score a goal
to achieve an objective

to score a hat trick
to have three successive favourable outcomes
refers to a bowler in cricket taking three wickets in three balls; such a feat being originally rewarded with the prize of a new hat

to score a point
to make a clever contribution in the course of debate

to score an own goal
to make a foolish mistake that counts against oneself
refers to soccer

to score points
to make a good impression

to score top points
to achieve the outstanding score; to be considered the best

to see the score
to appreciate the reality of a situation

to underscore something
to emphasise something
refers to typeface in printing and publishing

scratch

to be back to scratch
to have to start all over again
perhaps refers to the scratch mark in a boxing ring used to indicate an ability or willingness to fight, or perhaps refers to a starting line in a race from which competitors not receiving an advantage begin the race

to be up to scratch
to be of the required standard
perhaps refers to the scratch mark in a boxing ring used to indicate an ability or willingness to fight, or perhaps refers to a starting line in a race from which competitors not receiving an advantage begin the race

to start from behind scratch
to be faced with a handicap
refers to the starting mark (with no handicap advantage) in a race

to start from scratch
to commence something without the benefit of any past activity
refers to the starting mark (with no handicap advantage) in a race

sidelines

to sit on the sidelines
not to take part in the main action

sitting

to be a sitting duck
to be vulnerable to exploitation skate

to skate around some subject
by diversionary tactics to avoid discussing some subject

to skate on thin ice
to act in disregard of obvious danger; to require tact in dealing with a sensitive subject in conversation
Ralph Waldo Emerson (1803–82), *Prudence*, 'In skating over thin ice, our safety is in our speed'

skates

to get one's skates on
to hurry up

skittles

not to be all beer and skittles
not to be all pleasant and easy

somersault

to turn a complete somersault
to reverse one's established policy

splash

to make a splash
to create a sensation

sponge

to throw in the sponge
to concede defeat
refers to boxing

springboard

a springboard
a situation from which one is able to make a rapid advance

start

to have a head start
to have an advantage over others
refers to horse racing

to start from behind scratch
to be faced with a handicap
refers to the starting mark (with no handicap advantage) in a race

to start from scratch
to commence something without the benefit of any past activity
refers to the starting mark (with no handicap advantage) in a race

straps

to hit the straps
to really get going
refers to horses in harness

stretch

to enter the home stretch
to commence the last stage
refers to horse racing

stroke

a master stroke
particularly brilliant action

stumps

until stumps are drawn
until the end of the day's activities
refers to cricket

swim

it is a case of sink or swim
it is a case of success or failure with no other alternatives
refers to the 'testing' of so-called witches by throwing them into water to see if they would sink or swim

to be in the swim
to be a member of a group knowing what is going on

to swim against the tide
to take up a minority position

towel

to throw in the towel
to concede defeat
refers to boxing

track

track record
proven performance

tug

a tug of war
a dispute in which each protagonist desires a different course of action
refers to traditional fairground contest

turf

to be on one's own turf
to engage in one's own customary area of activity

volte

volte face
a reversal of previously held beliefs
French, 'a turning around'; the term 'volte' originally had use in both fencing and horsemanship

walkover

a walkover
an easy victory
refers to the winner walking over the finishing line for an unchallenged victory

warm

to warm up
to get ready

wicket

to be on a sticky wicket
to face some difficulties
refers to cricket

win

not to be here to win prizes
to be altruistic

to win by a long chalk
to win very conclusively
refers to scoring in a contest by making chalk marks on a score board

to win hands down
to win very convincingly
refers to a jockey riding confidently with hands low when a race is as good as won

to win some rounds
to be partly successful
refers to boxing

to win the booby prize
to do worse than all others

to win the prize in a canter
to win very easily
refers to horse racing

wooden

to get the wooden spoon
to come ingloriously last

refers to the custom of awarding a silver cup to the winner and a wooden spoon to the loser

Theatre

Abbott

to be an Abbott and Costello act
to involve two persons working together as a team

act

to be a hard act to follow
to be an impressive performance, not easily matched by the next person

to clean up one's act
to fix up the deficiencies in one's affairs

to get in on the act
to participate in some activity started by others

to get one's act together
to organise one's activities so as to make them efficient

aisles

to have an audience rolling in the aisles
to amuse an audience

barnstorm

to barnstorm
to travel around and actively promote one's cause or performance
refers to itinerant actors who performed in barns

bow

to bow out
to retire from some activity

to take a bow
to receive recognition

charade

to act out a charade
ostentatiously to pretend to be doing something; a pretence
refers to a parlour game of pretence

choreograph

to choreograph something
to organise the detail of who does what and when in a project

comedy

a comedy of errors
a series of separate mistakes in relation to some matter
refers to the title of a Shakespearean play

curtain

curtain raiser
introduction
refers to the theatre

the curtain rises on something
something is about to start
refers to the theatre

to ring down the curtain on something
to treat something as concluded

curtains

it's curtains!
this is the end!

dance

nothing to make a song or dance about
unexciting or unimportant

to lead someone a merry dance
to mislead a person
refers to the complex dances of earlier centuries when one person led another through complex steps

to make a song and dance about something
to create a fuss

danse

danse macabre
gruesome final step
French, 'ghastly dance'; now used to describe a gruesome literary or theatrical production (refers to fourteenth-century religious art depicting persons being led to the grave by death)

Frankenstein

to create a Frankenstein
to create something wicked and out of control
a reference to the fictional creator of a monster, in mistake for a reference to the monster itself; from the novel *Frankenstein: the Modern Prometheus* (1818), by Mary Wollstonecraft Shelley (1797–1851), second wife of British poet, Percy Bysshe Shelley (1792–1822)

gallery

to play to the gallery

to do something that appeals to unrefined opinion rather than something that is right
refers to the theatre

house

to bring the house down
to obtain rapturous applause
refers to the theatre

limelight

to be in the limelight
to be exposed to public attention
refers to an invention by Thomas Drummond (1797–1840) in 1826 by which a bright light was produced from combustion of hydrogen and oxygen on a surface of lime; came to be used in the theatre to beam a powerful light on one person to the exclusion of others

part

to play one's part
to cooperate or carry out one's obligations under some arrangement
refers to the theatre; Shakespeare, *As You Like It*, I:vii, 'All the world's a stage … and one man in his time plays many parts'

rehearsal

dress rehearsal
a preliminary practice or experience before the real thing

scenario

scenario
an imagined or postulated arrangement
refers to the theatre

scene

to make a scene
to create a fuss
refers to the theatre

to quit the scene
to depart
refers to the theatre

to set the scene for something
to get things ready for something
refers to the theatre

scenes

behind the scenes
out of public view or awareness
refers to the theatre

seat

to be on the edge of one's seat
to be very excited or anxious regarding what is currently happening

show

the show must go on
despite difficulties the action in contemplation has to proceed
refers to the theatre

to get the show on the road
to commence a planned activity
refers to a travelling circus

to give the show away
indiscreetly to reveal sensitive information
perhaps refers to revealing the plot of a theatre play

to steal the show
to have the maximum appeal to those watching
refers to the theatre

sideshow

a sideshow
an unimportant adjunct
refers to a carnival

sixty-four

a sixty-four thousand dollar question
a pertinent but very difficult question
refers to a radio quiz show in which an initial $1000 prize doubled with the successful answering of progressively more difficult questions

spotlight

to steal the spotlight
to become the centre of attention
refers to the theatre

to turn the spotlight on something
to draw public attention to something

stage

the stage is set
something is about to happen
refers to the theatre

to be centre stage
to have everyone's attention
refers to the theatre

to be on a world stage
to be prominent in international affairs
refers to the theatre

to stage manage something
to arrange how something happens
refers to the theatre

steal

to steal someone's thunder
to take credit for another person's good work
refers to a dispute over the copying of a machine invented by dramatist John Dennis (1657–1734) to reproduce the sound of thunder during a play

strings

to pull strings
to use one's special influence with those in a position to make favourable decisions which might otherwise not be forthcoming
refers to the actions of a puppeteer in directing the action

tricks

a whole bag of tricks
a series of articles or a series of artificial devices

upstage

to upstage someone
to deprive someone of the glory that would otherwise have been enjoyed by that person
refers to the theatre

wings

to wait in the wings
to be prepared to stay unobtrusive till the appropriate time for action arrives
refers to the theatre

Transport

alley

to be up one's alley
to be right within a person's expertise or area of interest

to rush into a blind alley
to make a precipitate move that does not lead one anywhere

avenue

avenue
method of approach

backfire

to backfire
to be counterproductive

baggage

to carry baggage
to handicap oneself

box

to be in the box seat
to be in a very powerful position to control activity
refers to the driver's seat in a horse-drawn carriage

brake

to put the brake on someone
to stop or slow down a person

buggy

the horse-and-buggy days
long ago

bus

the wheels are back under the bus
normal activity has been resumed

to jump on the bus
to join an activity already well under way

to miss the bus
to fail to exploit an opportunity

busman

a busman's holiday
leisure time spent in a way not significantly different from one's normal business activities

cab

to be the first cab off the rank
to be the first chosen or tried out

caravan

the caravan will roll on
the activity will continue

carried

to be carried away
to be excited by something imaginative

cart

to put the cart before the horse
to do things in the wrong order
Rudyard Kipling (1865–1936), *The Conundrum of the Workshops*, 'We know the tail must wag the dog, for the horse is drawn by the cart'

to upset the applecart
to engage in conduct disturbing a peaceful state of affairs and thereby to cause discomfort

class

a second-class citizen
a person not treated as an equal

to be first class
to be of the highest standard

coach

an opening wide enough to drive a coach and four through
an excellent opportunity to demonstrate the major errors or absurdities of something
the saying seems sometimes also to have referred to six horses: Sir Stephen Rice (1673–1715), as quoted by W. King, *State of the Protestants of Ireland* (1672), 'I will drive a coach and six horses through the Act of Settlement'

to drive a coach and horses through something
to demonstrate the major errors or absurdities of something
Sir Stephen Rice (1673–1715), as quoted by W. King, *State of the Protestants of Ireland* (1672), 'I will drive a coach and six horses through the Act of Settlement'

collision

to be on a collision course
to be headed for a clash with an opponent

Cook

a Cook's tour
a guided tour of inspection
refers to Thomas Cook, who established the world's first travel/tourist company, and the first commercial guided tours

Coventry

to send someone to Coventry
ostentatiously and collectively to ignore a person by way of punishment
refers to the refusal of the citizens of Coventry (UK) to have any social contact whatsoever with royalist soldiers in the English Civil War

creek

to be up the creek
to be mistaken completely

to be up the creek without a paddle
to be in trouble

cylinders

to spark on all cylinders
to work extremely well

derail

to derail some strategy
to cause a strategy to fail

drift

to drift apart
to lose contact or to change feelings once held in common

drive

an opening wide enough to drive a coach and four through
an excellent opportunity to demonstrate the major errors or absurdities of something
the saying seems sometimes also to have referred to six horses: Sir Stephen Rice (1673–1715), as quoted by W. King, *State of the Protestants of Ireland* (1672), 'I will drive a coach and six horses through the Act of Settlement'

to drive a coach and horses through something
to demonstrate the major errors or absurdities of something
Sir Stephen Rice (1673–1715), as quoted by W. King, *State of the Protestants of Ireland* (1672), 'I will drive a coach and six horses through the Act of Settlement'

driver

a back-seat driver
a person seeking to exercise control when it is not that person's responsibility

to be in the driver's seat
to be in charge

garage

garage sale
sale of miscellaneous assets at cheap prices

gear

to be in top gear
to be making excellent progress
refers to mechanics

geared-up

to be geared up to do something
to have equipment, labour, and know-how in place adequate for some task
refers to mechanics

grade

to be on the down grade
to be of deteriorating quality

to downgrade
to put into a lower category or priority

grind

to grind to a halt
to have an activity gradually cease to function despite expectations that it would continue

haul

for the long haul
as a long-term proposition

juggernaut

juggernaut
large overpowering force
Sanskrit: 'world protector'; a title of Krishna in Hinduism

L-plates

to have L-plates
to be new to a task
refers to learner's plates on the vehicle of a novice driver

lane

life in the fast lane
existence full of exciting, high-pressure activity

to go down memory lane
to reminisce

level best
making all possible effort
perhaps refers to railways

mileage

to get some mileage out of something
to benefit from something

miles

to be miles apart
to have great philosophical differences

to be miles away
to have one's mind on other matters

passport

to be a passport to success
to be a means of achieving success

pedestrian

pedestrian
uninspired
refers to travelling by foot

poles

to be poles apart
to have ideas that are very different

post

a staging post
a designated stopping or resting place on a journey
refers to the place at which the horses drawing a stagecoach were changed over

to go post haste
to go very fast
refers to urgent postal messages (originally carried on horseback)

power

under one's own power
without external help

railroad

to railroad something through
to rush people into accepting a proposal

rails

to run off the rails
to depart significantly from the intended course of action

railway

what a way to run a railway!
the way things are done is disgraceful
refers to a cartoon

ride

to get a magic carpet ride to something
to be given an easy and fortunate passage to an objective
refers to the magic carpet (of Oriental legend) that transported its owners wherever they wished

to get an armchair ride
to be given a particularly easy time

to go along for the ride
to seek to benefit from a project in which others contribute the effort

to take someone for a ride
to deceive a person

road

a middle-of-the-road solution
a solution near the middle of a range of possibilities

a road hog
an inconsiderate motorist
refers to gluttonous swine

fork in the road
time or place for decision

one for the road
a final drink before leaving

road blocks

difficulties

the royal road to success
the way of attaining success without effort

this is the end of the road for someone
a person will have no further opportunity to do something

to come to the end of the road
to come to the point where hope and endeavour are finished

to enter a long road
to commence a task that will take a long time

to face a rocky road ahead
to be likely to encounter difficulties

to get the show on the road
to commence a planned activity
refers to a travelling circus

to go down a particular road
to adopt a particular strategy

to happen down the road
to happen later

to road-test something
to try something out under real conditions

to set someone on the right road
to show a person how to go about doing something

roads

all roads lead to Rome
all alternatives will have the same outcome
refers to roads radiating from the great imperial capital to all parts of the Roman empire

to be at the cross-roads
to need to choose between several mutually exclusive alternatives

seat

a back-seat driver
a person seeking to exercise control when it is not that person's responsibility

to be in the box seat
to be in a very powerful position to control activity
refers to the driver's seat in a horse-drawn carriage

to be in the driver's seat
to be in charge

to take a back seat
not to involve oneself actively

sidetracked

to be sidetracked
to be diverted from one's main task
refers to railways

steam

full-steam ahead!
get going as fast as possible!
refers to a steam engine (especially in a ship or train)

to develop a head of steam
to gain momentum
refers to a steam engine or boiler

to let off steam
to engage in noisy or robust activity as a form of relaxation
refers to release of pressure from a boiler

to lose steam
to slow down
refers to a steam engine or boiler

to run out of steam
to lose one's energy and enthusiasm
refers to steam engines

under one's own steam
without external help
refers to a steam engine (especially in a ship)

stop

a whistlestop tour
a hurried (especially ceremonial) visit to many places
refers to a train journey

to come to a full stop
to cease activity completely

street

a one-way street
a flow of activity in only one direction

not to be in the same street as someone
not to be of comparable quality

the man in the street
the average citizen

to be in Queer street
to be in debt
origin obscure

to be up one's street
to be right within a person's expertise or area of interest

to walk in off the street

to come without prior arrangement or notification

streets

there is blood in the streets
much damage has been done to a cause

to be streets ahead
to outperform one's competitors by a wide margin

trail

to blaze a trail
to be the first person to do something
refers to marking a course to be followed by making blazes on a tree

train

to get on a gravy train
to take steps to become a recipient of benefits that are available but undeserved

to miss the train
to fail to exploit an opportunity

tram

to be on the wrong tram
to be completely mistaken as to the basic facts

truck

it fell off the back of a truck
(of an item of goods) it was stolen; (of a politically sensitive document) it was leaked to me

tunnel

to see the light at the end of the tunnel
to perceive relief at the imminent end of a period of prolonged difficulty

tunnel vision
an extremely narrow and inflexible way of considering issues

tyre

to carry a spare tyre
to be fat

U-turn

to do a U-turn
to reverse one's thinking

wagon

to be on the water wagon
to be teetotal

way

to stand in someone's way
to prevent a person achieving that person's goal

wheel

a big wheel
an important person

the squeaky wheel gets the oil
those complaining the most loudly will get their problems sorted out first

the wheel has turned
circumstances have changed and another party is now enjoying good fortune

the wheel has turned the complete/full circle
things are now back to where they were before

to be a fifth wheel
to be superfluous

to be a small cog in a large wheel
to be a relatively unimportant person in a large organisation

to put a spoke in someone's wheel
to interfere with another person's activity, so preventing its continuance

to put one's shoulder to the wheel
to make a strong effort

to reinvent the wheel
to waste resources doing something already accomplished

to wheel someone in
to bring a person of interest into discussions, plans, etc.

wheels

the wheels are back under the bus
normal activity has been resumed

the wheels fell off
the plan failed

the wheels have been turning
work has been going steadily on (contrast 'the wheel has turned')

to make the wheels go round
to cause something to happen

to oil the wheels
to make things go smoothly

to set the wheels in motion
to institute appropriate action

War and Military

ammunition

ammunition
arguments helpful to a case

armed

to be armed to the teeth
to carry many weapons
perhaps refers to carrying a knife in the teeth

armour

a chink in someone's armour
a weakness in someone's defences that creates an opportunity to do something that otherwise could not be done

a knight in shining armour
a person who comes to the rescue; a champion
derived from mediaeval tales of valiant knights rescuing those in distress

arms

to be up in arms against something
to express violent opposition to a proposal

arrow

another arrow in one's quiver
an additional reason

arrows

slings and arrows
adverse fortunes in life; hurtful experiences
Shakespeare, *Hamlet* III:i, 'Whether 'tis nobler in the mind to suffer / the slings and arrows of outrageous fortune, / or to take arms against a sea of troubles, / and by opposing end them?'

axe

an old battle-axe
a hostile woman

barrel

lock, stock and barrel
entirely
the lock, stock and barrel of a gun is the complete firearm

to look down the barrel of a gun
to be given little choice in a matter

barrels

with both barrels blazing
with great intensity

bastion

the last bastion
the only remaining defensive measure

bâton

to have a field marshal's bâton in one's kit
to be ambitious
variously attributed:
Louis XVIII (1755–1824), 'There is not one of you who has not in his knapsack the field marshal's bâton; it is up to you to bring it out' (speech to the Saint-Cyr cadets, 9 Aug. 1819, *Moniteur*, 10 Aug. 1819);
Napoleon I (1769–1821), 'Every French soldier carries in his cartridge-pouch the bâton of a marshal of France'; Mark Pattison (1813–84), 'Every private in the French army carries in his haversack the bâton of a marshal'

battle

a battle royal
a fight or argument with many simultaneous participants
refers to cockfighting

an old battle-axe
a hostile woman

to fight an uphill battle
to face difficulties or to have formidable opposition
refers to military battle

battleship

enough to sink a battleship
much more than sufficient

bearer

a standard bearer
a highly visible activist for a cause
military metaphor

bolt

to shoot one's bolt
to waste one's only opportunity; to have expended all one's effort
refers to an arrow, especially one for a crossbow

bomb

a bombshell
an unpleasant surprise

a time bomb

a source of serious problems that are certain to surface later on

to be a bomb
to be grossly defective

to put a bomb under someone
to induce a person to take some action

bombard

to bombard someone with something
to overwhelm a person with material or to assail a person persistently with words of argument or abuse

bow

shots across the bow
warnings
nautical metaphor

to draw a long bow
to state a conclusion that, although possible, is unlikely on the known facts
refers to archery

to have a second string to one's bow
to have an additional qualification appropriate to the task
refers to archery

breach

once more unto the breach
let us get on and undertake the task again
Shakespeare, *Henry V* III:i, 'Once more unto the breach, dear friends, once more; / Or close the wall up with our English dead!'

to stand in the breach
to fill a gap in the defences and bear the brunt of an attack or criticism
Shakespeare, *Henry V* III:i, 'Once more unto the breach, dear friends, once more; / Or close the wall up with our English dead!'

bridgehead

a bridgehead
an advance post set up to facilitate further access to some new market, etc.
military metaphor

broadside

a broadside
a short verbal attack
refers to all the guns situated or able to fire on one side of a ship

bullet

a magic bullet
a highly effective guaranteed remedy

to bite the bullet
to face up to the difficulties of a situation
refers to the use of biting on a bullet as a means of controlling one's reaction to pain in a surgical procedure without anaesthetic (for example, following a military battle)

to have a bullet that can be fired
to have available an effective weapon that can be used at will

bullets

a gun with no bullets
something incomplete and therefore useless for the desired purpose

burn

to burn one's bridges
to do something irreversible

camp

in our camp
in the group, representing our vested interest

camps

to have one's feet in both camps
to have good relations with two opponents

cannon

a loose cannon on the deck
a person or factor out of control and likely to cause trouble
nautical metaphor

catapult

to catapult
(of sales, etc.) to increase rapidly

to catapult to fame
to achieve fame unexpectedly quickly

catch

catch 22
a condition or consequence that precludes success; a dilemma where the victim cannot win
title of a 1961 novel by Joseph Heller in which a man pleads insanity to escape war service, but whose plea of insanity demonstrates his inherent sanity

cocked

to go off half-cocked

to act without adequate thought or preparation
refers to a gun at the half-ready

columnist
a fifth columnist
a person using a position of trust to work for a rival cause
refers to an extra body of supporters claimed by General Mola as being within Madrid when he besieged the city with four columns of nationalist forces during the Spanish Civil War in 1936

command
to be in command
to be on top of a situation

commanding
to be in a commanding position
to have a strategic advantage

corps
esprit de corps
a feeling of camaraderie and concern for the good name of some organisation of which one is a member
French, 'vital breath of a body'

cudgels
to take up the cudgels for someone
to defend a person
refers to a thick short stick used as a weapon

dagger
cloak-and-dagger activity
secret activity
originally referred to as 'cloak-and-sword' comedies (Spanish: *comedias de capa y espada*) — plays by seventeenth-century Spanish dramatists involving swashbuckling adventure; later adapted to refer to intrigue and secrecy ('cloak and dagger')

daggers
to look daggers at someone
to look at a person in a way that indicates great animosity
Shakespeare, *Hamlet* III:ii, 'I will speak daggers to her, but use none'

decimate
to decimate
to reduce in size greatly
strictly refers to reducing by one tenth — originally a punishment inflicted on Roman legions whereby one tenth of the soldiers were selected by lot and executed

decipher
to decipher something
to understand the significance of something

devastated
to be devastated
to be extremely disappointed

disaster
a pit of disaster
great and unexpected misfortune
a recipe for disaster
a certain way of achieving disaster

dispatches
to be mentioned in dispatches
to be favourably mentioned
refers to military recognition for bravery

ditch
to make a last-ditch stand
to make a brave effort to stave off final defeat
King William III (1650–1702), 'There is one way never to see it lost ... and that is to die in the last ditch' (quoted by Burnet, *History of His Own Times*,1715)

draw
to be quick on the draw
to act precipitately
refers to drawing a firearm

drum
to beat a drum for someone
to propagate another person's cause
to beat one's drum
to publicise immodestly one's own attributes
to drum someone out of some organisation
to terminate in ignominy a person's employment or membership
refers to the ceremonial cashiering in the army to the beating of parade drums
to drum-up support
actively to seek out support
to march to a different drum
to show an independent approach
military metaphor

dynamite
to be dynamite

to cause outrage or to have the potential to lead to danger or controversy

to play with dynamite

to invite trouble by virtue of one's risky conduct

explode

to explode

(of a person) to express rage

field

a field day

a very enjoyable and successful occasion

refers (originally) to an army's practice manoeuvres

a minefield

a source of great hidden danger or of difficulties not obvious at first

to be in the field

to be out in the working environment as opposed to headquarters, a laboratory, etc.

to have a field marshal's bâton in one's kit

to be ambitious

variously attributed:

Louis XVIII (1755–1824), 'There is not one of you who has not in his knapsack the field marshal's bâton; it is up to you to bring it out' (speech to the Saint-Cyr cadets, 9 Aug. 1819, *Moniteur*, 10 Aug. 1819);

Napoleon I (1769–1821), 'Every French soldier carries in his cartridge-pouch the bâton of a marshal of France'; Mark Pattison (1813–84), 'Every private in the French army carries in his haversack the bâton of a marshal'

to hold the field

not to be superseded

fire

a baptism of fire

the commencement of an operation that presents great difficulty

refers to religious ceremonial washing as an initiation ceremony; metaphorical use (as here) attributed to Napoleon III in referring to to a soldier's first battle

sure-fire

guaranteed

refers to firearms

to draw fire

to act in a way that attracts criticism

to fire a parting shot/shaft

to make a defiant or cutting gesture or remark on leaving

sometimes also referred to as a 'Parthian shot/shaft' — refers to missiles shot backwards by fleeing Parthian horsemen

to fire a salvo at someone

to present a series of criticisms to a person

refers to simultaneous discharge of firearms in a battle or as a salute (Italian *salva*, 'salutation')

to fire a volley at someone

to send a series of angry messages to someone

refers to a volley of missiles in battle; Alfred, Lord Tennyson (1809–92), *The Charge of the Light Brigade*, 'Cannon to right of them, cannon to left of them, cannon in front of them, volley'd and thunder'd'

to hang fire

to take no immediate action

refers to use of old guns in which there was a delay between ignition and firing of the charge

to hold fire

to defer criticising or attacking

to hold one's fire

to delay proposed action

fired

to have a bullet that can be fired

to have available an effective weapon that can be used at will

firing

to be in the firing line

to be among the first to be under attack

flak

to attract flak

to attract criticism

refers to anti-aircraft fire — abbrev. of German *fliegerabwehrkanone* (lit. 'aviator-defence-gun')

foot

to start off on the right foot

to commence an operation with great care to do it correctly

refers to marching

forces

to join forces

to cooperate with one another in order to achieve a common objective

fort

to hold the fort
to be in charge during the temporary absence of a superior
Philip Paul Bliss (1838–76), *The Charm*, 'Hold the fort, for I am coming'

gauntlet

to run the gauntlet
to be subjected to criticism
from Swedish *gantlopp* ('laneway') in reference to a military punishment inflicted on delinquents made to run between two files of soldiers, as used in Thirty Years' War, Holy Roman Empire, 1618–48

to throw down the gauntlet
to issue a challenge
refers to the glove worn by a knight; OFr *gantelet* (diminutive of 'glove')

ground

to cut the ground from under someone's feet
to withdraw support unexpectedly and, in the process, to cause embarrassment; OR to demolish a person's case and cause defeat, especially by anticipating that person's arguments or plans

to gain ground
to advance one's position relative to others
originally military; Shakespeare *Hamlet* IV:iv, 'we go to gain a little patch of ground'

to give ground
to make some concessions or to retreat or to concede some arguments
refers to military battle

to have the high ground
to have an advantage in moral terms
refers to military battle

to keep an ear to the ground
to be well informed as to current developments
refers to listening for distant sound by applying one's ear to the ground

to prepare one's ground
to get ready for a confrontation
refers to military battle

to stand one's ground
to maintain a stance in the face of opposition
refers to military battle

guard

new guard
changed regime

to catch someone off guard
to surprise a person
refers to fencing

to slip under one's guard
to cause a mistake to be made despite care being taken to prevent this
refers to fencing

gun

a gun with no bullets
something incomplete and therefore useless for the desired purpose

a scatter-gun approach
an effort going here, there and everywhere, instead of being properly targeted

smoking gun
damning evidence

to be a gun for hire
to be a person willing to undertake assignments for a fee

to hold a gun at someone's head
to put pressure on a person to make a particular decision regardless of that person's desires in the matter

to look down the barrel of a gun
to be given little choice in a matter

to outgun someone
to assert superiority over another person by use of more powerful devices

guns

to be going great guns
to be making very successful progress

to be great guns at something
to be very skilled at something

to bring out one's biggest guns
to use the most impressive persons or arguments

to spike someone's guns
to sabotage (or negate the effect of) an opponent's devices

to stick to one's guns
to continue to hold certain beliefs notwithstanding opposition by others
refers to military battle

to turn one's guns on someone
to direct an attack or criticism at a person

with all guns blazing
using all available devices

hatchet

to bury the hatchet
to abandon hostilities
refers to tradition of North American indigenous peoples to symbolise cessation of hostilities

to do a hatchet job
to destroy some existing activity or to ruin a person's credibility

hero

to make a hero of oneself
to do something for personal glorification

hilt

to the hilt
to the maximum extent
refers to swords

land

to ascertain the lie of the land
to establish the pertinent facts and opinions

line

to be in the firing line
to be among the first to be under attack

to be out of line
to adopt a stance not held by others
military metaphor

to fall into line
to conform with others
military metaphor

to put one's reputation on the line
to take a public stance in the realisation that there is a risk that one's reputation will suffer if one is proved wrong

to step out of line
to infringe accepted rules of behaviour
military metaphor

lock

lock, stock and barrel
entirely
the lock, stock and barrel of a gun is the complete firearm

march

in the course of a day's march
while carrying out one's normal activities
military metaphor

to march to a different drum
to show an independent approach
military metaphor

to steal a march on someone
to anticipate another person's actions and get in ahead
military metaphor

marching

to get one's marching orders
to be told to leave
military metaphor

marines

tell it to the marines
such nonsense is not believable
although now referring to a very unlikely tale, it originally applied to an unlikely tale that was, in fact, true — refers to King Charles II believing the unlikely (but true) tale of flying fish because the marines (the maritime regiment) testified that it was so

minefield

a minefield
a source of great hidden danger or of difficulties not obvious at first

order

the order of the day
the customary behaviour

orders

to get one's marching orders
to be told to leave
military metaphor

overkill

overkill
more action than really required for the purpose

packdrill

no names, no packdrill
the identities of the parties will be kept confidential to protect them
military metaphor

pan

a flash in the pan
something that begins promisingly but does not last
refers to the priming of old guns

petard

to be hoist with one's own petard
to have one's own case used against one
refers to being blown up by one's own petard (bomb); Shakespeare, *Hamlet*

III:iv, 'for 'tis sport to have the engineer hoist with his own petard'

point

to refuse point blank
to refuse outright
refers to pointing at the white spot (blank, French blanc) in the centre of an archery target

potshot

to take a potshot at someone
to make an opportunistic disparaging remark about a person
refers to shooting game for food and not in accordance with the rules of the sport

powder

to keep one's powder dry
to retain key arguments or resources in reserve for use later
refers to gunpowder in battle

prisoners

to take no prisoners
to be utterly ruthless
military metaphor

ranks

to break ranks
to identify oneself as having separate interests or views from the rest of a group
military metaphor

to close ranks
to sink minor differences in order to present a unified front to a common enemy
military metaphor

read

to read between the lines
to appreciate the true significance of something not put into words

retreat

to beat a retreat
to abandon some project
military metaphor

to retreat into one's shell
to become shy and introverted
refers to the action of tortoises and other animals when threatened

rocket

to give someone a rocket
to reprimand a person severely

to put a rocket under someone
to induce a person to take some action

to skyrocket
(of a price or value) to increase greatly in a short time

sabre

sabre-rattling
threatening war or violence

salvo

to fire a salvo at someone
to present a series of criticisms to a person
refers to simultaneous discharge of firearms in a battle or as a salute (Italian *salva*, 'salutation')

shell

to be shell-shocked
to be stunned by unexpected bad news
refers to psychological disturbance following exposure to wartime bombardment (esp. refers to World War I)

shoot

shoot!
go on, speak!

to shoot from the hip
to speak without careful assessment of the situation

to shoot one's bolt
to waste one's only opportunity; to have expended all one's effort
refers to an arrow, especially one for a crossbow

to shoot one's mouth off
to speak without thinking

to shoot oneself in the foot
to act in a foolish way and thus harm one's own cause

to shoot someone down in flames
utterly to destroy another person's arguments
refers to loss of aircraft in battle

to shoot something out of the water
to destroy something

to shoot the messenger
to blame the person who brings news of an undesired happening instead of the person really responsible for that happening

shooter

a straight shooter
a person who is frank and outspoken

a trouble-shooter
a person good at finding and then rectifying faults

shooting

the whole shooting match
the whole lot

shot

a big shot
an important person

a shot in the dark
a hopeful attempt at the unknown; a sheer guess

a siting shot
an initial move designed to establish facts for use in a later action
military metaphor

opening shot
first step in an activity expected to last a long time
military metaphor

that is a long shot
there is only a remote possibility

to be a sitting shot
to be a person whose actions make one very vulnerable to criticism

to be shot to pieces
to have one's case seriously damaged

to be shot to ribbons
(of an argument) to be utterly discredited

to beat by a long shot
to defeat very convincingly

to fire a parting shot
to make a defiant or cutting gesture or remark on leaving
sometimes also referred to as a 'Parthian shot/shaft' — refers to missiles shot backwards by fleeing Parthian horsemen

to give one's best shot
to make the best attempt possible

to have a shot at someone
to use subtly chosen words implying friendly criticism but designed to embarrass another person

to have a shot at something
to attempt to achieve something

to take a potshot at someone
to make an opportunistic disparaging remark about a person
refers to shooting game for food and not in accordance with the rules of the sport

shots

shots across the bow
warnings
nautical metaphor

to call the shots
to have the direction over a project

sights

to lower one's sights
to reduce one's ambition
military metaphor

to set one's sights on something
to aim to achieve something
military metaphor

signal

to send a smoke signal
to give an indication
refers to a means of communication used by North American indigenous peoples

slings

slings and arrows
adverse fortunes in life; hurtful experiences
Shakespeare, *Hamlet* III:i, 'Whether 'tis nobler in the mind to suffer / the slings and arrows of outrageous fortune, / or to take arms against a sea of troubles, / and by opposing end them?'

smoke

when the smoke clears
when sufficient time has passed to see what is going on

smokescreen

to set up a smokescreen
deliberately to confuse an issue by disguising its salient features

soldier

to be a brave soldier
courageously to do one's duty

to soldier on
to carry on despite difficulties

spearhead

to spearhead something
to lead a movement

spurs

to win one's spurs
to gain recognition after a period of effort
refers to the earning of a knighthood in battle

standoff

a Mexican standoff
a situation where neither of two parties is making a move
refers to poker

streets

there is blood in the streets
much damage has been done to a cause

striking

to be within striking distance
to be fairly close

stripes

to earn one's stripes
to deserve promotion
refers to military rank

sword

those who live by the sword shall die by the sword
those that are rough with others must accept the likelihood of unfavourable treatment in return
Matthew 26:52, 'All they that take the sword shall perish by the sword'

to be a two-edged sword
to involve both advantages and disadvantages of similar significance
Psalms 149:6, 'Let the high praises of God be in their mouth, and a two-edged sword in their hand'

to fall on one's sword
voluntarily to sacrifice one's position as a result of a sense of responsibility for an error
refers to suicide of Roman soldiers

to have a sword of Damocles hanging over one
to be in imminent danger despite normal activity going on all around one
refers to Damocles who had the sword of Dionysius hanging, by a slender thread, over his head — as a symbol of perpetual risk in life; the story is told in Cicero, *Tusculanae Disputationes*

to hold a sword at someone's throat
to assert undue pressure on another person in an endeavour to achieve a result that would otherwise not be forthcoming

swords

to cross swords with someone
to have a disagreement with another person

target

a moving target
an objective subject to constant revision

target
objective
the literal target is the one aimed at with arrows, darts, bullets, etc.; figuratively it refers to intangible sales targets and the like

to zero in on a target
to move directly towards one's objective

torpedo

to torpedo something
to make something suddenly ineffective
refers to genus of electric ray (fish), *Torpedo*, that has numbing effect on prey (Latin *torpere*, 'to be sluggish')

tower

to be a tower of strength
to be a person who supports and comforts another

trenches

to be back in the trenches
to be made to carry out menial tasks
military metaphor

trigger

to be trigger-happy
to be impetuous
refers to firing guns

to be quick on the trigger
to respond to something very quickly with little aforethought
refers to firing guns

trigger
factor responsible for certain events occurring at that particular time

trooper

to be a real trooper
to be a person willing to try anything

vanguard

to be in the vanguard of something
to be among the first to do something
derived from French *avant-garde* ('forward guard')

victory

a Pyrrhic victory

a win that costs more than if there had been a loss

refers to the Battle at Asculum in 279 BC at which King Pyrrhus of Epirus defeated the Romans

volley

to fire a volley at someone

to send a series of angry messages to someone

refers to a volley of missiles in battle; Alfred, Lord Tennyson (1809–92), *The Charge of the Light Brigade*, 'Cannon to right of them, cannon to left of them, cannon in front of them, volley'd and thunder'd'

war

the cold war

the unfriendly relations between the communist nations and the rest of the world

phrase first used by Bernard M. Baruch (1870–1965) in a speech before the South Carolina legislature, although Baruch said that the phrase was suggested to him by H. B. Swope, former editor of the New York *World*; Baruch, 16 April 1947, 'Let us not be deceived — we are today in the midst of a cold war'

to be on the war path

to be on the lookout for faults that can be criticised

to build up a war chest

to accumulate cash in readiness for some move

warfare

paper warfare

an excessive amount of correspondence or excessive bureaucracy

warhorse

a warhorse

an experienced and dependable campaigner in war, politics, sport, and other contests

weapons

to use all the weapons at one's disposal

to utilise all available advantages

Part III
Thesaurus

Abuse

give someone an inch and that person will take an ell
make a small concession to a person and that person will abuse it by taking much more
derived from old measure of length (ell) originally based on the length of the forearm (the Old English word *eln* being cognate with the Latin *ulna*–a long bone of the forearm)

give someone an inch and that person will take a mile
make a small concession to a person and that person will abuse it by taking much more

to feel the rough side of someone's tongue
to be verbally abused by a person

to get one's head blown off
to be abused very soundly

to get the rounds of the kitchen
(of a husband) to be subject to personal abuse by his wife

to give someone a piece of one's mind
to abuse another person

to kick someone around
to abuse a person

Achievement

a bird in the hand is worth two in the bush
a benefit currently available is more valuable than a seemingly much larger benefit that might or might not be achieved in the future

a crusade
an aggressive campaign to achieve some political or social objective
refers to the wars undertaken in the Middle Ages in an attempt to secure the rights of Christians to visit the Holy Land (from Latin *crus*, 'cross')

a feather in one's cap
a meritorious personal achievement
refers to the practice in a number of cultures of adding a feather to the headgear of a person in recognition of a significant personal achievement

a giant
a person whose ability and achievements exceed that of most other people
Genesis 6:4, 'There were giants in the earth in those days'

a Goliath
a giant or a person whose ability and achievements exceed that of most other people
refers to *1 Samuel* 17:23 ff

a milestone
a significant stage or achievement in a life or a history
refers to markers along a road indicating distance in miles

a recipe for disaster
a certain way of achieving disaster

a warm inner glow
satisfaction at some achievement
Joseph Conrad (1857–1924), *Youth*, 'the heat of life ... that glow in the heart that with every year grows dim, grows cold'

gateway to something
method of achieving something

heartburn
distress or regret at some disappointment
originally referred to passion, as in *Luke* 24:32, 'Did not our hearts burn within us, while he talked with us by the way?'

it is no use crying over spilt milk
there is nothing to be gained by lamenting over an irredeemable error

it was touch and go
there were considerable risks — - the objective was achieved, but only just
perhaps refers to the touching of the wheels of two moving vehicles

one cannot make bricks without straw
one cannot achieve results in the absence of adequate resources
Exodus 6:7 'Ye shall no more give the people straw to make bricks ... let them go and gather straw for themselves'

one would give one's eye teeth for something
a person would very much like to achieve some objective

refers to the (valued) canine teeth directly under the eye

pie in the sky
a hoped for result unlikely to be achieved

something has done the trick
something has achieved the desired purpose
refers to playing cards

the crowning point
the height of a person's achievement

the river found its mark
equilibrium between two pressures has been achieved

there are many ways to cook eggs
there are many ways to achieve an objective

there is more than one way to skin a cat
this can be achieved in a variety of ways

to achieve a flying start
to get operational very quickly

to be a passport to success
to be a means of achieving success

to be hell bent on something
to be very determined to achieve something, regardless of the adverse consequences

to be only a gleam in someone's eyes
not yet conceived, let alone achieved

to be unable to take a trick
to be unable to achieve success in anything
refers to playing cards

to be up against a brick wall
to be unable to achieve anything because of intractable opposition or apathy

to catapult to fame
to achieve fame unexpectedly quickly

to deliver the goods
to achieve the objective; to supply what is required

to drive someone from pillar to post
to send a person to a series of places in a vain attempt to achieve something
originally a term from royal tennis, referring to the balls being struck and banging about structures in the (indoors) court

to gain a foothold
to achieve a position from which further advances can readily be made

to get a magic carpet ride to something
to be given an easy and fortunate passage to an objective
refers to the magic carpet (of Oriental legend) that transported its owners wherever they wished

to get something under one's belt
to add to one's experience by achieving something worthwhile

to get the worst of all worlds
to get a series of disadvantages without achieving any corresponding advantages

to have a shot at something
to attempt to achieve something

to have one's heart set on something
to be very keen to achieve something

to have one's work cut out to do something
to have a difficult task to achieve something

to have the runs on the board
to have a demonstrable record of achievement
refers to scoring in cricket

to head someone in the right direction
to assist a person to achieve something

to heave a sigh of relief
to express satisfaction at the achievement of a solution to a difficult problem
John Keats (1795–1821), *I stood tip-toe upon a little hill*, 'born of the very sigh that silence heaves'

to hit the mark
to achieve one's object or to make the correct decision
refers to archery

to hold a knife/sword at someone's throat
to assert undue pressure on another person in an endeavour to achieve a result that would otherwise not be forthcoming

to join forces
to cooperate with one another in order to achieve a common objective

to kill two birds with one stone
to achieve a second objective in the course of achieving the first objective

to land something
to achieve something
refers to angling

to let blood
to allow some harm as the price for achieving some greater benefit
refers to surgical removal of a patient's blood

to mend fences
to achieve a reconciliation

to pip someone at the post
to achieve something only just ahead of a rival
refers to the winning post in horse racing

to pull something off
to achieve success in some enterprise

to put one's back into something
to work hard at achieving some goal

to salvage something out of the wreck
to achieve some minor benefits out of a disastrous situation
refers to shipwrecks

to score a goal
to achieve an objective

to set a hare running
to initiate an activity to achieve a related and desired effect
refers to hunting

to set one's sights on something
to aim to achieve something
military metaphor

to shadow box
to go through the motions without achieving or intending to achieve anything
refers to training for boxing by punching at one's own moving shadow

to stand in someone's way
to prevent a person achieving that person's goal

to steamroll something through
to use enormous force to achieve an objective
refers to a steamroller — a large earth-flattening machine

to throw one's cap/hat into the air
to express joy; OR to celebrate some achievement

to throw one's weight around
to assert one's real or assumed authority excessively

to walk away with a profit
to achieve a profit on concluding a project

to waste one's breath
to talk and request something without achieving anything

without any cards to play
without the means to achieve something
refers to playing cards

Activity

a backwater
a place of little activity

a busman's holiday
leisure time spent in a way not significantly different from one's normal business activities

a clarion call
a strong signal that is an unmistakable invitation to do something

a cobbler should stick to his last
a person should confine himself or herself to activities for which that person has been trained

a honeymoon
a short period enjoyed by a newcomer to some activity before that person's performance is criticised
refers to the holiday time (originally one 'moon' or month) immediately after a marriage ceremony

a logjam
a stoppage of activity caused by input in greater volume than allowed for
refers to a crowded mass of cut logs in a river

a mug's game
an activity that wise persons eschew
perhaps refers to the practice of representing faces (often humorous) on drinking mugs

a one-way street
a flow of activity in only one direction

a standard bearer
a highly visible activist for a cause

military metaphor

a watershed
an occasion dividing two distinct phases of activity
refers to the geographical division between the headwaters of adjacent river systems

across the board
over the whole range of activity

behind someone's back
in a way that deliberately conceals an activity from a person

blueprint
a master plan for some activity or a model that others can copy
refers to a detailed architectural or engineering drawing — originally consisting of white lines on a blue background

cloak-and-dagger activity
secret activity
originally referred to as 'cloak-and-sword' comedies (Spanish: *comedias de capa y espada*) — plays by seventeenth-century Spanish dramatists involving swashbuckling adventure; later adapted to refer to intrigue and secrecy ('cloak and dagger')

distant fields look greener
activities of which one has no experience seem more attractive than is really the case
Psalms 23:1, 'The Lord is my shepherd ... he shall feed me in a green pasture'

early in the piece
at an early stage of some activity

fun and games
light-hearted amusement and games (esp. flirtatious and/or naughty)

I'll soon stop that person's little game
that person's activities are not tolerated and I will ensure that they cease

in the course of a day's march
while carrying out one's normal activities
military metaphor

it is a long time between drinks
activity is occurring only very spasmodically

it takes two to tango
some activities cannot be carried out single-handedly
refers to a dance

kingmaker
person engaging in behind-the-scenes activities to promote another person to a particular leadership position

life in the fast lane
existence full of exciting, high-pressure activity

monkey business
mischievous or underhand activity

nimble-footed
quick to change the direction of one's activities when circumstances warrant

opening shot
first step in an activity expected to last a long time
military metaphor

someone's number is up
a person's period of activity or influence is about to expire; OR one is about to die

stamping ground
one's favourite place for certain activities

the bird is carved
the necessary action has been taken

the caravan will roll on
the activity will continue

the coast is clear
there are no observers to one's activity around

the wheels are back under the bus
normal activity has been resumed

the whole gamut
the whole range of some activity
refers to the whole range of notes in music

the world is one's oyster
one has enormous scope for activity
Shakespeare, *The Merry Wives of Windsor*, II:ii, 'Why, then the world's mine oyster'

to appoint a poacher to be gamekeeper
to engage, perhaps foolishly, a formerly dishonest person to a position where that person's specialised knowledge can assist the prevention of similar dishonest activity by others

to be at fever pitch
to be in a state of excited activity

to be in full swing
to be very active and going as well as possible

to be in the box seat
to be in a very powerful position to control activity
refers to the driver's seat in a horse-drawn carriage

to be in the doldrums
to be depressed or to show no activity
refers to a region of little wind near the equator, becalming sailing ships

to be in the thick of things
to get involved at the centre of some activity

to be off like a bride's nightie
to act promptly

to be on a treadmill
to be involved in some unpleasant ongoing activity that cannot readily be stopped

to be on one's own turf
to engage in one's own customary area of activity

to be on someone's cabbage patch
to engage in a competitive activity in a territory regarded by someone already there as rightfully belonging exclusively to that person

to be riveted to one's seat
to find the activity being watched very exciting and worthy of full attention

to be tied down
to have responsibilities precluding alternative activities

to be up to one's freckles in something
to be very deeply involved in something

to bow out
to retire from some activity

to call it a day
to cease involvement with some activity

to catch someone in the net
unexpectedly to involve a particular person in the course of activity designed to involve many others

to close the book on something
to terminate an activity

to come to a full stop
to cease activity completely

to do a hatchet job
to destroy some existing activity or to ruin a person's credibility

to drag someone kicking and screaming to do something
to force a person into some action that the person is most reluctant to undertake

to get in on the act
to participate in some activity started by others

to get one's act together
to organise one's activities so as to make them efficient

to get the show on the road
to commence a planned activity
refers to a travelling circus

to give the game away
to cease involvement with some activity; OR to reveal the nature of a hidden activity or plan

to go for the doctor
to go all out or to make a desperate bid for something

to go to sleep
to become inactive

to grind to a halt
to have an activity gradually cease to function despite expectations that it would continue

to gum up the works
to cause an activity to cease by preventing normal functioning of the necessary processes

to have a sword of Damocles hanging over one
to be in imminent danger despite normal activity going on all around one
refers to Damocles who had the sword of Dionysius hanging, by a slender thread, over his head — as a symbol of perpetual risk in life; the story is told in Cicero, *Tusculanae Disputationes*

to have a tiger by the tail
to be involved in an activity that is much more dangerous than one had realised

to have one's fingers in many different pies
to be engaged in a variety of separate activities

to have to run fast just to stand still
competition is such that merely to maintain one's relative position one needs to make positive progress

to hedge one's bets
to insure against a losing bet or investment by also investing on the opposite outcome
to jump on the bus
to join an activity already well under way
to keep off someone's patch
not to interfere with or compete against another person in that person's customary area of activity
to keep one's eye on someone
to supervise a person
to keep one's eye on something
to monitor a situation
to keep one's hand in
to engage in activities that reinforce skills that one has previously acquired
to keep the ball rolling
to take advantage of the existing momentum or to participate actively
to keep the home fires burning
to maintain normal domestic activity during the temporary absence of the main provider of the household
to leap in
to commence an activity without considering the wisdom of doing so or the best way to proceed
to let off steam
to engage in noisy or robust activity as a form of relaxation
refers to release of pressure from a boiler
to lower the boom
to bring to account and punish
to make a wigwam for a goose's bridle
to do something unspecified
nonsense said to children
to make sparks fly
to inflame or cause friction in a situation
Job 5:7, 'Man is born unto trouble, as the sparks fly upward'
to nip something in the bud
to stop some activity in its early stages when stopping it is still relatively easy
refers to the first signs of growth in plants
to pick up the pieces
to resume previous activities to the maximum extent possible after some setback
to plough new ground
to engage laboriously in an untried activity
to plough on
methodically and painstakingly to continue with an activity
to pull the plug
to terminate an activity suddenly
refers to electricity
to put a spoke in someone's wheel
to interfere with another person's activity, so preventing its continuance
to put something on 'hold'
to put something aside for the time being with a view to resuming activity later on
refers to the telephone
to put up the shutters
to cease an established activity
to run around in circles
to engage in excited but useless activity
to see a man about a dog
to do something unspecified
to set a hare running
to initiate an activity to achieve a related and desired effect
refers to hunting
to shut up shop
to cease an established activity
to start from behind scratch
to be faced with a handicap
refers to the starting mark (with no handicap advantage) in a race
to start the ball rolling
to commence and advance enthusiastically an activity
to stick to one's game
to confine oneself to activities in areas in which one has knowledge and expertise
to take a back seat
not to involve oneself actively
to try one's hand at something
to attempt a new activity, especially by way of experiment
to twiddle one's thumbs
not to be involved in any worthwhile activity

Advantage

a free kick
an advantageous opportunity accorded to a person
refers to football

a lame dog
a person under some disadvantage needing attention and assistance

a land of milk and honey
a country in which everything is in abundant supply
Exodus 3:8, '... to bring them up out of that land unto a good land ... flowing with milk and honey'

a mixed bag
some advantages and some disadvantages

bargaining chips
benefits that can be conceded in negotiations to obtain some advantage

leech
person taking undue advantage of others
refers to the blood-sucking activities of leeches

the boot is on the other foot
the advantage is reversed

the cure is worse than the complaint/disease
the remedy involves more disadvantages than if it were not applied
Francis Bacon (1561–1626), *Of Seditions and Troubles*, 'The remedy is worse than the disease'

the early bird gets the worm
a person who acts ahead of others gets an advantage over them

the upside
the advantage

to be a two-edged sword
to involve both advantages and disadvantages of similar significance
Psalms 149:6, 'Let the high praises of God be in their mouth, and a two-edged sword in their hand'

to be in a commanding position
to have a strategic advantage

to be quick on one's feet
cleverly to take advantage of a situation

to be right behind the eight ball
to be in a position of extreme disadvantage
refers to US game of pool in which the ultimate objective is to pot the black ball (which is numbered 8)

to cut both ways
to involve both advantages and disadvantages of similar significance

to draw first blood
to get an early advantage

to expose one's flank
to leave oneself open to the possibility of having advantage taken

to feather one's own nest
improperly to appropriate things for oneself (especially in financial transactions)

to fill a vacuum
to take advantage of an opportunity not acted on by others

to gain the upper hand
to attain, after some effort, an advantage over another person

to get the jump on someone
to get an advantage over a person

to get the worst of all worlds
to get a series of disadvantages without achieving any corresponding advantages

to give someone the edge
to give a person an advantage over others

to have a head start
to have an advantage over others
refers to horse racing

a leading edge
an advantage through possession of the latest technology or knowledge
refers to the foremost edge of an aircraft's wings

to have someone over a barrel
to take advantage of someone's weakened position in relation to oneself

to have the high ground
to have an advantage in moral terms
refers to military battle

to hijack a debate
to involve oneself in discussion on some matter and turn that discussion to one's advantage

to jump at the opportunity

enthusiastically to take immediate advantage of a good chance

to keep the ball rolling
to take advantage of the existing momentum or to participate actively

to kick a man when he is down
to take unfair advantage of a person already in difficulty

to make a rod for one's own back
to make a handicap for oneself

to play right into someone's hands
to act so as to give a person an unintended advantage

to run with something
to take advantage of some current development
refers to rugby

to see something through rose-coloured spectacles
to appreciate only the advantages and to disregard completely the disadvantages

to squeeze the last drop out of something
to get the maximum advantage out of some favourable situation

to squeeze the lemon dry
to get the maximum advantage out of some favourable situation
Sir Eric Geddes (1875–1937), 'The Germans ... are going to pay every penny; they are going to be squeezed, as a lemon is squeezed — until the pips squeak. My only doubt is not whether we can squeeze hard enough, but whether there is enough juice.' (10 December 1918)

to strike while the iron is hot
to take advantage of a situation that cannot last
refers to the work of blacksmiths and farriers; John Dryden (1631–1700), *Aenis*, 'We must beat the iron while it is hot, but we may polish it at leisure'

to take something lying down
to accept a disadvantage without protest

to take up the slack
to take advantage of surplus capacity
refers to working with ropes

to throw out the baby with the bathwater
to discard a major benefit in the course of obtaining a comparatively minor advantage

to use all the weapons at one's disposal
to utilise all available advantages

to want the best of both worlds
unreasonably to desire to get some advantage without incurring a corresponding disadvantage

what one loses on the swings one gains on the roundabouts
there are advantages and disadvantages that offset each other
Patrick Reginald Chalmers (1872–1942), *Green Days and Blue Days: Roundabouts and Swings*, 'what's lost upon the roundabouts we pulls up on the swings!'

Agreement

a bone of contention
the subject matter of violent disagreement
probably refers to dogs fighting over a bone

a sweetheart deal
an agreement negotiated in private to the special benefit of those involved in the negotiations

bedfellow
collaborator

that washes with me
I agree

to be an Abbott and Costello act
to involve two persons working together as a team

to be at odds with someone
to disagree with a person

to be of one mind
(of several people) to be agreed

to come to the party
to agree to someone's terms

to add/compare apples with oranges
to lump unconnected things together quite illogically

to compare apples with apples
to make a valid comparison

to cross swords with someone

to have a disagreement with another person
to lock someone into some arrangement
to create an agreement which cannot be broken by one of the parties
to ram something down someone's throat
to pressure another person into accepting an idea with which that person does not agree
to see eye to eye with someone
to agree
Isaiah 52:8, 'For they shall see eye to eye, when the Lord shall bring again Zion'
to set the seal on something
to confirm absolutely that something is agreed
to sign on the dotted line
to confirm one's agreement

Aim

a crusade
an aggressive campaign to achieve some political or social objective
refers to the wars undertaken in the Middle Ages in an attempt to secure the rights of Christians to visit the Holy Land (from Latin *crus*, 'cross')
a gun with no bullets
something incomplete and therefore useless for the desired purpose
a moving target
an objective subject to constant revision
an unholy alliance
a working relationship for a nefarious purpose between unlikely partners
any stick to beat a dog
any excuse will do if it serves one's purpose
it was touch and go
there were considerable risks —- the objective was achieved, but only just
perhaps refers to the touching of the wheels of two moving vehicles
one would give one's eye teeth for something
a person would very much like to achieve some objective
refers to the (valued) canine teeth directly under the eye
overkill
more action than really required for the purpose
something has done the trick
something has achieved the desired purpose
refers to playing cards
target
objective
the literal target is the one aimed at with arrows, darts, bullets, etc.; figuratively it refers to intangible sales targets and the like
the devil can cite scripture for his purpose
a person can quote a respectable or hostile authority while advocating a disreputable cause of that person's own
Shakespeare, *The Merchant of Venice* I:ii, 'The devil can cite scripture for his purpose'
there are many ways to cook eggs
there are many ways to achieve an objective
to beat someone to the punch
to get to some objective ahead of some keen rival
refers to boxing
to deliver the goods
to achieve the objective; to supply what is required
to earmark
to allocate to a specific purpose
refers to marking animals
to engage in pump priming
to spend public money with the aim of attracting parochial electoral support
refers to priming a water pump
to get a magic carpet ride to something
to be given an easy and fortunate passage to an objective
refers to the magic carpet (of Oriental legend) that transported its owners wherever they wished
to go down a particular track
to make decisions aimed at a particular goal
to go for the gold
to aim for victory

refers to Olympic medals

to hit the mark
to achieve one's object or to make the correct decision
refers to archery

to join forces
to cooperate with one another in order to achieve a common objective

to kill two birds with one stone
to achieve a second objective in the course of achieving the first objective

to leave someone out in the cold
to be excluded, ignored or neglected

to pull oneself together
by gathering one's faculties and strength, to rouse oneself to a renewed effort

to score a goal
to achieve an objective

to set one's sights on something
to aim to achieve something
military metaphor

to stake a claim
to indicate one's desire to obtain something
refers to placing a series of stakes in the ground as a sign of claiming a place for gold mining

to steamroll something through
to use enormous force to achieve an objective
refers to a steamroller — a large earth-flattening machine

to want something both ways
to desire two mutually exclusive objectives

to zero in on a target
to move directly towards one's objective

Alternative

all roads lead to Rome
all alternatives will have the same outcome
refers to roads radiating from the great imperial capital to all parts of the Roman empire

to be between the devil and the deep blue sea
to be faced with two equally unpalatable alternatives that cannot both be avoided

if the mountain will not come to Muhammad then Muhammad will go to the mountain
on recognising that one has insufficient power to effect one's most desired solution one decides to make do with the next best alternative
refers to the story of Muhammad humbly submitting to the greater power of God when Mt Safa did not obey the prophet's command to come to him

in another vein
as an alternative way of looking at things

it is a toss up
either alternative is equally acceptable
refers to the tossing of a coin

the horns of a dilemma
two unpalatable alternatives between which a choice must be made
dilemma: Greek for 'two assumptions'

to be at the cross-roads
to need to choose between several mutually exclusive alternatives

to be between Scylla and Charybdis
to be faced with two equally unpalatable alternatives that cannot both be avoided
refers to the voyage of Ulysses

to be in two minds
to be undecided between two alternatives

to be tied down
to have responsibilities precluding alternative activities

to fall between two stools
not to fit neatly into either of two available alternatives, and to waver between them

to have other irons in the fire
to have the opportunity to do something else as an alternative
Francis Beaumont (1584–1616) & John Fletcher (1579–1625), *The Faithful Friends* I:ii, 'It is always good when a man has two irons in the fire'

to pre-empt some issue

deliberately to do something that has the effect of limiting the range of alternative approaches to a matter
refers to the right of certain persons (originally the Crown) to buy certain things before others have an opportunity

to shop around
to explore alternatives
to signpost something
to give an indication of the alternatives available
to sit on the fence
to refuse to choose between two alternatives
to take stock
to contemplate the alternatives
to want to have one's cake and eat it too
to want two mutually exclusive alternatives
to weigh two alternative propositions in the balance
to assess the relative significance of two alternative propositions
Daniel 5:27, 'Thou art weighed in the balances and art found wanting'
variations on a theme
alternative approaches of a similar nature
refers to artistic themes

Anger

fireworks
a spectacular display or effect (including anger, panic, confusion, etc.)
I will have that person's guts for garters
I am extremely angry and dissatisfied with that person
to be a red rag to a bull
to be something that makes a person very angry and very excited
refers to the erroneous belief that the colour red, rather than the motion of waving, excites a bull
to be after someone's blood
to be keen to make a person the victim of an angry confrontation
to be purple with rage
to be very angry
to bite one's lip
to control emotion such as anger or mirth
to blow one's top
to show anger
refers to a volcano
to blow up
(of a person) to express rage
to explode
(of a person) to express rage
to fire a volley at someone
to send a series of angry messages to someone
refers to a volley of missiles in battle; Alfred, Lord Tennyson (1809–92), *The Charge of the Light Brigade*, 'Cannon to right of them, cannon to left of them, cannon in front of them, volley'd and thunder'd'
to fly off the handle
to show irrational anger
to foam at the mouth
to show extreme uncontrollable anger
refers to a rabid animal; Washington Irving (1783–1859), 'Fall down in convulsions [and] foam at the mouth'
to hit the roof
to be very angry
to jump up and down
to show excitement or anger or frustration
to kick the cat
to take out one's anger on some innocent party
to make someone's blood boil
to make a person very angry
to raise someone's hackles
to make a person angry
refers to feathers raised in anger on the back of the neck of certain birds; also, by analogy, refers to hairs raised in anger on the neck of dogs
to see blood
to be very angry
refers to a frenzy excited in some animals by the sight of blood
to see red
to become very angry

Annoyance

an eager beaver

a person with great drive and enthusiasm even if this causes annoyance to others

refers to the industriousness of the beaver, and adapted as World War II US expression for a very keen person who habitually volunteered

to be a thorn in someone's flesh
to be a constant annoyance or affliction

2 Corinthians 12:7, 10: 'There was given to me a thorn in the flesh ... I will glory in my infirmities'

to breathe down someone's neck
to cause annoyance to another person by remaining in that person's vicinity or by supervising that person too closely; OR to be narrowly behind another person in some competitive situation

to drive someone up the wall
by one's actions, to cause extreme annoyance to the point of desperation

to get on someone's nerves
by one's behaviour to cause annoyance to a person

to get someone's back up
to annoy or antagonise a person

to get under someone's skin
to cause intense annoyance to another person; OR to arouse interest in another person

may refer to the itching caused by certain parasitic creatures in or under the skin

to have the patience of a saint
to endure annoyances with particular calm

to kick heads in
to demonstrate extreme annoyance at, or dislike of, certain persons

to kick someone in the teeth
to inflict a grave or humiliating setback, criticism, or punishment upon a person

to rub someone up the wrong way
to annoy a person with actions that fail to recognise that person's current mood

Approval

a seal of approval
confirmation that something is satisfactory

to frown on something
to disapprove of some matter

to get the nod
to receive approval

to give a thumbs up
to approve or grant permission

refers to sign given by Roman emperor sparing a life

to give one's blessing to something
to indicate one's approval of something

to look at someone sideways
silently and politely to indicate one's disapproval

to shake one's head
to indicate disbelief or wonder or disapproval

Shakespeare, *Macbeth* III:iv, 'Never shake thy gory locks at me'

Argument

a battle royal
a fight or argument with many simultaneous participants

refers to cockfighting

a circuit-breaker
an event that breaks the tension in a dispute

refers to electrical circuits

a political football
a political issue that is being exploited for political point-scoring and gamesmanship, rather than being debated on its merits

ammunition
arguments helpful to a case

an argument holding water
a debating point of substance

eyeball to eyeball
confronting each other and taking account of each other's reactions

flip side

the arguments for the other point of view

mealy-mouthed
afraid of giving offence, not outspoken, hypocritical

myopia
an inability to see the longer term consequences of actions
refers to short-sightedness

not to have a leg to stand on
to have one's arguments completely demolished; OR to be without acceptable excuse or explanation

not to have any legs
(of an argument) to be unacceptable

shifting sands
arguments that are constantly being changed

that argument is wearing a bit thin
that case has been heard so often that it is losing its effect
refers to clothes or similar beginning to fail from continued use

the empty can makes the most noise
the least worthy arguments often attract the most publicity

the other side of the coin
the arguments for the opposite point of view

the thread
the connecting link of a set of arguments

to act as a devil's advocate
to put a point of view that one does not hold in order to draw out the best arguments regarding a proposition
refers to a church official vetting a candidate for sainthood (and ultimately to the testing of Job by Satan, *Job* 1:9 ff)

to argue the toss
to dispute a decision
refers to the tossing of a coin

to be after someone's blood
to be keen to make a person the victim of an angry confrontation

to be an open-and-shut case
to be an unarguable proposition

to be on shaky ground
not to have strong arguments

to be shot to ribbons
(of an argument) to be utterly discredited

to belt someone over the head
to override someone's views or arguments, often involving the use of heavy pressure

to bring out one's biggest guns
to use the most impressive persons or arguments

to buy into some argument
to seek to participate in some discussion

to confront someone head on
to meet and face up to someone in a hostile and direct fashion

to drive a wedge between two persons
to set out to cause a division between two persons
refers to the use of wedges in timber work

to expose holes
to expose weaknesses in an argument

to face the music
to accept responsibility when confronted by one's critics
refers to the theatre

to give ground
to make some concessions or to retreat or to concede some arguments
refers to military battle

to have an ace up one's sleeve
to hold an impressive counter-argument in reserve
refers to card games; from Latin *as* ('unity', that is 'one' or 'a single point')

to hijack a debate
to involve oneself in discussion on some matter and turn that discussion to one's advantage

to hold water
(of an argument) to be soundly based

to keep one's powder dry
to retain key arguments or resources in reserve for use later
refers to gunpowder in battle

to lead someone up the garden path
to mislead a person by deliberately fallacious arguments

to lock antlers/horns with someone
to have an argument with another person
refers to fighting between male horned animals

to parry some argument
to deflect some argument
refers to fencing

to play every card in the pack
to try very hard and use every conceivable argument
refers to playing cards

to prepare one's ground
to get ready for a confrontation
refers to military battle

to score a point
to make a clever contribution in the course of debate

to shoot someone down in flames
utterly to destroy another person's arguments
refers to loss of aircraft in battle

to tackle someone head on
to confront a person directly

to take off the gloves
to fight mercilessly or to debate with great ferocity
refers to bare-knuckle fighting before the introduction of the 'Marquis of Queensberry rules'

to take the wind out of someone's sails
to upset a person by anticipating that person's actions or by using arguments which that person was proposing to use
refers to a tactical manoeuvre in sailing whereby one boat blocks or 'takes' the wind advantage of another

to talk one's book
to present arguments that, although plausible, are really designed to foster one's vested interest

to tip the balance
to be further information or argument that results in an issue, that could have been decided either way, being determined in a particular way

to use every trick in the book
to try very hard and use every conceivable argument

to weigh in with a particular argument
to produce a strong argument

to wheel someone in
to bring a person of interest into discussions, plans, etc.

what is sauce for the goose is sauce for the gander
arguments that apply in one case also apply in another

Beginning

see Start

Behaviour

a carbon copy
an exact imitation
refers to the practice of producing a copy of a document by typing the original with carbon paper beneath, thus simultaneously making a copy

a watchdog
a person or organisation monitoring behaviour

an article of faith
a fundamental belief on which certain behaviour is based

fireworks
a spectacular display or effect (including anger, panic, confusion, etc.)

guiding light
a principle or example to follow in any activity
Exodus 13:21, 'And the Lord went before them by day in a pillar of a cloud, to lead them the way; and by night in a pillar of fire, to give them light'

horseplay
boisterous and undignified behaviour
John Dryden (1631–1700), 'He [Collier] is too much given to horseplay in his raillery'

I fear the Greeks even when they bear gifts
I am suspicious of generous behaviour from traditional opponents
Virgil (70–19 BC), *Aeneid* II:49, *Timeo Danaos et dona ferentis* ('I fear the Greeks even when they bring gifts'), in reference to the Trojan horse

if the shoe fits then wear it
if a general proposition describes your specific circumstances, then consider that it applies to you

not to put a foot wrong
to behave impeccably
refers to dancing steps
the order of the day
the customary behaviour
to be a bad egg
to be a dishonest or disreputable person
to be a Svengali
to be a person who controls another
refers to George du Maurier's *Trilby*
to be beyond the pale
to be socially unacceptable, especially for unacceptable standards or behaviour
'the Pale' originally (fourteenth century and later) referred to that part of Ireland under British rule (Latin *palus* 'a stake', marking a fence or boundary)
to be left with a nasty taste in one's mouth
to be appalled or very disappointed at another person's unethical behaviour to one
to blow the whistle on someone
to report a person's improper behaviour to the authorities or to publicise it
to get on someone's nerves
by one's behaviour to cause annoyance to a person
to keep one's eye on someone
to supervise a person
to keep one's eye on something
to monitor a situation
to lay it on the line
to make clear what the accepted rules of behaviour are
to lead with one's chin
by one's brash behaviour to virtually invite one's opponents to take action against one
refers to boxing
to make an exhibition of oneself
to behave in a way that invites ridicule
to make feathers fly
to cause a flurry of consternation and vigorous activity
refers to the fighting of cock birds
to play monkey tricks on someone
to engage in discreditable behaviour affecting a person
to pull one's socks up
to set out to improve or correct one's inadequate behaviour or performance
to ruffle someone's feathers
to engage in behaviour that irritates another person
to set tongues wagging
to behave in a way that encourages scandal mongers
to sow wild oats
to indulge in foolish behaviour while a young adult
to step out of line
to infringe accepted rules of behaviour
military metaphor
to teach someone a lesson
to inflict something unpleasant on a person in the hope that it will lead to a change in that person's behaviour
to watch one's step
to be on the lookout for danger or to set out to improve one's behaviour
transparent
(of behaviour, processes, etc.) to be easily discerned, to be obvious, to be evident

Belief

a bible basher
a person who makes unwelcome attempts to force religious beliefs on others
a doubting Thomas
a person who refuses to believe claims in the absence of proof
John 20:25, 'But he [Thomas] said … except I shall see in his hands the print of the nails … I will not believe'
a gut feeling
a belief based purely on intuition and unsupported by facts or evidence
a soul brother
a person of similar ideals
an article of faith
a fundamental belief on which certain behaviour is based
anyone could be forgiven for believing that
it is understandable that people would believe that

he is your man
he conforms to an ideal
Ev. S. Joann. 19:5 (Vulgate Bible): *Ecce Homo* ('Behold the man')

I'll eat my hat if so-and-so happens
I do not believe that so-and-so will happen

the fold
the body of believers
refers to an enclosure for sheep; *John* 10:16, 'Other sheep I have, which are not of this fold'

to be someone after one's own heart
to be a person who shares one's beliefs
1 Samuel 13:14 'A man after his own heart'

to be too big for one's boots
to have an unwarranted belief in one's capabilities or status

to be wide of the mark
to have a belief that is far removed from the true position
refers to archery

to believe in the tooth fairy
to be particularly gullible
refers to the mythical figure who exchanges children's milk teeth for a small sum of money

to go to the barricades for something
to believe in something very strongly and to be willing to go to great lengths in support of that belief

to preach to the converted
to say something to those who already believe in it

to put someone in the pillory
to hold a person up to ridicule for that person's beliefs
refers to a form of punishment involving public humiliation

to sacrifice something on the altar of some belief
to give up some benefit as a matter of principle

to sail under false colours
to pretend that one's real character or beliefs are different from what they really are
refers to a ship concealing its true identity

to shake one's head
to indicate disbelief or wonder or disapproval
Shakespeare, *Macbeth* III:iv, 'Never shake thy gory locks at me'

to show one's true colours
to disclose one's real character or beliefs
nautical metaphor

to stick to one's guns
to continue to hold certain beliefs notwithstanding opposition by others
refers to miltary battle

to take something as gospel
to believe that something is true

Utopian
ideally perfect
refers to the mythical island in Sir Thomas More's *Utopia* (Greek *ou topos*: 'no place')

volte face
a reversal of previously held beliefs
French, 'a turning around'; the term 'volte' originally had use in both fencing and horsemanship

Benefit

a bird in the hand is worth two in the bush
a benefit currently available is more valuable than a seemingly much larger benefit that might or might not be achieved in the future

a mare's nest
a discovery with illusory benefits

a milch cow
an easy and plentiful source of some desired benefit

bargaining chips
benefits that can be conceded in negotiations to obtain some advantage

every cloud has a silver lining
there are consolations and potential benefits even in seemingly adverse situations

fruitless
yielding no benefit

heads I win, tails you lose
whichever way this matter goes I will benefit at your expense
refers to the tossing of a coin

manna from heaven
unexpected benefits
derived from Hebrew *man-hu* ('what is this?'); *Exodus* 16:15, 'It is manna: for they wist not what it was. And Moses said unto them: this is the bread which the Lord hath given you to eat'

mirage
illusory benefit

that is just sour grapes
those are disparaging remarks made only because that person is peeved and resentful at someone else's better fortune
derived from Aesop's fable of 'the fox and the grapes' about expressing deliberate disparagement of a desired but unattainable object; 'sour grapes' also occurs in *Ezekiel* 18:2, 'the fathers have eaten sour grapes, and the children's teeth are set on edge'

the melody lingers on
the benefit of past actions remains

to be cream on top of the milk
to be an additional benefit in an already satisfactory scenario

to be icing on top of the cake
to be an additional benefit in an already satisfactory scenario

the salt of the earth
special people who make a vital contribution to society
Matthew 5:13, 'Ye are the salt of the earth'

to cast pearls before swine
to confer valuable benefits on someone who neither recognises nor appreciates them
Matthew 7:6, 'Neither cast ye your pearls before swine'

to get on a gravy train
to take steps to become a recipient of benefits that are available but undeserved

to get some mileage out of something
to benefit from something

to go along for the ride
to seek to benefit from a project in which others contribute the effort

to hand over something on a silver platter
to provide a valuable benefit for virtually nothing
refers to first-class service

to hand someone a poisoned chalice
to confer a seeming benefit on a person that will turn out to be a significant detriment

to laugh all the way to the bank
to appreciate one's good fortune

to learn a lesson
to benefit from one's experience

to let blood
to allow some harm as the price for achieving some greater benefit
refers to surgical removal of a patient's blood

to look a gift horse in the mouth
to be suspicious about a benefit that has been volunteered
Samuel Butler (1612–80), *Hudibras*, 'He ne'er consider'd it, as loth to look a gift horse in the mouth'; refers to the examination of a horse's teeth for an accurate assessment of its age

to mortgage the future
to get benefits now but at a cost in due course
refers to a charge over property recognised by the law

to pick someone's brain
to get the benefit of another person's knowledge and experience

to ride on the back of someone
without effort to benefit from the prior efforts of others

to ride on the sheep's back
to benefit from the production of wool

to rub off on someone
to benefit a person through an association that increases that person's skills

to sacrifice something on the altar of some belief
to give up some benefit as a matter of principle

to salvage something out of the wreck
to achieve some minor benefits out of a disastrous situation
refers to shipwrecks

to start from scratch
to commence something without the benefit of any past activity

refers to the starting mark (with no handicap advantage) in a race

to throw out the baby with the bathwater
to discard a major benefit in the course of obtaining a comparatively minor advantage

to throw someone a lifeline
to give significant assistance to a person

vulture
person benefiting from another's misfortune

windfall
unexpected good fortune
refers to fruit falling from a tree without having to be picked

Bigness

a big bang
a sudden major change in the environment

a big shot
an important person

a big wheel
an important person

a bird in the hand is worth two in the bush
a benefit currently available is more valuable than a seemingly much larger benefit that might or might not be achieved in the future

golden handshake
a large payment in connection with, or as an inducement to, retirement

a landslide
an electoral result involving victory or defeat by a very large margin

a mansize job
a large task

a mosaic
something with a large number of different aspects to it

a sausage machine
the turning out of large volumes without particular thought

a storm in a teacup
a controversy about a minor matter but one that looms large in the minds of the parties

a toehold
an opportunity small in itself but with the potential to lead to bigger things
refers to climbing trees, rockfaces, etc.

in for a penny, in for a pound
once something is commenced it ought to be finished; OR if one is willing to take a small risk then one might as well take a bigger one

more chiefs than Indians
a disproportionately large number of supervisors

not to be Robinson Crusoe
to be one of a large number of people with a common problem
refers to Daniel Defoe's *Robinson Crusoe*

someone's eyes are bigger than that person's stomach
a person is unrealistic in regard to that person's ability to cope with something

speak softly and carry a big stick
be polite to your potential enemies but maintain an active and visible defensive and offensive capability
from a speech by US President Theodore Roosevelt in 1901

the big smoke
the big city

the lion's share
the biggest portion

to be a big fish in a little pond
to be a person holding an important office but in an unimportant organisation

to be a money spinner
to produce large profits easily and quickly

to be a small cog in a large wheel
to be a relatively unimportant person in a large organisation

to be the thin end of the wedge
to be a small action or thing that has the potential to cause much larger undesirable consequences
refers to wedges used for splitting wood

to be the tip of the iceberg
to be only a very small portion of a much larger but less obvious whole

to be too big for one's boots
to have an unwarranted belief in one's capabilities or status

to be too big for one's breeches
to have an exaggerated idea of one's own importance
to be unable to keep people away with a big stick
to be faced with a large crowd or much demand
to bring out one's biggest guns
to use the most impressive persons or arguments
to crawl out of the woodwork
(referring to something unwelcome) to emerge from hiding or obscurity
to have a leg in
to have an opportunity which has the potential to lead to bigger things
to have deep pockets
to have large financial resources and to be willing to use them if the circumstances seem right
to scratch the surface
to deal with only a small portion of a much larger whole
to pay a king's ransom
to pay a very large sum
to pay something back with interest
to return a small favour with a bigger favour; or to extract retribution of greater value than the circumstances warrant
to pick the eyes out of something
to choose the most valuable items from among a large number
to stand over someone with a big stick
to intimidate a person in order to get that person to act in a particular way
to steamroll something through
to use enormous force to achieve an objective
refers to a steamroller — a large earth-flattening machine
to swarm out
to appear in large numbers from within
refers to bees or wasps'
to wield a big stick
to assert power

Care

a bull in a china shop
a careless person likely to cause great damage
he must have a long spoon that sups with the devil
great care is needed when negotiating with disreputable parties
Shakespeare apparently alludes to an old proverb in *The Tempest* II:ii, 'Mercy! mercy! this is a devil … I will leave him, I have no long spoon!'
not to just pick something out of a hat
to choose carefully, after weighing all the considerations
refers to choosing by lot by choosing things unseen from a hat
to hand-pick someone
to choose a person carefully for that person's individual attributes
to keep a weather eye out for something
to look out with particular care
nautical metaphor; refers to the eye that is turned towards the wind
to look to one's laurels
to be careful not to lose one's reputation for some skill
refers to laurel wreaths presented to winners of events at the ancient Olympics
to need to watch one's back
to find it necessary to take care in case others act against one's interests
to slip under one's guard
to cause a mistake to be made despite care being taken to prevent this
refers to fencing
to smell out something
to discover something by careful investigation
to start off on the right foot
to commence an operation with great care to do it correctly
to think twice before doing something
to consider with particular care
to tread lightly
to be careful
to watch one's P's and Q's
to be very careful

perhaps refers to pints and quarts of beer on a hotel slate, or perhaps to easily confused printer's type

Chance

be a devil!
take a chance!

the final throw of the dice
one last, desperate gamble

the hand of fate
chance

to be in the lap of the gods
to be a matter of apparent chance beyond human control
refers to wax tablets inscribed with requests and placed on the knees of statues of Greek gods

to be the luck of the draw
to be a chance result
refers to card games or a raffle

to cross someone's path
to meet another person by chance

to cruel someone's pitch
to spoil a person's chances

to have one's beady eyes on something
to await the chance to acquire something to which one is not properly entitled

to jump at the opportunity
enthusiastically to take immediate advantage of a good chance

to look for a needle in a haystack
to attempt something with a very small chance of success

to take pot luck
to take whatever happens by chance to be available
refers to a cooking pot of food

Change

a big bang
a sudden major change in the environment

a chameleon
a person without character who changes stance repeatedly to reflect the current circumstances

a leopard cannot change its spots
each person is born with certain unalterable characteristics
Jeremiah 13:23, 'Can the Ethiopian change his skin, or the leopard his spots?'

a new broom
a changed regime that is likely to alter the status quo

a road to Damascus experience
a sudden, dramatic conversion
refers to the sudden conversion of Paul (Saul) — *Acts* 9:3, 'And as he journeyed, he came to Damascus: and suddenly there shined around him a light from heaven: And he fell to the earth'

a rolling stone gathers no moss
a person who keeps changing jobs will not have a successful career
Tusser, *Five Hundred Points of Good Husbandrie* (1573), 'The stone that is rolling can gather no moss. / For master and servant oft changing is loss'

a sacred cow
an institution, person, idea, custom, etc. treated as being immune from criticism and change
refers to Hindu veneration of the cow

a sea-change
a significant transformation
Shakespeare, *The Tempest* I:ii, 'Nothing of him that doth fade / but doth suffer a sea-change / into something rich and strange

new guard
changed regime

nimble-footed
quick to change the direction of one's activities when circumstances warrant

seamless
unified, continuous, uninterrupted, imperceptible
John 19: 23, ' ... and also his [Jesus'] coat; now the coat was seamless, woven from the top throughout'

shifting sands
arguments that are constantly being changed

stiff cheese!
circumstances that might be unwelcome but will not be altered, and in respect of which no great sympathy is felt

that takes on added colour
there are now further facts that alter the appearance of a matter
the cold wind of change
the unpleasant realities of new circumstances
the devil one knows is better than the devil one does not know
the status quo is more comfortable than change
the ink is hardly dry
this involves indecent haste
refers to acting promptly, as soon as a document is signed
the tide has turned
conditions have changed
the wheel has turned
circumstances have changed and another party is now enjoying good fortune
to be a breath of fresh air
to be a pleasant change from the past
to be a stormy petrel
a person who disturbs a pleasant state of affairs by agitating for change
refers to the bird (petrel) that flies low over water during a storm and appears to be alternately touching one foot and then the other to the surface of the water as though walking upon it; the bird is sometimes thought to be the harbinger of a storm, and is named after St Peter who walked upon the stormy waters of Lake Gennesareth
to be carved in granite/marble
to be virtually unalterable
to be cast in bronze
to be virtually unalterable
to be in a rut
to lead a dull life, with no change from long-established habits
to be in a state of flux
to be subject to continuous change
to change one's mind
to alter the views that one had previously formed
to change one's tune
to alter one's publicly expressed views
to change tack
to alter one's direction
refers to sailing
to change the whole picture
to alter the major assumptions on which some assessment was based
to cry 'wolf'
repeatedly to raise an unjustified concern with the result that one will be ignored when the circumstances change and a real threat emerges
refers to a story of a boy who cried 'wolf' (from *Aesop's Fables*)
to defend one's bailiwick
to protect one's power, influence, or authority in regard to a particular activity
refers to a region under the jurisdiction of a particular bailiff
to die a natural death
by virtue of changed circumstances or the effluxion of time to be no longer relevant
to drift apart
to lose contact or to change feelings once held in common
to have a change of heart
to form a new view in place of a strongly held prior view
to leave one's mark on something
to be responsible for permanently altering the way something is operated
refers to the practice of illiterate persons making their 'mark' upon documents — usually signified by the sign of the cross preceded or followed by the person's name
to pass on the bâton
to hand over to a successor
to play it by ear
to develop one's strategy to always fit in with circumstances as they change from time to time
refers to playing music without the benefit of a written score
to put a new face on something
to alter the way something should be regarded
to rearrange the deckchairs on the Titanic
to take an initiative that is quite useless because it does not take much greater change into account
refers to the liner *Titanic* which struck an iceberg and sank in 1912
to set something in concrete
to make something virtually unalterable

to swap horses in mid-stream
to change that upon which one is reliant during the course of a project

to teach someone a lesson
to inflict something unpleasant on a person in the hope that it will lead to a change in that person's behaviour

to throw a few stones on the roof and see who comes out
to attempt to change a boring situation or resolve a stalemate

to tinker at the edges
to make minor or cosmetic changes without affecting the substance
refers to the common assumption that a tinker was an unreliable tradesman

to wither on the vine
by virtue of changed circumstances or the effluxion of time to be no longer relevant
John 15:5, 6, 'I am the vine, ye are the branches ... if a man abideth not in me, he is cast forth as a branch and is withered'

Commencement

see Start

Confusion

a dogfight
a confused fight, especially between aeroplanes

a tower of Babel
a noisy and confused assembly
Genesis 11:9, 'Therefore is the name of it called Babel; because the Lord did there confound the language of all the earth' (from which the word 'babble' is also derived)

all hell broke loose
great confusion erupted
John Milton (1608–74) *Paradise Lost*, 'Wherefore with thee came not all hell broke loose?'

to be all at sea
to be confused as to what is going on and what to do next

to be at sixes and sevens
to be confused, concerned and undecided
refers to a dispute between the Merchant Taylors and the Skinners over order of precedence in an annual London procession (who was to be sixth and who was to be seventh); in 1484 it was decided that henceforth the two guilds should alternate between 'sixes' and 'sevens' in consecutive years

to be bushed
to be lost or exhausted or puzzled or confused

to be in a fog
to be in a state of confusion

to get into a knot
to get into state of confusion

to lose one's head
to become agitated or confused
Rudyard Kipling (1865–1936), *If*, 'If you can keep your head when all about you are losing theirs ... '

to muddy the waters
deliberately to confuse an issue by creating a diversion

to set up a smokescreen
deliberately to confuse an issue by disguising its salient features

to watch one's P's and Q's
to be very careful
perhaps refers to pints and quarts of beer on a hotel slate, or perhaps to easily confused printer's type

Correctness

a step in the right direction
the first in a series of measures designed to correct some problem

golden mean
a moderate compromise between two extremes
from mathematics: the division of a straight line into two portions so that the ratio of the smaller to the larger equals the ratio of the larger to the whole

it is on the tip of my tongue
the right word has momentarily escaped me

a step in the right direction
the first in a series of measures designed to correct some problem

just what the doctor ordered

exactly right
mark my words
you will find out that I am right
one looks for elephants in elephant country
one needs to search in the right place
to be in the right ballpark
to be approximately correct
refers to baseball
to be up to the mark
to be of the right standard
refers to the official assay mark on gold and silver, originally put on at the Goldsmiths' Hall, London
to have one's heart in the right place
to have good intentions, to mean well
to head someone in the right direction
to assist a person to achieve something
to hit the bull's eye
to be extremely accurate in an activity; to score
derived from archery
to hit the mark
to achieve one's object or to make the correct decision
refers to archery
to hit the nail right on the head
astutely to come to the correct conclusion
to hold water
(of an argument) to be soundly based
to play one's cards right
to approach a matter sensibly
refers to playing cards
to play to the gallery
to do something that appeals to unrefined opinion rather than something that is right
refers to the theatre
to pull one's socks up
to set out to improve or correct one's inadequate behaviour or performance
to see daylight
to discern the way ahead towards the right answer
to set someone on the right road
to show a person how to go about doing something
to start off on the right foot
to commence an operation with great care to do it correctly
refers to marching
to strike the right key
to make comments that set the appropriate tone in a speech or conversation
refers to music
to strike the right note
to say or do something appropriate to a situation
refers to music

Courage

a David and Goliath battle
a struggle between two parties who are not evenly matched
refers to *1 Samuel* 17:23 ff
a stiff upper lip
obstinate courage in the face of pain or adversity
chicken-hearted
showing little courage
to be a brave soldier
courageously to do one's duty
to be a man of steel
to be a person with moral courage
to be in [or of] good heart
to be cheerful, especially in adversity
to brave the water
to enter a venture with courage and determination
to have a heart of oak
to be brave
refers to a famous sea song and naval march from the pantomime, *Harlequin's Invasion* (1759), by Garrick and Boyce.
to make a last-ditch stand
to make a brave effort to stave off final defeat
King William III (1650–1702), 'There is one way never to see it lost ... and that is to die in the last ditch' (quoted by Burnet, *History of His Own Times*,1715)
to present a happy face to the world
bravely to gloss over one's problems and to appear contented to others
to put a brave face on it
to face adversity cheerfully

to put one's head on the block
to have the courage of one's convictions
refers to execution by decapitation
to stick one's neck out
to have the courage of one's convictions or to take a calculated risk
refers to execution by decapitation

Criticism

a honeymoon
a short period enjoyed by a newcomer to some activity before that person's performance is criticised
refers to the holiday time (originally one 'moon' or month) immediately after a marriage ceremony
an Aunt Sally
a person who can readily be singled out and criticised as the proxy for a group
refers to an old game in which objects were thrown at the figure of the head of a woman
people in glass houses should not throw stones
those who are less than perfect are foolish to criticise others
John 8:7, 'He that is without sin among you, let him first cast a stone at her' (refers to ancient condemnation and punishment of people by stoning)
the pot calling the kettle black
criticising another person without realising one's own even greater shortcomings
to act as a sounding board
to give, on request, constructive criticisms of ideas tentatively held
refers, originally, to a board placed behind a speaker (esp. a preacher) to reflect the speaker's voice forwards to the congregation or audience
to attract flak
to attract criticism
refers to anti-aircraft fire — abbrev. of German *Fliegerabwehrkanone* (lit. 'aviator-defence-gun')
to be a sitting shot
to be a person whose actions make one very vulnerable to criticism
to be in the hot seat
to hold a position requiring one to answer criticism or accusations
to be like water off a duck's back
(of advice or criticism) to be completely ignored
to be on the war path
to be on the lookout for faults that can be criticised
to bite one's tongue
to resist from criticising
to bulldoze some proposal through
to ensure the passage of some measure in complete disregard of criticism or opposition
to cover oneself
to create evidence so that if one is criticised or accused later on one can clear one's name
to draw fire
to act in a way that attracts criticism
to engage in back-biting
to criticise in a trivial, annoying unfriendly manner
to face the music
to accept responsibility when confronted by one's critics
refers to the theatre
to fire a salvo at someone
to present a series of criticisms to a person
refers to simultaneous discharge of firearms in a battle or as a salute (Italian *salva*, 'salutation')
to get off someone's back
to leave a person alone to carry on without constant criticism
to give someone a bit of stick
to criticise a person mildly
to have a shot at someone
to use subtly chosen words implying friendly criticism but designed to embarrass another person
to have a thick skin
to be impervious to criticism
to have the hide of a rhinoceros
to be unaffected by, and unresponsive to, valid criticism
to hold fire
to defer criticising or attacking
to leave oneself wide open
to act in such a way that one's opponents will find much that can be easily criticised

refers to a bodily posture that is vulnerable to attack

to nail one's colours to the mast
publicly to declare one's position and to maintain it in the face of criticism
nautical metaphor

to nitpick
to criticise a person in respect of very minor matters
refers to the removal of lice eggs (nits) from the hair of an animal or person

to pour vitriol on something
to criticise something sharply
refers to sulphuric acid or to the caustic sulphates of various elements

to run the gauntlet
to be subjected to criticism
from Swedish *gantlopp* ('laneway') in reference to a military punishment inflicted on delinquents made to run between two files of soldiers, as used in Thirty Years' War, Holy Roman Empire, 1618–48

to stand in the breach
to fill a gap in the defences and bear the brunt of an attack or criticism
Shakespeare, *Henry V* III:i, 'Once more unto the breach, dear friends, once more; / Or close the wall up with our English dead!'

to turn one's guns on someone
to direct an attack or criticism at a person

Danger

a minefield
a source of great hidden danger or of difficulties not obvious at first

pitfall
unsuspected danger
refers to capturing animals by inducing them to fall into a pit

slippery path
dangerous course of action

someone's head is on the block
a person is in danger of being condemned; OR a person is in danger of having an appointment terminated
refers to execution by decapitation

to be a wolf in sheep's clothing
to be a hypocrite; to be dangerous although masquerading as something harmless
Matthew 7:15, 'Beware of false prophets, which come to you in sheep's clothing, but inwardly they are ravening wolves'

to be on a knife edge
to be in danger; OR to be a very close result

to be on the razor's edge
to be critically balanced; OR to be in danger

to bell the cat
to do some dangerous but highly useful mission
refers to a fable in which none of the mice was willing to put a warning bell on a cat

to fight fire with fire
to counter a dangerous situation by making an equally dangerous move

to founder on the shoals of something
to come to grief because of unexpected dangers
refers to a ship running aground in undetected shallow water

to have a sword of Damocles hanging over one
to be in imminent danger despite normal activity going on all around one
refers to Damocles who had the sword of Dionysius hanging, by a slender thread, over his head — as a symbol of perpetual risk in life; the story is told in Cicero, *Tusculanae Disputationes*

to have a tiger by the tail
to be involved in an activity that is much more dangerous than one had realised

to kick the communist can
to take every opportunity to exacerbate fear of communism in others

to play with fire
to invite trouble by meddling with dangerous matters

to push someone over the brink/edge
by a small action to cause the absolute ruin (financially or emotionally) of someone already in peril

to put one's head in the noose
to expose oneself to great danger likely to lead to one's downfall
refers to death by hanging

to put one's head into the lion's mouth
recklessly to expose oneself to great danger
refers to circus performance

to ride out the storm
to come safely through some dangerous situation
nautical metaphor

to sail close to the wind
to take a considered risk; to test the limits of what is possible or acceptable
refers to sailing in a manner such that sails remain filled while keeping the boat headed as near as possible into the wind

to see red lights flashing
to be conscious of the danger
refers to the 'stop' signal on roads and rail, or perhaps to lights on an emergency vehicle

to skate on thin ice
to act in disregard of obvious danger; to require tact in dealing with a sensitive subject in conversation
Ralph Waldo Emerson (1803–82), *Prudence*, 'In skating over thin ice, our safety is in our speed'

to walk a tightrope
to do something very dangerous in which one cannot afford to deviate from the required course of action

to watch one's step
to be on the lookout for danger; OR to set out to improve one's behaviour

Decision

a landmark ruling
a decision marking an important change or development in the state of affairs'

fork in the road
time or place for decision

if the mountain will not come to Muhammad then Muhammad will go to the mountain
on recognising that one has insufficient power to effect one's most desired solution one decides to make do with the next best alternative
refers to the story of Muhammad humbly submitting to the greater power of God when Mt Safa did not obey the prophet's command to come to him

the jury is still out
no decision has yet been made; OR there has not yet been an indication as to how the matter is viewed in the community

the wheels of justice grind slowly
it takes a long time to get a decision from the courts of law
Friedrich von Logau (1604–55), *Sinngedichte* (translated by H. W. Longfellow), 'Though the mills of God grind slowly, yet they grind exceeding small; though with patience he stands waiting, with exactness grinds he all'

to argue the toss
to dispute a decision
refers to the tossing of a coin

to be at sixes and sevens
to be confused, concerned and undecided
refers to a dispute between the Merchant Taylors and the Skinners over order of precedence in an annual London procession (who was to be sixth and who was to be seventh); in 1484 it was decided that henceforth the two guilds should alternate between 'sixes' and 'sevens' in consecutive years

to be at the cutting edge of something
to be in a position where important decisions are made

to be in two minds
to be undecided between two alternatives

to be out of someone's hands
to be up for decision by a different person
Ecclesiaticus 2:11, 'We will fall into the hands of the Lord, and not into the hands of men: for as his majesty is, so is his mercy'

to bite one's fingernails
anxiously to await a decision

to cross the Rubicon
to make an irreversible decision in regard to some commitment
refers to Caesar's crossing of the Rubicon River in Gaul in 49 BC thus declaring war on Pompey

to draw a line in the sand

to indicate clearly the limits of acceptability beyond which people should not go

to go down a particular track
to make decisions aimed at a particular goal

to have something to chew on
to have firm facts on which to base a decision

to hit the bull's eye
to be extremely accurate in an activity; to score
derived from archery

to hit the mark
to achieve one's object or to make the correct decision
refers to archery

to hold a gun at someone's head
to put pressure on a person to make a particular decision regardless of that person's desires in the matter

to hold the power to do something in the hollow of one's hand
to have the right to make crucial decisions
Isaiah 40:12, ' ... who hath measured the waters in the hollow of his hand ... '

to lose one's nerve
to abandon, out of fear, a decision to do something

to need the wisdom of Solomon
to require great sagacity when faced with a difficult decision
refers to King Solomon's ingenious solution to an apparently insoluble dilemma as described in *1 Kings* 3:16–28

to pin someone down
to find a person willing to accept blame or responsibility; OR to force a person to announce a decision or concede a point
refers to wrestling

to pull strings
to use one's special influence with those in a position to make favourable decisions which might otherwise not be forthcoming
refers to the actions of a puppeteer in directing the action

to rake over old coals
to seek to reopen a matter decided on long ago

to tip the balance/scales
to be further information or argument that results in an issue, that could have been decided either way, being determined in a particular way
refers to balance scales

to toss up
to decide on a fairly arbitrary basis
refers to the tossing of a coin

when the crunch comes
when the inevitable conclusion is reached

Development

a thought in the back of one's mind
an undeveloped idea

a wild card
(in general) an unexpected unpredictable development; OR (in playing cards) a card of a value specified by the player holding it; OR (in sport) a player or a team given entrance to a competition by the organisers, even if the entry is not strictly merited; OR (in computing) a character that will match any other character in a search string

an ugly duckling
an unprepossessing person or thing, the characteristics of which change in time to become attractive
refers to a cygnet in a brood of ducks in a children's story of that name by Hans Christian Andersen

framework
outline of a proposal, upon which further details can be developed

the bottom line
the conclusion that matters or the net effect of a series of developments
refers to the last line is a series of calculations or accounts

to be a turn-up for the books
to be a surprising development
refers to bookmaking and gambling

to blossom
(of a person's attributes) to develop

to develop a head of steam
to gain momentum
refers to a steam engine or boiler

to find one's feet

to develop one's skills in a previously unfamiliar situation

to keep an ear to the ground
to be well informed as to current developments
refers to listening for distant sound by applying one's ear to the ground

to mark time
to do nothing while awaiting developments
refers to marching

to play it by ear
to develop one's strategy to always fit in with circumstances as they change from time to time
refers to playing music without the benefit of a written score

to run with something
to take advantage of some current development
refers to rugby

to see the big picture
to have the vision and imagination enabling a project to be developed as part of a bigger whole

to see which way the cat jumps
to await developments

Difficulty

a baptism of fire
the commencement of an operation that presents great difficulty
refers to religious ceremonial washing as an initiation ceremony; metaphorical use (as here) attributed to Napoleon III in referring to to a soldier's first battle

a can of worms
a collection of complex intertwined problems

a David and Goliath battle
a struggle between two parties who are not evenly matched
refers to *1 Samuel* 17:23 ff

a fair-weather friend
a person purporting to be a friend who offers no support in difficult times

a hard nut to crack
a difficult problem to be solved; OR someone not easily influenced

a hiccup
a temporary minor holdup

a minefield
a source of great hidden danger or of difficulties not obvious at first

a prima donna
a person with an exaggerated opinion of that person's own importance making relations with others needlessly difficult
Italian, 'first lady'

a problem child
a source of unnecessary difficulty

a sixty-four thousand dollar question
a pertinent but very difficult question
refers to a radio quiz show in which an initial $1000 prize doubled with the successful answering of progressively more difficult questions

a sticky patch
a period fraught with difficulties

any port in a storm
anything that helps to avoid difficulties is welcome

blood, sweat, and tears
hard work and much effort
Winston Churchill, House of Commons, 13 May 1940, 'I have nothing to offer but blood, toil, tears, and sweat'

elbow grease
hard manual work
old jocular saying, in existence for several centuries, referring to the vigorous use of the elbow in rubbing, polishing, scrubbing, etc.

no sweat
this presents no difficulty

ready-made
easily fabricated or available without difficulty

road blocks
difficulties

Rome was not built in a day
complicated things require time

search for the Holy Grail
work towards a difficult goal
refers to a vessel or platter supposedly used by Christ at the Last Supper and featuring in the Arthurian legends

stumbling block
an impediment or difficulty preventing the easy completion of some project; OR a dilemma involving a moral issue

1 Corinthians 8:9, 'But take heed lest by any means this liberty of yours become a stumbling block to them that are weak'

this is hard to take
it is difficult to face up to the reality of this

the show must go on
despite difficulties the action in contemplation has to proceed
refers to the theatre

the very best of British luck
you will have a hard time of it, but you carry my best wishes

there's the rub
that is where a difficulty arises
Hamlet III:i, 'To sleep: perchance to dream: ay there's the rub'; the term is also used in bowls

to back someone into a corner
to leave a person no option

to batten down the hatches
to get ready for expected difficulties
nautical metaphor

to be a cross that one has to bear
to be a difficulty that one has to endure
Luke 14:27, 'And whosoever doth not bear his cross, and come after me, cannot be my disciple'

to be a fish out of water
to be in difficulty by virtue of being in a strange environment

to be a handful
to be difficult to manage
P. G. Wodehouse (1881–1975), 'Bailey will find her rather a handful. Does she ever sit still, by the way?'

to be a hard act to follow
to be an impressive performance, not easily matched by the next person

to be between a rock and a hard place
to be faced with two equally difficult and uncomfortable choices

to be in a hole
to experience some difficulties

to be in a jam
to be in difficulties

to be in a pickle
to be in difficulties
Shakespeare, *The Tempest* V:i, 'How cam'st thou in this pickle?'

to be in a quagmire
to be in great difficulty

to be in a stew
to be in a difficult situation; OR to be in an anxious, agitated, or confused state

to be in deep/hot water
to be in great difficulty

to be in the same boat
to share a common set of difficulties

to be in the soup
to be in great difficulties

to be no bed of roses
to be difficult or uncomfortable
Robert Louis Stevenson (1850–94), *Virginibus Puerisque* I:i, 'Marriage is like life in this — that it is a field of battle, and not a bed of roses'

to be no fun
to be difficult; to be lacking in levity

to be on a sticky wicket
to face some difficulties
refers to cricket

to be out of one's depth
to find that some issue is too complicated or too difficult

to be out of the woods
the previous difficulties have been overcome

to be parts of a jigsaw
to be elements in the solution of something complex
refers to a jigsaw puzzle

to be pushing uphill
to face difficulties

to be sheer murder
to be extremely unpleasant or difficult; OR to be an inglorious defeat

to be the hard core
to be the central and most difficult problem

to be up a gum tree
to be in difficulty; OR at the end of one's resources

to bite the bullet
to face up to the difficulties of a situation
refers to the use of biting on a bullet as a means of controlling one's reaction to pain in a surgical procedure without anaesthetic (for example, following a military battle)

to carry baggage
to handicap oneself

to catch someone in a bind

to find a person in a difficulty from which that person cannot readily extricate himself or herself

to face a rocky road ahead
to be likely to encounter difficulties

to fall on one's feet
surprisingly to succeed despite difficulties

to fight an uphill battle
to face difficulties or to have formidable opposition
refers to military battle

to get around some difficulty
to use an approach that overcomes some difficulty

to give someone hell
to make life extremely difficult for a person

to grab the devil by the tail
to face up to difficulties

to grasp the nettle
to deal with an unpleasant difficulty by decisive action
Aaron Hill (1685–1750), 'Tender-hearted stroke a nettle, / And it stings you for your pains; / Grasp it like a man of mettle, / And it soft as silk remains'

to have a dream run
to encounter no difficulties

to have a hard row to hoe
to have a difficult assignment
refers to agriculture; James Russell Lowell (1819–91), *The Biglow Papers*, 'You've a darned long row to hoe'

to have a job in front of one
to have all or much of a difficult task still to be completed

to have lead in one's saddlebags
to work with a handicap
refers to horse-racing handicaps in which lead in the saddlebags makes winning more difficult

to have one hand tied behind one's back
to work with a handicap

to have one's work cut out to do something
to have a difficult task to achieve something

to have the cards stacked against one
to be faced with many difficulties frustrating a project
refers to playing cards

to have the odds stacked against one
to be faced with many difficulties frustrating a project
refers to betting

to heave a sigh of relief
to express satisfaction at the achievement of a solution to a difficult problem
John Keats (1795–1821), *I stood tip-toe upon a little hill*, 'born of the very sigh that silence heaves'

to iron out something
to sort out a difficult problem

to jump a hurdle
to overcome a problem or difficulty

to kick a man when he is down
to take unfair advantage of a person already in difficulty

to leave someone in the lurch
to desert a person who is in difficulties
refers to the score in certain games — especially cribbage

to make a good fist of something
to make a good attempt at, or to succeed in, a difficult task

to need the wisdom of Solomon
to require great sagacity when faced with a difficult decision
refers to King Solomon's ingenious solution to an apparently insoluble dilemma as described in *1 Kings* 3:16–28

to penetrate someone's thick skull
to make a person understand something difficult or acknowledge something unwelcome

to plot a safe course through troubled waters
to make a plan that overcomes certain difficulties
nautical metaphor

to put one's thinking cap on
to concentrate on finding a solution to a difficult problem

to put something into the 'too-hard' basket
to defer consideration of a difficult issue

to put the jigsaw together

to solve a problem by placing together a number of separate facts
refers to a jigsaw puzzle

to run into heavy weather
to encounter difficulties
nautical metaphor

to sharpen one's axe
to get ready for a difficult task

to sink deeper into the mud/mire
to get into even greater difficulty

to skirt around the difficulties
to proceed with care and avoid problems

to smell trouble
to perceive difficulties

to soldier on
to carry on despite difficulties

to strike a snag
to encounter a difficulty
refers to angling

to take the bull by the horns
to come to grips with the realities of a difficult problem

to take the rough with the smooth
to accept the hardships of life along with its pleasant features

to tip-toe around the difficulties
to act with discretion and care to conceal difficulties, or to prevent problems occurring

to tread a fine/thin line
cautiously to take action in circumstances where either too much or too little will cause difficulties

to wear one's crown of thorns
to have one's own difficulties
John 19:2, 'And the soldiers plaited a crown of thorns, and put it on his [Jesus'] head'

Disappointment

a damp squib
disappointingly ineffective action
refers to fireworks that fail to go off

someone's face fell
someone registered obvious disappointment

someone's jaw dropped
someone registered obvious astonishment and/or disappointment

to be a bitter pill to swallow
to be a great humiliation or disappointment that has to be endured

to be a severe blow
to be a great disappointment

to be devastated
to be extremely disappointed

to be left with a nasty taste in one's mouth
to be appalled or very disappointed at another person's unethical behaviour to one

Displeasure

a damp squib
disappointingly ineffective action
refers to fireworks that fail to go off

someone would turn in his or her grave
someone would have been very surprised or displeased if he or she had known while still alive

I will have that person's guts for garters
I am extremely angry and dissatisfied with that person

someone's face fell
someone registered obvious disappointment

someone's jaw dropped
someone registered obvious astonishment and/or disappointment

to be a bitter pill to swallow
to be a great humiliation or disappointment that has to be endured

to be a severe blow
to be a great disappointment

to be at the end of one's tether
to be frustrated because one is at the very limit of one's resources of knowledge, authority, or patience
refers to tethering of animals with a rope

to be cut to pieces
to be very upset; OR to be completely overrun and defeated

to be devastated
to be extremely disappointed

to be left with a nasty taste in one's mouth

to be appalled or very disappointed at another person's unethical behaviour to one

to be someone's bLte noire
to be a person whose ideas and actions cause upset and loathing in another person
French, *bLte noire* ('black beast')

to bite someone's head off
rudely and excessively to express displeasure at a person

to break someone's heart
to act in a way causing great upset to another person
Psalms 69:21, 'Thy rebuke hath broken my heart; I am full of heaviness'; Shakespeare *Hamlet* I:ii, 'But break my heart ... ')

to give someone a black look
to indicate one's displeasure with a person

to go through the roof
(of a person) to be very upset; OR (of prices) to escalate greatly

to knit one's brows
to indicate one's displeasure

to make a noise about something
to complain or express dissatisfaction about something

to open up a festering sore
to upset a person by drawing attention to a long-standing grievance apparently forgotten

to put someone's nose out of joint
to upset another person

to take the wind out of someone's sails
to upset a person by anticipating that person's actions or by using arguments which that person was proposing to use
refers to a tactical manoeuvre in sailing whereby one boat blocks or 'takes' the wind advantage of another

to throw brickbats at someone
to express displeasure with a person
refers to portions of brick, esp. ones used as missiles

to tread on someone's corns/toes
to upset another person by interfering in that person's area of responsibility

to upset the applecart
to engage in conduct disturbing a peaceful state of affairs and thereby to cause discomfort

to vote with one's feet
to express one's attitude by one's physical movement towards or away from something

to wave a finger at someone
to indicate mild displeasure at another person's actions

Ease

a milch cow
an easy and plentiful source of some desired benefit

a walkover
an easy victory
refers to the winner walking over the finishing line for an unchallenged victory

distant fields look greener
activities of which one has no experience seem more attractive than is really the case
Psalms 23:1, 'The Lord is my shepherd ... he shall feed me in a green pasture'

it's a breeze
it is easy

money for jam
remuneration easily earned

to be small beer
to be quite unimportant

ready-made
easily fabricated or available without difficulty

stumbling block
an impediment or difficulty preventing the easy completion of some project; OR a dilemma involving a moral issue
1 Corinthians 8:9, 'But take heed lest by any means this liberty of yours become a stumbling block to them that are weak'

to be a laid-down misPre
to be very easily accomplished and/or to be certain of outcome
refers to card playing where one player undertakes not to win any tricks while playing with the disadvantage of having that player's cards exposed to observation by others

to be a money spinner

to produce large profits easily and quickly

to be a piece of cake

to be very easy or greatly to one's liking

to be able to do something standing on one's head

to be able to do something very easily

to be able to do something with one hand behind one's back

to be able to do something very easily

to be able to eat someone for breakfast

to be able to outwit a person very easily

to be child's play

to be easy or to require only elementary skills and knowledge

to be in clover

to enjoy a life of ease and luxury

refers to grazing animals in rich pasture

to be money for old rope

to be an easily made profit

to be plain sailing

to be quite straightforward and very easy

refers to navigation by means of a 'plane chart' on which meridians and parallels of latitude are represented by equidistant straight lines

to be putty in someone's hands

to be far too easily influenced by another person

refers to material able to be fashioned into various shapes

to chase every hare

to be easily sidetracked

to die hard

stubbornly to refuse to give up a belief or theory; not to give up easily

to get an armchair ride

to be given a particularly easy time

to have a mind of one's own

not to be easily influenced

to have nerves of steel

not to be easily frightened

to leave oneself wide open

to act in such a way that one's opponents will find much that can be easily criticised

refers to a bodily posture that is vulnerable to attack

to nip something in the bud

to stop some activity in its early stages when stopping it is still relatively easy

refers to the first signs of growth in plants

to roll off the tongue

to be said very easily

to run rings around someone

to outwit another person easily

to serve something up to someone on a plate

to make something especially easy for a particular person

to smooth the path for someone

to use one's influence to make arrangements so that a person's task will be easier or more readily accomplished

Isaiah 40:3, 'Prepare ye the way of the Lord; make smooth in the desert a highway for our God'

to streamline

to organise better by simplification

to take something in one's stride

to cope with something easily

refers to a horse jumping an obstacle

to win the prize in a canter

to win very easily

refers to horse racing

transparent

(of behaviour, processes, etc.) to be easily discerned, to be obvious, to be evident

Electoral

a clean sweep

a complete clearing out; OR winning all available prizes or awards

a landslide

an electoral result involving victory or defeat by a very large margin

neck and neck

(of contestants) with little between them

refers to a winning margin in horse racing

not to pull any punches

to be brutally frank

refers to boxing

the swing of the pendulum

the alternation of prospects, fortune, or experience

to be a cliff-hanger
to be very exciting with the result in doubt
refers to episodes of early serial films that ended with the hero in a hazardous plight to attract cinema-goers to the next episode

to be level pegging
(of contestants) to have little between them
refers to cribbage

to engage in pump priming
to spend public money with the aim of attracting parochial electoral support
refers to priming a water pump

to get rolled
to be outvoted

to hop onto the bandwagon
to subscribe to an emerging majority opinion

to keep one's head
to remain calm in a crisis or unexpectedly to retain an elected or appointed position
Rudyard Kipling (1865–1936), *If*, 'If you can keep your head when all about you are losing theirs ... '

to vote with one's feet
to express one's attitude by one's physical movement towards or away from something

underdog
a person or team that is likely to lose a contest and therefore likely to be the object of sympathy

Employment

a dead-end position
a job with no prospects of advancement

feather bedding
(in industrial relations) creating unnecessary jobs solely to increase employment; OR (in economics) assisting an inefficient industry by government grants or excessive tariff protection

glass ceiling
an unstated but definite limit (resulting from prejudice) to promotion in employment

golden shackles
financial arrangements designed to discourage employees changing from one employer to another

rising star
person making good progress in that person's career

someone's job is on the line
a person's career path is under consideration; AND/OR that person's present position is at risk

to drum someone out of some organisation
to terminate in ignominy a person's employment or membership
refers to the ceremonial cashiering in the army to the beating of parade drums

to have one's fingers in the till
to steal from one's employer

to hold someone's hand
to give detailed on-the-job training and supervision

to know the ropes
to know how to do one's job
nautical metaphor

to move on to greener pastures
to move to a better environment; to commence a new, better career
Psalms 23:1, 'The Lord is my shepherd: therefore can I lack nothing. he shall feed me in a green pasture: and lead me forth beside the waters of comfort'

to swing the lead
to cheat an employer by not working while being paid to do so or by malingering; to avoid work or some other task by concocting a plausible excuse for not doing it, or by pretending to be ill
originally referred to a leadsman lazily swinging the line, rather than getting on with taking soundings

to tickle the peter
to rob one's employer
refers to slang term for cash box

to turn an honest penny
to earn money by hard work

End

a big bang
a sudden major change in the environment

a clean sweep
a complete clearing out; OR winning all available prizes or awards

a dead-end position
a job with no prospects of advancement

a logjam
a stoppage of activity caused by input in greater volume than allowed for
refers to a crowded mass of cut logs in a river

a photo finish
a close result in a contest
refers to horse racing

at five minutes to midnight
almost at the last moment

at the end of the day
in due course, or at the conclusion of a project

cold turkey
the sudden cessation of drugs to an addict and, by extension, the sudden cessation of any habitually pleasurable activity
probably refers to the appearance of the skin of drug addicts experiencing withdrawal symptoms (similarity to the skin of a plucked cold turkey)

cut it out!
stop doing that!

danse macabre
gruesome final step
French, 'ghastly dance'; now used to describe a gruesome literary or theatrical production (refers to fourteenth-century religious art depicting persons being led to the grave by death)

dead and buried
(of some issue) definitely concluded, especially so long ago as to be nearly forgotten

death of a thousand cuts
a slow, unpleasant ending

from a to z
from start to finish

from alpha to omega
from start to finish
refers to the first and last letters of the Greek alphabet

from go to whoa
from start to finish
refers to the commands given to horses

horses are out of the barn
it is now too late

I'll soon stop that person's little game
that person's activities are not tolerated and I will ensure that they cease

in for a penny, in for a pound
once something is commenced it ought be finished; OR if one is willing to take a small risk then one might as well take a bigger one

in the wash-up
when everything is finalised

it's not over until the fat lady sings
it is not finished yet
probably refers to operatic performances, but during a radio broadcast made by the present author, a listener suggested that the metaphor refers to Kate Smith singing the US national anthem

one for the road
a final drink before leaving

quietly to fold up one's tent
surreptitiously to abandon a previously cherished stance
Henry Wadsworth Longfellow (1807–82), *The Day is Done*, 'The cares that infest the day shall fold their tents, like the Arabs, and as silently steal away'

someone's head is on the block
a person is in danger of being condemned; OR a person is in danger of having an appointment terminated
refers to execution by decapitation

stalemate
a final result in which neither party to a dispute is victorious
refers to chess

that wraps it up
that completes all the required tasks in this project

the bottom line
the conclusion that matters or the net effect of a series of developments
refers to the last line is a series of calculations or accounts

the buck stops here
I accept full responsibility

hand-lettered sign on desk of US President Harry S. Truman (Phillips, *The Truman Presidency*, Ch. 12)

the clock is ticking
time is running out

the final countdown
the last stages of something
refers to the launch of space vehicles

the final (or last) straw
the latest step that, when added to a large number of seemingly harmless previous steps, sets off a significant event resulting from the cumulative effect
see 'the straw that broke the camel's back'

the sands are running out
the time available for some action is nearly at an end
refers to an hour-glass of running sand

the sun has set on something
something has concluded

the tail end of something
the very end of something

this is the end of the road for someone
a person will have no further opportunity to do something

to abandon ship
to abrogate one's responsibilities or to abandon a project
refers to the order given when a ship is about to sink

to bale out of something
to abandon an enterprise in anticipation of disaster
refers to emergency parachute jump from an aeroplane

to be all over bar the shouting
to be virtually finished

to be in at the death
to be present at the conclusion of something
refers to fox hunting — when the fox is caught and killed

to be in at the kill
to be present at the climatic finish to something
refers to hunting

to be on a treadmill
to be involved in some unpleasant ongoing activity that cannot readily be stopped

to be on one's death bed
(of a person, organisation or piece of equipment) to be about to cease effectiveness

to be only a gleam in someone's eyes
not yet conceived, let alone achieved

to be out on one's ear
to be ejected from a situation or place or to have one's services abruptly terminated

to be out the door
to have one's position terminated

to be stopped in one's tracks
suddenly and unexpectedly to be prevented from carrying on with a project

to be the sting in the tail
to be the unexpected unpleasant conclusion

to be up a gum tree
to be in difficulty; OR at the end of one's resources

to beat a retreat
to abandon some project
military metaphor

to break one's duck
to end a spell that had no results
refers to cricket in which a 'duck' represents no score

to break the back of a task
to complete the bulk of the work

to bury the hatchet
to abandon hostilities
refers to tradition of North American indigenous peoples to symbolise cessation of hostilities

to call it a day
to cease involvement with some activity

to call off the dogs
to abandon a pursuit or inquiry
refers to hunt master calling off the dogs if they are on the wrong scent

to cast prudence to the winds
to cease being careful or wise

to chop someone off at the socks
to stop someone's proposals prematurely

to close the book on something
to terminate an activity

to come to a full stop
to cease activity completely

to come to a head
to reach culmination
medical metaphor; refers to abscess formation

to come to a sticky end
to endure an unpleasant fate

to come to the end of the road
to come to the point where hope and endeavour are finished

to crystallise
to emerge in its final form

to cut corners
to lower one's standards in order to complete something more quickly

to deal the final hand
to take steps that conclude a matter
refers to playing cards

to dot the i's and cross the t's
to be meticulous in completing documentation

to drum someone out of some organisation
to terminate in ignominy a person's employment or membership
refers to the ceremonial cashiering in the army to the beating of parade drums

to dry up
to cease

to fall by the wayside
to be abandoned and to therefore drop out; to fail to stay the course
Matthew 13:4, 'And when he sowed, some seeds fell by the wayside, and the fowls came and gobbled them up'

to fetter someone
to stop a person acting on that person's own initiative

to finish with a bang
to conclude something in grand style

to get on stream
to now operate successfully following the end of a settling-in period

to get rid of the dead wood
to terminate the services of unsatisfactory personnel
refers to pruning of bushes

to get up off one's butt
to cease being apathetic
refers to US slang for the buttocks

to give someone the boot
to terminate a person's appointment

to give the game away
to cease involvement with some activity; OR to reveal the nature of a hidden activity or plan

to grind to a halt
to have an activity gradually cease to function despite expectations that it would continue

to hold the pen poised
to be ready to consummate a deal

to jettison some proposal
to abandon some proposal as worthless or impracticable

to kill some proposal stone dead
to take action that stops a proposal completely
refers to death by stoning

to lay some theory to rest
to abandon some theory as being no longer appropriate
refers to death –as in 'laying out' (preparing a corpse for disposal), or as in 'laying someone to rest' (at a funeral)

to lose heart
to be discouraged

to lose one's nerve
to abandon, out of fear, a decision to do something

to lose one's touch
to cease to be familiar with, or adept at, something

to lower the boom
to bring to account and punish

to make a last-ditch stand
to make a brave effort to stave off final defeat
King William III (1650–1702), 'There is one way never to see it lost ... and that is to die in the last ditch' (quoted by Burnet, *History of His Own Times*,1715)

to nip something in the bud
to stop some activity in its early stages when stopping it is still relatively easy
refers to the first signs of growth in plants

to pass on the bâton
to hand over to a successor

to peg out
to die
refers to the final act in a game of cribbage

to play the last card in the pack
to be forced to use one's last expedient

refers to playing cards

to play the trump card
to make a final move, thereby defeating one's opponents
refers to playing cards

to put a wall around someone
to stop a person associating with others

to put something to bed
finally to dispose of something

to put the brake on someone
to stop or slow down a person

to put up the shutters
to cease an established activity

to rake over old coals
to seek to reopen a matter decided on long ago

to receive the coup de grâce
to be finished off by an opponent
French, 'mercy stroke'

to ring down the curtain on something
to treat something as concluded

to run into a dead end
to get nowhere in an investigation

to run its course
to come to a natural end

to see the light at the end of the tunnel
to perceive relief at the imminent end of a period of prolonged difficulty

to shelve some proposal
to abandon some proposal

to shut up shop
to cease an established activity

to sound the death knell of something
to indicate the impending end of something
refers to the knell (sound) of a bell rung at a funeral; Shakespeare, *Macbeth* II:i, 'The bell invites me ... it is a knell that summons thee to heaven or to hell'

to stem the haemorrhage/bleeding
to put a stop to the financial losses of a project

to stitch up a deal
successfully to conclude a deal

to strangle some discussion
to cut off some unfinished discussion

to throw someone to the lions
to sacrifice or condemn a person to that person's fate
refers to execution or bloodsport by throwing persons to be eaten by lions

to tie something up
to finalise the arrangements for something

to tie up the loose ends
to complete the minor outstanding items of some substantially finished project

to turn a complete somersault
to reverse one's established policy

to turn up trumps
to finish up better than expected or to experience unexpected good luck
refers to playing cards

to walk away with a profit
to achieve a profit on concluding a project

to wield the knife
to terminate the services of one or more persons or to prune expenditure

to wrap up a deal
to bring a deal to a successful conclusion

until stumps are drawn
until the end of the day's activities
refers to cricket

when the crunch comes
when the inevitable conclusion is reached

when the music stops
suddenly and soon
refers to an imminent crisis leading to some resolution of a matter, as in a game of musical chairs

where the axe falls
who suffers the consequences

Enthusiasm

a fire in someone's belly
ambition or driving force producing great enthusiasm

a shot in the arm
something to revive a person's enthusiasm
refers to medical injections

an eager beaver

a person with great drive and enthusiasm even if this causes annoyance to others
refers to the industriousness of the beaver, and adapted as World War II US expression for a very keen person who habitually volunteered

bright-eyed and bushy-tailed
naVve but enthusiastic

deafening silence
great apathy and lack of enthusiasm

half-hearted
unenthusiastic

heart and soul
with great energy
Matthew 22:36–40, 'Thou shalt love the Lord thy God with all thy heart and with all thy soul and with all thy mind'

I would give my right arm for something
I am very keen to acquire something

keepers of the flame
persons entrusted to maintain old traditions and keen to do so
refers to those entrusted with keeping a sacred flame of remembrance alight

larger than life
exaggerated; more than normal

lukewarm
unenthusiastic although not hostile

not to break someone's door down
to be unenthusiastic about someone's goods or services

not to care a hoot
not to show the slightest concern or enthusiasm

one's heart is not in some cause
one has little enthusiasm for some cause

the lifeblood
the main or essential ingredient; OR the person or factor instilling enthusiasm

they fell over themselves to do something
they showed great keenness while doing something

to be a live wire
to be an enthusiast
refers to electrical wires

to be after someone's blood
to be keen to make a person the victim of an angry confrontation

to be after someone's scalp
to be keen to penalise a person
refers to the savage practice of removing the scalp of a killed person as a trophy

to be bitten with something
to become very enthusiastic over something

to be close to one's heart
to be a project about which one is very keen

to be dying to do something
to be extremely keen to do something

to be hot on a subject
to be knowledgeable and enthusiastic about a subject

to be in someone's blood
to be something about which a person is inherently very knowledgeable or keen

to be itching to go
to be highly enthusiastic and keen to start

to be on one's soap box
to hold forth on an issue about which one feels keenly
refers to orators standing on soap boxes (strong wooden boxes) as a platform

to be the life and soul of the party
to be the prime enthusiast for a cause
Shakespeare, *A Midsummer Night's Dream*, 'My love, my life, my soul, fair Helena!'

to beat someone to the punch
to get to some objective ahead of some keen rival
refers to boxing

to break one's neck to do something
to be particularly keen
refers to reckless enthusiasm

to carry a torch for someone
to harbour (perhaps secret and unrequited) desires for love and marriage
refers to the torch of love

to galvanise someone into action
forcefully to shock or rouse someone into action
refers to Luigi Galvani (1737–98), Italian physiologist, whose name was applied to the shock received from a direct electric current

to get one's teeth into something
to tackle a task with enthusiasm

to give something a blood transfusion
to give something new enthusiasm
to go hammer and tongs
to do something with great energy
refers to energetic work of a blacksmith
to grab an opportunity with both hands
to seize an opportunity with great enthusiasm
to have one's heart in something
to be enthusiastic about and committed to a cause
to have one's heart set on something
to be very keen to achieve something
to jump at the opportunity
enthusiastically to take immediate advantage of a good chance
to jump into the ring
enthusiastically to join in a contest or challenge
refers to the practice of jumping into a boxing ring to make a challenge
to leap at an idea
to accept a suggestion enthusiastically
to lose heart
to be discouraged
to make a beeline for something
to go straight to something with great enthusiasm or to head for some goal by the most direct route
to pour cold water on some idea
to be unenthusiastic about some proposal or scornful of its apparent weaknesses
to pull oneself together
by gathering one's faculties and strength, to rouse oneself to a renewed effort
to rebound with a vengeance
to return to an issue with great enthusiasm
to run out of steam
to lose one's energy and enthusiasm
refers to steam engines
to start the ball rolling
to commence and advance enthusiastically an activity
to take a shine to someone
to be keen on a person
to want someone's hide
to be keen to penalise a person
with much fanfare
with great enthusiasm and public acclaim
with open arms
enthusiastically

Equality

a David and Goliath battle
a struggle between two parties who are not evenly matched
refers to *1 Samuel* 17:23 ff
a Goliath
a giant or a person whose ability and achievements exceed that of most other people
refers to *1 Samuel* 17:23 ff
a level playing field
competition on equal terms
a second-class citizen
a person not treated as an equal
to be between the devil and the deep blue sea
to be faced with two equally unpalatable alternatives that cannot both be avoided
it is a toss up
either alternative is equally acceptable
refers to the tossing of a coin
only a cigarette paper between them
virtually equal or close together
only a postage stamp between them
virtually equal or close together
only a tissue between them
virtually equal or close together
the river found its mark
equilibrium between two pressures has been achieved
to be between Scylla and Charybdis
to be faced with two equally unpalatable alternatives that cannot both be avoided
refers to the voyage of Ulysses
to be between a rock and a hard place

to be faced with two equally difficult and uncomfortable choices

to be line ball

to be equal or to be a matter about which it is very difficult to make a definitive decision one way or the other

refers to sport (especially tennis)

to compete on all fours with someone

to strive on equal terms

refers to the four limbs of the body

to fight fire with fire

to counter a dangerous situation by making an equally dangerous move

Excess

a holier-than-thou attitude

excessive righteousness

daylight robbery

the charging of grossly excessive prices

delivered in spades

to a considerable degree; in large numbers

feather bedding

(in industrial relations) creating unnecessary jobs solely to increase employment; OR (in economics) assisting an inefficient industry by government grants or excessive tariff protection

highway robbery

the charging of grossly excessive prices

refers to robbery by armed brigands on the highways

paper warfare

an excessive amount of correspondence or excessive bureaucracy

penny-pinching

excessively mean

red tape

excessively bureaucratic procedures

refers to bureaucrats and lawyers securing their briefs with red tape; the term is said to have been coined by Charles Dickens (1812–70), but popularised by Thomas Carlyle (1795–1881)

someone has swallowed a dictionary

a person uses excessively long words

that takes the cake

that is quite absurd or outrageous or excessively cheeky

to be a sticky beak

to show excessive curiosity into matters not of one's concern

to be above water

(of securities) to have a market value in excess of the cost price

to be babes in the wood

to be excessively naVve and inexperienced and thus ripe for exploitation

based on the folk legend of the babes in the wood of Wayland Hall, Norfolk

to be dressed up to the nines

to be attired in garments of the highest standard

perhaps a corruption of 'to then eyen' ('to the eyes'); Thomas Hardy (1840–1928), 'She's dressed up to the nines for some grand party'

to be on one's high horse

to be excessively pompous

refers to persons of high rank riding on tall horses; John Brown (1715–66), *Letter to Garrick*, 'Altogether upon the high horse'

to be tied to someone's apron strings

to be excessively influenced by one's mother

to be too frightened to say 'boo' to a goose

to be excessively shy

to be wet behind the ears

to be excessively naVve and inexperienced

to burn the candle at both ends

to exhaust one's resources through working excessive hours'

to charge like a wounded bull

to impose excessive prices

a play on words; not a simile

to cost an arm and a leg

to be excessively expensive

to eat one's head off

to eat excessively

to go overboard

to act foolishly and in an excessive way

to hang onto someone's coat-tails

to rely excessively on another's initiatives and achievements

to kill the goose that lays the golden eggs
through excessive greed, to sacrifice future gains for a short-term advantage
based on a Greek fable about a man who killed the goose that laid golden eggs; his aim was to collect the whole stock of eggs at once but, in doing so, he ended his future supply

to make heavy weather of something
to struggle excessively with a relatively simple task
nautical metaphor

to make noise enough to wake the dead
to be excessively noisy

to pay through the nose
to pay an excessive price
refers to an onerous tax imposed by the Danes in Ireland in the ninth century whereby those who refused to pay had their noses slit

to read the riot act
to reprimand persons who are excessively noisy or otherwise misbehaving
refers to the police reading out to a rowdy crowd extracts from a law requiring the crowd's dispersement

to talk the hind leg off a donkey
to talk excessively

Expectation

a gambit
(in a competitive situation) an opening move that involves short-term losses in the expectation of long-term gains
Italian *gambetto*, literally 'tripping up'

drawcard
feature expected to attract a crowd

front runner
person expected to win; OR someone who performs well only when holding an advantage

not to hold one's breath for something
to give up all expectation

opening shot
first step in an activity expected to last a long time
military metaphor

the calm before the storm
the quiet period before an expected or inevitable crisis

there are black clouds on the horizon
bad news is expected

to batten down the hatches
to get ready for expected difficulties
nautical metaphor

to be a tall order
to be an unreasonable expectation

to be in cloud-cuckoo land
to be mad or to have unrealistic expectations
'cloud-cuckoo land' was an imaginary city built in the air by the birds (according to the *Nephelococcygia* of *The Birds* by Aristophanes) — hence any utopian fantastic scheme

to be more than flesh can stand
to be more than a person reasonably can be expected to endure

to be more than one bargained for
to be more than one expected

to be successful beyond one's wildest dreams
to be far more successful than one could have expected

to beat the odds
to do better than could reasonably have been expected
refers to betting on horse races or similar

to cast one's bread upon the waters
to give generously because one will eventually be rewarded for one's generosity
Ecclesiastes 11:1, 'Cast thy bread upon the waters: for thou shalt find it after many days'

to catch someone with his pants/trousers down
to act when another person least expects it

to count one's chickens before they are hatched
to treat as fact the expected results of a future proposal
originally attributed to Erasmus (1466–1536) in slightly different form

to defy gravity
to go up when the expectation is to go down
to fall through
not to eventuate as expected
to grind to a halt
to have an activity gradually cease to function despite expectations that it would continue
to have Buckley's chance
to have no expectation at all
a pun, a reference to what follows 'Buckley' in 'Buckley & Nunn', the name of a well-known former Melbourne retailer
to live on borrowed time
to live longer than expected
to loom on the horizon
to be expected but not immediately
to raise the spectre of something
to draw attention to the expectation of something worrying refers to a ghost or apparition
to see the colour of someone's eyes
to see how a person matches expectations or requirements
to seek the pot of gold at the end of the rainbow
to have naVve expectations
refers to the proverbial belief in the existence of a pot of gold at the end of a rainbow
to turn up trumps
to finish up better than expected or to experience unexpected good luck
refers to playing cards
to wait for the other shoe to drop
to await the seemingly imminent and inevitable
refers to a person being disturbed by a neighbour who drops one shoe on the floor, the listener then being frustrated when the sound of the other shoe being dropped is not heard
to wear one's heart on one's sleeve
to lack the reserve expected of one
refers to the fashion of wearing a sign of romantic attachment on one's sleeve; Shakespeare *Othello* I:i, 'But I will wear my heart upon my sleeve'

Expense

a Pyrrhic victory
a win that costs more than if there had been a loss
refers to the Battle at Asculum in 279 BC at which King Pyrrhus of Epirus defeated the Romans
a Rolls-Royce solution
a high quality but excessively expensive way of doing something
a white elephant
an expensive and useless luxury
refers to gifts of sacred elephants by the King of Siam to persons then ruined by the expense of their upkeep
a white knight
a person voluntarily coming to the assistance of another person at considerable personal cost
derived from mediaeval tales of valiant knights rescuing those in distress, white being associated with purity and goodness
garage sale
sale of miscellaneous assets at cheap prices
heads I win, tails you lose
whichever way this matter goes I will benefit at your expense
refers to the tossing of a coin
not to be worth the candle
to be too expensive in relation to the true value; AND/OR not to be worth the effort required
the law of the jungle
the principle that those having power will use it at the expense of all others
Rudyard Kipling (1865–1936), *The Law of the Jungle*, 'Now this is the law of the jungle — as old and as true as the sky; and the wolf that shall keep it may prosper, but the wolf that shall break it must die'
the sky is the limit
there is no restriction upon what can be done
to be above water
(of securities) to have a market value in excess of the cost price
to be on the house
to be free of cost
to buy something for a song

to buy something very cheaply
to cost an arm and a leg
to be excessively expensive
to cut costs to the bone
to economise strictly
to hedge one's bets
to insure against a losing bet or investment by also investing on the opposite outcome
to hit someone hard
greatly to affect a person emotionally; OR to cost a person a lot of money
to hold the purse strings
to have control of expenditure
refers to a drawstring closing a purse
to mortgage the future
to get benefits now but at a cost in due course
refers to a charge over property recognised by the law
to wield the knife
to terminate the services of one or more persons or to prune expenditure

Experience

a blessing in disguise
an unwelcome but salutary experience
James Hervey (1696–1743), *Reflections on a Flower Garden*, 'Ee'en crosses from his sov'reign hand are blessings in disguise'
a green chum
an inexperienced person
Shakespeare, *Antony & Cleopatra* I:v, 'my salad days, when I was green in judgment'
a nightmare
an unpleasant experience
a past master
an expert with long experience
derived from freemasonry
a trap for young players
a significant likelihood of the inexperienced or naVve making mistakes
a warhorse
an experienced and dependable campaigner in war, politics, sport, and other contests
an old head on young shoulders
experience, knowledge, and maturity in a young person
distant fields look greener
activities of which one has no experience seem more attractive than is really the case
Psalms 23:1, 'The Lord is my shepherd ... he shall feed me in a green pasture'
hard-bitten
toughened by experience
refers to horses that are 'hard' in the mouth or bite (and thus difficult to control)
hard-boiled
toughened by experience
refers to cooking (esp. eggs)
off the top of one's head
impromptu, based on experience or intuition, but without detailed consideration
to be babes in the wood
to be excessively naVve and inexperienced and thus ripe for exploitation
based on the folk legend of the babes in the wood of Wayland Hall, Norfolk
to be in a hole
to experience some difficulties
to be in a tight corner
to have little or no chance of escape from a difficult situation
to be in uncharted waters
to be the first to experience something
nautical metaphor
to be someone's bread and butter
to be a person's livelihood or to be a person's everyday experience
to be wet behind the ears
to be excessively naVve and inexperienced
to broaden someone's mind
to expose a person to a greater variety of experiences and interests than that person had previously experienced
to cut one's teeth on something
to get one's first experience by doing something
to feel the draught
to experience unfavourable conditions
to hide one's light under a bushel
to keep others in ignorance of one's skills and experience

Luke 11:33, 'No man, when he hath lighted a candle, putteth it in a secret place, neither under a bushel'

to learn a lesson
to benefit from one's experience

to pick someone's brain
to get the benefit of another person's knowledge and experience

to put someone through the mill
to make someone endure significant hardship through severe practical experience

to reap as one has sown
to experience the consequences of one's own actions

Galatians 6:7, 'Whatsoever a man soweth, that shall he also reap'

to teach one's grandmother how to suck eggs
to try to tell a much more experienced person something very obvious to that person

to turn up trumps
to finish up better than expected or to experience unexpected good luck

refers to playing cards

Expertise

a backroom boy
someone who works behind the scenes

Lord Beaverbrook (24 April 1941), 'to whom must praise be given ... to the boys in the backroom' (referring to the anonymous laboratory workers who contributed so much to scientific warfare and war production in World War II)

a past master
an expert with long experience

derived from freemasonry

father knows best
as an expert, I know better than you do what is most suitable for you

not to be someone's cup of tea
not to be to a person's liking; OR to be outside a person's expertise or area of interest

to be slipping
to be losing one's cunning or expertise

to be up one's alley
to be right within a person's expertise or area of interest

to hang up one's shingle
to go into business offering expert personal services

refers to an external notice advertising one's name and qualifications

to stick to one's game
to confine oneself to activities in areas in which one has knowledge and expertise

Fact

a goldmine
a source of much wealth or of many facts

a gut feeling
a belief based purely on intuition and unsupported by facts or evidence

a siting shot
an initial move designed to establish facts for use in a later action

military metaphor

a tell-tale sign
a visible indication revealing true facts despite efforts at concealment

it will all come out in the wash
the facts will emerge as work proceeds

put that in your pipe and smoke it
contemplate that fact if you can!

a strong rebuke given to an adversary; R. H. Barham (1788–1845), *Lay of St Odille*, 'So put that in your pipe, my Lord Otto, and smoke it!'

showdown
a final test or confrontation after declaring one's position

refers to poker

that takes on added colour
there are now further facts that alter the appearance of a matter

the affair blew up
certain unwelcome facts have become publicly available

the penny dropped
a person has just realised a fact that should have been obvious

refers to old-fashioned pay toilets

to ascertain the lie of the land

to establish the pertinent facts and opinions

to balance the picture
to quote facts or arguments in contradiction

to be old hat
to be old-fashioned; OR well known to the point of tedium

to be on the wrong tram
to be completely mistaken as to the basic facts

to bring a fact home to someone
to make a person recognise a fact despite that person's inclination to the contrary

to count one's chickens before they are hatched
to treat as fact the expected results of a future proposal
originally attributed to Erasmus (1466–1536) in slightly different form

to drag someone by the head and ears
to force a person to reveal the true facts

to draw a long bow
to state a conclusion that, although possible, is unlikely on the known facts
refers to archery

to flush out the facts
to ascertain, after some effort, the truth of some matter

to fly blind
to do something in ignorance of the relevant facts
refers to pilots flying without visual guidance (and relying on instruments)

to have one's wires crossed
to be mistaken about key facts
refers to a short-circuit in electrical wiring

to have something to chew on
to have firm facts on which to base a decision

to put the jigsaw together
to solve a problem by placing together a number of separate facts
refers to a jigsaw puzzle

to send someone away with a flea in the ear
to give a person frank, but unwelcome, facts
perhaps refers to fleas trapped in the armour of ancient knights, or perhaps from the discomfort felt by a dog with a flea in its ear; or perhaps, figuratively, to any lingering irritation in the ear

to sift
to examine closely and assess the components appropriately

to strengthen someone's hand
to give a person additional authority or greater moral support or more facts to support that person's case

to take something at face value
(of alleged facts) to accept something without question or challenge

to take something with a grain of salt
to regard the facts in a statement with considerable scepticism

to throw in one's six pennies'/two cents' worth
modestly to supply one's own facts or views

to wake up to something
to realise a fact or its significance

to whitewash
to attempt to conceal the guilt or mistakes of a person
refers to the use of whitewash on a wall to conceal blemishes

when the balloon goes up
when the adverse facts come to light

when the chips are down
when all facts are known and taken into consideration

Factor

a bottleneck
a factor obstructing an even flow

a catalyst
a factor causing something to happen
in chemistry, a catalyst is strictly, a factor that facilitates (but does not initiate) a chemical reaction

a stereotype
(of a group) a general impression of the characteristics that is assumed to apply to all members of that group
refers to the plates formerly used in printing

chicken and egg

a situation involving two factors each of which causes the other, making it impossible to decide which came first

the lifeblood
the main or essential ingredient; OR the person or factor instilling enthusiasm

to be a magnet
to be an attractive person or thing to which other persons or things are drawn

to cloud one's mind
to allow irrelevant or extraneous factors to affect one's impartiality or judgment

to make or break someone
to be a factor leading either to a person's success or to that person's failure, with no intermediate position

to paint a black picture
to state a set of unfavourable factors

to present a rosy picture
to state a set of favourable factors

to see which way the wind is blowing
to establish the factors relevant to a situation
John Seldon (1584–1654), 'Take a straw and throw it up into the air, you shall see by that which way the wind is'

to tip the balance/scales
to be further information or argument that results in an issue, that could have been decided either way, being determined in a particular way
refers to balance scales

trigger
factor responsible for certain events occurring at that particular time

Failure

a bloodbath
catastrophic losses

a case of rats leaving a sinking ship
the desertion of an enterprise in anticipation of imminent failure

a damp squib
disappointingly ineffective action
refers to fireworks that fail to go off

a flash in the pan
something that begins promisingly but does not last
refers to the priming of old guns

a gambit
(in a competitive situation) an opening move that involves short-term losses in the expectation of long-term gains
Italian *gambetto*, literally 'tripping up'

a game of cat and mouse
negotiations between two parties of unequal bargaining power during which the stronger makes some temporary concessions to the weaker without, however, affecting the latter's eventual total defeat

a landslide
an electoral result involving victory or defeat by a very large margin

a Pyrrhic victory
a win that costs more than if there had been a loss
refers to the Battle at Asculum in 279 BC at which King Pyrrhus of Epirus defeated the Romans

a roller-coaster ride
a series of successes followed by failures

a South Sea bubble
an unrealistic financial venture that is bound to result in total loss
refers to a notorious financial scandal involving the South Sea Company (UK) in 1720

checkmate
defeat
refers to chess

it is a case of sink or swim
it is a case of success or failure with no other alternatives
refers to the 'testing' of so-called witches by throwing them into water to see if they would sink or swim

stalemate
a final result in which neither party to a dispute is victorious
refers to chess

that is money down the drain
money has been wastefully lost on a failed project

the dice are loaded against someone

a person is unlikely to succeed in something
refers to cheating in gambling with dice

the wheels fell off
the plan failed

to back the wrong horse
to have faith in, give support to, and/or invest in a project that proves to be unsuccessful
refers to betting on racehorses

to bang one's head against a brick wall
to fight an unwinnable case

to be a dead duck
to have failed; OR or to be in a hopeless situation

to be done like a dinner
to be defeated and humiliated

to be on the ropes
to be facing defeat
refers to boxing

to be one in the eye for someone
to represent an unexpected and unwelcome defeat

to be sheer murder
to be extremely unpleasant or difficult; OR to be an inglorious defeat

to be slipping
to be losing one's cunning or expertise

to beat by a long shot
to defeat very convincingly

to become a vegetable
to lose one's ability to respond to many external stimuli, especially those that normally contribute to the quality of life; to lead a monotonous life with no animation

to burn one's fingers
to suffer (esp. loss of money) through foolishness or meddling
refers to taking chestnuts from a fire

to chase a corpse
to harp on something long ago resolved or a lost cause

to derail some strategy
to cause a strategy to fail

to draw a blank
to be unsuccessful
refers to playing cards

to eat crow
to act in a humiliating fashion to achieve a desired outcome
from an incident in New England (North America) in the Anglo–American War of 1812–14

to eat someone alive
to defeat a person soundly

to fall to the ground
to fail
Matthew 10:29, 'Are not two sparrows sold for a farthing? And one of them shall not fall on the ground without your Father ... '

to fly out the window
to become irretrievably and wastefully lost

to force someone on to that person's knees
to inflict a humiliating defeat on a person

to get off the canvas
to recover after near defeat
refers to boxing

to give someone a bath
to defeat a person comprehensively

to go down the tube
to fail

to hold a winning hand
to be in an unbeatable position to defeat others
refers to playing cards

to hold all the aces
to be in an unbeatable position to defeat others
refers to playing cards; from Latin *as* ('unity', that is 'one' or 'a single point')

to hold the trump card
to be in an unbeatable position to defeat others
refers to playing cards

to kiss something good-bye
to give something up as permanently lost

to kiss the ground
to revere or bless the land; OR to be overthrown

to lick one's wounds
to adjust oneself to defeat
refers to a dog cleaning its own wounds

to lose face
to experience embarrassment by an affront to one's dignity

to lose money hand over fist

to lose money very fast and comprehensively
to lose one's shirt
to make heavy financial losses
Luke 6:29 (RSV), '... and from him who takes away your coat do not withhold even your shirt'
to make a last-ditch stand
to make a brave effort to stave off final defeat
King William III (1650–1702), 'There is one way never to see it lost ... and that is to die in the last ditch' (quoted by Burnet, *History of His Own Times*,1715)
to make or break someone
to be a factor leading either to a person's success or to that person's failure, with no intermediate position
to meet one's Waterloo
to receive a decisive defeat
refers to Napoleon's fate at the Battle of Waterloo (1815)
to miss the boat/bus/train
to fail to exploit an opportunity
to miss the sharks while netting the minnows
to succeed in minor aspects but fail in the ones that really matter
to nurse one's bruises/wounds
to adjust oneself to defeat
to overstep the mark
to fail to observe the proprieties
refers to gaining an unfair advantage in a contest (originally the mark between two fighters)
to play the trump card
to make a final move, thereby defeating one's opponents
refers to playing cards
to raise the stake
to increase the amount of potential gain or loss in a project
refers to gambling
to rub it in
to humiliate another person by emphasising that person's defeat
to save face
to avoid humiliation or loss of reputation
to sink slowly in the west
to fail gradually
refers to the setting of the sun in the western sky
to stem the haemorrhage/bleeding
to put a stop to the financial losses of a project
to throw good money after bad
to waste further money in a vain attempt to recover money already lost
to throw in the sponge/towel
to concede defeat
refers to boxing
to tighten the noose
to get closer to inflicting defeat
refers to death by hanging
to trump someone
to defeat a person
refers to playing cards
to turn the corner
to commence being successful after initial failures
to wipe the floor with someone
to inflict a humiliating defeat on a person

Falsity

a false dawn
an incident giving rise to unjustified hope
refers to a transient light that precedes the true dawn by about an hour
a tall story
an interesting but untrue and unbelievable tale
a white lie
a false statement uttered in a good cause
some mud will stick
reputations will be hurt even after accusations are proved false
to cook the books
fraudulently to maintain false records of financial transactions
to dream up some story
to concoct a false story naVvely or maliciously
to lie through one's teeth
to tell blatant untruths
to nail a lie
to expose an untruth
to pull someone's leg
to tell a false but plausible story as an act of humour
to sail under false colours

to pretend that one's real character or beliefs are different from what they really are
refers to a ship concealing its true identity
to speak with a forked tongue
to utter halftruths with the intention of misleading the listener
to swallow the line
to accept as truth the story being proffered
refers to angling

Frankness

a straight shooter
a person who is frank and outspoken
not to pull any punches
to be brutally frank
refers to boxing
to come out into the open
to start being frank
to hit someone right between the eyes
to be brutally frank
refers to fighting
to lay one's cards on the table
to be utterly frank and open or to honestly disclose one's position
refers to playing cards
to make no bones about it
to be brutally frank
to send someone away with a flea in the ear
to give a person frank, but unwelcome, facts
perhaps refers to fleas trapped in the armour of ancient knights, or perhaps from the discomfort felt by a dog with a flea in its ear; or perhaps, figuratively, to any lingering irritation in the ear
to shoot from the hip
to speak without careful assessment of the situation
to speak one's mind
to express one's views frankly and forcefully

Fright

in fear and trembling
in a state of apprehension
Philippians 2:12, 'Work out your own salvation with fear and trembling'
to frighten hell out of someone
to cause great alarm to a person
to frighten the horses
to scare people off by one's ill-considered tactics
Mrs Patrick Campbell (1865–1940), quoting oral tradition, 'I don't mind where people make love, so long as they don't do it in the street and frighten the horses'
to have a threat hanging over one's head
to fear some intimated unpleasant action
refers to Damocles who had the sword of Dionysius hanging, by a slender thread, over his head — as a symbol of perpetual risk in life; the story is told in Cicero, *Tusculanae Disputationes*
to have nerves of steel
not to be easily frightened
to lose one's nerve
to abandon, out of fear, a decision to do something
to make someone's flesh creep
to frighten a person with something horrific
to jump nearly out of one's skin
to receive a fright
to put the fear of God into someone
to frighten a person into behaving properly
Ecclesiates 12:13, 'Fear God, and keep his commandments; for this is the whole duty of man'
to scare the pants off someone
to frighten a person greatly
to tremble in one's shoes
to be afraid

Future

a bird in the hand is worth two in the bush

a benefit currently available is more valuable than a seemingly much larger benefit that might or might not be achieved in the future

a crystal ball
accurate knowledge of the future
refers to ancient means of divining the future

to bat on
to continue an activity
refers to cricket

to be destined for the scrapheap
to face a future in which one will have no meaningful role

to conduct a post mortem on something
to review past actions with a view to learning lessons for the future
Latin, *post mortem*, 'after the death'

to count one's chickens before they are hatched
to treat as fact the expected results of a future proposal
originally attributed to Erasmus (1466–1536) in slightly different form

to have a cloud hanging over one's head
there is doubt as to one's future
refers to the pillar of cloud (God) passing judgment on the Hebrews; the pillar of cloud is described in *Exodus* 13:21 *et seq.*

to keep someone's seat warm
to hold a position temporarily with a view to another person's taking it over permanently in the near future

to keep something up one's sleeve
secretly to retain something in reserve for use in the future or at a later stage of negotiations
refers to playing cards or magicians

to mortgage the future
to get benefits now but at a cost in due course
refers to a charge over property recognised by the law

to pigeon-hole
to put aside for further consideration in the distant future
refers to placing something in a small hole, like the small hole in a dovecot for the pigeons to walk in and out

to put something into cold storage
to put something aside to be dealt with at some indeterminate future time

to telegraph one's punches
by one's actions to give advance warning of one's future plans
refers to sending an advance message

to wash one's hands of something
emphatically to decline future responsibility
Matthew 27:24, 'He [Pilate] took water and washed his hands in full view of the crowd. "My hands are clean of this man's blood," he declared'

Happiness and Enjoyment

a field day
a very enjoyable and successful occasion
refers (originally) to an army's practice manoeuvres

all their Christmases came at once
they were overjoyed

in halcyon days
in past happier times
Shakespeare, *Henry V, Part 1*, I:ii, 'Expect St Martin's summer, halcyon days'; refers to the fourteen days about the winter solstice when winds were calm, and to the mythical bird said to breed in a floating nest at that time

to be in a seventh heaven
to be ecstatically happy in a state of bliss
refers to the highest state of heavenly bliss in Judaism, Christianity, and Islam

to be in clover
to enjoy a life of ease and luxury
refers to grazing animals in rich pasture

to be on cloud nine
to be very happy

to be on the crest of a wave
to enjoy success that might not last

to be on top of the world
to be very happy

to be rapt in something
to be thoroughly involved with something and enjoying it immensely
shortened form of 'enraptured'

to have a ball
to have an enjoyable time

to have a run for one's money
to at least get some enjoyment out of an otherwise abortive exercise
refers to betting on horse racing

to jump for joy
to express great satisfaction

to lap it up
to enjoy the attention

to laugh one's head off
to enjoy something greatly

to make the beast with two backs
to engage in sexual intercourse
Shakespeare, *Othello* I:i, 'Your daughter and the Moor are now making the beast with two backs'

to play the field
to distribute one's favours among more than one person

to throw one's cap/hat into the air
to express joy; OR to celebrate some achievement

to turn handstands
to express great joy

to walk on air
to be joyful

to warm the cockles of someone's heart
to delight a person
refers to the cockle shell which looks like a heart; the formal name for bivalve molluscs (such as cockles) is *cardium* (Latin for 'heart')

Harm

a muckraker
a person who sets out to publicise features harming another person's reputation

not to touch a hair on someone's head
not to harm a person
Matthew 10:30, 'the very hairs of your head are all numbered'

one cannot make an omelette without breaking eggs
the desired end dictates the means even if they cause harm to others

the final (or last) straw
the latest step that, when added to a large number of seemingly harmless previous steps, sets off a significant event resulting from the cumulative effect
see 'the straw that broke the camel's back'

the straw that broke the camel's back
the latest step that, when added to a large number of seemingly harmless previous steps, sets off a sudden significant event resulting from the cumulative effect

to be a wolf in sheep's clothing
to be a hypocrite; to be dangerous although masquerading as something harmless
Matthew 7:15, 'Beware of false prophets, which come to you in sheep's clothing, but inwardly they are ravening wolves'

to cut one's nose off to spite one's face
to act in pique in a way that harms only oneself

to keep something on an even keel
to ensure that something is kept balanced and stable
nautical metaphor

to let blood
to allow some harm as the price for achieving some greater benefit
refers to surgical removal of a patient's blood

to save one's bacon
to escape harm
refers to the value attached to bacon as a stored food

to shoot oneself in the foot
to act in a foolish way and thus harm one's own cause

to stab someone in the back
deliberately and surreptitiously to harm a person who regarded one as a friend

Hope

a chink of light
a small hope of a solution or breakthrough

a false dawn
an incident giving rise to unjustified hope
refers to a transient light that precedes the true dawn by about an hour

a fat chance
little hope

a laundry list
a large set of demands

a light in the sky
a sign of great hope

a slough of despond
a feeling of hopelessness
refers to a swamp; John Bunyan (1628–88), *The Pilgrim's Progress* Pt I, 'The name of the slough was despond'

not a dog's chance
virtually no hope at all

not the ghost of a chance
no hope at all
Katherine Mansfield (1888–1923), 'he hadn't a ghost of a chance, he hadn't an earthly'

pie in the sky
a hoped for result unlikely to be achieved

the one bright spot on the horizon
the only hopeful aspect

things look black
there is little hope of success or prosperity or a favourable outcome

to clasp/grasp at straws
desperately to resort to any expedient in a hopeless situation
refers to a drowning person

to fish for compliments
to drop hints in the hope that one will receive praise or recognition

to fly a kite
to issue uncovered cheques in the hope that they will be covered before clearance; OR to test public reaction to a measure in contemplation by leaking broad details of it to the media

to have a snowflake's chance in hell
to have no hope or possibility at all

to keep one's fingers crossed
to hope for a good outcome
refers to making the sign of the Christian cross to protect against ill-fortune

to pull something out of the fire
to salvage something in a seemingly hopeless situation

to sow seeds
to propagate ideas in the hope that they will be adopted

to teach someone a lesson
to inflict something unpleasant on a person in the hope that it will lead to a change in that person's behaviour

to throw a sprat to catch a mackerel
to risk a little in the hope of gaining much

to touch wood
to hope that our good luck will not go away
refers to ancient belief in sacred power of certain trees, especially oak, ash, hazel, hawthorn and willow

Idea

a brainwave
a suddenly occurring bright idea

a copycat
a person who imitates another person's ideas

a dinosaur
someone or something with incredibly outmoded ideas

a pipeline to someone
an intermediary used as a means of communicating ideas to a person

a swelled head
an exaggerated idea of one's abilities or status

a thought in the back of one's mind
an undeveloped idea

brainchild
inspired original idea

I buy that
I accept that idea

moonshine
unrealistic ideas

the idea has legs
this notion seems a good one

to act as a sounding board
to give, on request, constructive criticisms of ideas tentatively held

refers, originally, to a board placed behind a speaker (esp. a preacher) to reflect the speaker's voice forwards to the congregation or audience

to be bankrupt of ideas
to be bereft of ideas

to be poles apart
to have ideas that are very different

to be someone's bLte noire
to be a person whose ideas and actions cause upset and loathing in another person
French, *bLte noire* ('black beast')

to be the cradle of something
to be the place where some idea was first nurtured

to be too big for one's breeches
to have an exaggerated idea of one's own importance

to brainstorm
to pool thoughts in the course of a session designed to generate fresh ideas and especially to build up on the ideas of others

to disseminate ideas
to spread ideas to a wide audience
literally, 'to scatter seeds in various places'

to dust some idea off
to revive some proposal

to encapsulate some idea
to reduce the essential points of a complicated proposal to a small number of words

to go to someone's head
to cause a person to get an exaggerated idea of that person's abilities or status

to have a blank canvas
freedom to create anything
refers to an artist's canvas

to knock an idea on the head
utterly to reject a proposal

to leap at an idea
to accept a suggestion enthusiastically

to pour cold water on some idea
to be unenthusiastic about some proposal or scornful of its apparent weaknesses

to put several heads together
to confer and pool ideas

to put pen to paper
to set out one's ideas in written form

to ram something down someone's throat
to pressure another person into accepting an idea with which that person does not agree

to sow seeds
to propagate ideas in the hope that they will be adopted

to speak the same language
to have a good understanding and similar ideas

to stand on someone's shoulders
to build up on another person's ideas

to steal someone's clothes
to plagiarise another person's ideas

to test the water
to try out an idea in a small way

to throw something out of the window
to reject completely an idea or proposal

to turn someone's head
to cause a person to get an exaggerated idea of that person's abilities or status

young Turks
members of an organisation who hold ideas regarded as too revolutionary
refers to an early twentieth-century revolutionary political party in what was to become Turkey

Inference

the answer is a lemon
there is no appropriate answer to that sort of proposition

to bark up the wrong tree
to reach an incorrect conclusion and/or to pursue an erroneous course of action

to draw a long bow
to state a conclusion that, although possible, is unlikely on the known facts
refers to archery

to get the wrong sow by the ear
to reach an incorrect conclusion

to hit the nail right on the head

astutely to come to the correct conclusion

to jump to a conclusion
to infer something without proper consideration

to make up one's mind
to reach a conclusion after contemplating a matter

to put two and two together to reach a conclusion (usually obvious) by combining isolated pieces of information

Interest

a nine-day wonder
an exciting event, but one that will cease to arouse interest when the novelty has worn off
old English proverb: 'a wonder lasts nine days, and then the puppy's eyes are open'; Shakespeare was probably alluding to this proverb (or similar) in *Henry VI Pt III*, III:ii, 'That would be ten days' wonder, at the least / That's a day longer than a wonder lasts'

a sweetheart deal
an agreement negotiated in private to the special benefit of those involved in the negotiations

a tall story
an interesting but untrue and unbelievable tale

birds of a feather flock together
persons of like interests gather in the same place
Samuel Rutherford (?1600–61), 'Fowls of a feather flock together'

in our camp
in the group, representing our vested interest

kindred spirit
person with similar interests and eccentricities
John Keats (1795–1821), *O Solitude!*, 'Almost the highest bliss of human-kind, / when to thy haunts two kindred spirits flee'

not to be someone's cup of tea
not to be to a person's liking; OR to be outside a person's expertise or area of interest

not to care a pin for something
not to have the slightest interest in something

on our side of the fence
in the group representing our vested interest

someone's guardian angel
someone's friend, watching over them and advancing their interests
Shakespeare, *Hamlet* IV:i, 'Angels and ministers of grace defend us!'

to be on one's hobby horse
to dominate a conversation by insisting on talking about subjects in which one has an obsessive interest
refers to a person who dressed with a figure of a horse around the waist or on the head in Morris dancing — hence a figure of fun, a jester, a buffoon

to be up one's alley
to be right within a person's expertise or area of interest

to bore someone to death
to weary a person greatly by dull and uninteresting conversation or by lack of action

to bore someone to tears
to weary a person by dull and uninteresting conversation or by lack of action

to bore the pants off someone
to weary a person by dull and uninteresting conversation

to break ranks
to identify oneself as having separate interests or views from the rest of a group
military metaphor

to broaden someone's mind
to expose a person to a greater variety of experiences and interests than that person had previously experienced

to compare notes
to exchange information about some subject of mutual interest

to have a finger in the pie
to have an interest in a project, especially an officious involvement

to have an axe to grind
to have a vested interest; to pursue a personal objective

to need to watch one's back
to find it necessary to take care in case others act against one's interests

to talk one's book
to present arguments that, although plausible, are really designed to foster one's vested interest

to throw one's hat into the ring
publicly to announce one's interest in some position
refers to custom of throwing one's hat into a ring to indicate a willingness to take part in a boxing challenge

to wear a particular hat
to act in a particular capacity or for a particular vested interest

to whet one's appetite
to arouse one's curiosity, interest, or desire

Interference

a logjam
a stoppage of activity caused by input in greater volume than allowed for
refers to a crowded mass of cut logs in a river

a palace revolt
the overthrow of those in authority by their subordinates

a stitch in time saves nine
preventive maintenance saves money in the long run

nothing is sacred
nothing is safe from interference

pull your head in!
do not interfere in this! you are advised to withdraw from this situation

stumbling block
an impediment or difficulty preventing the easy completion of some project; OR a dilemma involving a moral issue
1 Corinthians 8:9, 'But take heed lest by any means this liberty of yours become a stumbling block to them that are weak'

to be stopped in one's tracks
suddenly and unexpectedly to be prevented from carrying on with a project

to block someone's path
to interfere with a person's opportunity to advance

to break down the barriers
to do away with the prejudice preventing something

to cloud one's mind
to allow irrelevant or extraneous factors to affect one's impartiality or judgment

to get the red light
to be forbidden to do something
refers to the 'stop' signal on roads and rail

to go over someone's head
to bypass lower levels of authority and approach someone more senior instead; OR to be beyond a person's ability to understand

to hold someone on a short leash
to give a person very little freedom
refers to a lead used to restrain coursing hounds

to keep off someone's patch
not to interfere with or compete against another person in that person's customary area of activity

to keep one's cotton-picking fingers off something
not to interfere (in a meddlesome fashion) with something

to keep someone in a strait jacket
to deny a person any discretionary powers at all
refers to a restraining 'jacket' used to control violent or insane persons

to let blood
to allow some harm as the price for achieving some greater benefit
refers to surgical removal of a patient's blood

to poke one's nose into something
to interfere

to put a leg-rope on someone
to give a person very little freedom
refers to a restraining rope on cattle on other animals

to put a spoke in someone's wheel
to interfere with another person's activity, so preventing its continuance

to put one's foot down
to assert one's authority and insist on something

to queer the pitch for someone
to spoil the opportunity a person has to do something

to spike someone's guns

to sabotage (or negate the effect of) an opponent's devices
to stand in someone's way
to prevent a person achieving that person's goal
to strengthen someone's hand
to give a person additional authority or greater moral support or more facts to support that person's case
to take the gilt off the gingerbread
to strip something of its main attraction
to throw a spanner into the works
to cause an unexpected complication
to tie someone's hands
to prevent a person from acting as that person sees fit
to tie someone's hands behind that person's back
to make it impossible for a person to act at all
to tread on someone's corns/toes
to upset another person by interfering in that person's area of responsibility
to wipe the slate clean
to forgive past indiscretions

Involvement

a lone wolf
a person who prefers to act without involving others
the cure is worse than the complaint/disease
the remedy involves more disadvantages than if it were not applied
Francis Bacon (1561–1626), *Of Seditions and Troubles*, 'The remedy is worse than the disease'
to be a black-and-white issue
to involve very clear distinctions
Ben Jonson (1573–1637), *Every Man in his Honour*, 'I have it here in black and white'
to be a two-edged sword
to involve both advantages and disadvantages of similar significance
Psalms 149:6, 'Let the high praises of God be in their mouth, and a two-edged sword in their hand'
to be in something up to one's armpits
to be involved very deeply in something
to be in the thick of things
to get involved at the centre of some activity
to be on a treadmill
to be involved in some unpleasant ongoing activity that cannot readily be stopped
to be the centre of the spider's web
to control an operation that involves numerous and/or complex ingredients
to be up to one's ears in something
to be involved very deeply in something
to be up to one's elbows in something
to be very busy and involved with something
to be up to one's neck in something
to be very deeply involved in something
to be up to the eyeballs in something
to be involved very deeply in something
to butt in
to involve oneself, uninvited, in someone else's conversation
refers to the aggressive action of animals with the head
to call it a day
to cease involvement with some activity
to catch someone in the net
unexpectedly to involve a particular person in the course of activity designed to involve many others
to cover one's tracks
to hide the evidence of one's involvement
to cut both ways
to involve both advantages and disadvantages of similar significance
to give the game away
to cease involvement with some activity; OR to reveal the nature of a hidden activity or plan
to have a finger in something

to be involved in something

to have a tiger by the tail
to be involved in an activity that is much more dangerous than one had realised

to hedge one's bets
to insure against a losing bet or investment by also investing on the opposite outcome

to hijack a debate
to involve oneself in discussion on some matter and turn that discussion to one's advantage

to leave someone high and dry
to isolate a person from a desired involvement; to withdraw all support from a person
nautical metaphor referring to a boat stranded out of water

to raise merry hell
to cause an uproar by outlandish, reckless, or larrikinish behaviour
in the eighteenth century there were clubs of reckless young men, known as 'hell-fire clubs', who were said to 'raise merry hell'

to see the back of someone
to know that a person is no longer involved in something

to start the ball rolling
to commence and advance enthusiastically an activity

to take a back seat
not to involve oneself actively

to twiddle one's thumbs
not to be involved in any worthwhile activity

uneasy lies the head that wears a crown
leadership involves some risks and some burdens (esp. the risk of being deposed)
Shakespeare, *Henry IV*, Part 2, III:i, 'Uneasy lies the head that wears a crown'

Judgment

beauty is in the eye of the beholder
some things are matters for subjective judgments
Shakespeare *Love's Labour Lost* II:i, 'Beauty is bought by judgment of the eye'

in someone's eyes
in a person's judgment

to cloud one's mind
to allow irrelevant or extraneous factors to affect one's impartiality or judgment

to fall flat on one's face
to fail or to be seriously embarrassed by a bad error of judgment

to fall in love with something
to have lost detachment in assessing the merits of some matter

to have an open mind
to be willing to assess evidence on its merits and without prejudging it

to judge a book by its cover
foolishly to go only by superficial appearances

to put money on the table
to back one's judgment in a tangible way or to demonstrate one's sincerity

to put one's money where one's mouth is
to back one's boasting by putting assets at risk

to twist someone's arm
to coerce another person to do something against that person's will or better judgment

Knowledge

a crystal ball
accurate knowledge of the future
refers to ancient means of divining the future

a down-to-earth solution
a realistic solution

a rich vein of gold
much useful information; a good source of something desirable

a skeleton in the closet/cupboard
an unpleasant truth the knowledge of which has been deliberately suppressed
William Makepeace Thackeray (1811–63), *The Newcomes* (1855), ' … they have a skelton or two in their closets as well as their neighbours'

an old head on young shoulders
experience, knowledge, and maturity in a young person

as soon as someone's back was turned
at the moment it became possible to do something without a person's knowledge

father knows best
as an expert, I know better than you do what is most suitable for you

fools rush in where angels fear to tread
unsophisticated persons take unwise risks in circumstances where more knowledgeable persons would exercise caution
Alexander Pope (1688–1744), *An Essay on Criticism* 1:625, 'For fools rush in where angels fear to tread'

hard-headed
realistic

someone would turn in his or her grave
someone would have been very surprised or displeased if he or she had known while still alive

heaven only knows
it is not known to me or anyone else

it hits one
one suddenly realises something

it's a small world
it is surprising to meet people one knows in unexpected places

not to have the foggiest notion
to know nothing at all about the subject

on the radar screen
in someone's consciousness

still waters run deep
a person with a quiet manner might have many unrecognised characteristics — both good and bad
W. H. Auden (1907–73), *Twelve Songs VIII*, 'Still waters run deep, my dear, there's never smoke without fire'

the left hand does not know what the right hand is doing
a person or an organisation is not aware of inconsistencies in conduct
Matthew 6:3, 'But when you give alms, do not let your left hand know what your right hand is doing'

the penny dropped
a person has just realised a fact that should have been obvious
refers to old-fashioned pay toilets

the pot calling the kettle black
criticising another person without realising one's own even greater shortcomings

the word is out
it is now known

to be a full bottle on something
to be very knowledgeable about a subject

to be at the end of one's tether
to be frustrated because one is at the very limit of one's resources of knowledge, authority, or patience
refers to tethering of animals with a rope

to be child's play
to be easy or to require only elementary skills and knowledge

to be geared up to do something
to have equipment, labour, and know-how in place adequate for some task
refers to mechanics

to be hot on a subject
to be knowledgeable and enthusiastic about a subject

to be in someone's blood
to be something about which a person is inherently very knowledgeable or keen

to be in the swim
to be a member of a group knowing what is going on

to be old hat
to be old-fashioned; OR well known to the point of tedium

to bring a fact home to someone
to make a person recognise a fact despite that person's inclination to the contrary

to buy a pig in a poke
to buy goods of unknown quality
refers to the practice of selling a person a cat (purported to be a pig) in a bag (or poke); if the person opened the bag and looked inside, that person 'let the cat out of the bag'

to cock one's eye at someone
to glance knowingly at a person

to draw a long bow

to state a conclusion that, although possible, is unlikely on the known facts

refers to archery

to drop names

to slip names of celebrities allegedly known to the speaker into a conversation in an attempt to impress

to hand on the torch

to pass on the traditions and aspirations of life

Lucretius (94?–55 BC), ' … the generations of living creatures are changed and like the runners relay the torch of life'

to have a tiger by the tail

to be involved in an activity that is much more dangerous than one had realised

to have eyes at/in the back of one's head

to know more of what is going on than is generally realised

to have one's feet firmly on the ground

to be very practical

to have one's fingers on the pulse

to know what is going on

medical/nursing metaphor

to know something in one's heart of hearts

to know something — although reluctant to admit it, even to oneself

Shakespeare, *Hamlet* III:ii, 'In my heart's core, ay, in my heart of heart'

to know something inside out

to know something very thoroughly

to know the ropes

to know how to do one's job

nautical metaphor

to know where one stands

to know what one supports or how one is affected

to know which way to turn

to know which strategy to adopt or where to seek assistance

to pick someone's brain

to get the benefit of another person's knowledge and experience

to put one's reputation on the line

to take a public stance in the realisation that there is a risk that one's reputation will suffer if one is proved wrong

to see the back of someone

to know that a person is no longer involved in something

to see the light

to understand the real situation

refers to the conversion of Saul (Paul) on the road to Damascus, *Acts* 9:3, 4 'And suddenly there shined round about him a light from heaven: and he fell to the earth'

to shrug one's shoulders

to indicate that one does not know or care, or that one is unable or unwilling to assist

to spread the gospel

to propagate principles or attitudes that one believes to be true

Mark 16:15, 'Go ye into the world and preach the gospel to every creature'

to stick to one's game

to confine oneself to activities in areas in which one has knowledge and expertise

to wake up to something

to realise a fact or its significance

under someone's nose

in a person's immediate area of responsibility or in circumstances where that person should have known something

what is this — a bunch of grapes or a bowl of goldfish?

surely you know what this is?

when the chips are down

when all facts are known and taken into consideration

with 20/20 hindsight

with the benefit of knowing what happened

refers to American system of expressing perfect visual acuity

Leadership

kingmaker

person engaging in behind-the-scenes activities to promote another person to a particular leadership position

the blind leading the blind

persons without the necessary skills for a task purporting to impart those skills to others

Matthew 15:14, 'And if the blind lead the blind, both shall fall into the ditch'

the high priest of something
the leading advocate of something
refers to religious leaders

to be at the head of the pack
to be the best of many, or the *de facto* leader

to be at the top of the tree
to be a leading member of one's profession

to be the leading light
to be the most important person in a venture
Exodus 13:21, 'And the Lord went before them by day in a pillar of a cloud, to lead them the way; and by night in a pillar of fire, to give them light'

to knock someone off that person's perch
to displace a person from a leadership position in some competitive situation

to set the pace
to give a lead in regard to a rate of progression
refers to horse racing and foot racing

to spearhead something
to lead a movement

too many cooks spoil the broth
more than one leader can confuse and harm a project

Likelihood

a bull in a china shop
a careless person likely to cause great damage

a cancer
an evil that is likely to spread

a death wish
the contemplation or commission of action so foolish that it is likely to lead to utter disaster

a loose cannon on the deck
a person or factor out of control and likely to cause trouble
nautical metaphor

a new broom
a changed regime that is likely to alter the status quo

a pipedream
a fanciful notion, wished for but unlikely
probably derived from smoking opium in pipes

an unholy alliance
a working relationship for a nefarious purpose between unlikely partners

heir apparent
the person likely to succeed another

it is pointing in the right direction
it is proceeding towards success

pie in the sky
a hoped for result unlikely to be achieved

straws in the wind
small but significant indicators of future events
John Seldon (1584–1654), 'Take a straw and throw it up into the air, you shall see by that which way the wind is'

there is blood in the water
something is likely to cause a person to go into a frenzy

to be on the cards
to be likely

to be short-sighted
not to recognise the likely consequences

to draw a long bow
to state a conclusion that, although possible, is unlikely on the known facts
refers to archery

to face a rocky road ahead
to be likely to encounter difficulties

to look for a needle in a haystack
to attempt something with a very small chance of success

to give someone enough rope to hang himself or herself
to give a person the opportunity to do something that is likely to get that person into severe trouble

to leap-frog something
to overtake something, with the likelihood of, in turn, being overtaken
refers to a game in which participants jump over each other in turn

to spin a yarn
to tell an amusing or unlikely story
a play on words referring to spinning yarn for cloth

where there is smoke there is fire
if there is a hint of trouble, then it is highly likely that there really is trouble
W. H. Auden (1907–73), *Twelve Songs* VIII, 'Still waters run deep, my dear, there's never smoke without fire'

Membership

a black sheep
a disreputable member of an otherwise reputable group
a blueblood
a person of high birth
refers to the appearance of the blood of certain Spanish noble families — supposed to be more of a blue colour due to a lack of Moorish blood
a clean sweep
a complete clearing out; OR winning all available prizes or awards
esprit de corps
a feeling of camaraderie and concern for the good name of some organisation of which one is a member
French, 'vital breath of a body'
every galah in the petshop
everybody
flagship
most important member of a group of related entities
refers to the ship carrying an admiral's flag
fresh blood
newly joined members of some organisation
pariah
social outcast
refers to members of a low caste in India
the great unwashed
the general public
the lowest common denominator
the highest level of taste found among all the members of some target audience
this mathematical phrase is used despite the fact that 'the highest common multiple' would be more logical
to be a cuckoo in the nest
to purport to be a member of a group of people although having no such right and, in the process, to usurp the rights of those entitled to be there
refers to a cuckoo depositing its eggs in the nests of other birds
to be at the top of the tree
to be a leading member of one's profession
to be in the swim
to be a member of a group knowing what is going on
to be in the wilderness
to be out of office against one's will
Numbers 14:33, 'And your children shall wander in the wilderness forty years'
to be on some organisation's books
to be a member or client of some organisation
to drum someone out of some organisation
to terminate in ignominy a person's employment or membership
refers to the ceremonial cashiering in the army to the beating of parade drums
to fall between the cracks
to be ineligible for something because one does not fit neatly into any of several relevant categories
to fall on one's sword
voluntarily to sacrifice one's position as a result of a sense of responsibility for an error
refers to suicide of Roman soldiers
to get a guernsey
to be given the opportunity to do something
refers to the jumpers worn by members of football teams
to introduce new blood
to recruit new members to some organisation
to keep up with the Joneses
to maintain a lifestyle beyond one's means in order to match that of some neighbourhood role model
refers to keeping pace with Jones amid pomp, but whether this relates to the metaphor is problematical: William Wordsworth (1770–1850), *Jones! As from Calais* (1807), 'Jones! as from Calais southward you and I went pacing side by side, this public way streamed with the pomp of a too-credulous day'
to shepherd some group

to marshal the members of some group

young Turks
members of an organisation who hold ideas regarded as too revolutionary
refers to an early twentieth-century revolutionary political party in what was to become Turkey

Misleading

a house of cards
an organisation that gives a misleading impression of solidity

to lead someone a merry dance
to mislead a person
refers to the complex dances of earlier centuries when one person led another through complex steps

to lead someone up the garden path
to mislead a person by deliberately fallacious arguments

to pull the wool over someone's eyes
to deceive or deliberately mislead another person
derived from the inability of some sheep to see clearly if wool is across their eyes

to speak with a forked tongue
to utter halftruths with the intention of misleading the listener

to throw dust into someone's eyes
to deceive a person by presenting inaccurate or misleading information
Koran: 'Neither didst thou, O Muhammad, cast dust into their eyes; but it was God who confounded them'

to throw someone off the scent
to deceive a person by giving out misleading indications
refers to fox hunting

Mistake

a comedy of errors
a series of separate mistakes in relation to some matter
refers to the name of a Shakespearean play

a loose cannon on the deck
a person or factor out of control and likely to cause trouble
nautical metaphor

a slip of the tongue
incorrect words uttered accidentally

a trap for young players
a significant likelihood of the inexperienced or naVve making mistakes

glaring error
patently obvious mistake

Murphy's law
the principle that everything that can go wrong will go wrong

not to be a hanging matter
to be only a minor mistake

sacrificial lamb
somebody unfairly made to suffer for the mistakes of others
Exodus 29:41, 'Sacrifice the other lamb at twilight ... an offering made to the Lord by fire'

something is rotten in the state of Denmark
the situation is corrupt and unacceptable
Shakespeare, *Hamlet* III:iv, 'Something is rotten in the state of Denmark'

to bark up the wrong tree
to reach an incorrect conclusion and/or to pursue an erroneous course of action

to be off-beam
to be mistaken

to be on the wrong tack
to be using an inaccurate procedure or policy likely to lead to error
refers to sailing

to be on the wrong track
to be heading towards an incorrect conclusion

to be on the wrong tram
to be completely mistaken as to the basic facts

to be on the wrong wavelength
to be incorrect in one's thinking
refers to radio reception

to be up the creek
to be mistaken completely

to be wide of the mark
to have a belief that is far removed from the true position
refers to archery

to catch someone flat-footed
to take someone unawares or making mistakes
to clean up a mess
to sort out mistakes or neglect
to drive a coach and horses through something to demonstrate the major errors or absurdities of something
Sir Stephen Rice (1673–1715), as quoted by W. King, *State of the Protestants of Ireland* (1672), 'I will drive a coach and six horses through the Act of Settlement'
to fall flat on one's face
to fail or to be seriously embarrassed by a bad error of judgment
to get the wrong sow by the ear
to reach an incorrect conclusion
to have an eagle eye
to be able very readily to notice small mistakes or fine details missed by others
to have hold of the wrong end of the pineapple
to be utterly mistaken
to have one's wires crossed
to be mistaken about key facts
refers to a short-circuit in electrical wiring
to hold the wrong end of the stick
to be completely mistaken about something
to lose face
to experience embarrassment by an affront to one's dignity
to put one's foot in it
to make a foolish mistake
to put one's reputation on the line
to take a public stance in the realisation that there is a risk that one's reputation will suffer if one is proved wrong
to put the cart before the horse
to do things in the wrong order
Rudyard Kipling (1865–1936), *The Conundrum of the Workshops*, 'We know the tail must wag the dog, for the horse is drawn by the cart'
to save face
to avoid humiliation or loss of reputation
to slip under one's guard
to cause a mistake to be made despite care being taken to prevent this
refers to fencing
to sow the wind and reap the whirlwind
to make bad mistakes and to suffer the even worse consequences
Hosea 8:7, 'They have sown the wind, and they shall reap the whirlwind'

Money

a cash cow
a source of ready money
a licence to print money
a lucrative government-conferred monopoly or privilege
Lord Thomson of Fleet (1894–1977), 'It's just like having a licence to print your own money' (after the opening of Scottish commercial television, as recorded in Braddon, *Roy Thomson of Fleet Street*)
a Rolls-Royce solution
a high quality but excessively expensive way of doing something
a stitch in time saves nine
preventive maintenance saves money in the long run
he who pays the piper calls the tune
a person contributing money or resources to a project is entitled to control it
he wouldn't give you the shine off his suit
he is very mean
that person wouldn't give you the steam off his or her sausages
that person is very mean
in for a penny, in for a pound
once something is commenced it ought be finished; OR if one is willing to take a small risk then one might as well take a bigger one
money for jam
remuneration easily earned
not for love or money
definitely not
not to be made of money
not to be wealthy
not to have a bean
to have no money

penny-pinching
excessively mean
pin money
an allowance to a wife for her personal use
probably refers to money for purchase of hair pins and other decorative pins
that is money down the drain
money has been wastefully lost on a failed project
the choice is between eating well or sleeping well
one can invest for maximum yield or maximum security, but not both
the hip-pocket nerve
the assessment of issues by their financial effects on one
the money is rolling in
the scheme is very profitable
to be a money spinner
to produce large profits easily and quickly
to be in the black
to have money
refers to the black ink used to indicate a credit in a manuscript accounting ledger
to be in the red
to owe money
refers to the red ink used to indicate a liability in a manuscript accounting ledger
to be out of pocket
to have lost money in a transaction
to be unable to rub two pennies together
to be very poor
to build up a war chest
to accumulate cash in readiness for some move
to burn one's fingers
to suffer (esp. loss of money) through foolishness or meddling
refers to taking chestnuts from a fire
to button up one's purse
to refuse to spend money
to cost a pretty penny
to be very expensive
to engage in cherry picking
(in business) to accept only the potentially most lucrative deals
to engage in pump priming
to spend public money with the aim of attracting parochial electoral support
refers to priming a water pump
to have a run for one's money
to at least get some enjoyment out of an otherwise abortive exercise
refers to betting on horse racing
to have deep pockets
to have large financial resources and to be willing to use them if the circumstances seem right
to have money burning a hole in one's pocket
to be impatient to spend or invest available funds
to have money flowing out of one's ears
to be very rich
to hit someone hard
greatly to affect a person emotionally; OR to cost a person a lot of money
to hold out a fistful of dollars
to offer money by way of inducement
to hold the purse strings
to have control of expenditure
refers to a drawstring closing a purse
to line one's pockets
to make, improperly and secretly, a profit out of some transaction
to lose money hand over fist
to lose money very fast and comprehensively
to pork barrel
to spend taxpayers' money in one area in order to attract political support
refers to times of slavery in America when pork was provided to slaves gathered around the pork barrel
to put money on the table
to back one's judgment in a tangible way or to demonstrate one's sincerity
to put one's money where one's mouth is
to back one's boasting by putting assets at risk
to save a bundle
to save much money
to see the colour of someone's eyes
to see how a person matches expectations or requirements
to throw good money after bad
to waste further money in a vain attempt to recover money already lost

to tighten the purse strings
to reduce outlays
refers to a drawstring closing a purse

to turn an honest penny
to earn money by hard work

to turn one's chips in
to convert one's assets or entitlements into cash

to wield the knife
to terminate the services of one or more persons or to prune expenditure

Monitoring

a watchdog
a person or organisation monitoring behaviour

to have a crow's eye
to be cunning or alert

to keep an eye on the ball
to monitor a fast-changing situation

to keep one's eye on someone
to supervise a person

to keep one's eye on something
to monitor a situation

to keep tabs on something
to monitor something

Naïveté

a lamb led to slaughter
a naïve person allowing himself or herself to be exploited
Isaiah 53:5, 'He was oppressed, and he was afflicted, yet he opened not his mouth: he is brought as a lamb to the slaughter'

a trap for young players
a significant likelihood of the inexperienced or naïve making mistakes

bright-eyed and bushy-tailed
naïve but enthusiastic

not to have been born yesterday
not to be naïve

that is strictly for the birds
that is trivial nonsense appealing only to the naïve and the gullible

to be babes in the wood
to be excessively naïve and inexperienced and thus ripe for exploitation
based on the folk legend of the babes in the wood of Wayland Hall, Norfolk

to be green
to be naïve
Shakespeare, *Antony & Cleopatra* I:v, 'my salad days, when I was green in judgment'

to be off the planet
to be extremely naïve or uninformed

to be wet behind the ears
to be excessively naïve and inexperienced

to dream up some story
to concoct a false story naïvely or maliciously

to have come down in the last shower
to be naïve
refers to someone having just arrived with the last shower of rain

to seek the pot of gold at the end of the rainbow
to have naïve expectations
refers to the proverbial belief in the existence of a pot of gold at the end of a rainbow

Nonsense

a load of rubbish
blatant nonsense

hogwash
nonsense
refers to 'hog wash' — meaning kitchen swill for pigs (and therefore worthless)

mumbo jumbo
blatant nonsense
refers to a deity worshipped by primitive tribes

tell it to the marines
such nonsense is not believable
although now referring to a very unlikely tale, it originally applied to an unlikely tale that was, in fact, true — refers to King Charles II believing the unlikely (but true) tale of flying fish because the marines (the maritime regiment) testified that it was so

that is strictly for the birds
that is trivial nonsense appealing only to the naïve and the gullible

to be eye wash
to be nonsense
that has nothing to do with the price of fish
that is quite irrelevant

Opinion

a prima donna
a person with an exaggerated opinion of that person's own importance making relations with others needlessly difficult
Italian, 'first lady'
heresy
views different from those held by the majority
originally referred only to church orthodoxy, but now generalised metaphorical use
spectrum
wide range of different opinions or backgrounds
the jury is still out
no decision has yet been made; OR there has not yet been an indication as to how the matter is viewed in the community
the other side of the coin
the arguments for the opposite point of view
the tide is running in favour of some proposition
public opinion supports some proposition
to act as a devil's advocate
to put a point of view that one does not hold in order to draw out the best arguments regarding a proposition
refers to a church official vetting a candidate for sainthood (and ultimately to the testing of Job by Satan, *Job* 1:9 ff)
to ascertain the lie of the land
to establish the pertinent facts and opinions
to be a lone voice crying out in the wilderness
to be the only person stating unpopular views
John 1:23, 'I am the voice of one crying in the wilderness'
to be a thorn in someone's side
to be a constant annoyance or affliction
2 Corinthians 12:7, 10: 'There was given to me a thorn in the flesh ... I will glory in my infirmities'
to be full of hot air
to make unsubstantiated empty statements; to be bombastic
to be on the other side of the fence
to have an opposing point of view or position
to belt someone over the head
to override someone's views or arguments, often involving the use of heavy pressure
to break ranks
to identify oneself as having separate interests or views from the rest of a group
military metaphor
to bridge a gulf
to overcome a wide divergence in views
Luke 16:26, 'Between us and you there is a great gulf fixed'
to change one's mind
to alter the views that one had previously formed
to change one's tune
to alter one's publicly expressed views
to claim that something is the best thing since sliced bread
to have a high opinion of the importance or novelty of an invention or practice
to echo someone's words
to repeat another person's views as though they were one's own
to get words in edgeways
to manage to interrupt a conversation or monologue in order to say something oneself
to have a change of heart
to form a new view in place of a strongly held prior view
to know one's mind
to form and adhere to an opinion
to polarise
to cause people to identify themselves as belonging to groups holding opposing views
refers to electromagnetic poles

to pull one's horns in
to retreat from previously stated views
refers to fighting between male horned animals
to put someone back in his/her box/place
to make it clear to a person that that person's views are not welcome
to sail against the wind
to oppose the views currently being held by others
to sing a particular song
to state particular views
to speak one's mind
to express one's views frankly and forcefully
to take a sounding
to ascertain people's views
nautical metaphor referring to ascertaining the depth of water
to throw in one's six pennies'/two cents' worth
modestly to supply one's own facts or views
you can get lost
I intend to take no notice whatsoever of you or your views
you can jump in the lake
I intend to take no notice whatsoever of you or your views

Opportunity

a chink in someone's armour
a weakness in someone's defences that creates an opportunity to do something that otherwise could not be done
a chink in the wall
an opportunity to do something that otherwise could not be done
a chink of light
a small hope of a solution or breakthrough
a foot in the door
the opportunity to do business
a free kick
an advantageous opportunity accorded to a person
refers to football
golden opportunity
an unparalleled chance or occasion
a toehold
an opportunity small in itself but with the potential to lead to bigger things
refers to climbing trees, rockfaces, etc.
a trap for young players
a significant likelihood of the inexperienced or naïve making mistakes
a window of opportunity
an opportunity temporarily available
an ocean full of fish
plenty of opportunity
an opening wide enough to drive a coach and four through
an excellent opportunity to demonstrate the major errors or absurdities of something
the saying seems sometimes also to have referred to six horses: Sir Stephen Rice (1673–1715), as quoted by W. King, *State of the Protestants of Ireland* (1672), 'I will drive a coach and six horses through the Act of Settlement'
at five minutes to midnight
almost at the last moment
the doors of the Ritz are open to all
despite rhetoric to the contrary wealthy people have many advantages over poor people
refers to the Ritz Hotel, London, founded in 1906 by César Ritz
this is the end of the road for someone
a person will have no further opportunity to do something
to be a crack in the wall
to represent a small opportunity that can be exploited
to block someone's path
to interfere with a person's opportunity to advance
to blow something
unintentionally to destroy some opportunity
to carve out a niche for oneself
deliberately to create an opportunity to use one's talents effectively
to close the door on someone
to deny another person a desired opportunity
to close the gate

to deny an opportunity that was previously available

to dip one's toe in the water
gently to explore an opportunity

to feed the dogs while they are barking
to do something while the opportunity is available

to fill a vacuum
to take advantage of an opportunity not acted on by others

to find one's niche
to find the opportunity to use one's talents

to get a guernsey
to be given the opportunity to do something
refers to the jumpers worn by members of football teams

to get only one bite at the cherry
to receive no further opportunity

to give someone enough rope to hang himself or herself
to give a person the opportunity to do something that is likely to get that person into severe trouble

to grab an opportunity with both hands
to seize an opportunity with great enthusiasm

to have a leg in
to have an opportunity which has the potential to lead to bigger things

to have other irons in the fire
to have the opportunity to do something else as an alternative
Francis Beaumont (1584–1616) & John Fletcher (1579–1625), *The Faithful Friends* I:ii, 'It is always good when a man has two irons in the fire'

to have the ball at one's feet
to have unlimited opportunity
refers to football games

to keep one's eyes open for something
to be on the lookout for an opportunity to do something

to knock on doors
to seek out opportunities

to miss the boat/bus/train
to fail to exploit an opportunity

to open doors
to create opportunities

to dip one's toe in the water
gently to explore an opportunity

to queer the pitch for someone
to spoil the opportunity a person has to do something

to run with the ball
to make the most of the opportunity
refers to rugby

to shut the door on someone
to deny another person a desired opportunity

to turn back the clock
to have another opportunity to do something that should have been done already; or to attempt to undo something that cannot be undone

willing bride
(commerce) keen partner

your race is run
you have had your opportunity
Hebrews 12:1, 'Let us run ... the race that is set before us'

Past

a past master
an expert with long experience
derived from freemasonry

a warhorse
an experienced and dependable campaigner in war, politics, sport, and other contests

in halcyon days
in past happier times
Shakespeare, *Henry V*, *Part 1*, I:ii, 'Expect St Martin's summer, halcyon days'; refers to the fourteen days about the winter solstice when winds were calm, and to the mythical bird said to breed in a floating nest at that time

the chickens are coming home to roost
the consequences of a person's past actions are now being felt by that person
Robert Southey (1774–1843), *The Curse of Kehama* (1810), 'Curses are like young chickens, they always come home to roost'

the melody lingers on
the benefit of past actions remains

to be a breath of fresh air

to be a pleasant change from the past

to conduct a post mortem on something
to review past actions with a view to learning lessons for the future
Latin, *post mortem*, 'after the death'

to even the score
to respond by way of retribution for some past action of another person

to mend bridges
to restore a broken-up relationship

to start from scratch
to commence something without the benefit of any past activity
refers to the starting mark (with no handicap advantage) in a race

to wipe the slate clean
to forgive past indiscretions

Pleasure

a willing horse
a cheerful worker

fun and games
light-hearted amusement and games (esp. flirtatious and/or naughty)

not to be all beer and skittles
not to be all pleasant and easy

the cheering could be heard a block away
there was great rejoicing

the party is over
the previous pleasant arrangements have been discontinued

to be a breath of fresh air
to be a pleasant change from the past

to be a stormy petrel
a person who disturbs a pleasant state of affairs by agitating for change
refers to the bird (petrel) that flies low over water during a storm and appears to be alternately touching one foot and then the other to the surface of the water as though walking upon it; the bird is sometimes thought to be the harbinger of a storm, and is named after St Peter who walked upon the stormy waters of Lake Gennesareth

to be a tonic
to cheer someone up

to be full of beans
to be very cheerful

to be in [or of] good heart
to be cheerful, especially in adversity

to be meat and drink
to be very pleasurable; or to be basic, familiar, and essential to one's experience of life'
Matthew 25:35, 'For I was an hungred, and ye gave me meat: I was thirsty and ye gave me drink'; Shakespeare, 'It is meat and drinke to me to see a clowne'

music to one's ears
comments that one is very pleased to hear
Shakespeare, *Romeo and Juliet* II:i, 'How silver-sweet sound lovers' tongues by night, / like softest music to attending ears!'

to be on a path strewn with roses
to lead a very pleasant life

to be tickled pink
to be very pleased
Oliver Goldsmith (1730–74), *She Stoops to Conquer*, 'the very pink of perfection'

to bounce back
to resume a cheerful existence after some setback

to bring the house down
to obtain rapturous applause
refers to the theatre

to cast a cloud over something
to spoil the pleasure of an occasion

to drain every ounce out of something
to get the maximum use or pleasure out of something

to give someone heart
to cause a person to cheer up

to have an audience rolling in the aisles
to amuse an audience

to have someone in stitches
greatly to amuse a person

to kill oneself laughing
to be greatly amused

to lick one's chops
to look forward to something with pleasurable anticipation
refers to salivation in anticipation of food

positively purring
(of a person) very pleased; (of an engine) running very smoothly
refers to a cat's purring

to take the rough with the smooth

to accept the hardships of life along with its pleasant features

Possibility

a middle-of-the-road solution
a solution near the middle of a range of possibilities

as soon as someone's back was turned
at the moment it became possible to do something without a person's knowledge

bedrock price
lowest possible price

catch 22
a condition or consequence that precludes success; a dilemma where the victim cannot win
title of a 1961 novel by Joseph Heller in which a man pleads insanity to escape war service, but whose plea of insanity demonstrates his inherent sanity

on the deathknock
at the last possible moment
refers to the mythical figure of 'Death' knocking on the door to claim a victim

one can't get a quart into a pint pot
one cannot do the impossible

one can't make a silk purse out of a sow's ear
it is impossible to manufacture something of a high standard from inferior raw materials
Malcolm Bradbury (1932–), 'For the mass of men, you can't make a silk purse out of a sow's ear'

that has put paid to it
the project can no longer proceed
refers to the counting house and an account being labelled as 'paid' (meaning 'settled'); thus, the matter is settled and finished

that is a long shot
there is only a remote possibility

the game is up
the plan is no longer able to succeed

there is more than one way to skin a cat
this can be achieved in a variety of ways

to be a crack in the wall
to represent a small opportunity that can be exploited

to be a grey area
to be in an undefined position straddling two or more possibilities
refers to something being neither black nor white

to be able to do something standing on one's head
to be able to do something very easily

to be able to do something with one hand behind one's back
to be able to do something very easily

to be able to eat someone for breakfast
to be able to outwit a person very easily

to be able to lay one's hands on something
to be able to locate something

to be able to spot trouble a mile away
to be able to perceive problems before they actually occur

to conjure up something
to produce something in circumstances where this seemed impossible

to draw a long bow
to state a conclusion that, although possible, is unlikely on the known facts
refers to archery

to draw blood from a stone
to do the impossible

to exhaust the field
to use up all the possibilities

to have a good nose for business
to be able to identify profitable business situations

to have a snowflake's chance in hell
to have no hope or possibility at all

to have an eagle eye
to be able very readily to notice small mistakes or fine details missed by others

to have broad shoulders
to be able to cope well with responsibility

to have one's foot on something

to be about to acquire something or to be able to acquire something

perhaps refers to limbering-up exercises before Roman footraces in which competitors were said to 'have their foot in (or on)' — meaning that they were ready to begin the task

to lurk in the shadows

to have a low profile at the moment, but with the possibility of becoming much more conspicuous at any time

to move heaven and earth

to do everything possible

Revelation 21:1, 'And I saw a new heaven and a new earth, for the first heaven and the first earth had passed away'; a reference to the apocalyptic vision of the greatest possible change to all creation

to paint oneself into a corner

foolishly to put oneself into a position from which escape is impossible

to produce something out of thin air

to get hold of something in circumstances where this seemed impossible

Shakespeare, *The Tempest* IV:i, ' ... are melted into air, into thin air'

to push water uphill

foolishly to attempt the impossible

to tie someone's hands behind that person's back

to make it impossible for a person to act at all

to try to square the circle

to attempt the impossible

refers to a classical problem in geometry, namely, to construct with a compass a square of the same area as a given circle

two can play at that game

it is possible to retaliate

Power

a figurehead

the ceremonial chief officer of some organisation without any real power

refers to the ornamental carving at the front of a ship

a game of cat and mouse

negotiations between two parties of unequal bargaining power during which the stronger makes some temporary concessions to the weaker without, however, affecting the latter's eventual total defeat

a Goliath

a giant or a person whose ability and achievements exceed that of most other people

refers to *1 Samuel* 17:23 ff

a tall poppy

a person with great power or responsibility and/or in receipt of high remuneration

a toothless tiger

an authority that has been given powers totally inadequate for its task

fiefdom

a sphere of operation in which a person exercises absolute control regardless of the wishes of others

if the mountain will not come to Muhammad then Muhammad will go to the mountain

on recognising that one has insufficient power to effect one's most desired solution one decides to make do with the next best alternative

refers to the story of Muhammad humbly submitting to the greater power of God when Mt Safa did not obey the prophet's command to come to him

juggernaut

large overpowering force

Sanskrit: 'world protector'; a title of Krishna in Hinduism

more power to your elbow

may your praiseworthy efforts continue and be strengthened one can't beat

City Hall

the ordinary citizen is powerless against bureaucracy

the law of the jungle

the principle that those having power will use it at the expense of all others

Rudyard Kipling (1865–1936), *The Law of the Jungle*, 'Now this is the law of the jungle — as old and as true as the sky; and the wolf that shall keep it may prosper, but the wolf that shall break it must die'

the power behind the throne

a person exercising the real authority but without having the official right to do so

William Pitt, Earl of Chatham (1708–78) ('Pitt the Elder'), 'There is something behind the throne greater than the king himself'

the top dog
the person in the most powerful position

refers to the dominant dog in a pack

to be in the box seat
to be in a very powerful position to control activity

refers to the driver's seat in a horse-drawn carriage

to flex one's muscles
to assert one's personality or powers

to have a long arm
to have far-reaching power

to hold the power to do something in the hollow of one's hand
to have the right to make crucial decisions

Isaiah 40:12, ' ... who hath measured the waters in the hollow of his hand ... '

to keep someone in a strait jacket
to deny a person any discretionary powers at all

refers to a restraining 'jacket' used to control violent or insane persons

to rule with a rod of iron
to keep strict discipline

Psalms 2:9, 'Thou shalt break them with a rod of iron; thou shalt dash them in pieces like a potter's vessel'

to snap one's fingers
to gesture contemptuously, especially in the expectation of immediate obedience

to trample someone under foot
by virtue of one's great power to treat a person's rights with contempt and not to give that person proper consideration

to tug one's forelock
to pay obeisance to someone

to want the organ-grinder, not the monkey
to wish to deal with the person in authority rather than an underling

refers to a street musician using a barrel-organ, often accompanied by a pet monkey

to wield a big stick
to assert power

tsar
a person exercising excessive power over others

under one's own power
without external help

Practicability

a broad church
an organisation willing to accept members with a wide variety of different views

a castle in Spain
a desirable imagining, but an impracticable proposition

a castle in the air
a desirable imagining, but an impracticable proposition

to be in an ivory tower
to be immersed in theoretical considerations and ignorant of the practical realities

Song of Solomon 7:4, 'Thy neck is as a tower of ivory'

to jettison some proposal
to abandon some proposal as worthless or impracticable

to pay lip service to some rules
to disregard some rules in practice while acknowledging them in words

to put someone through the mill
to make someone endure significant hardship through severe practical experience

to start with a blank sheet of paper
to commence an exercise without being bound by any established practices

to turn sour
to become unsatisfactory

Praise

a back-handed compliment
a polite expression seemingly of praise but really intended as an insult

more power to your elbow

may your praiseworthy efforts continue and be strengthened

to fish for compliments
to drop hints in the hope that one will receive praise or recognition

to get an elephant stamp
to receive praise

to get full marks for something
to receive the highest praise for something

to pull oneself up by one's bootstraps
to make a praiseworthy effort to better oneself unaided

to sing someone's praises
to commend a person exuberantly

Pretence

to act out a charade
ostentatiously to pretend to be doing something; a pretence
refers to a parlour game of pretence

to be mutton dressed up as lamb
foolishly to pretend to be younger

to play possum
to lie low; to feign unconsciousness or death
refers to the possum's habit of attempting to evade capture by feigning death

to sail under false colours
to pretend that one's real character or beliefs are different from what they really are
refers to a ship concealing its true identity

to sweep something under the carpet/rug
to pretend that some blemish does not exist

to touch a nerve
to mention a sensitive subject

to turn a blind eye to something
to pretend that something obvious does not exist
refers to action by Horatio, Lord Nelson (1758–1805), when disregarding Admiralty signals: 'I have only one eye — I have a right to be blind sometimes — I really do not see the signal!' (at the Battle of Copenhagen, reported in Southey, *Life of Nelson*, ch. 7)

Prevention

a bottleneck
a factor obstructing an even flow

a logjam
a stoppage of activity caused by input in greater volume than allowed for
refers to a crowded mass of cut logs in a river

a stitch in time saves nine
preventive maintenance saves money in the long run

cut it out!
stop doing that!

I'll soon stop that person's little game
that person's activities are not tolerated and I will ensure that they cease

stonewalling
deliberate obstruction or delaying tactics

stumbling block
an impediment or difficulty preventing the easy completion of some project; OR a dilemma involving a moral issue
1 Corinthians 8:9, 'But take heed lest by any means this liberty of yours become a stumbling block to them that are weak'

the fat is in the fire
action with certain unstoppable consequences has now been initiated

to be on a treadmill
to be involved in some unpleasant ongoing activity that cannot readily be stopped

to be stopped in one's tracks
suddenly and unexpectedly to be prevented from carrying on with a project

to break down the barriers
to do away with the prejudice preventing something

to chop someone off at the socks
to stop someone's proposals prematurely

to come to a full stop
to cease activity completely

to fetter someone
to stop a person acting on that person's own initiative

to fight bushfires
to deal with crises as they arise rather than take preventive action
to nip something in the bud
to stop some activity in its early stages when stopping it is still relatively easy
refers to the first signs of growth in plants
to put a spoke in someone's wheel
to interfere with another person's activity, so preventing its continuance
to put a wall around someone
to stop a person associating with others
to put the brake on someone
to stop or slow down a person
to shut the stable door after the horse has bolted
to take preventive action only after the relevant event
to slip through the net
to happen as an isolated case despite steps taken to prevent such events
to slip under one's guard
to cause a mistake to be made despite care being taken to prevent this
refers to fencing
to stand in someone's way
to prevent a person achieving that person's goal
to stem the haemorrhage/bleeding
to put a stop to the financial losses of a project
to tie someone's hands
to prevent a person from acting as that person sees fit

Price and Value

a bird in the hand is worth two in the bush
a benefit currently available is more valuable than a seemingly much larger benefit that might or might not be achieved in the future
a jewel
any highly valued person or thing
a listening post
a place where information of strategic value can be collected
military metaphor
a treasure trove
a valuable discovery
bedrock price
lowest possible price
daylight robbery
the charging of grossly excessive prices
fire sale
a forced sale, realising bargain prices
refers to the sale of goods damaged by fire
garage sale
sale of miscellaneous assets at cheap prices
highway robbery
the charging of grossly excessive prices
refers to robbery by armed brigands on the highways
not a mite
not at all
refers to a coin of small value — *Mark* 12:42, 'A certain poor widow ... threw in two mites, which make a farthing'
not to be worth a continental
to have no value
refers to currency notes of early US issue which quickly depreciated in value
not to be worth the candle
to be too expensive in relation to the true value; AND/OR not to be worth the effort required
something has no guts in it
something has no substance to it
to be above water
(of securities) to have a market value in excess of the cost price
to cast pearls before swine
to confer valuable benefits on someone who neither recognises nor appreciates them
Matthew 7:6, 'Neither cast ye your pearls before swine'
to charge a mint
to impose very high prices
to charge like a wounded bull
to impose excessive prices
a play on words; not a simile
to charge the earth
to impose very high prices
to earn peanuts

to get a reward that is far too small in relation to the value of the services rendered

to go through the roof
(of a person) to be very upset; OR (of prices) to escalate greatly

to hand over something on a silver platter
to provide a valuable benefit for virtually nothing
refers to first-class service

to head north
(of prices, etc.) to go up

to head south
(of prices, etc.) to go down

to lose one's right arm
to lose some highly valued assistance

to pay something back with interest
to return a small favour with a bigger favour; or to extract retribution of greater value than the circumstances warrant

to pay through the nose
to pay an excessive price
refers to an onerous tax imposed by the Danes in Ireland in the ninth century whereby those who refused to pay had their noses slit

to pick the eyes out of something
to choose the most valuable items from among a large number

to sell one's birthright for a mess of pottage
through foolishness to exchange something of substance for something of little value
Genesis 25:34, 'Then Jacob gave Esau bread and pottage of lentils ... thus Esau despised his birthright'

to sell someone a pup
to cheat a person in a transaction, especially by misrepresentation as to the true value of something

to skyrocket
(of a price or value) to increase greatly in a short time

yeoman service
valuable assistance over a long time
refers to an officer in an official household or military establishment

Pride and Humility

a Jezebel
a wicked shameless woman, especially one who wears heavy make-up
2 Kings 9:30, 'Jezebel heard of it; and she painted her face, and tired her head'

barefaced
shameless

to be done like a dinner
to be defeated and humiliated

to be in the doghouse
to be in disgrace

to be the apple of someone's eye
to be a much cherished person
refers to the pupil of the eye — 'the apple of the eye' as being the centre of visual perception and therefore especially cherished and much-valued

to cut tall poppies down to size
to diminish the self-importance of haughty persons

to hang one's head
to be ashamed of oneself; OR to be disappointed and lacking in morale
Shakespeare, *Henry VIII* III:i, 'Even the billows of the sea, / hung their heads and then lay by'

to put on airs and graces
to act in an affected manner

to rub it in
to humiliate another person by emphasising that person's defeat

to rub someone's nose in it
to humiliate a person by highlighting something embarrassing to that person

to swallow one's pride
to take action despite the humiliating nature of this course

Problem

a can of worms
a collection of complex intertwined problems

a step in the right direction
the first in a series of measures designed to correct some problem

a time bomb

a source of serious problems that are certain to surface later on

Bob's your uncle!
that solves the problem!
refers to the many preferments given in the nineteenth century by UK Prime Minister (Robert) Lord Salisbury to his nephew A. J. Balfour (and to a number of other relatives of the prime minister)

growing pains
problems encountered by virtue of expansion
refers to the pains sometimes felt in the limbs by children and adolescents

join the club!
you are only one of many people with similar problems

not to be Robinson Crusoe
to be one of a large number of people with a common problem
refers to Daniel Defoe's *Robinson Crusoe*

one's door is always open
people can take their problems to one at any time

teething trouble
problems in the early stages of a project
refers to a small child's discomfort when developing teeth

the sky fell in
a very serious problem arose
Matthew 24:29, 'Immediately after the distress of those days the sun will be darkened, and the moon will not give its light; the stars will fall from the sky, and the heavenly bodies will be shaken'

the squeaky wheel gets the oil
those complaining the most loudly will get their problems sorted out first

to be left holding the baby
to be forced to accept responsibility for someone else's problems

to be the hard core
to be the central and most difficult problem

to be up the creek without a paddle
to be in trouble

to come to grips with some problem
to be on the way to solving a problem

to cut the Gordian knot
to solve, especially by force, a virtually insoluble problem
refers to a complicated knot tied by Gordius and eventually cut by Alexander the Great

to escape by the skin of one's teeth
to only just avoid some disaster
Job 19:20, 'I am escaped with the skin of my teeth'

to fiddle at the edges
to do some relatively minor things that do not deal with the substance of a problem

to get stuck into some problem
to attempt to solve a problem with great vigour

to get to first base
to succeed in achieving the first stage in any undertaking
refers to baseball

to heave a sigh of relief
to express satisfaction at the achievement of a solution to a difficult problem
John Keats (1795–1821), *I stood tip-toe upon a little hill*, 'born of the very sigh that silence heaves'

to iron out something
to sort out a difficult problem

to jump a hurdle
to overcome a problem or difficulty

to jump that hurdle when one comes to it
to deal with a particular problem only when it becomes necessary to do so

to hold one's head just above water
to cope with problems but with little margin to spare or to stay solvent

to know where the shoe pinches
to realise from personal experience what the cause of some problem really is

to leave something up in the air
to have an unresolved problem

to make mountains out of molehills
to treat a minor problem as though it were a major disaster

to need something like a hole in the head
to be confronted with a completely undesired problem

to play the cards as they fall
to deal with problems as they arise
refers to playing cards
to present a happy face to the world
bravely to gloss over one's problems and to appear contented to others
to prey on one's mind
(of a problem) to keep worrying one
to put one's thinking cap on
to concentrate on finding a solution to a difficult problem
to take the bit between one's teeth
to face up to a problem
refers to riding or racing horses
to take the bull by the horns
to come to grips with the realities of a difficult problem
to try to square the circle
to attempt the impossible
refers to a classical problem in geometry, namely, to construct with a compass a square of the same area as a given circle

Punishment

a kick in the shins
an unexpected and undeserved setback
a scapegoat
a person who is forced to take the blame for something not that person's fault
Leviticus 16:10, 'But the goat, on which the lot fell to be the scapegoat ... to make an atonement'
draconian
excessively severe
refers to an especially harsh code of laws drawn up by the Athenian legislator, Drako (620 BC)
for one's sins
by way of punishment, as it were
those who live by the sword shall die by the sword
those that are rough with others must accept the likelihood of unfavourable treatment in return
Matthew 26:52, 'All they that take the sword shall perish by the sword'
heads will roll
transgressors will be punished
refers to execution by decapitation
to be a glutton for punishment
a person who is eager to work very hard even without the prospect of commensurate reward
Rudyard Kipling (1865–1936), 'He's honest, and a glutton for work'
to be for the high jump
to face dismissal or the end of one's career
refers to death by hanging
to get off scot-free
to go unpunished
refers to an exemption from tax; scot (from old norse *skot*) means tax
to kiss the rod
to accept punishment meekly
Shakespeare, *The Two Gentlemen of Verona* I:ii, 'and presently all humbled kiss the rod!'
to send someone to Coventry
ostentatiously and collectively to ignore a person by way of punishment
refers to the refusal of the citizens of Coventry (UK) to have any social contact whatsoever with royalist soldiers in the English Civil War
to thrash with a feather
to impose only a minor punishment for a very serious offence

Readiness

a cash cow
a source of ready money
off the peg
(of clothes) ready-made
ready-made
easily fabricated or available without difficulty
to batten down the hatches
to get ready for expected difficulties
nautical metaphor
to be at hand
to be in the vicinity, ready to help
to be up to concert pitch
to be ready
to clear the decks
to get ready for action
nautical metaphor
to draw a deep breath

to get ready for exertion or for emotional news

to gird up one's loins
to get ready for action
Job 38:3 'Gird up thy loins now like a man'

to grit one's teeth
to get ready to suffer pain

to hold the field
not to be superseded

to prepare one's ground
to get ready for a confrontation
refers to military battle

to set the scene for something
to get things ready for something
refers to the theatre

to sharpen one's axe
to get ready for a difficult task

to sharpen the knives
to get ready for a concerted attack on a person or principle

to spread one's wings
to test or develop one's abilities, to lead a life of greater scope than previously

to warm up
to get ready

Refusal and Rejection

a doubting Thomas
a person who refuses to believe claims in the absence of proof
John 20:25, 'But he [Thomas] said ... except I shall see in his hands the print of the nails ... I will not believe'

not to lift a finger to help someone
to refuse to assist

stick it up your guernsey!
I have absolutely no interest in you and what you saying!
refers to the jumpers worn by members of football teams

that is not to be sneezed at
that is so significant that it should not be rejected

to be a dog in the manger
spitefully to deny something to others, notwithstanding its uselessness to oneself
from *Aesop's Fables*

to be an ostrich
to refuse to face up to an unpleasant truth
refers to the reputed habit of ostriches in danger

to be like water off a duck's back
(of advice or criticism) to be completely ignored

to blackball someone
to reject a person as unsuitable
refers to a vote against someone by secretly placing a black ball in a box (as opposed to a white or red ball which indicated approval); the voting procedure was common in ancient Rome and Greece — hence 'ballot' (French, *ballotte*, 'a little ball')

to bury one's head in the sand
to refuse to face up to an unpleasant truth
refers to the reputed habit of ostriches in danger

to button up one's purse
to refuse to spend money

to close the gate
to deny an opportunity that was previously available

to cut the umbilical cord
to free a person from the excessive influence of another; OR to separate a person from an essential source of supplies

to draw the line at that
to refuse to go any further

to gather dust
not to be acted upon, but without being formally rejected

to go haywire
to function in a disordered and strange fashion
refers to difficulty in handling coils of hay-binding wire

to keep someone in a strait jacket
to deny a person any discretionary powers at all
refers to a restraining 'jacket' used to control violent or insane persons

to knock an idea on the head
utterly to reject a proposal

to leave someone out in the cold

to be excluded, ignored or neglected

to pass the buck

to shift responsibility to someone else

refers to the buckhorn knife passed around the table to indicate the dealer while playing poker

to plead the fifth amendment

to refuse to answer an unwelcome question

refers to the fifth amendment of the United States constitution, which provides protection against self-incrimination

to pull up the drawbridge

defensively to withdraw and refuse to cooperate'

refers to the drawbridge over a defensive moat around a castle

to refuse point blank

to refuse outright

refers to pointing at the white spot (blank, French blanc) in the centre of an archery target

to shut the door on someone

to deny another person a desired opportunity

to sit on the fence

to refuse to choose between two alternatives

to slam the door in someone's face

ostentatiously to refuse to have any dealings with a person

to throw a blanket over a proposal

to refuse to proceed with a proposal

to throw something out of the window

to reject completely an idea or proposal

to turn off the tap

to deny further access to supplies or information

to turn one's back on someone

to decline to assist or deal with a person

to wash one's hands of something

emphatically to decline future responsibility

Matthew 27:24, 'He [Pilate] took water and washed his hands in full view of the crowd. "My hands are clean of this man's blood," he declared'

wild horses would not cause me to do something

I refuse absolutely to do something

refers to a form of torture in which persons were dragged behind horses

Reputation

a black sheep

a disreputable member of an otherwise reputable group

a muckraker

a person who sets out to publicise features harming another person's reputation

by their fruits ye shall know them

their true nature will be revealed by their results

Matthew 7:20, 'wherefore by their fruits ye shall know them'

he must have a long spoon that sups with the devil

great care is needed when negotiating with disreputable parties

Shakespeare apparently alludes to an old proverb in *The Tempest* II:ii, 'Mercy! mercy! this is a devil ... I will leave him, I have no long spoon!'

sexy

highly marketable

some mud will stick

reputations will be hurt even after accusations are proved false

to blot one's copybook

to spoil one's previously good reputation or record

to crucify someone

to do severe damage unfairly to a person's reputation or credibility

Mark 15:13, 'And they cried out again, Crucify him'

to have a black mark against one's name

to have a tarnished reputation

to look to one's laurels

to be careful not to lose one's reputation for some skill

refers to laurel wreaths presented to winners of events at the ancient Olympics

to make a name for oneself

to earn a good reputation by virtue of some skill

to make something one's trade mark

to have a distinctive characteristic or way of doing things
to paint someone black
to ruin a person's reputation
to pin the tail on the donkey
to put the blame on a person who has with some effort been identified as responsible
refers to children's parlour game
to put one's reputation on the line
to take a public stance in the realisation that there is a risk that one's reputation will suffer if one is proved wrong
to rest on one's laurels
to use a reputation for success earned in earlier times as a substitute for current endeavour
refers to laurel wreaths presented to winners of events at the ancient Olympics
to undermine someone's position
to injure another person's reputation and influence by unfair and secret tactics
to wear sackcloth and ashes
humbly to demonstrate repentance
Esther 4:3, 'There was great mourning ... and many lay in sackcloth and ashes'

Responsibility

a tall poppy
a person with great power or responsibility and/or in receipt of high remuneration
charity begins at home
a person's first responsibility should be to that person's family
John Fletcher (1579–1625), *The Wild-Goose Chase*, 'Charity and beating begins at home'
one's opposite number
a person with similar responsibilities in another organisation
someone would run a mile
a person would do anything to escape that person's responsibilities
someone's fingerprints are all over this
it is obvious that a particular person was solely responsible for this
that is on your head
you will have to accept responsibility for that
Shakespeare, *Merchant of Venice*, IV:i, 'My deeds upon my head'
the ball is in someone's court
it is some other person's responsibility
refers to tennis
the buck stops here
I accept full responsibility
hand-lettered sign on desk of US President Harry S. Truman (Phillips, *TheTruman Presidency*, Ch. 12)
to abandon ship
to abrogate one's responsibilities or to abandon a project
refers to the order given when a ship is about to sink
to be a glutton for punishment
a person who is eager to work very hard even without the prospect of commensurate reward
Rudyard Kipling (1865–1936), 'He's honest, and a glutton for work'
to be in someone's bailiwick
to be some other person's responsibility
refers to a region under the jurisdiction of a particular bailiff
to be in someone's shoes
to have another person's responsibility
to be left holding the baby
to be forced to accept responsibility for someone else's problems
to be one's baby
to be one's area of responsibility; to be one's special object of devotion or doting
to be one's pigeon
to be one's area of responsibility
to be tied down
to have responsibilities precluding alternative activities
to dump something in someone's lap
to impose an unwelcome responsibility on another person
to engage in empire building
to set out to expand the size of the business or bureaucratic unit for which one is responsible, especially as a means of increasing one's own importance

to face the music
to accept responsibility when confronted by one's critics
refers to the theatre

to have blood on one's hands
to be the person responsible for someone else's predicament
Matthew 27:24, 'He [Pilate] took water and washed his hands in full view of the crowd. "My hands are clean of this man's blood," he declared'

to have broad shoulders
to be able to cope well with responsibility

to pass the buck
to shift responsibility to someone else
refers to the buckhorn knife passed around the table to indicate the dealer while playing poker

to pin someone down
to find a person willing to accept blame or responsibility; OR to force a person to announce a decision or concede a point
refers to wrestling

to put a burden on someone's shoulders
to impose responsibilities on a person

to shoot the messenger
to blame the person who brings news of an undesired happening instead of the person really responsible for that happening

to take a weight off someone's shoulder
to assist a person by relieving that person of some responsibility

to throw the ball back to someone
to return responsibility for something to another person

to tread on someone's corns/toes
to upset another person by interfering in that person's area of responsibility

to walk away from something
to abrogate one's responsibilities in regard to some matter

to wash one's hands of something
emphatically to decline future responsibility
Matthew 27:24, 'He [Pilate] took water and washed his hands in full view of the crowd. "My hands are clean of this man's blood," he declared'

under someone's nose
in a person's immediate area of responsibility or in circumstances where that person should have known something

uneasy lies the head that wears a crown
leadership involves some risks and some burdens (esp. the risk of being deposed)
Shakespeare, *Henry IV*, Part 2, III:i, 'Uneasy lies the head that wears a crown'

Result

a cocktail
a mixture of several components contributing to a result
refers to an aperitif; origin of name obscure

a landslide
an electoral result involving victory or defeat by a very large margin

a litmus test
a simple examination that reveals the true state of affairs
refers to a test with litmus paper to establish whether a solution is acid or alkaline

a patchwork quilt
a result arising from many uncoordinated inputs

a photo finish
a close result in a contest
refers to horse racing

a South Sea bubble
an unrealistic financial venture that is bound to result in total loss
refers to a notorious financial scandal involving the South Sea Company (UK) in 1720

all roads lead to Rome
all alternatives will have the same outcome
refers to roads radiating from the great imperial capital to all parts of the Roman empire

backwash
consequence

by their fruits ye shall know them
their true nature will be revealed by their results

Matthew 7:20, 'wherefore by their fruits ye shall know them'

chicken and egg
a situation involving two factors each of which causes the other, making it impossible to decide which came first

come hell or high water
regardless of the difficulties or obstacles

death blow
incident that results in the destruction of something

harvest
end result of labour

Matthew 8:37, 'The harvest truly is plenteous, but the labourers are few'

if the cap fits then wear it
if that description corresponds with your characteristics, then you are in that category

one can lead a horse to water, but one can't make it drink
one can give advice to a person but cannot ensure that it will be acted on

one cannot make bricks without straw
one cannot achieve results in the absence of adequate resources

Exodus 6:7 'Ye shall no more give the people straw to make bricks ... let them go and gather straw for themselves'

one has made one's bed and one will now have to lie on it
one has to bear the consequences of one's actions

one might as well be hanged for a sheep as for a lamb
further action will not increase the adverse consequences already in train

refers to the stealing of either sheep or lambs being capital crimes under old English law

one shudders to think what the outcome might be
there is great concern as to the outcome

pie in the sky
a hoped for result unlikely to be achieved

Rafferty rules
the complete absence of rules

origin obscure

slings and arrows
adverse fortunes in life; hurtful experiences

Shakespeare, *Hamlet* III:i, 'Whether 'tis nobler in the mind to suffer / the slings and arrows of outrageous fortune, / or to take arms against a sea of troubles, / and by opposing end them?'

smoking gun
damning evidence

stalemate
a final result in which neither party to a dispute is victorious

refers to chess

the answer is a lemon
there is no appropriate answer to that sort of proposition

the chickens are coming home to roost
the consequences of a person's past actions are now being felt by that person

Robert Southey (1774–1843), *The Curse of Kehama* (1810), 'Curses are like young chickens, they always come home to roost'

the fat is in the fire
action with certain unstoppable consequences has now been initiated

the final (or last) straw
the latest step that, when added to a large number of seemingly harmless previous steps, sets off a significant event resulting from the cumulative effect

see 'the straw that broke the camel's back'

the proof of the pudding is in the eating
the success of a venture will be measured by its results

the straw that broke the camel's back
the latest step that, when added to a large number of seemingly harmless previous steps, sets off a sudden significant event resulting from the cumulative effect

things look black
there is little hope of success or prosperity or a favourable outcome

to apply pressure on someone
to induce a person to do something that that person would otherwise not

do by implying adverse consequences if the person does not cooperate

to be a laid-down misPre

to be very easily accomplished and/or to be certain of outcome

refers to card playing where one player undertakes not to win any tricks while playing with the disadvantage of having that player's cards exposed to observation by others

to be a mixed blessing

to be an outcome with some desirable and some undesirable features

to be ahead by a country mile

to be in a comfortable lead

in the long distances of certain rural areas, a 'country mile' is jocularly believed to be a very long mile

to be black magic

to lack any scientific or logical basis

refers to witchcraft

to be hell bent on something

to be very determined to achieve something, regardless of the adverse consequences

to be on tenterhooks

anxiously to await some result

refers to cloth being stretched or 'tentered'; Latin: *tentus* ('stretched')

to be short-sighted

not to recognise the likely consequences

to be sidetracked

to be diverted from one's main task

refers to railways

to be the kiss of death

to be something intended to be helpful but resulting in total destruction

to be the luck of the draw

to be a chance result

refers to card games or a raffle

to bear fruit

to result in success

to break one's duck

to end a spell that had no results

refers to cricket in which a 'duck' represents no score

to count one's chickens before they are hatched

to treat as fact the expected results of a future proposal

originally attributed to Erasmus (1466–1536) in slightly different form

to cover one's hide

to provide excuses or take other evasive action in an attempt to avoid the adverse consequences of one's actions

to cry 'wolf'

repeatedly to raise an unjustified concern with the result that one will be ignored when the circumstances change and a real threat emerges

refers to a story of a boy who cried 'wolf' (from *Aesop's Fables*)

to dig one's own grave

to take action that results in an unintended disaster for oneself

to get brownie points

to receive credit for being very well behaved, or for meritorious achievement

refers to junior girl guide members; the metaphor is often used jocularly or sarcastically with respect to adults

to have egg on one's face

to be embarrassed by the results of one's own stupidity

to hedge one's bets

to insure against a losing bet or investment by also investing on the opposite outcome

to hide under someone's skirts

to let someone else take the consequences of one's actions

refers to childish seeking for protection

to hold a knife/sword at someone's throat

to assert undue pressure on another person in an endeavour to achieve a result that would otherwise not be forthcoming

to keep one's fingers crossed

to hope for a good outcome

refers to making the sign of the Christian cross to protect against ill-fortune

to let someone off the hook

to allow a person to escape the adverse consequences of that person's own actions

refers to angling

to nurse one's bruises/wounds

to adjust oneself to defeat

to open the floodgates

to take action that will have massive consequences

Shakespeare, *Othello* I:iii, 'My particular grief is of so flood-gate and o'erbearing nature that it engluts and swallows other sorrows'

to pay the price
to suffer the adverse consequences of one's acts or omissions

to prick up one's ears
suddenly to start paying attention to a conversation in progress as a result of a halfheard phrase
refers to horses and dogs

to raise merry hell
to cause an uproar by outlandish, reckless, or larrikinish behaviour
in the eighteenth century there were clubs of reckless young men, known as 'hell-fire clubs', who were said to 'raise merry hell'

to reap as one has sown
to experience the consequences of one's own actions
Galatians 6:7, 'Whatsoever a man soweth, that shall he also reap'

to reap the whirlwind
to suffer the adverse consequences of a bad act
Hosea 8:7, 'They have sown the wind, and they shall reap the whirlwind'

to score a hat trick
to have three successive favourable outcomes
refers to a bowler in cricket taking three wickets in three balls; such a feat being originally rewarded with the prize of a new hat

to seal someone's fate
to cause a certain final outcome adversely affecting a person'

to shake a tree
to do something to see what will result

to sow the wind and reap the whirlwind
to make bad mistakes and to suffer the even worse consequences
Hosea 8:7, 'They have sown the wind, and they shall reap the whirlwind'

to stew in one's juice
to suffer the adverse consequences of one's acts or omissions
Shakespeare, *Hamlet* III:iv, 'But to live in the rank sweat of an enseamed bed, stew'd in corruption'

to stir up a hornet's nest
to take action that results in unpleasant side-effects

to take a caning
to suffer the adverse consequences of one's acts or omissions

to throw one's weight around
to assert one's real or assumed authority excessively

to tip the balance/scales
to be further information or argument that results in an issue, that could have been decided either way, being determined in a particular way
refers to balance scales

to turn tail
to run away; OR to reverse oneself

Retirement

golden handshake
a large payment in connection with, or as an inducement to, retirement

in harness
to be constrained and in work

swan song
last appearance before retirement
refers to the ancient (but erroneous) belief that the swan sings beautifully before it dies; such a belief is referred to by Plato, Aristotle, Shakespeare, Spenser, and Coleridge (among others)

to bow out
to retire from some activity

to hang up one's boots
to retire

to step down
to retire from some position

today a rooster, tomorrow a feather duster
when circumstances change, an important person can, immediately, become unimportant

Revenge

to get one's own back on someone
to extract revenge

to pay someone back in that person's own coin
to retaliate in kind

to return the compliment
to reciprocate; OR to extract revenge
to take no prisoners
to be utterly ruthless
military metaphor
to thirst for blood
to be eager for revenge
two can play at that game
it is possible to retaliate

Reversal

one cannot teach an old dog new tricks
people become set in their ways irreversibly
the boot is on the other foot
the advantage is reversed
the die is cast
the course of action is irreversible
to back pedal
to reverse to some extent previously applied policies
refers to riding a cycle
to burn one's bridges
to do something irreversible
to cross the Rubicon
to make an irreversible decision in regard to some commitment
refers to Caesar's crossing of the Rubicon River in Gaul in 49 BC thus declaring war on Pompey
to do a U-turn
to reverse one's thinking
to do an about face
to reverse a previously enunciated policy
to let the genie out of the bottle
to cause something irreversible to take place
'genie' was adopted (to refer to a spirit released from a bottle) by the French translators of *Arabian Nights' Entertainments*
to turn a complete somersault
to reverse one's established policy
to turn around 180 degrees
completely to reverse a stance
to turn round
to reverse one's policy
to turn something on its ear/head
to reverse something
to turn the tables on someone
to cause the relative positions of oneself and another person to be reversed
refers to chess or draughts (and turning the table, or board, the other way around)
to turn the tide
to reverse the direction of something
volte face
a reversal of previously held beliefs
French, 'a turning around'; the term 'volte' originally had use in both fencing and horsemanship

Risk

a belt-and-braces approach
action backing up other action by way of excessive caution
refers to wearing a belt as well as braces
fools rush in where angels fear to tread
unsophisticated persons take unwise risks in circumstances where more knowledgeable persons would exercise caution
Alexander Pope (1688–1744), *An Essay on Criticism* 1:625, 'For fools rush in where angels fear to tread'
half a loaf is better than none
it is more advantageous to accept less than is really desired than risk missing out completely
John Heywood (1546), 'Throw no gift at the giver's head;/better is half a loaf than no bread
in for a penny, in for a pound
once something is commenced it ought be finished; OR if one is willing to take a small risk then one might as well take a bigger one
it is a case of sink or swim
it is a case of success or failure with no other alternatives
refers to the 'testing' of so-called witches by throwing them into water to see if they would sink or swim
it was touch and go
there were considerable risks — - the objective was achieved, but only just
perhaps refers to the touching of the wheels of two moving vehicles

nervous Nellies
persons unwilling to take any risks
not to put all one's eggs in the one basket
to spread one's risks
someone's job is on the line
a person's career path is under consideration; AND/OR that person's present position is at risk
to be sitting on a volcano
to be safe for the time being but exposed to the risk of a sudden great disaster
to chance one's arm
to take a great risk
refers to the stripes on the uniforms of non-commissioned officers
to enter treacherous waters
to engage in an enterprise with risks that are not obvious
nautical metaphor
to go out on a limb
to put oneself in an isolated or stranded position
to go through fire and water
to undertake all attendant risks
perhaps refers to ordeals of fire and water — ancient Anglo-Saxon ordeals of torture used to ascertain guilt or innocence
to jump in feet first
to take a calculated risk
to play Russian roulette
to engage in a dangerously unpredictable exercise
refers to an act of daring in which one squeezes the trigger of a revolver held to the head (after loading one chamber and spinning the cylinder — thus the one being fired is determined by chance)
to play it safe
to take no risks
to play with dynamite
to invite trouble by virtue of one's risky conduct
to push one's luck
having already done well in something, then to take risks which can prejudice everything
to put one's money where one's mouth is
to back one's boasting by putting assets at risk
to put one's reputation on the line
to take a public stance in the realisation that there is a risk that one's reputation will suffer if one is proved wrong
to stick one's neck out
to have the courage of one's convictions or to take a calculated risk
refers to execution by decapitation
to take a punt
to take a calculated risk
refers to gambling
to take the plunge
to make an irreversible initial action; to commit oneself to a course of action
refers to leaping into water
to throw a sprat to catch a mackerel
to risk a little in the hope of gaining much
uneasy lies the head that wears a crown
leadership involves some risks and some burdens (esp. the risk of being deposed)
Shakespeare, *Henry IV*, Part 2, III:i, 'Uneasy lies the head that wears a crown'

Sadness

heartache
sadness
William Blake (1757–1827), *To Hayley*, 'Thy friendship oft has made my heart to ache'
heartbreak
despair
Psalms 69:21, 'Thy rebuke hath broken my heart; I am full of heaviness'; Shakespeare *Hamlet* I:ii, 'But break my heart . . . '
one's heart bleeds for someone
one feels truly sad for a person's fate
derived from the Christian Church's veneration of the sacred heart of Jesus (*sacré couer*) which was symbolised by a bleeding heart — sacrificed for the sake of humanity
there is blood on the floor
this has caused great anguish
to beat one's breast

to express sorrow
refers to traditional expression of grief
to cast a shadow over something
to introduce a note of warning or sadness in regard to some matter
to cry one's eyes out
to express great sadness at a situation
to drive someone almost to tears
to act in such a way as to cause someone significant distress
to drown one's sorrows
to drink by way of solace and in an attempt to forget some misfortune
to set someone's teeth on edge
to cause a person intense irritation or discomfort
Ezekiel 18:2, 'The fathers have eaten sour grapes, and the children's teeth are set on edge'; Shakespeare, *Henry IV Pt 1* III:i, 'And that would set my teeth nothing on edge, nothing so much as mincing poetry'
to take something to heart
to learn to appreciate the significance of something; or to be much saddened by something
with a heavy heart
in sorrow
Johann Wolfgang von Goethe (1749–1832), *Gretchen am Spinnrad*, 'My peace is gone, my heart is heavy'
you can eat your heart out
I don't care if you are intensely aggrieved or jealous

Sameness

a nod is the same as a wink to a blind horse
fine distinctions are not appropriate here
Captain Marryat (1792–1848), *Peter Simple*, 'But you're a dutiful son, so I'll say no more about it — a nod's as good as a wink to a blind horse'
a round robin
(1) a series of cheques from A to B, from B to C, from C to A, and so on, leaving all of them in the same net position as before; (2) a document signed by members of an organisation which has the same effect as a resolution of a meeting; (3) a petition arranged with the names in a circle such that no name appears at the top; (4) a sporting tournament in which each competitor competes once with each of the others
refers to corruption of French *rond* ('round') and *ruban* ('a ribbon')
all roads lead to Rome
all alternatives will have the same outcome
refers to roads radiating from the great imperial capital to all parts of the Roman empire
birds of a feather flock together
persons of like interests gather in the same place
Samuel Rutherford (?1600–61), 'Fowls of a feather flock together'
Box and Cox
two persons who are never around at the same time
refers to the name of a play by J. M. Morton (1811–91), *Box and Cox* (adapted from the French)
by the same token
by the same argument, in a similar way
in one fell swoop
all at the same time
Shakespeare, *Macbeth* IV:iii, 'What! all my pretty chickens and their dam, at one fell swoop?'
not to be in the same street as someone
not to be of comparable quality
to all sing from the same hymnal
to act consistently with each other
refers to a book of hymns
to be able to chew gum and walk at the same time
to be able to do two relatively simple things simultaneously
used ironically to disparage a person of limited capacities
to be in harmony with someone
to work cooperatively and effectively together
to be in the same boat
to share a common set of difficulties
to be in the same league
to have comparable skills
refers to sporting competitions
to be in tune with someone

to think in a similar way to someone else

to be on the same wavelength
to think on similar lines
refers to radio reception

to be tarred with the same brush
to be damned merely because of one's association with another person
refers to treating cuts on sheep with a tarbrush

to be with it
to be fully informed and conversant with something, especially with modern trends, and to be part of such a movement

to follow suit
to do the same as others
refers to playing cards

to speak the same language
to have a good understanding and similar ideas

to speak the same language
to have a good understanding and similar ideas

under one roof
under the same management; OR in the same building

Satisfaction

a seal of approval
confirmation that something is satisfactory

a warm inner glow
satisfaction at some achievement
Joseph Conrad (1857–1924), *Youth*, 'the heat of life ... that glow in the heart that with every year grows dim, grows cold'

I will have that person's guts for garters
I am extremely angry and dissatisfied with that person

ironclad
firm or rigorous
refers to armour-plated naval vessels

lean and hungry
efficient
Shakespeare, *Julius Caesar* I:ii, 'Yond' Cassius has a lean and hungry look; he thinks too much: such men are dangerous'

to be a well-oiled piece of machinery
to be functioning very satisfactorily

to be cream on top of the milk
to be an additional benefit in an already satisfactory scenario

to be first class
to be of the highest standard

to be icing on top of the cake
to be an additional benefit in an already satisfactory scenario

to be on course
to be progressing satisfactorily towards one's goal

to get rid of the dead wood
to terminate the services of unsatisfactory personnel
refers to pruning of bushes

to heave a sigh of relief
to express satisfaction at the achievement of a solution to a difficult problem
John Keats (1795–1821), *I stood tip-toe upon a little hill*, 'born of the very sigh that silence heaves'

to hit a sour note
to say or do something inappropriate to a situation
refers to music

to jump for joy
to express great satisfaction

to make a noise about something
to complain or express dissatisfaction about something

to rub one's hands with glee
to express great satisfaction

Secrecy

a word in someone's ear
a confidential discussion

between you and me and the gatepost
confidentially

Chinese walls
a system to ensure that different parts of some organisation do not gain access to each other's confidential information

cloak-and-dagger activity
secret activity

originally referred to as 'cloak-and-sword' comedies (Spanish: *comedias de capa y espada*) — plays by seventeenth-century Spanish dramatists involving swashbuckling adventure; later adapted to refer to intrigue and secrecy ('cloak and dagger')

it is all done with mirrors
this is achieved by magic or illusion

low-down
confidential information relevant to something

no names, no packdrill
the identities of the parties will be kept confidential to protect them
military metaphor

something is in the wind
something is going on secretly

sub rosa
in strict confidence
Latin *sub rosa* 'under the rose' — refers to being under the rose (as a symbol of secrecy)

to be a closed book
to be a secret

to be tight-lipped
to keep confidences or to be uncommunicative

to ferret something out
by diligent research to discover some secret
refers to a ferret pursuing rabbits in their burrows

to have a card up one's sleeve
secretly to have information relevant to a transaction
refers to card games

to have a heart-to-heart talk
to have a confidential discussion on a highly personal matter
John Henry Newman (1801–90), 'Heart speaks to heart' (*cor ad cor loquitur*), motto on coat-of-arms as cardinal

to hold one's cards close to one's chest
to keep one's plans and strategies secret
refers to playing cards

to keep something dark
to keep something secret

to keep something under one's hat
to maintain a confidence

to keep something up one's sleeve
secretly to retain something in reserve for use in the future or at a later stage of negotiations
refers to playing cards or magicians

to keep something under wraps
to keep a matter confidential, especially pending an official announcement

to let the cat out of the bag
to reveal an embarrassing secret
refers to the practice of selling a person a cat (purported to be a pig) in a bag (or poke) — hence 'a pig in a poke'; if the person opened the bag and looked inside, that person 'let the cat out of the bag'

to line one's pockets
to make, improperly and secretly, a profit out of some transaction

to seal one's lips
to keep a confidence

to show one's slip
to reveal details which one meant to keep private
refers to women's petticoats

to tell tales out of school
to gossip mischievously and reveal secrets about others

to undermine someone's position
to injure another person's reputation and influence by unfair and secret tactics

wheels within wheels
secret machinations

Situation

a gambit
(in a competitive situation) an opening move that involves short-term losses in the expectation of long-term gains
Italian *gambetto*, literally 'tripping up'

a Mexican standoff
a situation where neither of two parties is making a move
refers to poker

a place in the sun
a favourable situation

a springboard
a situation from which one is able to make a rapid advance

a straight face
a facial expression that does not reveal one's thoughts in a humorous situation
a stranglehold
exclusive and complete control
refers to wrestling or fighting
catch 22
a condition or consequence that precludes success; a dilemma where the victim cannot win
title of a 1961 novel by Joseph Heller in which a man pleads insanity to escape war service, but whose plea of insanity demonstrates his inherent sanity
every cloud has a silver lining
there are consolations and potential benefits even in seemingly adverse situations
it is an ill wind that blows no good
even a seeming misfortune leads to some blessings
out of the frying pan into the fire
from one bad situation to an even worse one
something is rotten in the state of Denmark
the situation is corrupt and unacceptable
Shakespeare, *Hamlet* III:iv, 'Something is rotten in the state of Denmark'
that is the way the chips fall
that is the way that the benefits and detriments are distributed after an event
that is the way the cookie crumbles
that is the actual situation
the ice is melting
friendly relations are being restored
the nature of the beast
the reality of the situation
Revelation 13:17, ' ... he that had the mark, or the name of the beast, or the number of his name'
to add fuel to the fire
to make a bad situation worse
to be at the bottom of the food chain
to be at the lowest level in a hierarchy
to be in command
to be on top of a situation
to be in the dry dock
to be out of action while undergoing repairs
refers to ship repairs
to be quick on one's feet
cleverly to take advantage of a situation
to bite the bullet
to face up to the difficulties of a situation
refers to the use of biting on a bullet as a means of controlling one's reaction to pain in a surgical procedure without anaesthetic (for example, following a military battle)
to breathe down someone's neck
to cause annoyance to another person by remaining in that person's vicinity or by supervising that person too closely; OR to be narrowly behind another person in some competitive situation
to cross a bridge only when one comes to it
to await the crystallisation of a situation before sorting it out
to cry one's eyes out
to express great sadness at a situation
to feed the fire
to exacerbate a situation
to fight fire with fire
to counter a dangerous situation by making an equally dangerous move
to fish in troubled waters
to profit from a disturbed situation
refers to angling
to have a good nose for business
to be able to identify profitable business situations
to have the whip hand
to be in control of a situation
refers to the hand holding the whip in controlling horses, and perhaps slaves
to inflame a situation
to aggravate a situation
Shakespeare, *Julius Caesar* III:ii, 'It will inflame you, it will make you mad'
to keep an eye on the ball
to monitor a fast-changing situation
to keep one's eye on someone
to supervise a person
to keep one's eye on something
to monitor a situation
to keep up with the ball

to maintain awareness of a situation

to knock someone off that person's perch
to displace a person from a leadership position in some competitive situation

to pour oil on troubled waters
to calm down a situation

to pour petrol on the flames
to make a bad situation worse

to pull someone's chestnuts out of the fire
to retrieve a situation for someone else
refers to fable of a monkey getting roasting chestnuts out of a fire by using the cat's paw to achieve the desired result

to pull something out of the fire
to salvage something in a seemingly hopeless situation

to put a match to petrol
to cause an actual disaster out of a potentially disastrous situation

to put jam on someone's bread
to make a good situation even better

to put one's best face on something
to focus on the positive features surrounding a basically disastrous situation

to put someone in the picture
to fill a person in with the background of a situation

to ride out the storm
to come safely through some dangerous situation
nautical metaphor

to salvage something out of the wreck
to achieve some minor benefits out of a disastrous situation
refers to shipwrecks

to see the light
to understand the real situation
refers to the conversion of Saul (Paul) on the road to Damascus, *Acts* 9:3, 4 'And suddenly there shined round about him a light from heaven: and he fell to the earth'

to see the score
to appreciate the reality of a situation

to see which way the wind is blowing
to establish the factors relevant to a situation
John Seldon (1584–1654), 'Take a straw and throw it up into the air, you shall see by that which way the wind is'

to set someone's teeth on edge
to cause a person intense irritation or discomfort
Ezekiel 18:2, 'The fathers have eaten sour grapes, and the children's teeth are set on edge'; Shakespeare, *Henry IV Pt 1* III:i, 'And that would set my teeth nothing on edge, nothing so much as mincing poetry'

to squeeze the last drop out of something
to get the maximum advantage out of some favourable situation

to strike while the iron is hot
to take advantage of a situation that cannot last
refers to the work of blacksmiths and farriers; John Dryden (1631–1700), *Aenis*, 'We must beat the iron while it is hot, but we may polish it at leisure'

to squeeze the lemon dry
to get the maximum advantage out of some favourable situation
Sir Eric Geddes (1875–1937), 'The Germans ... are going to pay every penny; they are going to be squeezed, as a lemon is squeezed — until the pips squeak. My only doubt is not whether we can squeeze hard enough, but whether there is enough juice.' (10 December 1918)

to underplay some situation
to make something seem less significant than it is

Skill

a bush lawyer
a person without legal qualifications who has a reasonable, although not perfect, knowledge of the law, and who likes to make technical points in arguments

a chessmaster
a clever strategist

a dark horse
a person with unsuspected talents

Benjamin Disraeli (1804–81), *The Young Duke*, 'A dark horse, which had never been thought of, and which the careless St James had never even observed in the list, rushed past the grandstand in sweeping triumph'

a David and Goliath battle
a struggle between two parties who are not evenly matched
refers to *1 Samuel* 17:23 ff

a fat cat
a well-remunerated politician, public servant, or businessperson

a pea-and-thimble trick
a clever fraud committed in the presence of its victim without this being obvious at the time
refers to a sleight-of-hand trick played with three thimbles and a pea, the thimbles being moved about and observers being asked to guess under which thimble the pea is

a rabbit warren
a building with a maze of rooms and passages

that person couldn't knock the skin off a rice pudding
that person is weak or ineffective

that person's blood is worth bottling
that person is very clever or competent

it is all done with mirrors
this is achieved by magic or illusion

level best
making all possible effort
perhaps refers to railways

not to be the full two bob
not to be very intelligent
refers to slang term for two shillings

one needs to crawl before one can walk
skills are best developed in logical stages

one's long suit
one's main skills
refers to playing cards

the blind leading the blind
persons without the necessary skills for a task purporting to impart those skills to others
Matthew 15:14, 'And if the blind lead the blind, both shall fall into the ditch'

to be a bear of very little brain
to have little intelligence
refers to A. A. Milne's *Winnie-the-Pooh*

to be a chess game
to be a complex, skilful exercise involving moves and countermoves

to be able to chew gum and walk at the same time
to be able to do two relatively simple things simultaneously
used ironically to disparage a person of limited capacities

to be chief cook and bottlewasher
to perform a range of duties singlehandedly — ranging from important to menial

to be child's play
to be easy or to require only elementary skills and knowledge

to be going great guns
to be making very successful progress

to be hot stuff
to be skilful, or very passionate, or highly sexed

to be in the same league
to have comparable skills
refers to sporting competitions

to be quick on one's feet
cleverly to take advantage of a situation

to be the new kid on the block
to lack the experience of others

to find one's feet
to develop one's skills in a previously unfamiliar situation

to find one's niche
to find the opportunity to use one's talents

to have a crow's eye
to be cunning or alert

to have more degrees than a thermometer
to be too academic
a play on the word 'degree'

to hide one's light under a bushel
to keep others in ignorance of one's skills and experience
Luke 11:33, 'No man, when he hath lighted a candle, putteth it in a secret place, neither under a bushel'

to keep one's hand in
to engage in activities that reinforce skills that one has previously acquired

to look to one's laurels
to be careful not to lose one's reputation for some skill
refers to laurel wreaths presented to winners of events at the ancient Olympics

to make a name for oneself
to earn a good reputation by virtue of some skill

to raise something to a fine art form
to refine a thing or a process to the point where doing it is a highly skilled task

to rub off on someone
to benefit a person through an association that increases that person's skills

to score a point
to make a clever contribution in the course of debate

to send a boy on a man's errand
to engage a person to do a task beyond that person's capabilities

to separate the men from the boys
to distinguish between those with and without certain skills

to stick to one's knitting
to confine oneself to what one is used to doing

to take someone's measure
to sum up a person's character or skills

to try something out on the dog
to test the feasibility or safety of a dubious remedy or project

to wean someone off something
to induce a person to abandon some entrenched practice

tour de force
feat of skill or strength
French, 'feat of strength'

Slowness

at a snail's pace
very slowly
Shakespeare, *As You Like It*, II:vii, 'The whining schoolboy … creeping like snail unwillingly to school'

death of a thousand cuts
a slow, unpleasant ending

the mills of God grind slowly
retribution might be delayed but is inevitable
Friedrich von Logau (1604–55), *Sinngedichte* (translated by H. W. Longfellow), 'Though the mills of God grind slowly, yet they grind exceeding small; though with patience he stands waiting, with exactness grinds he all'

the wheels of justice grind slowly
it takes a long time to get a decision from the courts of law
Friedrich von Logau (1604–55), *Sinngedichte* (translated by H. W. Longfellow), 'Though the mills of God grind slowly, yet they grind exceeding small; though with patience he stands waiting, with exactness grinds he all'

to be slow off the mark
to be slow to start something
refers to the starting mark of a race

to drag one's feet
to be deliberately uncooperative or slow to act

to drag one's heels
to perform unduly slowly

to drag the chain
to perform unduly slowly
refers to a horse or bullock that is not pulling its weight, thus causing its chains to drag on the ground

to inch forward
to make slow progress
William Golding (1911–93), 'He inched along the path, with shuffling steps'

to lose steam
to slow down
refers to a steam engine or boiler

to sink slowly in the west
to fail gradually
refers to the setting of the sun in the western sky

to bleed to death slowly
to be heading in gradual steps towards total ruin

Smallness

a backwater
a place of little activity

a chink of light
a small hope of a solution or breakthrough

a fat chance
little hope

a fox hole
a small space of refuge and shelter (especially in battle)
Matthew 8:20, 'the foxes have holes, and the birds of the air have nests; but the son of man hath not where to lay his head'

a handful
a small number or amount

a pawn
a person of small importance who is manipulated by others
from Old French *poön*, *peon* ('foot soldier'); now applied to the smallest piece on the chess board

a storm in a teacup
a controversy about a minor matter but one that looms large in the minds of the parties

a toehold
an opportunity small in itself but with the potential to lead to bigger things
refers to climbing trees, rockfaces, etc.

a trickle
a small amount, in gradual stages

give someone an inch and that person will take an ell
make a small concession to a person and that person will abuse it by taking much more
derived from old measure of length (ell) originally based on the length of the forearm (the Old English word *eln* being cognate with the Latin *ulna*–a long bone of the forearm)

in for a penny, in for a pound
once something is commenced it ought be finished; OR if one is willing to take a small risk then one might as well take a bigger one

Lilliputian
small
refers to a place in *Gulliver's Travels* (1726) by Jonathon Swift (1667–1745)

not a jot
not even a small amount
refers to the Greek letter *iota* (i)

not to be a hanging matter
to be only a minor mistake

one's heart is not in some cause
one has little enthusiasm for some cause

people stayed away in droves
few people came
refers to a moving group of cattle, sheep, or other animals

pintsize
small

tall oaks from little acorns grow
even major enterprises have to have small beginnings
David Everett (1769–1813), *Lines Written for a School Declamation*, 'Large streams from little fountains flow, / tall oaks from little acorns grow'

the tail wagging the dog
a minor aspect with disproportionate effect on a major aspect

there is no room to swing a cat
this place is very small
refers to the swinging of a whip (a cat-o'-nine-tails) in the confined space of a ship's hull

to be a big fish in a little pond
to be a person holding an important office but in an unimportant organisation

to be a crack in the wall
to represent a small opportunity that can be exploited

to be a small cog in a large wheel
to be a relatively unimportant person in a large organisation

to be chicken feed
to be small and unimportant

to be the thin end of the wedge
to be a small action or thing that has the potential to cause much larger undesirable consequences
refers to wedges used for splitting wood

to be the tip of the iceberg
to be only a very small portion of a much larger but less obvious whole

to bend the rules
to overlook minor infractions of the rules

to chisel away at something
to reduce the size of something in a series of small stages

to cut no ice with someone
to have little effect on a person
perhaps refers to ice-skating

to decimate
to reduce in size greatly

strictly refers to reducing by one tenth — originally a punishment inflicted on Roman legions whereby one tenth of the soldiers were selected by lot and executed

to earn peanuts
to get a reward that is far too small in relation to the value of the services rendered

to encapsulate some idea
to reduce the essential points of a complicated proposal to a small number of words

to fiddle at the edges
to do some relatively minor things that do not deal with the substance of a problem

to have an eagle eye
to be able very readily to notice small mistakes or fine details missed by others

to hold someone on a short leash
to give a person very little freedom
refers to a lead used to restrain coursing hounds

to live from hand to mouth
being in poor financial circumstances to survive (with little safety margin)
refers to immediate consumption of whatever one has in one's hand

to look down the barrel of a gun
to be given little choice in a matter

to look for a needle in a haystack
to attempt something with a very small chance of success

to make mountains out of mole-hills
to treat a minor problem as though it were a major disaster

to miss the sharks while netting the minnows
to succeed in minor aspects but fail in the ones that really matter

to nitpick
to criticise a person in respect of very minor matters
refers to the removal of lice eggs (nits) from the hair of an animal or person

to scratch the surface
to deal with only a small portion of a much larger whole

to pay something back with interest
to return a small favour with a bigger favour; or to extract retribution of greater value than the circumstances warrant

to push someone over the brink
by a small action to cause the absolute ruin (financially or emotionally) of someone already in peril

to salvage something out of the wreck
to achieve some minor benefits out of a disastrous situation
refers to shipwrecks

to sell one's birthright for a mess of pottage
through foolishness to exchange something of substance for something of little value
Genesis 25:34, 'Then Jacob gave Esau bread and pottage of lentils ... thus Esau despised his birthright'

to test the water
to try out an idea in a small way

to thrash with a feather
to impose only a minor punishment for a very serious offence

to throw a sprat to catch a mackerel
to risk a little in the hope of gaining much

to throw out the baby with the bathwater
to discard a major benefit in the course of obtaining a comparatively minor advantage

to throw someone a few crumbs
to fob a person off with a few symbolic but unimportant concessions
Luke 16:21, 'a certain beggar ... desiring to be fed with the crumbs which fell from the rich man's table'

to tinker at the edges
to make minor or cosmetic changes without affecting the substance
refers to the common assumption that a tinker was an unreliable tradesman

two men and a dog
very few people

Speech

a nod and a wink

a sign that understanding has been reached in a matter that, in the interests of discretion, has not been discussed aloud

Captain Marryat (1792–1848), *Peter Simple*, 'But you're a dutiful son, so I'll say no more about it — a nod's as good as a wink to a blind horse'

a shaggy dog story

a laborious, far-fetched, amusing story

refers to the shaggy dog that originally featured in many of these stories

a word in someone's ear

a confidential discussion

a burning question

a much discussed question

not to mince words

to speak bluntly

not to put too fine a point on it

speaking bluntly

Charles Dickens (1812–70) *Bleak House* ch. 11, '"not to put too fine a point upon it" — a favourite apology for plain-speaking with Mr Snagsby'

shoot!

go on, speak!

speak softly and carry a big stick

be polite to your potential enemies but maintain an active and visible defensive and offensive capability

from a speech by US President Theodore Roosevelt in 1901

talk of the devil

here is the person we were just discussing

to bandy something about

to discuss something in a light-hearted manner

to bare one's soul

talkatively to give a revealing insight into oneself

to bite someone's nose off

to speak to a person with excessive aggression

to break the ice

to take the initiative in starting discussions

Francis Bacon (1561–1626), *Of Cunning*, 'In things that are tender and unpleasing, it is good to break the ice by some whose words are of less weight …'

to buy into some argument

to seek to participate in some discussion

to chew fat

to discuss a matter, often with grumbling and unhappiness

to draw a veil over something

pointedly to avoid discussing something

to drop names

to slip names of celebrities allegedly known to the speaker into a conversation in an attempt to impress

to find one's tongue

to overcome one's shyness and speak

to get down to brass tacks

to discuss the aspects that really matter

perhaps refers to Cockney rhyming slang ('brass tacks' = 'facts')

to get down to taws

to discuss the aspects that really matter

to have a bone to pick

to have a grievance that requires discussion

to have a heart-to-heart talk

to have a confidential discussion on a highly personal matter

John Henry Newman (1801–90), 'Heart speaks to heart' (*cor ad cor loquitur*), motto on coat-of-arms as cardinal

to have a loose tongue

to speak foolishly or indiscreetly

to have a nuclear ships policy

to neither confirm nor deny something

refers to the US policy of neither confirming nor denying whether a particular ship is carrying nuclear arms

to have a sharp tongue

to speak in a cutting and abrasive fashion

to hijack a debate

to involve oneself in discussion on some matter and turn that discussion to one's advantage

to keep one's mouth shut

not to discuss some matter

to lay a proposal on the table

to make a proposal available for discussion or to adjourn discussion on a proposal for an indefinite period

to open the batting

to be the first in a series of persons speaking or doing something
refers to cricket

to poke mullock at someone
to ridicule a person, or to rubbish that person's arguments
refers to the heap of rubbish at the top of a mineshaft

to pontificate
to speak as if with great authority and with an assumed air of infallibility
refers to the pope (or pontiff)

to shoot from the hip
to speak without careful assessment of the situation

to shoot one's mouth off
to speak without thinking

to skate around some subject
by diversionary tactics to avoid discussing some subject

to snap someone's head off
to speak to a person with excessive aggression

to speak one's mind
to express one's views frankly and forcefully

to speak the same language
to have a good understanding and similar ideas

to speak with a forked tongue
to utter halftruths with the intention of misleading the listener

to strangle some discussion
to cut off some unfinished discussion

to talk nineteen to the dozen
to speak very quickly

to talk one's book
to present arguments that, although plausible, are really designed to foster one's vested interest

to talk shop
to discuss business or professional matters on a social occasion

to talk the hind leg off a donkey
to talk excessively

to talk through one's hat
to say things that demonstrate the speaker's ignorance of the subject

to talk turkey
to talk realistically
origin obscure; North American slang

to waste one's breath
to talk and request something without achieving anything

were your ears burning?
we were discussing you
Pliny: 'When our ears do glow and tingle, some do talk of us in our absence'

Speed

at a break-neck pace
very fast
refers to horseriding at great speed

at a rate of knots
very fast
nautical metaphor; refers to the original measure of a ships's speed by noting the rate at which the ship passed a regular series of knots tied in a rope which was maintained in position beside the ship

before one can say 'Jack Robinson'
very quickly
origin of phrase is disputed, but dates from at least the eighteenth century

before one can say 'knife'
very quickly

by leaps and bounds
with surprisingly fast progress

fast and furious
in an exciting way, in quick succession

full-steam ahead!
get going as fast as possible!
refers to a steam engine (especially in a ship or train)

nimble-footed
quick to change the direction of one's activities when circumstances warrant

speed the plough!
let us get on with this as fast as possible!
George Chapman (?1559–?1634), *Bussy d'Ambois*, I:i, 'speed his plough!'

tailspin
a loss of control; a state of chaos
refers to a spin by an aircraft with the tail spiralling

to achieve a flying start
to get operational very quickly

to be a money spinner

to produce large profits easily and quickly

to be all systems 'go'
to be ready to proceed as fast as possible

to be quick on one's feet
cleverly to take advantage of a situation

to be quick on the draw
to act precipitately
refers to drawing a firearm

to catapult
(of sales, etc.) to increase rapidly

to come in thick and fast
to arrive quickly and in great volume

to cut corners
to lower one's standards in order to complete something more quickly

to go hot foot
to do something fast

to go post haste
to go very fast
refers to urgent postal messages (originally carried on horseback)

to have to fly
to need to leave in order to reach the next destination quickly

to keep an eye on the ball
to monitor a fast-changing situation

to lose money hand over fist
to lose money very fast and comprehensively

to take short cuts
to do something by a faster but less thorough method

Standard

a benchmark
a standard by which something is measured
refers to a mark (and associated bench) used in ancient building practices as a reference point for measuring and levelling

a hallmark
a standard
refers to the official assay mark on gold and silver, originally put on at the Goldsmiths' Hall, London

a yardstick
a standard by which something is measured
refers to a stick used for measuring a yard in distance

froth and bubble
superficially attractive but really insignificant items
'Life is mainly froth and bubble ... ' (folk rhyme)

guiding light
a principle or example to follow in any activity
Exodus 13:21, 'And the Lord went before them by day in a pillar of a cloud, to lead them the way; and by night in a pillar of fire, to give them light'

not to be in the race
to lack the required standard

one can't make a silk purse out of a sow's ear
it is impossible to manufacture something of a high standard from inferior raw materials
Malcolm Bradbury (1932–), 'For the mass of men, you can't make a silk purse out of a sow's ear'

the Plimsoll line
the standard
refers to the mark fixing the maximum load line of a merchant ship in water, and to Samuel Plimsoll MP (1824–98) who campaigned for safe shipping practices

the silly season
the holiday period, when hard news is scarce and journalistic standards are lowered

the touchstone
the standard
refers to a dark flinty stone used to assess samples of gold by comparing streaks left on it with those streaks left by known gold-containing standards

to be able to hear a pin drop
to experience silence

to be below par
to be less than the desired standard

to be beyond the pale
to be socially unacceptable, especially for unacceptable standards or behaviour
'the Pale' originally (fourteenth century and later) referred to that part of Ireland under British rule (Latin *palus* 'a stake', marking a fence or boundary)

to be up to scratch

to be of the required standard

perhaps refers to the scratch mark in a boxing ring used to indicate an ability or willingness to fight, or perhaps refers to a starting line in a race from which competitors not receiving an advantage begin the race

to be up to the mark

to be of the right standard

refers to the official assay mark on gold and silver, originally put on at the Goldsmiths' Hall, London

to beatify someone

to describe a person as worthy of honour

refers to a step in the process towards canonisation as a saint

to cut corners

to lower one's standards in order to complete something more quickly

to lift one's game

to raise the standard of one's performance

to move the goal posts

unfairly to alter the rules after some action (that relied on the old rules) has already started

refers to sporting games

to play the last card in the pack

to be forced to use one's last expedient

refers to playing cards

to scrape the bottom of the barrel

to be forced to use the last available resources; to lower one's standards because one is short of resources

to weed some group out

to get rid of some elements not meeting a desired standard

Start

a baptism of fire

the commencement of an operation that presents great difficulty

refers to religious ceremonial washing as an initiation ceremony; metaphorical use (as here) attributed to Napoleon III in referring to to a soldier's first battle

a big bang

a sudden major change in the environment

D-Day

the long-awaited time at which some action commences

refers to the Allied invasion of Europe in World War II

from a to z

from start to finish

from alpha to omega

from start to finish

refers to the first and last letters of the Greek alphabet

from go to whoa

from start to finish

refers to the commands given to horses

from the word 'go'

from the beginning

John 1:1, 'In the beginning was the word'

in for a penny, in for a pound

once something is commenced it ought be finished; OR if one is willing to take a small risk then one might as well take a bigger one

it is on for young and old

the excitement has started (esp. referring to fighting)

tall oaks from little acorns grow

even major enterprises have to have small beginnings

David Everett (1769–1813), *Lines Written for a School Declamation*, 'Large streams from little fountains flow, / tall oaks from little acorns grow'

the curtain rises on something

something is about to start

refers to the theatre

the rot set in

conditions started to deteriorate

to achieve a flying start

to get operational very quickly

to be back to scratch

to have to start all over again

perhaps refers to the scratch mark in a boxing ring used to indicate an ability or willingness to fight, or perhaps refers to a starting line in a race from which competitors not receiving an advantage begin the race

to be first off the mark

to start ahead of all others

refers to the starting mark of a race

to be itching to go

to be highly enthusiastic and keen to start

to be slow off the mark

to be slow to start something
refers to the starting mark of a race

to be the dawn of a new day
to be the start of a different regime

to be the first cab off the rank
to be the first chosen or tried out

to break the ice
to take the initiative in starting discussions
Francis Bacon (1561–1626), *Of Cunning*, 'In things that are tender and unpleasing, it is good to break the ice by some whose words are of less weight ...'

to come out into the open
to start being frank

to enter a long road
to commence a task that will take a long time

to enter the home stretch
to commence the last stage
refers to horse racing

to get in on the act
to participate in some activity started by others

to get the show on the road
to commence a planned activity
refers to a travelling circus

to get to first base
to succeed in achieving the first stage in any undertaking
refers to baseball

to go back to square one
to start all over again
refers to board games

to have L-plates
to be new to a task
refers to learner's plates on the vehicle of a novice driver

to jump the gun
to start before one is meant to
refers to a starting pistol in a race

to kick off
to start some action
refers to football

to leap in
to commence an activity without considering the wisdom of doing so or the best way to proceed

to move on to greener pastures
to move to a better environment; to commence a new, better career
Psalms 23:1, 'The Lord is my shepherd: therefore can I lack nothing. he shall feed me in a green pasture: and lead me forth beside the waters of comfort'

to move the goal posts
unfairly to alter the rules after some action (that relied on the old rules) has already started
refers to sporting games

to pass on the bâton
to hand over to a successor

to prick up one's ears
suddenly to start paying attention to a conversation in progress as a result of a halfheard phrase
refers to horses and dogs

to set sail
to commence a voyage

to show someone the ropes
to teach a beginner how to do something
nautical metaphor

to start from scratch
to commence something without the benefit of any past activity
refers to the starting mark (with no handicap advantage) in a race

to start from taws
to begin from the beginning

to start off on the right foot
to commence an operation with great care to do it correctly
refers to marching

to start the ball rolling
to commence and advance enthusiastically an activity

to start to bite
to start to be effective

to start with a blank sheet of paper
to commence an exercise without being bound by any established practices

to touch base with someone
to make an initial contact
refers to baseball

to turn the corner
to commence being successful after initial failures

Strategy

a chessmaster
a clever strategist

a listening post
a place where information of strategic value can be collected
military metaphor
opening gambit
the first in a series of strategic moves
usually refers to chess (see also *gambit*); Italian *gambetto*, literally 'tripping up'
to be in a commanding position
to have a strategic advantage
to derail some strategy
to cause a strategy to fail
to go down a particular road
to adopt a particular strategy
to hold one's cards close to one's chest
to keep one's plans and strategies secret
refers to playing cards
to play it by ear
to develop one's strategy to always fit in with circumstances as they change from time to time
refers to playing music without the benefit of a written score
zugzwang
a disadvantageous action being forced on one
chess term: German, *Zug* move + *Zwang* 'compulsion, obligation' = a compulsory move

Stupidity

a death wish
the contemplation or commission of action so foolish that it is likely to lead to utter disaster
a simple Simon
a foolish, gullible, or half-witted person
refers to a well-known nursery rhyme character (who met a pieman)
a wild-goose chase
a futile chase or search
refers to old game of 'follow-the-leader' on horses in which the objective was to follow a winding and difficult course without ever catching up
beadledom
stupid officiousness
refers to a church official (a beadle) appointed to deal with petty offenders
boneheaded
stupid
cock-eyed
stupid
hare-brained
wildly stupid
Benjamin Disraeli (1804–81), speech 1878, 'The hare-brained chatter of irresponsible frivolity'
that person has some palings off the fence
that person is mentally disturbed
if you gave that person a penny for that person's thoughts you would get change
that person is extremely stupid
not to be the full quid
not to be very intelligent
not to have an ounce of sense
to be stupid
people in glass houses should not throw stones
those who are less than perfect are foolish to criticise others
John 8:7, 'He that is without sin among you, let him first cast a stone at her' (refers to ancient condemnation and punishment of people by stoning)
to be mutton dressed up as lamb
foolishly to pretend to be younger
to be only ten pence in the shilling
to be slightly stupid
refers to 'old' shillings and pence when a shilling equalled twelve pence
to burn one's fingers
to suffer (esp. loss of money) through foolishness or meddling
refers to taking chestnuts from a fire
to earn a dunce's cap
to do something stupid
a 'dunce' being derived from the name of Duns Scotus (1265–1308) and his followers ('Dunsers') whose hair-splitting theology was later perceived to be opposed to learning and enlightenment; Thomas Fuller (1608–61), 'a dunce, void of learning but full of books'
to fly blind
to do something in ignorance of the relevant facts
refers to pilots flying without visual guidance (and relying on instruments)

to go overboard
to act foolishly and in an excessive way
to have a bird brain
to be stupid
to have a loose tongue
to speak foolishly or indiscreetly
to have egg on one's face
to be embarrassed by the results of one's own stupidity
to judge a book by its cover
foolishly to go only by superficial appearances
to look though the wrong end of the telescope
completely to miss the point
to make an ass of oneself
to act stupidly in public
to need to have one's head read
to engage in behaviour so foolish that a psychiatric examination seems called for
to paint oneself into a corner
foolishly to put oneself into a position from which escape is impossible
to play Russian roulette
to engage in a dangerously unpredictable exercise
refers to an act of daring in which one squeezes the trigger of a revolver held to the head (after loading one chamber and spinning the cylinder — thus the one being fired is determined by chance)
to push water uphill
foolishly to attempt the impossible
to put one's foot in it
to make a foolish mistake
to put one's foot in one's mouth
to say something foolish
to sell one's birthright for a mess of pottage
through foolishness to exchange something of substance for something of little value
Genesis 25:34, 'Then Jacob gave Esau bread and pottage of lentils ... thus Esau despised his birthright'
to shoot oneself in the foot
to act in a foolish way and thus harm one's own cause
to sign one's own death warrant
foolishly to do something that is inevitably bound to lead to utter disaster
to sow wild oats
to indulge in foolish behaviour while a young adult
why keep a dog and bark oneself?
it is silly to pay for assistance and then do things personally

Success

a breakthrough
major success in overcoming obstacles to knowledge or a proposal
a field day
a very enjoyable and successful occasion
refers (originally) to an army's practice manoeuvres
a flash in the pan
something that begins promisingly but does not last
refers to the priming of old guns
a gambit
(in a competitive situation) an opening move that involves short-term losses in the expectation of long-term gains
Italian *gambetto*, literally 'tripping up'
a highflyer
an ambitious and/or successful person
a landslide
an electoral result involving victory or defeat by a very large margin
a Pyrrhic victory
a win that costs more than if there had been a loss
refers to the Battle at Asculum in 279 BC at which King Pyrrhus of Epirus defeated the Romans
a roller-coaster ride
a series of successes followed by failures
a rolling stone gathers no moss
a person who keeps changing jobs will not have a successful career
Tusser, *Five Hundred Points of Good Husbandrie* (1573), 'The stone that is rolling can gather no moss. / For master and servant oft changing is loss'
a walkover
an easy victory

refers to the winner walking over the finishing line for an unchallenged victory

chalk it up!
the success was unexpected
refers to scoring in a contest by making chalk marks on a score board

front runner
person expected to win; OR someone who performs well only when holding an advantage

it is in the bag
the enterprise has succeeded or surely will succeed

it is mind over matter
one's resolve to overcome suffering will succeed

it is pointing in the right direction
it is proceeding towards success

more power to your elbow
may your praiseworthy efforts continue and be strengthened

stalemate
a final result in which neither party to a dispute is victorious
refers to chess

the proof of the pudding is in the eating
the success of a venture will be measured by its results

the royal road to success
the way of attaining success without effort

things look black
there is little hope of success or prosperity or a favourable outcome

to be a passport to success
to be a means of achieving success

to be going great guns
to be making very successful progress

to be home and hosed
to be assured of victory or success in a task
refers to horse racing (a jocular reference to a horse leading in a race being already home and hosed down)

to be on a winner
to have faith in, give support to and/or invest in a project which proves to be successful
refers to betting on racing

to be on the crest of a wave
to enjoy success that might not last

to be successful beyond one's wildest dreams
to be far more successful than one could have expected

to be unable to take a trick
to be unable to achieve success in anything
refers to playing cards

to bear fruit
to result in success

to bring home the bacon
to be successful
refers to bringing home a valued prize

to fight tooth and nail
to strive very hard to win

to get on stream
to now operate successfully following the end of a settling-in period

to get to first base
to succeed in achieving the first stage in any undertaking
refers to baseball

to go for the gold
to aim for victory
refers to Olympic medals

to have a cast-iron case
to be assured absolutely of victory in a dispute, an argument, or in legal proceedings

to have had a good innings
to have enjoyed satisfactory time and success in an undertaking; to have had a successful life
refers to cricket

to have someone by the throat
to have a decisive advantage such that victory is assured

to have someone on toast
to have someone at a disadvantage, to be able to do what one wishes to a person

to pull the rug out from under someone
unexpectedly to withdraw support

to hold a winning hand
to be in an unbeatable position to defeat others
refers to playing cards

to hold all the aces
to be in an unbeatable position to defeat others
refers to playing cards; from Latin *as* ('unity', that is 'one' or 'a single point')

to hold all the cards
to be assured of victory
refers to playing cards

to hold someone at bay
successfully to resist an attacker
James Thomson (1700–48), *Autumn*, 'He stands at bay, and puts his last weak refuge in despair' — description of a stag

to hold the trump card
to be in an unbeatable position to defeat others
refers to playing cards

to look for a needle in a haystack
to attempt something with a very small chance of success

to make a good fist of something
to make a good attempt at, or to succeed in, a difficult task

to make a killing
to be in a very successful business venture

to make or break someone
to be a factor leading either to a person's success or to that person's failure, with no intermediate position

to make the grade
to succeed

to miss the sharks while netting the minnows
to succeed in minor aspects but fail in the ones that really matter

to pass with flying colours
to be very successful in a test or contest
refers to ships returning to port with colours flying triumphantly

to pay off
to be successful; OR formally to complete a ship's period of active service

to play the trump card
to make a final move, thereby defeating one's opponents
refers to playing cards

to pull something off
to achieve success in some enterprise

to raise the stake
to increase the amount of potential gain or loss in a project
refers to gambling

to rest on one's laurels
to use a reputation for success earned in earlier times as a substitute for current endeavour
refers to laurel wreaths presented to winners of events at the ancient Olympics

to ride high
to be successful but vulnerable
refers to riding a horse while sitting high and upright — a posture likely to result in a fall

to ride the wave
to be successful for the time being
refers to surfing

to score a hat trick
to have three successive favourable outcomes
refers to a bowler in cricket taking three wickets in three balls; such a feat being originally rewarded with the prize of a new hat

to show dividends
to be successful

to smell blood
to divine imminent victory

to stitch up a deal
successfully to conclude a deal

to strike gold
to have one's efforts suddenly rewarded by great success
refers to gold-mining

to strike pay dirt
to become successful
refers to soil containing gold or other precious metal

to strike the right chord
to appeal successfully to someone's emotions
refers to music

to throw a sprat to catch a mackerel
to risk a little in the hope of gaining much

to turn the corner
to commence being successful after initial failures

to win by a long chalk
to win very conclusively
refers to scoring in a contest by making chalk marks on a score board

to win hands down
to win very convincingly
refers to a jockey riding confidently with hands low when a race is as good as won

to win some rounds
to be partly successful
refers to boxing

to win the prize in a canter
to win very easily
refers to horse racing

to wrap up a deal
to bring a deal to a successful conclusion

when one's ship comes in
when one's business venture is successfully completed; OR when luck arrives

Surprise

a bombshell
an unpleasant surprise

a thunderbolt
a surprise
Shakespeare, *Julius Caesar* IV:iii, 'Be ready, gods, with all your thunderbolts; / dash him to pieces

someone would turn in his or her grave
someone would have been very surprised or displeased if he or she had known while still alive

not to bat an eyelid
to fail to express any surprise

someone's eyes popped
a person expressed great surprise

the mind boggles
this is astonishing

to be an eye-opener
to be a surprise

to catch someone off guard
to surprise a person
refers to fencing

to catch someone on the hop
to take a person by surprise

to raise one's eyebrows
to show surprise or disbelief

to rub one's eyes
to express astonishment

to take one's breath away
to surprise greatly, or astonish

wouldn't it rot your socks!
what an unpleasant surprise!

Truth

a litmus test
a simple examination that reveals the true state of affairs
refers to a test with litmus paper to establish whether a solution is acid or alkaline

a skeleton in the closet/cupboard
an unpleasant truth the knowledge of which has been deliberately suppressed
William Makepeace Thackeray (1811–63), *The Newcomes* (1855), ' … they have a skelton or two in their closets as well as their neighbours'

a tall story
an interesting but untrue and unbelievable tale

a tell-tale sign
a visible indication revealing true facts despite efforts at concealment

apocryphal
fictitious but resembling truth and illustrating a point
Greek: *apocrypha*, 'hidden'

out of the mouths of babes and sucklings
(as indiscreetly revealed) the truth
Psalms 8:2, 'Out of the mouths of babes and sucklings hast thou ordained strength … '

to be an ostrich
to refuse to face up to an unpleasant truth
refers to the reputed habit of ostriches in danger

to be too close to home
to be too near the truth to be welcome

to beat about the bush
to fail to come to the point
refers to hunters flushing game from cover by beating of the vegetation in which animals are hidden

to bring something into focus
to put some matter into its proper context and explain its true significance

to bury one's head in the sand
to refuse to face up to an unpleasant truth
refers to the reputed habit of ostriches in danger

to cloak something

to disguise the true nature of something

to drag someone by the head and ears
to force a person to reveal the true facts

to flush out the facts
to ascertain, after some effort, the truth of some matter

to open someone's eyes to something
to alert another person to the truth of something
Matthew 9:30, 'And their eyes were opened'

to read between the lines
to appreciate the true significance of something not put into words

to sell someone a pup
to cheat a person in a transaction, especially by misrepresentation as to the true value of something

to separate the wheat from the chaff
to separate the worthy from the unworthy
Matthew 3:12, 'His winnowing fork is in his hand, and he will clear his threshing floor and gather his wheat into the granary, but the chaff he will burn with unquenchable fire'

to show one's true colours
to disclose one's real character or beliefs
nautical metaphor

to slide under the bar
not to arouse suspicion

to speak with a forked tongue
to utter halftruths with the intention of misleading the listener

to swallow the line
to accept as truth the story being proffered
refers to angling

to take something as gospel
to believe that something is true

to unmask someone
to reveal a person's true identity

Unexpected Happenings

a kick in the shins
an unexpected and undeserved setback

a pit of disaster
great and unexpected misfortune

a shaggy dog story
a laborious, far-fetched, amusing story
refers to the shaggy dog that originally featured in many of these stories

a wild card
(in general) an unexpected unpredictable development; OR (in playing cards) a card of a value specified by the player holding it; OR (in sport) a player or a team given entrance to a competition by the organisers, even if the entry is not strictly merited; OR (in computing) a character that will match any other character in a search string

an Aladdin's cave
a place full of unexpected treasure
refers to a character and events in *Arabian Nights' Entertainments*

chalk it up!
the success was unexpected
refers to scoring in a contest by making chalk marks on a score board

it's a small world
it is surprising to meet people one knows in unexpected places

manna from heaven
unexpected benefits
derived from Hebrew *man-hu* ('what is this?'); *Exodus* 16:15, 'It is manna: for they wist not what it was. And Moses said unto them: this is the bread which the Lord hath given you to eat'

not to be a magic pudding
not to represent an everlasting supply of something
from the name of a book by Norman Lindsay

the answer to a maiden's prayer
an unexpected but very welcome happening

to be a bolt from the blue

to be a totally unexpected event

to be one in the eye for someone
to represent an unexpected and unwelcome defeat

to be one out of the box
to be unexpectedly superb
refers to magician's trick

to be shell-shocked
to be stunned by unexpected bad news
refers to psychological disturbance following exposure to wartime bombardment (esp. refers to World War I)

to be stopped in one's tracks
suddenly and unexpectedly to be prevented from carrying on with a project

to be the sting in the tail
to be the unexpected unpleasant conclusion

to catapult to fame
to achieve fame unexpectedly quickly

to catch someone in the net
unexpectedly to involve a particular person in the course of activity designed to involve many others

to come out of the blue
to be totally unexpected

to cut the ground from under someone's feet
to withdraw support unexpectedly and, in the process, to cause embarrassment; OR to demolish a person's case and cause defeat, especially by anticipating that person's arguments or plans

to founder on the shoals of something
to come to grief because of unexpected dangers
refers to a ship running aground in undetected shallow water

to keep one's head
to remain calm in a crisis or unexpectedly to retain an elected or appointed position
Rudyard Kipling (1865–1936), *If*, 'If you can keep your head when all about you are losing theirs ... '

to open a Pandora's box
to do something that produces all sorts of undesired and unexpected side-effects
refers to the woman in Greek mythology who brought misery to the world; Pandora's box contained all human ills and, when opened, it released uncontrollable misery on humanity

to pull a rabbit out of the hat
to produce an unexpected and seemingly miraculous but highly desirable solution
refers to magician's trick

to pull the rug out from under someone
unexpectedly to withdraw support

to take a nose dive
to fall steeply, suddenly and unexpectedly

to throw a spanner into the works
to cause an unexpected complication

to turn up trumps
to finish up better than expected or to experience unexpected good luck
refers to playing cards

to turn white
to express shock at unexpected news

to vanish into thin air
unexpectedly to disappear
Shakespeare, *The Tempest* IV:i, ' ... are melted into air, into thin air'

windfall
unexpected good fortune
refers to fruit falling from a tree without having to be picked

Unrealistic Ideas

a South Sea bubble
an unrealistic financial venture that is bound to result in total loss
refers to a notorious financial scandal involving the South Sea Company (UK) in 1720

moonshine
unrealistic ideas

someone's eyes are bigger than that person's stomach
a person is unrealistic in regard to that person's ability to cope with something

to be in cloud-cuckoo land
to be mad or to have unrealistic expectations

'cloud-cuckoo land' was an imaginary city built in the air by the birds (according to the *Nephelococcygia* of *The Birds* by Aristophanes) — hence any utopian fantastic scheme

to bite off more than one can chew
to be over ambitious and thus unrealistic as to one's capabilities

to chase rainbows
to be quite unrealistic

to have one's head in the clouds
to be unrealistic

to shoot for the stars
to be unrealistic

to talk turkey
to talk realistically
origin obscure; North American slang

to want to jump all one's fences at once
unrealistically to want to solve all problems at once, rather than sequentially
refers to steeplechasing on horseback

Unwelcome

a bible basher
a person who makes unwelcome attempts to force religious beliefs on others

a blessing in disguise
an unwelcome but salutary experience
James Hervey (1696–1743), *Reflections on a Flower Garden*, 'Ee'en crosses from his sov'reign hand are blessings in disguise'

stiff cheese!
circumstances that might be unwelcome but will not be altered, and in respect of which no great sympathy is felt

the affair blew up
certain unwelcome facts have become publicly available

to be one in the eye for someone
to represent an unexpected and unwelcome defeat

to be too close to home
to be too near the truth to be welcome

to penetrate someone's thick skull
to make a person understand something difficult or acknowledge something unwelcome

to play gooseberry
to act as an unwelcome chaperon

to plead the fifth amendment
to refuse to answer an unwelcome question
refers to the fifth amendment of the United States constitution, which provides protection against self-incrimination

to put someone back in his/her box/place
to make it clear to a person that that person's views are not welcome

to rear its ugly head
to make an unwelcome appearance

to send someone away with a flea in the ear
to give a person frank, but unwelcome, facts
perhaps refers to fleas trapped in the armour of ancient knights, or perhaps from the discomfort felt by a dog with a flea in its ear; or perhaps, figuratively, to any lingering irritation in the ear

Waiting

hold your horses!
just wait a little!

to be on tenterhooks
anxiously to await some result
refers to cloth being stretched or 'tentered'; Latin: *tentus* ('stretched')

to bite one's fingernails
anxiously to await a decision

to cool one's heels
to be kept waiting

to cross a bridge only when one comes to it
to await the crystallisation of a situation before sorting it out

to have one's beady eyes on something
to await the chance to acquire something to which one is not properly entitled

to kick one's heels
to be kept waiting

to mark time

to do nothing while awaiting developments
refers to marching

to see which way the cat jumps
to await developments

to sweat it out
to await one's fate calmly

to wait for the other shoe to drop
to await the seemingly imminent and inevitable
refers to a person being disturbed by a neighbour who drops one shoe on the floor, the listener then being frustrated when the sound of the other shoe being dropped is not heard

to wait in the wings
to be prepared to stay unobtrusive till the appropriate time for action arrives
refers to the theatre

to wait two shakes of a lamb's tail
to wait just a few moments

to wait with bated breath
to be excited in anticipation of some event

Wealth

a banana republic
a country with a poor economy

a goldmine
a source of much wealth or of many facts

a pot of gold
wealth, especially a reward long wished-for

life raft
financial assistance sufficient to avert insolvency

not to be made of money
not to be wealthy

not to have a brass razoo
to be very poor
refers to an imaginary coin of trivial value

not to have the wherewithal to rub two sticks together
to be very poor

rags to riches
the transition from poverty to wealth

the doors of the Ritz are open to all
despite rhetoric to the contrary wealthy people have many advantages over poor people
refers to the Ritz Hotel, London, founded in 1906 by César Ritz

to be a gay dog
to lead an idle life while flaunting the symbols of wealth

to be born with a silver spoon in one's mouth
to be brought up by wealthy parents
refers to the traditional gift of a silver spoon (an 'apostle spoon') to a child at baptism — the child born of wealthy parents is assured of riches from the moment of birth and thus does not have to await baptism to receive a valuable gift

to have money flowing out of one's ears
to be very rich

to hold one's head just above water
to cope with problems but with little margin to spare or to stay solvent

to live from hand to mouth
being in poor financial circumstances to survive (with little safety margin)
refers to immediate consumption of whatever one has in one's hand

to stay afloat
to remain solvent

well-heeled
rich

Welcome

any port in a storm
anything that helps to avoid difficulties is welcome

the answer to a maiden's prayer
an unexpected but very welcome happening

the more the merrier
everyone is welcome

the red-carpet treatment
courtesies extended to a person to make that person feel important and welcome
refers to the welcome accorded a visiting dignitary

to be a sight for sore eyes
to be something welcome

to be better than a poke in the eye with a burnt stick
to be not particularly welcome, but better than other alternatives
to come in out of the cold
to be welcomed into a group
to kill the fatted calf
to demonstrate welcome and complete acceptance of another person
Luke 15:23. 'And bring hither the fatted calf and let us eat, and be merry'
to pipe someone on board
to welcome a person
nautical metaphor

Work and Effort

a dry hole
an exercise that, after much effort, proves fruitless
refers to drilling for oil
a fifth columnist
a person using a position of trust to work for a rival cause
refers to an extra body of supporters claimed by General Mola as being within Madrid when he besieged the city with four columns of nationalist forces during the Spanish Civil War in 1936
a scatter-gun approach
an effort going here, there and everywhere, instead of being properly targeted
a willing horse
a cheerful worker
an unholy alliance
a working relationship for a nefarious purpose between unlikely partners
bedfellow
collaborator
blood, sweat, and tears
hard work and much effort
Winston Churchill, House of Commons, 13 May 1940, 'I have nothing to offer but blood, toil, tears, and sweat'
donkey work
necessary but uninspiring routine work
refers to the laborious work done by a donkey
elbow grease
hard manual work
old jocular saying, in existence for several centuries, referring to the vigorous use of the elbow in rubbing, polishing, scrubbing, etc.
to be flat out like a lizard drinking
to be hard at work
a play on words, not strictly a simile
good chemistry
an ability to work closely together
harvest
end result of labour
Matthew 8:37, 'The harvest truly is plenteous, but the labourers are few'
it is neck or nothing
a desperate effort is called for
refers to a winning margin in horse racing
it will all come out in the wash
the facts will emerge as work proceeds
more power to your elbow
may your praiseworthy efforts continue and be strengthened
Parkinson's law
the principle that work expands to match the work capacity available
title of a book (1957) by Prof. C. Northcote Parkinson
put your back into it!
work energetically!
search for the Holy Grail
work towards a difficult goal
refers to a vessel or platter supposedly used by Christ at the Last Supper and featuring in the Arthurian legends
the royal road to success
the way of attaining success without effort
the wheels have been turning
work has been going steadily on (contrast 'the wheel has turned')
to be a busy bee
to work with great diligence
to be a happy ship
to have a contented workforce
to be at the coal face
to be in the place where the real work is done
to be chief cook and bottlewasher
to perform a range of duties single-handedly — ranging from important to menial
to be geared up to do something

to have equipment, labour, and know-how in place adequate for some task
refers to mechanics

to be in the field
to be out in the working environment as opposed to headquarters, a laboratory, etc.

the salt of the earth
special people who make a vital contribution to society
Matthew 5:13, 'Ye are the salt of the earth'

to beaver away
to work diligently at some task
refers to the industriousness of the beaver

to break the ice
to take the initiative in starting discussions
Francis Bacon (1561–1626), *Of Cunning*, 'In things that are tender and unpleasing, it is good to break the ice by some whose words are of less weight ...'

to burn the candle at both ends
to exhaust one's resources through working excessive hours'

to burn the midnight oil
to work late into the night
Francis Quarles (1592–1644), *Emblems*, 'We spend our midday sweat, our midnight oil; / we tire the night in thought, the day in toil'

to compete on all fours with someone
to strive on equal terms
refers to the four limbs of the body

to do the leg work
to carry out the part of a project that requires actually physically walking around and collecting information, etc.

to fight tooth and nail
to strive very hard to win

to gain the upper hand
to attain, after some effort, an advantage over another person

to go along for the ride
to seek to benefit from a project in which others contribute the effort

to go the extra mile
to work beyond the call of duty
Matthew 5:41, 'Whosoever shall compel thee to go a mile, go with him twain'

to have too much on one's plate
to be unable to cope with one's workload

to inundate
to overload with replies, etc.

to keep one's head
to remain calm in a crisis or unexpectedly to retain an elected or appointed position
Rudyard Kipling (1865–1936), *If*, 'If you can keep your head when all about you are losing theirs ... '

to keep one's nose to the grindstone
to work with particular diligence
refers to having one's head down low while working on a grindstone sharpening tools

to keep out of someone's hair
to let someone get on with that person's work in his or her own way

to play the last card in the pack
to be forced to use one's last expedient
refers to playing cards

to pull one's fingers out
to cease indolence and get on with a job with alacrity

to pull one's weight
to do one's proper share of the work requiring to be done
refers to rowing

to pull oneself up by one's bootstraps
to make a praiseworthy effort to better oneself unaided

to pull oneself up by one's own shoelaces
to make a superhuman effort

to pull out all stops
to make maximum effort
refers to organ playing at maximum volume

to pull together
to work in harmony
refers to rowing

to put one's back into something
to work hard at achieving some goal

to put one's best foot forward
to make a special effort

to put one's shoulder to the wheel
to make a strong effort

to ride on the back of someone

without effort to benefit from the prior efforts of others
to roll up one's sleeves
to get on with a job energetically
to snow someone under
to overload a person with work
to spark on all cylinders
to work extremely well
to steal someone's thunder
to take credit for another person's good work
refers to a dispute over the copying of a machine invented by dramatist John Dennis (1657–1734) to reproduce the sound of thunder during a play
to stir a finger
to make some minimum effort
to strike a blow
to begin or resume work
to strike a blow for some principle
to work towards the attainment of some principle
to strike at the roots of something
to work towards the destruction of something
to strike gold
to have one's efforts suddenly rewarded by great success
refers to gold-mining
to swing the lead
to cheat an employer by not working while being paid to do so or by malingering; to avoid work or some other task by concocting a plausible excuse for not doing it, or by pretending to be ill
originally referred to a leadsman lazily swinging the line, rather than getting on with taking soundings
to take the rough with the smooth
to accept the hardships of life along with its pleasant features
to win one's spurs
to gain recognition after a period of effort
refers to the earning of a knighthood in battle
to work hand in glove with someone
to work in close cooperation with a person or to be in collusion with a person to the detriment of others
to work one's fingers to the bone
to work very hard
to work overtime at something
to spend a lot of time and effort at doing something
shoulder to shoulder
in close proximity

Worry

a headache
a cause for worry
a new lease of life
the prospect of a better existence from now on, or of better functioning after repair
not to lose any sleep over something
not to worry about some matter
to drive someone out of that person's mind
to produce insanity in a person
often used jocularly, with exaggeration
to prey on one's mind
(of a problem) to keep worrying one
to raise the spectre of something
to draw attention to the expectation of something worrying refers to a ghost or apparition
to send a chill down someone's neck
to be worrying news
to spend a sleepless night
to worry about something

Appendices

APPENDIX ONE

'Yes, Prime Minister'

The following extract is from the 'Conflict of Interest' episode of 'Yes, Prime Minister', the popular BBC television series. It features a discussion between Sir Desmond Glazebrook, a leading banker who is keen to become governor of the Bank of England, and James Hacker, the British prime minister.

Glazebrook: City's a funny place, Prime Minister. You know, if you spill the beans you open up a whole can of worms. I mean, how can you let sleeping dogs lie if you let the cat out of the bag? You bring in a new broom and if you're not very careful you find you've thrown the baby out with the bathwater. Change horses in the middle of the stream, next thing you know you're up the creek without a paddle.

Hacker: And then what happens?

Glazebrook: Well! Obviously the balloon goes up. They hit you for six. An own goal, in fact.

From the script by Jonathan Lynn and Antony Jay; reproduced with the permission of BBC Enterprises Limited

APPENDIX TWO

Some Figurative Computer Terms

back door
a hole in the security of a system that has been deliberately left in place by its designers to give them a measure of control over it

card
a small circuit board, designed to provide expanded capability to a computer, plugged into one of its expansion slots

handshaking
the exchange of information between two modems linked by telephone at the start of a data transfer, and the resulting agreement about the protocol to be used for this transfer

hardware
the physical components of a computer, as distinct from the programs used to give it instructions

software
the programs used to give a computer instructions, as distinct from its physical components

Trojan horse
a malicious program designed to destroy data or cause other harm but which is disguised as something useful — for example, a game, or even as a program intended to find and destroy viruses

APPENDIX THREE

Material for Party Games

The lists in this book can also be used as the raw material for various party games and similar pursuits. Twelve illustrations are set out below:

1. A keyword (for example, 'horse', 'ball', 'head', 'water', etc.) is selected. The object of the game is to see how many different metaphors using this particular keyword (whether included in this book or not) each player can recall within a short time limit. For example, for the keyword 'horse', metaphors might include: 'to swap horses in mid-stream', 'a dark horse', and so on.
2. A category (for example, 'cricket', 'colours', 'domestic pets', 'numerals', etc.) is selected. The object of the game is to see how many different metaphors using words from this category (whether included in this book or not) each player can recall within a short time limit. For example, from cricket, 'to go in to bat for someone' or 'to have the runs on the board'.
3. A subject area (for example, 'defeat', 'price', 'knowledge', 'responsibility', etc.) is selected. The object of the game is to see how many different metaphors relating to this particular subject area (whether included in this book or not) each player can recall within a short time limit. For example, to convey 'defeat', metaphors might include 'checkmate' or 'to be on the ropes'.
4. The initial words (for example, 'To beard … ') of some well-known metaphors are quoted. The object of the game

is to provide the concluding words ('... the lion in his den').

5. A general topic is selected. The object of the game is to evolve the best paragraph using a certain minimum number of metaphors (say, ten). This would need to have regard to factors such as humour, originality, and plausibility. (For an example of such a piece, see the passage at the front of this book.) If desired, the players of this game could be given access to copies of the book while drafting their paragraphs.
6. One or two pages of the current issue of a daily newspaper are designated. The object of the game is to see how many different metaphors each player can recognise on these pages. An element of luck as well as skill can be introduced by giving different pages to different players (say, the corresponding pages of successive issues).
7. A number of specific metaphors are selected. The object of the game is to best translate them into bureaucratic language. For example, 'to flog a dead horse' could become 'to impose flagellation measures on an equine quadruped which is permanently devoid of its original capacities'.
8. The above game can also be played in reverse, with the players being given the bureaucratic versions and required to work out, within a short time limit, what the corresponding customary 'plain English' expressions are.
9. The names of well-known persons are designated. The object of the game is to evolve appropriate 'last words' for each, based on metaphors. For example, for Albert Einstein: 'To an observer on earth, my clock will appear to have stopped'.
10. A series of definitions is given – for example, 'to strive very hard to win', 'to be quite ineffective', 'to be afraid or dejected', 'to be a member of a group knowing what is going on', 'to fight an unwinnable case', and so on. The object of the game is to match each definition with a

well-known metaphor. For example, to take the phrases given above:

to strive very hard to win – *to fight tooth and nail*

to be quite ineffective – *to labour mightily and produce a mouse*

to be afraid or dejected – *to have one's heart in one's boots*

to be a member of a group knowing what is going on – *to be in the swim*

to fight an unwinnable case – *to bang one's head against a brick wall*

11. The above game is rather difficult. An easier version involves producing two lists of, say, twenty items each, both in random order. One list consists of metaphors and the other of definitions. The object of the game is to match up the items in the two lists as quickly as possible.

12. One or two pages of the current issue of a daily newspaper are designated. The object of the game is to produce, within a specified time limit, fresh headlines for as many articles on these pages as possible – using the metaphors which best fit in with the articles concerned. Judging would need to take into account the suitability and effectiveness of the metaphors chosen.

Afterword

One enthusiastic reader of an earlier edition of this book, Sharon Benson of Ottawa, Ontario, Canada, has provided an overview of how she used it. It is reproduced below with her permission, as it may be helpful to others working in similar fields.

She is a writer who works in the corporate and promotional realm. Her company helps businesses to communicate with other businesses and with customers or prospective customers. She also assists organisations wishing to relay information to their stakeholders. Typically, her output includes advertising copy, brochures, annual reports, speeches, films and videos.

> I can imagine that you would be interested in feedback on your book. The research and assemblage of all these metaphorical expressions must have been a Herculean task; rest assured that your efforts have not gone unappreciated!
>
> I've never tried to describe the process I go through when writing, but generally here's how I might use your book when creating copy for a client. I use a process called mind-mapping when I write. Meaning, I develop a core idea and then let my mind wander along whatever roads it wishes to travel in order to develop that idea. The dictionary, thematic and thesaurus structure of your book all help when I reach a dead end.

For example, I recently created a corporate overview for a technology based firm where I used the headline 'Stop, Look and Listen' to introduce prospective customers to a disparate product line that includes security alarm systems and asset management tools.

I played with lines such as 'right up your alley' and 'middle of the road' within the body copy and then looked in your book for expressions that conveyed the intent of each product. The result? Crisp, creative copy that thrilled the client and made me look good.